C000161123

Ordnance Survey

STREET ATLAS
East Kent

Contents

III   *Key to map symbols*

IV-V   *Key to map pages*

VI   *Administrative and post code boundaries*

1   *Street maps*

206   *Town plans of Bromley and Dartford*

207   *Town plans of Gravesend and Royal Tunbridge Wells*

208   *Town plans of Sevenoaks and Tonbridge*

209   *Index of hospitals, railway stations, schools, shopping centres, street names and universities*

PHILIP'S

First edition published 1989
Third edition published 1994
First colour edition published 1997
Reprinted 1998 by

Ordnance Survey®   and   George Philip Ltd
Romsey Road,   an imprint of Reed Consumer Books Ltd
Maybush,   Michelin House, 81 Fulham Road,
Southampton SO16 4GU   London SW3 6RB
                                 and Auckland, Melbourne

ISBN 0-540-07483-7 (hardback)
ISBN 0-540-07276-1 (wire-o)

© Crown copyright 1997
© George Philip Ltd 1997

All rights reserved. No part of this publication may be reproduced,
stored in a retrieval system or transmitted, in any form or by any
means, electronic, mechanical, photocopying, recording or otherwise,
without the permission of the Publishers and the copyright owner.

To the best of the Publishers' knowledge, the information in this atlas
was correct at the time of going to press. No responsibility can be
accepted for any errors or their consequences.

The representation in this atlas of a road, track or path is no evidence
of the existence of a right of way.

**The mapping between pages 1 and 208 (inclusive) in this atlas is
derived from Ordnance Survey® OSCAR® and Land-Line® data,
and Landranger® mapping.**

Ordnance Survey, OSCAR, Land-Line and Landranger are registered
trade marks of Ordnance Survey, the National Mapping Agency of
Great Britain.

Printed and bound in Spain by Cayfosa

Motorway (with junction number)	
Primary routes (dual carriageway and single)	
A roads (dual carriageway and single)	
B roads (dual carriageway and single)	
Minor through road (dual carriageway and single)	
Minor roads	
Roads under construction	
Railways	
Tramway, miniature railway	
Rural track, private road or narrow road in urban area	
Gate or obstruction to traffic (restrictions may not apply at all times or to all vehicles)	
All paths, bridleways, byway open to all traffic, road used as a public path	
The representation in this atlas of a road, track or path is no evidence of the existence of a right of way	

45
140
Adjoining page indicators

Dover Castle   **Non-Roman antiquity**

ROMAN FORT   **Roman antiquity**

Acad	**Academy**	Mon	**Monument**
Cemy	**Cemetery**	Mus	**Museum**
C Ctr	**Civic Centre**	Obsy	**Observatory**
CH	**Club House**	Pal	**Royal Palace**
Coll	**College**	PH	**Public House**
Ex H	**Exhibition Hall**	Resr	**Reservoir**
Ind Est	**Industrial Estate**	Ret Pk	**Retail Park**
Inst	**Institute**	Sch	**School**
Ct	**Law Court**	Sh Ctr	**Shopping Centre**
L Ctr	**Leisure Centre**	Sta	**Station**
LC	**Level Crossing**	TH	**Town Hall/House**
Liby	**Library**	Trad Est	**Trading Estate**
Mkt	**Market**	Univ	**University**
Meml	**Memorial**	YH	**Youth Hostel**

British Rail station	
Private railway station	
Bus, coach station	
Ambulance station	
Coastguard station	
Fire station	
Police station	
Casualty entrance to hospital	
Church, place of worship	
H	**Hospital**
i	**Information centre**
P	**Parking**
PO	**Post Office**
The Canterbury High School	**Important buildings, schools, colleges, universities and hospitals**
	County boundaries
Great Stour	**Water name**
	Stream
	River or canal (minor and major)
	Water
	Tidal water
	Woods
	Houses

■ The dark grey border on the inside edge of some pages indicates that the mapping does not continue onto the adjacent page

■ The small numbers around the edges of the maps identify the 1 kilometre National Grid lines

The scale of the maps is 5.52 cm to 1 km (3¹/₂ inches to 1 mile)

0		¹/₄		¹/₂		³/₄		1 mile
0	250m		500m		750m		1 Kilometre	

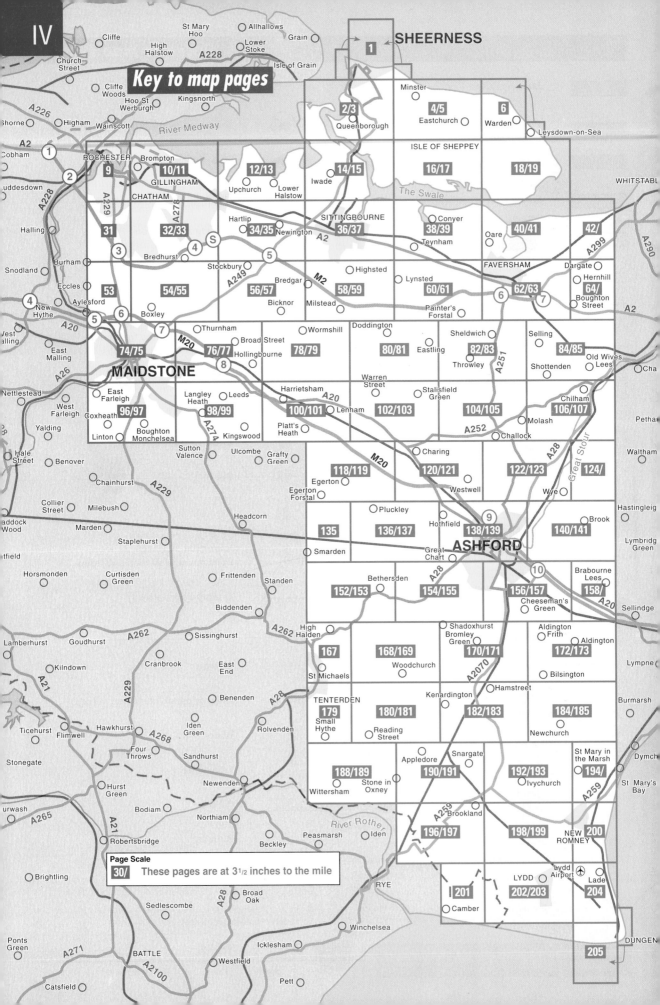

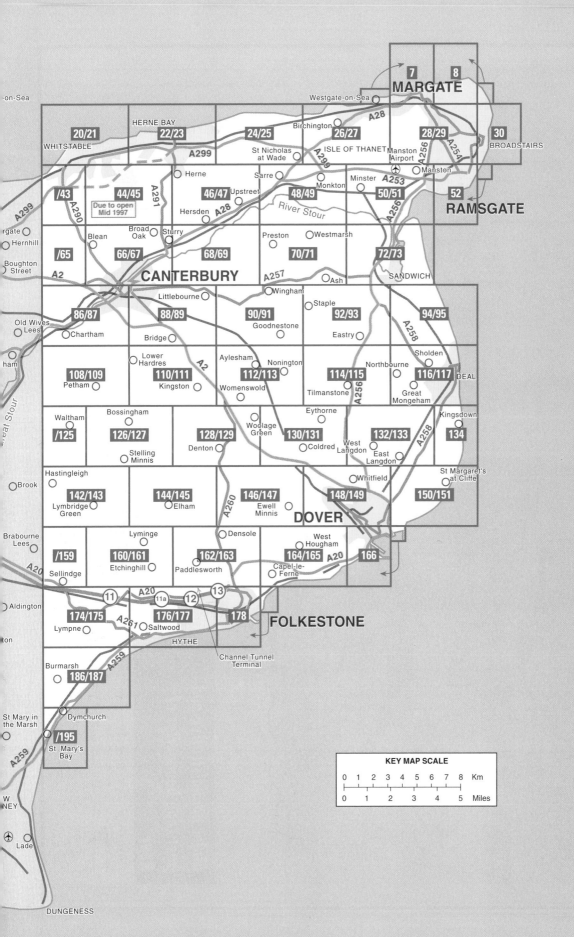

KEY MAP SCALE

0 1 2 3 4 5 6 7 8 Km

0 1 2 3 4 5 Miles

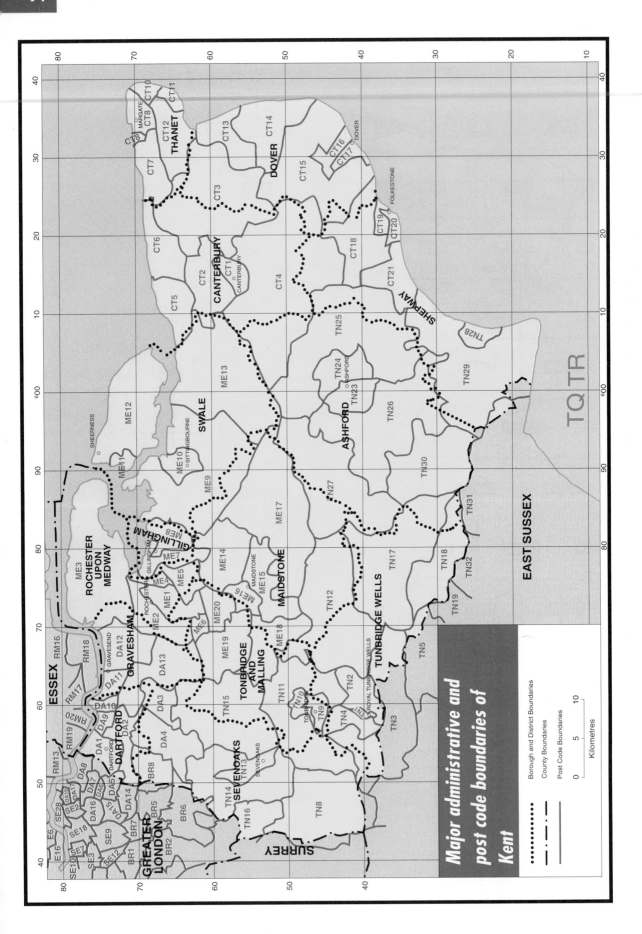

Major administrative and
post code boundaries of
Kent

Borough and District Boundaries

County Boundaries

Post Code Boundaries

Kilometres

0   5   10

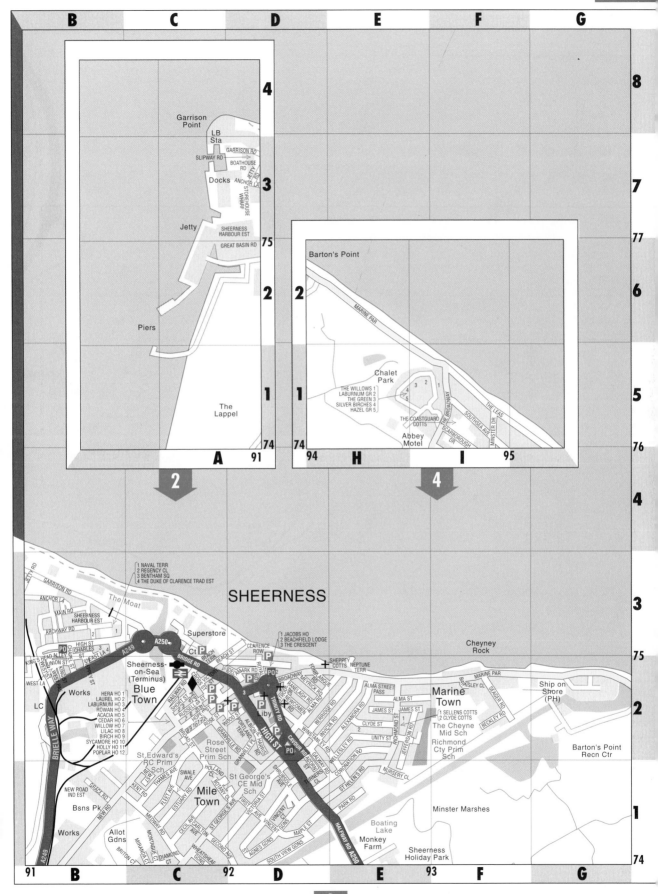

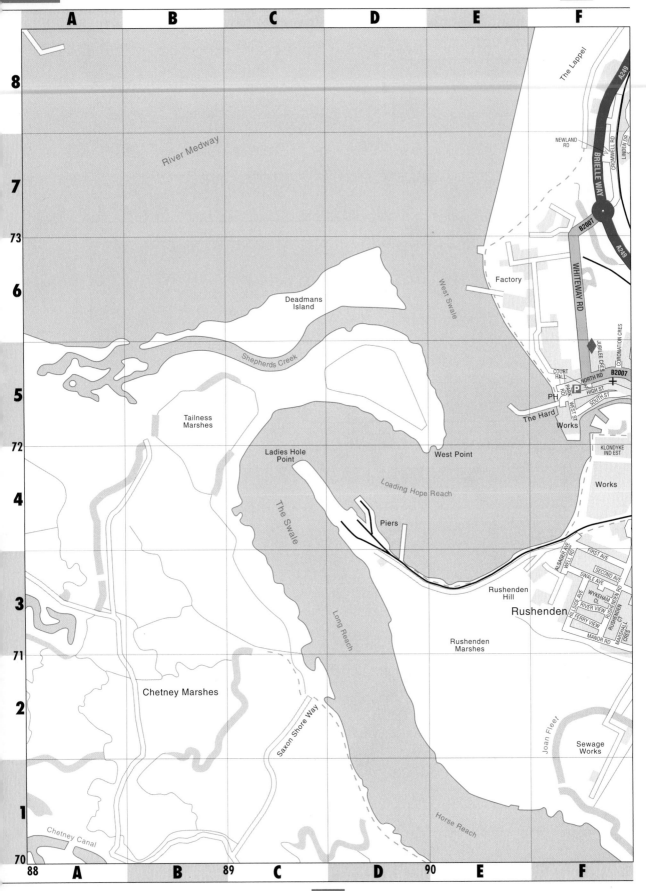

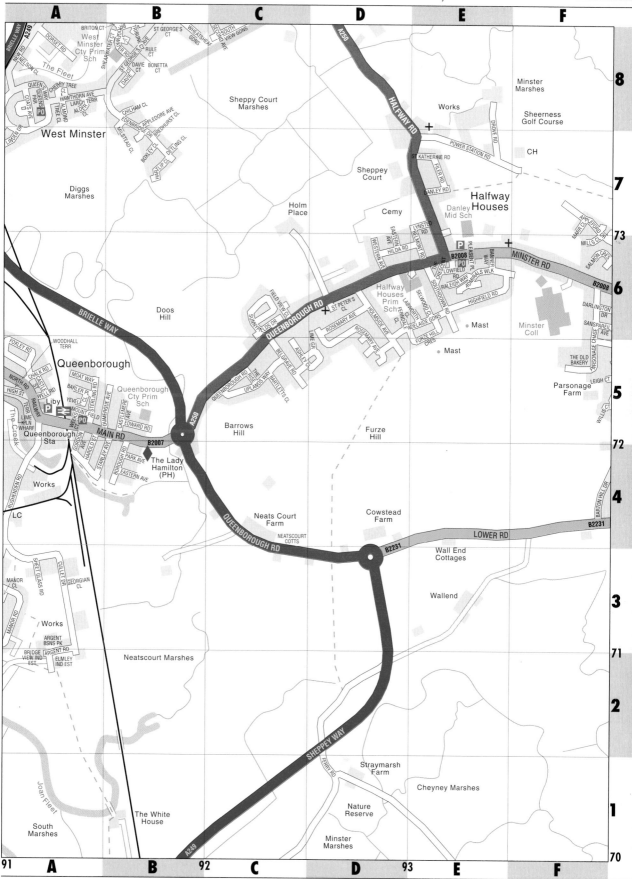

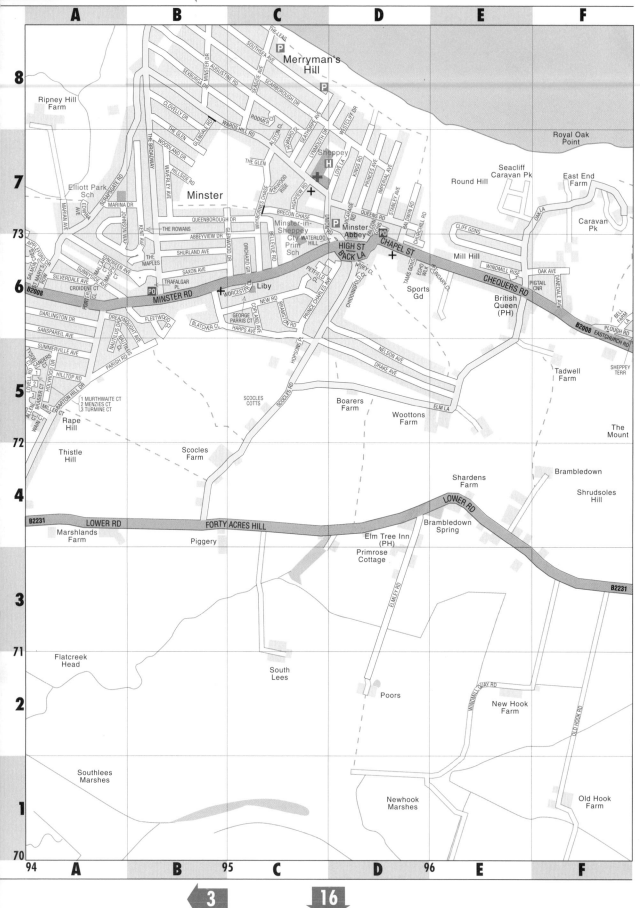

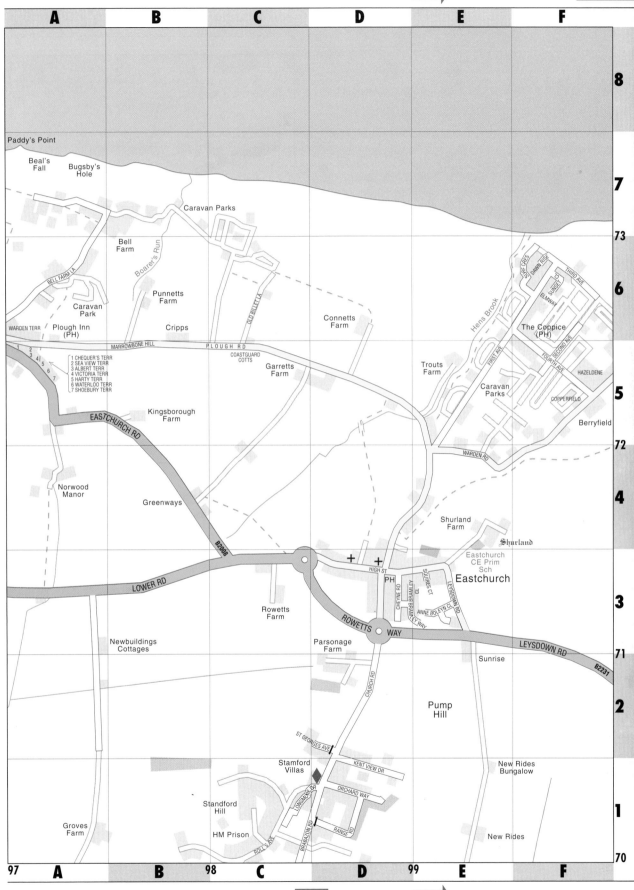

A   B   C   D   E   F

8

Paddy's Point

Beal's
Fall

Bugsby's
Hole

7

73

Caravan Parks

6

Bell
Farm

Boarer's Run

Bell Farm La

SURF CRES

DAWN RISE

THIRD AVE

SUNSET

ELMWAY

Punnetts
Farm

Caravan
Park

Plough Inn
(PH)

WARDEN TERR

OLD BILLETT LA

Connetts
Farm

The Coppice
(PH)

SECOND AVE

Hens Brook

Cripps

MARROWBONE HILL   P L O U G H RD

COASTGUARD
COTTS

Trouts
Farm

FIRST AVE

FOURTH AVE

HAZELDENE

5

EASTCHURCH RD

1   2
3 4 5
6   7

1 CHEQUER'S TERR
2 SEA VIEW TERR
3 ALBERT TERR
4 VICTORIA TERR
5 HARTY TERR
6 WATERLOO TERR
7 SHOEBURY TERR

Garretts
Farm

Caravan
Parks

COPPERFIELD

Berryfield

72

Kingsborough
Farm

WARDEN RD

Norwood
Manor

Greenways

B2008

Shurland
Farm

Shurland

4

LOWER RD

Eastchurch
CE Prim
Sch

HIGH ST

PH

Eastchurch

SQUIRES CT

BRAMLEY CL

Rowetts
Farm

CHEYNE RD

ANNE BOLEYN CL

LEYSDOWN RD

3

Newbuildings
Cottages

Parsonage
Farm

ROWETTS   WAY

LEYSDOWN RD

B2231

71

CHURCH RD

Sunrise

Pump
Hill

2

ST GEORGES AVE

Stamford
Villas

KENT VIEW DR

New Rides
Bungalow

LONGMORE DR

ORCHARD WAY

Standford
Hill

BRABAZON RD

RANGE   RD

1

Groves
Farm

HM Prison

ROLLS AVE

New Rides

70

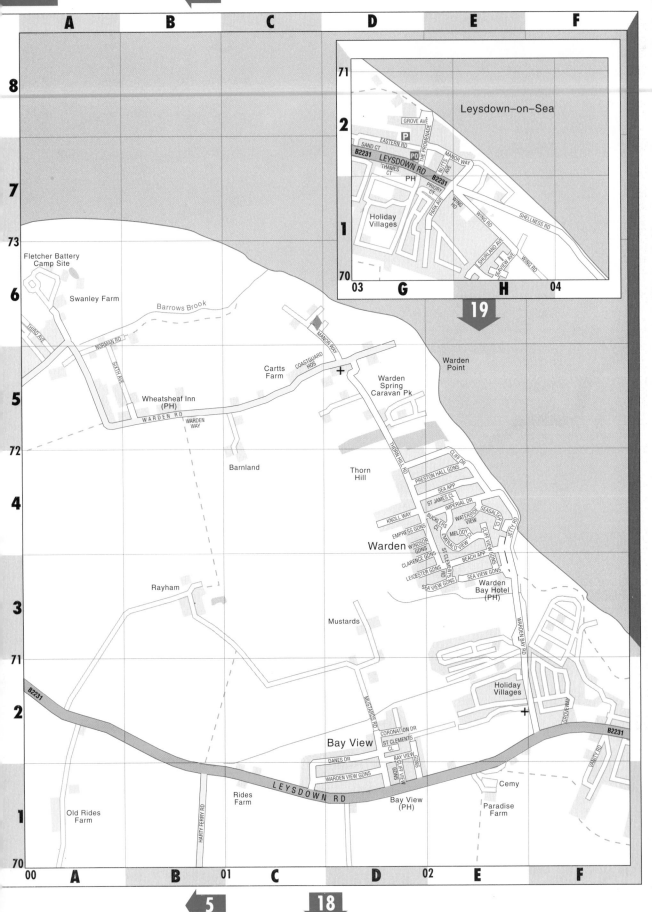

A   B   C   D   E   F

8

7

73

6

72

5

4

71

3

2

70

1

Fletcher Battery
Camp Site

Swanley Farm

THIRD AVE

NORMAN RD

SIXTH AVE

Barrows Brook

Wheatsheaf Inn
(PH)

WARDEN RD

WARDEN WAY

Barnland

Rayham

Cartts Farm

COASTGUARD HOS

MANOR WAY

Warden
Spring
Caravan Pk

Thorn Hill

THORN HILL RD

Warden
Point

PRESTON HALL GDNS

CLIFF DR

SEA APP

KNOLL WAY

ST JAMES CL

IMPERIAL DR

WATERSIDE VIEW

SEASALTER CL

BUCKLERS CL

MELODY

EMPRESS GDNS

EMERALD VIEW

CLIFF VIEW GDNS

JETTY RD

Warden

WINDSOR GDNS

ST CLEMENTS RD

BEACH APP

CLARENCE GDNS

LEICESTER GDNS

SEA VIEW GDNS

SEA VIEW GDNS

Warden
Bay Hotel
(PH)

Mustards

WARDEN BAY RD

Holiday
Villages

GROVE WAY

B2231

B2231

MUSTARDS RD

CORONATION DR

Bay View

ST CLEMENTS CL

DANES DR

BAY VIEW GDNS

CLIFF VIEW GDNS

WARDEN VIEW GDNS

LEYSDOWN RD

Bay View
(PH)

Cemy

Paradise
Farm

VANITY RD

Old Rides
Farm

HARTY FERRY RD

Rides
Farm

Inset: Leysdown-on-Sea

71

2

1

70

03   G   H   04

Leysdown-on-Sea

GROVE AVE

EASTERN RD

SAND CT

B2231

LEYSDOWN RD

THAMES CT

PH

THE PROMENADE

MANOR WAY

NUTTS AVE

B2231

PRIORY CV

PARK AVE

WING RD

WING RD

SHELLNESS RD

Holiday
Villages

SHURLAND AVE

SEAVIEW AVE

WING RD

19

00   A   B   01   C   D   02   E   F

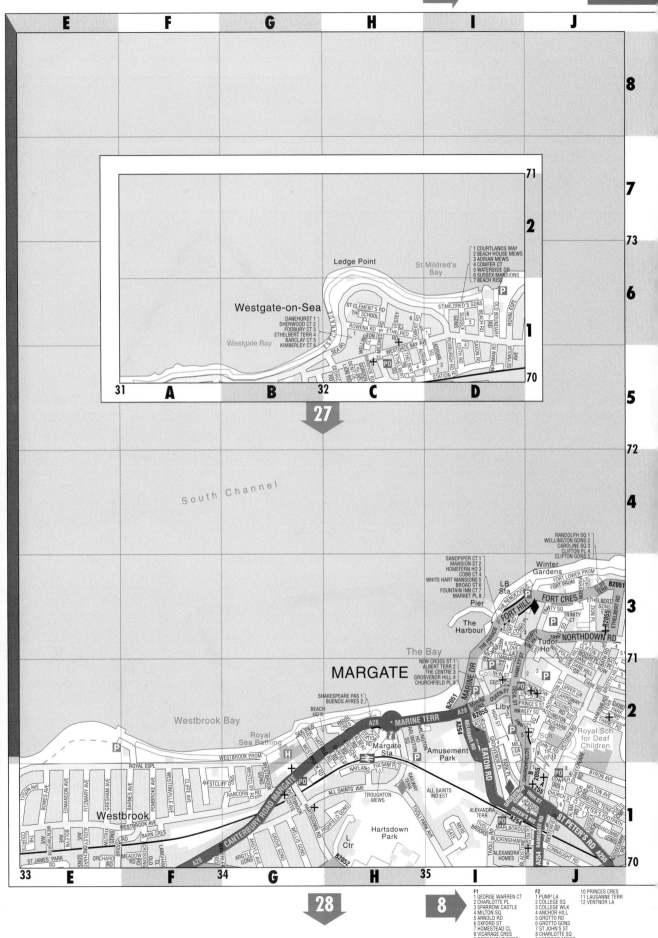

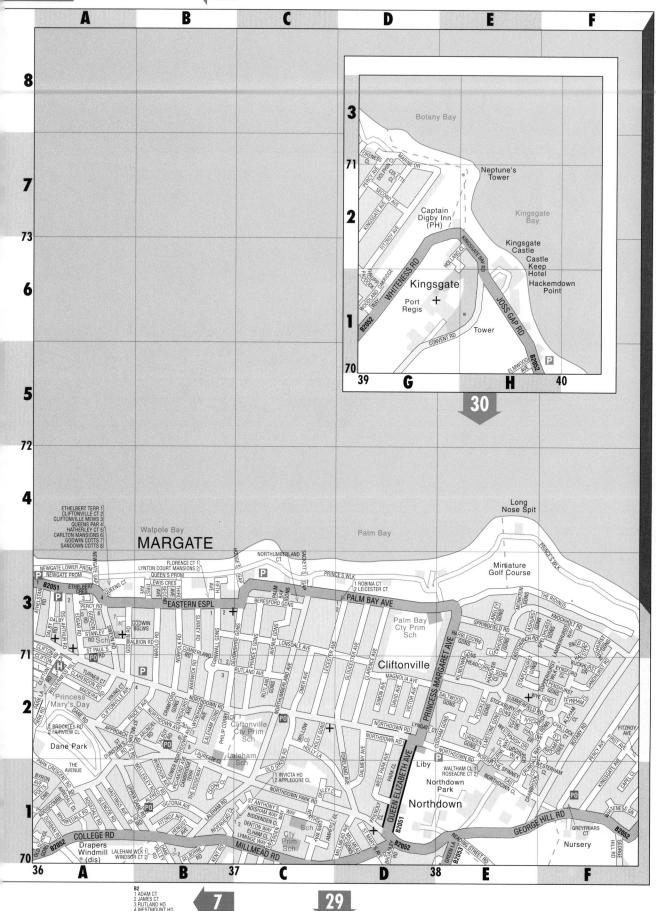

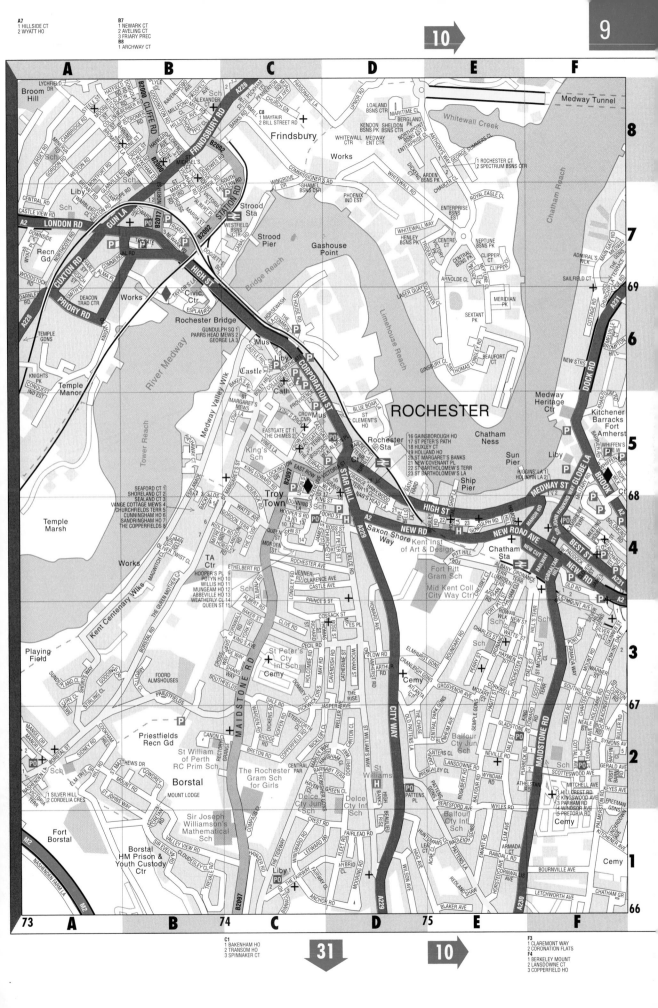

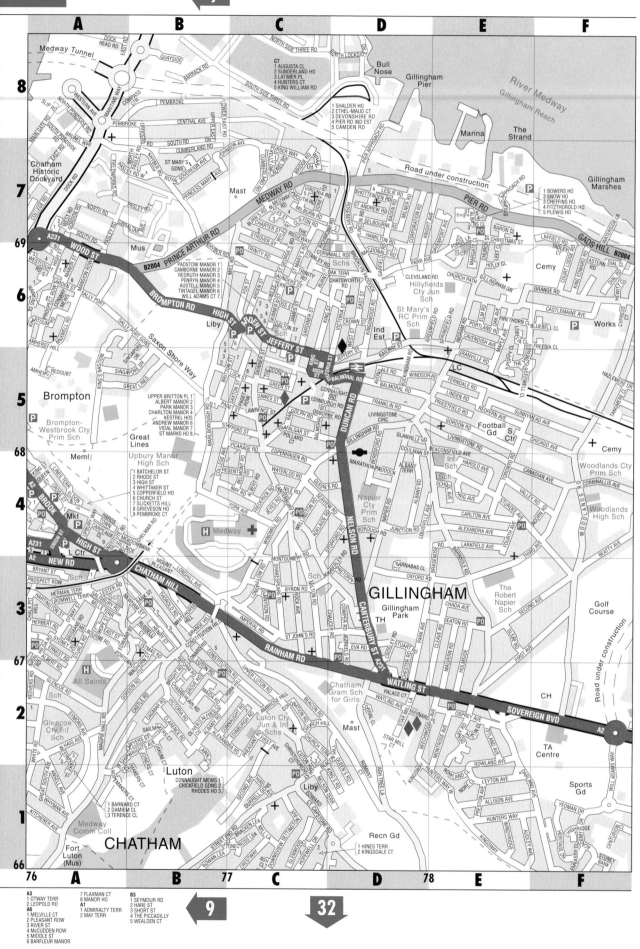

A3
1 OTWAY TERR
2 LEOPOLD RD
A6
1 MELVILLE CT
2 PLEASANT ROW
3 RIVER ST
4 McCUDDEN ROW
5 MIDDLE ST
6 BARFLEUR MANOR

7 FLAXMAN CT
8 MANOR HO
A7
1 ADMIRALTY TERR
2 MAY TERR

B3
1 SEYMOUR RD
2 HARE ST
3 SHORT ST
4 THE PICCADILLY
5 WEALDEN CT

12

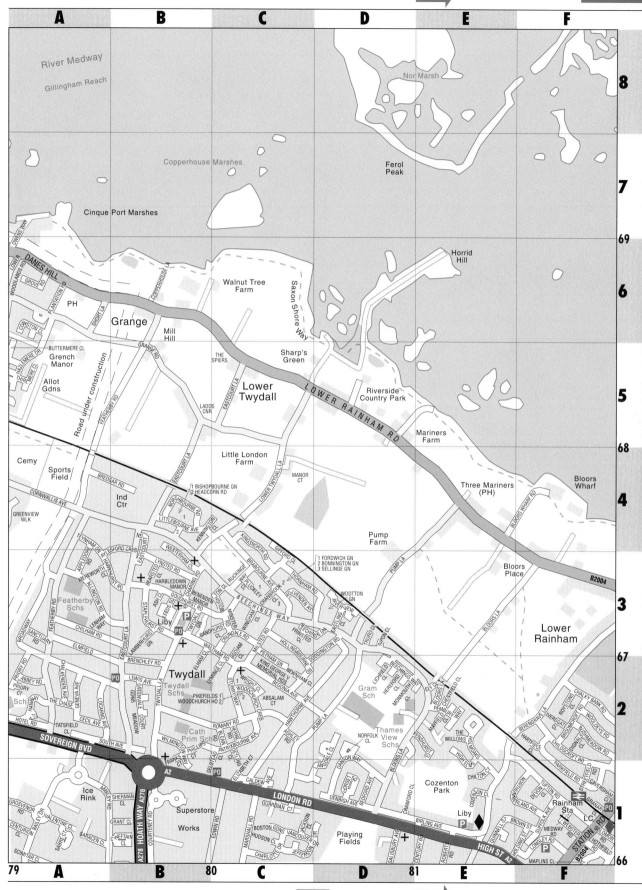

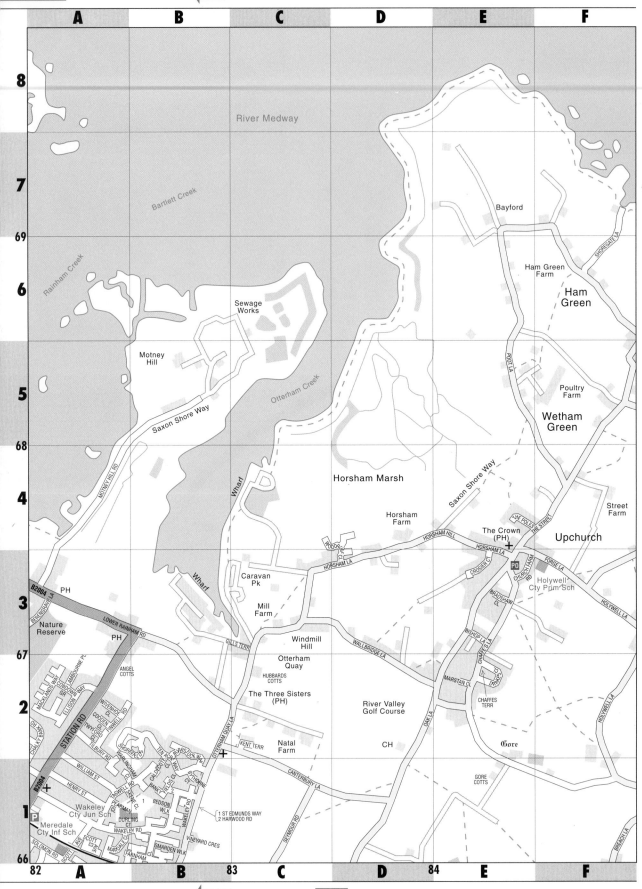

A　　B　　C　　D　　E　　F

8

7

69

6

River Medway

Bartlett Creek

Rainham Creek

Sewage
Works

Motney
Hill

5

Otterham Creek

68

Saxon Shore Way

4

Horsham Marsh

Wharf

Horsham
Farm

Saxon Shore Way

Bayford

Ham Green
Farm

Ham
Green

POOT LA

Poultry
Farm

Wetham
Green

SHOREGATE LA

Street
Farm

Upchurch

THE STREET

Ye Poles St

The Crown
(PH)

HORSHAM HILL

Horsham Hill

HORSHAM LA

CROSIER CT

Holywell
Cty Prim Sch

PO

CHURCH FARM

FORGE LA

HOLYWELL LA

3

B2004

BERENGRAVE LA

PH

Nature
Reserve

PH

LOWER RAINHAM RD

MOTNEY HILL RD

Wharf

WOODS PL

Caravan
Pk

Mill
Farm

Windmill
Hill

Otterham
Quay

WALLBRIDGE LA

BISHOP LA

BRADSHAW CL

CHAFFES LA

MARSTAN CL

OAK LA

TO DINES

67

GILLS TERR

HUBBARDS
COTTS

The Three Sisters
(PH)

River Valley
Golf Course

CHAFFES
TERR

Gore

HOLYWELL LA

2

B2004

STATION RD

MACKLANDS WAY
GR

COBBROWN CL
GR

ELLISON CL

LAMBOURNE PL

ANGEL
COTTS

WIVENHOE RD

GOODES CL
KINNELL CL

PWYFORD CL

TEN ACRE WAY

SHOREFIELD RD

OTTERHAM QUAY LA

KENT TERR

Natal
Farm

CANTERBURY LA

CH

GORE
COTTS

CHALKY RD

ELM BANK RD

TILBURY RD

WARINGHAM RD

CALLDECOTT RD

RESNE CL

BANKY FIELDS CL

BT THORNE

WAKELEY RD

SEYMOUR RD

1

P

Wakeley
Cty Jun Sch

WILLIAM ST

HENRY ST

TASWELL RD

PEARMAN

DURLING
CT

BEDSON
WLK

WAKELEY RD

1 ST EDMUNDS WAY
2 HARWOOD RD

1

2

Meredale
Cty Inf Sch

SOLOMON RD

AVE

SCOTT

SCOTT

MARDALE CL

FARNHAM

SMARDEN WLK

VINEYARD CRES

BROACH LA

66

82　　A　　B　　83　　C　　D　　84　　E　　F

| A | B | C | D | E | F |

Milfordhope Creek

Greenborough Marshes

Slaughterhouse Point

8

Milfordhope Marsh

Stangate Creek

The Shade

7

Twinney Creek

69

Barksore Marshes

River Medway

6

Halstow Creek

Funton Creek

Callows House

Twinney Wharf

5

Twinney Acre

68

FROG FARM COTTS

Saxon Shore Way

Funton Brickworks

Frog Farm

Funton

4

Sewage Works

Saxon Shore Way

Great Barksore Farm

GREENWAYS

Stray Farm

Little Barksore

Tiptree Hill

3

PO

THE GREEN

CURLEW NE

HERON

LAPWING DR

THE STREET

BURNTWICK DR

CLELAND

CROUCH HILL

VICARAGE LA

THE CRESCENT

PH

WESTMOR

Lower Halstow

Holywell

Green Farm

LANDRAIL RD

SCHOOL LA

CUMBERLND DR

67

Tiptree

WESTFIELD COTTS

Elm Farm

2

BREACH LA

Lower Halstow Cty Prim Sch

Callum Hill

STICKFAST LA

The Laurels

WARDWELL LA

Boxted Farm

1

BOXTED LA

HIGH OAK HILL

BELMOR AVE

Great Norwood

Hawes Wood

66

| A | B | C | D | E | F |

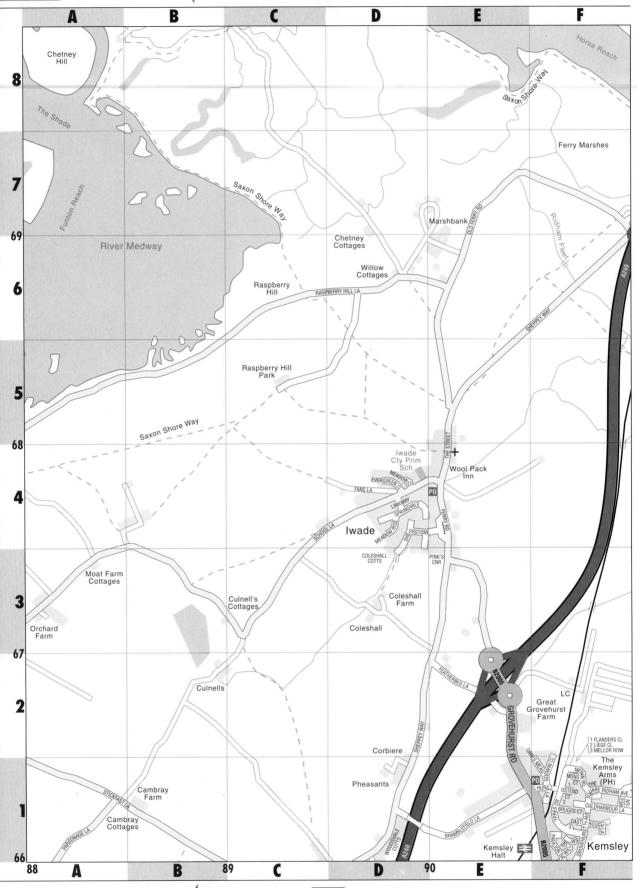

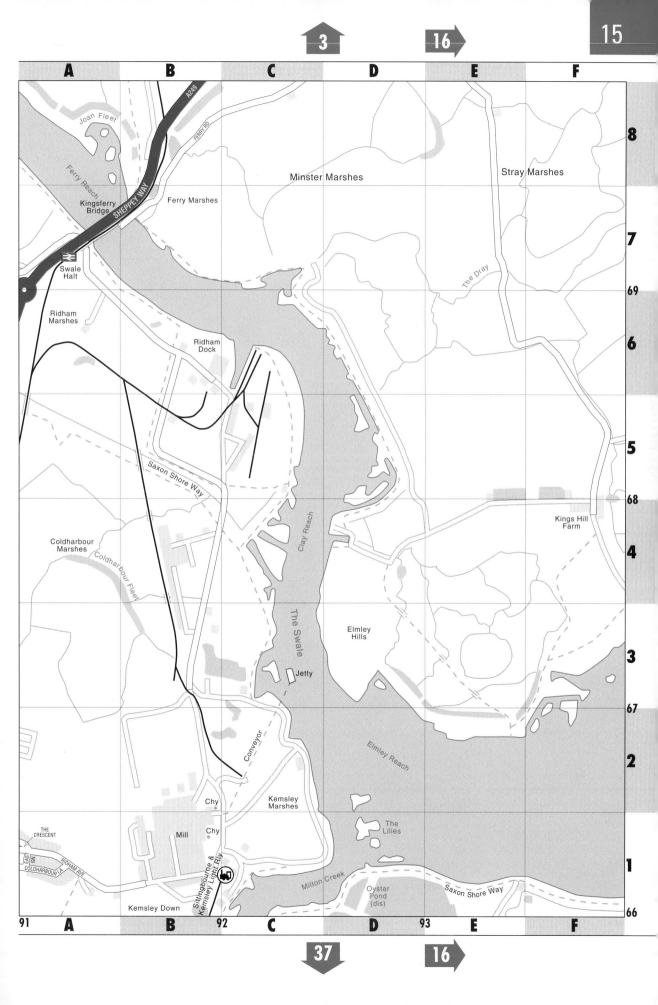

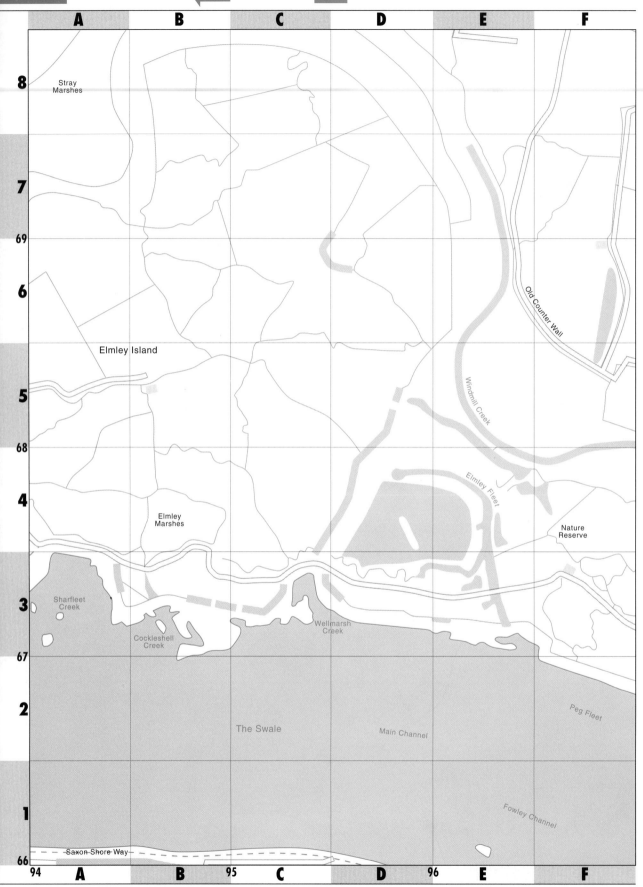

Stray
Marshes

Old Counter Wall

Elmley Island

Windmill Creek

Elmley Fleet

Elmley
Marshes

Nature
Reserve

Sharfleet
Creek

Wellmarsh
Creek

Cockleshell
Creek

Peg Fleet

The Swale

Main Channel

Fowley Channel

Saxon Shore Way

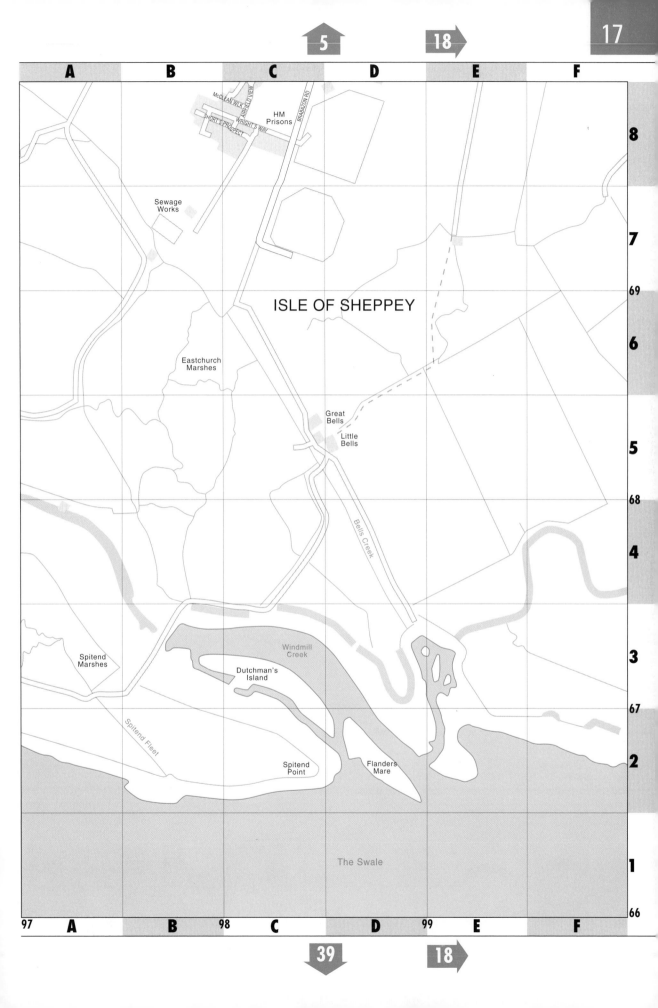

ISLE OF SHEPPEY

17 6

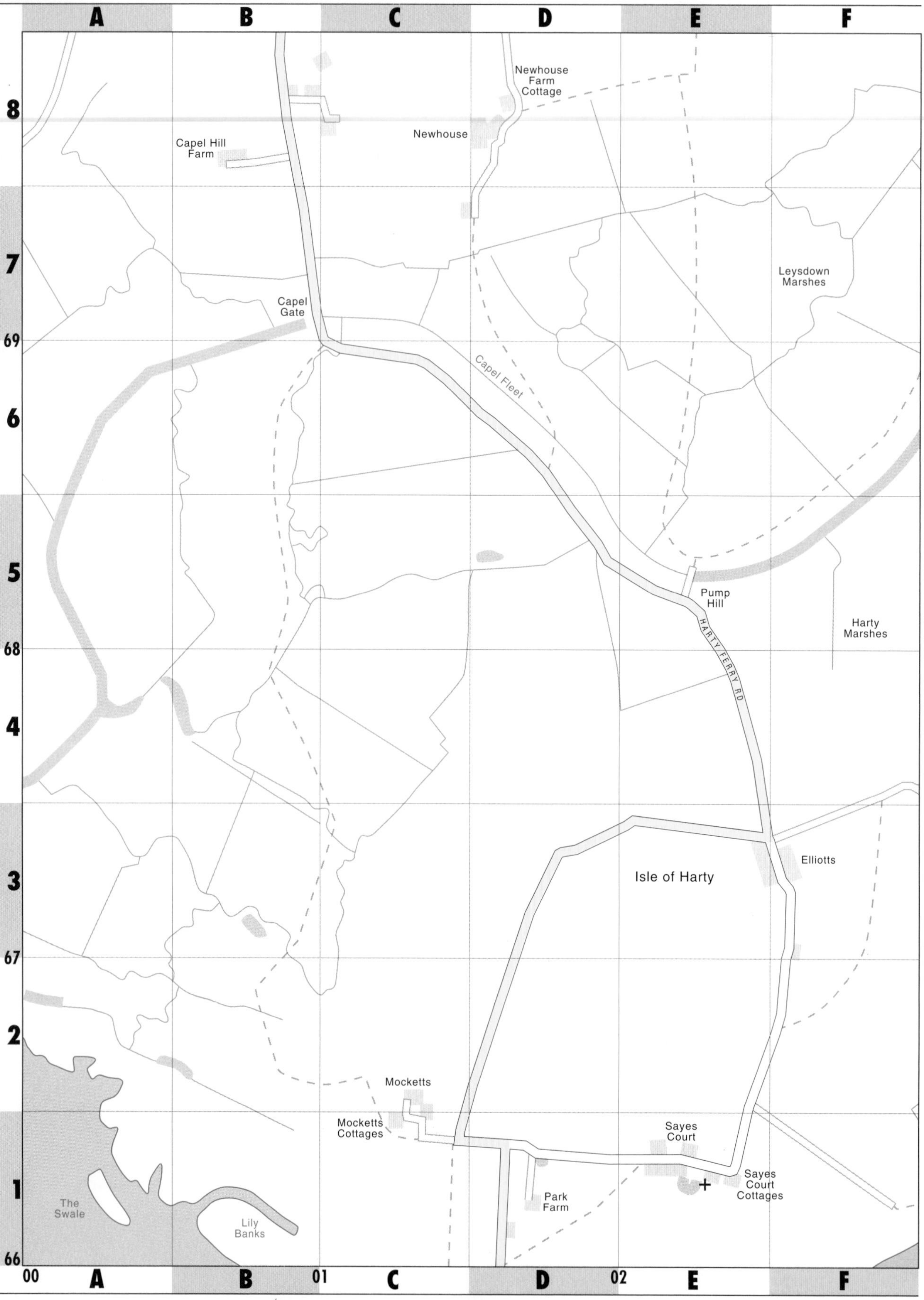
A B C D E F
8
7
69
6
5
68
4
3
67
2
1
66
00
01
02
Newhouse Farm Cottage
Newhouse
Capel Hill Farm
Capel Gate
Leysdown Marshes
Capel Fleet
Pump Hill
HARTY FERRY RD
Harty Marshes
Elliotts
Isle of Harty
Mocketts
Mocketts Cottages
Sayes Court
Sayes Court Cottages
Park Farm
The Swale
Lily Banks

17 40

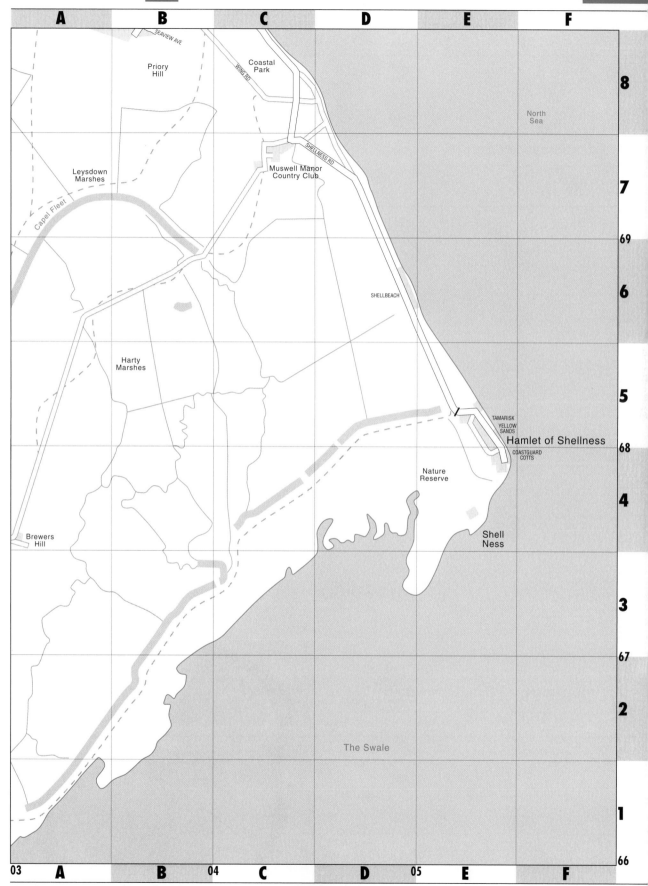

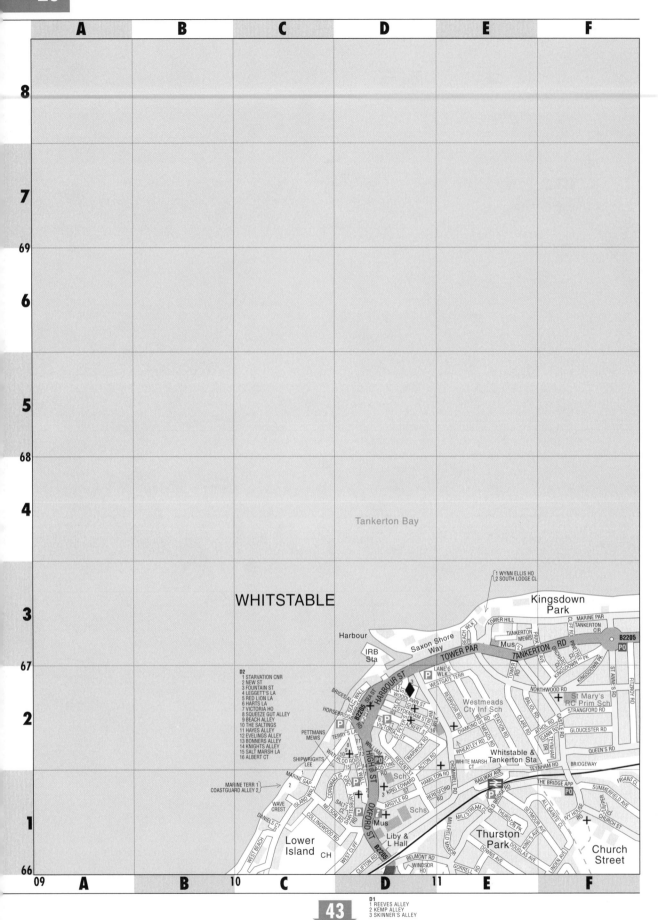

	A	B	C	D	E	F

WHITSTABLE

Tankerton Bay

Kingsdown Park

1 WYNN ELLIS HO
2 SOUTH LODGE CL

Harbour

Saxon Shore Way

TOWER HILL
TANKERTON MEWS

MARINE PAR
TANKERTON CIR

B2205
PO

IRB Sta

TOWER PAR

TANKERTON RD

D2
1 STARVATION CNR
2 NEW ST
3 FOUNTAIN ST
4 LEGGETT'S LA
5 RED LION LA
6 HARTS LA
7 VICTORIA HO
8 SQUEEZE GUT ALLEY
9 BEACH ALLEY
10 THE SALTINGS
11 HAYES ALLEY
12 EVELINGS ALLEY
13 BONNERS ALLEY
14 KNIGHTS ALLEY
15 SALT MARSH LA
16 ALBERT CT

LANE'S WLK
WEST GATE TERR

HARBOUR ST

Westmeads Cty Inf Sch

St Mary's RC Prim Sch

NORTHWOOD RD

STRANGFORD RD

GLOUCESTER RD

PETTMANS MEWS

TERRY'S LA

Whitstable & Tankerton Sta

QUEEN'S RD

SHIPWRIGHTS LEE

WHITE MARSH

BRIDGEWAY

MARINE GAP

MARINE TERR 1
COASTGUARD ALLEY 2

HIGH ST

Schs

RAILWAY AVE

THE BRIDGE APP
PO

WAVE CREST

KING EDWARD ST

Schs

FRIARS CL

SUMMERFIELD AVE

DANIELS CL

ARGYLE RD

Mus

THURSTON PARK

Thurston Park

OXFORD ST

Liby & L Hall

Church Street

WEST BEACH

Lower Island
CH

WEST CLIFF

CLIFTON RD

BELMONT RD

WINDSOR HO

B2205

CHURCH ST

D1
1 REEVES ALLEY
2 KEMP ALLEY
3 SKINNER'S ALLEY

A **B** **C** **D** **E** **F**

8

7

69

6

5

68

4

COASTGUARD
COTTS

Saxon Shore Way

1 LINCOLN CL
2 DELMAR CL
3 SWAKELEY WLK

KITE FARM

Seaview
Caravan & Chalet
Park

MORRIS AVE
AUSTIN AVE
CROSSLEY AVE
HUMBER AVE
SUNBEAM AVE
RILEY AVE
CRESTA CL

Sewage
Works

Swalecliffe

Tankerton

PRIEST & SOW
CNR

MARINE CRES

PLOUGH LA

COLEWOOD RD

WHITSTABLE RD

3

MARINE PAR

TANKERTON
CT

B2205

PRIES

PRINCESS RD

BROOK RD

ST AUGUSTINE RD

EDGAR

RUSSET DR

WOODMAN AVE

TYLER WAY

B2205

PO

P

TANKERTON RD

SEAFIELD RD

HERNE BAY RD

PRINCESS

BROOK CL

EMMERSON GDNS

TASSELL'S

SWALECLIFFE COURT DR

ST JOHN'S RD

GOODWIN AVE

Works

67

ELLIS RD

BENNELLS AVE

ST SWITHIN'S RD

NEWTON RD

BRIDGEFIELD RD

KEMP RD

BURNAN RD

ELM WOOD

ELM WOOD CL

CHURCH WAY

Liby

RECTORY GDNS

Swalecliffe
Cty Prim Sch

BADDLESMERE RD
GRAYSTONE RD
MANOR RD
PIER AVE
LISA CT
NORTHWOOD RD
WYNN RD

H

SOUTHWOOD RD

PALACE

SWALECLIFFE RD

PO

LONGFIELD CL

A299

2

Whitstable &
Tankerton

QUEENS RD

Chestfield & Swalecliffe
Sta

Bodkin
Farm

Purchas
Wood

THANET WAY

REEVES WAY

CH
Superstore

LAVENDER

MAYDOWNS RD

NACHOLS LA

OAKWOOD DR

HAM SHADES LA

FOXGROVE RD

ENTICOTT

CHAUCER AVE

FLETCHER RD

MARLOW CL

HIGHGATE

BECKET

THE HEATH

John Wilson
BSNS PK

HARVEY DR

PRIMROSE WAY

CHESTFIELD RD

SHARE AND COULTER RD

ALMOND

SADDLERS MEWS

CHURCHWOOD DR

May
Downs

1

FRIARS CL
NURSERY CL
HILLSIDE RD
BRIDEWELL PK
CLOVER RISE
RICHMOND RD

RIDGEWAY

LAXTON

FERN CL

GREEN LEAS
THE LEAS
FAIRWAY
BEECHCROFT
LONGACRE

THE RIDINGS
CHARNWOOD

Chestfield

Woodcroft

Ash
Plantation

South
Tankerton

CHURCH ST
BARTLETT RD
GRASMERE RD
A299

Highgate
Lodge

POLO WAY

THE RUSSETS
THE LEAS

MOLEHILL RD

66

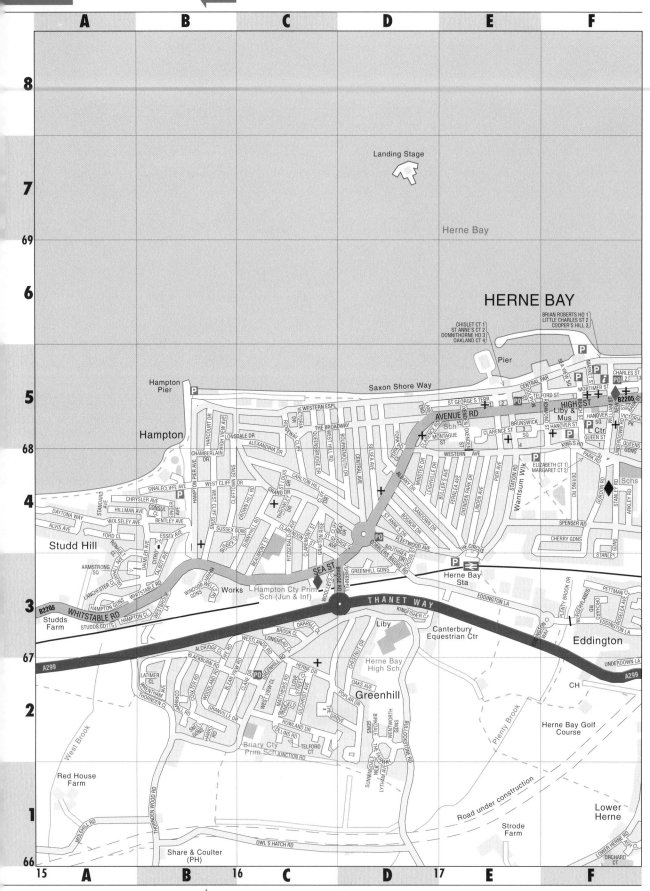

Landing Stage

Herne Bay

HERNE BAY

BRIAN ROBERTS HO 1
LITTLE CHARLES ST 2
COOPER'S HILL 3

CHISLET CT 1
ST ANNE'S CT 2
DONNITHORNE HO 3
OAKLAND CT 4

Pier

Hampton
Pier

Saxon Shore Way

CHARLES ST

Hampton

AVENUE RD
Liby
& Mus
HIGH
ST

Studd Hill

Hampton Cty Prim
Sch (Jun & Inf)

SEA ST

Works

WHITSTABLE RD

B2205

Herne Bay
Sta

Eddington

Studds
Farm

STUDDS COTTS

A299

THANET WAY

Liby

Canterbury
Equestrian Ctr

Greenhill

Herne Bay
High Sch

Herne Bay Golf
Course

Briary Cty
Prim Sch

A299

West Brook

Red House
Farm

Road under construction

Lower
Herne

Strode
Farm

OWL'S HATCH RD

Share & Coulter
(PH)

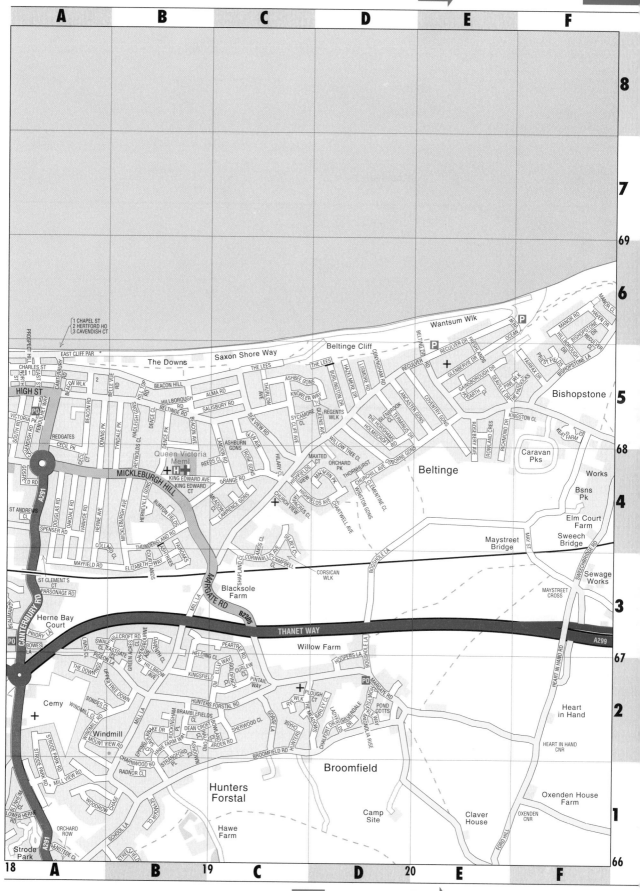

23

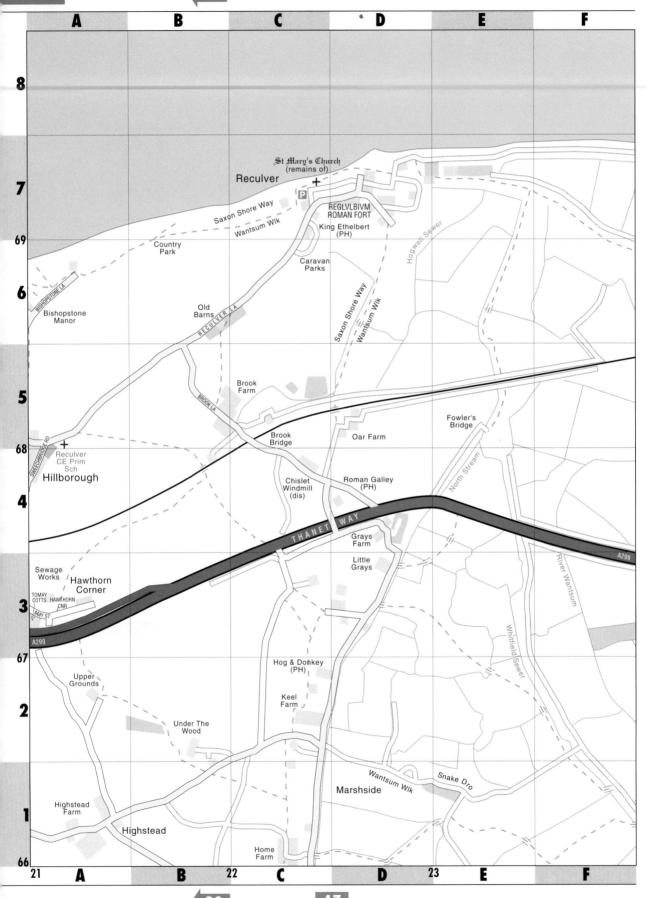

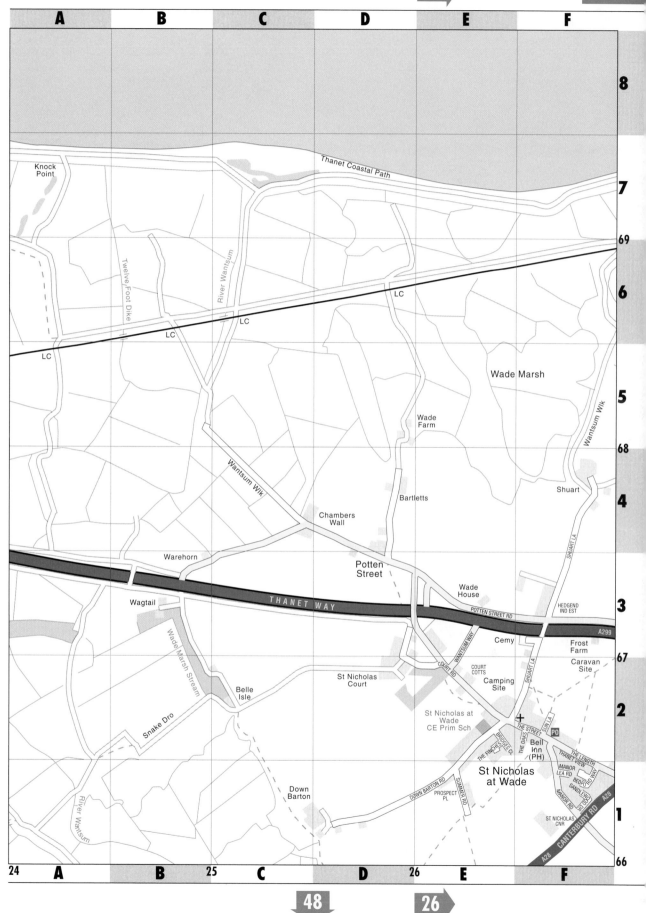

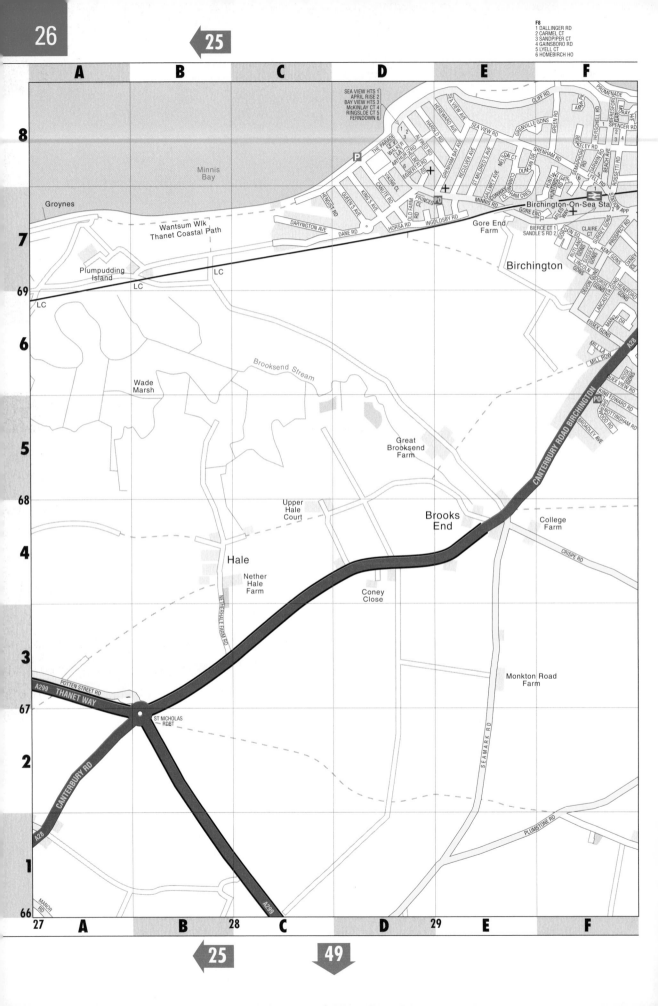

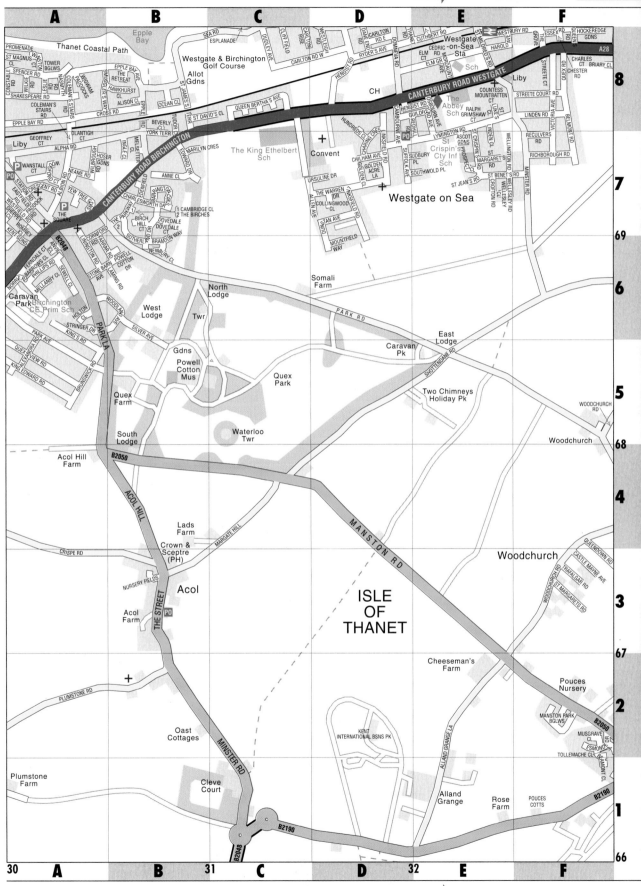

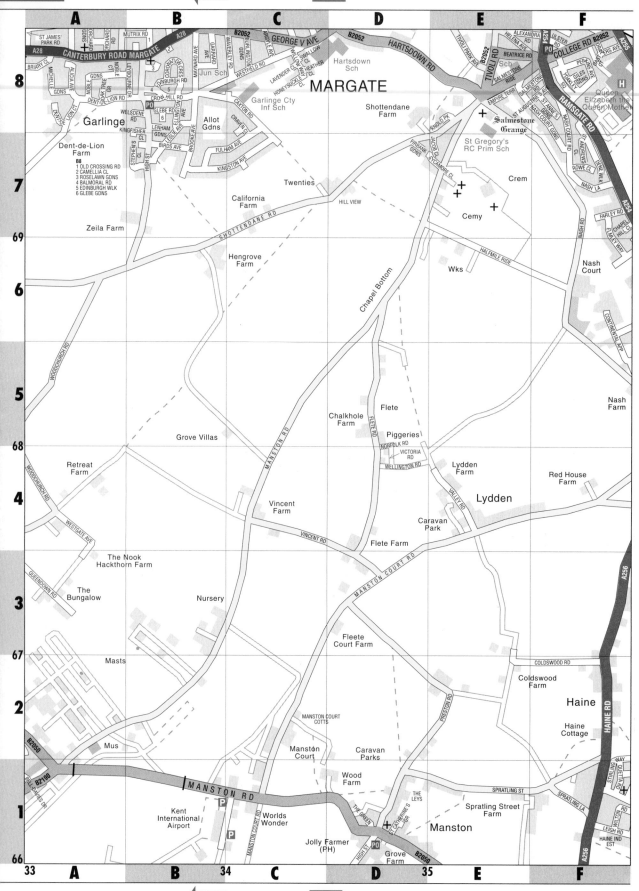

MARGATE

Dent-de-Lion
Farm
B8
1 OLD CROSSING RD
2 CAMELLIA CL
3 ROSELAWN GDNS
4 BALMORAL RD
5 EDINBURGH WLK
6 GLEBE GDNS

Garlinge

Zeila Farm

California
Farm

Twenties

HILL VIEW

Hengrove
Farm

Chapel Bottom

Wks

Nash
Court

Salmestone
Grange

St Gregory's
RC Prim Sch

Crem

Cemy

Nash
Farm

Flete

Chalkhole
Farm

Piggeries

Grove Villas

Retreat
Farm

Vincent
Farm

Lydden
Farm

Lydden

Red House
Farm

Caravan
Park

Flete Farm

The Nook
Hackthorn Farm

Nursery

The
Bungalow

Fleete
Court Farm

Coldswood
Farm

Masts

Haine

Haine
Cottage

Mus

Manston Court
Cotts

Manston
Court

Caravan
Parks

Wood
Farm

Spratling Street
Farm

Kent
International
Airport

Worlds
Wonder

THE
LEYS

Manston

Jolly Farmer
(PH)

Grove
Farm

Haine Ind
Est

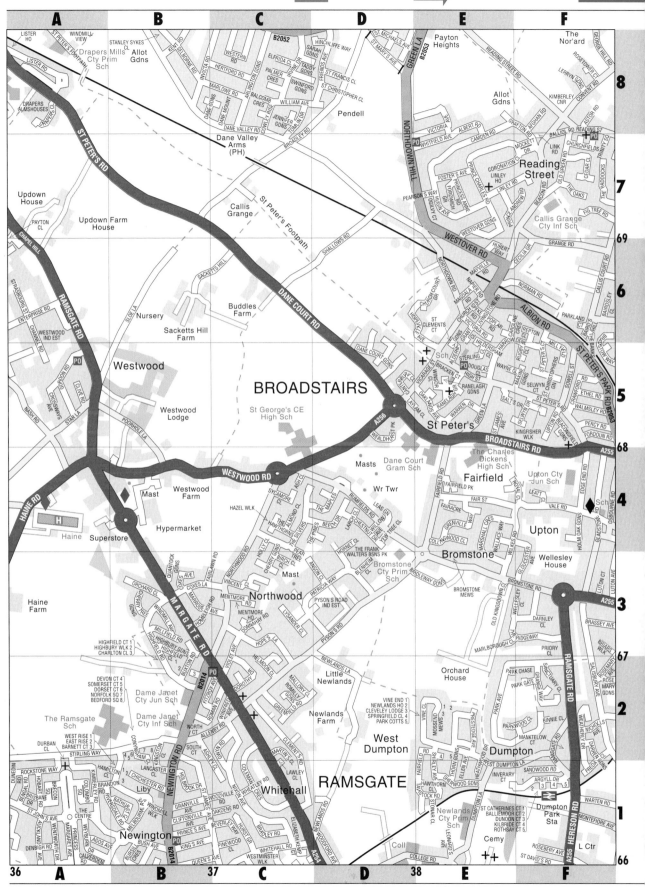

North
Foreland

North Foreland
Golf Course

CH

Kingsgate
Coll

Hunton
House

B2052

NORTH FORELAND HILL

CRESCENT RD

Reading St

Elmwood
Farm

Stella Maris
Convent

Masts

VILLIERS HO 1
YARDLEY HO 2
GLENAVON HO 3
FORELAND PARK HO 4
STONE HO 5

NORTH FORELAND RD

NORTH FORELAND AVE

ST ANNE'S RD

CLIFF PROM

CLIFF RD

The
Foreland
Sch

BISHOP'S AVE

CASTLE AVE

QUEEN'S AVE

KING'S AVE

SEA VIEW RD

LANTHORNE RD

ELIZABETH CT

PLACE GDNS

PARK RD

Stone Bay
Sch

CORNWALLIS
GDNS

KNIGHT'S AVE

STONE RD

WINGS CT

CHEVIOT RD

Thanet Coastal Path

EASTERN ESPL

East Cliff

Mus

1 THANET CL
2 STAINES PL
3 FERN CT

DICKENS RD

WILLOW CT
ROWAN CT

1 LLOYD RD 1
2 CLARENDON MEWS
3 MANOR RD

Broadstairs Sta

Liby

CAERNARVON
GDNS

RECTORY RD

NELSON PL

SHUTTLE RD

COPPERFIELD

BROADSTAIRS

Bleak
House

Slipway

ALBION ST

B4
1 CHURCH RD
2 CHURCH SQ
3 UNION SQ
4 ELDON PL
5 ST MARY'S RD
6 SEAVIEW COTTS
7 PROSPECT PL
8 CROFT'S PL
9 SERENE PL
10 RAGLAN PL
11 DUNDONALD RD
12 SERENE CT
13 CHARLOTTE ST
14 BUCKINGHAM RD
15 CHANDOS SQ
16 CHANDOS RD
17 YORK AVE
18 JUBILEE CT
19 WROTHAM AVE

POTHE BROADWAY

A255

HIGH ST

QUEEN'S RD

YORK ST

B2052

Pier
Mus

Viking
Bay

RAMSGATE RD

A255

Thanet Coll

1 UPPER APPROACH RD
2 APPROACH RD

The
Holy Cross
RC High Sch

Bradstow
Sch

GRANVILLE RD

WEST CLIFF RD

SEAPOINT RD

Louisa Bay

1 GRANVILLE AVE
2 WEST CLIFF AVE
3 QUEENS GDNS
4 CHARLESTON CT
5 SEAVIEW CT

PALMERSTON
AVE

South Cliff

6 VIKING CT
7 BRAESIDE

LEYBOURN
RD

WESTERN ESPL

Dumpton
Point

DUMPTON PARK DR

DUMPTON GAP RD

MINSTER CL

Gap House
Sch

Dumpton
Bay

SEACROFT RD

SOUTH CLIFF PAR

DETLING AVE

CLIFFSIDE DR

OCEAN VIEW

Holy Trinity
CE Prim
Sch

MONTEFIORE AVE

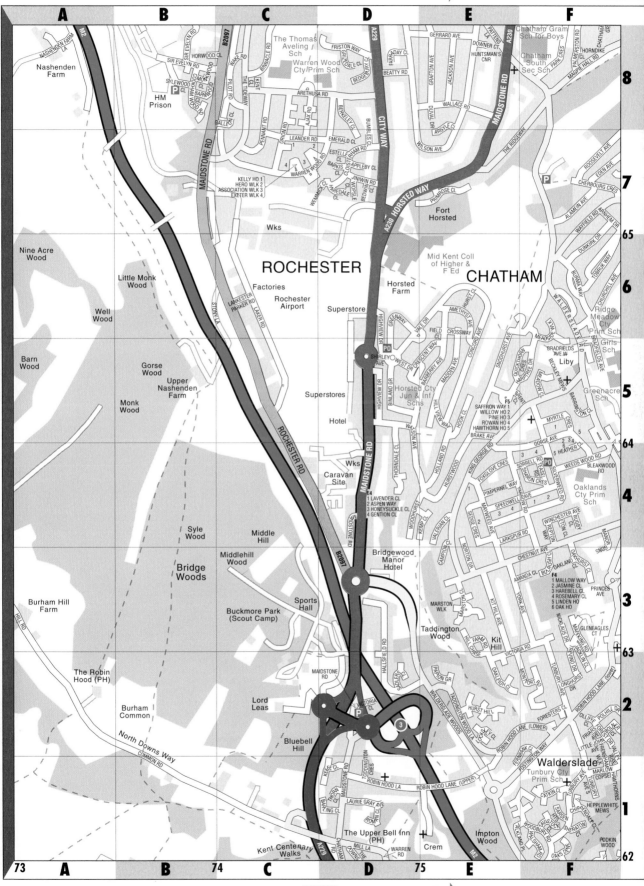

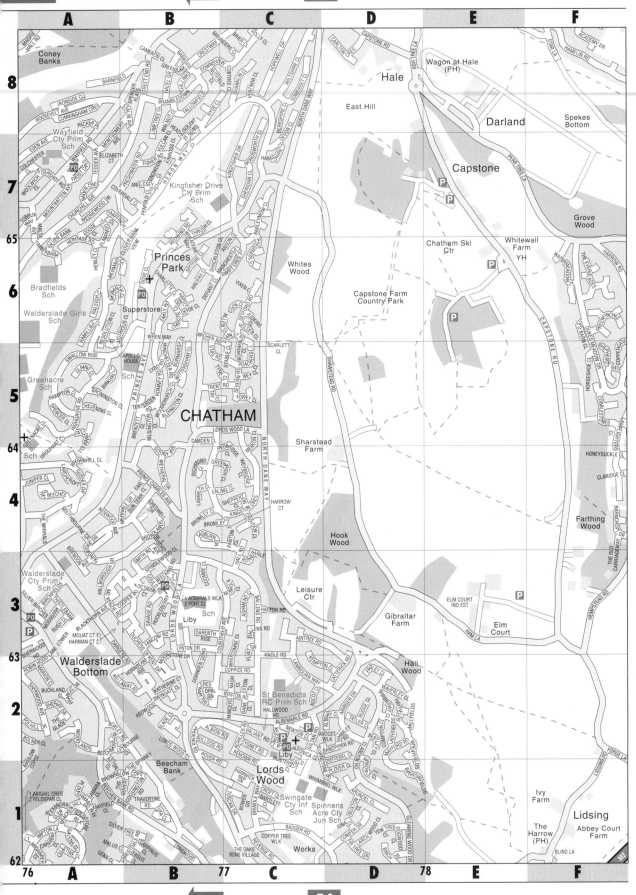

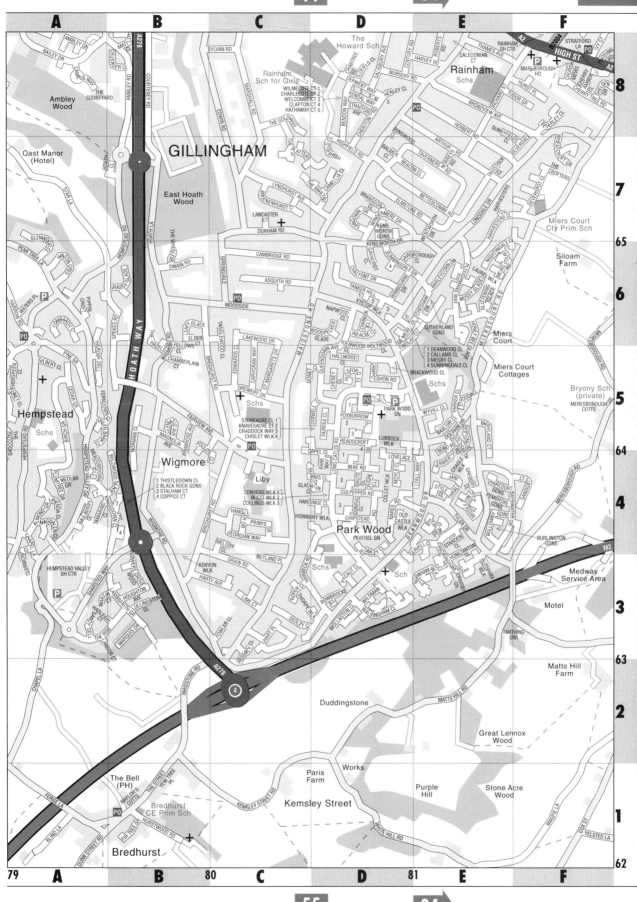

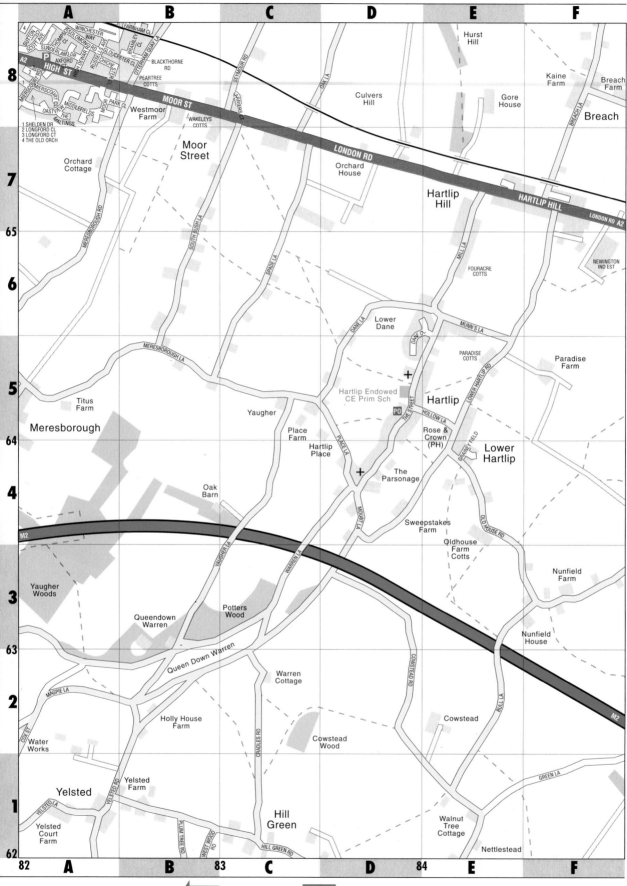

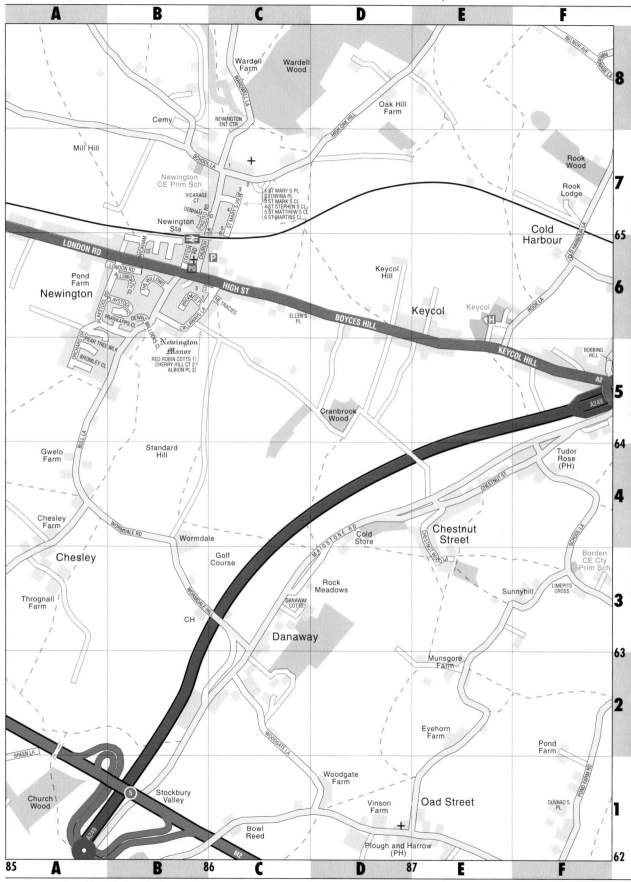

A **B** **C** **D** **E** **F**

8

Wardell Farm
Wardell Wood

Oak Hill Farm

HIGH OAK HILL

BELNOR AVE

Rook Wood

7

Cemy

NEWINGTON ENT CTR

WARDELL LA

Rook Lodge

Mill Hill

SCHOOL LA

Newington CE Prim Sch

VICARAGE CT

1 ST MARY'S PL
2 EDWINA PL
3 ST MARK'S CL
4 ST STEPHEN'S CL
5 ST MATTHEW'S CL
6 ST MARTINS CL

Cold Harbour

65

OLD HARBOUR LA

DENHAM RD

HALSTED RD

ST MARY'S VIEW

Newington Sta

LONDON RD

WICKHAM CL

CHURCH LA

STATION RD

PO

P

HIGH ST

Keycol Hill

6

Pond Farm

Newington

ALLSWORTH RD

LONDON RD

THE WILLOWS

PLAYSTOOL RD

BROCK'S PL

THE TRACIES

2

3

THE TRACIES

ELLEN'S PL

BOYCES HILL

Keycol

Keycol

H

ROOK LA

PLAYSTOOL RD

PLUMSTOOL RD

FRANKAPPS CL

DENWG

WILLOWS CL

CALLAWAYS LA

Newington Manor

RED ROBIN COTTS 1
CHERRY HILL CT 2
ALBION PL 3

KEYCOL HILL

BOBBING HILL

A2

ORCHARD DR

PEAR TREE WLK

BROMLEY CL

Cranbrook Wood

A249

5

Gwelo Farm

BULLA LA

Standard Hill

Tudor Rose (PH)

64

CHESTNUT ST

4

Chesley Farm

WORMDALE RD

Wormdale

MAIDSTONE RD

Cold Store

CHESTNUT WD LA

Chestnut Street

SCHOOL LA

Borden CE Cty Prim Sch

Chesley

Golf Course

Sunnyhill

LIMEPITS CROSS

3

Thrognall Farm

WORMDALE HILL

CH

Rock Meadows

DANAWAY COTTS

Danaway

Munsgore Farm

63

2

Eyehorn Farm

Pond Farm

POND FARM RD

GREEN LA

WOODGATE LA

5

Church Wood

Stockbury Valley

A249

Woodgate Farm

Vinson Farm

Oad Street

DUVARD'S PL

1

Bowl Reed

M2

Plough and Harrow (PH)

62

A **B** **C** **D** **E** **F**

85   86   87

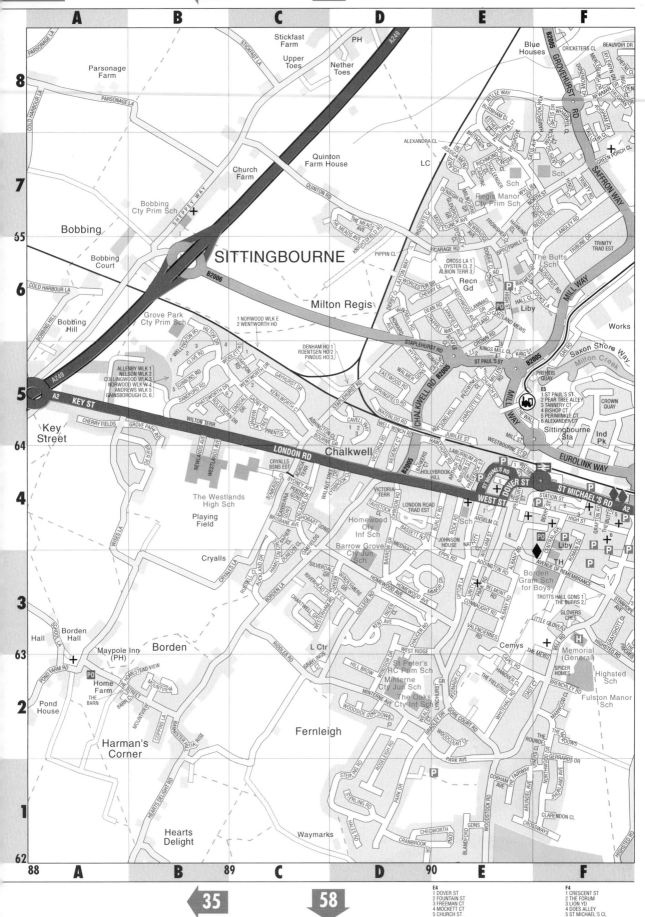

SITTINGBOURNE

E4
1 DOVER ST
2 FOUNTAIN ST
3 FREEMAN ST
4 MOCKETT CT
5 CHURCH ST
6 PEMBURY CT
7 THE CLOISTERS
8 MIDDLETON CT

F4
1 CRESCENT ST
2 THE FORUM
3 LION YD
4 DOES ALLEY
5 ST MICHAEL'S CL
6 BANKS YD

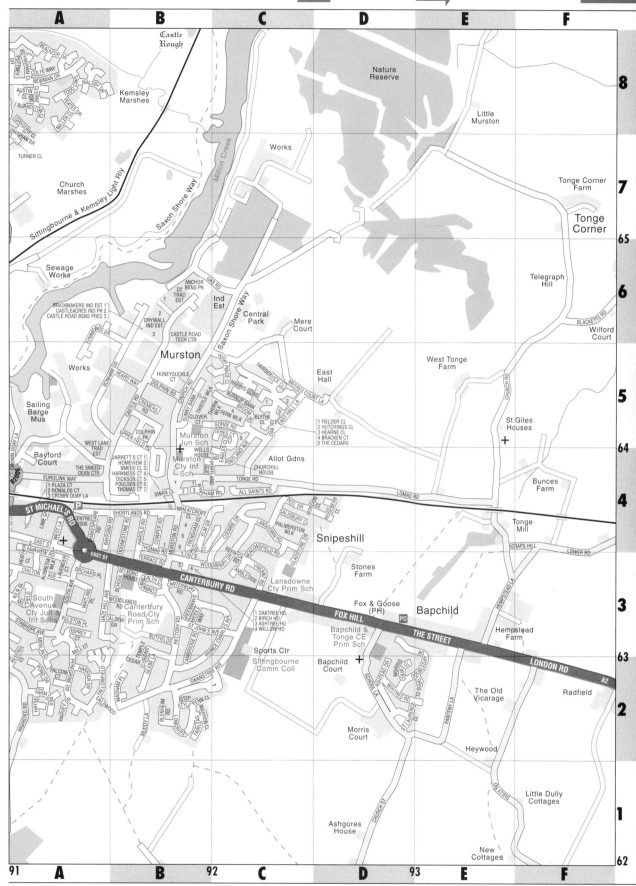

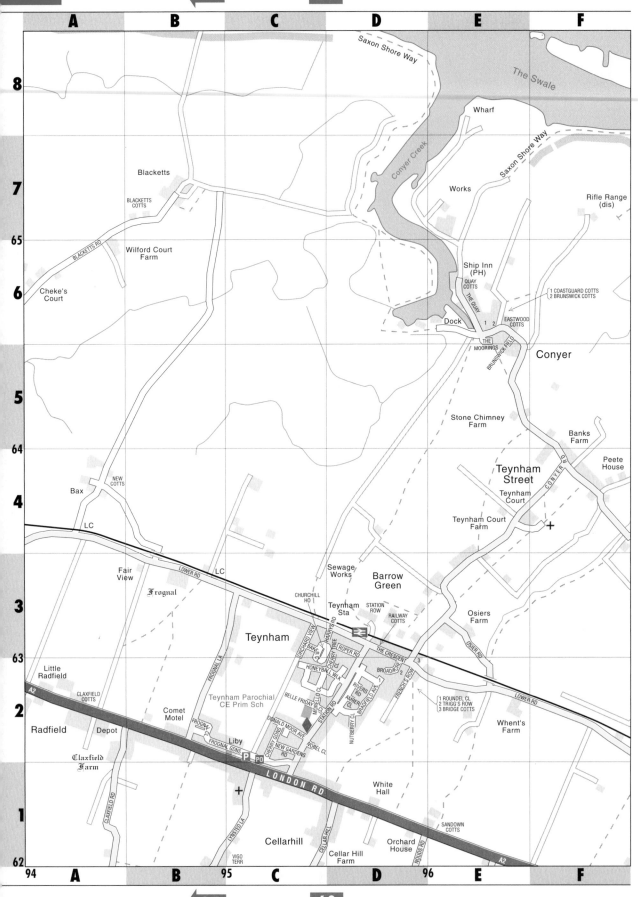

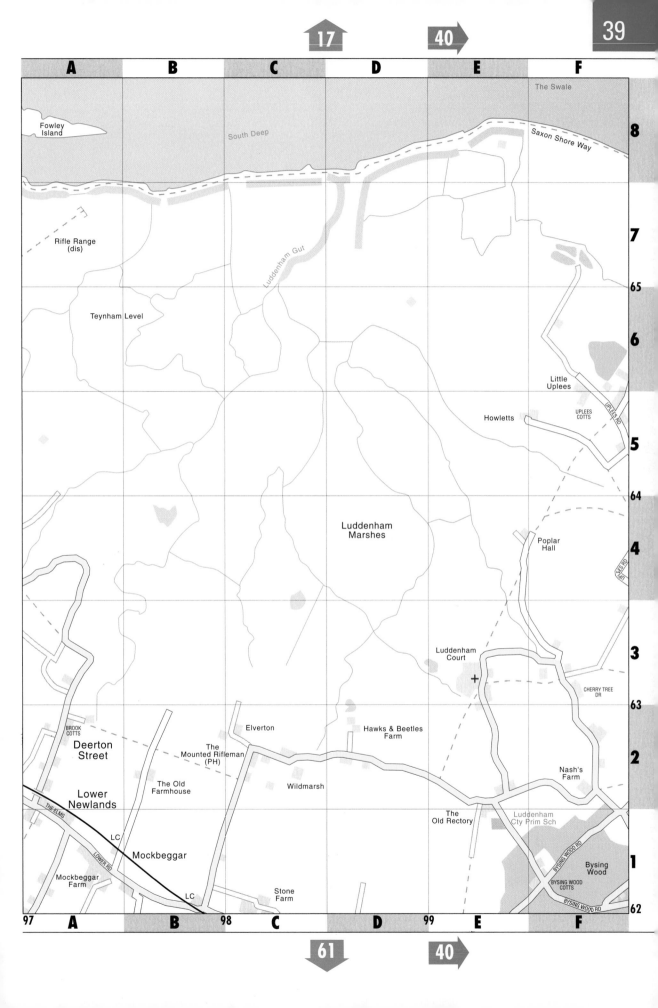

The Swale

Fowley Island

South Deep

Saxon Shore Way

8

Rifle Range (dis)

7

Luddenham Gut

65

Teynham Level

6

Little Uplees

UPLEES COTTS

UPLEES RD

Howletts

5

64

Luddenham Marshes

Poplar Hall

4

UPLEES RD

Luddenham Court

3

+

CHERRY TREE DR

63

BROOK COTTS

Elverton

Hawks & Beetles Farm

Nash's Farm

2

Deerton Street

The Mounted Rifleman (PH)

Lower Newlands

The Old Farmhouse

Wildmarsh

The Old Rectory

Luddenham Cty Prim Sch

THE ELMS

LC

Mockbeggar

LUDDENHAM WOOD RD

Bysing Wood

1

LOWER RD

Mockbeggar Farm

Stone Farm

LC

BYSING WOOD COTTS

62

BYSING WOOD RD

39
18

A B C D E F

8

The Ferry Inn
(PH)

HARTY FERRY RD

7

Uplees
Marshes

The Swale

65

6

Gate House
Bungalow

Nature
Reserve

Saxon Shore Way

5

Oare
Marshes

Nagden
Marshes

64

HARTY
FERRY
COTTS

UPLEES RD

4

Broomfield
Farm

Court
Lodge
Farm

Norman's
Hill

Shipwright's
Arms
(PH)

Faversham Creek

UPLEES RD

Hollowshore

3

CHURCH RD

Pheasant
Farm

Oare Creek

Wharf

Ham
Marshes

Oare

RUSSEL PL

Works

63

HARRISON
TERR

COLEGATES CT

PO

COLEGATES RD

PH

THE STREET

Ham Farm

2

COLEGATES RD

MOUNT PLEASANT

B2045

Works

Gravel
Works

JOHN HALL CL

Piggery

SEAGAR RD

Windmill
(dis)

ORE RD

Gate
House

HAM RD

FAVERSHAM

Saxon Shore Way

1

WESTERN LINK

Works

MAITLAND CT

WYGHT CT

WELLS WAY

SHERWOOD

The
Brents

GOLDFINCH CL

FOSTALL RD

SPRINGHEAD RD

LARKSFIELD RD

BROCK RD

UPPER BRENTS

BRENTS
IND EST

Wharf

Faversham Creek

Works

Sewage
Works

62

BYSING WOOD RD

B2045

WILDISH

IVORY CL

BLAXLAND CL

JOHNSON CL

BYSING WOOD RD

CHURCHILL WAY

Davington
Cty Prim
Sch

ABBEY FIELDS

00 A B 01 C D 02 E F

39
62

41

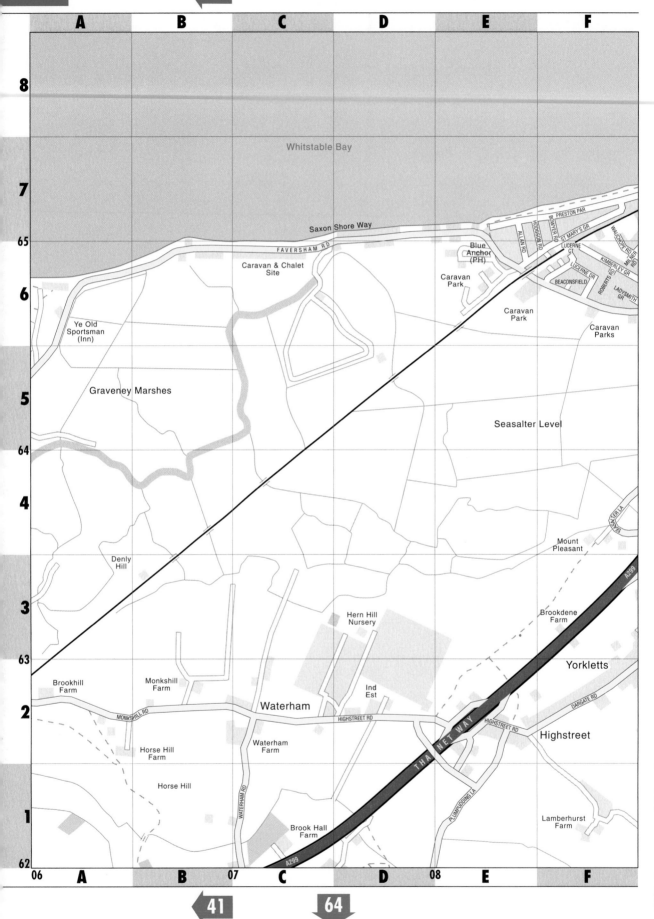

8

7

65

Whitstable Bay

Saxon Shore Way

FAVERSHAM RD

Caravan & Chalet
Site

Blue
Anchor
(PH)

PRESTON PAR

ALLAN RD

HODGSON RD

BOWYER RD

ST MARY'S GR

LUCERNE
CT

LUCERNE DR

BEACONSFIELD

KIMBERLEY GR

ROBERTS RD

WALMORE RD

RIDER
MILL RD

LADYSMITH
GR

6

Caravan
Park

Caravan Park

Caravan
Parks

Ye Old
Sportsman
(Inn)

Graveney Marshes

5

Seasalter Level

64

4

Denly
Hill

Mount
Pleasant

SEASALTER LA

A299

3

Hern Hill
Nursery

Brookdene
Farm

63

Yorkletts

Brookhill
Farm

Monkshill
Farm

Ind
Est

Waterham

THANET WAY

HIGHSTREET RD

DARGATE RD

2

MONKSHILL RD

HIGHSTREET RD

Highstreet

Horse Hill
Farm

Waterham
Farm

WATERHAM RD

PLUMPUDDING LA

1

Horse Hill

Brook Hall
Farm

Lamberhurst
Farm

62

A299

41   64

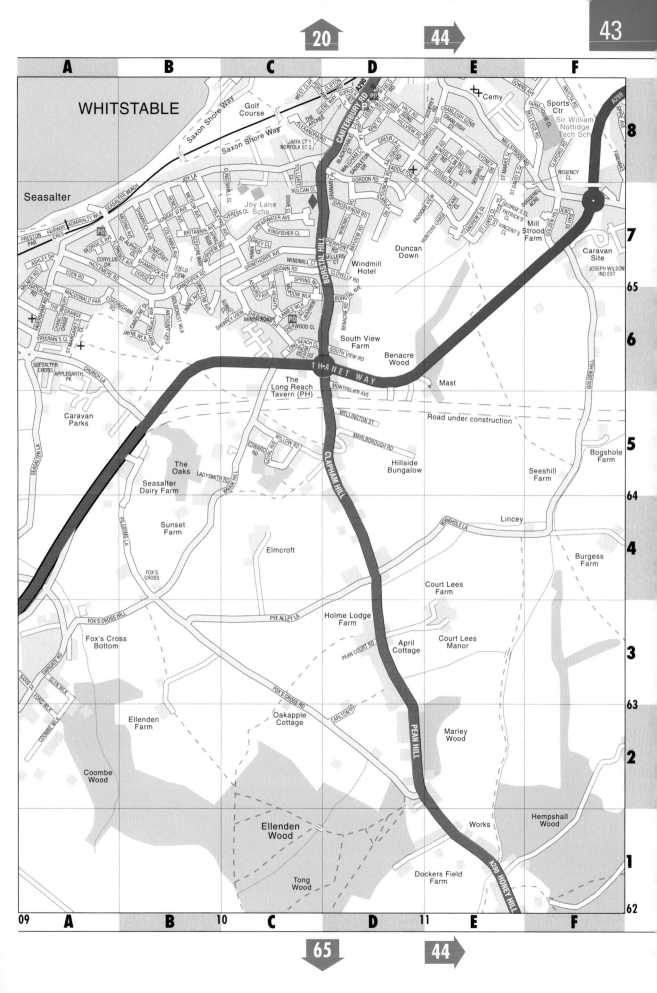

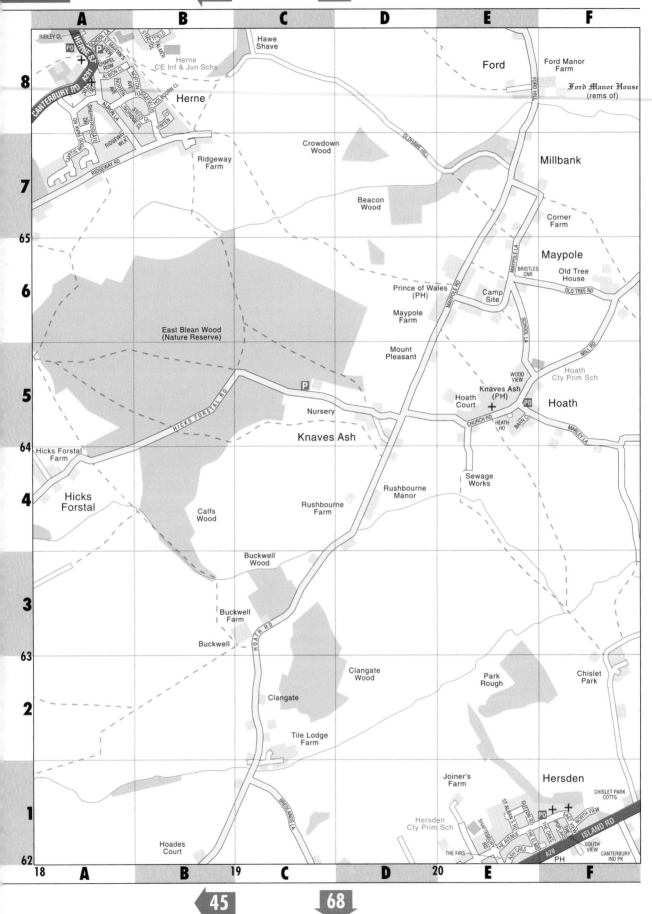

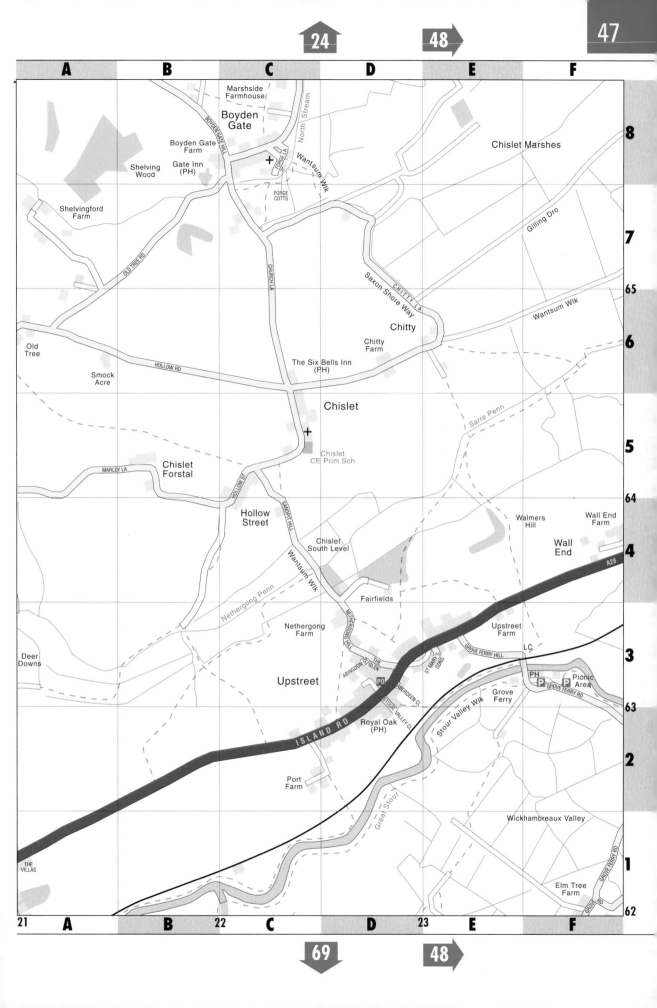

A B C D E F

8
7
65
6
5
64
4
3
63
2
1
62

Marshside Farmhouse

Boyden Gate

Boyden Gate Farm

Gate Inn (PH)

Shelving Wood

Shelvingford Farm

North Stream

Forge La

Forge Cotts

Boyden Gate Hill

Wantsum Wlk

Chislet Marshes

Gilling Dro

Church La

Old Tree Rd

Chitty La

Saxon Shore Way

Wantsum Wlk

Chitty

Old Tree

Smock Acre

Hollow Rd

The Six Bells Inn (PH)

Chitty Farm

Chislet

Sarre Penn

Marley La

Chislet Forstal

Chislet CE Prim Sch

Hollow St

Hollow Street

Sandpit Hill

Chislet South Level

Walmers Hill

Wall End Farm

Wall End

A28

Wantsum Wlk

Nethergong Penn

Fairfields

Deer Downs

Nethergong Hill

Nethergong Farm

The Abingdon Glen

St Glen

Upstreet

St Mary's Gdns

Upstreet Farm

Grove Ferry Hill

LC

PH
P
P
Picnic Area

Grove Ferry Rd

Grove Ferry

Island Rd

PO

Aberdeen Cl

Stour Valley Cl

Royal Oak (PH)

Stour Valley Wlk

63

Port Farm

Great Stour

Wickhambreaux Valley

The Villas

Elm Tree Farm

Grove Ferry Rd

Grove Ferry Rd

21 22 23

47 25

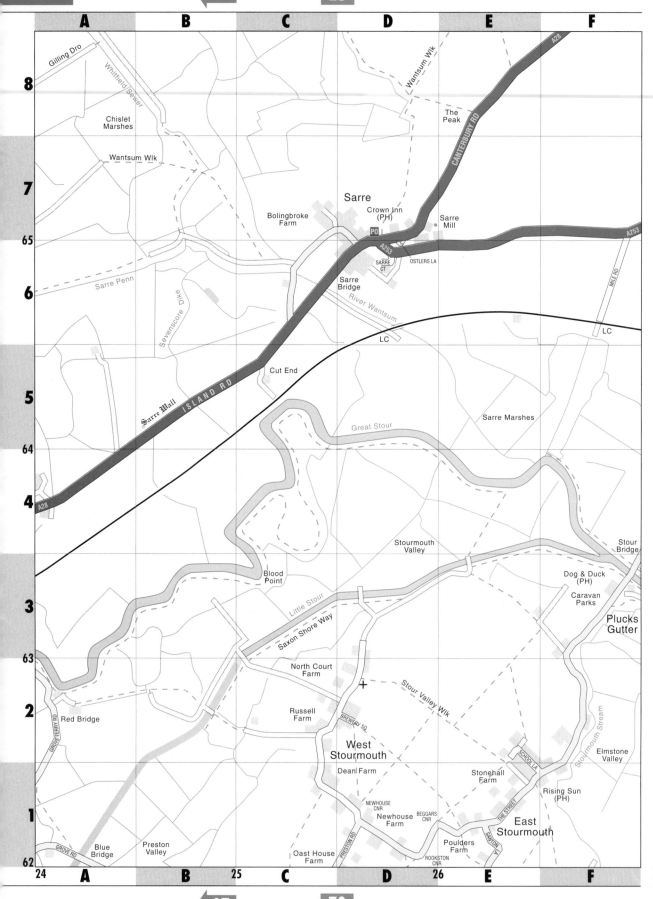

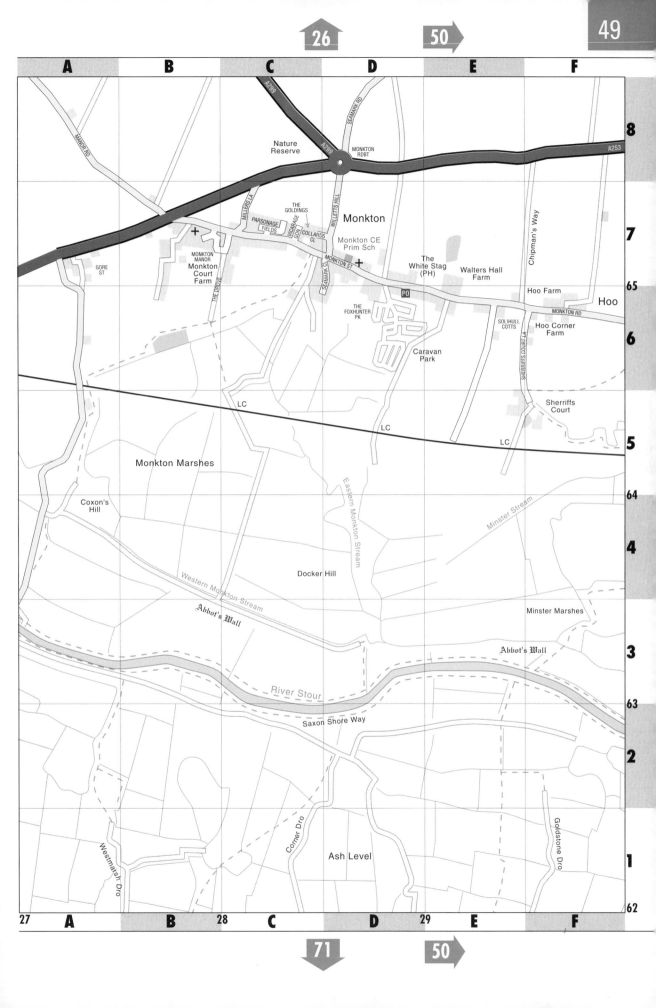

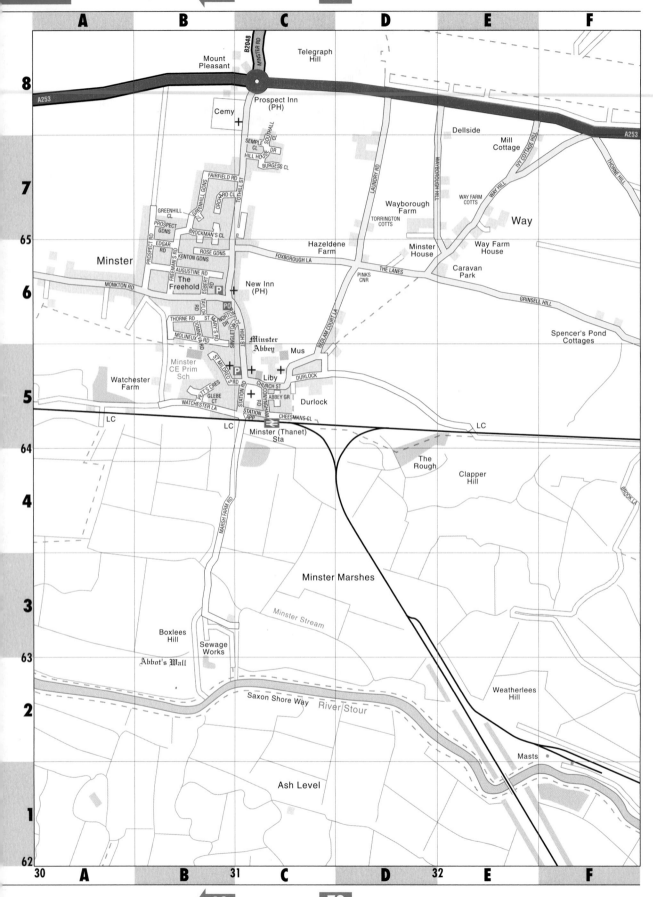

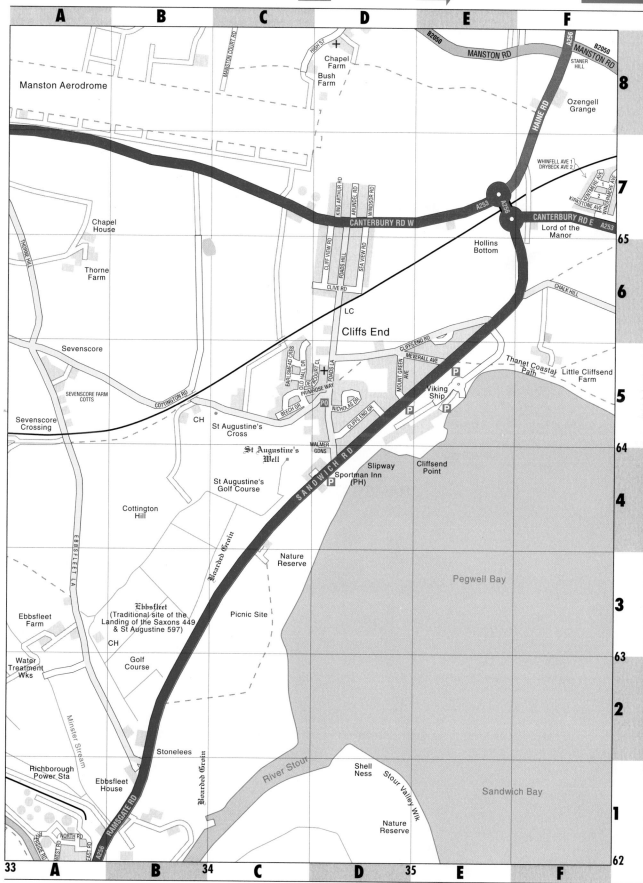

B2050 MANSTON RD A256 B2050 MANSTON RD

STANER HILL

8

Manston Aerodrome

Chapel Farm

Bush Farm

High St

Ozengell Grange

HAINE RD

Chapel House

Thorne Hill

King Arthur Rd

Arundel Rd

Windsor Rd

WHINFELL AVE 1
DRYBECK AVE 2

KENTMERE AVE

WINDERMERE AVE

KIRKSTONE AVE

7

CANTERBURY RD W A253 A256 CANTERBURY RD E A253

Thorne Farm

Cliff View Rd

Roads Hill

Sea View Rd

Clive Rd

Hollins Bottom

Lord of the Manor

65

CHALK HILL

6

Sevenscore

LC

Cliffs End

Cliffs End Rd

Meverall Ave

Thanet Coastal Path

Little Cliffsend Farm

Sevenscore Farm Cotts

Sevenscore Crossing

Cottington Rd

Earlsmead Cres

Old Hall Dr

Old Dell

Court Cl

Primrose Way

Foads La

Mount Green Ave

Viking Ship

P

P

P

5

CH

St Augustine's Cross

Beech Gr

Nicholas Dr

Cliffs End Gr

64

St Augustine's Well

Walmer Gdns

Sandwich Rd

Sportman Inn (PH)

Slipway

Cliffsend Point

St Augustine's Golf Course

PO

P

Cottington Hill

Boarded Groin

Nature Reserve

Pegwell Bay

4

Ebbsfleet
(Traditional site of the Landing of the Saxons 449 & St Augustine 597)

Picnic Site

3

Ebbsfleet Farm

CH

Golf Course

63

Water Treatment Wks

2

Minster Stream

Stonelees

Boarded Groin

River Stour

Shell Ness

Stour Valley Wlk

Sandwich Bay

1

Richborough Power Sta

Ebbsfleet House

RAMSGATE RD

A256

Nature Reserve

WEST RD

NORTH RD

EAST RD

62

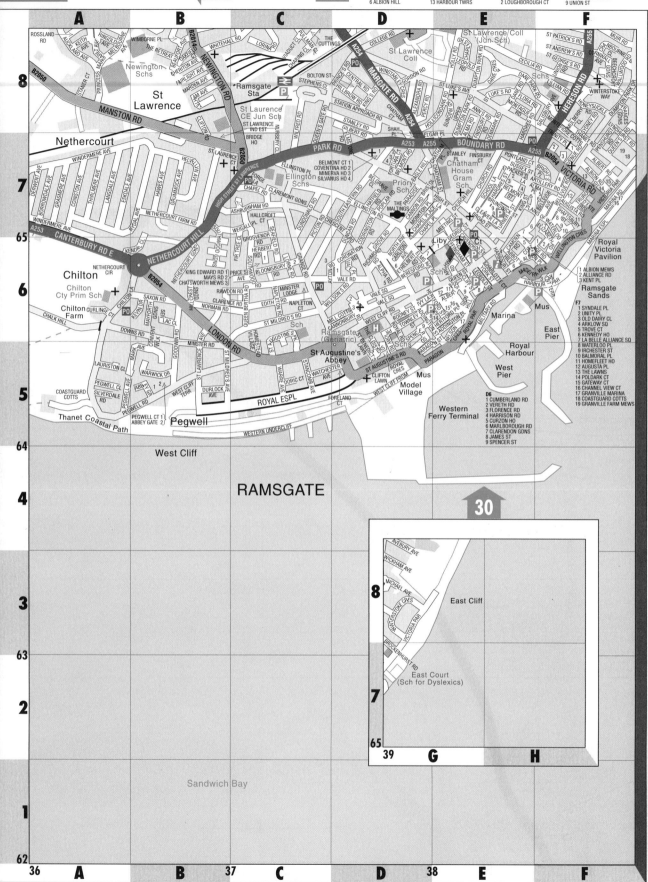

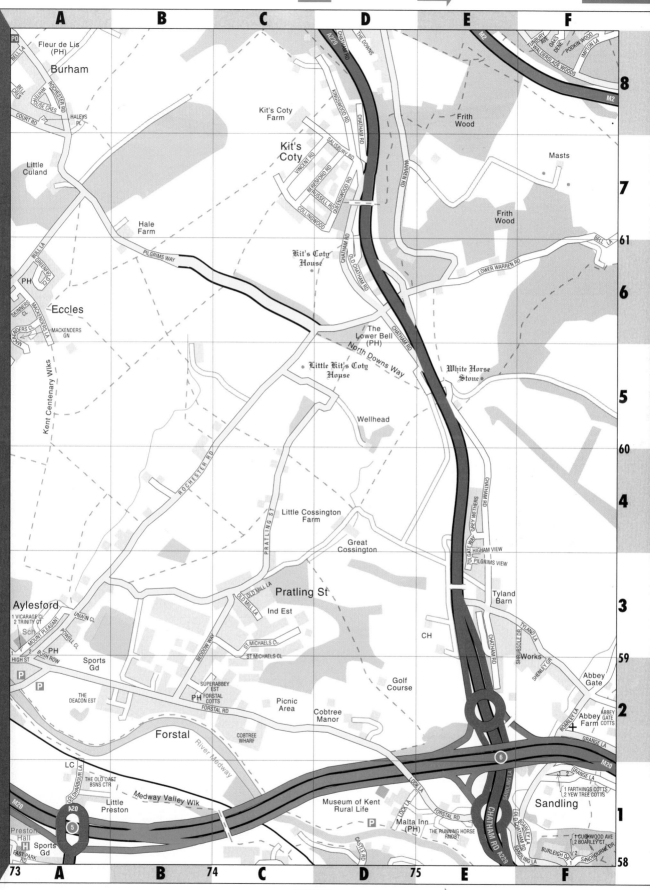

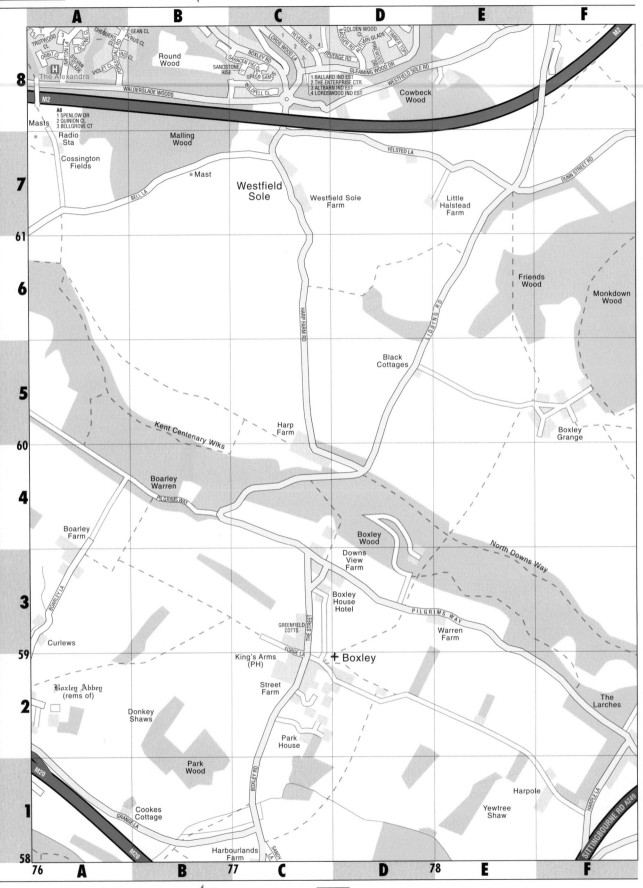

A   B   C   D   E   F

8

The Alexandra
The Alexandra

2 Trotwood Cl
1 Orbit Cl
Clare Cl
Chequers Cl
Pyrus Cl
Gean Cl
Hampton La
Sylvan Cl
Forestdale Rd
Violet Cl
Iris Cl
Clare Cl

Round
Wood

Saracen Field
Sandstone
Rise
Green Sand
Wildfell Cl

Lords Wood La
Boxley Rd
Revenge Rd
Golden Wood Cl
Badger Rd
Autumn Glade
Timber Tops
Pinewood Dr
Revenge Rd
Gleaming Wood Dr
Westfield Sole Rd

1 BALLARD IND EST
2 THE ENTERPRISE CTR
3 ALTBARN IND EST
4 LORDSWOOD IND EST

Cowbeck
Wood

M2

WALDERSLADE WOODS

M2

A8
1 SPENLOW DR
2 QUINION CL
3 BELLGROVE CT

Masts

Radio
Sta

Malling
Wood

YELSTED LA

DUNN STREET RD

Cossington
Fields

7

• Mast

BELL LA

**Westfield
Sole**

Westfield Sole
Farm

LIDSING RD

Little
Halstead
Farm

Friends
Wood

Monkdown
Wood

61

6

HARP FARM RD

Black
Cottages

Boxley
Grange

5

Kent Centenary Wlks

Harp
Farm

60

Boarley
Warren

4

PILGRIMS WAY

Boxley
Wood

North Downs Way

Boarley
Farm

BOARLEY LA

Downs
View
Farm

Boxley
House
Hotel

PILGRIMS WAY

Warren
Farm

3

Curlews

Greenfield
Cotts

THE STREET

FORGE LA

59

King's Arms
(PH)

+ **Boxley**

Boxley Abbey
(rems of)

2

Donkey
Shaws

Street
Farm

The
Larches

Park
House

BOXLEY RD

M20

Park
Wood

Harpole

1

M20

Cookes
Cottage

GRANGE LA

Yewtree
Shaw

HARP LE LA

SITTINGBOURNE RD A249

58

76   A   B   77   C   D   78   E   F

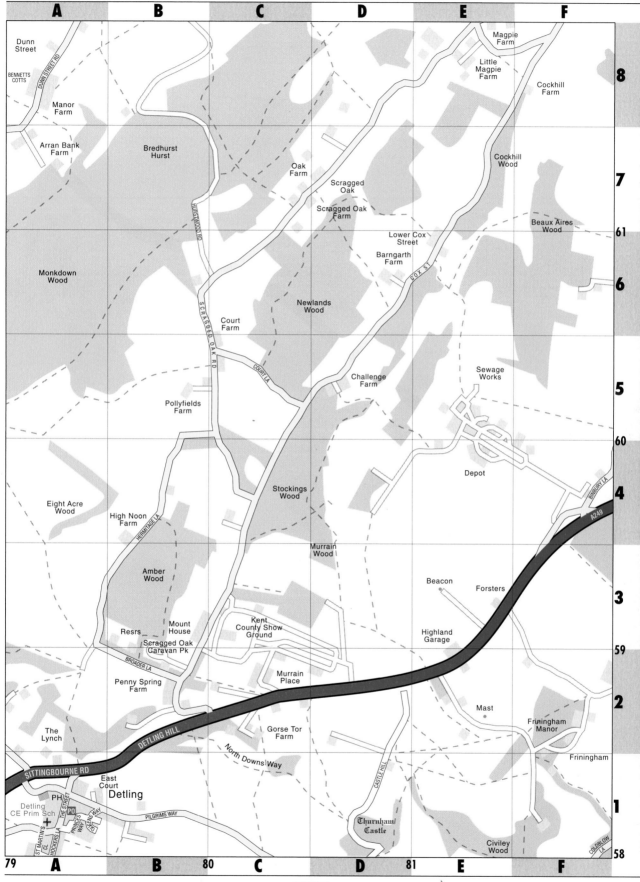

A B C D E F

8

Dunn
Street

BENNETTS
COTTS

Manor
Farm

Arran Bank
Farm

Bredhurst
Hurst

Oak
Farm

Scragged
Oak

Scragged Oak
Farm

Magpie
Farm

Little
Magpie
Farm

Cockhill
Farm

Cockhill
Wood

Beaux Aires
Wood

7

61

Monkdown
Wood

Court
Farm

Newlands
Wood

Lower Cox
Street

Barngarth
Farm

COX ST

6

Pollyfields
Farm

Challenge
Farm

Sewage
Works

5

60

Eight Acre
Wood

High Noon
Farm

Stockings
Wood

Murrain
Wood

Depot

BINBURY LA

A249

4

Amber
Wood

Beacon

Forsters

3

Resrs

Mount
House

Scragged Oak
Caravan Pk

Kent
County Show
Ground

Highland
Garage

59

BROADER LA

Penny Spring
Farm

Murrain
Place

Mast

Friningham
Manor

Friningham

2

The
Lynch

DETLING HILL

Gorse Tor
Farm

North Downs Way

CASTLE HILL

1

SITTINGBOURNE RD

East
Court

Detling

Pilgrims Way

Thurnham
Castle

Civiley
Wood

COLDBLOW LA

58

PH

Detling
CE Prim Sch

ST MARTIN'S CL

HOCKERS

PRINCES WAY

THE STREET

PO

THE SEED WAY

PILGRIMS WAY

79 A B 80 C D 81 E F

HURSTWOOD RD

SCRAGGED OAK RD

COURT LA

HERMITAGE LA

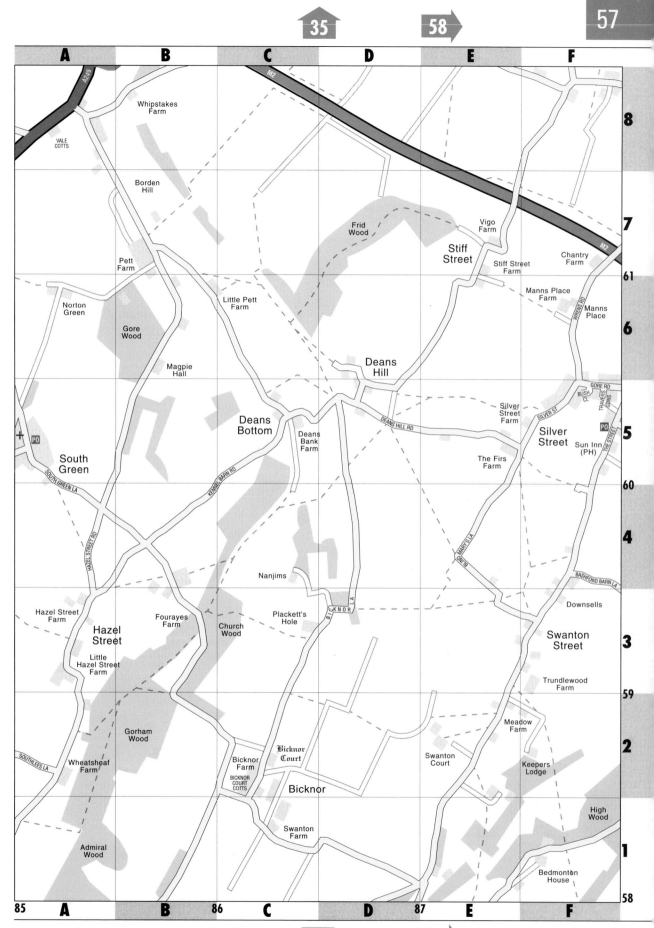

A B C D E F

8
7
61
6
5
60
4
59
3
2
1
58

Whipstakes Farm

VALE COTTS

Borden Hill

M2

Pett Farm

Norton Green

Gore Wood

Little Pett Farm

Magpie Hall

Frid Wood

Stiff Street

Vigo Farm

Stiff Street Farm

Chantry Farm

Manns Place Farm

WRENS RD

Manns Place

Deans Hill

Deans Bottom

Deans Bank Farm

DEANS HILL RD

Silver Street Farm

SILVER ST

GORE RD

BUSH CL

TRAVERS GDNS

Silver Street

PO

Sun Inn (PH)

THE STREET

PO

South Green

SOUTH GREEN LA

HAZEL STREET RD

KEMBLE BARN RD

The Firs Farm

Nanjims

BLIND MARY'S LA

BASHFORD BARN LA

Downsells

Hazel Street Farm

Hazel Street

Fourayes Farm

Church Wood

Plackett's Hole

BICKNOR LA

Swanton Street

Little Hazel Street Farm

Trundlewood Farm

SOUTHLEES LA

Gorham Wood

Wheatsheaf Farm

Bicknor Farm

Bicknor Court

Meadow Farm

Swanton Court

Keepers Lodge

BICKNOR COURT COTTS

Bicknor

High Wood

Admiral Wood

Swanton Farm

Bedmonton House

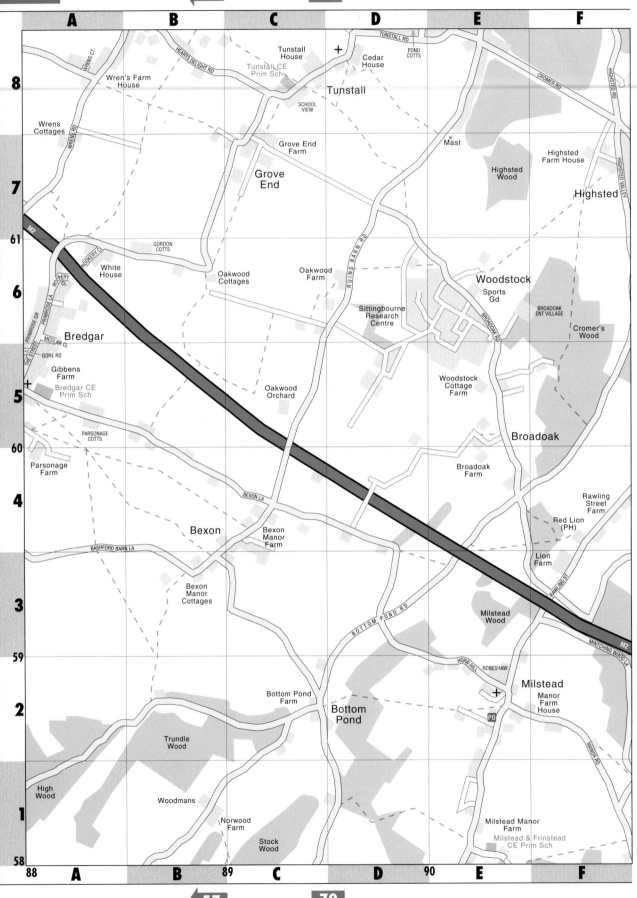

A   B   C   D   E   F

8

WRENS CT

Wren's Farm
House

Tunstall
House

Tunstall CE
Prim Sch

Cedar
House

TUNSTALL RD

POND
COTTS

CROMER RD

HIGHSTED RD

Wrens
Cottages

WRENS RD

HEARTS DELIGHT RD

SCHOOL
VIEW

Tunstall

Mast

Highsted
Wood

Highsted
Farm House

Highsted

HIGHSTED VALLEY

7

Grove End
Farm

Grove
End

61

M2

GORDON
COTTS

ROOKERY CL

White
House

Oakwood
Cottages

Oakwood
Farm

RUINS BARN RD

Woodstock

Sports
Gd

BROADOAK ENT VILLAGE

Cromer's
Wood

6

ROOKERY CL

PRIMROSE LA

PRIMROSE GR

Bredgar

Sittingbourne
Research
Centre

BROADOAK RD

MEDLAR CL

THE STREET

GORE RD

Gibbens
Farm

Bredgar CE
Prim Sch

Oakwood
Orchard

Woodstock
Cottage
Farm

Broadoak

5

PARSONAGE
COTTS

Broadoak
Farm

Rawling
Street
Farm

60

Parsonage
Farm

BEXON LA

Red Lion
(PH)

Lion
Farm

4

BASHFORD BARN LA

Bexon

Bexon
Manor
Farm

RAWLING ST

Milstead
Wood

Bexon
Manor
Cottages

BOTTOM POND RD

Milstead

3

MINTCHING WOOD LA

M2

59

HORN HILL

ROBESHAW

Manor
Farm
House

Bottom Pond
Farm

Bottom
Pond

PO

MANOR RD

2

Trundle
Wood

High
Wood

Woodmans

Norwood
Farm

Stock
Wood

Milstead Manor
Farm

Milstead & Frinstead
CE Prim Sch

1

58

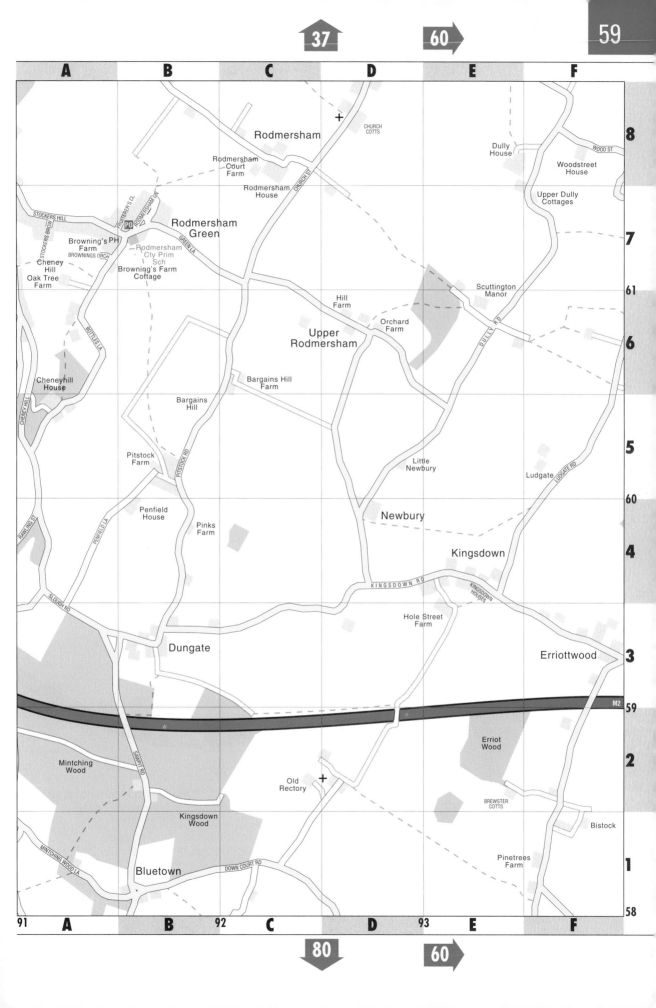

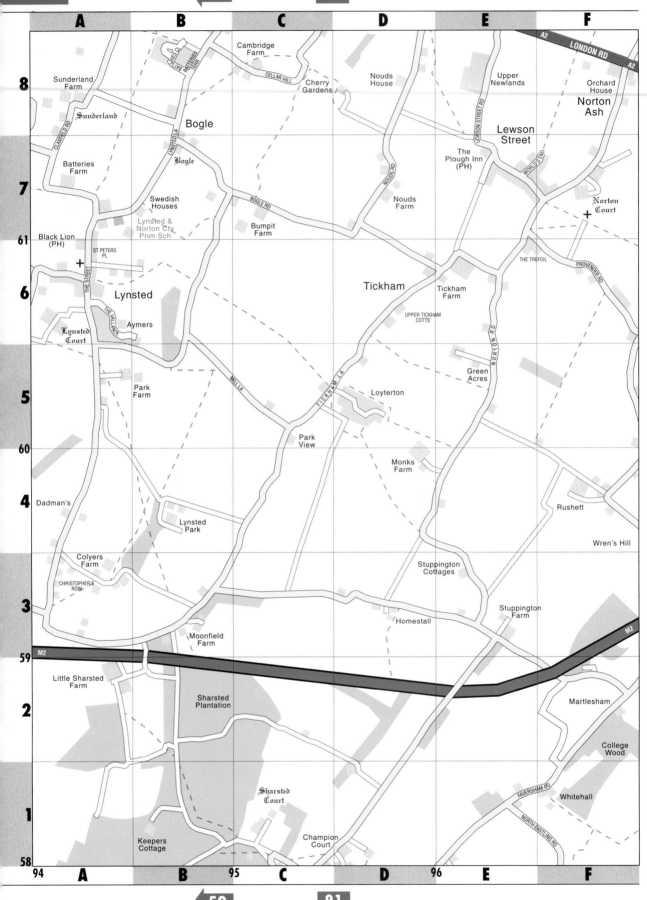

A B C D E F

8
Sunderland Farm
Sunderland
Cambridge Farm
CELLAR HILL
Cherry Gardens
Nouds House
Upper Newlands
Orchard House
Norton Ash
LONDON RD
A2

Bogle
Batteries Farm
Bogle
Lewson Street
The Plough Inn (PH)

7
Swedish Houses
BOGLE RD
Bumpit Farm
Nouds Farm
Norton Court

61
Lynsted & Norton Cty Prim Sch
Black Lion (PH)
ST PETERS PL
THE TREFOIL
PROVENDER RD

6
Lynsted
Tickham
Tickham Farm
THE VALLANCE
Aymers
UPPER TICKHAM COTTS

Lynsted Court

5
Park Farm
MILL LA
TICKHAM LA
Loyterton
Green Acres
NORTON RD

60
Park View
Monks Farm

4
Dadman's
Lynsted Park
Rushett
Wren's Hill

3
Colyers Farm
CHRISTOPHER'S ROW
Stuppington Cottages
Homestall
Stuppington Farm
M2

59
Moonfield Farm
M2

2
Little Sharsted Farm
Sharsted Plantation
Martlesham

College Wood

1
Sharsted Court
Whitehall
FAVERSHAM RD
NORTH EASTLING RD

58
Keepers Cottage
Champion Court

94 A B 95 C D 96 E F

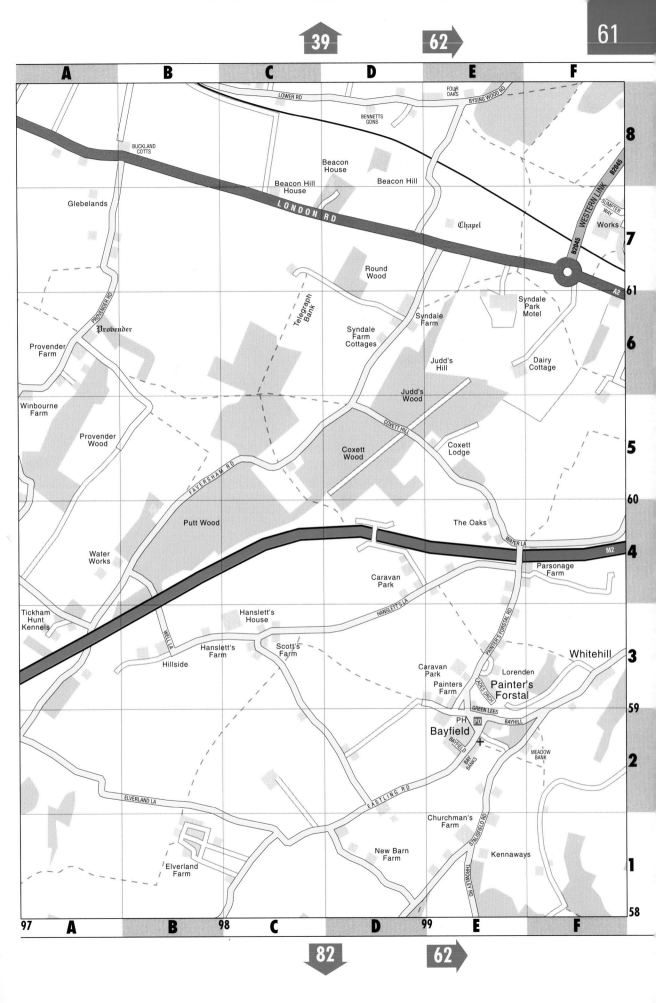

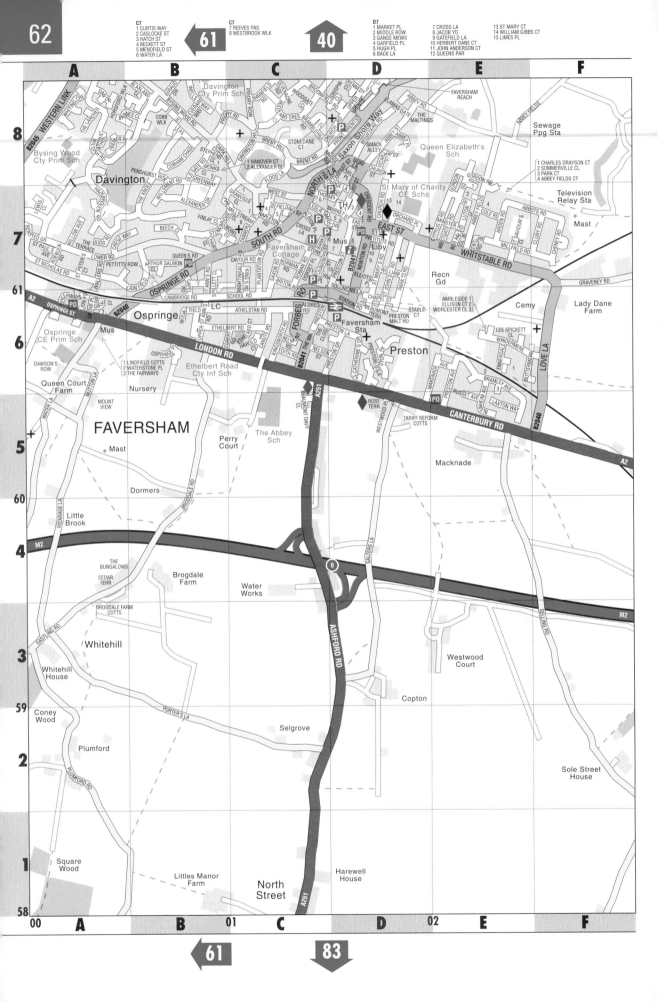

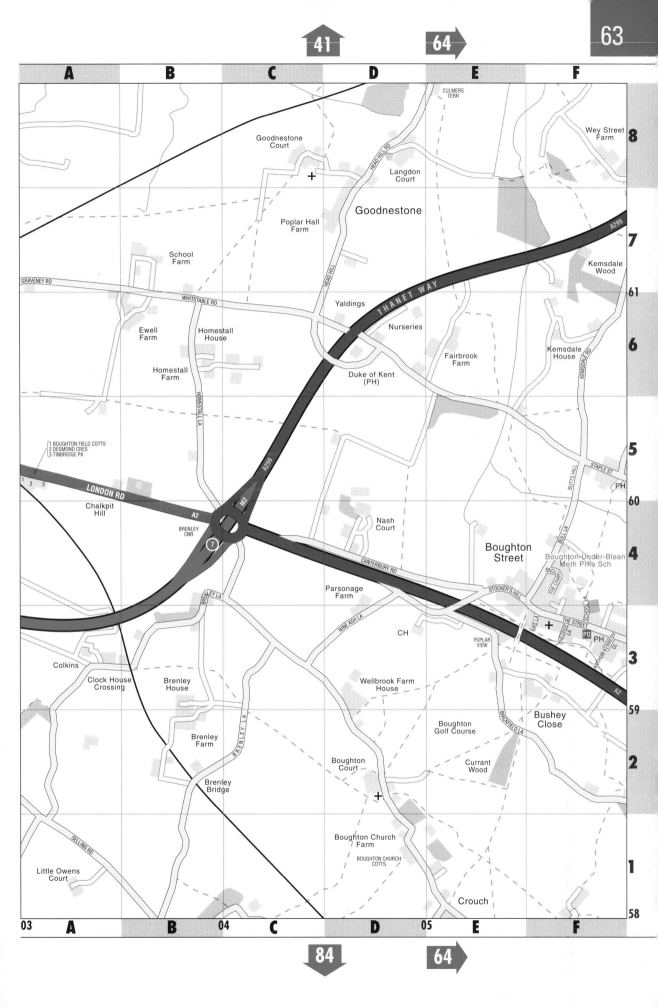

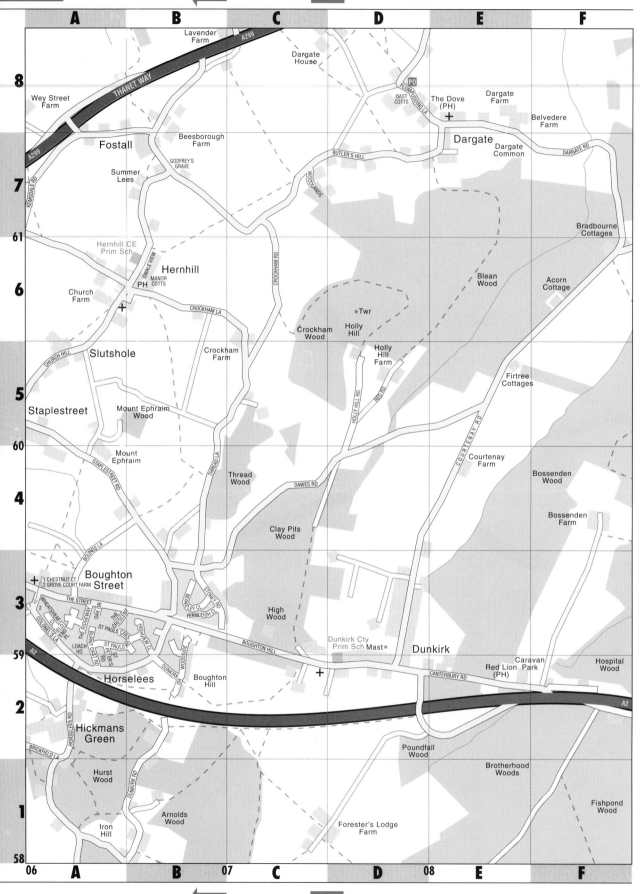
A   B   C   D   E   F

8

Lavender Farm

A299 THANET WAY

Dargate House

PO

Wey Street Farm

OAST COTTS

The Dove (PH)

Dargate Farm

Belvedere Farm

A299

Fostall

Beesborough Farm

GODFREY'S GRAVE

BUTLER'S HILL

Dargate

Dargate Common

DARGATE RD

Summer Lees

7

KEMSDALE RD

WOODLANDS

Bradbourne Cottages

61

Hernhill CE Prim Sch

SWALE VIEW

CROCKHAM RD

Blean Wood

Acorn Cottage

6

Church Farm

Hernhill

PH   MANOR COTTS

CROCKHAM LA

•Twr

Crockham Wood

Holly Hill

FIRTREE

Firtree Cottages

CHURCH HILL

Slutshole

Crockham Farm

Holly Hill Farm

RED RD

5

Staplestreet

Mount Ephraim Wood

HOLLY HILL RD

COURTENAY RD

60

STAPLESTREET RD

Mount Ephraim

THREAD LA

Courtenay Farm

Bossenden Wood

4

Thread Wood

DAWES RD

Bossenden Farm

BOUNDS LA

Clay Pits Wood

3

1 CHESTNUT CT
2 GROVE COURT FARM

Boughton Street

STONEY RD

BERKLEY CL

FERNLEIGH CL

High Wood

Dunkirk

WHEATSHEAF CL
THE TERRACE

THE RIDGEWAY

OAK DR

THE PRESENT

ST PAULS CRES

HIGHVIEW CL

Dunkirk Cty Prim Sch Mast•

59

A2

COLONEL'S LA

CLOSE

LOACH HO

ST PETER'S

DUNKIRK RD

OSPGOOM

ST PAULS

BOUGHTON HILL

Red Lion (PH)

Caravan Park

Hospital Wood

Horselees

Boughton Hill

CANTERBURY RD

2

HORSE LEES RD

A2

Hickmans Green

Poundfall Wood

BRICKFIELD LA

DUNKIRK RD

Hurst Wood

Brotherhood Woods

1

Iron Hill

Arnolds Wood

Forester's Lodge Farm

Fishpond Wood

58

Meadow Grange Nursery

Butler's Court Wood

DENSTROUDE LA

Denstroude

Brook Lodge

A290

HONEY HILL

Honey Hill

Blean Bird Park

Clay Hill

Honey Hill Farm

Royal Oak (PH)

WOODLANDS

Parsonage Farm

BLEAN COMM A290

Denstroude Farm

Nature Reserve

Mincing Wood

Little Den Lees

Crawford's Rough

Great Den Lees

North Bishopden Wood

Grimshill Wood

Crooked Oak

Church Wood

Nature Reserve

NEW RD

Manson Wood

Homestall Wood

Landing Strip

Willows Wood

DENSTEAD LA

Stumps Farm

Staines Farm

Plough Inn (PH)

Harbledown Lodge

GLEMSFORD COTTS

Upper Harbledown

NEW COTTS

THE GREEN

LITTLE MEADOW

PO

PROSPECT COTTS

Poldhurst Farm

A2050

A2

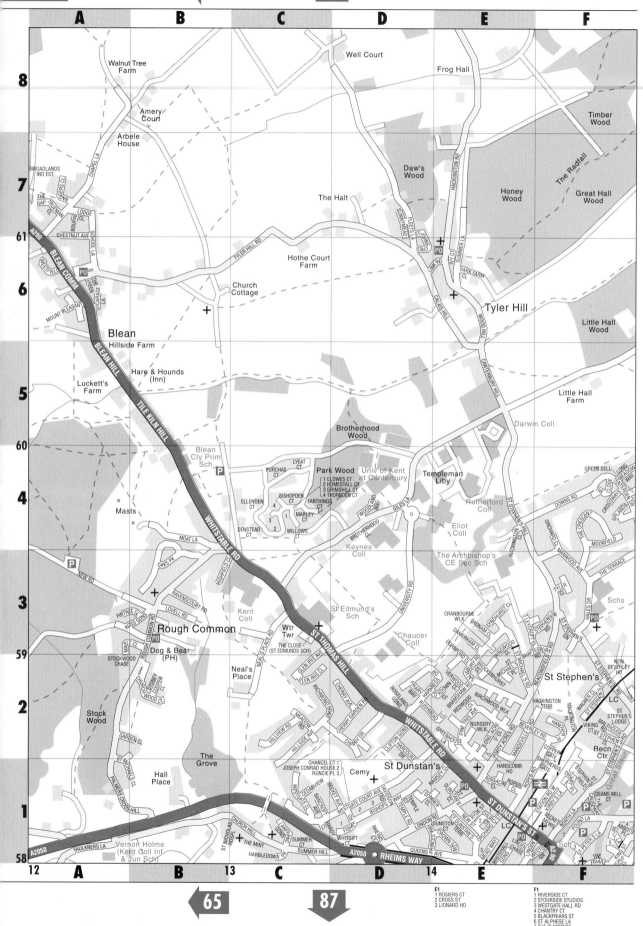

E1
1 ROSIERS CT
2 CROSS ST
3 LIONARD HO

F1
1 RIVERSIDE CT
2 STOURSIDE STUDIOS
3 WESTGATE HALL RD
4 CHANTRY CT
5 BLACKFRIARS ST
6 ST ALPHEGE LA
7 THE CLOISTERS

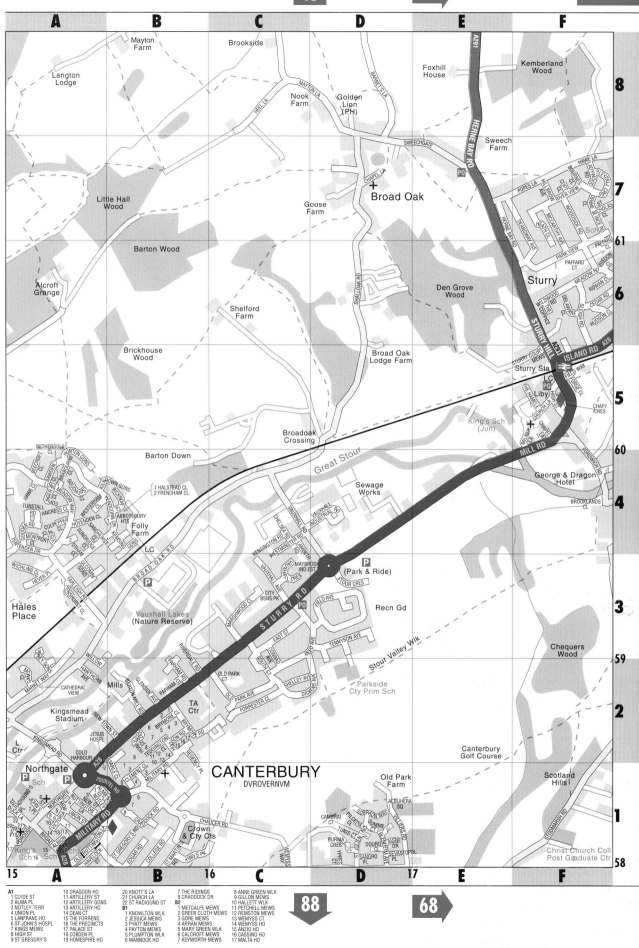

A1
1 CLYDE ST
2 ALMA PL
3 NOTLEY TERR
4 UNION PL
5 LANFRANC HO
6 ST JOHN'S HOSPL
7 KINGS MEWS
8 HIGH ST
9 ST GREGORY'S

10 DRAGOON HO
11 ARTILLERY ST
12 ARTILLERY GDNS
13 ARTILLERY HO
14 DEAN CT
15 THE FORRENS
16 THE PRECINCTS
17 PALACE ST
18 COBDEN PL
19 HOMESPIRE HO

20 KNOTT'S LA
21 CHURCH LA
22 ST RADIGUND ST
B1
1 KNOWLTON WLK
2 JESSICA MEWS
3 PYATT MEWS
4 PAYTON MEWS
5 PLUMPTON WLK
6 MANNOCK HO

7 THE RIDINGS
8 CRADDOCK DR
B2
1 METCALFE MEWS
2 GREEN CLOTH MEWS
3 GORE MEWS
4 ARRAN MEWS
5 MARY GREEN WLK
6 CALCROFT MEWS
7 KEYWORTH MEWS

8 ANNE GREEN WLK
9 GILLON MEWS
10 HALLETT WLK
11 PETCHELL MEWS
12 REMSTON MEWS
13 WEMYSS CT
14 WEMYSS HO
15 ANZIO HO
16 CASSINO HO
17 MALTA HO

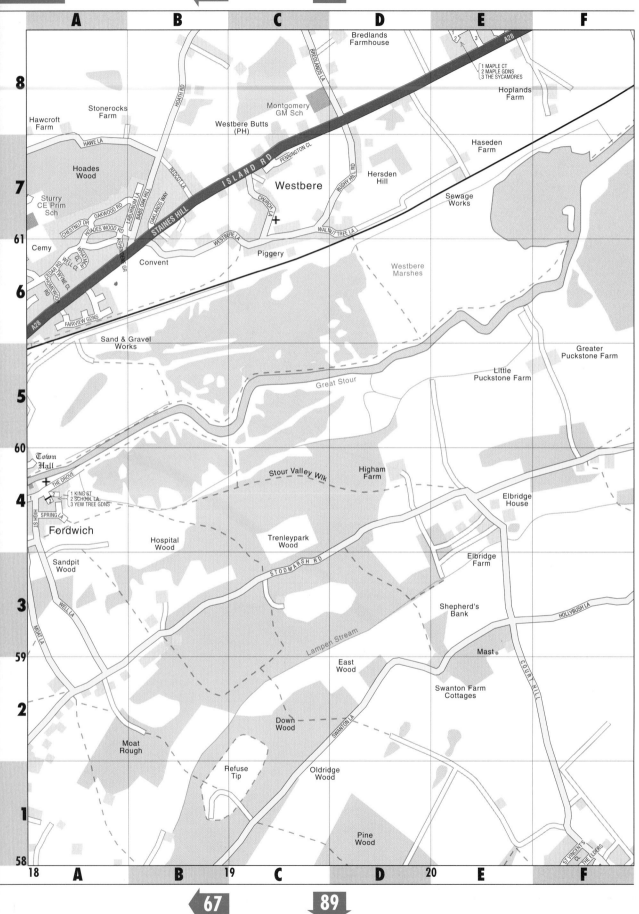

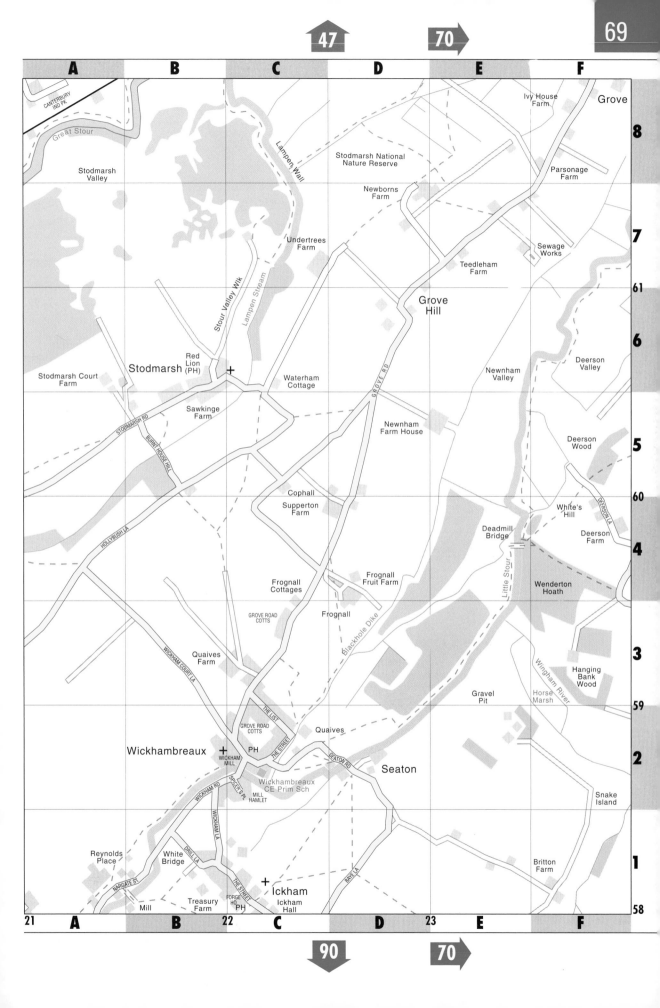

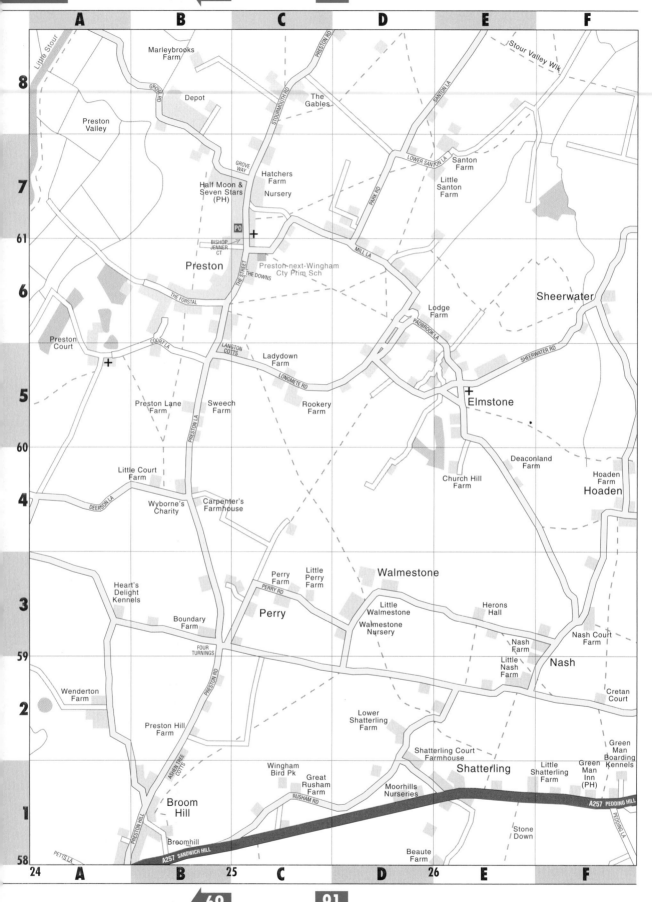

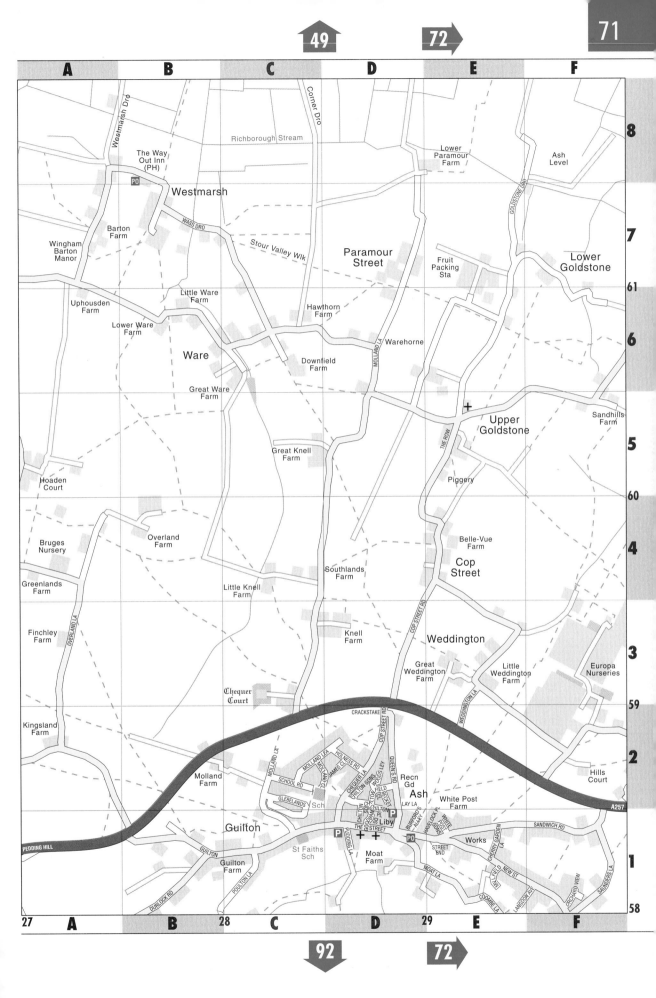

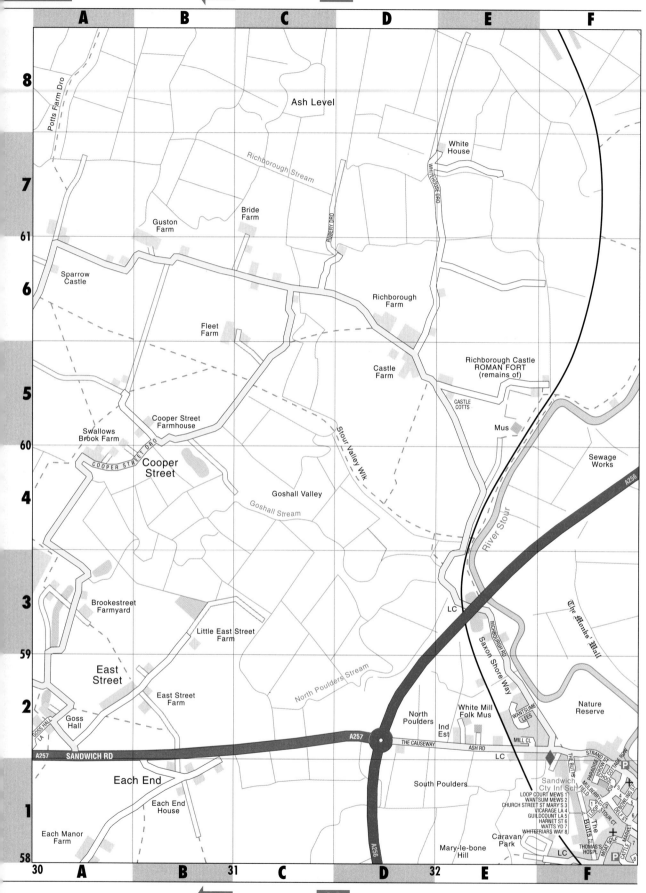

A B C D E F

8

7

61

6

5

60

4

3

59

2

1

58

30 A 31 B C D 32 E F

Ash Level

White House

Richborough Stream

WHITEHOUSE DRO

Potts Farm Dro

Guston Farm

Bride Farm

RUBERY DRO

Sparrow Castle

Richborough Farm

Fleet Farm

Castle Farm

Richborough Castle
ROMAN FORT
(remains of)

CASTLE COTTS

Mus

Cooper Street Farmhouse

Swallows Brook Farm

COOPER STREET DRO

Cooper Street

Stour Valley Wlk

Sewage Works

A256

Goshall Valley

Goshall Stream

River Stour

The Monks Wall

Brookestreet Farmyard

Little East Street Farm

LC

Saxon Shore Way

RICHBOROUGH RD

East Street

North Poulders Stream

Nature Reserve

Goss Hall

East Street Farm

North Poulders

Ind Est

White Mill Folk Mus

WANTSUME LEES

MILL CL

GOSS HALL LA

SANDWICH RD

A257

A257 SANDWICH RD

THE CAUSEWAY

ASH RD

LC

Each End

South Poulders

Sandwich Cty Inf Sch

LOOP COURT MEWS 1
WANTSUM MEWS 2
CHURCH STREET ST MARY'S 3
VICARAGE LA 4
GUILDCOUNT LA 5
HARNET ST 6
WATTS YD 7
WHITEFRIARS WAY 8

Each End House

A256

Mary-le-bone Hill

Caravan Park

ST THOMAS'S HOSP

LC

Each Manor Farm

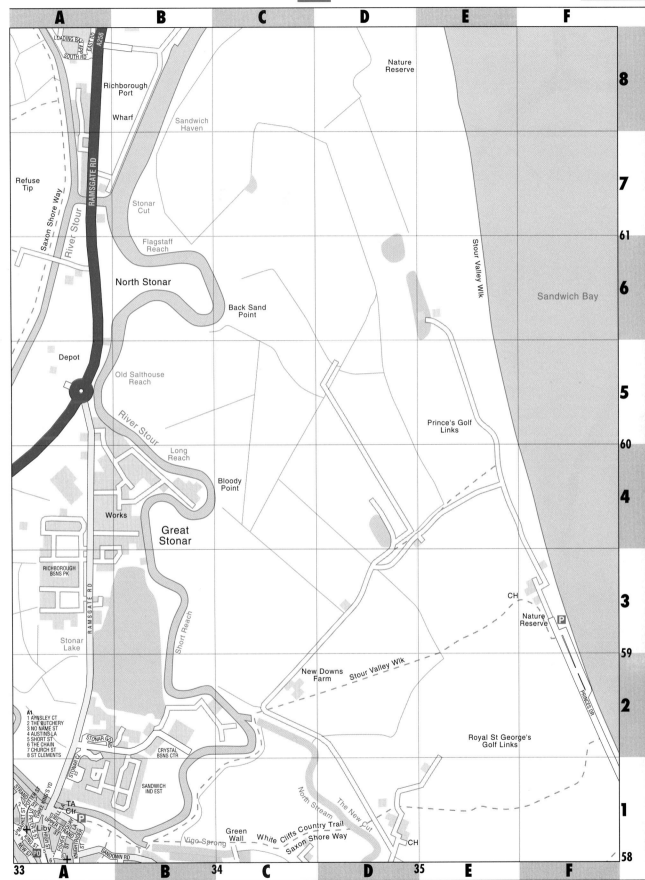

A   B   C   D   E   F

8
7
61
6
5
60
4
3
59
2
1
58

LOADING BAY
SOUTH RD
EAST RD
A256

Richborough
Port

Wharf

Sandwich
Haven

Nature
Reserve

Refuse
Tip

Saxon Shore Way

River Stour

RAMSGATE RD

Stonar
Cut

Flagstaff
Reach

North Stonar

Back Sand
Point

Stour Valley Wlk

Sandwich Bay

Depot

Old Salthouse
Reach

River Stour

Long
Reach

Bloody
Point

Prince's Golf
Links

Works

Great
Stonar

Short Reach

RICHBOROUGH
BSNS PK

RAMSGATE RD

Stonar
Lake

CH

Nature
Reserve

P

PRINCES DR

A1
1 AYNSLEY CT
2 THE BUTCHERY
3 NO NAME ST
4 AUSTINS LA
5 SHORT ST
6 THE CHAIN
7 CHURCH ST
8 ST CLEMENTS

New Downs
Farm

Stour Valley Wlk

STONAR CL

CRYSTAL
BSNS CTR

SANDWICH
IND EST

Royal St George's
Golf Links

STRAND ST
GALLOWS
UPPER STRAND ST
NEW ST
THREE KINGS YD
FISHER ST
DELF ST
KING ST
SANDOWN RD
STONAR CL
THE MINT'S YD
HIGH ST
UPPER STRAND LA
KNIGHTRIDER
MARKET ST
ST PETER'S ST
NEW ST
KING'S AVE

TA
Ctr
P

Liby

PO

Vigo Sprong

Green
Wall

White Cliffs Country Trail

Saxon Shore Way

North Stream

The New Cut

CH

33   34   C   D   35   E   F

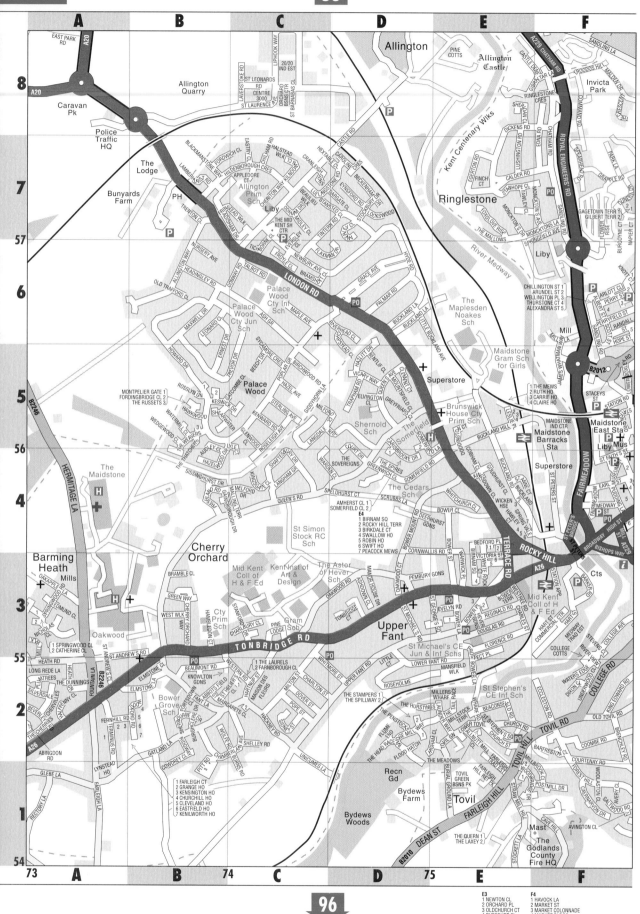

E3	F4
1 NEWTON CL	1 HAVOCK LA
2 ORCHARD PL	2 MARKET ST
3 OLDCHURCH CT	3 MARKET COLONNADE
4 RYECOURT CL	4 MARKET BLDGS
5 WHITE ROCK PL	5 ROYAL STAR ARC
6 VICTORIA CT	6 MIDDLE ROW

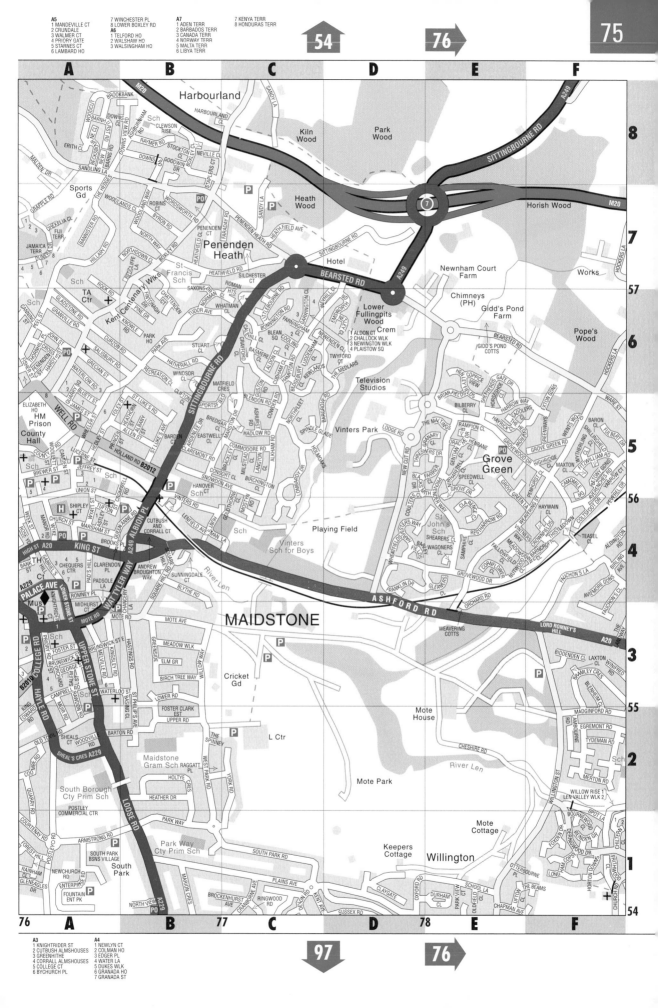

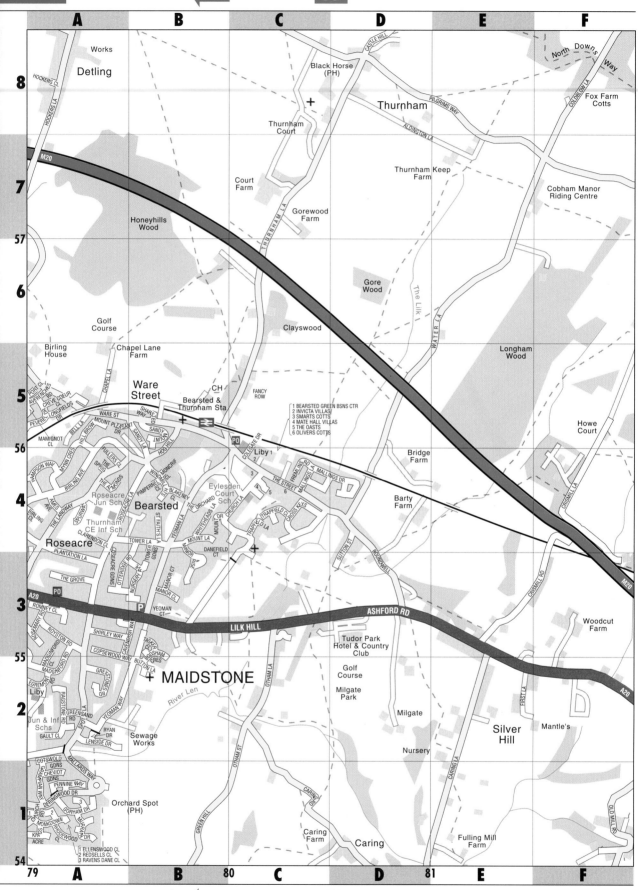

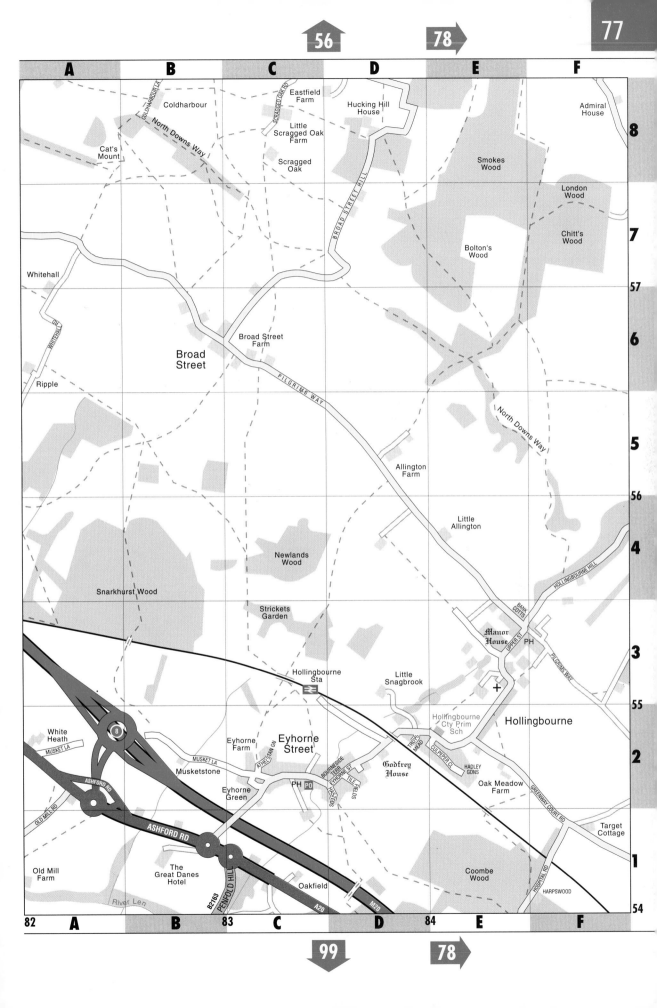

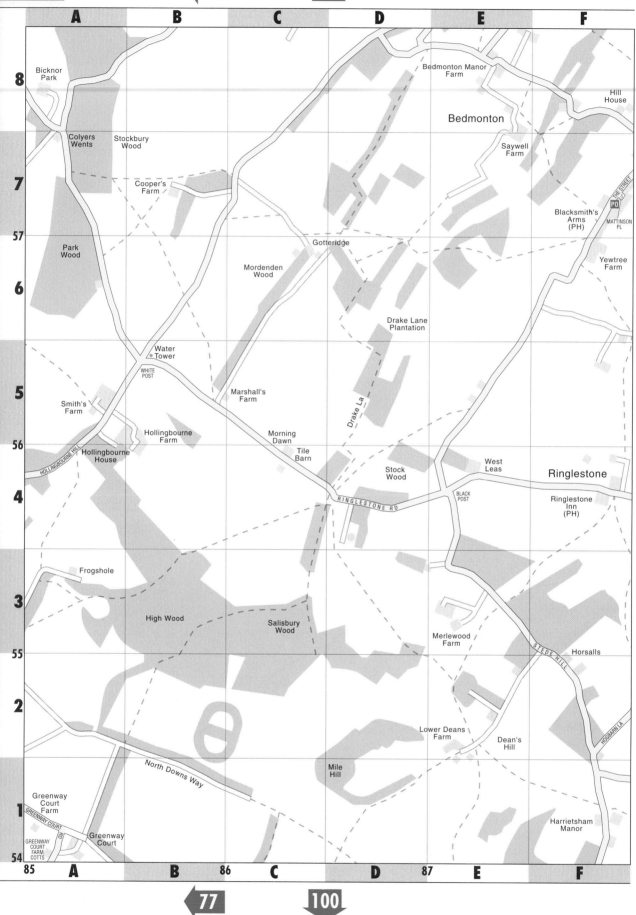

Bicknor
Park

Colyers
Wents

Stockbury
Wood

Cooper's
Farm

Park
Wood

Bedmonton Manor
Farm

Bedmonton

Hill
House

Saywell
Farm

Blacksmith's
Arms
(PH)

THE STREET

PO

MATTINSON
PL

Gotteridge

Mordenden
Wood

Yewtree
Farm

Drake Lane
Plantation

Water
Tower

WHITE
POST

Marshall's
Farm

Drake La

Smith's
Farm

Hollingbourne
Farm

Morning
Dawn

Tile
Barn

Stock
Wood

West
Leas

Ringlestone

Hollingbourne
House

HOLLINGBOURNE HILL

RINGLESTONE RD

BLACK
POST

Ringlestone
Inn
(PH)

Frogshole

High Wood

Salisbury
Wood

Merlewood
Farm

STEDE HILL

Horsalls

Lower Deans
Farm

Dean's
Hill

HOGBARN LA

North Downs Way

Mile
Hill

Greenway
Court
Farm

GREENWAY COURT RD

Greenway
Court

GREENWAY
COURT
FARM
COTTS

Harrietsham
Manor

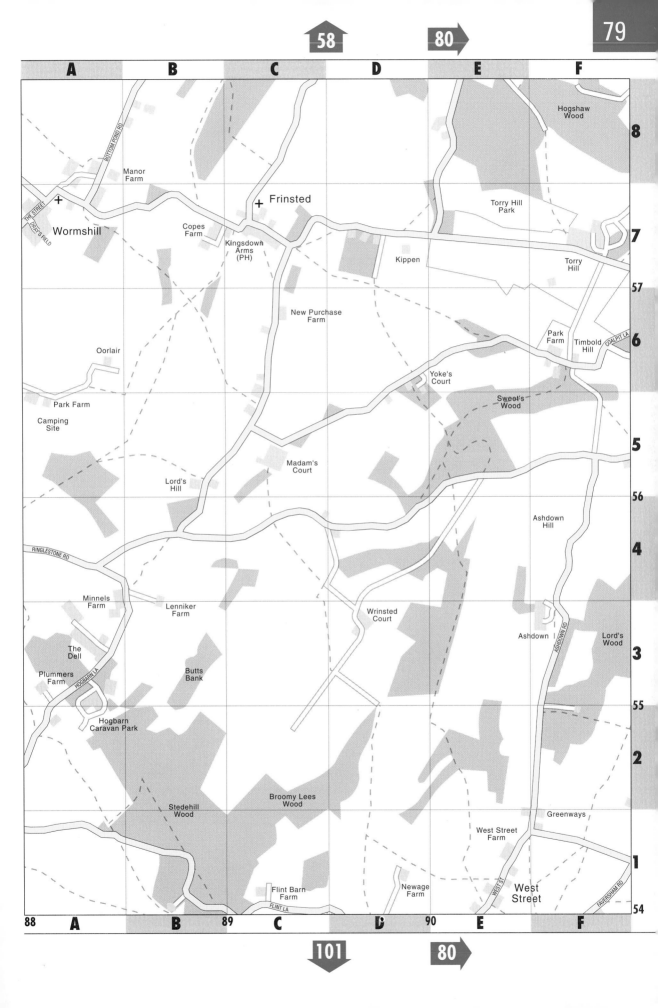

A | B | C | D | E | F

8

BOTTOM POND RD

Hogshaw Wood

Manor Farm

THE STREET

+ Wormshill

DRAY'S FIELD

+ Frinsted

Torry Hill Park

7

Copes Farm

Kingsdown Arms (PH)

Kippen

Torry Hill

57

New Purchase Farm

Park Farm

Timbold Hill

COALPIT LA

6

Oorlair

Yoke's Court

Sweet's Wood

Park Farm

Camping Site

5

Lord's Hill

Madam's Court

Ashdown Hill

56

RINGLESTONE RD

4

Minnels Farm

Lenniker Farm

Wrinsted Court

Ashdown

ASHDOWN RD

Lord's Wood

The Dell

HOGBARN LA

Butts Bank

3

Plummers Farm

55

Hogbarn Caravan Park

2

Stedehill Wood

Broomy Lees Wood

Greenways

West Street Farm

1

Flint Barn Farm

FLINT LA

Newage Farm

WEST ST

West Street

FAVERSHAM RD

54

79
59

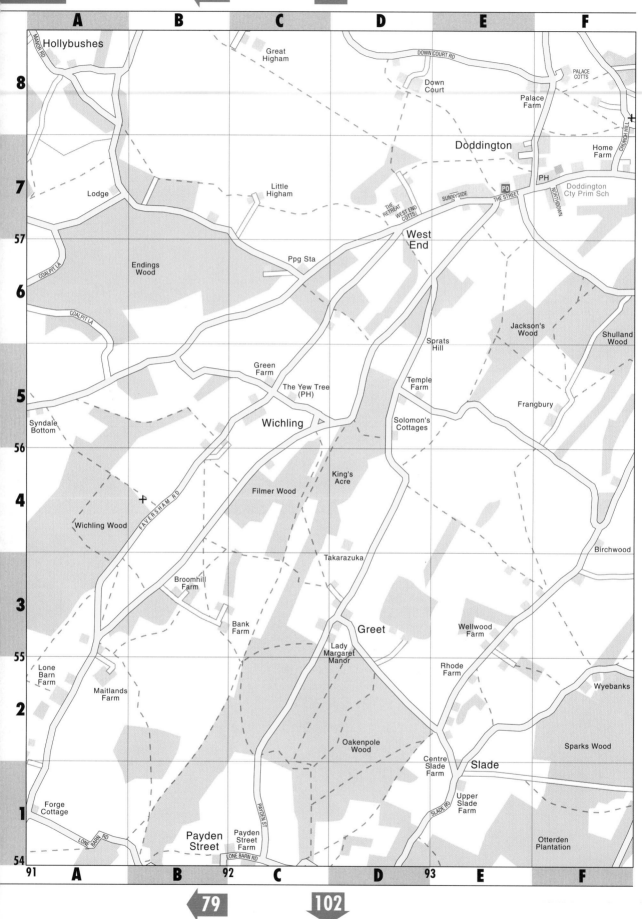

79
102

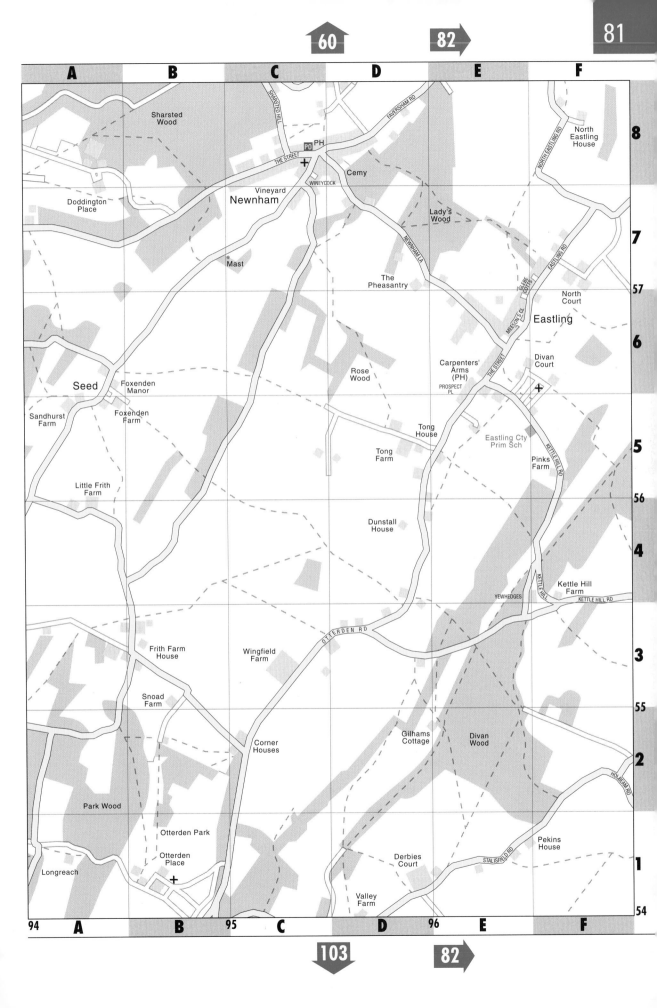

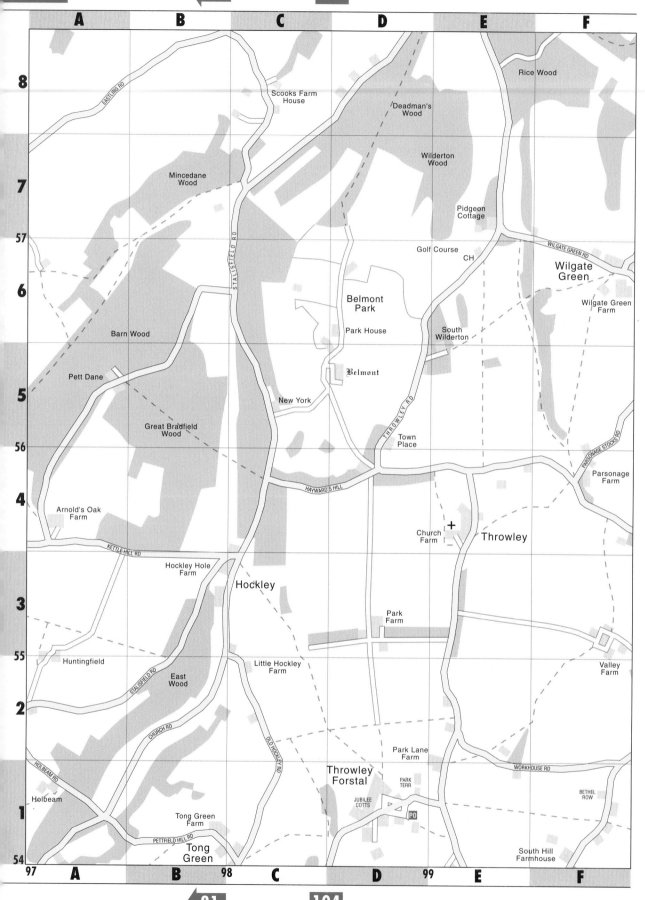

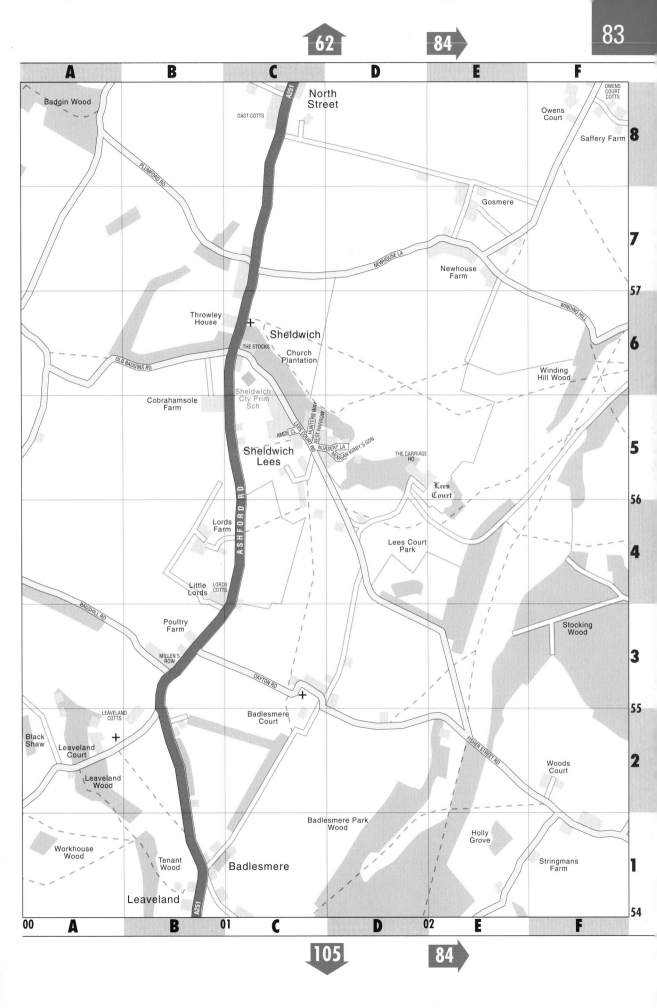

62

84

A B C D E F

Badgin Wood

OWENS COURT COTTS

North Street

OAST COTTS

Owens Court

Saffery Farm

8

PLUMFORD RD

Gosmere

7

NEWHOUSE LA

Newhouse Farm

WINDING HILL

57

Throwley House

Sheldwich

6

OLD BADGINS RD

THE STOCKS

Church Plantation

Winding Hill Wood

Cobrahamsole Farm

Sheldwich Cty Prim Sch

HUNTERS WAY

WEST HARROW

5

ASHFORD RD

Sheldwich Lees

AMOS CL

LEES COURT RD

NURSERY LA

MORGAN KIRBY'S GDN

THE CARRIAGE HO

Lees Court

56

Lords Farm

Lees Court Park

4

Little Lords

LORDS COTTS

Stocking Wood

BAGSHILL RD

Poultry Farm

3

MILLEN'S ROW

DAYTON RD

55

LEAVELAND COTTS

Badlesmere Court

FISHER STREET RD

Black Shaw

Leaveland Court

Woods Court

2

Leaveland Wood

Badlesmere Park Wood

Holly Grove

Workhouse Wood

Tenant Wood

Badlesmere

Stringmans Farm

1

Leaveland

A251

54

00 A B 01 C D 02 E F

105

84

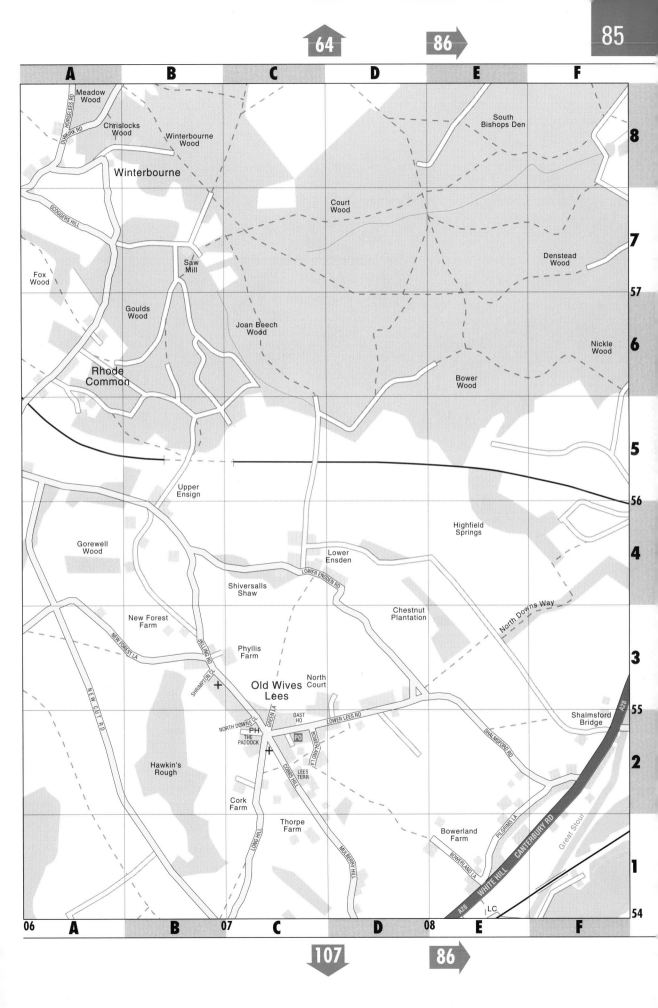

A B C D E F

8 7 57 6 5 56 4 3 55 2 1 54

Meadow Wood
Chrislocks Wood
Winterbourne Wood
Winterbourne
South Bishops Den
HORSELEES RD
DUNKIRK RD
SCOGGERS HILL
Court Wood
Denstead Wood
Fox Wood
Saw Mill
Goulds Wood
Joan Beech Wood
Nickle Wood
Rhode Common
Bower Wood
Upper Ensign
Highfield Springs
Gorewell Wood
Lower Ensden
LOWER ENSDEN RD
North Downs Way
Shiversalls Shaw
Chestnut Plantation
New Forest Farm
NEW FOREST LA
SELLING RD
SHRIMPTON CL
Phyllis Farm
Old Wives Lees
North Court
Shalmsford Bridge
A28
NEW CUT RD
GREEN LA
NORTH DOWNS CL
OAST HO
Lower Lees Rd
SHALMSFORD RD
PH
THE PADDOCK
PO
BOWERLAND LA
Hawkin's Rough
LEES TERR
COBBS HILL
Cork Farm
LONG HILL
Thorpe Farm
MULBERRY HILL
Bowerland Farm
BOWERLAND LA
PILGRIMS LA
WHITE HILL
CANTERBURY RD
Great Stour
A28
LC

06 A B 07 C D 08 E F

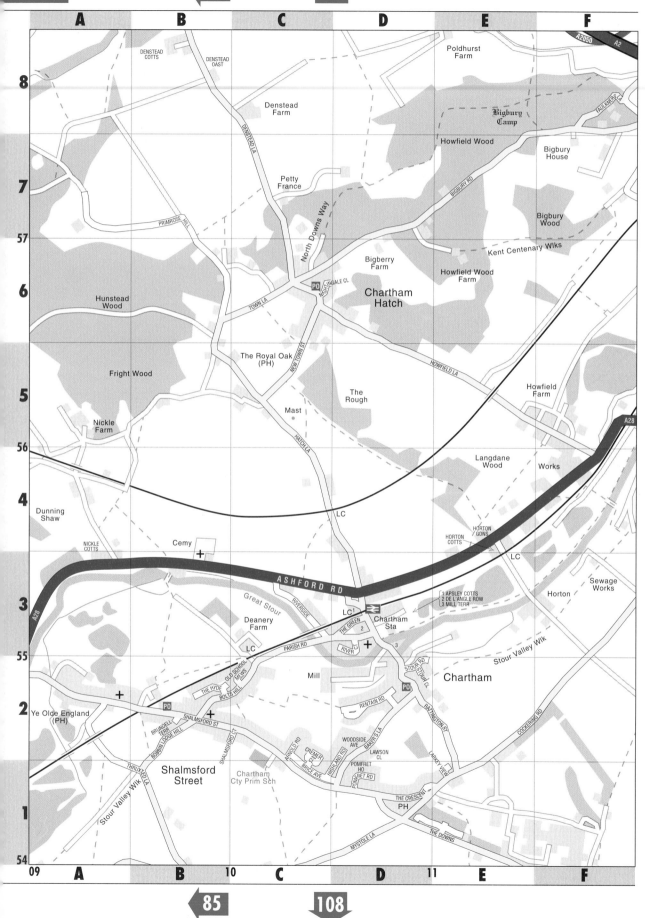

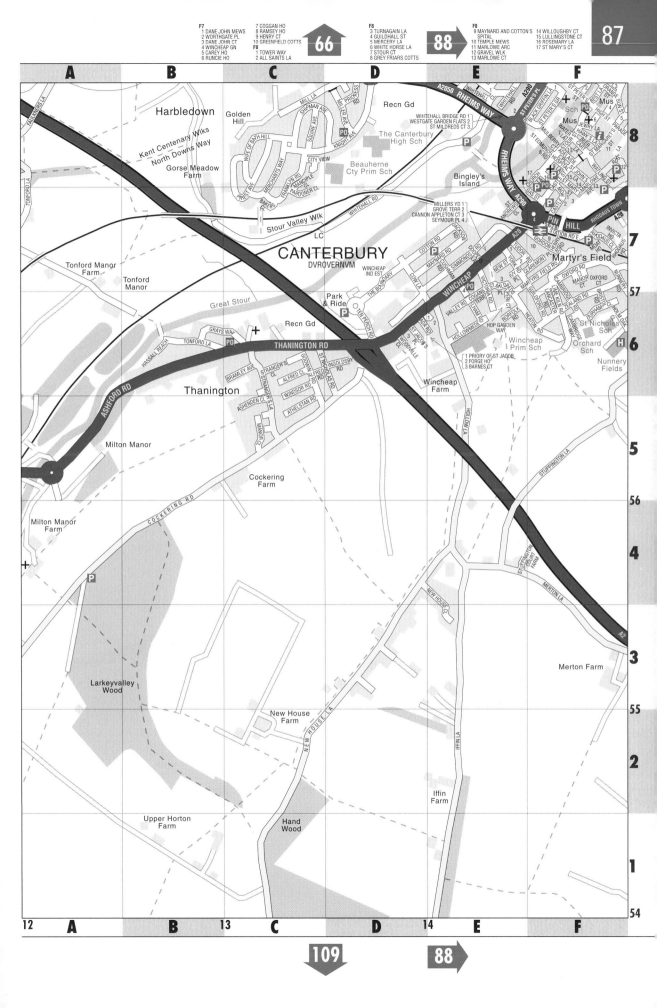

88

A8
1 BUTCHERY LA
2 LONGMARKET
3 IRON BAR LA
4 BURGATE LA
5 LADY WOOTON'S GN
6 CHURCH ST (ST PAULS)

7 ALMSHOUSES

87

67

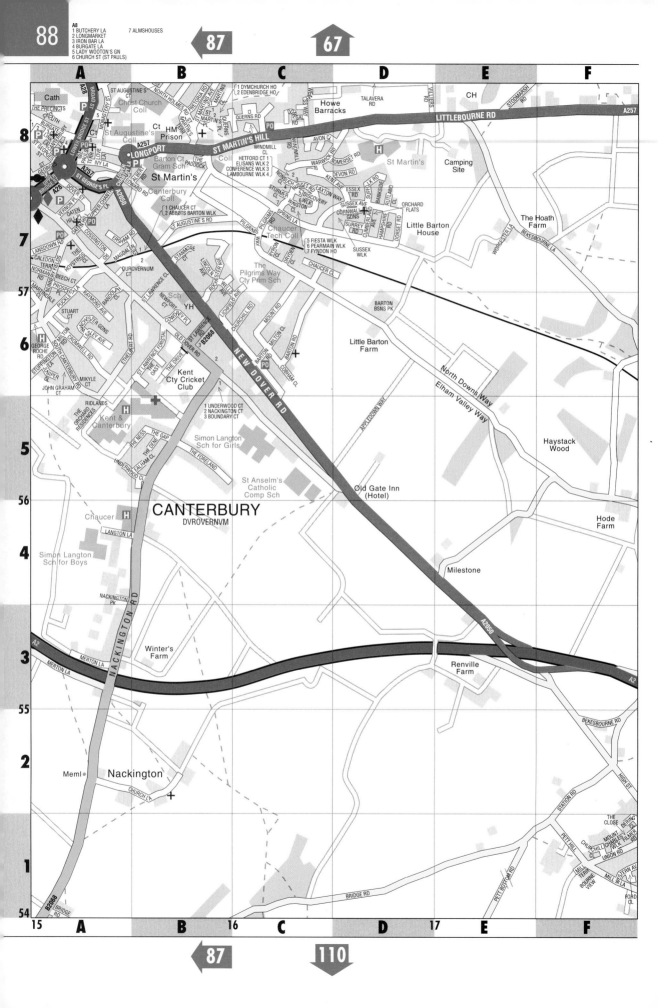

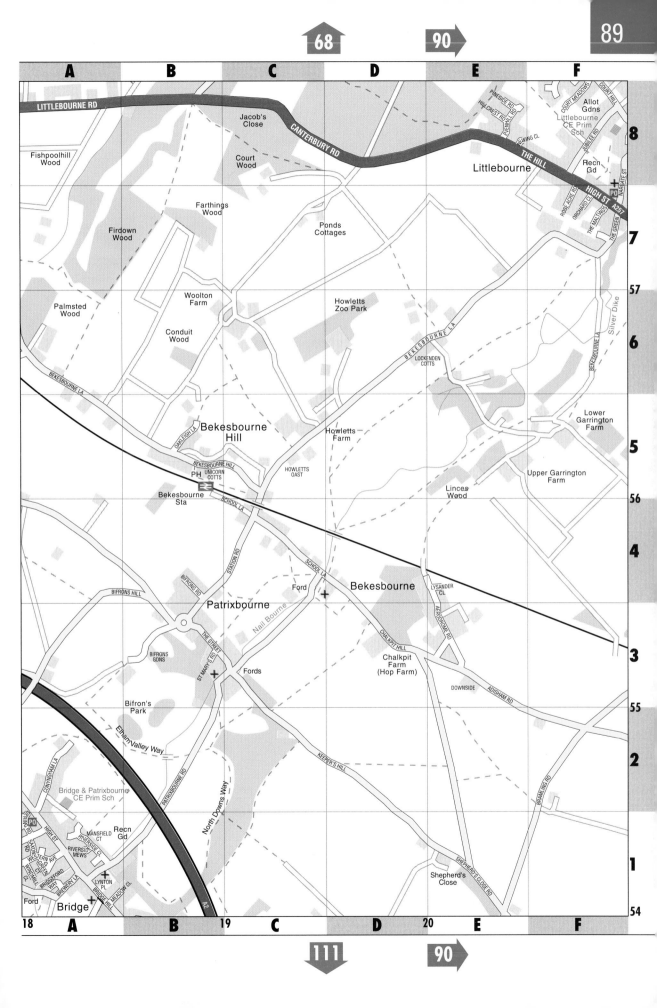

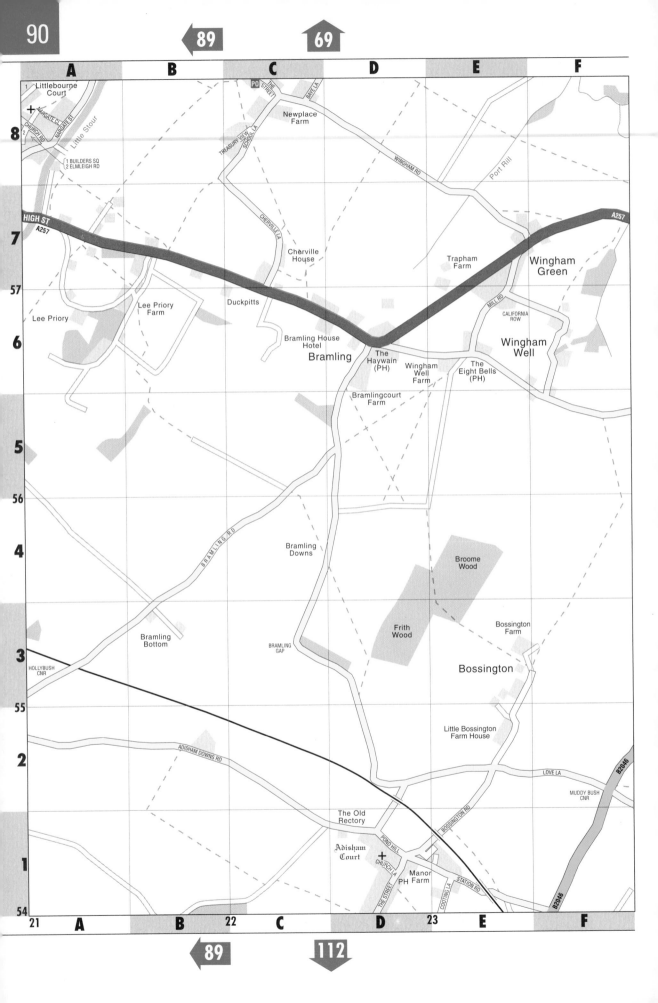

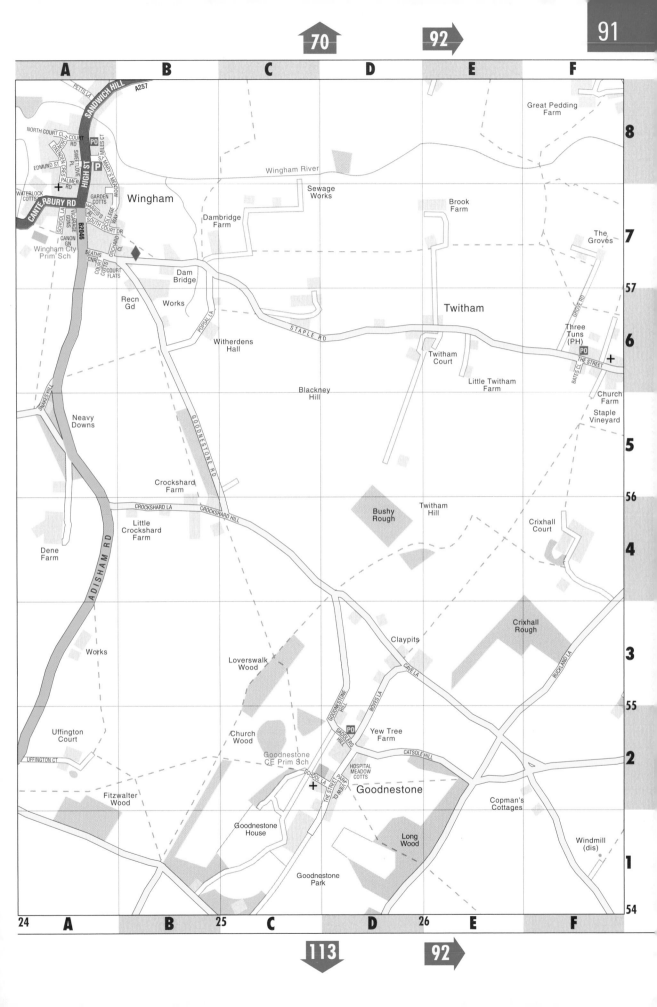

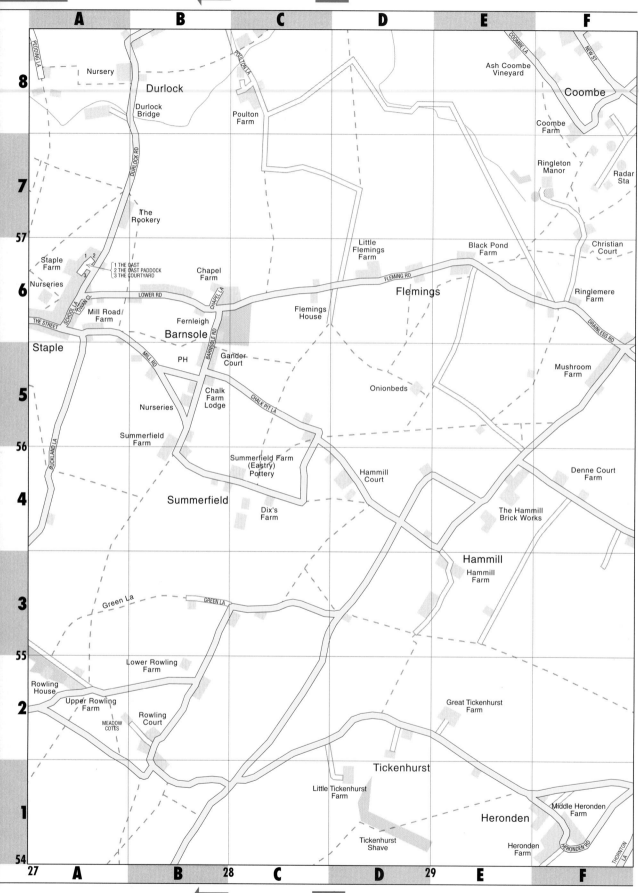

Nursery

Durlock

Durlock
Bridge

Poulton
Farm

Ash Coombe
Vineyard

Coombe

Coombe
Farm

Ringleton
Manor

Radar
Sta

The
Rookery

Little
Flemings
Farm

Black Pond
Farm

Christian
Court

Staple
Farm

Nurseries

Chapel
Farm

Flemings

Ringlemere
Farm

1 THE OAST
2 THE OAST PADDOCK
3 THE COURTYARD

LOWER RD

FLEMING RD

Mill Road
Farm

Fernleigh

Barnsole

Flemings
House

DRAINLESS RD

Staple

THE STREET

PH

Gander
Court

Mushroom
Farm

Nurseries

Chalk
Farm
Lodge

CHALK PIT LA

Onionbeds

Summerfield
Farm

Denne Court
Farm

Summerfield Farm
(Eastry)
Pottery

Hammill
Court

Summerfield

Dix's
Farm

The Hammill
Brick Works

Hammill

Hammill
Farm

Green La

GREEN LA

Lower Rowling
Farm

Rowling
House

Upper Rowling
Farm

Great Tickenhurst
Farm

MEADOW
COTTS

Rowling
Court

Tickenhurst

Little Tickenhurst
Farm

Middle Heronden
Farm

Heronden

Heronden
Farm

Tickenhurst
Shave

HERONDEN RD

THORNTON LA

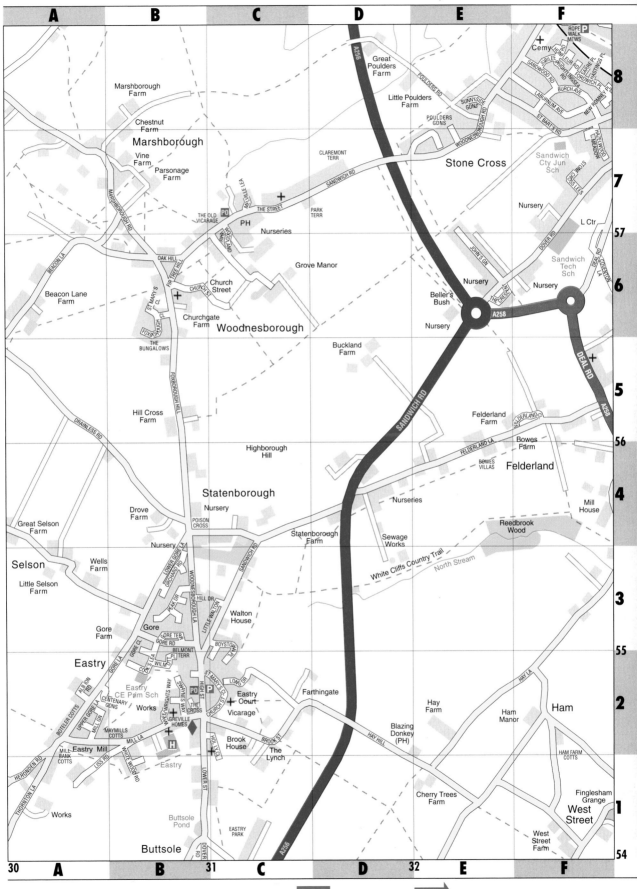

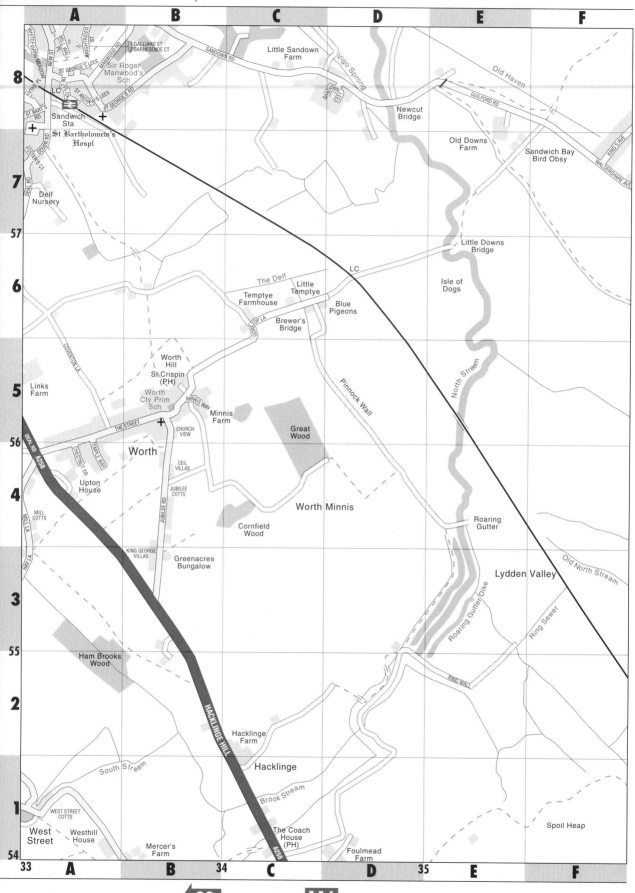

Royal
St George's
Golf Links

Sandwich Bay

KING'S AVE

COASTGUARD
COTTS

Sandwich Bay
Estate

NORTH RD

PRINCES DR

WALDERSHARE AVE

SHAWDON AVE

FRANCIS AVE

CAMBRIDGE AVE

DICKSON'S
CNR

Lyddcourt
Stile

Lydden

Mary Bax's
Stone

Royal Cinque Ports Golf Links

White Cliffs Country Trail

Saxon Shore Way

Chequers
(PH)

Caravan
Park

Old North Stream

Tennants
Hills

Walnut Tree
Farm

Sandhills

REDHOUSE WAY

CH

GOLF RD

Penfold Sewer

Spoil
Heap

Sandown Castle
(remains of)

1 CASTLE WLK
2 CANUTE WLK

CANUTE RD

SANDOWN RD

THE MARINA

ETHELBERT RD

GOLF CT 1
LINKS CT 2

8

7

57

6

5

56

4

3

55

2

1

54

36   37   38

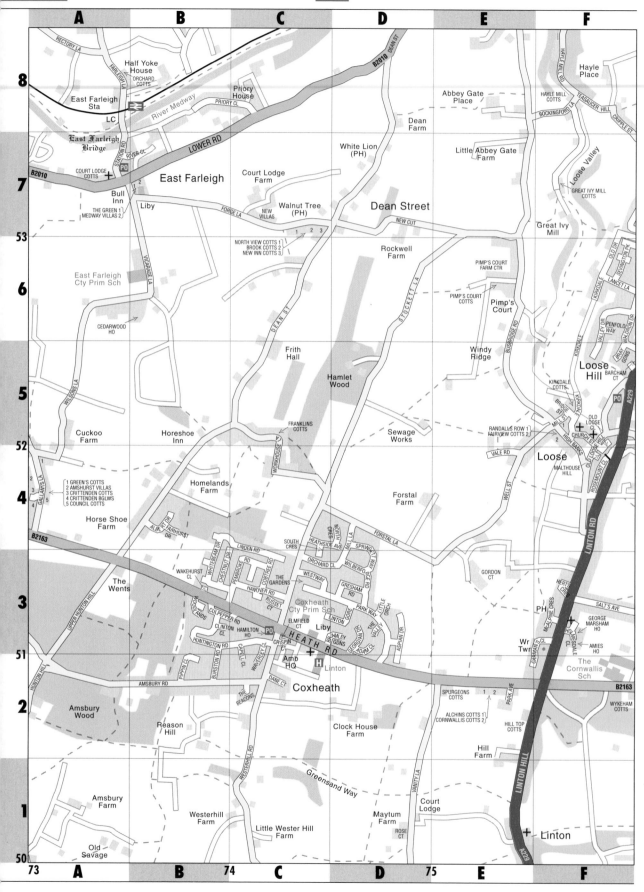

A B C D E F

8

7

53

6

5

52

4

3

51

2

1

50

RECTORY LA
Half Yoke House
ORCHARD COTTS
East Farleigh Sta
LC
East Farleigh Bridge
River Medway
Priory House
PRIORY CL
Dean Farm
Abbey Gate Place
Hayle Place
HAYLE MILL RD
HAYLE MILL COTTS
TEASAUGER HILL
BOCKINGFORD LA
CRIPPLE ST
B2010
LOWER RD
B2010
DEAN ST
Dean Farm
White Lion (PH)
Little Abbey Gate Farm
Loose Valley
B2010
COURT LODGE COTTS
PO
East Farleigh
Court Lodge Farm
Great Ivy Mill
GREAT IVY MILL COTTS
Bull Inn
STATION RD
RIVER CL.
Liby
FORGE LA
NEW VILLAS
Walnut Tree (PH)
Dean Street
NEW CUT
Great Ivy Mill
THE GREEN 1
MEDWAY VILLAS 2
VICARAGE LA
NORTH VIEW COTTS 1
BROOK COTTS 2
NEW INN COTTS 3
Rockwell Farm
STOCKETT LA
PIMP'S COURT FARM CTR
East Farleigh Cty Prim Sch
DEAN ST
PIMP'S COURT COTTS
Pimp's Court
KIRKDALE
OLD DR
SELINGTON DR
LANCET LA
KIRKDALE
CEDARWOOD HO
Frith Hall
Windy Ridge
BUSBRIDGE RD
VALLEY DR
PENFOLD WAY
WINDSON DR
GRAY GDNS
Hamlet Wood
Loose Hill
KIRKDALE COTTS
BARCHAM CT
WILSONS LA
Horeshoe Inn
FRANKLINS COTTS
Sewage Works
BRIDGE STILE
MILL LA
KIRKDALE
OLD LODGE
HIGH BANKS
PO
A229
Cuckoo Farm
WORKHOUSE LA
VALE RD
CHURCH ST
OLD LODGE CL
Loose
MALTHOUSE HILL
1 GREEN'S COTTS
2 AMSHURST VILLAS
3 CRITTENDEN COTTS
4 CRITTENDEN BGLWS
5 COUNCIL COTTS
Homelands Farm
WELL ST
Forstal Farm
ROSEMOUNT CL
GALLANTS LA
Horse Shoe Farm
ALBERT DR
R FAIRHURST
NORTH CRES
MILL LA
HEATHSIDE AVE
FORSTAL LA
GORDON CT
LINTON RD
HERTS DR
SALT'S AVE
B2163
The Wents
WAKEHURST CL
WHITEBEAM DR
CHESTNUT DR
PEMBROKE RD
CUBTREE RD
SOUTH CRES
ORCHARD CL
SPRINGFIELD WAY
WILBERFORCE RD
McALPINE CRES
PH
GEORGE MARSHAM HO
Wr Twr
UPPER HUNTON HILL
WOODLANDS
CULPEPPER RD
HANOVER RD
RUSSET CT
WESTWAY
GRESHAM RD
PARK WAY
LITTLE ORCH
LINTON
VALLEY DR
GEORGIAN CL
ASPEN DR
AMIES HO
MEADOW RD
The Cornwallis Sch
CLINTON CL
HAMILTON HO
PO
HEATH RD
Coxheath Cty Prim Sch
Liby
BEMLEY GDNS
CARMAN'S CL
HUNTON HILL
PIPPIN CL
BURSTON RD
CAPELL CL
WAVERLEY CL
CRISPIN
Amb HQ
H
Linton
ELMFIELD CT
LINTON HILL
LINTON RD
AMSBURY RD
THE BEACONS
DANE CT
Coxheath
SPURGEONS COTTS
PARK AVE
WYKEHAM COTTS
Amsbury Wood
Reason Hill
Clock House Farm
ALCHINS COTTS 1
CORNWALLIS COTTS 2
HILL TOP COTTS
WESTERHILL RD
GREENSAND WAY
VANITY LA
Hill Farm
Amsbury Farm
Westerhill Farm
Little Wester Hill Farm
Maytum Farm
Court Lodge
ROSE CT
Linton
Old Savage
A229

73 A B 74 C D 75 E F

D7
1 ROCHESTER HO
2 CANTERBURY HO
3 CAMBRIDGE HO
4 WINCHESTER HO
5 SALISBURY HO

D8
1 MEDWAY HO
2 DARENTH HO
3 THAMES HO
4 STOUR HO
5 ROTHER HO

E7
1 SWALE HO
2 TRENT HO
3 SHROPSHIRE TERR
4 HUNTINGDON WLK
5 DERWENT HO
6 INVERNESS HO

7 GLASGOW HO
8 ABERDEEN HO
9 TEES HO
10 TYNE HO

E8
1 HARDWICK HO
2 NEATH CT

3 CUCKMERE HO
4 TAMAR HO
5 HUMBER HO
6 ORWELL HO
7 WAVENEY HO
8 WELLAND HO

F5
1 CAPETOWN HO
2 JOHANNESBURG HO
3 HERON APARTMENTS
4 LIVINGSTONE WLK
5 NELSON HO
6 BALMORAL HO

F6
1 AINTREE HO
2 ASCOT HO
3 CHEPSTOW HO
4 FOLKSTONE CL
5 TITCHFIELD CL
6 FONTWELL CL

7 DONCASTER CL
8 HAVANT WLK
9 PLUMPTON WLK
10 FAREHAM WLK
11 DENSTEAD WLK
12 ANDOVER WLK
13 GROOMBRIDGE SQ

75

98

97

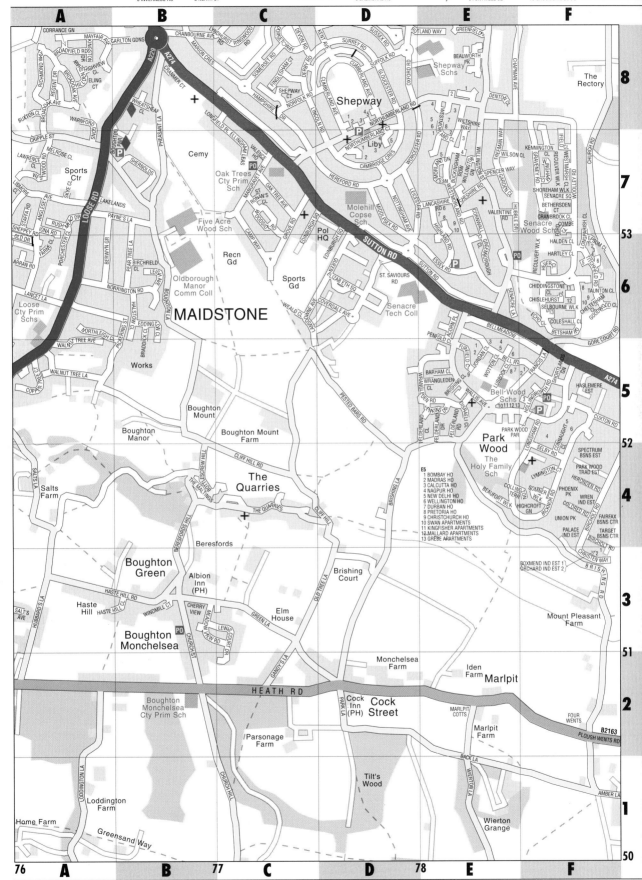

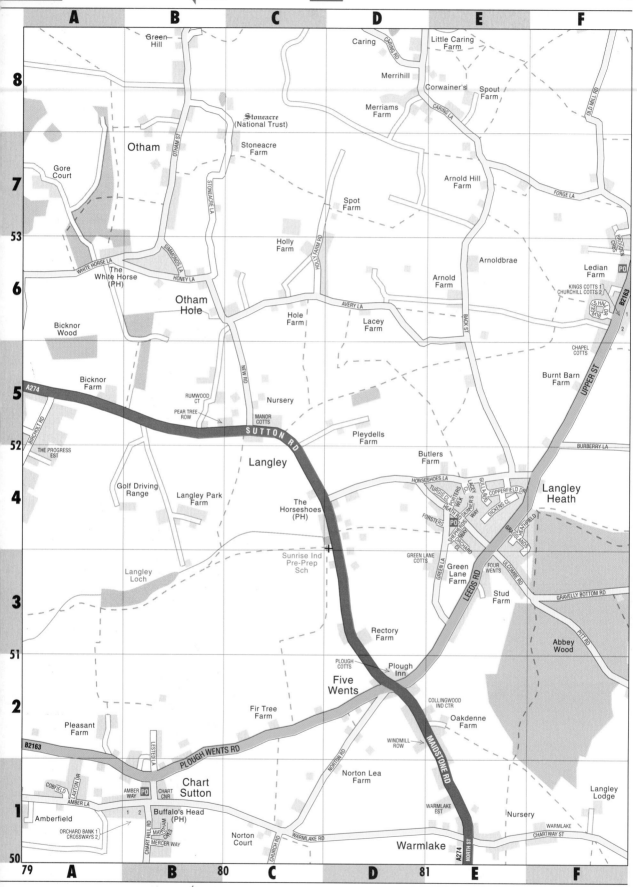

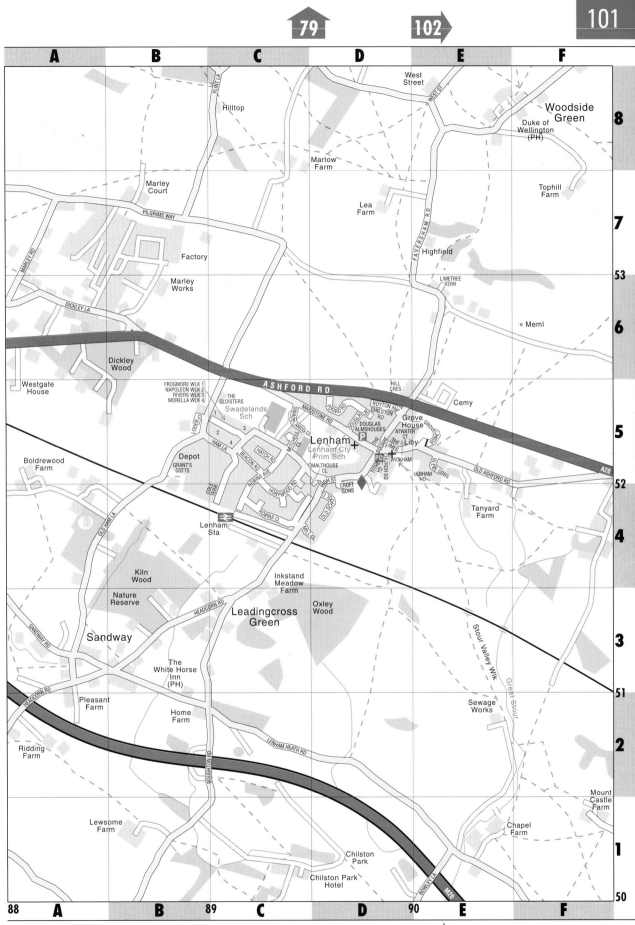

A B C D E F

8
7
53
6
5
52
4
3
51
2
1
50

Woodside Green

West Street

Duke of Wellington (PH)

Hilltop

FLINT LA

Marlow Farm

Tophill Farm

Marley Court

Lea Farm

FAVERSHAM RD

WEST ST

PILGRIMS WAY

MARLEY RD

Factory

Highfield

LIMETREE TERR

Marley Works

Meml

DICKLEY LA

Dickley Wood

ASHFORD RD

Cemy

Westgate House

FROGMORE WLK 1
NAPOLEON WLK 2
RIVERS WLK 3
MORELLA WLK 4

THE CLOISTERS

MAIDSTONE RD

FORD RD
CHILSTON RD
ROYTON AVE

HILL CRES

Grove House

GROVE RD

Boldrewood Farm

LOWER CL

Swadelands Sch

MICHELL'S LANDS CL

DOUGLAS RD

Lenham

Douglas Almshouses

ATWATER CT

Liby

Cemy

HAM LA

Depot

GRANT'S COTTS

BEACON RD

HATCH RD

MICHELLS CL

Lenham Cty Prim Sch

P

THE SQUARE

THE LIMES

WICKHAM PL

Lenham Ho

THE GDNS

OLD ASHFORD RD

A20

OLD MILL LA

COLE TERR

ROBINS AVE

HONYWOOD RD

HIGH ST

MALTHOUSE CL

CROFT GDNS

PO

Lenham Sta

ROBINS CL

OLD SCH CT

MILL CL

Tanyard Farm

Kiln Wood

Nature Reserve

HEADCORN RD

Inkstand Meadow Farm

Leadingcross Green

Oxley Wood

Stour Valley Wlk

Great Stour

Sewage Works

Sandway

SANDWAY RD

The White Horse Inn (PH)

Home Farm

HEADCORN RD

Pleasant Farm

BOUGHTON RD

LENHAM HEATH RD

Ridding Farm

Lewsome Farm

Chilston Park

Chilston Park Hotel

BOWLEY LA

M20

Mount Castle Farm

Chapel Farm

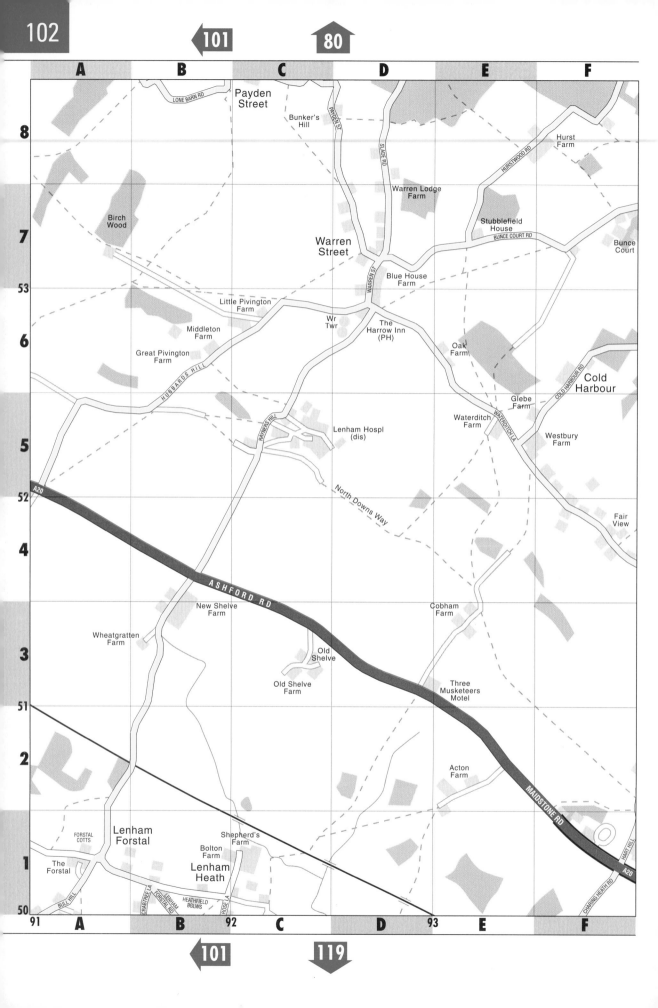

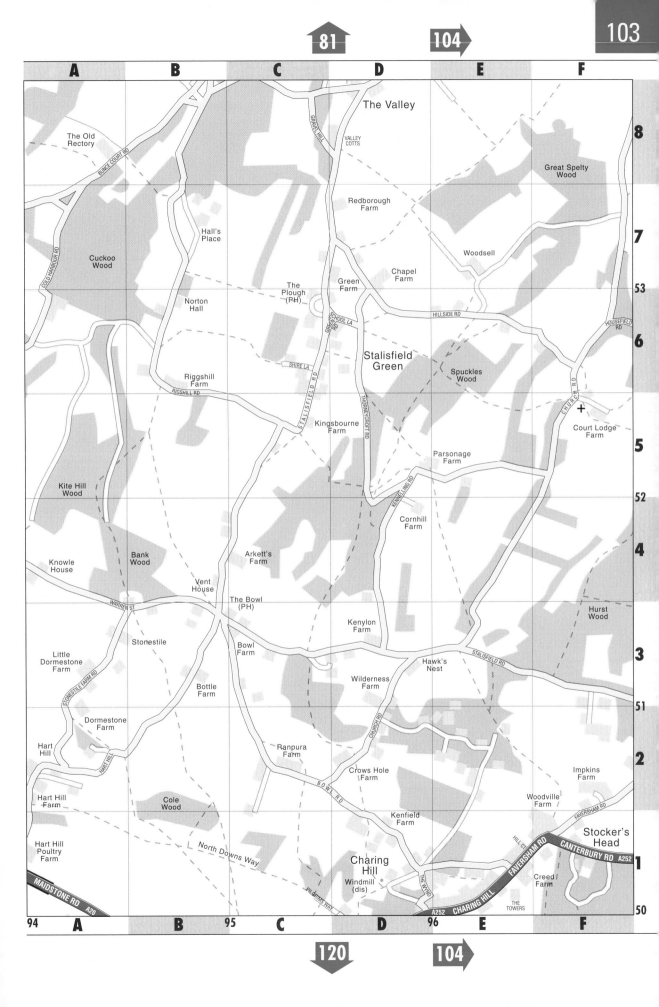

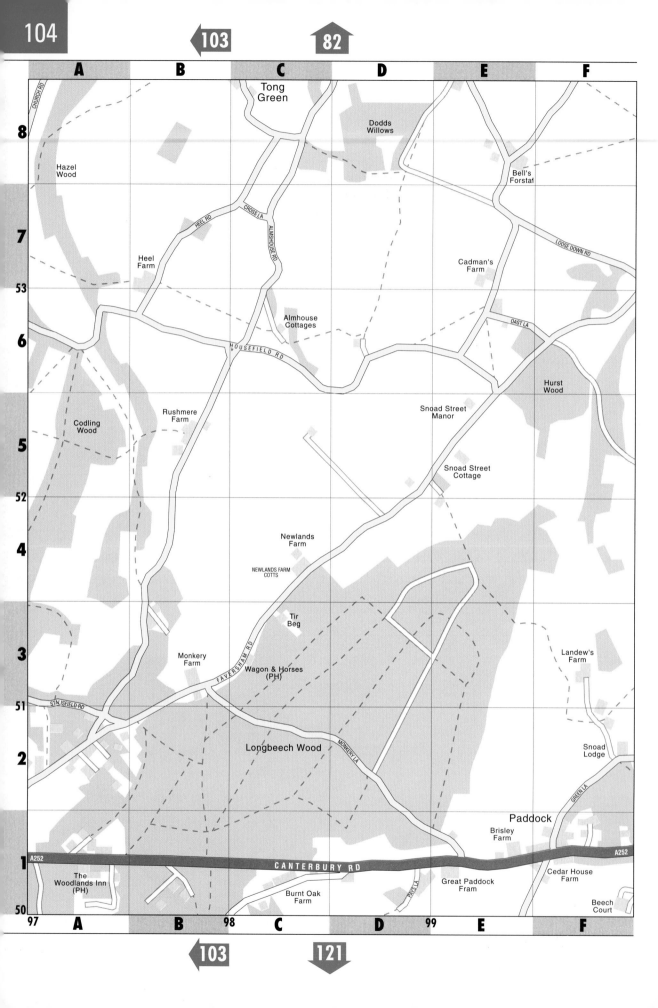

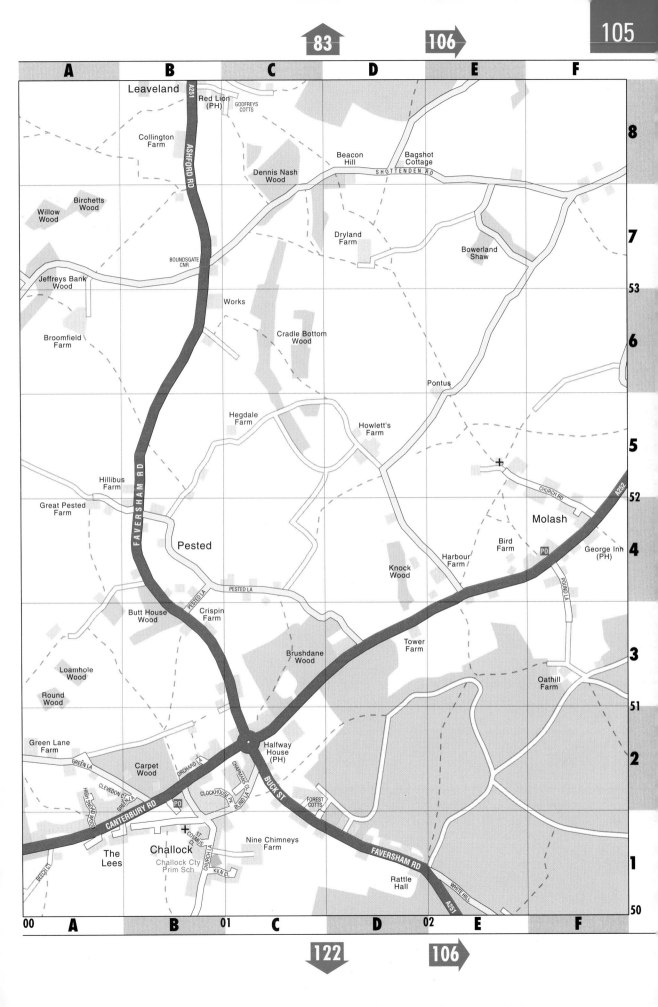

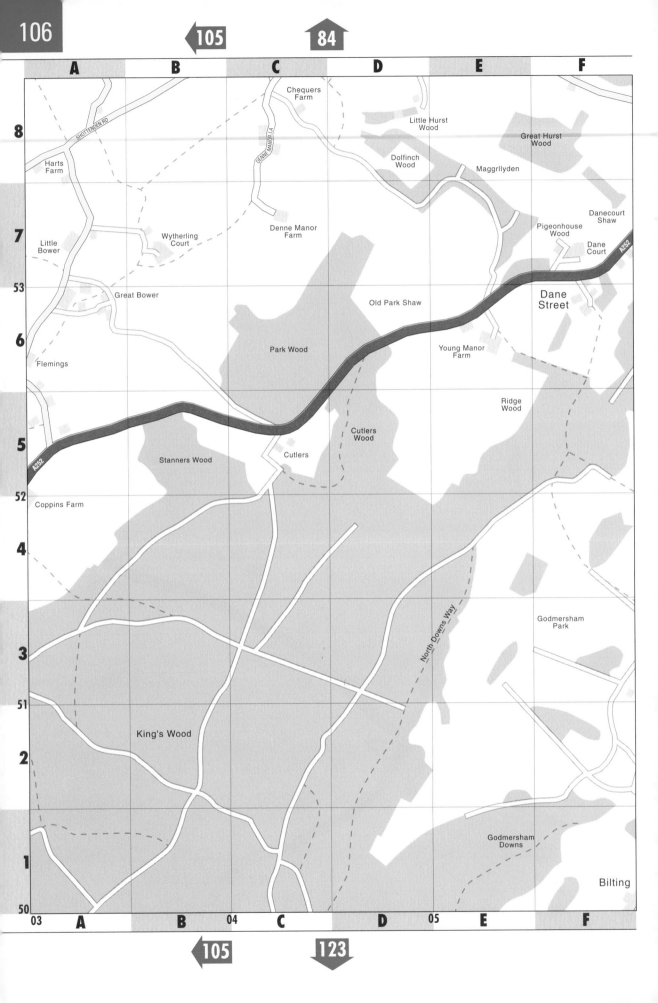

A   B   C   D   E   F

8

Chequers Farm

Little Hurst Wood

Great Hurst Wood

Harts Farm

SHOTTENDEN RD

DENNE MANOR LA

Dolfinch Wood

Maggrllyden

7

Little Bower

Wytherling Court

Denne Manor Farm

Pigeonhouse Wood

Danecourt Shaw

Dane Court

A252

53

Great Bower

Old Park Shaw

Dane Street

6

Flemings

Park Wood

Young Manor Farm

Ridge Wood

A252

5

Coppins Farm

Stanners Wood

Cutlers

Cutlers Wood

52

4

3

North Downs Way

Godmersham Park

51

King's Wood

2

1

Godmersham Downs

Bilting

50

03   A   B   04   C   D   05   E   F

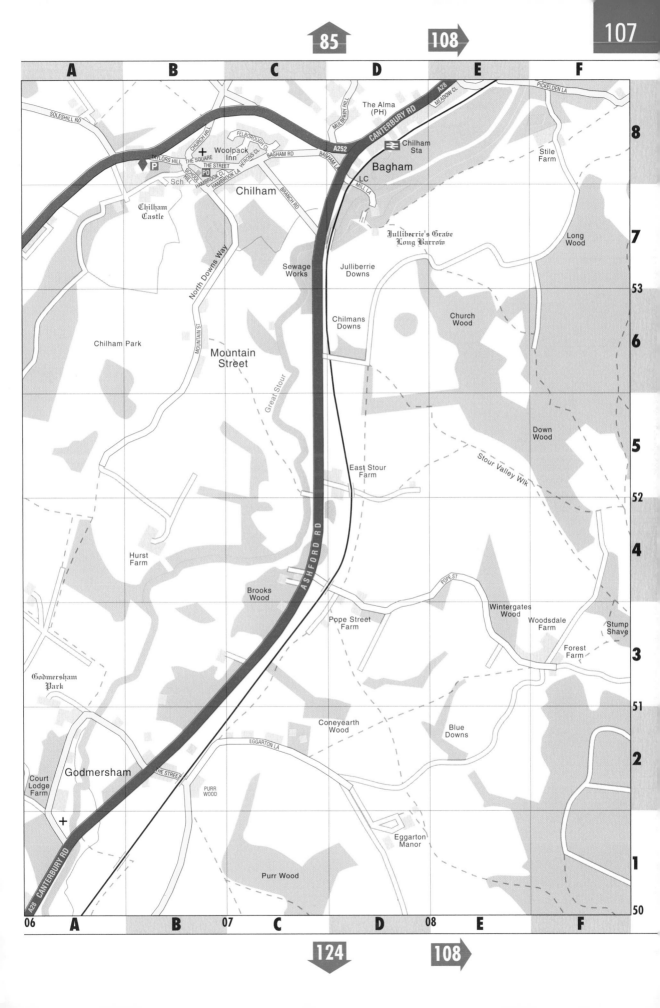

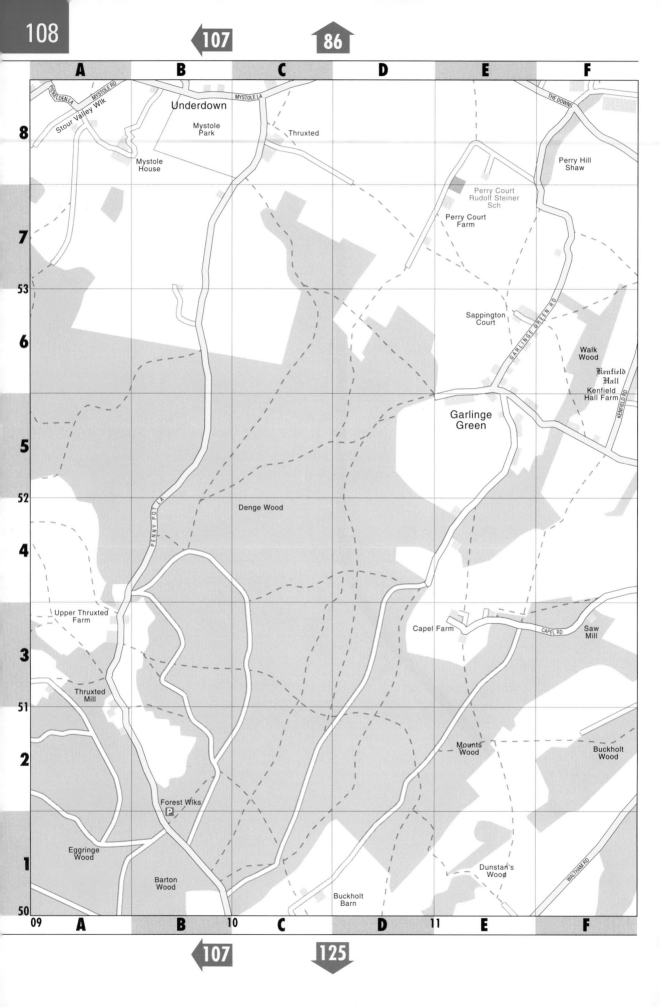

A   B   C   D   E   F

PICKELDEN LA

MYSTOLE RD

Stour Valley Wlk

MYSTOLE LA

Underdown

Mystole
Park

Thruxted

THE DOWNS

8

Mystole
House

Perry Hill
Shaw

Perry Court
Rudolf Steiner
Sch

Perry Court
Farm

7

53

Sappington
Court

GARLINGE GREEN RD

Walk
Wood

6

Kenfield
Hall

Kenfield
Hall Farm

KENFIELD RD

Garlinge
Green

5

52

PENNY POT LA

Denge Wood

4

Upper Thruxted
Farm

Capel Farm

CAPEL RD

Saw
Mill

3

51

Thruxted
Mill

Mounts
Wood

Buckholt
Wood

2

Forest Wlks

P

1

Eggringe
Wood

Dunstan's
Wood

WALTHAM RD

Barton
Wood

Buckholt
Barn

50

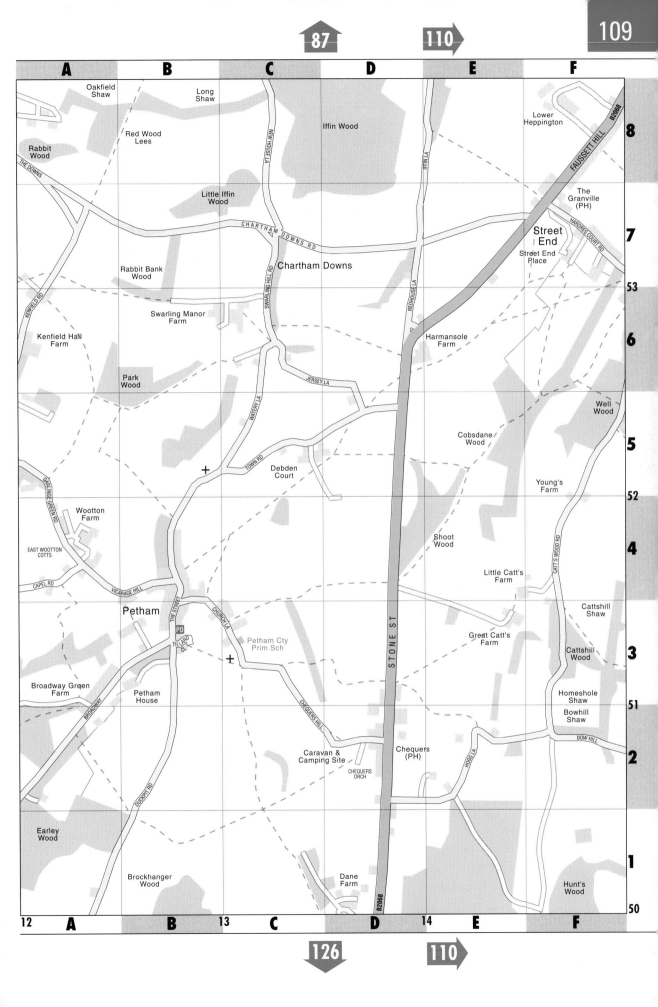

A B C D E F

8

7

53

6

5

52

4

3

51

2

1

50

WHITE HILL CT

BRIDGE RD

Whitehill
Wood

Middle
Pett
Farm

Warren
Wood

North Court
Farm

Little
Pett
Farm

Redhill
Wood

The
Shave

Lower
Hardres

BUTTS CT

SCHOOL LA

Little
Eaton
Farm

Lenhall
Farm

PO
BUTTS
MEADOW
PH

Stockfield
Wood

Avenue
Wood

Pett
Bottom

The Duck
(PH)

Cook's
Farm

TAPLEYS HILL

PETT BOTTOM RD

CROWS CAMP RD

Gorsley
Wood

Peaceful
Retreat
Farm

HARDRES COURT RD

PILOT'S FARM RD

Pilot's
Wood

Broxhall
Farm

Broxhall
Wood

BROXHALL RD

Langham
Park
Farm

St Andrew's
Wood

WOODGATE

PHEASANTS HALL RD

Bursted
Manor

BOW HILL

Upper
Hardres
Court

Hardres
Court
Farm

BURSTED HILL

Bursted
Wood

Park
Rough

Reed
Farm

The
Manor
House

REED MILL LA

Westwood
Farm

Marley
Wood

15 A B 16 C D 17 E F

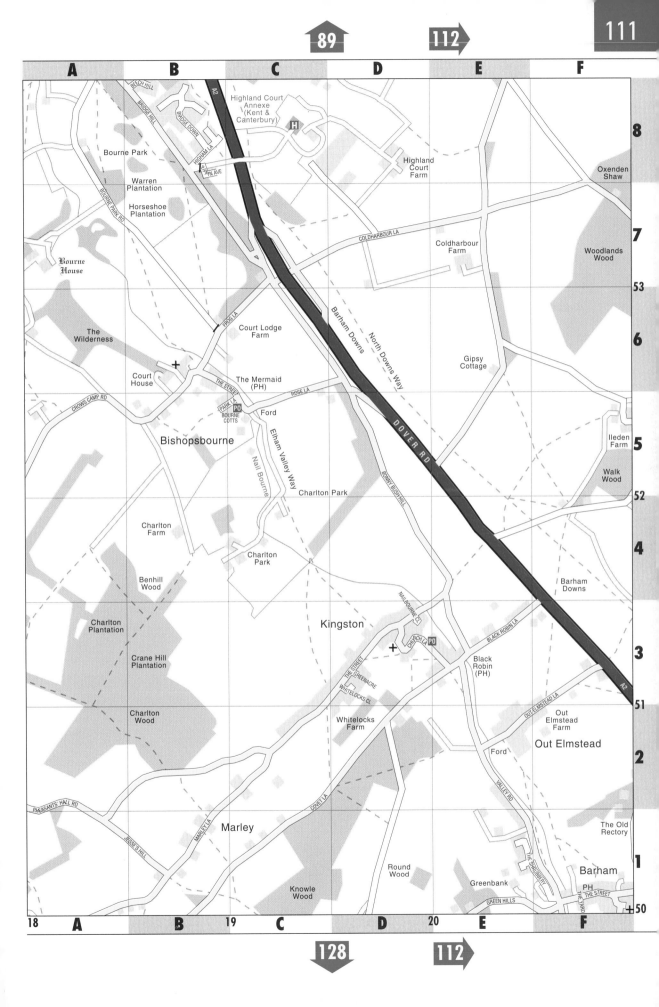

111
90

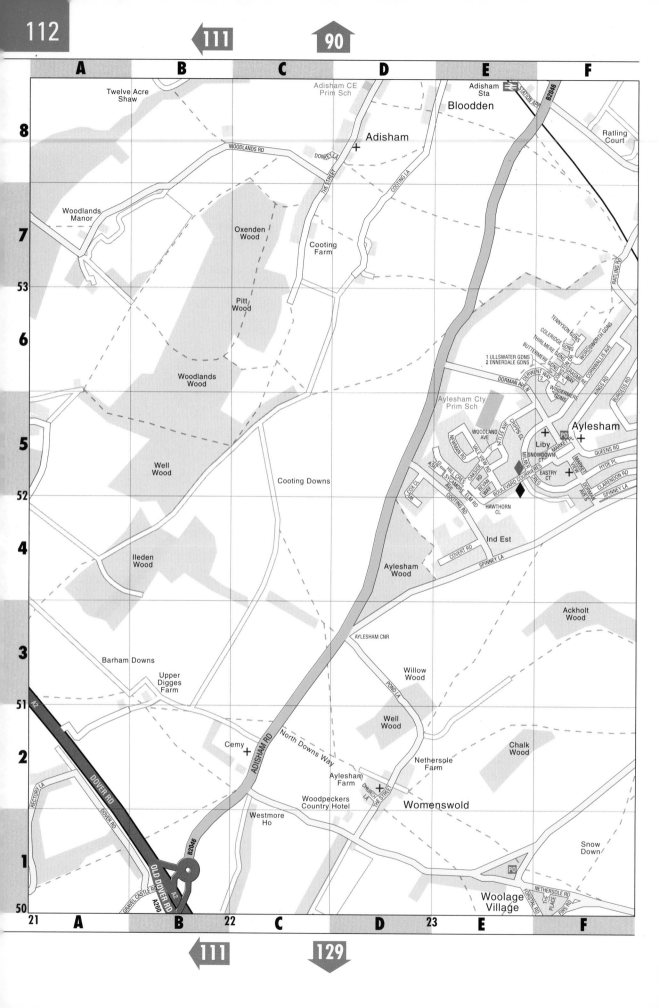

Twelve Acre Shaw

Adisham CE Prim Sch

Bloodden

Adisham Sta

Ratling Court

WOODLANDS RD

DONKEY LA

Adisham

THE STREET

COOTING LA

Woodlands Manor

Oxenden Wood

Cooting Farm

STATION APP

B2046

Pitt Wood

RATLING RD

Tennyson Gdns

Coleridge Gdns

Wordsworth Gdns

Thirlmere Gdns

Buttermere Gdns

Grasmere

Cornwallis Ave

Kings Rd

Burgess Rd

1 ULLSWATER GDNS
2 ENNERDALE GDNS

Woodlands Wood

DORMAN AVE N

Derwent Way

Windermere Gdns

Aylesham Cty Prim Sch

Aylesham

Newman Rd

Woodland Ave

Vale View Rd

Mytlee Ave

Chips Cl

Snowdown Ct

PO

Liby

Market

Well Wood

Queens Rd

Cox Cl

Aspen

Hill Cres

Oakside

Sycamore

Elm Rd

Bean Way

Milner Cres

BOULEVARD COURRIERES

Eastry Ct

Market View

Dorman Ave S

Hyde Pl

Clarendon Rd

Spinney La

Cooting Downs

Cooting Rd

Hawthorn Cl

Ackholt Wood

Ileden Wood

Aylesham Wood

Ind Est

COVERT RD

SPINNEY LA

AYLESHAM CNR

Barham Downs

Willow Wood

Upper Digges Farm

POND LA

A2

Well Wood

Chalk Wood

RECTORY LA

DOVER RD

Cemy

ADISHAM RD

North Downs Way

Nethersole Farm

Aylesham Farm

THE STREET

CHURCH LA

Womenswold

DOVER RD

B2046

Woodpeckers Country Hotel

Westmore Ho

Snow Down

GRAVEL CASTLE RD

A2

OLD DOVER RD

A260

PO

NETHERSOLE RD

FORSTAL RD

THE PLACE

FIRS RD

Woolage Village

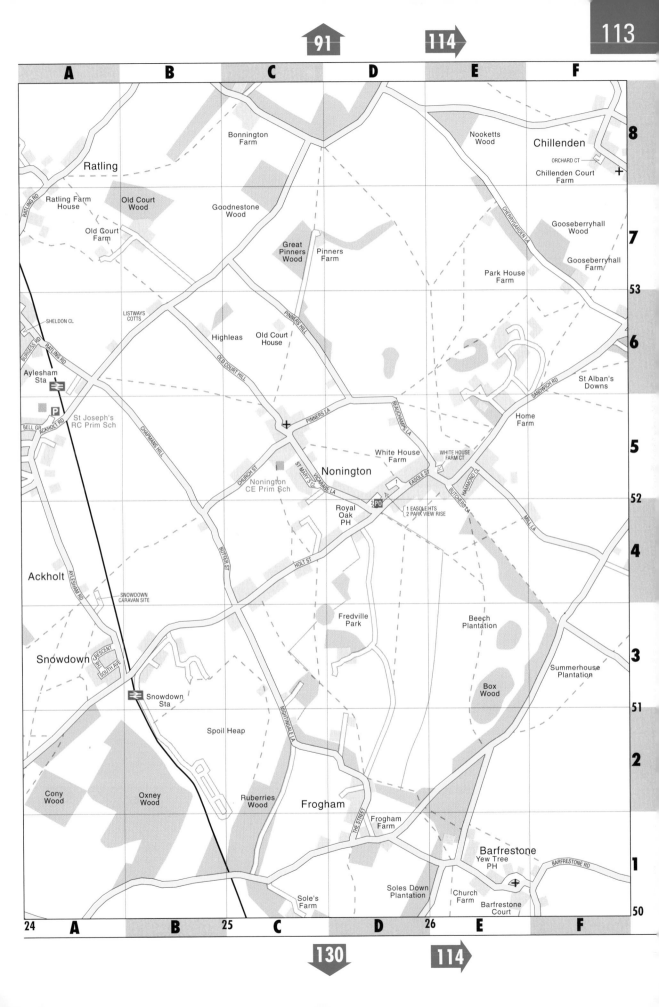

← 113
92

| | A | B | C | D | E | F |

8

YEW TREE FARM

SHORT ST

Griffin's Head (PH)

War Meml

Home Wood

Knowlton

7

The Warren

Home Farm

CUCKOLDS CNR

Knowlton Court

Knowlton Park

Black La

THORNTON LA

SANDWICH RD

53

The Grove

Manorial Earthworks

Shingleton Wood

6

Dover Lodge Cottages

Shingleton Farm

Venson Farm

St Alban's Downs

Round Wood

Shingleton Cottages

Thorntonhill Cottages

5

Kelk Hill

Shingleton Cottages

Thornton Farm

Thornton

Kittington Cottages

52

Brown Pudding Plantation

Thornton Wood

Garden Wood

4

The Downs

PIKE RD

Dane Court

SCHOOL RD

Kittington Farm

3

Beeches Farm

51

Craythorne Firs

2

POPLAR DR

CYPRESS GR

ROMAN WAY

SWEETBRIAR LA

BEECH DR

ASH GR

CHERRY GR

Spoil Heap

Burgess Hill

Works

BARVILLE RD

PO

ST JOHNS RD

FAIRVIEW RD

CHAUCER RD

OAK GR

ARCH RD

MILNER RD

MILNER

ADELAIDE RD

TERRACE RD

Elvington

1

Sports Gd

ELMTON LA

WIGMORE LA

SANDWICH RD

BARFRESTONE RD

50

| 27 | A | B | 28 | C | | D | 29 | E | | F |

← 113
131

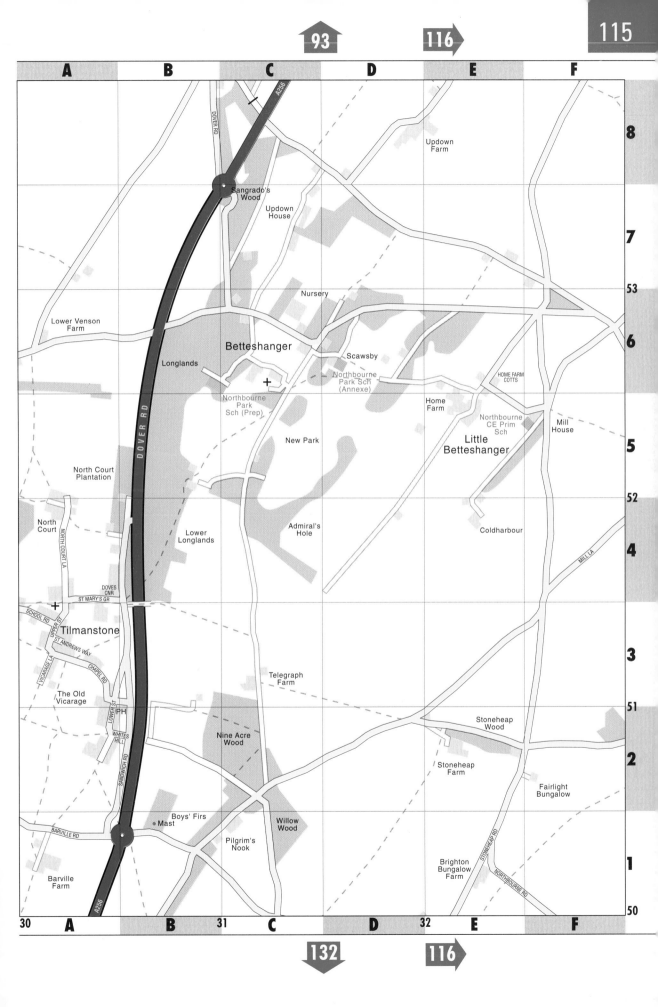

A B C D E F

8

7

53

6

Updown
Farm

Sangrado's
Wood

Updown
House

Lower Venson
Farm

Nursery

Betteshanger

Scawsby

Longlands

Northbourne
Park Sch
(Annexe)

HOME FARM
COTTS

Northbourne
Park
Sch (Prep)

Home
Farm

Northbourne
CE Prim
Sch

Mill
House

DOVER RD

New Park

Little
Betteshanger

5

North Court
Plantation

52

NORTH COURT LA

North
Court

Lower
Longlands

Admiral's
Hole

Coldharbour

MILL LA

4

DOVES
CNR

ST MARY'S GR

SCHOOL RD

UPPER ST

Tilmanstone

ST ANDREWS WAY

VICARAGE LA

CHAPEL RD

Telegraph
Farm

3

The Old
Vicarage

LOWER ST

PH

51

WHITES
HILL

Nine Acre
Wood

Stoneheap
Wood

SANDWICH RD

Stoneheap
Farm

2

Fairlight
Bungalow

Boys' Firs
Mast

Willow
Wood

STONEHEAP RD

BARVILLE RD

Pilgrim's
Nook

Brighton
Bungalow
Farm

NORTHBOURNE RD

1

Barville
Farm

A256

50

30 A 31 B C 32 D E F

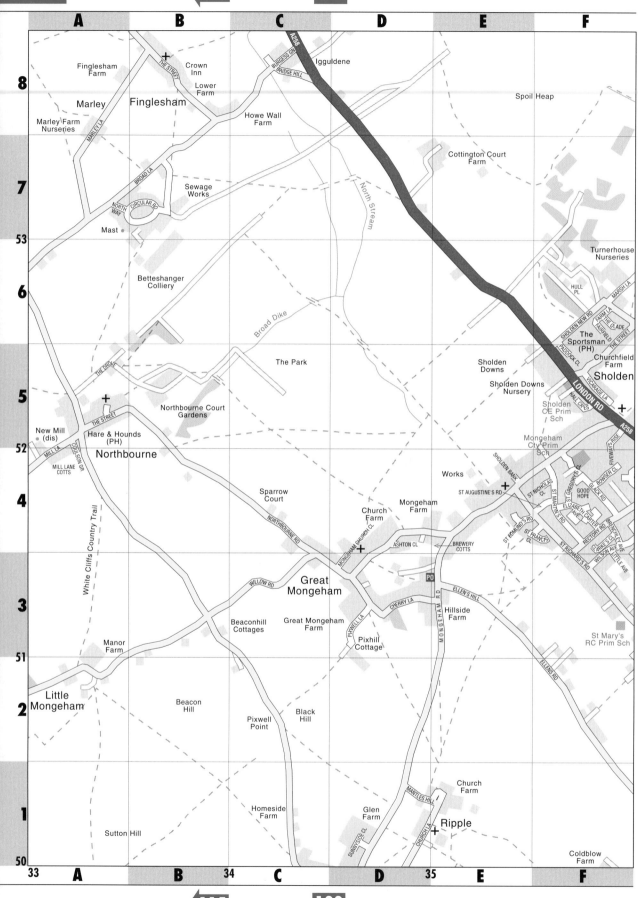

101

135

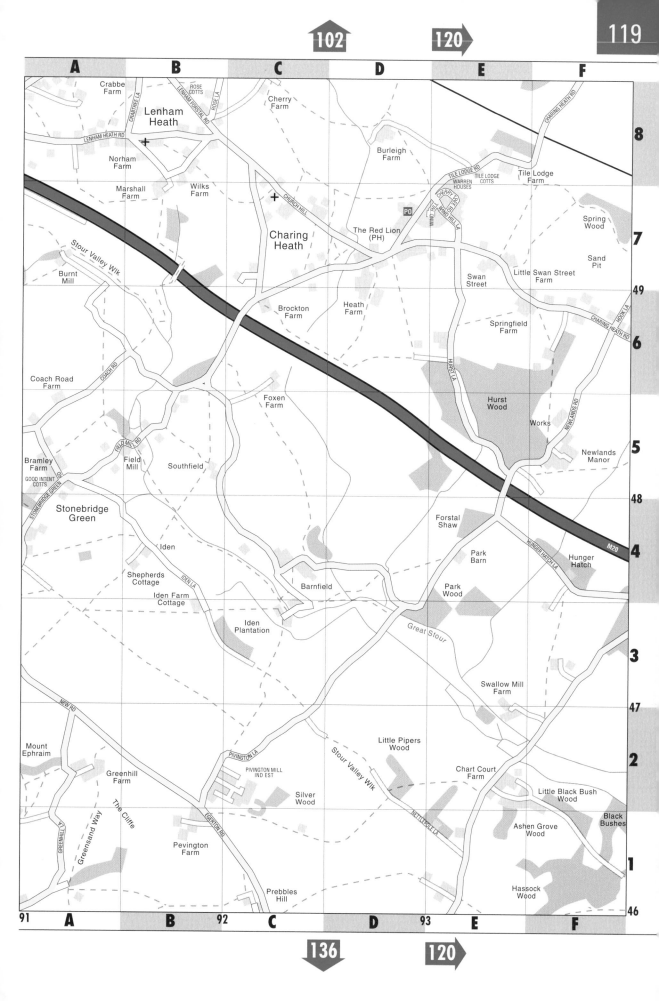

119
103

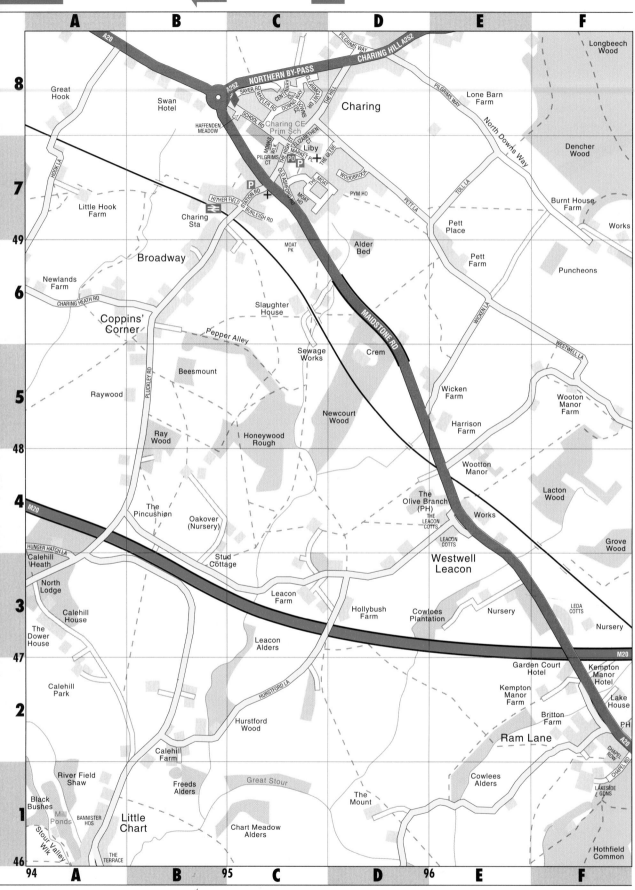

119
137

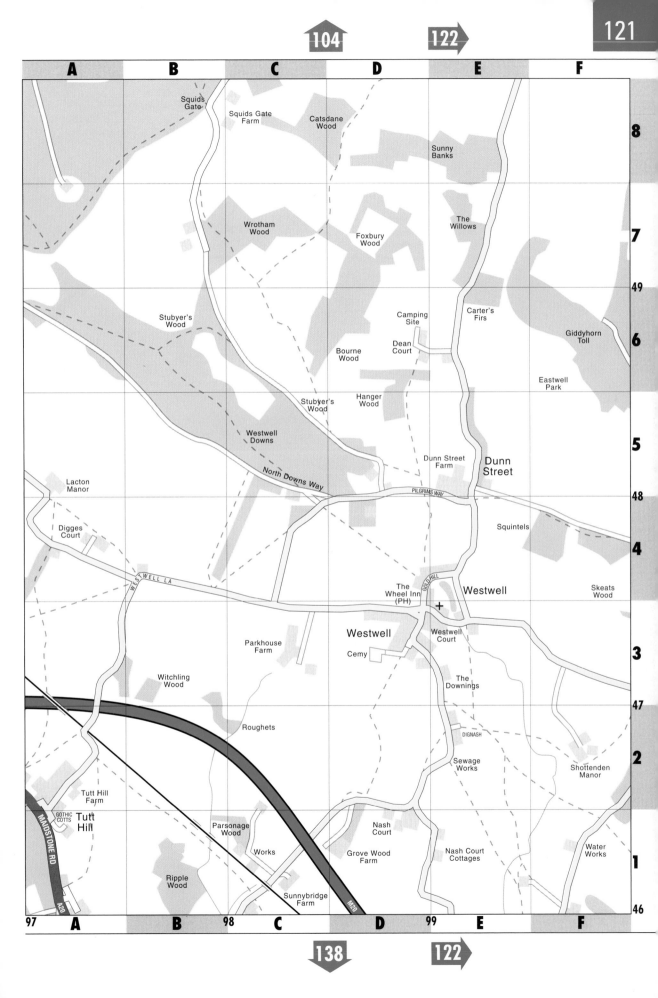

A   B   C   D   E   F

8

Squids
Gate
Squids Gate
Farm
Catsdane
Wood
Sunny
Banks

7
Wrotham
Wood
The
Willows
Foxbury
Wood

49

Carter's
Firs
6
Stubyer's
Wood
Camping
Site
Giddyhorn
Toll
Bourne
Wood
Dean
Court
Eastwell
Park

Stubyer's
Wood
Hanger
Wood

5
Westwell
Downs
Dunn Street
Farm
Dunn
Street

North Downs Way

Lacton
Manor
PILGRIMS WAY

48

Digges
Court
Squintels

4
WESTWELL LA
GOLF HILL
Skeats
Wood
The
Wheel Inn
(PH)
Westwell

Parkhouse
Farm
Westwell
Court

3
Westwell
Cemy
Witchling
Wood
The
Downings

47
Roughets
DIGNASH

2
Sewage
Works
Shottenden
Manor
Tutt Hill
Farm

GOTHIC
COTTS
Tutt
Hill
Parsonage
Wood
Nash
Court
Water
Works

1
Works
Grove Wood
Farm
Nash Court
Cottages
Ripple
Wood

MAIDSTONE RD
Sunnybridge
Farm
M20

46

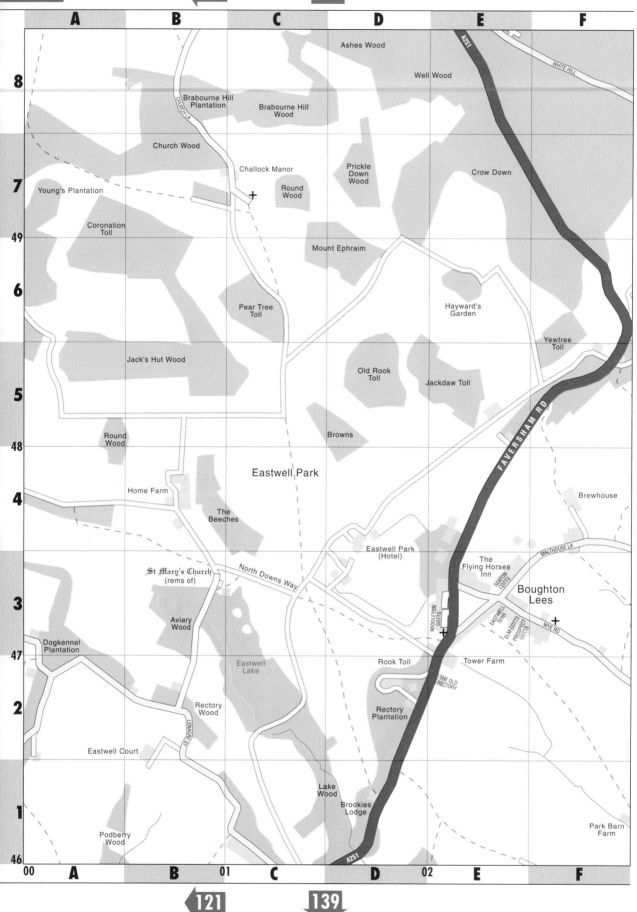

A   B   C   D   E   F

8

Ashes Wood

Well Wood

WHITE HILL

Brabourne Hill
Plantation

Brabourne Hill
Wood

CHURCH LA

7

Church Wood

Challock Manor

Young's Plantation

Round
Wood

Prickle
Down
Wood

Crow Down

A251

49

Coronation
Toll

Mount Ephraim

6

Pear Tree
Toll

Hayward's
Garden

Yewtree
Toll

Jack's Hut Wood

Old Rook
Toll

Jackdaw Toll

5

FAVERSHAM RD

48

Round
Wood

Browns

Eastwell Park

4

Home Farm

Brewhouse

The
Beeches

Eastwell Park
(Hotel)

MALTHOUSE LA

St Mary's Church
(rems of)

North Downs Way

The
Flying Horses
Inn

Boughton
Lees

3

Aviary
Wood

MIDDLETON COTTS

SEATON COTTS

EASTWELL TERR

ELM COTTS   PROSPECT COTTS

WYE RD

47

Dogkennel
Plantation

Eastwell
Lake

Rook Toll

Tower Farm

THE OLD RECTORY

2

LENACRE ST

Rectory
Wood

Rectory
Plantation

Eastwell Court

1

Lake
Wood

Brookies
Lodge

Park Barn
Farm

Podberry
Wood

46

00   A   B   01   C   D   02   E   F

A251

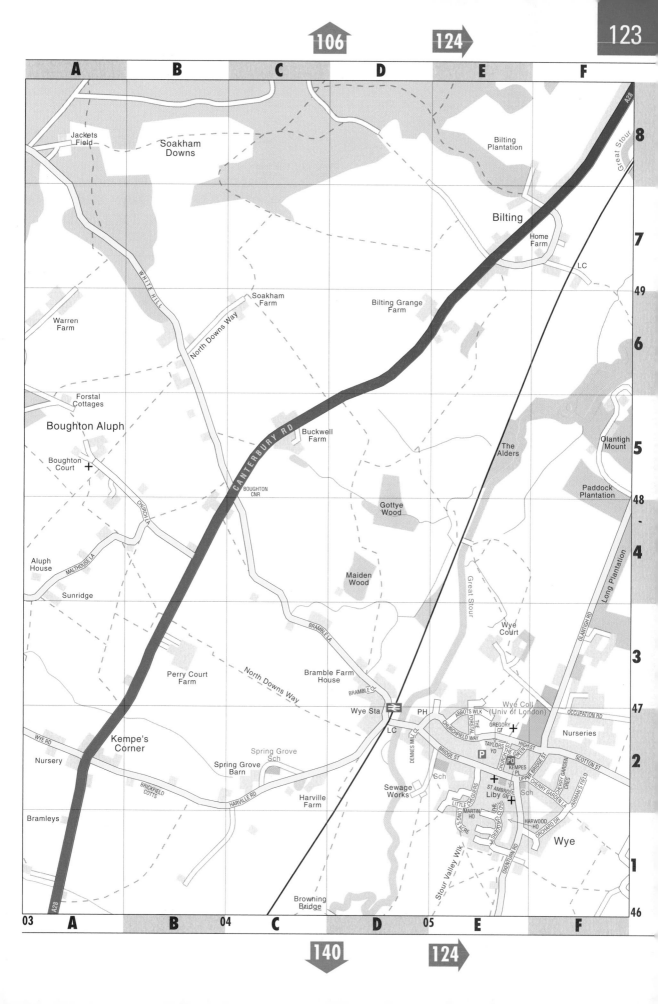

A B C D E F

8

7

49

6

5

48

4

3

47

2

1

46

Jackets Field

Soakham Downs

Bilting Plantation

Bilting

Home Farm

LC

Warren Farm

White Hill

North Downs Way

Soakham Farm

Bilting Grange Farm

Forstal Cottages

Boughton Aluph

Buckwell Farm

Canterbury Rd

The Alders

Olantigh Mount

Boughton Court

Boughton CNR

Paddock Plantation

Gottye Wood

Church La

Aluph House

Malthouse La

Maiden Wood

Great Stour

Long Plantation

Sunridge

Bramble La

Wye Court

Olantigh Rd

Perry Court Farm

North Downs Way

Bramble Farm House

Bramble Ct

Wye Sta

PH

Wye Coll (Univ of London)

Occupation Rd

Nurseries

Wye Rd

Kempe's Corner

LC

Churchfield Way

Arbots Wlk

The Forstal

The Green

Gregory Ct

High St

Scotton St

Nursery

Spring Grove Sch

Spring Grove Barn

Dennes Mill Cl

Bridge St

Taylors Yd

Church St

Kempes Pl

Upper Bridge St

Cherry Garden La

Cherry Garden Cres

Nathan's Field

Brickfield Cotts

Harville Rd

Harville Farm

Sewage Works

Sch

P

PO

Liby Gn

St Ambrose

Sch

Wye

Bramleys

Little Crouchers

Long's Acre

Martin Ho

The Cross

Subway

Oxenturn Rd

Harwood Ho

Orchard Dr

A28

Stour Valley Wlk

Browning Bridge

Great Stour

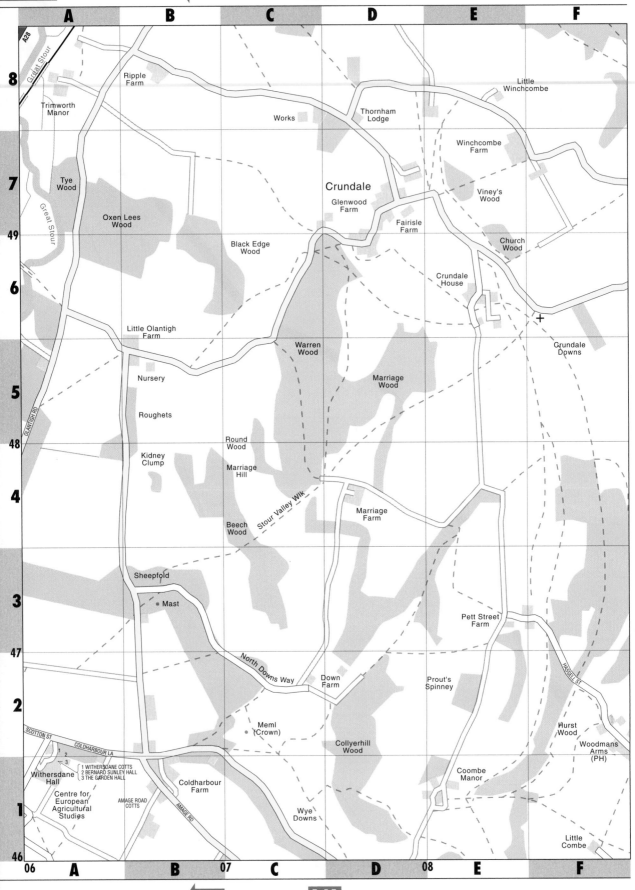

A · B · C · D · E · F

8

Great Stour
A28
Ripple Farm
Trimworth Manor
Works
Thornham Lodge
Little Winchcombe
Winchcombe Farm

7

Tye Wood
Crundale
Glenwood Farm
Viney's Wood

Great Stour
Oxen Lees Wood
Fairisle Farm

49

Black Edge Wood
Church Wood

6

Crundale House

Little Olantigh Farm
Crundale Downs

OLANTIGH RD
Warren Wood

Nursery
Marriage Wood

5

Roughets

Round Wood

48

Kidney Clump
Marriage Hill

4

Stour Valley Wlk
Beech Wood
Marriage Farm

Sheepfold

3

· Mast
Pett Street Farm

47

North Downs Way
Down Farm
Prout's Spinney
HASSEL ST

2

Meml (Crown)
Collyerhill Wood
Hurst Wood
Woodmans Arms (PH)

SCOTTON ST
COLDHARBOUR LA
Coombe Manor

1 WITHERSDANE COTTS
2 BERNARD SUNLEY HALL
3 THE GARDEN HALL

Withersdane Hall
Coldharbour Farm
1
Centre for European Agricultural Studies
AMAGE ROAD COTTS
AMAGE RD
Wye Downs
Little Combe

46

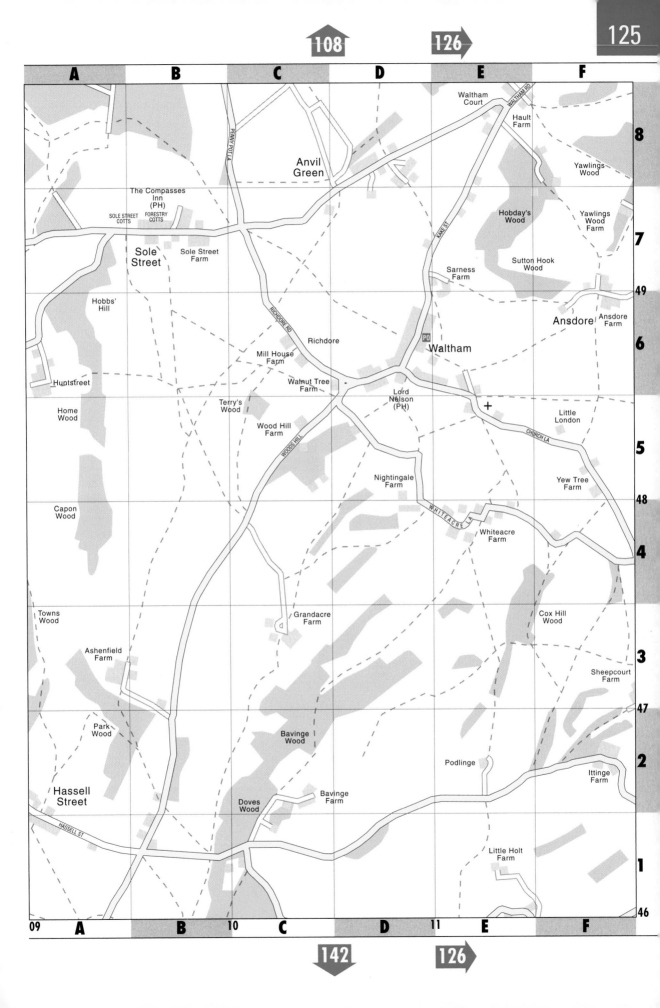

A   B   C   D   E   F

8

Waltham
Court

WALTHAM RD

Hault
Farm

Yawlings
Wood

Anvil
Green

KANE ST

Hobday's
Wood

Yawlings
Wood
Farm

7

The Compasses
Inn
(PH)

SOLE STREET
COTTS

FORESTRY
COTTS

Sole
Street

Sole Street
Farm

PENNY POT LA

Sutton Hook
Wood

49

Sarness
Farm

Hobbs'
Hill

Ansdore

Ansdore
Farm

RICHDORE RD

Richdore

PO

Waltham

6

Mill House
Farm

Huntstreet

Walnut Tree
Farm

Lord
Nelson
(PH)

+

Little
London

Home
Wood

Terry's
Wood

CHURCH LA

Wood Hill
Farm

WOODS HILL

5

Nightingale
Farm

Yew Tree
Farm

48

Capon
Wood

WHITEACRE LA

Whiteacre
Farm

4

Towns
Wood

Grandacre
Farm

Cox Hill
Wood

Ashenfield
Farm

Sheepcourt
Farm

3

47

Park
Wood

Bavinge
Wood

Podlinge

Ittinge
Farm

2

Hassell
Street

Doves
Wood

Bavinge
Farm

HASSELL ST

Little Holt
Farm

1

46

09   A   B   10   C   D   11   E   F

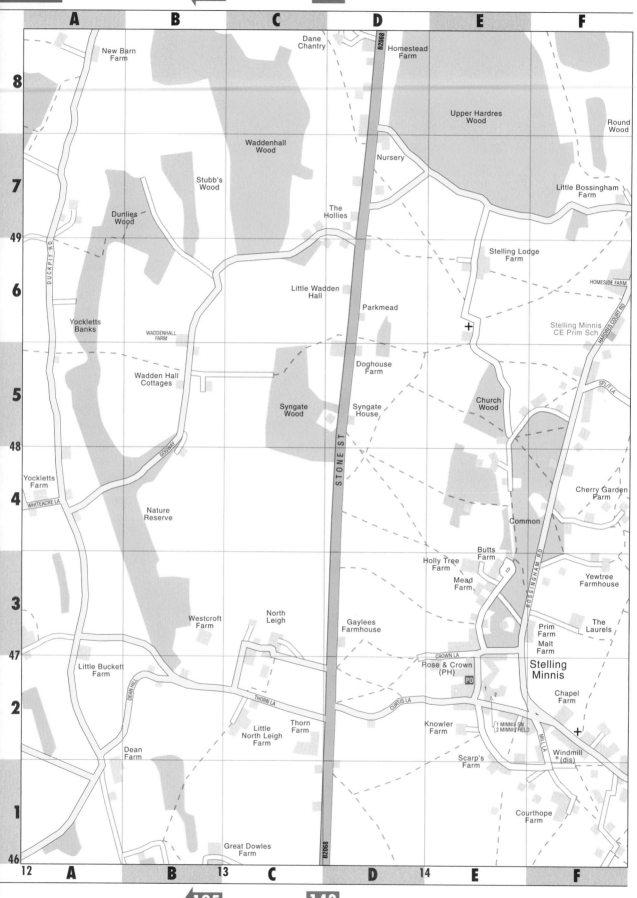

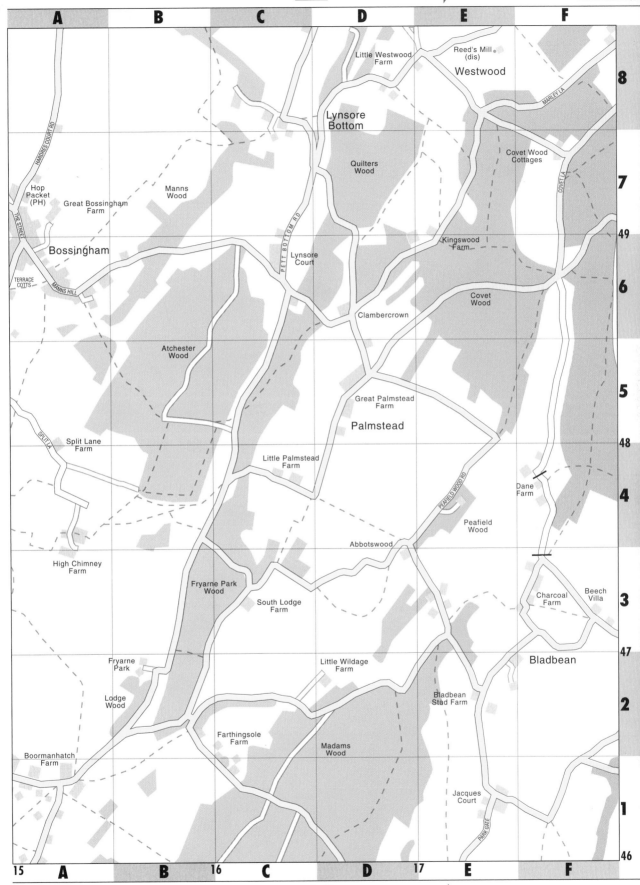

A B C D E F

8

Little Westwood
Farm

Reed's Mill
(dis)

Westwood

Lynsore
Bottom

Covet Wood
Cottages

7

Hop
Packet
(PH)

Manns
Wood

Quilters
Wood

HARDRES COURT RD

Great Bossingham
Farm

MARLEY LA

COVET LA

49

THE STREET

Bossingham

Kingswood
Farm

PETT BOTTOM RD

Lynsore
Court

6

TERRACE
COTTS

MANNS HILL

Clambercrown

Covet
Wood

Atchester
Wood

5

Great Palmstead
Farm

Palmstead

SPLIT LA

Split Lane
Farm

48

Little Palmstead
Farm

Dane
Farm

4

PEAFIELD WOOD RD

Peafield
Wood

High Chimney
Farm

Abbotswood

Charcoal
Farm

Beech
Villa

Fryarne Park
Wood

3

South Lodge
Farm

47

Bladbean

Fryarne
Park

Little Wildage
Farm

Lodge
Wood

Bladbean
Stud Farm

2

Farthingsole
Farm

Boormanhatch
Farm

Madams
Wood

Jacques
Court

1

PARK GATE

46

15 A B 16 C D 17 E F

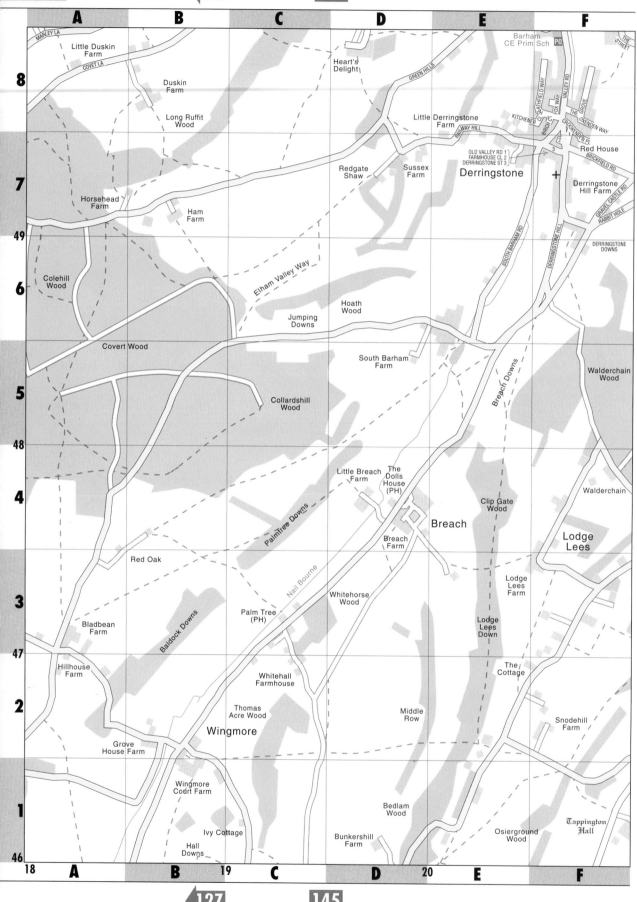

129
113

A B C D E F

8

7

49

6

5

48

4

3

47

2

1

46

24 A B 25 C D 26 E F

Leighgate Bottom

Three Barrows Down

Lower Soles Wood

LONG LA

Stafflands Wood

North Downs Way

LONG LA

Golgotha

SHEPHERDSWELL RD

Long Lane Farm

West Court Downs

LC

Crossways

WESTCOURT LA

GLEN

PENFOLD GDNS

EYTHORNE RD

MEADOW VIEW RD

BERNAR GDNS

Shepherdswell or Sibertswold

MILL LA

HACKLING DANE

Shepherds Well Sta

MOTORWELL DR

STATION RD

HILL AVE

THE GRANGE

ST ANDREWS GDNS

SIBERTS CT

THE TERRACE

APPROACH RD

Bricklayers Arms (PH)

THE OAKLEYS

PO

WHITTINGTON TERR

CHURCH HILL

MILLFIELDS

MOON HILL

Puckland Wood

West Court Farm

Botolph Street Farm

MOORLAND RD

Sibertswold CE Prim Sch

Upton Court Farm

Halfway Street

COLDRED RD

Coxhill Farm

Diamond Farm

COXHILL

Hope Wood

Claysole Wood

Upton Wood

A2

DOVER RD

CHURCH RD

47

Five Oaks

Lyddenhill Wood

LYDDEN HILL

A2

COLDRED HILL

129
147

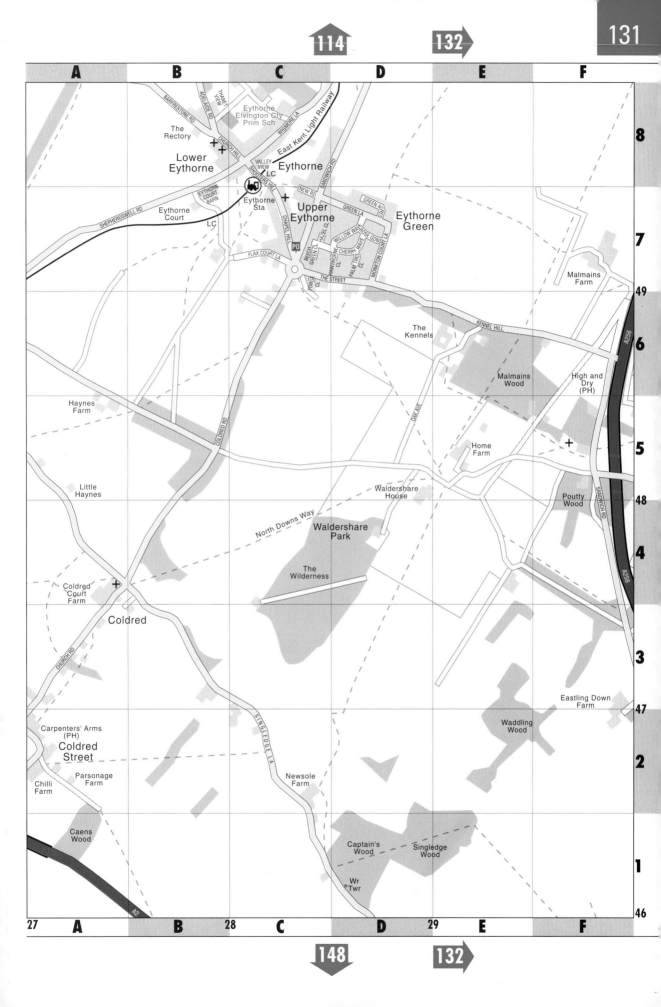

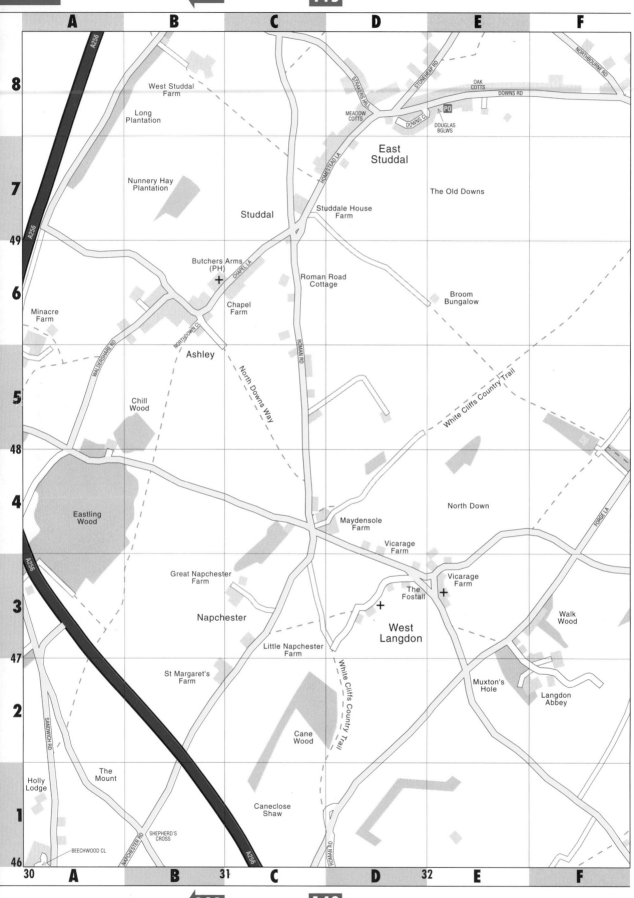

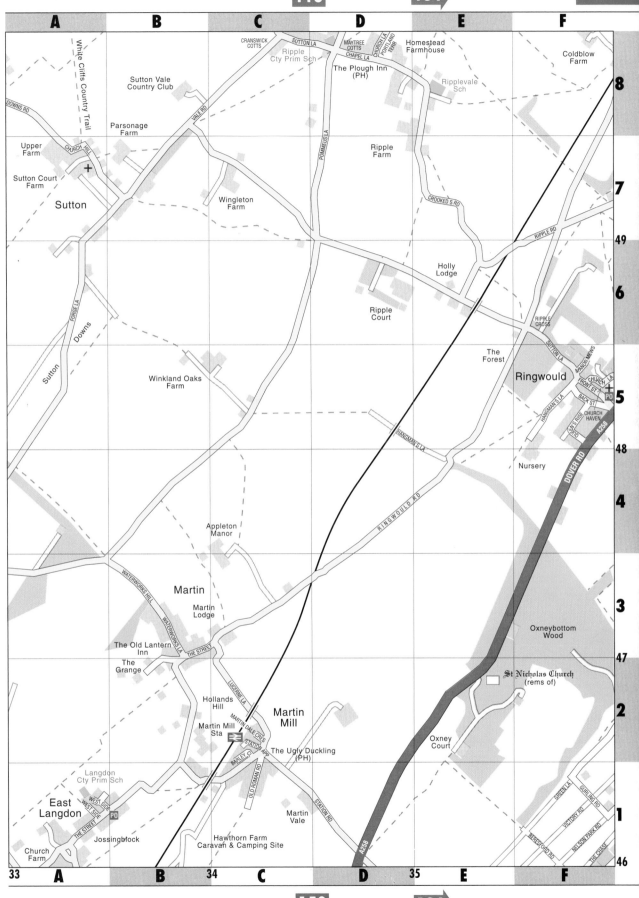

White Cliffs Country Trail

Downs Rd

Upper Farm

Sutton Court Farm

Sutton

Church Hill

Forge La

Sutton Downs

Parsonage Farm

Sutton Vale Country Club

Vale Rd

Wingleton Farm

Cranswick Cotts

Ripple Cty Prim Sch

Sutton La

Maytree Cotts

Chapel La

Church La

Portland Terr

The Plough Inn (PH)

Homestead Farmhouse

Pommeus La

Ripple Farm

Ripplevale Sch

Coldblow Farm

Crooked S Rd

Holly Lodge

Ripple Rd

Ripple Court

The Forest

Ripple Cross

Sutton La

Manor Mews

Ringwould

Church

Front St

Back St

Old St Yn's Rise

Hangman's La

Church Haven

PO

Winkland Oaks Farm

Hangman's La

Ringwould Rd

Nursery

Dover Rd

A258

Appleton Manor

Waterworks Hill

Martin

Martin Lodge

Waterworks La

The Old Lantern Inn

The Grange

The Street

Oxneybottom Wood

St Nicholas Church (rems of)

Lucerne La

Hollands Hill

Martin Dale Cres

Martin Mill

Martin Mill Sta

Station App

The Ugly Duckling (PH)

Barley Cl

Oxney Court

Langdon Cty Prim Sch

East Langdon

West Side

West Side

PO

The Street

Old Roman Rd

Station Rd

Martin Vale

Green La

Gurling Rd

Victory Rd

Nelson Park Rd

Beresford Rd

The Chase

Church Farm

Jossingblock

Hawthorn Farm Caravan & Camping Site

A258

33 34 35 46 47 48 49

133
117

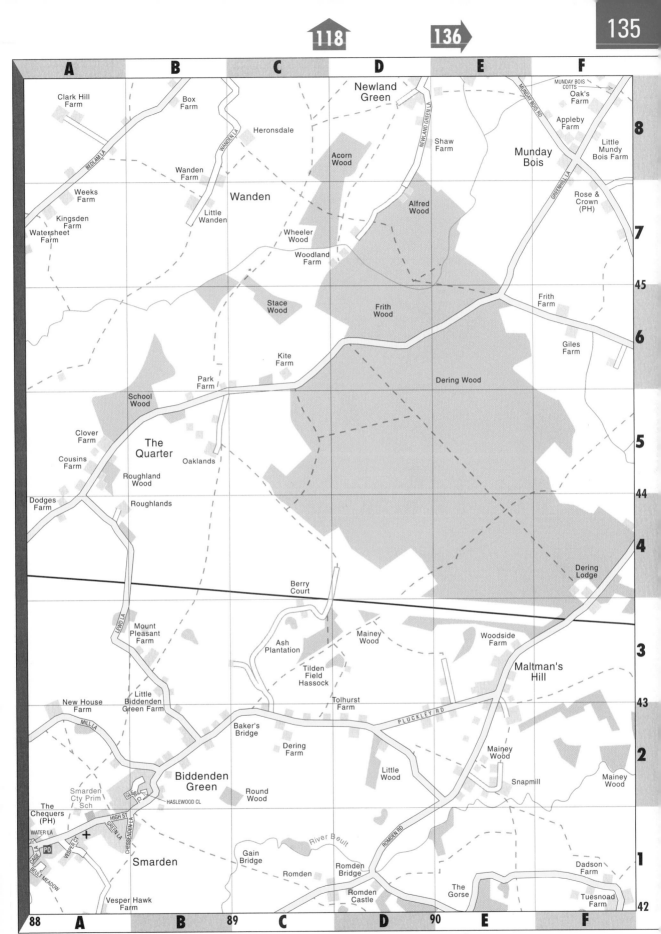

A B C D E F

8

Clark Hill Farm

Box Farm

Newland Green

MUNDAY BOIS COTTS

Oak's Farm

Heronsdale

Shaw Farm

Appleby Farm

Little Mundy Bois Farm

BEDLAM LA

Wanden Farm

WANDEN LA

Acorn Wood

Munday Bois

GREENHILL LA

Weeks Farm

Wanden

Alfred Wood

Rose & Crown (PH)

7

Kingsden Farm

Little Wanden

Wheeler Wood

NEWLAND GREEN LA

MUNDAY BOIS RD

Watersheet Farm

Woodland Farm

Frith Farm

45

Stace Wood

Frith Wood

Giles Farm

6

Kite Farm

Dering Wood

Park Farm

School Wood

Clover Farm

The Quarter

Oaklands

5

Cousins Farm

Roughland Wood

Dodges Farm

Roughlands

44

4

Dering Lodge

Berry Court

Mount Pleasant Farm

Mainey Wood

Woodside Farm

3

LEWD LA

Ash Plantation

Maltman's Hill

Tilden Field Hassock

New House Farm

Little Biddenden Green Farm

Tolhurst Farm

43

MILL LA

Baker's Bridge

PLUCKLEY RD

Mainey Wood

2

Dering Farm

GLEB.. RD

Biddenden Green

Snapmill

Mainey Wood

Smarden Cty Prim Sch

HASLEWOOD CL

Round Wood

Little Wood

HIGH ST

The Chequers (PH)

GREEN LA

CHESSENDEN LA

ROMDEN RD

WATER LA

+

River Beult

Dadson Farm

1

PO

VESPER CT

BEULT MEADOW

Smarden

Gain Bridge

Romden

Romden Bridge

Romden Castle

The Gorse

Tuesnoad Farm

Vesper Hawk Farm

42

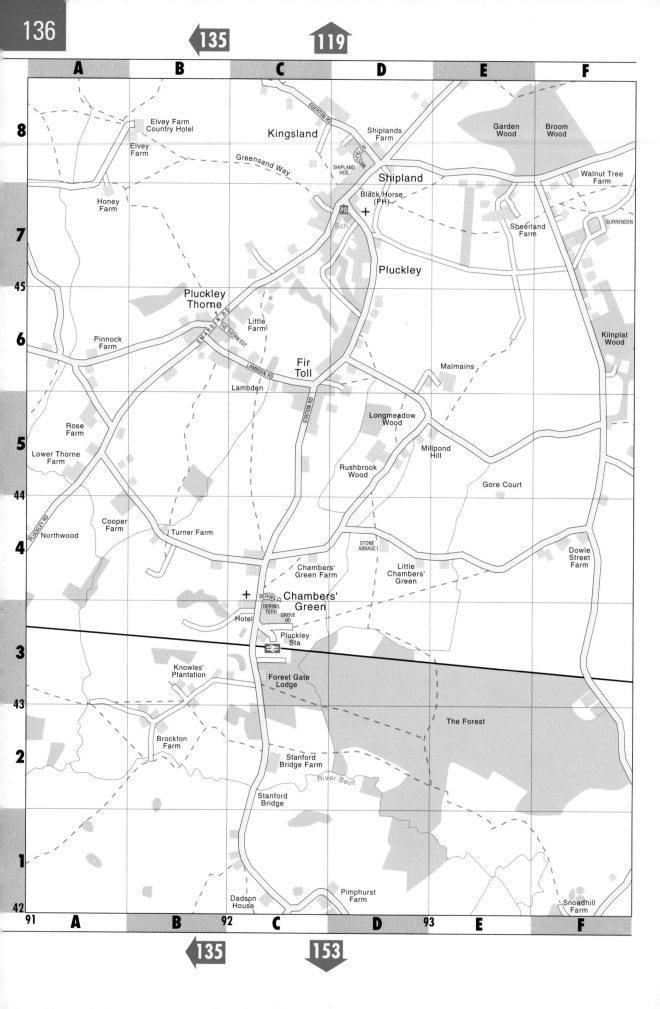

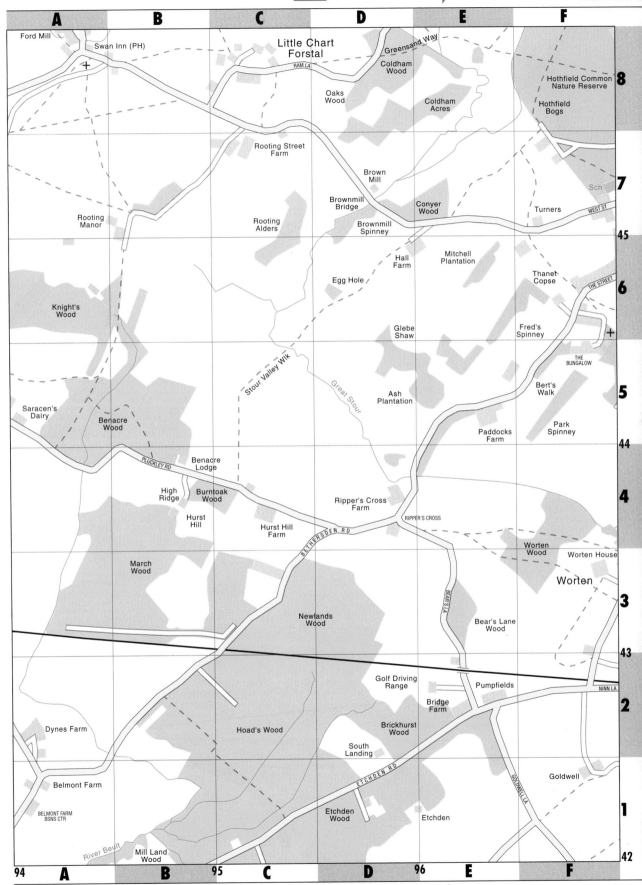

A **B** **C** **D** **E** **F**

Ford Mill

Swan Inn (PH)

Little Chart
Forstal

RAM LA

Greensand Way

Coldham
Wood

8

Hothfield Common
Nature Reserve

Oaks
Wood

Coldham
Acres

Hothfield
Bogs

Rooting Street
Farm

Brown
Mill

Sch

7

Brownmill
Bridge

Conyer
Wood

Turners

WEST ST

Rooting
Manor

Rooting
Alders

Brownmill
Spinney

45

Hall
Farm

Mitchell
Plantation

Thanet
Copse

THE STREET

6

Egg Hole

Knight's
Wood

Glebe
Shaw

Fred's
Spinney

THE
BUNGALOW

Stour Valley Wlk

Great Stour

Ash
Plantation

Bert's
Walk

5

Saracen's
Dairy

Benacre
Wood

Paddocks
Farm

Park
Spinney

44

PLUCKLEY RD

Benacre
Lodge

High
Ridge

Burntoak
Wood

Ripper's Cross
Farm

4

Hurst
Hill

Hurst Hill
Farm

BETHERSDEN RD

RIPPER'S CROSS

Worten
Wood

Worten House

March
Wood

BEARS LA

Worten

3

Newlands
Wood

Bear's Lane
Wood

43

Golf Driving
Range

Pumpfields

NINN LA

2

Bridge
Farm

Dynes Farm

Hoad's Wood

Brickhurst
Wood

Goldwell

South
Landing

GOLDWELL LA

Belmont Farm

ETCHDEN RD

BELMONT FARM
BSNS CTR

Etchden
Wood

Etchden

1

River Beult

Mill Land
Wood

42

A20

P

8

Ripple
Court

Beechbrook
Farm

Castle
Farm

M20

Foxenhill
Toll

Beechbrook

Crouchers
Manor

Kingsland

Beechbrook
Wood

SAMDYHURST LA

CH

Sch

COMMON
WAY

7

Tollhill
Wood

SCHOOL RD
PLANTATION CL
COACH DR
SACKVILLE CL
TUFTON RD
BEECH DR

45

PO

Hothfield

Yonsea
Farm

Depot

MAIDSTONE RD

Mill
House

Woodside

WESTWELL LA

POTTERS CL

Potters
Corner

THANET TERR
THE STREET

Home
Farm

PH

POTTERS
CNR

PARK DR

MEADOW VIEW

6

The
Larches

WATERFALL RD

Broomfield
Wood

Potters Corner
Wood

Hoad's Wood

Nursery

Marble
Wood

Eyesend
Plantation

Mansion
Copse

Pigsbrook
Wood

GODINTON LA

Eyesend

ASHGROVE
ALMONDS CL
ORCHARD CL
FARRIER CL
DENSOLE WLK
WARREN VIEW

The
Warren

5

Godinton
Plantation

Balls
Wood

Balls
Wood

Lodge
Wood

A20

ORIEL RD

44

West
Lodge

Petts
Hole

ORCHARD DR

4

Godinton

Godinton
Park

Chestnut Tell
Plantation

LONG WLK

MANOR WAY

Worten
Mill

Swinford
Manor
Sch

Jubilee
Plantation

GREENSAND WAY

Loudon
Wood

Chimneys
(PH)

LOUDON CT

A28

B2074

Worten Home
Farm

Great Stour

Stour Valley Wlk

River
Spinney

Godinton
Cty Prim
Sch

LOUDON PATH

LOUDON WAY

CEDAR CL

EAST LODGE RD

LIME CL

POPLAR CL

HORSHAM CL

HILTON RD

BRIDGE RD

3

Willow
Bed

CHART AVE

THE FORGE

LOCKHOLT CL

SPRINGWOOD DR

THE SPRINGWOOD

STANLEY

CHESTNUT CL

CYPRESS AVE

JUNIPER CL

CHART RD

St GEORGE'S
BSNS CTR

STAFFORD

43

MAPLE CL

ROWAN CL

YEW CL

VIBURNUM CL

BRUNSWICK RD

COBBS WOOD
IND EST

HANDOVER CL

BRUNSWICK IND CTR

NINN LA

2

Depot

Ninn Lodge
Farm

Godinton
Park

Bucksford
Manor

B2229

BEAVER LA

LENACRE RD

BROOKFIELD
IND PK

Riverside
Sch

MONTPELIER
BSNS PK

JEFFERSON CL

DENCORA WAY

Bucksford
Bridge

CHART RD

Buxford
Mill

Singleton
Lake

BUCKSFORD LA

BROOKFIELD RD

RIVERVIEW

STOUR CL

CYGNET WAY

FORD WAY

MILLBROW LA

CRESSFIELD

B2229

1

Great
Chart

PH

THE STREET
THE STOKE
THE PADDOCKS
CORONATION DR
MIDDLE CL

SINGLETON RD

THORPES WAY

HAYMAKERS CL

A28

Playing
Field

COVERT 1
EGGRINGE 2
HONEYFIELD 3
SILECROFT CT 4
BROUGHTON CT 5
OAKENPOLE 6
HUNTSWOOD 7

LONG
BEECH

MILLBROOK MEADOW

OAKLANDS

BAILEY'S FIELD

ARLINGTON

HACKL

42

97

98

99

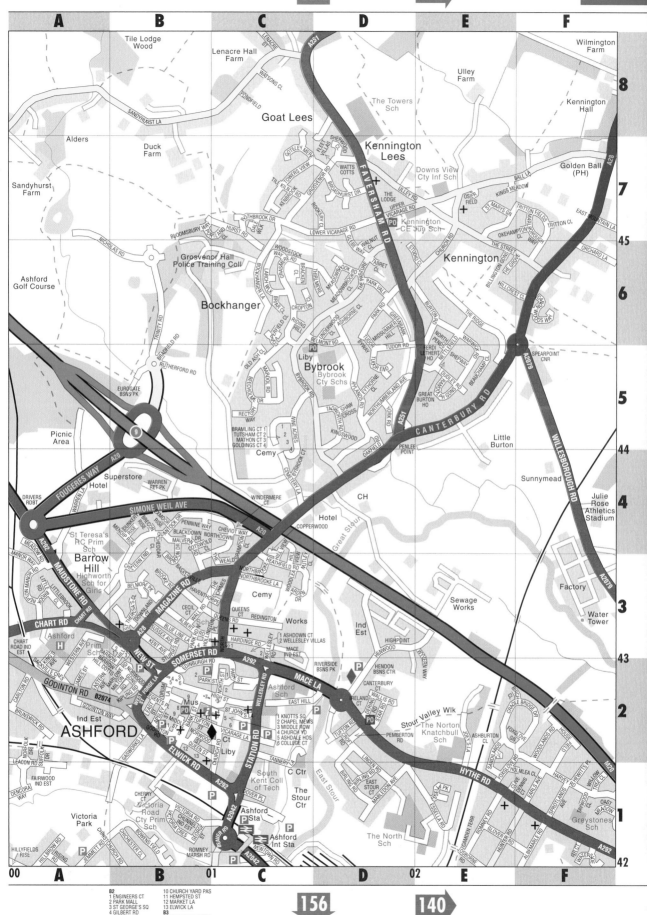

B2
1 ENGINEERS CT
2 PARK MALL
3 ST GEORGE'S SQ
4 GILBERT RD
5 NEW RENTS
6 CASTLE ST
7 KINGS PAR
8 COUNTY SQ
9 TUFTON WLK
10 CHURCH YARD PAS
11 HEMPSTED ST
12 MARKET LA
13 ELWICK LA
B3
1 BARROW HILL TERR
2 BARROWHILL PL
3 GRAVEL WLK
4 WOLSELEY PL

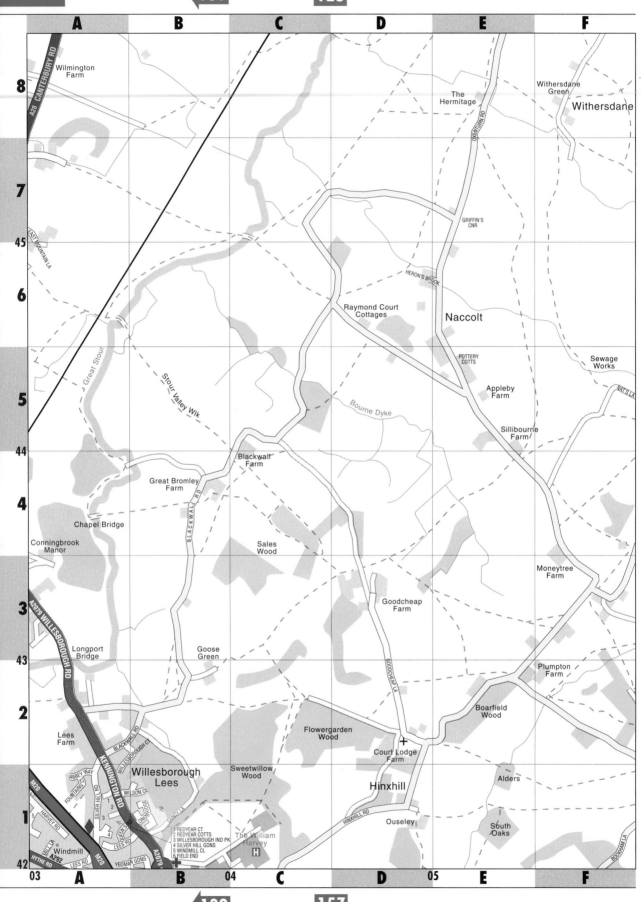

A B C D E F

8
Wilmington Farm
Withersdane Green
The Hermitage
Withersdane

7

45
GRIFFIN'S CNR

6
HERON'S BROOK
Raymond Court Cottages
Naccolt

5
Stour Valley Wlk
Bourne Dyke
POTTERY COTTS
Appleby Farm
Sewage Works
Sillibourne Farm
VAT'S LA

44
Blackwall Farm

4
Great Bromley Farm
Chapel Bridge
Sales Wood
Moneytree Farm

Conningbrook Manor

3
A2079 WILLESBOROUGH RD
Longport Bridge
Goose Green
Goodcheap Farm
Plumpton Farm

43
Boarfield Wood

2
Lees Farm
Flowergarden Wood
Court Lodge Farm
Alders

Willesborough Lees
Sweetwillow Wood
Hinxhill

1
Windmill
1 REDYEAR CT
2 REDYEAR COTTS
3 WILLESBOROUGH IND PK
4 SILVER HILL GDNS
5 WINDMILL CL
6 FIELD END
The William Harvey
Ouseley
South Oaks

42
03 A B 04 C D 05 E F

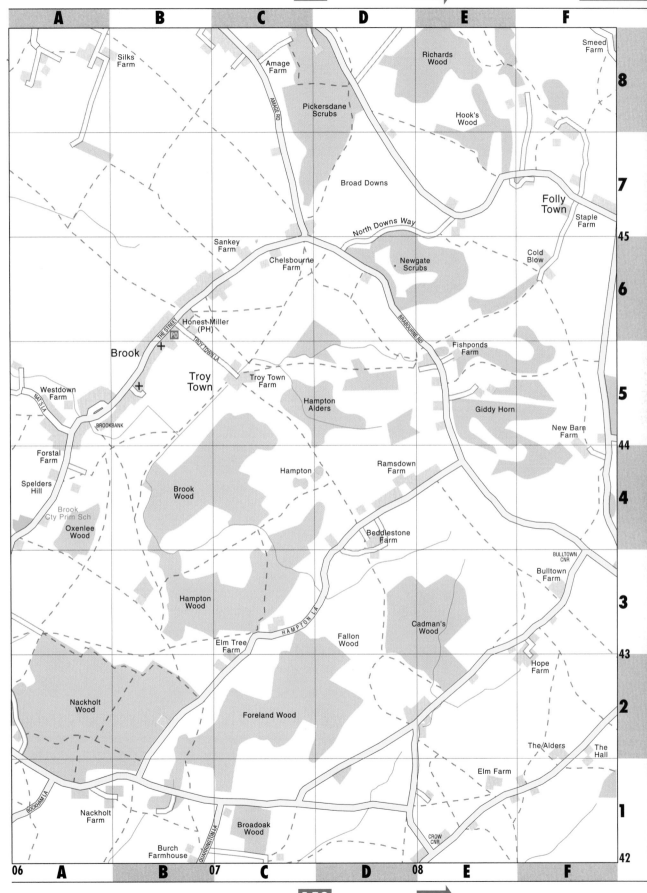

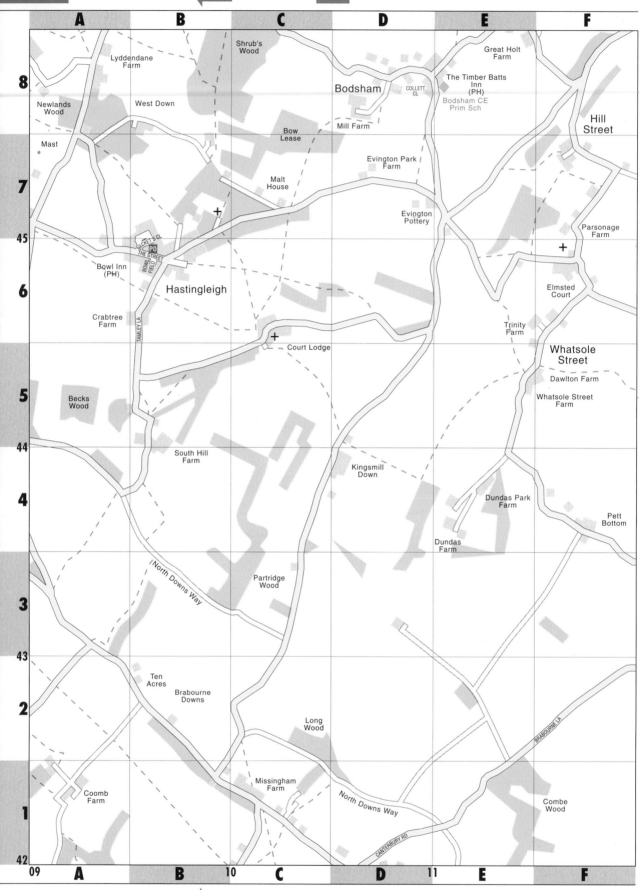

143
127

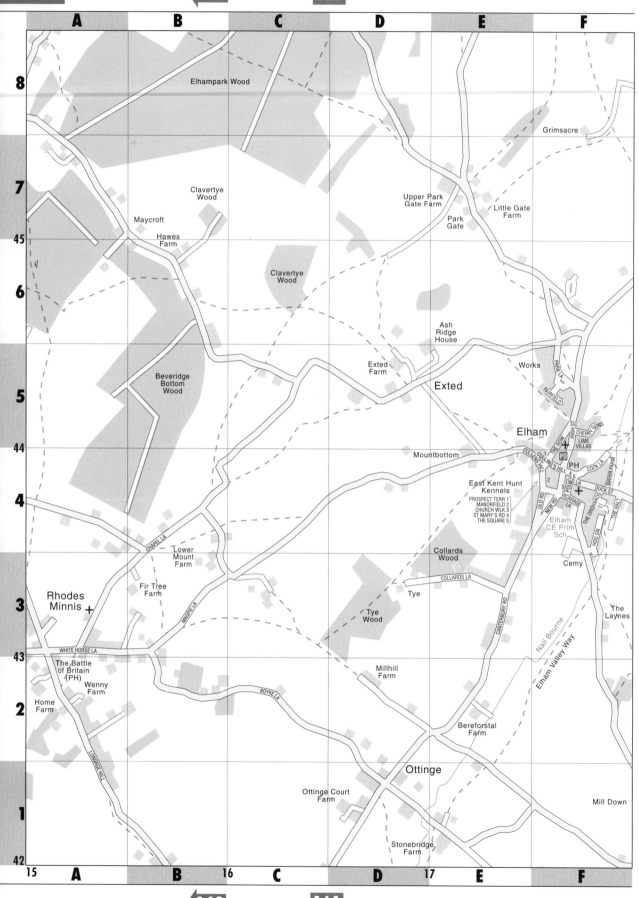

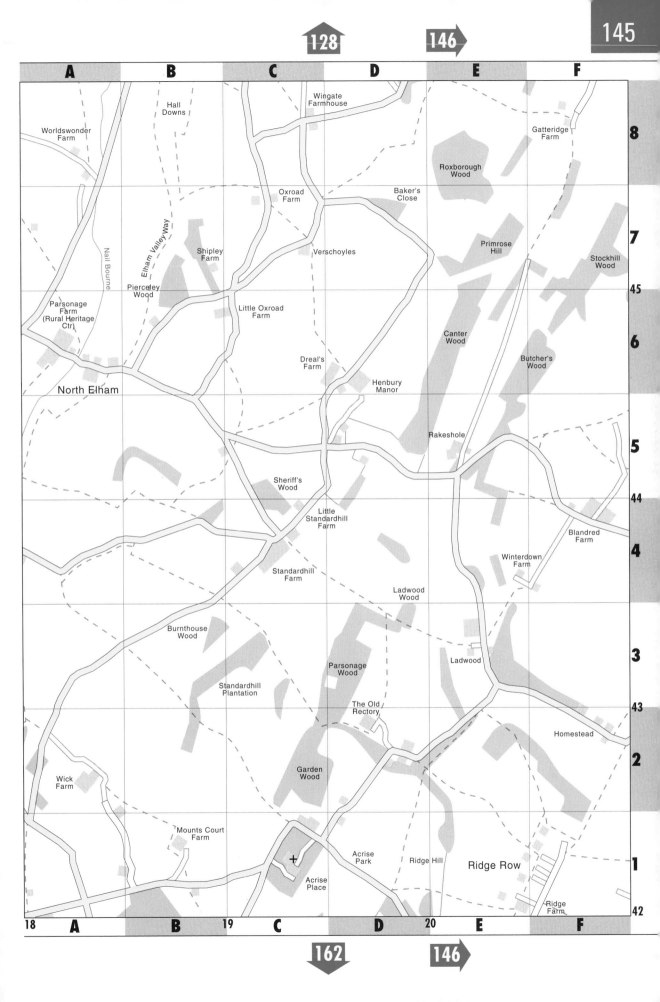

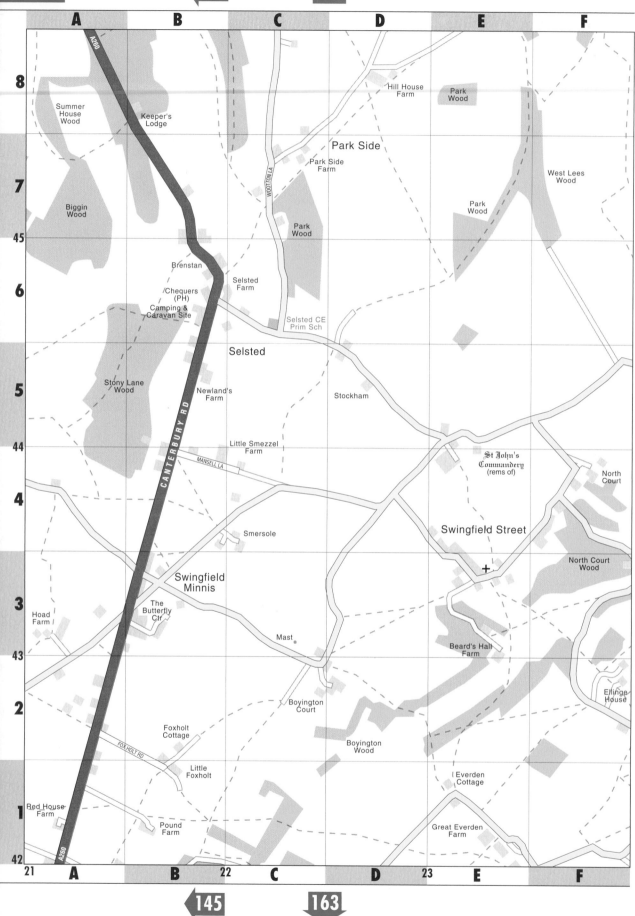

145
129

A   **B**   **C**   **D**   **E**   **F**

8

7

45

6

5

44

4

3

43

2

1

42

Summer House Wood

Keeper's Lodge

Biggin Wood

Hill House Farm

Park Wood

Park Side

Park Side Farm

West Lees Wood

WOOTTON LA

Park Wood

Park Wood

Brenstan

Chequers (PH)

Selsted Farm

Camping & Caravan Site

Selsted CE Prim Sch

Stony Lane Wood

Selsted

Newland's Farm

Stockham

CANTERBURY RD

St John's Commandery (rems of)

North Court

Little Smezzel Farm

MANSELL LA

Smersole

Swingfield Street

North Court Wood

Hoad Farm

Swingfield Minnis

The Butterfly Ctr

Mast

Beard's Hall Farm

Ellinge House

Foxholt Cottage

Boyington Court

FOX HOLT RD

Little Foxholt

Boyington Wood

Everden Cottage

Red House Farm

A260

Pound Farm

Great Everden Farm

21   **A**   **B**   **22**   **C**   **D**   **23**   **E**   **F**

145
163

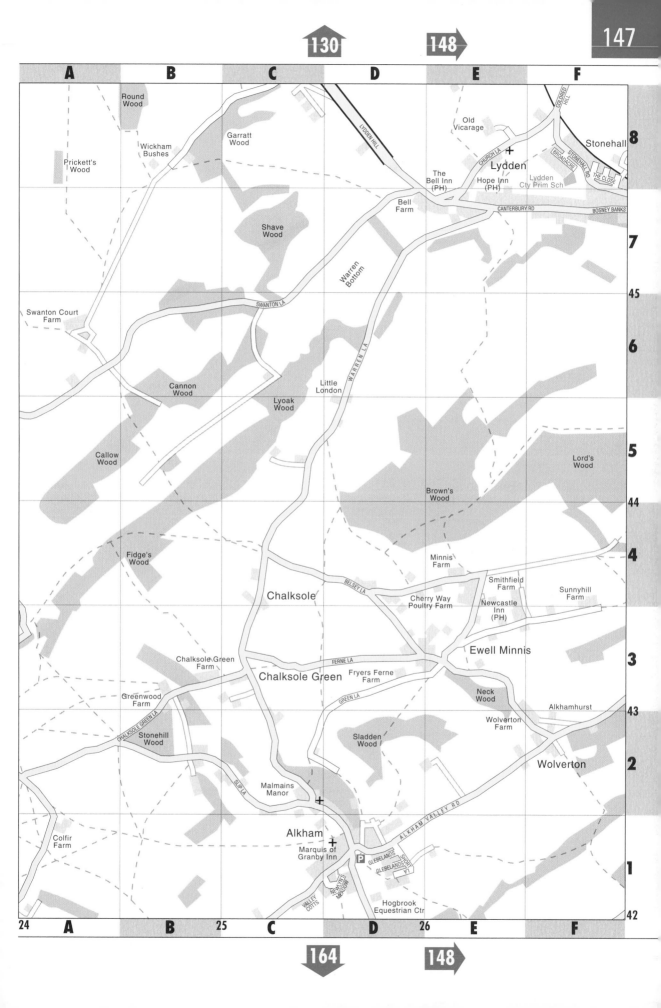

130
148

A B C D E F

Round Wood

Prickett's Wood

Wickham Bushes

Garratt Wood

LYDEN HILL

Old Vicarage

CHURCH LA

Lydden

CORONED HILL

Stonehall

STONEHALL RD

BROADACRE

THE CLOSE

8

The Bell Inn (PH)

Hope Inn (PH)

Lydden Cty Prim Sch

Bell Farm

CANTERBURY RD

BOSNEY BANKS

Shave Wood

7

Warren Bottom

45

Swanton Court Farm

SWANTON LA

6

Cannon Wood

Little London

WARREN LA

Lyoak Wood

Callow Wood

Lord's Wood

5

Brown's Wood

44

Fidge's Wood

Minnis Farm

4

Chalksole

BELSEY LA

Smithfield Farm

Sunnyhill Farm

Cherry Way Poultry Farm

Newcastle Inn (PH)

Chalksole Green Farm

Ewell Minnis

3

FERNE LA

Chalksole Green

Fryers Ferne Farm

Neck Wood

Alkhamhurst

43

Greenwood Farm

GREEN LA

Wolverton Farm

CHALKSOLE GREEN LA

Stonehill Wood

Sladden Wood

Wolverton

2

SLIP LA

Malmains Manor

Colfir Farm

ALKHAM VALLEY RD

Alkham

Marquis of Granby Inn

P

GLEBELANDS

GLEBELANDS

1

NEWLYNS MEADOW

VALLEY COTTS

Hogbrook Equestrian Ctr

42

24 A B 25 C D 26 E F

164
148

147 131

A B C D E F

8
7
45
6
5
44
4
3
43
2
42

A2

Singledge Farm

Lenacre Court Farm

ORCHARD CL

THE PIER LA

GUILFORD AVE

Temple Farm

Lenacre Wood

LENACRE AVE

Whitfield

NURSERY LA

CASTLE DR

Stonehall

STONEHALL RD

BUSHEY BANKS

GREEN LA

SINGLEDGE LA

SINGLEDGE AVE

Little Watersend

Woodville Hall

LONDON RD

Bassingham Court

Temple Ewell

DOWNHILL CL

TEMPLE SIDE

TEMPLE CL

GREEN LA

Motel

A256

Great Watersend Farm

WATERSEND

TEMPLAR RD

MILL ST

HIGH ST

BROOKSIDE

LONDON ROAD TEMPLE EWELL

WELLINGTON RD

PARK RD

THE AVENUE

Lousyberry Wood

Whitfield Valley

HENNIKER CL

CHURCH HILL

Prim Sch

LOWER RD

MALVERN MEADOW

MALVERN RD

EGERTON RD

Manor Farm

REDVERS COTTS

WOODSIDE CL

WHITFIELD HILL

Old Park Wood

Ghost Hill

Scotland Common

Kearsney Sta

COURT LA

COURT DR

KEARSNEY AVE

LABURNUM CL

Playing Field

Bushy Ruff House

KEARSNEY CT

Kearsney Abbey

BEECHWOOD RD

PAVILION MEADOW

COURT HO

LEAHURST CT

The Minnis

Abbey Lake

BUSHY RUFF COTTS

ABBEY RD

CHISNAL

CHISNAL RD

ORCHARD VILLAS

River Dour

LONDON ROAD (RIVER)

Oldpark Hill

ALKHAM RD

CHILTON AVE

Kearsney

Coxhill Mount

COXHILL CRES

COXHILL GDNS

CHILTON WAY

RIVER ST

PO

River St Prim Sch

BERESFORD RD

LOWER RD

RIVER DALE

Water Mill

KINGSTON CL

Mill

A256

ALKHAM VALLEY RD

Chilton Farm

Frandham Wood

BADGERS RISE

MEADWAY

River Cty Prim Sch

DOVE LEA GDNS

BY LAN

VALLEY RD

MAXIMERING RD

DOUR SIDE

LEWISHAM RD

River Meadow

RIVER MEADOW

MINNIS LA

The Common

COWPER RD

LICKHURST CT

ORCHARD RD

WEST ST

LYNDHURST RD

HAWTHORN

BRIAR RD

MILL CL

CRABBLE RD

RIVER CT

River Down Wood

HAZELDOWN RD

CROVE HILL

THE SPINNEY

THE RIDGEWAY

RIVER DR

River Minnis

CUSWIN

WESTDEAN CL

WOODLAND RD

Crabble

Football Gd

River Minnis Farm

River Bottom Wood

DEANWOOD RD

CRABBLE LA

Gorse Hill

Coombe Down

Gorsehill Wood

Oak Wood

ABBEY RD

Ind Est

HOLMESTONE RD

POULTON CLOSE

BANSTEAD

COOMBE RD

ST RADIGUND'S RD

BARWICK RD

BEAUFOY TERR

Ind Est

27 A 28 B C 28 D 29 E F

A B C D E F

8

CHAPEL RD
THE DROVE
McPHERSON RD
CHURCH WHITFIELD RD
CHURCH WHITFIELD
Little Pineham Farm
Pineham
Poison Down
Enifer Down

Parsonage Farm
Great Pineham Farm
Limekiln Down

7

Whitfield
WITLEY WLK
FARNCOMBE WAY
BURGESS CL
Whitfield City Prim Sch
ARCHER'S COURT RD
Gifford's Covert

45

Light Hill
Pineham Rd
EAST LANGDON RD

6

WHITFIELD RDBT
WHITE CLIFFS BSNS PK
Radio Sta
Mast
Superstore
HONEYWOOD PARKWAY
Bsns Pk
Gustoncourt Farm
NEW COTTS
Guston
THE STREET
THE LANE

5

KHARTOUM SQ
HONEYWOOD RD
Transport Mus
Old Park
Archers Court Sch
North Downs Way
White Cliffs Country Trail
Copthorne
Chance Inn (PH)

44

MARSDEN GDNS
OLD PARK CL
FULBERT RD
ROKESLEY RD
Buckland Valley
DOVER RD
Frith Farm
MARTIN'S RD

4

Playing Field
The Powell Sch (Prim)
Melbourne City Prim Sch
Green Lane Hill
NATAL RD
DURBAN CRES
JOHANNESBURG RD
Whiting Farm
Mast
Shaft
Duke of York's Royal Military Sch
Recn Gd

3

ARMOURERS WLK
DODD'S LA
MANGERS PL
FRIARS WAY
WEAVERS WAY
SQUIRES WAY
PILGRIMS WAY
OLD PARK WAY
SHIPMANS WAY
KNIGHTS WAY
MONKS WAY
ROOSEVELT RD
WINNAN WAY
CLEVELAND RD
1 WINNIPEG CL
2 PERTH WAY
Long Hill
Guston CE Prim Sch
South Foreland
TANGIER CT
CORUNNA CT
BURGOYNE HTS
GIBRALTAR SQ
DUNKIRK SQ
LUCKNOW CL
ALAMEIN CL
KOHIMA
NAMUR PL
ANZIO CRES
CASSINO
CORUNNA CT

43

LONDON RD (RIVER)
CRABBLE HILL
CRABBLE AVE
PIONEER RD
BROOKFIELD RD
GLENFIELD
RUTLAND RD
NAPIER RD
HOBART CRES
CHRISTCHURCH WAY
PARFITT WAY
EVISON CL
Mast
The Danes Recn Gd
Buckland
Cemy
Cemys
DANES CT
OLD CHARLTON RD
Fort Burgoyne (Casemated Barracks)
FORT BURGOYNE RD

2

ST ANDREW TERR
MINNIS TERR
CRABBLE MEADOWS
ST GEORGES RD
HILLSIDE RD
BUCKLAND AVE
BROOKFIELD PL
SPRINGFIELD RD
HEATHFIELD AVE
ALFRED RD
NIGHTINGALE RD
MAYFIELD AVE
BARTON RD
Prim Sch
St Edmund's RC Sch
DOVER
Connaught Park
Connaught Barracks

1

St Radigund's
St Radigund's City Prim Sch
DALMATIA CT
MARJAN CL
COOMBE VALLEY RD
BOWMAN CT
PRIMROSE RD
RANDOLPH RD
MASONS RD
PROSPECT PL
LONDON RD
VICTORIA RD
TA Ctr
Jun Sch
THE GROVE
BARTON RD
FRITH RD
CHARLTON GN
St Richard's RC Prim Sch
St Gram Sch for Girls
SALISBURY RD
PARK AVE
CASTLE AVE
CONNAUGHT RD
1 CRAFFORD ST
2 GODWYNE CT
3 RICHMOND CT
4 CASTLEMOUNT RD
Connaught Barracks
Edinburgh Hill
UPPER RD
CASTLE HILL RD

42

BEAUFOY RD
MARJAN CL
MACDONALD RD
COOMBE CL
Buckland
1 PRIMROSE PL
2 KNIGHTS CT
3 CASTLEVIEW CT
4 CHARLES LISTER CT
5 KINGSFORD CT
6 HERBERT ST
YH
A256
Dover Gram Sch
Castlemount Sch
Dover Castle
Bleriot Meml
EAST NORMAN RD
A2
JUBILEE WAY

30 A B 31 C 32 E F 42

B2
1 ST ANNE'S CT
2 OSPREY CT
3 MAYFIELD CT

B3
1 FITZWALTER CT
2 WELLINGTON GDNS
3 BRUNSWICK GDNS
4 WASHINGTON CL
5 BOSTON CL
6 TORONTO CL
7 HUDSON CL
8 MONTREAL CL

C1
1 ALEXANDRA PL
2 BARTON VIEW TERR
3 LEIGHTON CT
4 ST ALPHEGE RD
5 SHOOTER'S HILL
6 BARTHOLOMEW ST
7 CHURCHILL ST
8 PAUL'S PL
9 MATTHEW'S PL
10 WARDEN CT

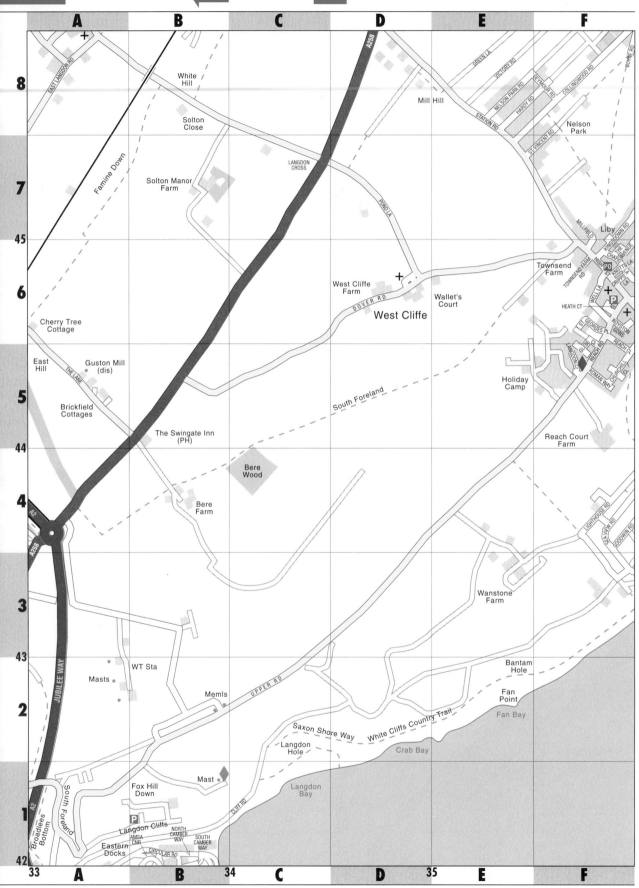

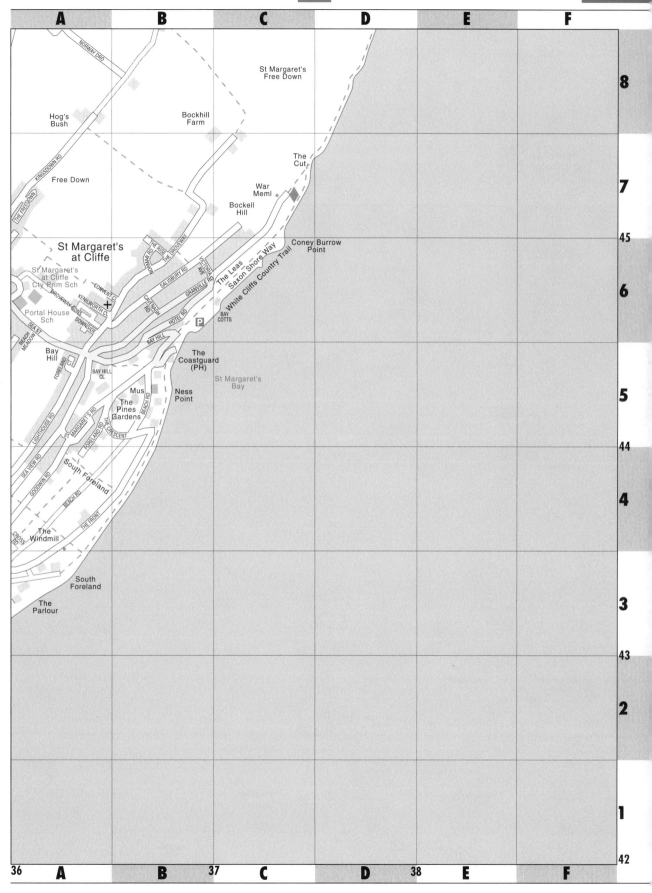

St Margaret's
Free Down

Hog's
Bush

Bockhill
Farm

The Cut

Free Down

War
Meml

Bockell
Hill

Coney Burrow
Point

St Margaret's
at Cliffe

The Leas

Saxon Shore Way

St Margaret's
at Cliffe
Cty Prim Sch

White Cliffs Country Trail

Portal House
Sch

BAY
COTTS

Bay
Hill

The
Coastguard
(PH)

St Margaret's
Bay

Mus

Ness
Point

The
Pines
Gardens

South Foreland

The
Windmill

South
Foreland

The
Parlour

NORWAY DRO

KINGSDOWN RD

THE FREEDOWN

THE RISE

MANNON RD

THE DROVEWAY

SALISBURY RD

VICTORIA AVE

GRANVILLE RD

CONVENT CL

DROVEWAY GDNS

KENILWORTH CL

DOWNSIDE

CAVENAGH RD

HOTEL RD

BAY HILL

BEACH RD

SEA ST

BEACH MEADOW

FORELAND CT

BAY HILL CL

LIGHTHOUSE RD

MARGARET'S RD

FORELAND RD

THE CRESCENT

SEA VIEW RD

GOODWIN RD

BEACH RD

THE FRONT

CROSS RD

36   37   38

42 43 44 45

A   B   C   D   E   F

1 2 3 4 5 6 7 8

135

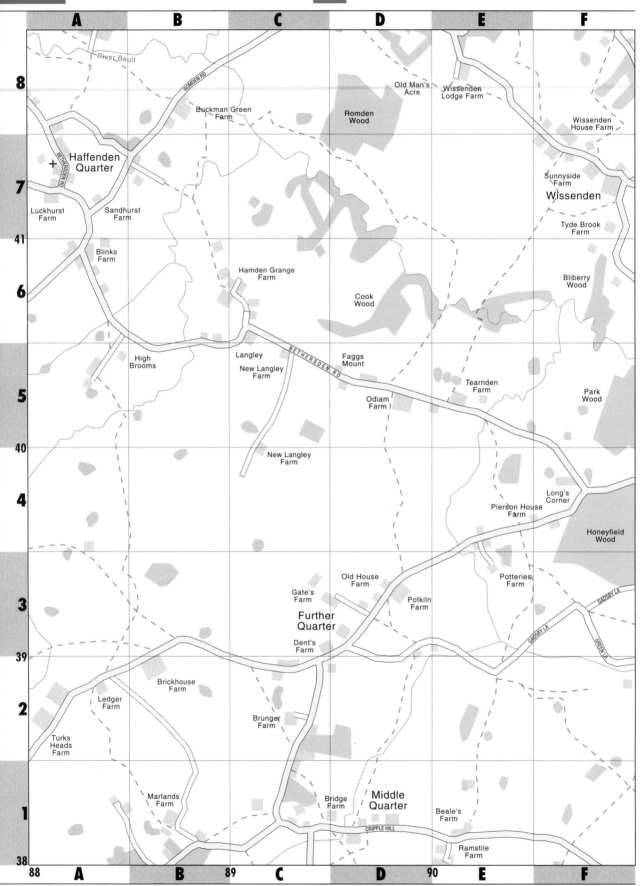

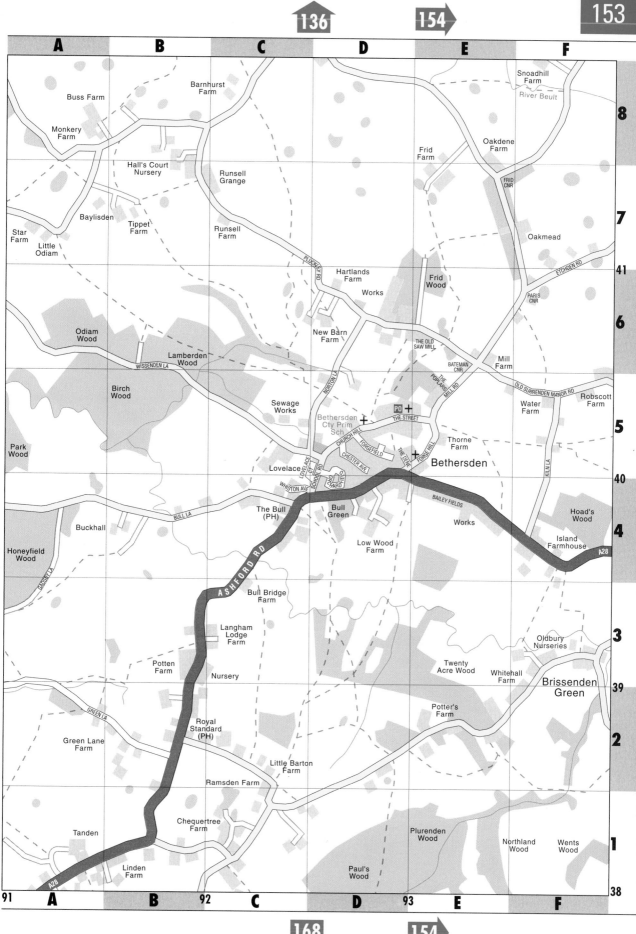

153
137

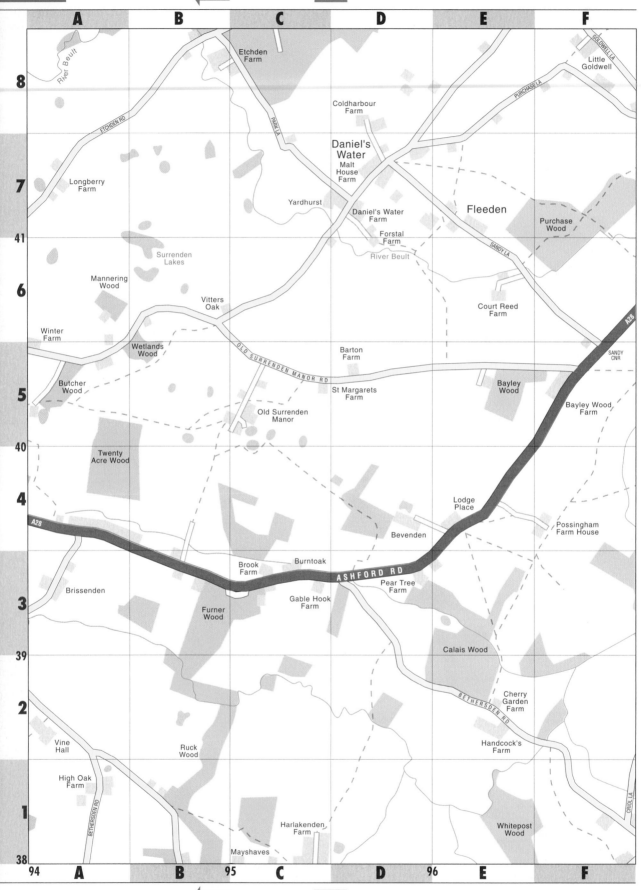

153
169

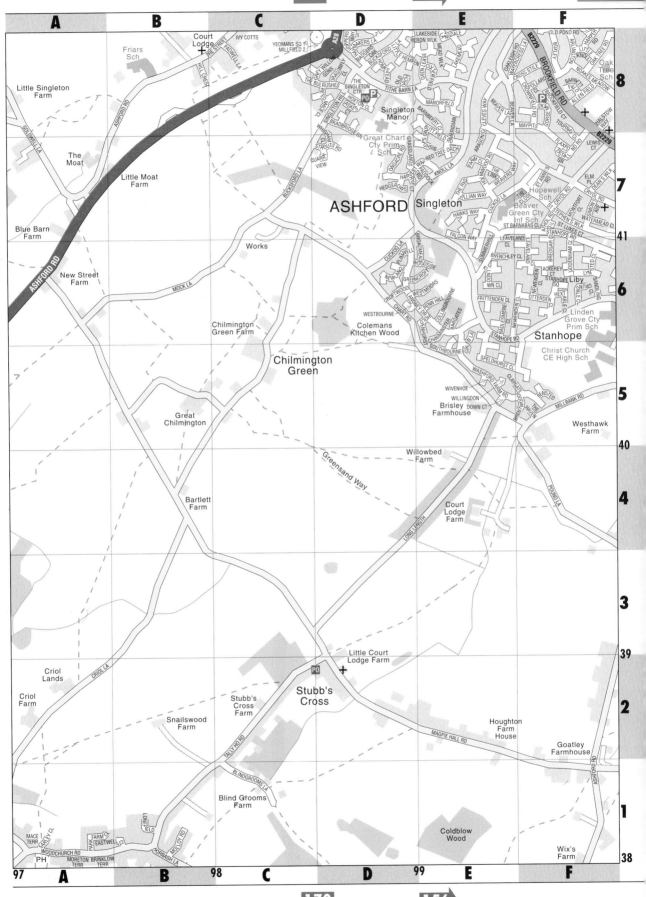

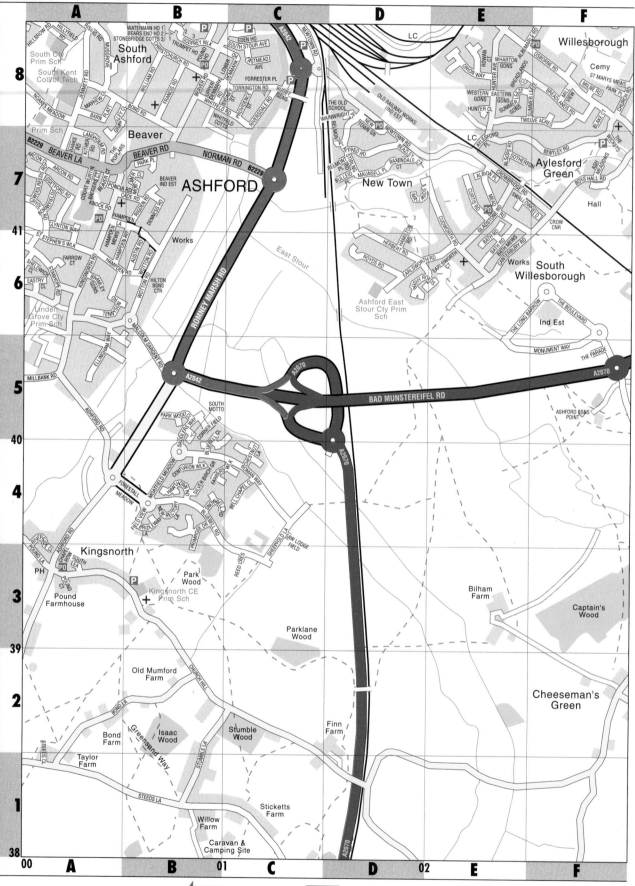

155
139

A   B   C   D   E   F

8

7

41

6

5

40

4

39

3

2

1

38

South City
Prim Sch
South Kent
Coll of Tech

WILLBROW RD
HILLYFIELD
RD
FISH RD
MUSGROVE

WATERMAN HO 1
BEARS END HO 2
STONEBRIDGE COTTS 3

South
Ashford

South Ashford

CHRISTCHURCH RD
WILLIAM RD
FRANCIS RD

GODFREY WLK
TRUMPET HO
EDEN HO
SOUTH STOUR AVE
DENMARK
RD
PSTMEAD
AVE

FORRESTER PL

Beaver

NOAH'S MEADOW
MAYHEW CT
BARN
PLATT
LANGTON LA RD
KITHER RD
BANKS RD

BEAVER LA
ARCON CL
ARCON RD
ESSEFORD RD
COURT WURTIN
BAGGERS RD
POMERO RD
KNOCK RD
CRYOL RD

BEAVER RD
NORMAN RD

B2229

ASHFORD
Works

B2229

East Stour

THE OLD
SCHOOL
WAINWRIGHT

LC

Old Railway Works
(IND EST)

NEW
TOWN GN

New Town

Willesborough

ORION WAY
HUNTER AVE
WESTERN
GDNS
HUNTER CL

WHARTON
GDNS
EASTERN
GDNS
SUMMER
GDNS

OSBORNE RD
BROADLANDS
TWELVE ACRES

Cemy
ST MARYS MEWS
MILNE RD

LC
ALBION PL
ALCOVE RD

Aylesford
Green

Hall

South
Willesborough

Ind Est

THE LONG BARROW
MONUMENT WAY
THE BOULEVARD
THE PARADE

A2070

Ashford BSNS
POINT

5

Kingsnorth

PH

Pound
Farmhouse

Park
Wood

Kingsnorth CE
Prim Sch

REED CRES

SAW LODGE
FIELD

Parklane
Wood

Bilham
Farm

Captain's
Wood

Cheeseman's
Green

Old Mumford
Farm

CHURCH HILL

Bond
Farm
Isaac
Wood

Greensand Way

Stumble
Wood

STUMBLE LA

Finn
Farm

Taylor
Farm

STEEDS LA

Willow
Farm

Sticketts
Farm

Caravan &
Camping Site

A2070

155
171

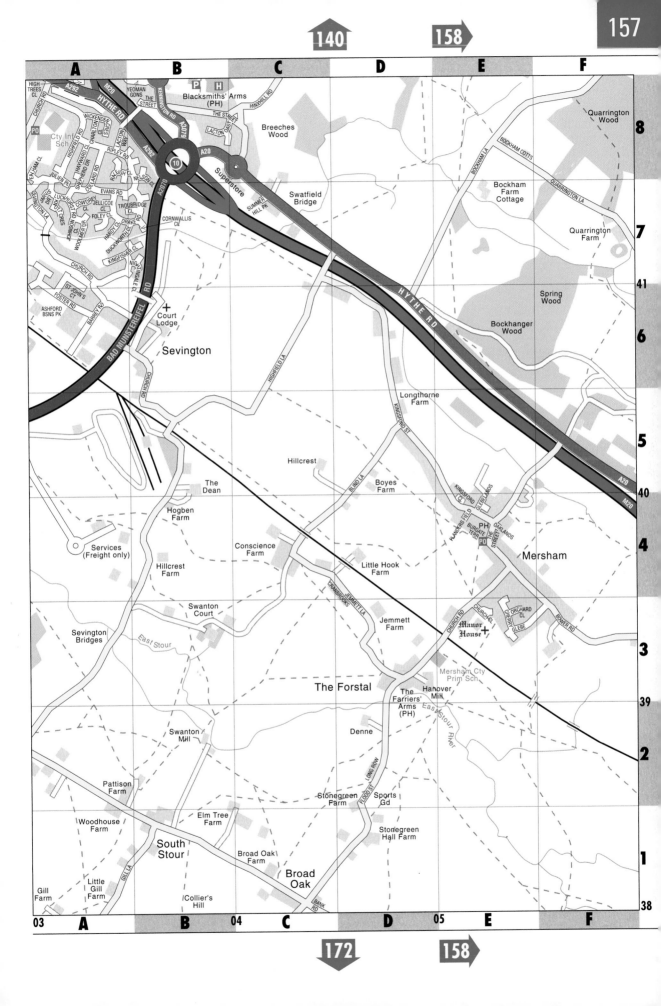

157 141

A B C D E F

8

7

41

6

5

40

4

3

39

2

1

38

Fallon Farmhouse

Fords Water

Waterside Farm

Bircholt Wood

Bircholt Forstal

BIRCHOLT FORSTAL

Seeley Farm

California Farm

Gains Cottage

QUARRINGTON LA

Bircholt Court

MANOR POUND LA

Deer Park

Brockham Farm

Chapel Farm

CANTERBURY RD

POUND LA

Jacob's Platation

Pemsey Farm

Brabourne Lees

LEES RD

MOUNTBATTEN WAY

BRAMLEY CL

PROSPECT WAY

MOUNTBATTEN WAY

PO

THE LEES CL

THE WARREN

Hatch Park

Mersham-le-Hatch

Court Farmhouse

BRIDGE RD

MAUSE FIELD

Barrack Wood

Joe Farm

THE CHESTNUTS

Woolpack Hill

SANDY PL

GALL RD

KNATCHBULL WAY

WARREN HTS

Warren Hill

RIDGEWAY TERR

THE RIDGEWAY

Ridgeway

The Woolpack (PH)

CAROLAND CL

RAMSTONE CL

Smeeth Cty Prim Sch

PLAIN RD

MANOR LEAZE

A20

M20

Ridgeway

CHURCH RD

Bog Farm

Fishpond Wood

Lodge House

LILYVALE COTTS

Lily Vale

Home Farm

Church Farm

Scott's Hall Plantation

STOCK LA

The Paddocks

Smeeth

HYTHE RD

Lily Vale Farm

Washington

BOWER RD

STATION RD

Evegate

Scott's Hall

Water Farm

Little Stock Farm

Evegate Manor

Park Wood

Apple Barn

COOPER'S LA

A20

Park Wood Cottage

Sellindge Converter Station

CHURCH LA

East Stour River

M20

Evegate Mill

Works

157 173

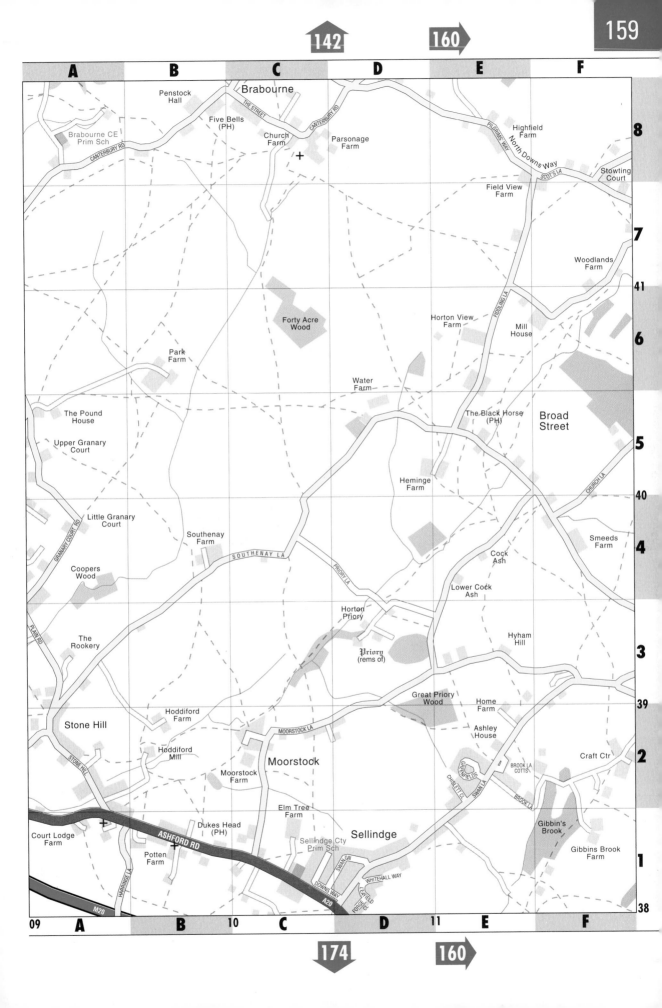

Brabourne

Penstock Hall

Five Bells (PH)

Church Farm

Parsonage Farm

CANTERBURY RD

THE STREET

Brabourne CE Prim Sch

CANTERBURY RD

PILGRIMS WAY

North Downs Way

SCOT'S LA

Highfield Farm

Stowting Court

Field View Farm

Woodlands Farm

Forty Acre Wood

Horton View Farm

Mill House

FIDDLING LA

Park Farm

Water Farm

The Black Horse (PH)

Broad Street

The Pound House

Upper Granary Court

Heminge Farm

CHURCH LA

Little Granary Court

GRANARY COURT RD

Southenay Farm

SOUTHENAY LA

Smeeds Farm

Cock Ash

Coopers Wood

PRIORY LA

Lower Cock Ash

Hyham Hill

PLAIN RD

The Rookery

Horton Priory

Priory (rems of)

Great Priory Wood

Home Farm

Hoddiford Farm

Stone Hill

MOORSTOCK LA

Ashley House

Craft Ctr

STONE HILL

Hoddiford Mill

Moorstock Farm

Moorstock

GREENFIELDS

CHISLETT C

SWAN LA

BROOK LA COTTS

BROOK LA

Elm Tree Farm

Court Lodge Farm

ASHFORD RD

Dukes Head (PH)

Sellindge Cty Prim Sch

Sellindge

Gibbin's Brook

HARRINGE LA

Potten Farm

SWAN GN

WHITEHALL WAY

Gibbins Brook Farm

DOWNS WAY

A20

LEAFIELD C

FORGE CL

M20

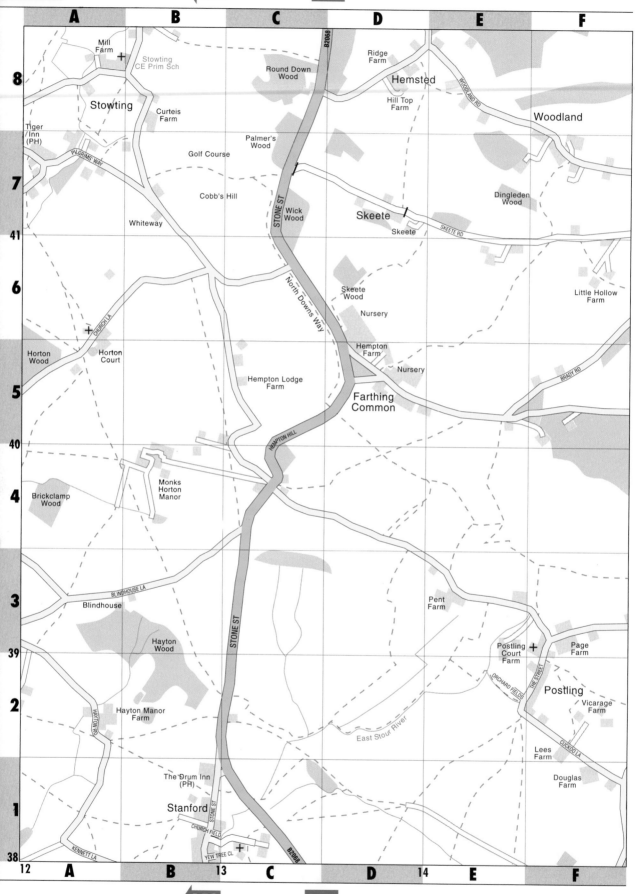

A B C D E F

8

Mill Farm

Stowting CE Prim Sch

Round Down Wood

Ridge Farm

Hemsted

Hill Top Farm

Woodland

Stowting

Curteis Farm

Tiger Inn (PH)

PILGRIMS' WAY

Palmer's Wood

Golf Course

WOODLAND RD

7

Cobb's Hill

Wick Wood

Skeete

Dingleden Wood

Whiteway

STONE ST

Skeete

SKEETE RD

41

6

North Downs Way

Skeete Wood

Nursery

Little Hollow Farm

CHURCH LA

Horton Wood

Horton Court

Hempton Lodge Farm

Hempton Farm

Nursery

BRADY RD

5

Farthing Common

40

HEMPTON HILL

Brickclamp Wood

Monks Horton Manor

4

BLINDHOUSE LA

Blindhouse

Pent Farm

3

STONE ST

Hayton Wood

Postling Court Farm

Page Farm

39

THE STREET

ORCHARD FIELDS

Postling

2

HAYTON RD

Hayton Manor Farm

Vicarage Farm

CUCKOO LA

East Stour River

Lees Farm

The Drum Inn (PH)

Douglas Farm

1

STONE ST

Stanford

CHURCH FIELD

KENNETT LA

YEW TREE CL

B2068

38

12 A B 13 C D 14 E F

B2068

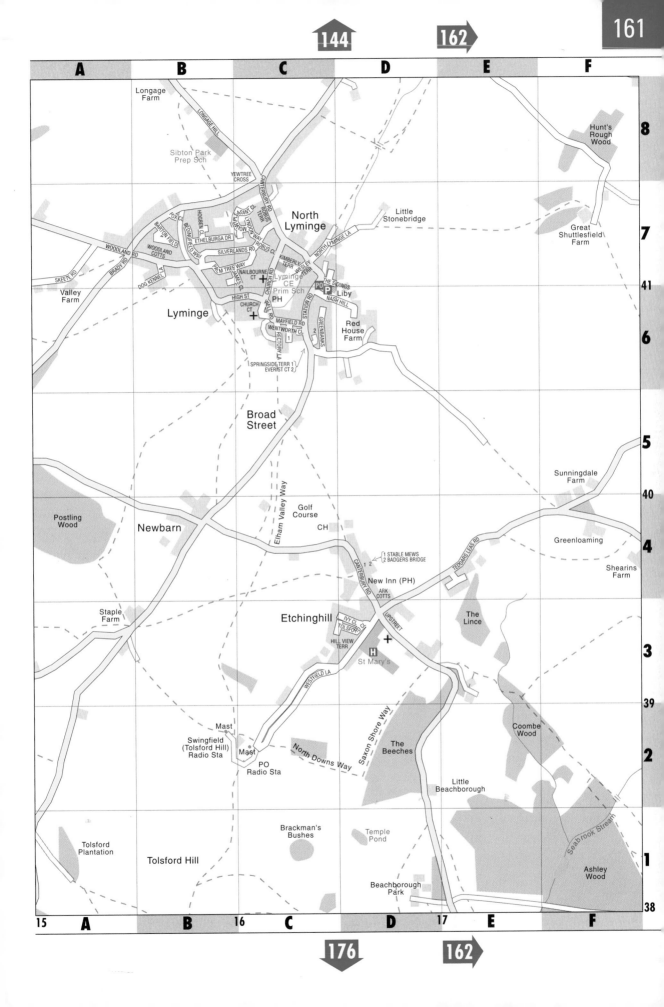

A B C D E F

8
7
41
6
5
40
4
39
3
2
1
38

Longage Farm

Sibton Park Prep Sch

YEWTREE CROSS

LONGAGE HILL

CANTERBURY RD

North Lyminge

Little Stonebridge

Hunt's Rough Wood

Great Shuttlesfield Farm

WOODLAND RD

SKEETS RD

BRADY RD

DOG KENNEL

BARTON FIELD
FOX CL
HOGBEN CL
BEDINGFIELD WAY
PLEASANT CL
LYNTON TERR
ROBUS TERR
ETHELBURGA DR
ROBUS CL
SILVERLANDS RD
WOODLAND WAY
WOODLAND COTTS
PALM TREE WAY
NAILBOURNE CT
JAMES PL
KIMBERLY TERR
WESLEY TERR
NORTH LYMINGE LA

Lyminge CE Prim Sch
THE SIDINGS

Liby
NASH HILL

Valley Farm

Lyminge

HIGH ST
CHURCH RD
NELL RD
CHURCH CT
PH
WENTWORTH CL
RECTORY LA
MAYFIELD RD
STATION RD
GREENBANKS

PO
P

Red House Farm

SPRINGSIDE TERR 1
EVERIST CT 2

Broad Street

Elham Valley Way

Golf Course
CH

Sunningdale Farm

Greenloaming

Postling Wood

Newbarn

1 STABLE MEWS
2 BADGERS BRIDGE

Shearins Farm

CANTERBURY RD

New Inn (PH)
ARK COTTS

EDGARS LEAS RD

The Lince

Staple Farm

Etchinghill

IVY CL
TOLSFORD CL
HILL VIEW TERR
UPSTREET

St Mary's
H

WESTFIELD LA

Saxon Shore Way

Coombe Wood

Mast

Swingfield (Tolsford Hill) Radio Sta

Mast
PO Radio Sta

North Downs Way

The Beeches

Little Beachborough

Seabrook Stream

Tolsford Plantation

Tolsford Hill

Brackman's Bushes

Temple Pond

Beachborough Park

Ashley Wood

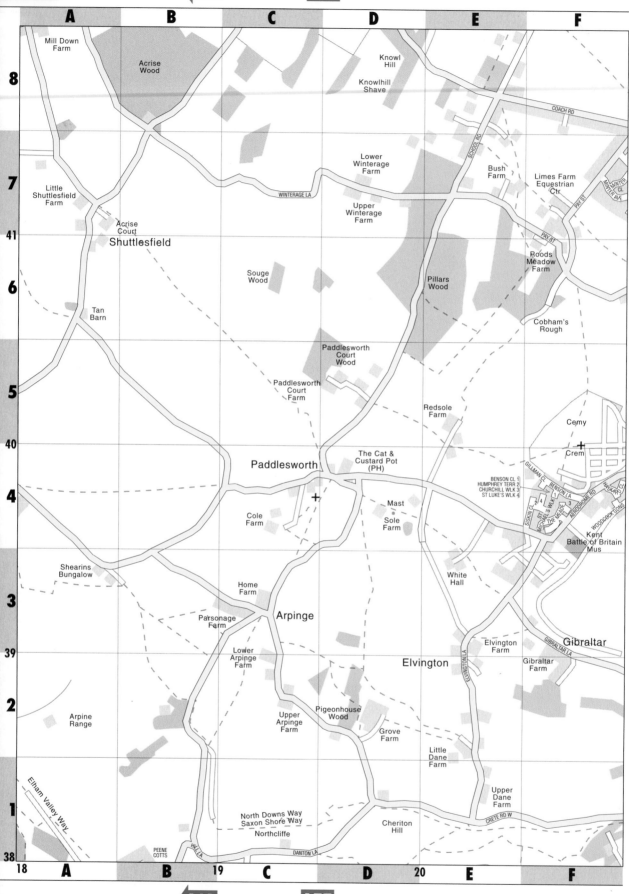

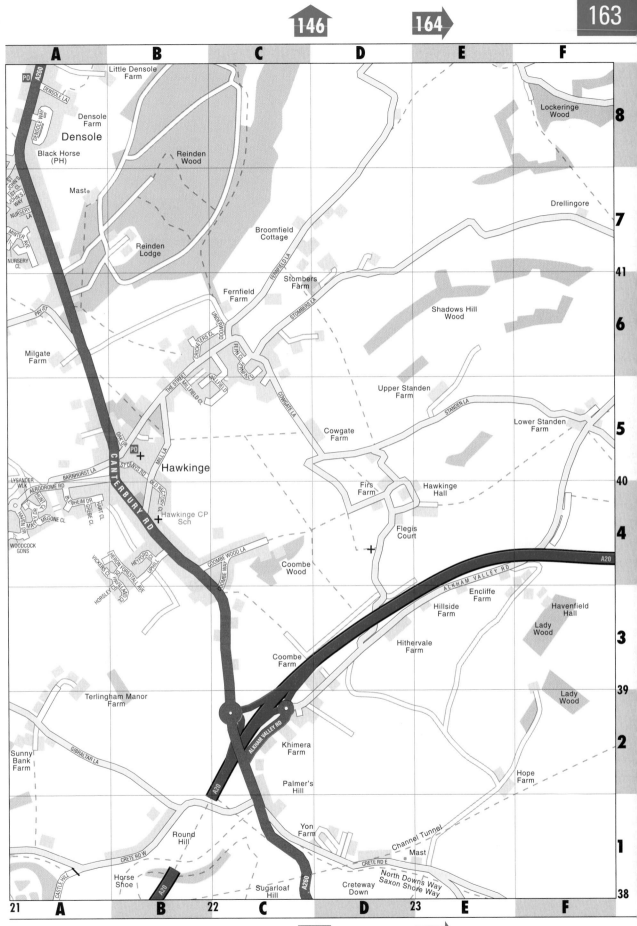

163
147

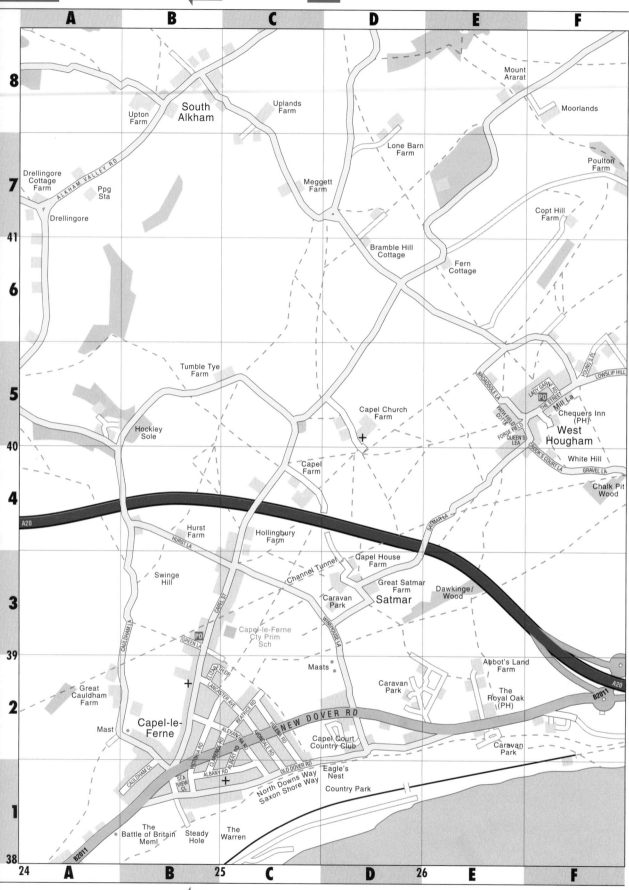

163

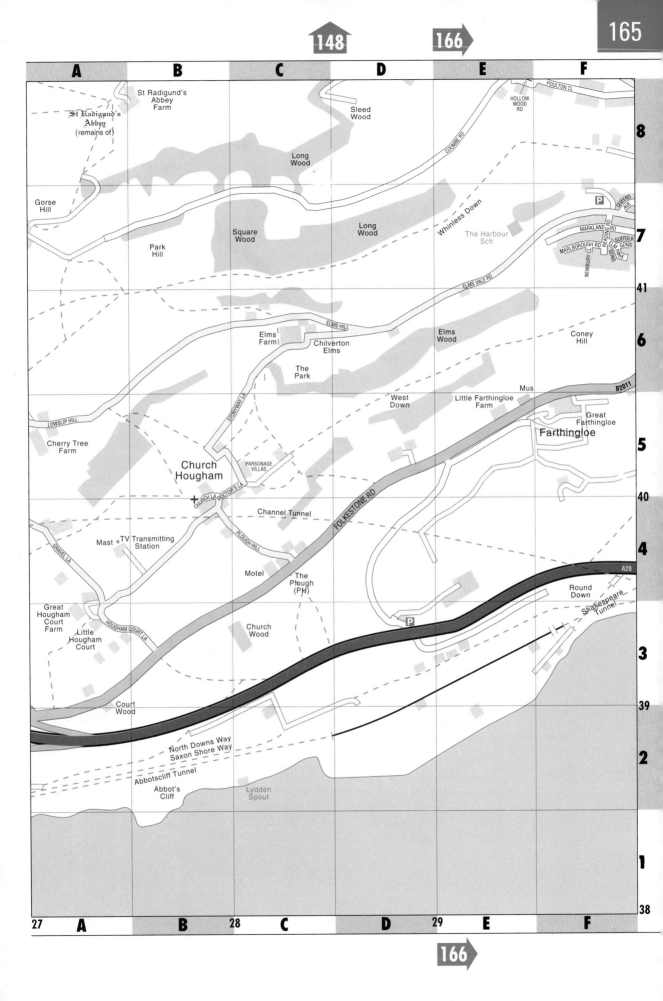

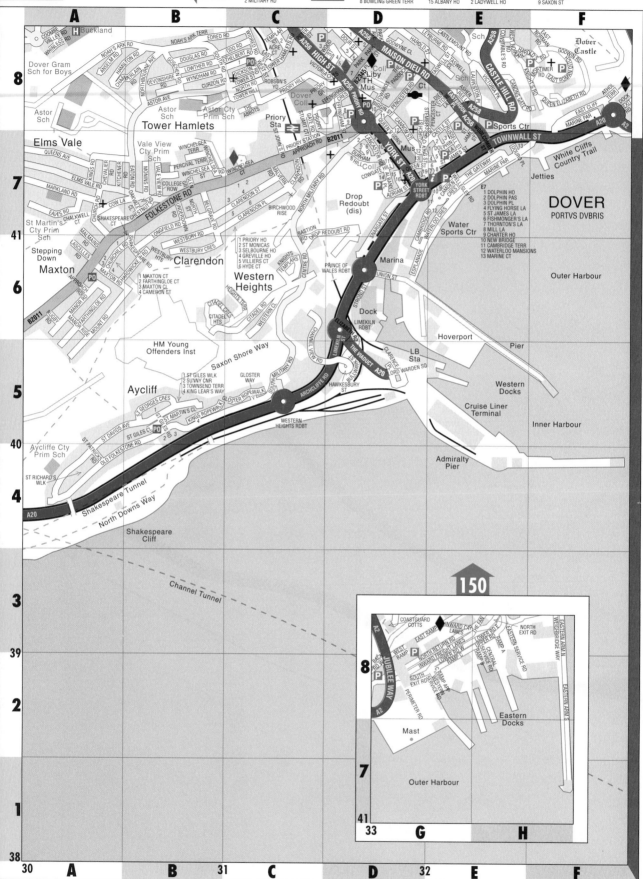

C8
1 TOWER HAMLETS ST
2 DE BURGH ST
3 CHARLTON CTR
D7
1 CHRISTCHURCH CT
2 MILITARY RD

D7
3 LANCASTER HO
4 STEMBROOK CT
5 CORNWALL HO
6 WINDSOR HO
7 EDINBURGH HO
8 BOWLING GREEN TERR

9 DURHAM CL
10 YORK HO
11 PRINCES ST
12 MARKET SQ
13 GAOL LA
14 GORELY HO
15 ALBANY HO

16 CHAPEL PL
17 BATTLE OF BRITAIN HOMES
18 CHAPEL LA
19 BENCH ST
D8
1 HEWITT RD
2 LADYWELL HO

4 GOODFELLOW WAY
4 MAISON DIEU PL
5 ROYAL VICTORIA PL
6 PARK MEWS
7 LADYWELL
8 NORMAN ST
9 SAXON ST

10 PRIORY ST
11 WORTHINGTON ST
12 NEW ST

DOVER
PORTVS DVBRIS

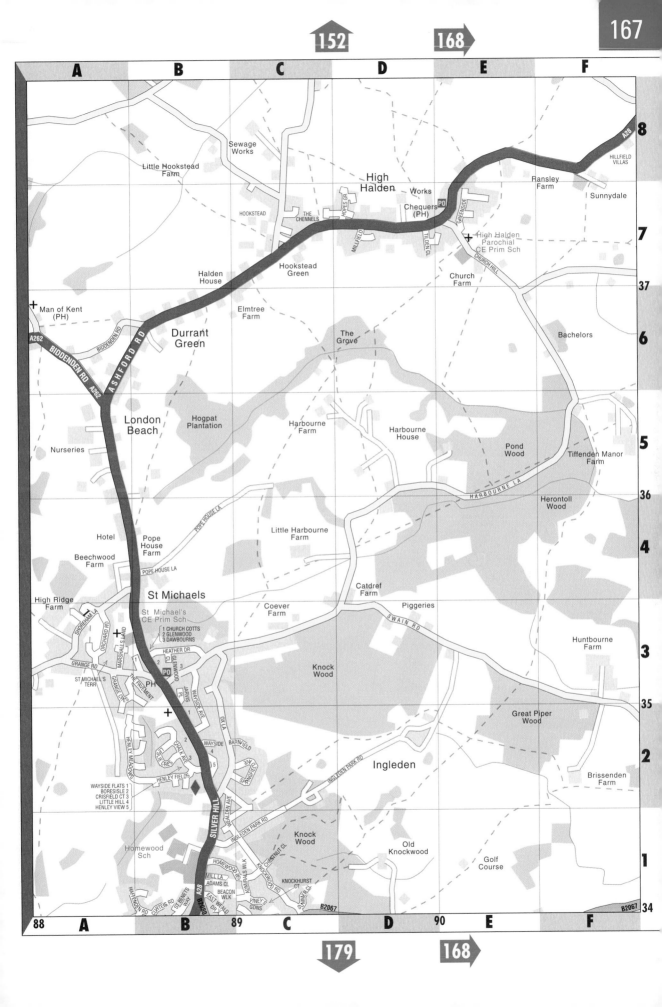

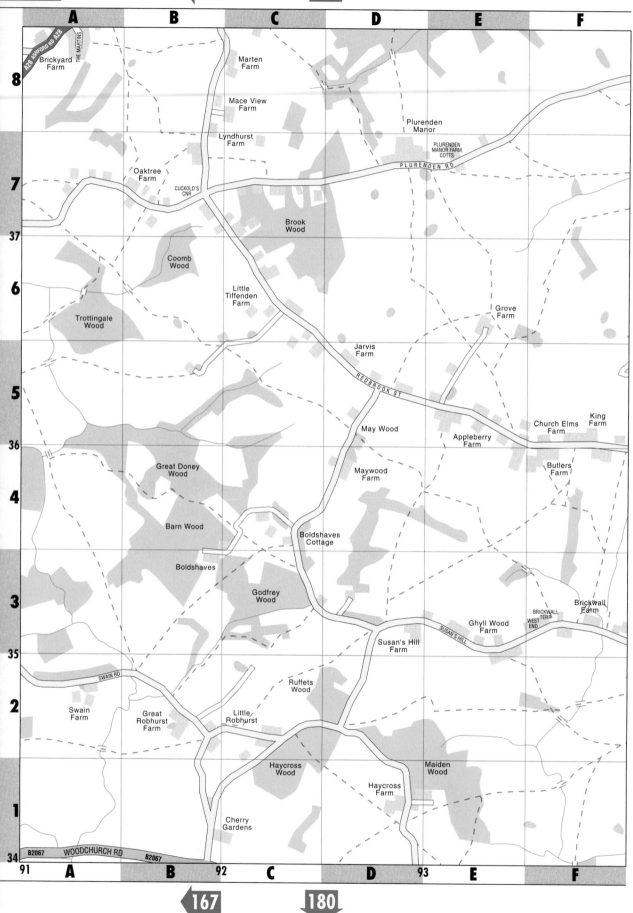

A · B · C · D · E · F

A28 ASHFORD RD A28
THE MARTINS
Brickyard Farm

Marten Farm

Mace View Farm

Plurenden Manor

Lyndhurst Farm

PLURENDEN MANOR FARM COTTS

Oaktree Farm

PLURENDEN RD

CUCKOLD'S CNR

Brook Wood

Coomb Wood

Little Tiffenden Farm

Grove Farm

Trottingale Wood

Jarvis Farm

REDBROOK ST

May Wood

Church Elms Farm

King Farm

Appleberry Farm

Great Doney Wood

Maywood Farm

Butlers Farm

Barn Wood

Boldshaves Cottage

Boldshaves

Godfrey Wood

BRICKWALL TERR WEST END

Brickwall Farm

Ghyll Wood Farm

SUSAN'S HILL

Susan's Hill Farm

SWAIN RD

Ruffets Wood

Swain Farm

Great Robhurst Farm

Little Robhurst

Haycross Wood

Maiden Wood

Haycross Farm

Cherry Gardens

B2067 WOODCHURCH RD B2067

91 · A · B · 92 · C · D · 93 · E · F

8 7 37 6 5 36 4 3 35 2 1 34

8

Coxland
Wood

St Peter's Way

Shadoxhurst

Kenilworth
Farm

THE STREET

DUCK LA

MAYNE CL

Nursery

Woodside
Farm

HORNASH LA

Works

Alex
Farm

7

Hillcrest
Farm

Great Turrels
Wood

Upper Toke's
Wood

CHURCH LA

Forty Acre
Wood

37

Nursery

Manor
Farm

Bromley
Green

Nickley
Wood

Bambridge Wood

6

NICKLEY WOOD RD

Poplar
Farm

BROMLEY GREEN RD

Kennels

Moat
Farm

Dering
Wood

Bromley Green
Farm

Little
Hurst

Courthope
Wood East

5

Jenkey
Farm

Long Hurst

HAMSTREET RD

36

Capel Wood

Bayland
Wood

4

Birchett
Wood

Longrope
Wood

Capel
House

CAPEL RD

Sugarloaf

3

Sir Edward Street's
Wood

St Thomas'
Cross

Spot House
Farm

35

Forest Walks

2

Parsonage
Farm

P

Picnic
Site

Orlestone

Burnt
Oak

Court
Lodge

MALTHOUSE LA

ASHFORD RD

Tucker
Farm

1

Fifty Acre Wood

Faggs
Wood

Apsley
Wood

A2070

Lord's Wood

34

Adams Wood

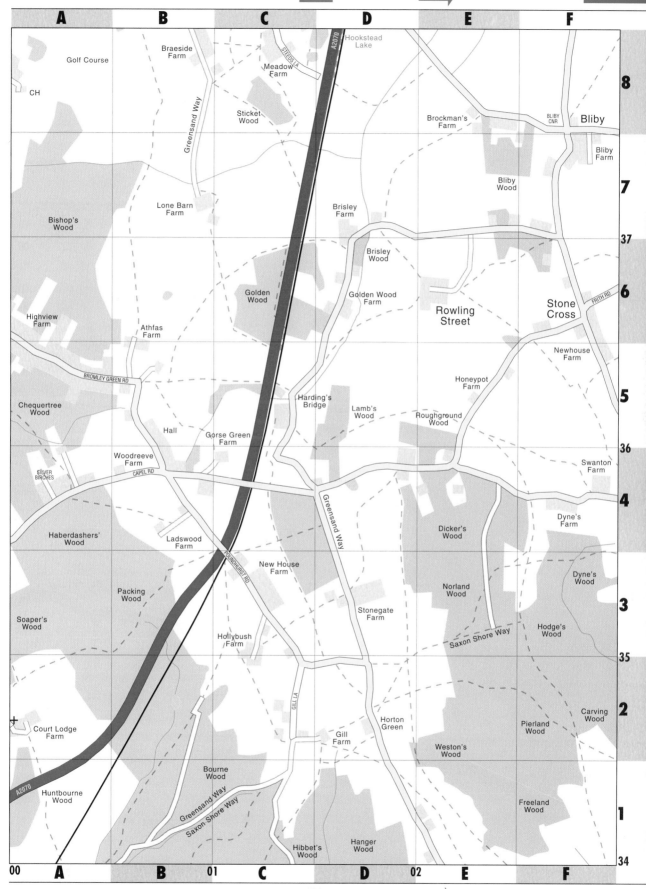

Golf Course

CH

Braeside
Farm

Meadow
Farm

Hookstead
Lake

Sticket
Wood

Brockman's
Farm

BLIBY
CNR

Bliby

Bliby
Farm

Bliby
Wood

7

37

Greensand Way

Lone Barn
Farm

Bishop's
Wood

Brisley
Farm

Brisley
Wood

Golden
Wood

Golden Wood
Farm

Rowling
Street

Stone
Cross

FRITH RD

6

Highview
Farm

Athfas
Farm

Newhouse
Farm

Honeypot
Farm

5

Chequertree
Wood

BROMLEY GREEN RD

Hall

Gorse Green
Farm

Harding's
Bridge

Lamb's
Wood

Roughground
Wood

Swanton
Farm

36

Woodreeve
Farm

CAPEL RD

SILVER
BIRCHES

Ladswood
Farm

Dyne's
Farm

4

Haberdashers'
Wood

POUNDHURST RD

New House
Farm

Greensand Way

Dicker's
Wood

Dyne's
Wood

Packing
Wood

Soaper's
Wood

Stonegate
Farm

Norland
Wood

Hodge's
Wood

Saxon Shore Way

35

3

Hollybush
Farm

GILL LA

Horton
Green

Pierland
Wood

Carving
Wood

2

Court Lodge
Farm

Gill
Farm

Weston's
Wood

Bourne
Wood

Freeland
Wood

A2070

Huntbourne
Wood

Greensand Way

Saxon Shore Way

Hibbet's
Wood

Hanger
Wood

1

34

171
157
171
184

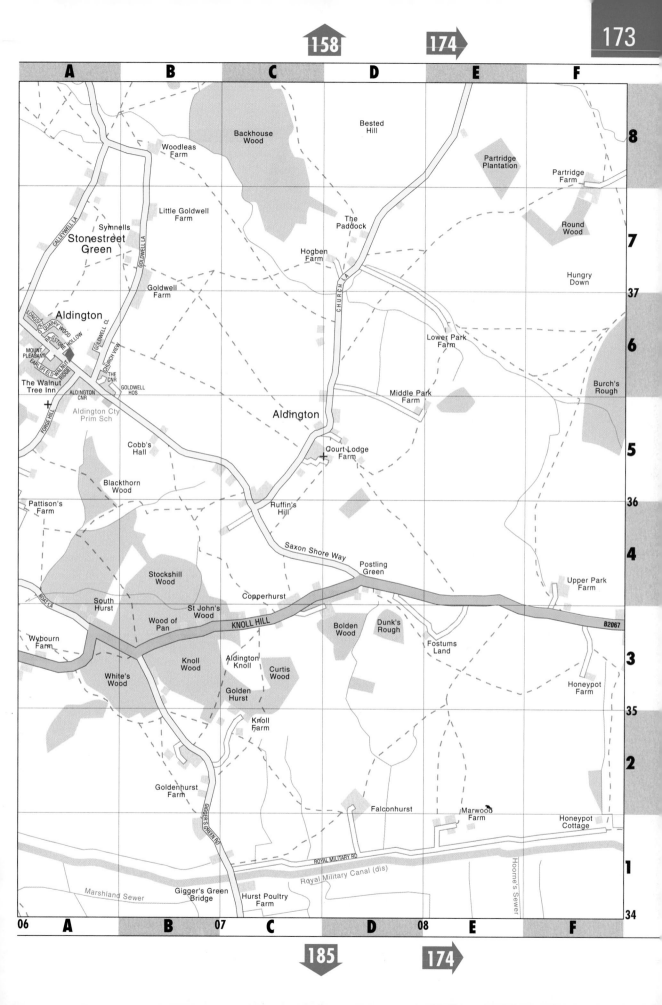

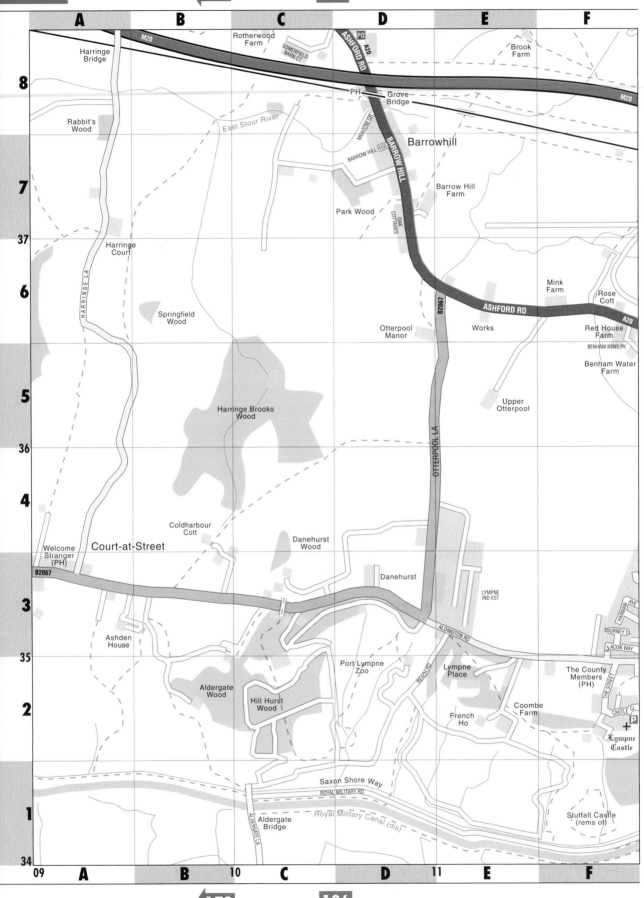

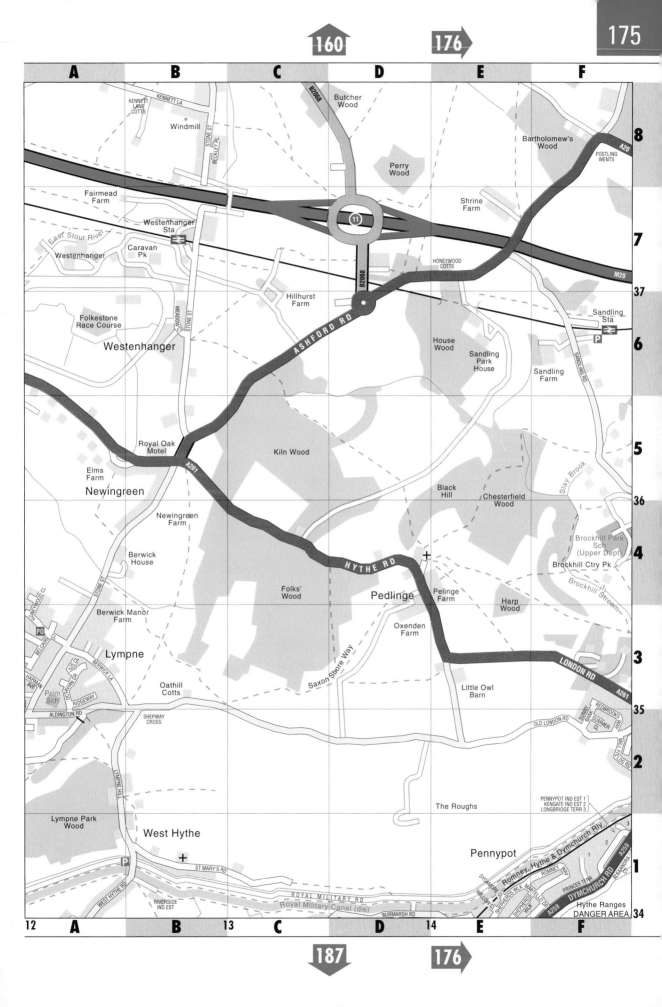

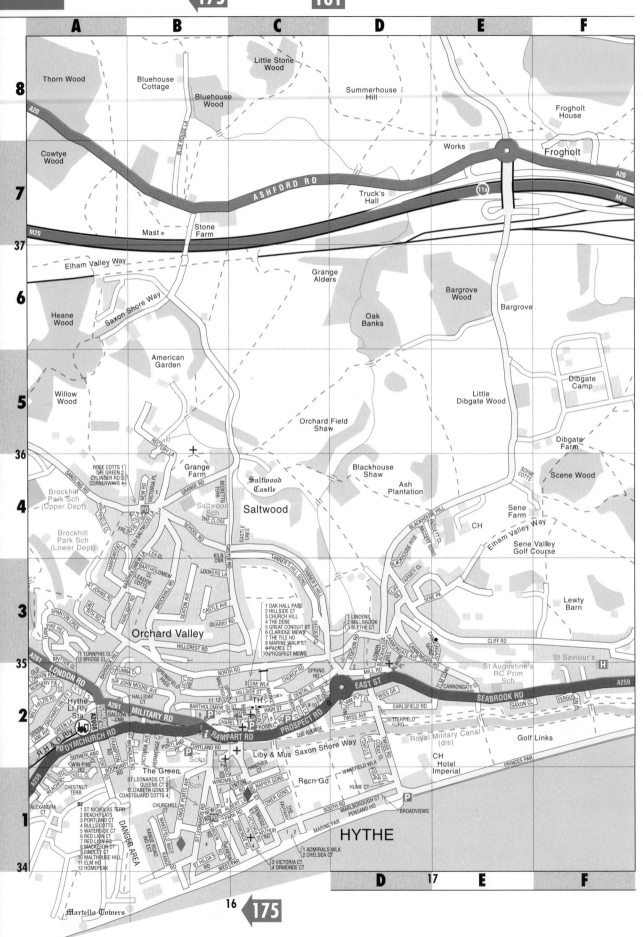

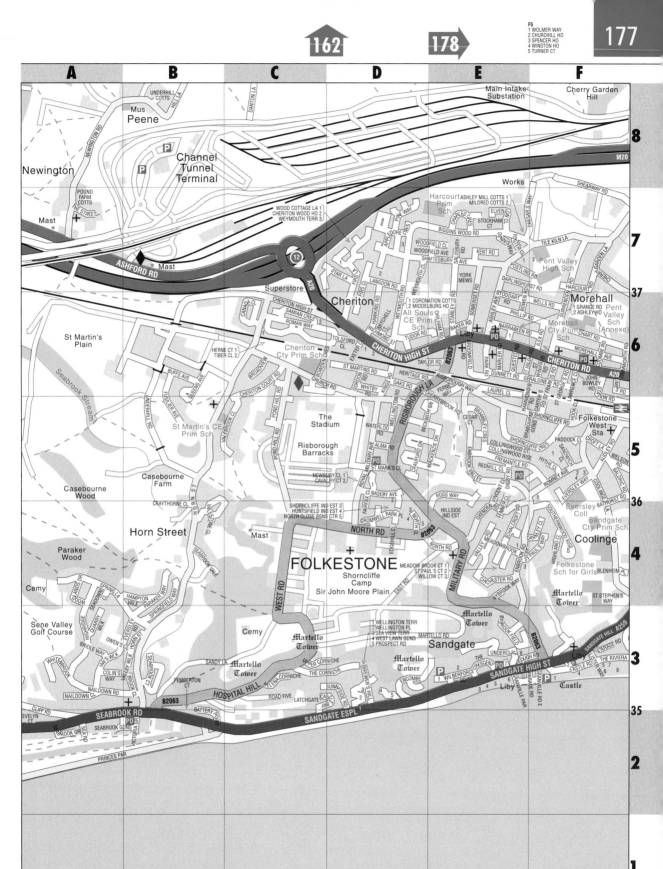

178 →

E3
1 HILLSIDE
2 SOUTHOVER CT
3 HOMEVALE HO
4 TOWER CT
5 SIR JOHN MOORE CT
6 RIVIERA CT
7 NORTH LA
8 WHITE CT

F3
1 MARTELLO TERR
2 LACHLAN WAY
3 JAMES MORRIS CT
4 CASTLE CL
5 VARNE LODGE
6 VARNE CT
7 BEACH MARINE
8 ZARENA CT

177
163

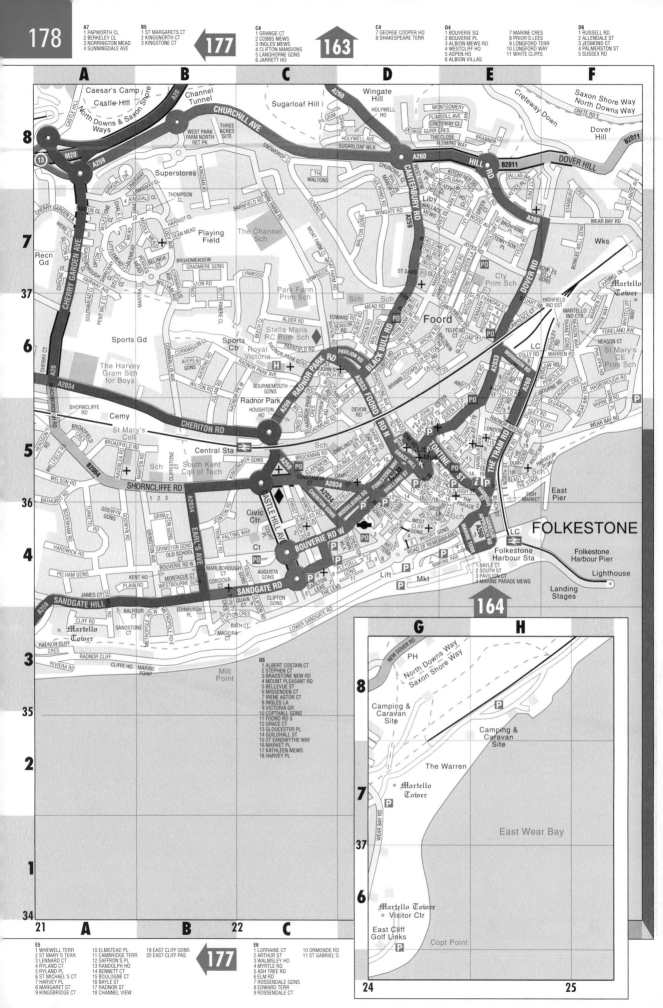

164

177

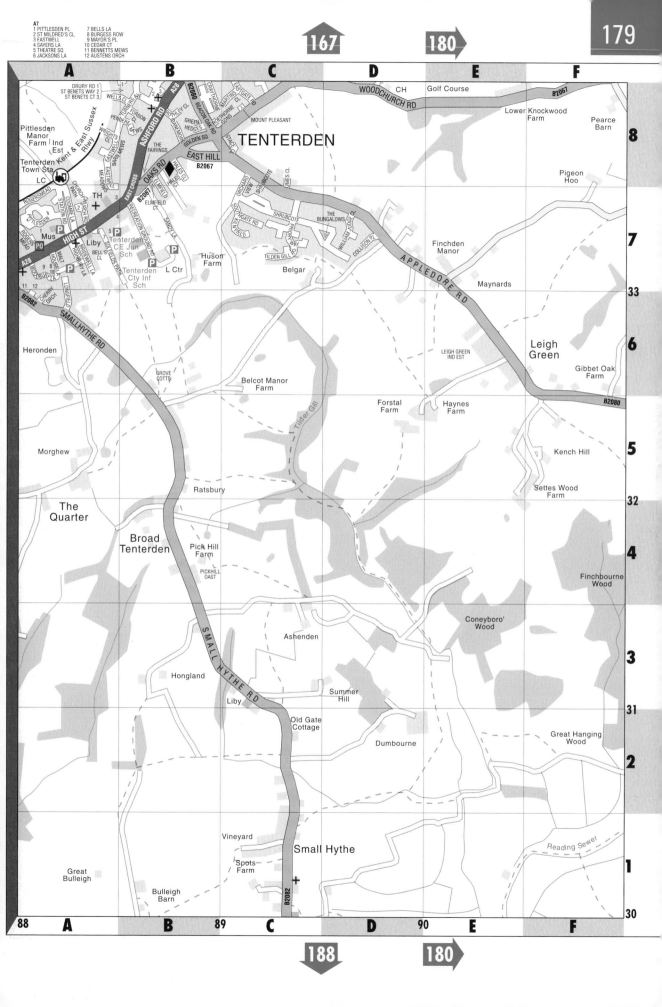

167
180

A7
1 PITTLESDEN PL
2 ST MILDRED'S CL
3 EASTWELL
4 SAYERS LA
5 THEATRE SQ
6 JACKSONS LA
7 BELLS LA
8 BURGESS ROW
9 MAYOR'S PL
10 CEDAR CT
11 BENNETTS MEWS
12 AUSTENS ORCH

A   B   C   D   E   F

WOODCHURCH RD   CH   Golf Course   B2067

DRURY RD 1
St BENETS WAY 2
St BENETS CT 3

Lower Knockwood Farm   Pearce Barn

Pittlesden Manor Farm Ind Est

Kent & East Sussex Rlwy

ASHFORD RD

B2080

TENTERDEN

8

Pigeon Hoo

Tenterden Town Sta   LC

THE FAIRINGS

OAKS RD   EAST HILL   B2067

EAST CROSS

ELMFIELD CT   B2067

ELMFIELD

The Bungalows

APPLEDORE RD

Finchden Manor

7

Rogersmead   Station Rd   Coombe La   Pittlesden

Mus   P0   HIGH ST   A28   TH

Liby   Tenterden CE Jun Sch   P

Tenterden Cty Inf Sch   L Ctr

CHERRY ORCH   LONGFIELD

Huson Farm

SHRUBCOTE   SOUTHGATE RD   ORCHARD VIEW   SWAIN FIELD   WILLIAM JUDGE CL   COLLISON PL

Belgar   TILDEN GILL

Maynards

33

Leigh Green IND EST

A28   WOODS   11 12

SMALLHYTHE RD   B2082

Heronden

GROVE COTTS

Belcot Manor Farm

Tilder Gill

Forstal Farm   Haynes Farm

Leigh Green

Gibbet Oak Farm

6

33

B2080

Morghew

Ratsbury

Kench Hill

5

Settes Wood Farm

32

The Quarter

Broad Tenterden

Pick Hill Farm

PICKHILL OAST

Finchbourne Wood

4

SMALL HYTHE RD

Ashenden

Coneyboro' Wood

3

Hongland

Liby

Summer Hill

Old Gate Cottage

Dumbourne

Great Hanging Wood

31

2

Great Bulleigh

Vineyard

Spots Farm

Small Hythe

B2082

Reading Sewer

1

Bulleigh Barn

30

88   A   B   89   C   D   90   E   F

188
180

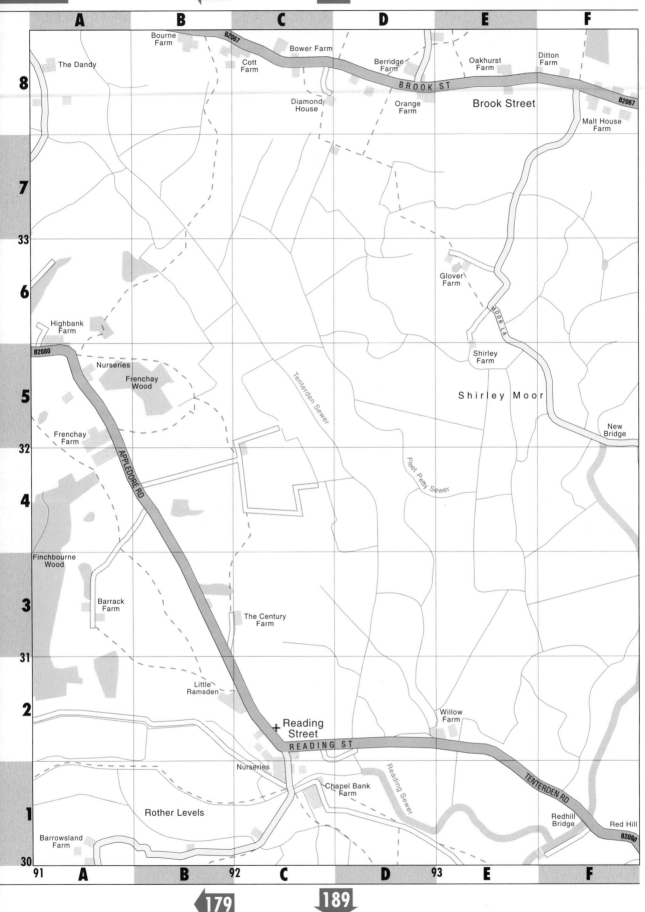

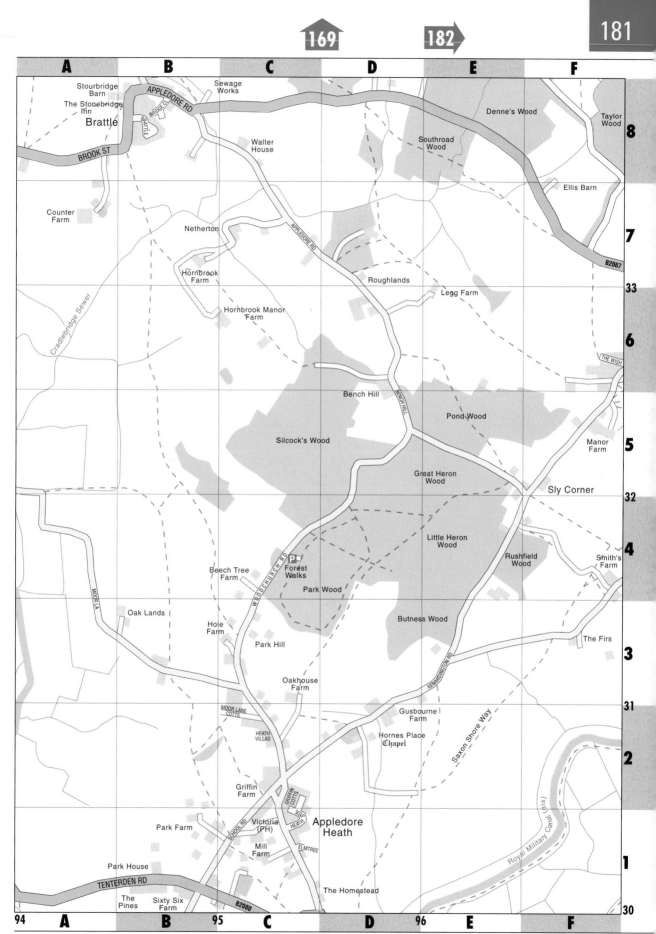

A B C D E F

Stourbridge Barn
The Stonebridge Inn
Brattle
Sewage Works
APPLEDORE RD
BRIDGE CL
BRATTLE
BROOK ST

Denne's Wood
Taylor Wood
8

Walter House
Southroad Wood

Counter Farm
Netherton
APPLEDORE RD
Ellis Barn
7

Hornbrook Farm
Roughlands
Legg Farm
33

Hornbrook Manor Farm
6

THE WISH

Bench Hill
BENCH HILL
Pond Wood
Manor Farm
5

Silcock's Wood
Great Heron Wood
Sly Corner
32

Little Heron Wood
Rushfield Wood
Smith's Farm
4

Beech Tree Farm
WOODCHURCH RD
P
Forest Walks
Park Wood
Butness Wood
The Firs
3

Oak Lands
MOOR LA
Hole Farm
Park Hill
KENARDINGTON RD

Oakhouse Farm
31

MOOR LANE COTTS
HEATH VILLAS
Gusbourne Farm
Saxon Shore Way
2

Griffin Farm
GRIFFIN COTTS
Hornes Place Chapel

Park Farm
SCHOOL RD
Victoria (PH)
GRIFFIN HEATH
Appledore Heath

Mill Farm
ELMTREE
Royal Military Canal (dis)
1

Park House
The Homestead
TENTERDEN RD
The Pines
Sixty Six Farm
B2080
30

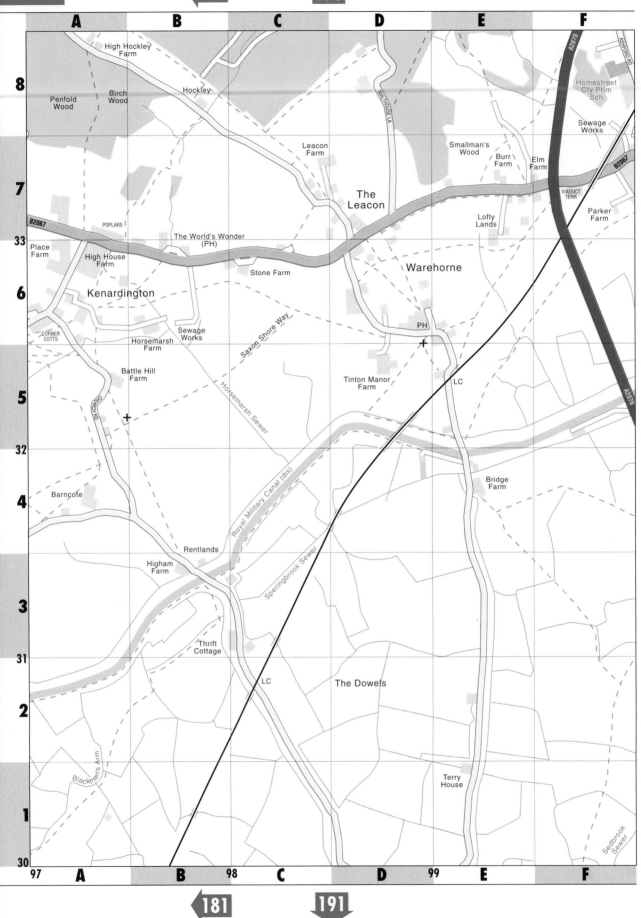

A B C D E F

8

Penfold
Wood

High Hockley
Farm

Birch
Wood

Hockley

Leacon
Farm

Smallman's
Wood

Burr
Farm

Elm
Farm

Homestreet
Cty Prim
Sch

Sewage
Works

7

The
Leacon

Lofty
Lands

Parker
Farm

VIADUCT
TERR

B2067

33

B2067

Place
Farm

POPLARS

The World's Wonder
(PH)

Warehorne

High House
Farm

Stone Farm

6

Kenardington

PH

CORNER
COTTS

Horsemarsh
Farm

Sewage
Works

Saxon Shore Way

LC

Battle Hill
Farm

Tinton Manor
Farm

Horsemarsh Sewer

5

OLD ROMNEY RD

A2070

32

Bridge
Farm

Barncote

Royal Military Canal (dis)

Rentlands

4

Speringbrook Sewer

Higham
Farm

3

Thrift
Cottage

31

LC

The Dowels

2

Blackman's Arm

Terry
House

1

Sedbrook
Sewer

30

97 A B 98 C D 99 E F

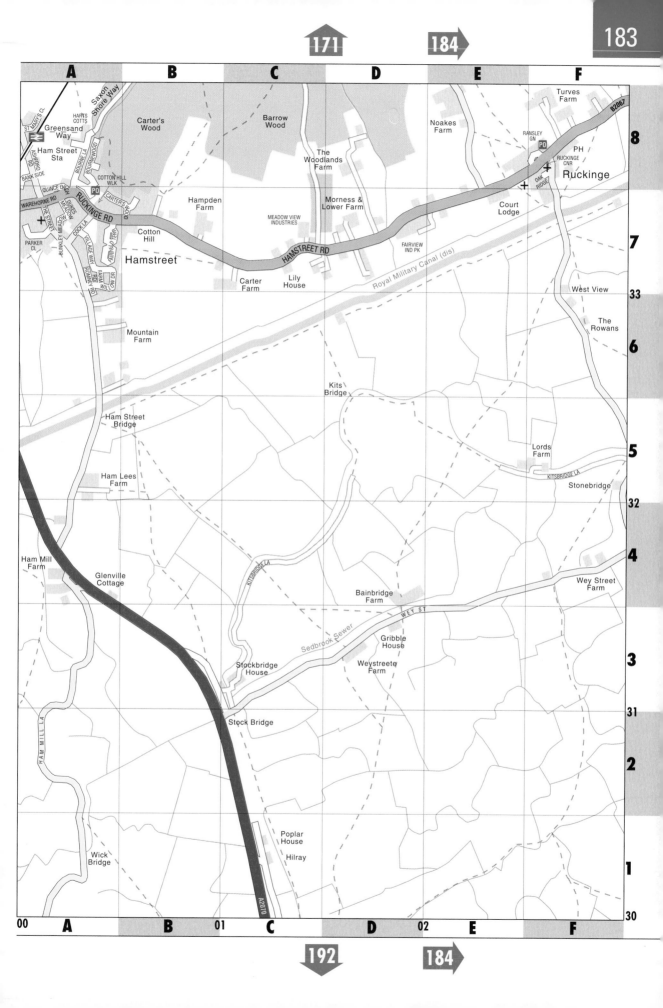

A B C D E F

ST MARY'S CL.
Greensand Way
Saxon Shore Way
Carter's Wood
Barrow Wood
HARTS COTTS
Ham Street Sta
Turves Farm
B2067
Noakes Farm
Ransley GN
PO
PH
RUCKINGE CNR
8
ASHFORD RD
BANK SIDE
BOURNE LA
BOURNEWOOD
COTTON HILL WLK
PO
The Woodlands Farm
Oak Ridge
Ruckinge
QUINCE ORCH
RUCKINGE RD
CARTER'S WOOD
Hampden Farm
Morness & Lower Farm
Court Lodge
WAREHORNE RD
DUKES MEADOW
THE STREET
MEADOW VIEW INDUSTRIES
PARKER CL
COCK LA
Cotton Hill
HAMSTREET RD
FAIRVIEW IND PK
West View
7
BRINKLEY MEADOW
VILLAGE WAY
PARTRIDGE LA
Hamstreet
HAMSTREET RD
Royal Military Canal (dis)
33
FARM WLK
ROMNEY RD
WILLOW DR
Carter Farm
Lily House
The Rowans
Mountain Farm
Kits Bridge
6
Ham Street Bridge
Lords Farm
5
Ham Lees Farm
KITSBRIDGE LA
Stonebridge
32
Ham Mill Farm
KITSBRIDGE LA
Wey Street Farm
4
Glenville Cottage
Bainbridge Farm
WEY ST
Sedbrook Sewer
Gribble House
3
Stockbridge House
Weystreete Farm
HAM MILL LA
Stock Bridge
31
2
A2070
Poplar House
Wick Bridge
Hilray
1
30

00 A B 01 C D 02 E F

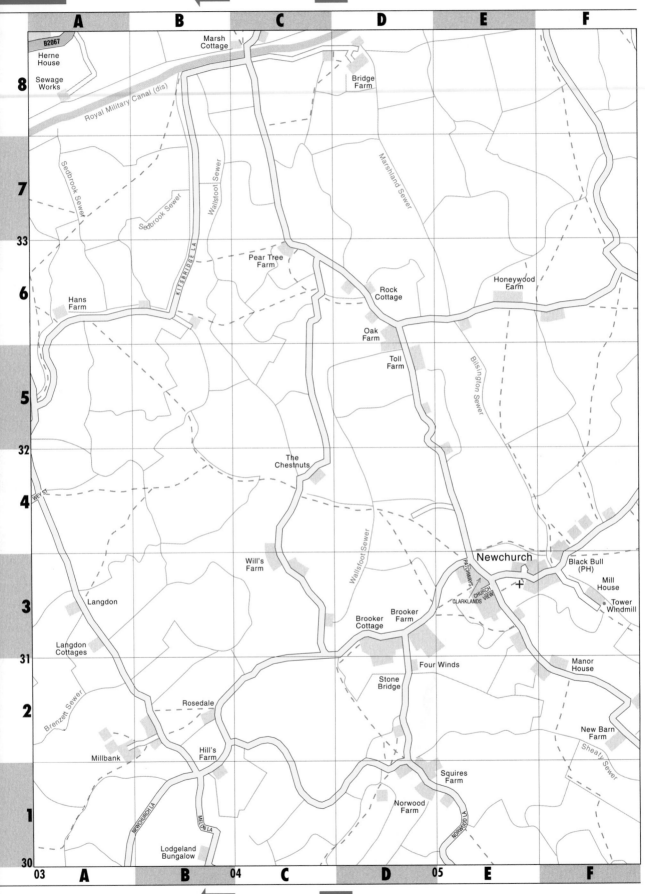

B2067

Herne House

Sewage Works

Royal Military Canal (dis)

Marsh Cottage

Bridge Farm

Sedbrook Sewer

Sedbrook Sewer

Wallstoot Sewer

KITSBRIDGE LA

Marshland Sewer

Pear Tree Farm

Rock Cottage

Honeywood Farm

Hans Farm

Oak Farm

Toll Farm

Bilsington Sewer

The Chestnuts

Wallsfoot Sewer

WEY ST

Will's Farm

Newchurch

Black Bull (PH)

Mill House

Langdon

PATCHWAY'S

CHURCH VIEW

CLARKLANDS

Tower Windmill

Brooker Cottage

Brooker Farm

Langdon Cottages

Four Winds

Manor House

Brenzett Sewer

Rosedale

Stone Bridge

Millbank

Hill's Farm

New Barn Farm

Sheaty Sewer

Squires Farm

NEWCHURCH LA

MELON LA

Norwood Farm

NORWOOD LA

Lodgeland Bungalow

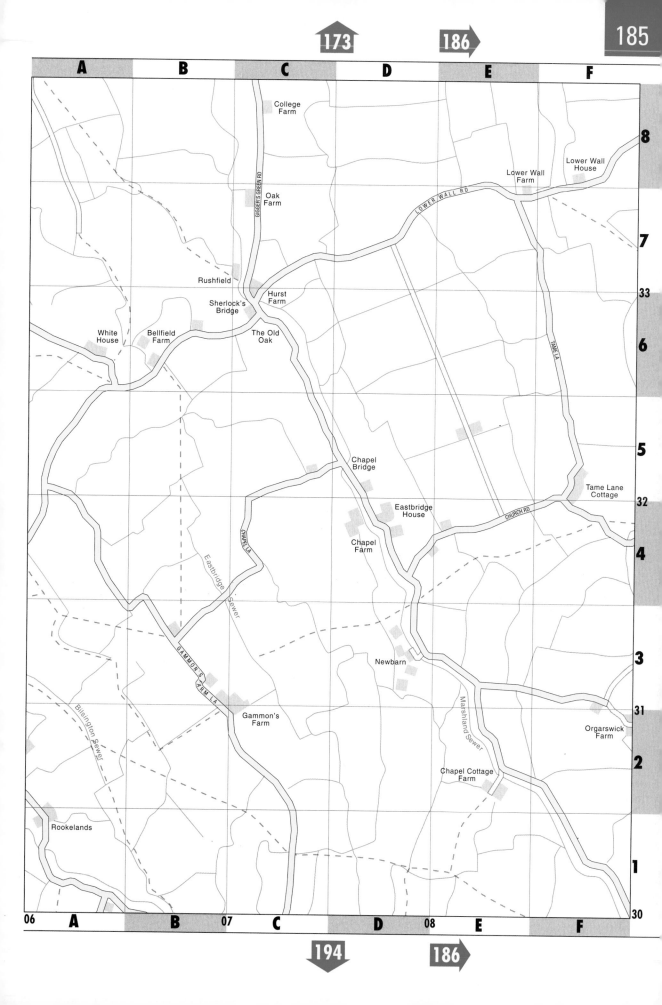

A   B   C   D   E   F

College
Farm

8

GIGGER'S GREEN RD

Oak
Farm

LOWER WALL RD

Lower Wall
Farm

Lower Wall
House

7

Rushfield

Sherlock's
Bridge

Hurst
Farm

33

White
House

Bellfield
Farm

The Old
Oak

TAME LA

6

Chapel
Bridge

5

CHAPEL LA

Eastbridge Sewer

Chapel
Bridge

Tame Lane
Cottage

32

Eastbridge
House

CHURCH RD

Chapel
Farm

4

GAMMON'S FARM LA

Bilsington Sewer

Newbarn

Marshland Sewer

3

Gammon's
Farm

31

Orgarswick
Farm

2

Chapel Cottage
Farm

Rookelands

1

30

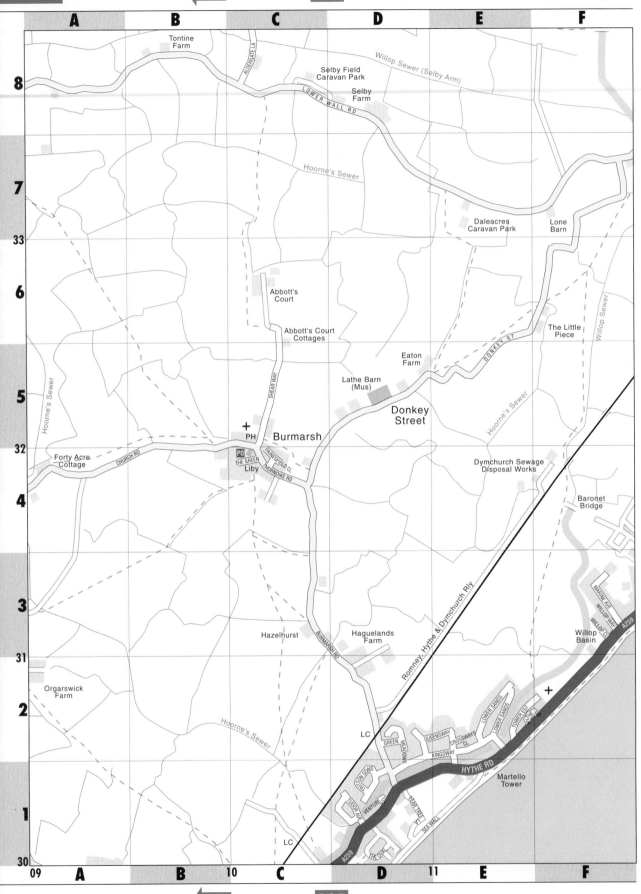

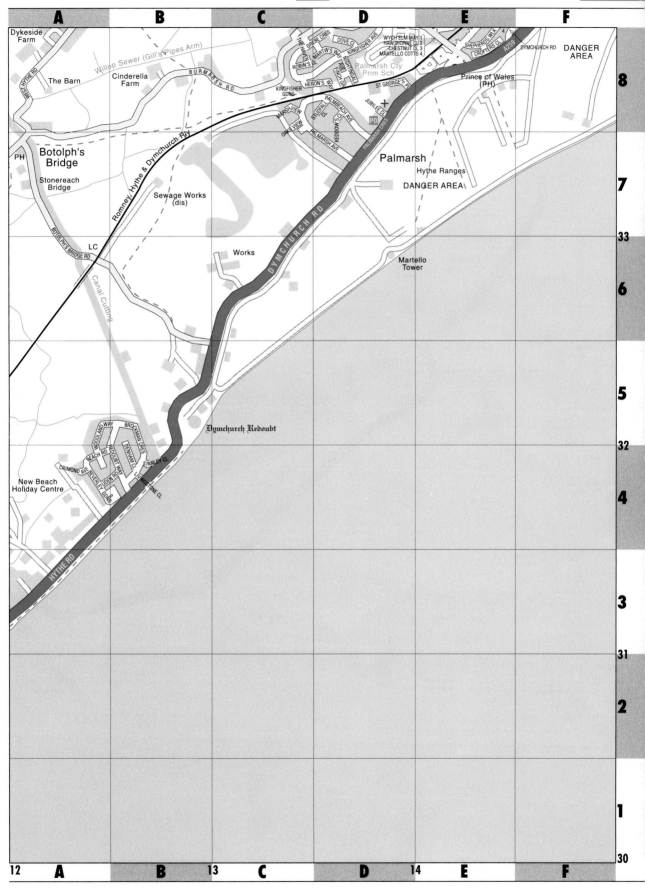

Dykeside Farm
The Barn
Cinderella Farm
Willop Sewer (Gill's Pipes Arm)
BURMARSH RD
WEST HYTHE RD

THE HAVEN
GREBE CRES
ROBIN'S CL
KINGFISHER GDNS
MARSH VIEW
OAKS VIEW
DOVE CL
KINGFISHER AVE
MARTW'S WAY
NIGHTINGALE
HERON'S WAY
STUDFALL CL
PALMBEACH AVE
PALMARSH AVE
KEDDOW'S CL

WYCH ELM WAY 1
HAWTHORNE CL 2
CHESTNUT CL 3
MARTELLO COTTS 4
SHEPHERDS WLK
CROFTERS CL
DYMCHURCH RD
A259

DANGER AREA

Palmarsh City Prim Sch
St GEORGE'S PL
PALMARSH CRES
JUBILEE CL
PO

Prince of Wales (PH)

Palmarsh
Hythe Ranges
DANGER AREA

Botolph's Bridge
PH
Stonereach Bridge
Romney, Hythe & Dymchurch Rly
Sewage Works (dis)
BOTOLPH'S BRIDGE RD
LC
Canal Cutting

DYMCHURCH RD

Works

Martello Tower

Dymchurch Redoubt

WOODLAND WAY
BROADMAN CRES
BEACH RD
REDOUBT WAY
CRIMOND AVE
BEVERLEY GDNS
UDER RW
DENHAM CL
STANLEY CL
LIVINGSTONE CL

New Beach Holiday Centre

HYTHE RD

8
7
33
6
5
32
4
3
31
2
1
30

12   A   B   13   C   D   14   E   F

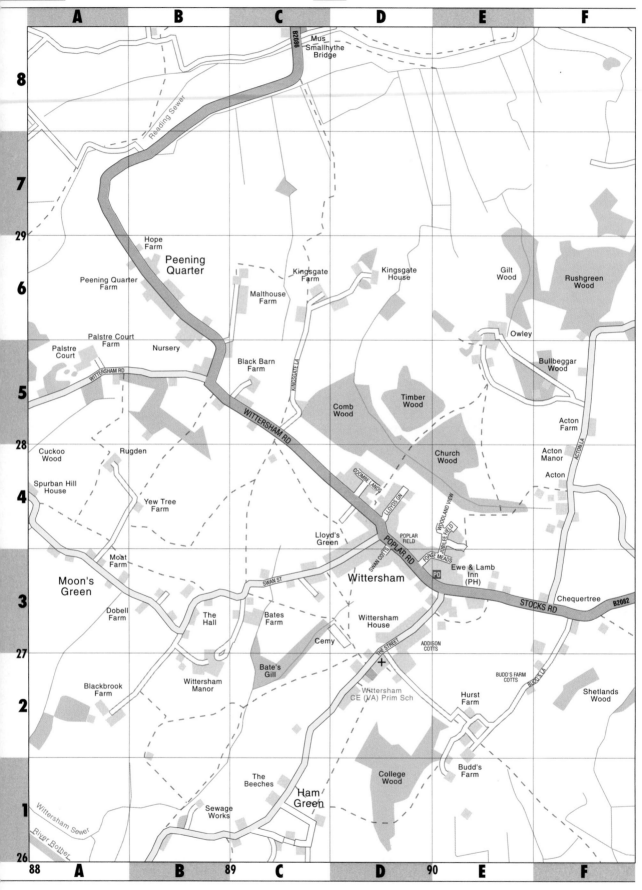

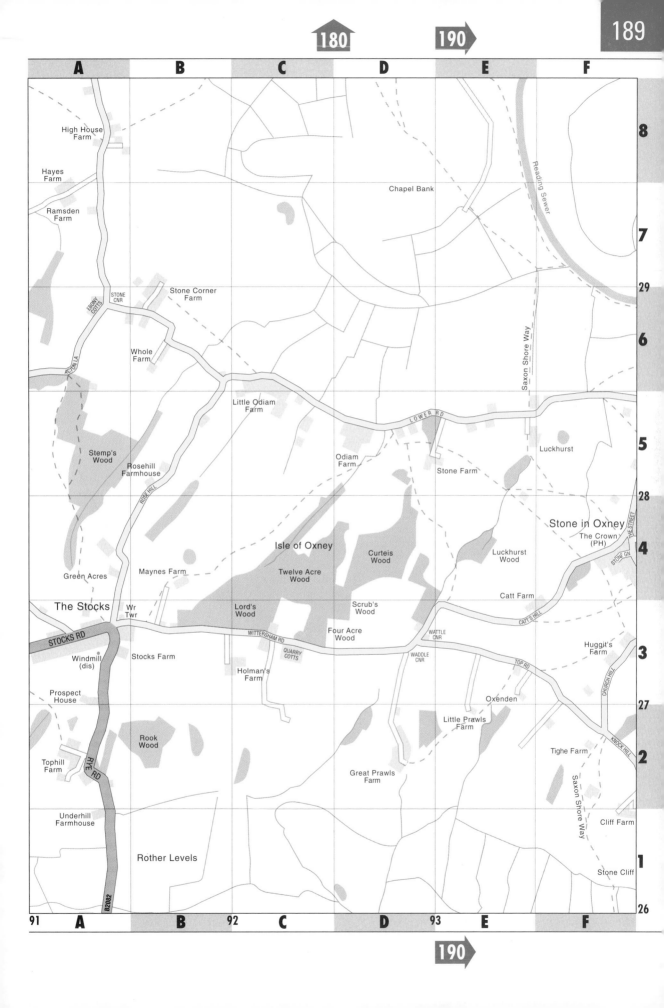

180
190

A **B** **C** **D** **E** **F**

High House Farm

Hayes Farm

Ramsden Farm

Chapel Bank

Reading Sewer

STONE CNR

EBONY COTTS

Stone Corner Farm

Whole Farm

ACTON LA

Saxon Shore Way

Little Odiam Farm

LOWER RD

Luckhurst

Stemp's Wood

Rosehill Farmhouse

ROSE HILL

Odiam Farm

Stone Farm

Stone in Oxney

THE STREET

Isle of Oxney

Curteis Wood

Luckhurst Wood

The Crown (PH)

STONE GN

Green Acres

Maynes Farm

Twelve Acre Wood

Catt Farm

Catt Farm

The Stocks

Wr Twr

Lord's Wood

Scrub's Wood

CATT'S HILL

Huggit's Farm

STOCKS RD

Windmill (dis)

Stocks Farm

WITTERSHAM RD

QUARRY COTTS

Four Acre Wood

WATTLE CNR

WADDLE CNR

TOP RD

CHURCH HILL

Prospect House

Holman's Farm

Oxenden

Little Prawls Farm

RYE RD

Rook Wood

Tighe Farm

KNOCK HILL

Tophill Farm

Great Prawls Farm

Saxon Shore Way

Cliff Farm

Underhill Farmhouse

Rother Levels

Stone Cliff

B2082

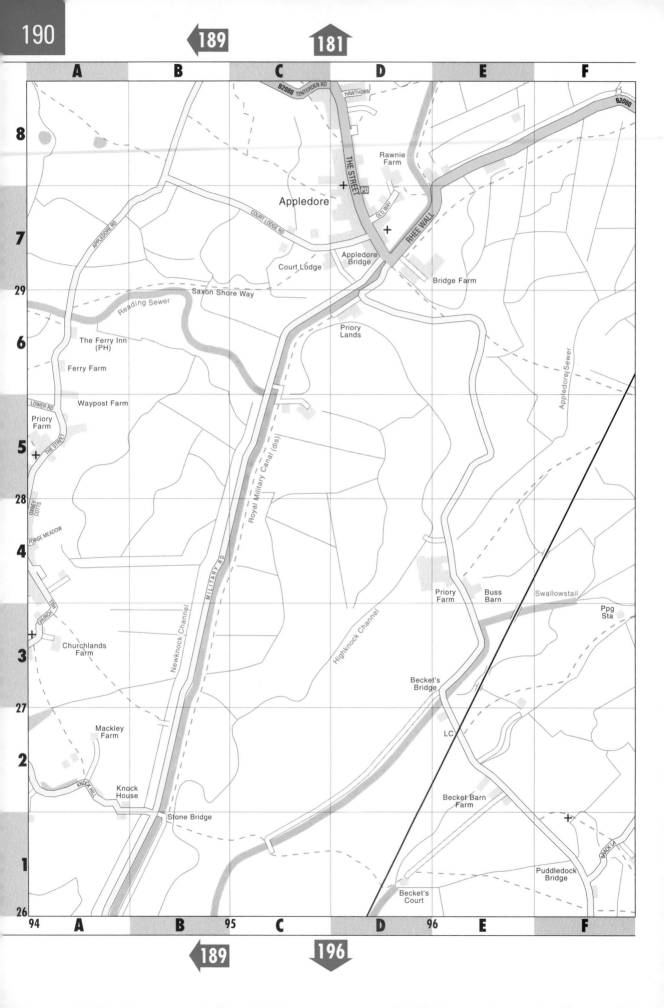

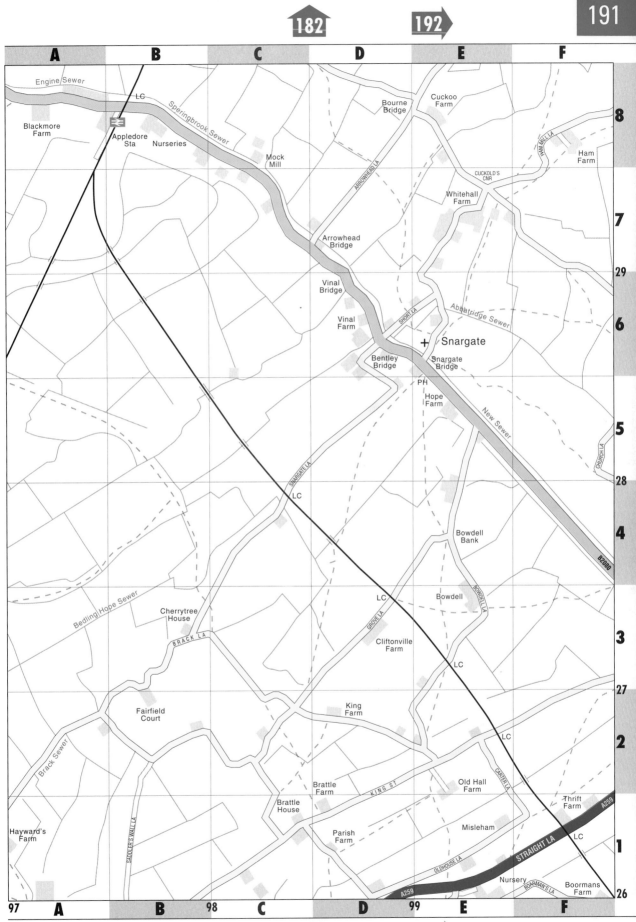

182
192

Engine Sewer
LC
Blackmore Farm
Appledore Sta
Nurseries
Speringbrook Sewer
Mock Mill
Bourne Bridge
Cuckoo Farm
Ham Mill La
Ham Farm
CUCKOLD'S CNR
Whitehall Farm
Arrowhead La
Arrowhead Bridge
Vinal Bridge
Abbatridge Sewer
Vinal Farm
Short La
Snargate
New Sewer
Church La
Bentley Bridge
Snargate Bridge
PH
Hope Farm
Bowdell Bank
B2080
Snargate La
LC
Bedling Hope Sewer
Cherrytree House
Bowdell
Bondell La
LC
LC
Brack La
Cliftonville Farm
Grove La
LC
Fairfield Court
King Farm
LC
Brack Sewer
Carter La
Saddlers Wall La
Brattle Farm
King St
Old Hall Farm
Thrift Farm
A259
Brattle House
Hayward's Farm
Parish Farm
Misleham
Straight La
LC
Oldhouse La
A259
Nursery
Boorman's La
Boormans Farm

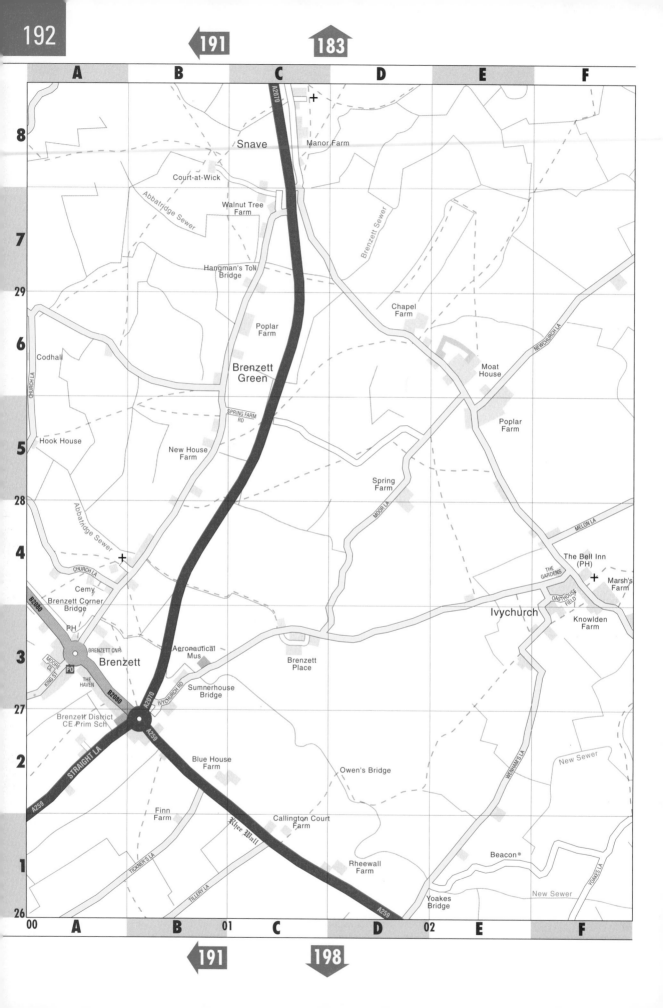

184
194
199
194

A   B   C   D   E   F

8

7

29

6

5

28

4

3

27

2

1

26

03   A   B   04   C   D   05   E   F

Lodgeland Farm

Little Appledore

Melon Farm

MELON LA

Brenzett Sewer

NEWCHURCH LA

Golding Cottage

Melon Farm

Melon Lane Bridge

Home Farm

YOAKES LA

Yoakes Court Farm

Five Vents Bridge

FIVE VENTS LA

Sunnyside Farm

Sheaty Sewer

Willow Farm

Popton Bridge

NORWOOD LA

ROOKERY BUSH LA

North Fording Farm

CHITTENDEN'S LA

Goose Farm

Honeychild Manor

Tonbridge Farm

Springfield

HOPE LA

Beechcroft Farm

New Sewer

193
185

193
200

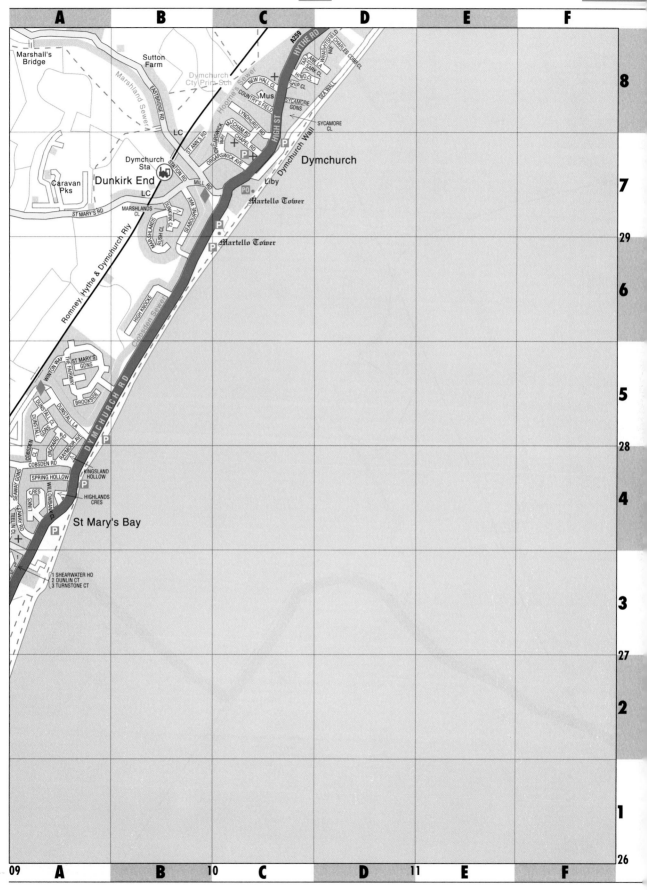

Marshall's Bridge

Sutton Farm

Marshland Sewer

EASTBRIDGE RD

Dymchurch Cty Prim Sch

COUNTRY'S FIELD

Hoorne Sewer

A259

HYTHE RD

WRAIGHTSFIELD

HYTHE RD

CHARLES COBB CL

NINE

TARR...

ARK CL

LARK CL

SARK CL

HIND CL

SHIP CL

NEW HALL CL

LYNDHURST RD

MITCHAM RD

ORGARSWICK WAY

CHAPEL RD

SYCAMORE GDNS

SEA WALL

Mus

HIGH ST

SYCAMORE CL

Dymchurch

Dymchurch Wall

LC

ST ANN'S RD

SUTTON RD

MILL RD

Dymchurch Sta

Dunkirk End

Caravan Pks

St Mary's Rd

ORGARSWICK AVE

SEABOURNE WAY

DUNKIRK CL

MARSHLANDS CL

MARSHLANDS

RUSH CL

Romney, Hythe & Dymchurch Rly

HIGH KNOCKE

Cobsden Sewer

DYMCHURCH RD

PO

Liby

Martello Tower

Martello Tower

Martello Tower

29

8

7

6

WINTON WAY

THE FAIRWAY

ST MARY'S GDNS

BROOKSIDE

DUNSTALL LA

DUNSTALL CL

DUNSTALL

ORCHARD

RAYMOOR AVE

RD

COBSDEN CL

COBSDEN RD

SPRING HOLLOW

SEWAY GDNS

LINKS RD

WILLOWBANK CL

FEELIN CL

CRES

St Mary's Bay

Kingsland Hollow

HIGHLANDS CRES

1 SHEARWATER HO
2 DUNLIN CT
3 TURNSTONE CT

1
2
3

5

28

4

3

27

2

1

26

A B C D E F

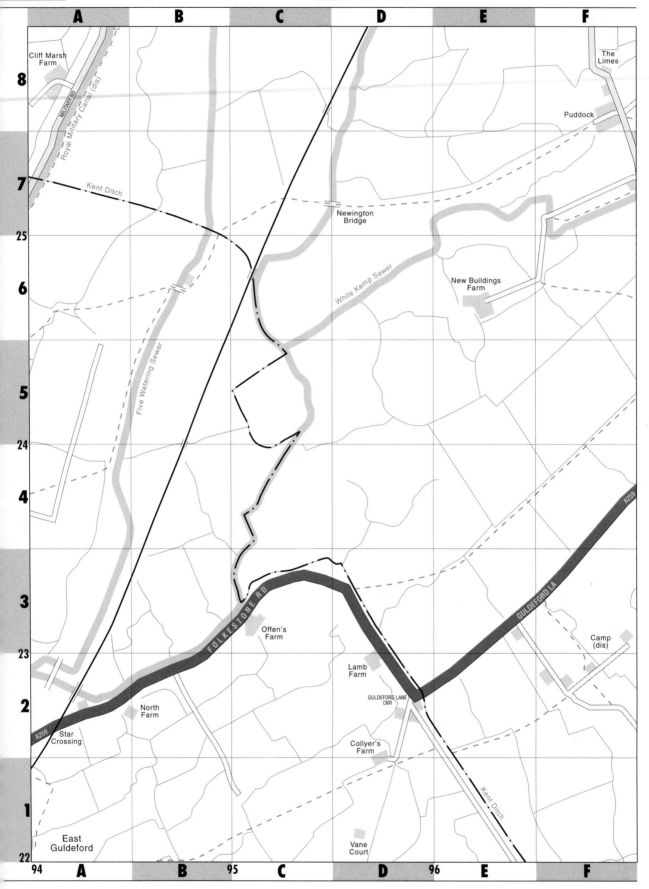

A   B   C   D   E   F

8

Cliff Marsh
Farm

The Limes

Puddock

7

Kent Ditch

Newington
Bridge

Royal Military Canal (dis)

MILITARY RD

25

6

White Kemp Sewer

New Buildings
Farm

Five Watering Sewer

5

24

4

A259

GULDEFORD LA

3

FOLKESTONE RD

Offen's
Farm

Camp
(dis)

23

Lamb
Farm

2

North
Farm

GULDEFORD LANE
CNR

A259

Star
Crossing

Collyer's
Farm

Kent Ditch

1

East
Guldeford

Vane
Court

22

94   A   B   95   C   D   96   E   F

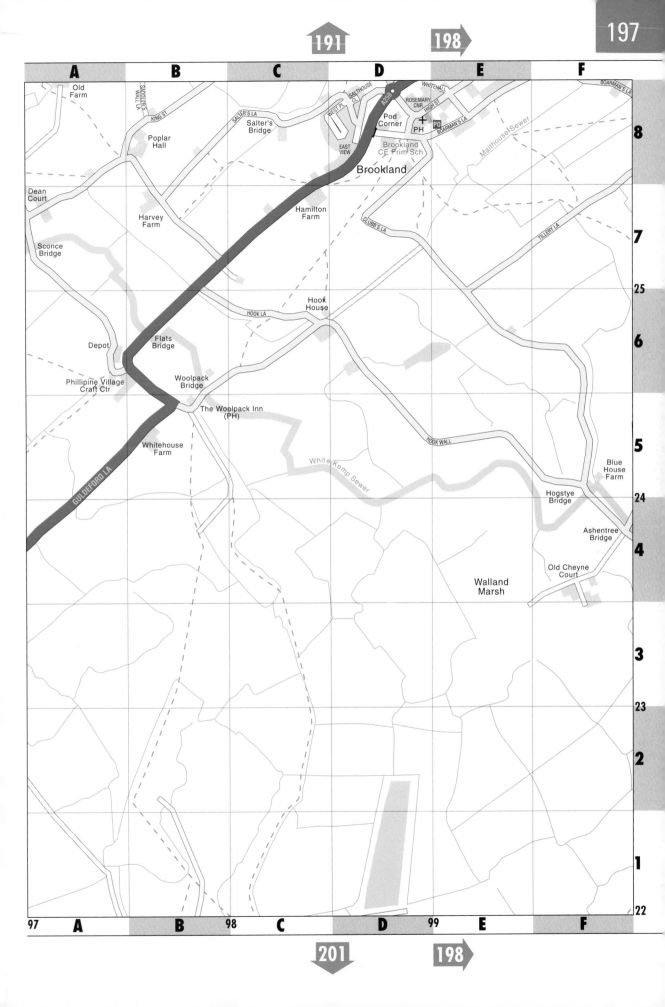

A B C D E F

8

7

25

6

5

24

4

3

23

2

1

22

Tickner's La

Barnland Farm

Tillery La

LC

Barnhouse La

Narrowbush La

LC

LC

Mountain La

Ashentree La

St Thomas's Innings

LC

Washington La

Coldharbour Farm

Prospect Farm

Eighteen Acre La

Bush Farm

Beggarsbush La

A259

New Sewer

Oakes La

Vine Cottage

Sycamore House

A259

Sycamore Farm

Millbank La

Court Lodge

Coldharbour Bridge

White Kemp Sewer

White's House

LC

Coldharbour La

Old Romney Bridge

Wheelsgate

Cutter's Bridge

Bow Bridge

Midley Cottages

LC

Baynham Farm

Baynham Petty Sewer

Hawthorn Cnr

Scott's Marsh House

Newland Bungalow

Newland Farm Cottage

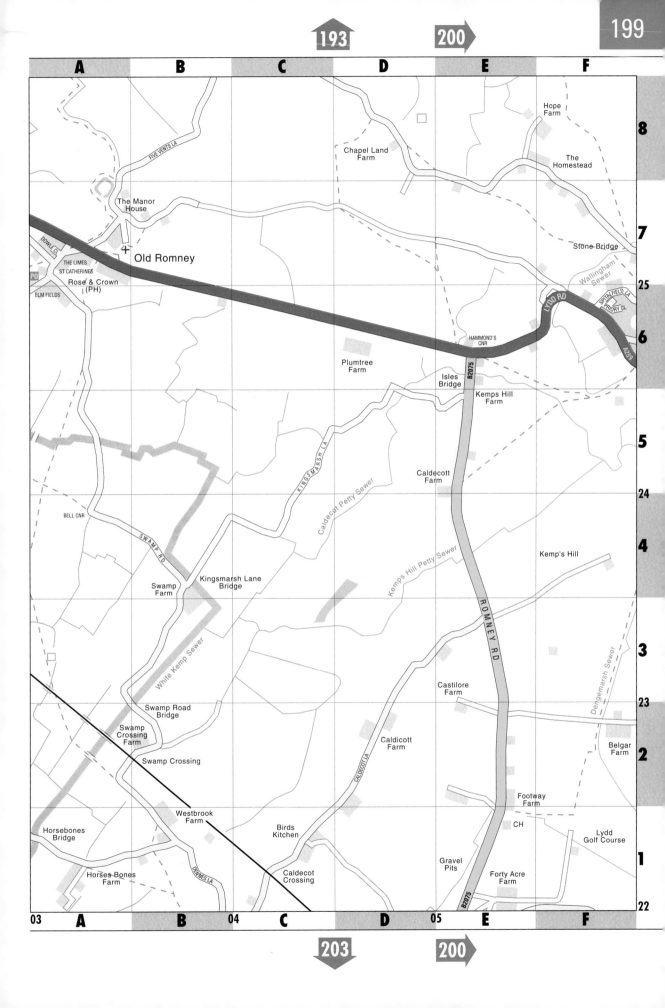

A B C D E F

8

Hope Farm

Chapel Land Farm

The Homestead

7

The Manor House

Stone Bridge

Wallingham Sewer

FIVE VENTS LA

DOWLE CL

THE LIMES
ST CATHERINES

Old Romney

PO

Rose & Crown
(PH)

ELM FIELDS

25

LYDD RD

SPITALFIELD LA

PRIORY CL

6

HAMMOND'S
CNR

A259

Plumtree Farm

Isles Bridge

B2075

Kemps Hill Farm

5

KINGSMARSH LA

Caldecot Petty Sewer

Caldecott Farm

24

BELL CNR

SWAMP RD

Kemps Hill Petty Sewer

Kemp's Hill

4

Swamp Farm

Kingsmarsh Lane Bridge

White Kemp Sewer

ROMNEY RD

Dengemarsh Sewer

3

Swamp Road Bridge

Castilore Farm

23

Swamp Crossing Farm

Caldicott Farm

Belgar Farm

2

Swamp Crossing

CALDECOT LA

Footway Farm

Westbrook Farm

Birds Kitchen

CH

Lydd Golf Course

Horsebones Bridge

Gravel Pits

1

Horses Bones Farm

BRANES LA

Caldecot Crossing

B2075

Forty Acre Farm

22

A B C D E F

8

7

25

6

5

24

4

3

23

2

1

22

GLOUCESTER MEWS
ELLESMERE MEWS
CLARENDON MEWS
ELLIS DR
ST MARY'S RD
RICHMOND DR
BRUSSENDEN CL
DYMCHURCH RD
Warren House
Warren Farm
Warren Inn (PH)

1 MELBURY MEWS
2 PEMBROKE MEWS
3 WINDSOR MEWS
4 RYSWICK MEWS

Littlestone Golf Course

New Romney Schs
Southlands Comm Comp Sch
New Romney Main Sewer

Romney Warren Golf Course
Littlestone Tower

BROADLANDS AVE
BROADLANDS CRES
WALNER GDNS
CANNON ST
FAIRFIELD RD
GEORGE ST
CHANTHERINE LA
CHANTHERINE LA
ASHFORD LA
WALNER LA
FAIRFIELD CL
CAVENDISH RD
MADEIRA RD

COCKREED

PRESCOTT HO
FAIRFIELD RD
Liby
NORTH ST
WEST ST
HIGH ST
TH
SUSSEX RD
SPITALFIELD LA
SUSSEX RD
ST JOHN'S RD
PO
QUEEN'S RD
LYDD RD A259
Cemy
CHURCH RD
CHURCH APP
CHURCH LA

STATION RD
B2071
THE CHURCHLANDS
THE CHURCHLANDS
ENGLISH CL
GREENLY CL
WELLS CL
IMBERT CL
CLARY RD
LEAROYD RD
STATION APP
CAREY
TOONEY RD
WILLS AVE

Mountfield Row
New Romney Sta
Ind Est

1 SPRINGWOOD CT
2 CHURCHLANDS HO
3 WILES HO
4 DERVILLE HO
5 ASHDOWN CRES

1 GOLDEN SQ
2 MALTHOUSE COTTS
3 ROME HOUSE CNR
4 ROME RD
5 ST LAWRENCE CT
6 VICTORIA ST

NEW ROMNEY

MARLBOROUGH DR
THE FAIRWAY
WARREN RD
THE INNINGS
BLENHEIM RD
LINKS WAY
ST NICHOLAS RD
ANNE ROPER CL
CHERRY GDNS
ST ANDREW'S RD
ORCHARD DR
BLENHEIM RD
CH
CH
LANGPORT RD
PO
LITTLESTONE RD
QUEEN'S RD
METHERAVE CL
PARK RD
B2071
THE SALTINGS
MARINE PAR
CLOVELLY
Littlestone-on-Sea

VICTORIA RD W
VICTORIA RD
ARMADA CL
GRAND PAR
COAST RD

THE APARTMENTS 1
GRAND CT 2
MULBERRY CT 3

Caravan Park
Caravan Park

Sewage Works

CLARKE RD
CHANNEL WATCH
P
IRB Sta

Romney Salts

MEEHAN RD
ADIE RD
ADIE RD
DUNES RD
HARDY RD
ALFRED RD
MEEHAN RD S
COAST DR
MERRITT RD

Romney, Hythe & Dymchurch Railway

Jolly Fisherman (PH)
PO
P

Greatstone Prim Sch
BALDWIN RD
THE PARADE
ROBERTS RD
BALLARD RD
SEAVIEW RD
LC
LC
Greatstone-on-Sea

Dengemarsh Sewer
Mockmill Sewer
Northlade

06   07   08

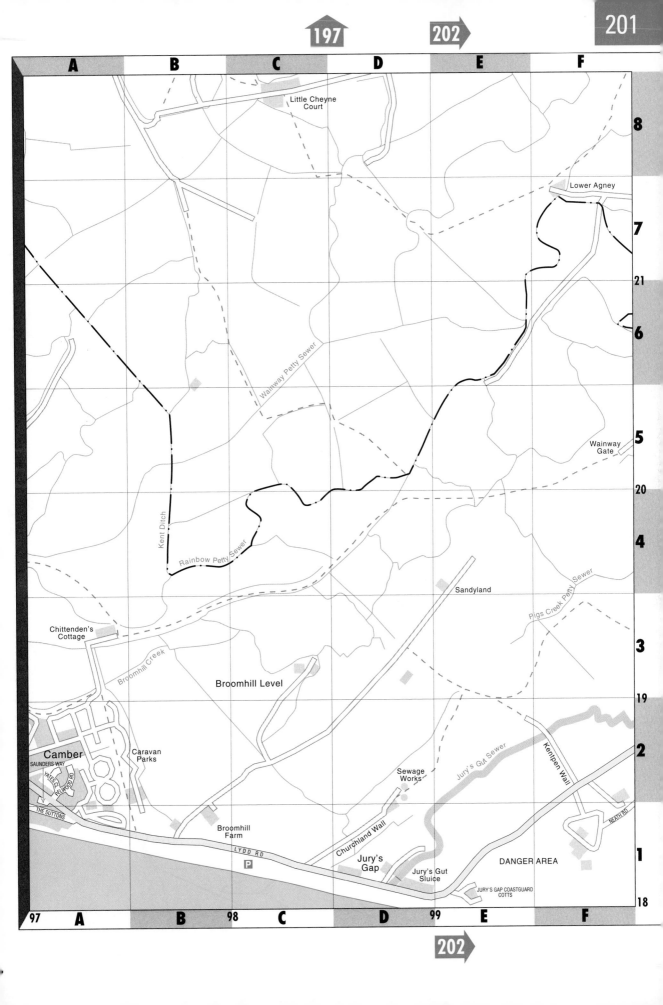

A B C D E F

8
7
21
6
5
20
4
3
19
2
1
18

Little Cheyne Court

Lower Agney

Wainway Petty Sewer

Wainway Gate

Kent Ditch

Rainbow Petty Sewer

Sandyland

Pigs Creek Petty Sewer

Chittenden's Cottage

Broomhill Creek

Broomhill Level

Camber

SAUNDERS WAY

YATES CL

BELMOND RD

THE SUTTONS

Caravan Parks

Broomhill Farm

LYDD RD

P

Sewage Works

Churchland Wall

Jury's Gap

Jury's Gut Sluice

Jury's Gut Sewer

Kenipen Wall

NEATH RD

DANGER AREA

JURY'S GAP COASTGUARD COTTS

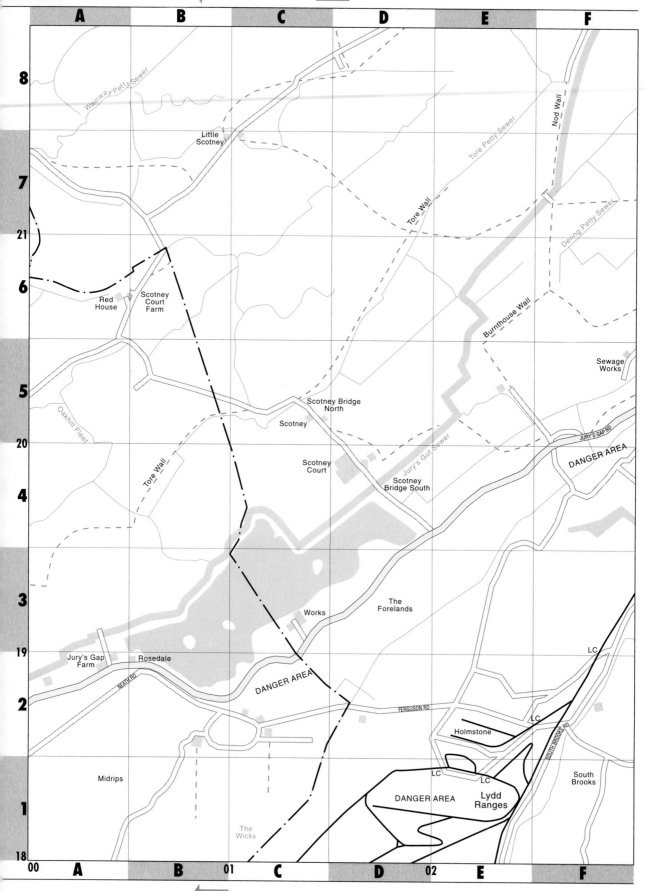

Wainway Petty Sewer

Tore Petty Sewer

Nod Wall

Dering Petty Sewer

Little Scotney

Tore Wall

Burnthouse Wall

Sewage Works

Red House

Scotney Court Farm

Oakhill Fleet

Scotney Bridge North

Scotney

JURY'S GAP RD

DANGER AREA

Tore Wall

Scotney Court

Jury's Gut Sewer

Scotney Bridge South

LC

The Forelands

Works

Jury's Gap Farm

Rosedale

NEATH RD

DANGER AREA

FERGUSON RD

LC

Holmstone

SOUTH BROOKS RD

Midrips

LC

LC

South Brooks

DANGER AREA

Lydd Ranges

The Wicks

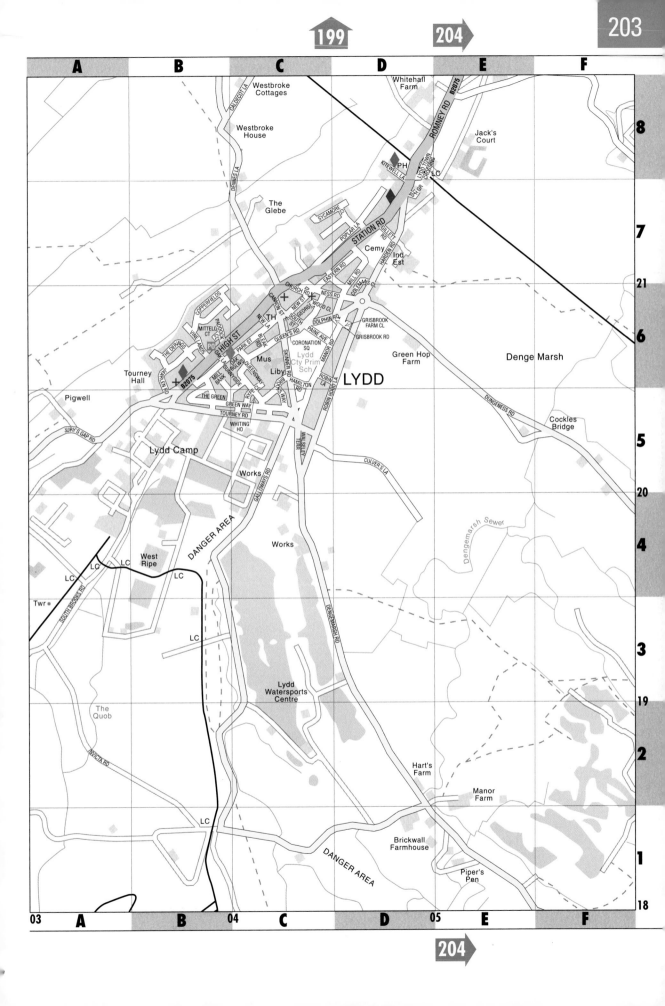

203
200

A   B   C   D   E   F

8

Romney Sands
Holiday Village

LC

Romney Sands
Sta

Caravan
Park   1
        2
        3

LA ROCCO 1
LA TAUSCO 2
LA GALAMINA 3

BEACHMONT CL

PRIOR RD

Mockmill Sewer

Lydd
Airport

CHANNON RD

DERVILLE RD

THE PARADE

7

WALLER RD

LEONARD RD

COLEVILLE CRES

21

BEATRICE
MEWS

6

The Ship
(PH)

HULL RD

TOBY RD

LCs

P

TAYLOR RD

FORT CL

Lade

LADE FORT
COTTS

LC

FORT LYNE

FORT LYNE S

Romney, Hythe & Dymchurch Railway

WILLIAMSON RD

LLOYDS CL SOUTH

SAXTON RD

PLEASANCE RD N

5

COAST DR

20

Works

4

Boulderwall
Farm

PLEASANCE ROAD CENTRAL

3

Conveyor

DUNGENESS RD

KERTON RD

Lydd-on-Sea

19

Halfway
Bush

2

PLEASANCE RD S

Mast

BATTERY RD

Denge
Marsh

Coastguard
Cottages

1

Walkers Outland
(RSPB Reserve)

18

06   A   B   07   C   D   08   E   F

203
205

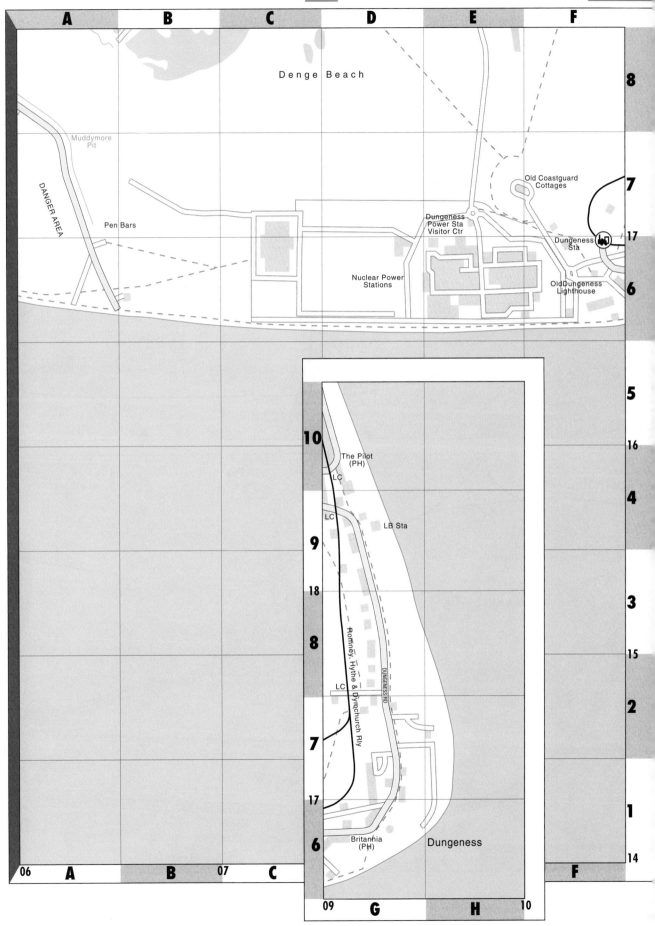

Denge Beach

Muddymore
Pit

DANGER AREA

Pen Bars

Old Coastguard
Cottages

Dungeness
Power Sta
Visitor Ctr

Dungeness
Sta

Nuclear Power
Stations

Old Dungeness
Lighthouse

The Pilot
(PH)

LC

LC

LB Sta

9

18

Romney, Hythe & Dymchurch Rly

DUNGENESS RD

LC

7

17

6

Britannia
(PH)

Dungeness

06   A   B   07   C   F

09   G   H   10

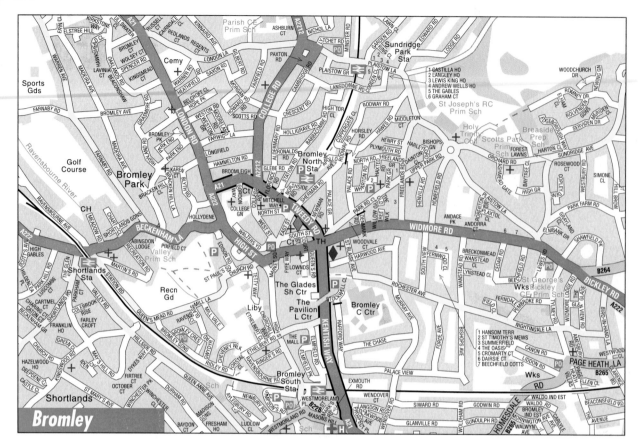

Bromley

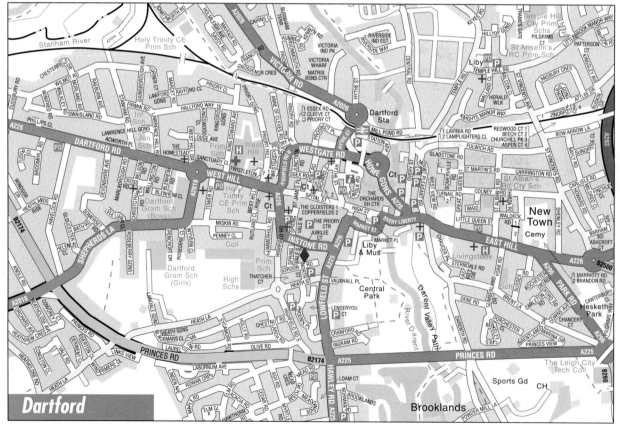

Dartford

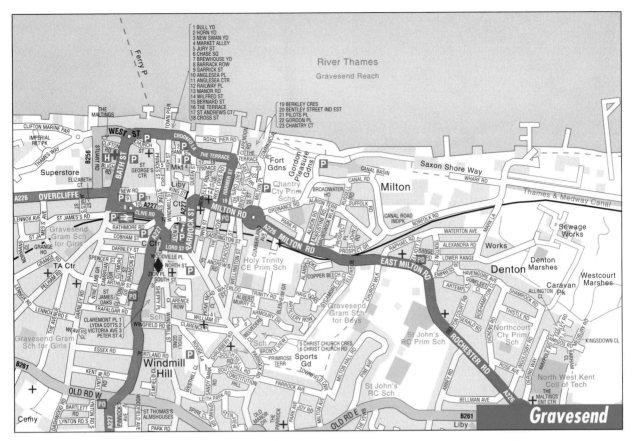

Gravesend

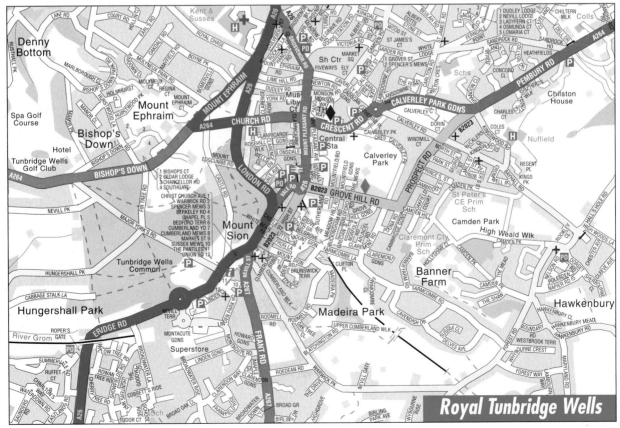

Royal Tunbridge Wells

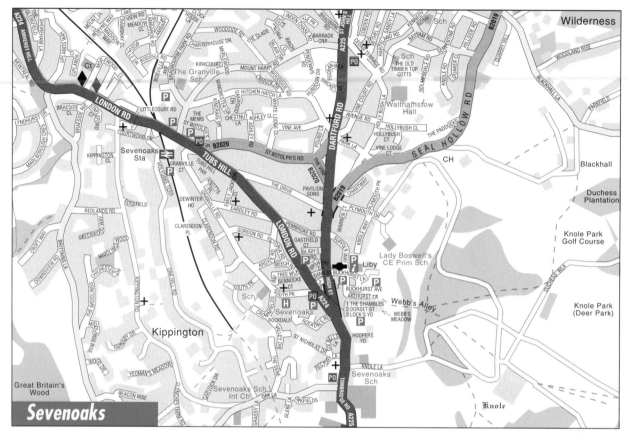

Sevenoaks

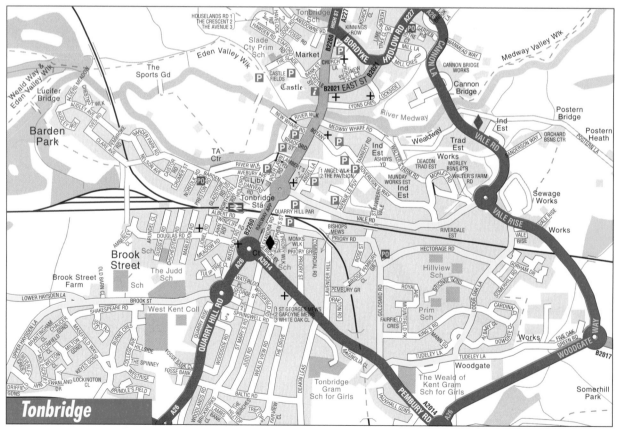

Tonbridge

Street names are listed alphabetically and show the locality, the Postcode District, the page number and a reference to the square in which the name falls on the map page

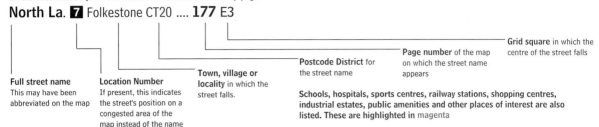

North La. 7 Folkestone CT20 .... 177 E3

Full street name
This may have been abbreviated on the map

Location Number
If present, this indicates the street's position on a congested area of the map instead of the name

Town, village or locality in which the street falls.

Postcode District for the street name

Page number of the map on which the street name appears

Grid square in which the centre of the street falls

Schools, hospitals, sports centres, railway stations, shopping centres, industrial estates, public amenities and other places of interest are also listed. These are highlighted in magenta

Abbreviations used in the index

App **Approach**	Cl **Close**	Espl **Esplanade**	N **North**	S **South**
Arc **Arcade**	Comm **Common**	Est **Estate**	Orch **Orchard**	Sq **Square**
Ave **Avenue**	Cnr **Corner**	Gdns **Gardens**	Par **Parade**	Strs **Stairs**
Bvd **Boulevard**	Cotts **Cottages**	Gn **Green**	Pk **Park**	Stps **Steps**
Bldgs **Buildings**	Ct **Court**	Gr **Grove**	Pas **Passage**	St **Street, Saint**
Bsns Pk **Business Park**	Ctyd **Courtyard**	Hts **Heights**	Pl **Place**	Terr **Terrace**
Bsns Ctr **Business Centre**	Cres **Crescent**	Ho **House**	Prec **Precinct**	Trad Est **Trading Estate**
Bglws **Bungalows**	Dr **Drive**	Ind Est **Industrial Estate**	Prom **Promenade**	Wlk **Walk**
Cswy **Causeway**	Dro **Drove**	Intc **Interchange**	Ret Pk **Retail Park**	W **West**
Ctr **Centre**	E **East**	Junc **Junction**	Rd **Road**	Yd **Yard**
Cir **Circus**	Emb **Embankment**	La **Lane**	Rdbt **Roundabout**	

20/20 Ind Est. ME16 .... 74 C8
Abbeville Ho. ME1 .... 9 C4
Abbey Cl. Deal CT14 .... 117 A5
Abbey Cl. Minster ME12 .... 4 D6
Abbey Fields. ME13 .... 62 E7
Abbey Fields Ct. ME13 .... 62 E7
Abbey Gate. CT11 .... 52 B5
Abbey Gate Cotts. ME20 .... 53 F2
Abbey Gdns. CT2 .... 67 A2
Abbey Gr. Minster, Thanet CT12 .. 50 C5
Abbey Gr. Ramsgate CT11 .... 52 B5
Abbey Pl. ME13 .... 62 D8
Abbey Rd. Faversham ME13 ..... 62 D8
Abbey Rd. Gillingham ME8 ...... 11 A2
Abbey Rd. Kearsney CT16 ...... 148 D4
Abbey Rd. River CT15 & CT17 .. 148 D1
Abbey Sch The. CT8 .... 27 E8
Abbey St. ME13 .... 62 D8
Abbey Way. TN24 .... 140 A1
Abbeyview Dr. ME12 .... 4 B6
Abbot's Hill. CT11 .... 52 E6
Abbots Barton Wlk. CT1 .... 88 B7
Abbots Field. ME16 .... 74 B2
Abbots Pl. CT1 .... 66 F1
Abbots Rd. ME13 .... 62 F7
Abbots The. CT17 .... 166 C8
Abbots Wlk. TN25 .... 123 E2
Abbotsbury Hts. CT2 .... 67 B4
Abbott Rd. CT20 .... 178 E6
Abbotts Cl. ME1 .... 9 B3
Aberdeen Cl. CT3 .... 47 D3
Aberdeen Ho. 8 ME15 .... 97 E7
Abigail Cres. ME5 .... 32 A1
Abingdon Gr. CT3 .... 47 D3
Abingdon Rd. ME16 .... 74 C4
Abinger Dr. ME5 .... 32 D2
Absalam Ct. ME8 .... 11 C2
Acacia Ho. ME12 .... 1 C2
Acacia Terr. ME10 .... 36 C4
Academy Dr. ME7 .... 10 F1
Achilles Rd. ME5 .... 32 C2
Ackerey Ct. TN23 .... 155 F6
Ackholt Rd. CT3 .... 113 A5
Acol Hill. CT7 .... 27 B4
Acorn Pl. ME15 .... 97 E6
Acorn Rd. ME7 .... 10 F4
Acorn St. ME12 .... 1 D1
Acre Cl. ME4 .... 9 E1
Acre Ct. CT17 .... 166 C8
Acre The. CT16 .... 148 F8
Acton La. TN30 .... 188 B4
Acton Rd. CT5 .... 20 D2
Ada Rd. CT1 .... 87 D6
Adam Cl. ME17 .... 96 D3
Adam Ct. 1 ME4 .... 8 B2
Adams Cl. TN30 .... 167 B1
Adbert Dr. ME15 .... 96 B4
Addelam Cl. CT14 .... 117 A4
Addelam Rd. CT14 .... 117 A4
Addington Pl. CT11 .... 52 E6
Addington Rd. Margate CT9 ..... 7 J2
Addington Rd.
   Sittingbourne ME10 .... 36 E3

Addington Sq. CT9 .... 7 J2
Addington St. Margate CT9 .... 7 J2
Addington St. Ramsgate CT11 ... 52 D6
Addiscombe Gdns. CT9 .... 7 J1
Addiscombe Rd. CT9 .... 8 A1
Addison Cotts. TN30 .... 188 D3
Adelaide Dr. ME10 .... 36 C4
Adelaide Gdns.
   Halfway Houses ME12 .... 3 E6
Adelaide Gdns. CT1 .... 52 E6
Adelaide Gdns. 16
Adelaide Pl. CT1 .... 87 F8
Adelaide Rd. Elvington CT15 .. 114 B1
Adelaide Rd. Gillingham ME7 .. 10 C4
Aden Terr. 1 ME14 .... 75 A7
Adie Rd. TN28 .... 200 D3
Adie Rd N. TN28 .... 200 D4
Adisham CE Prim Sch. CT3 ... 112 D8
Adisham Downs Rd.
   CT3 & CT4 .... 90 B2
Adisham Dr. ME16 .... 74 B7
Adisham Gn. ME10 .... 36 F8
Adisham Rd. Bekesbourne CT4 .. 89 E3
Adisham Rd. Wingham CT3 ..... 91 A4
Adisham Sta. CT3 .... 112 E8
Adisham Way. CT9 .... 8 C1
Admiral's Wlk. ME4 .... 9 F7
Admirals Wlk.
   Halfway Houses ME12 .... 3 E6
Admirals Wlk. Hythe CT21 ..... 176 C1
Admirals Wlk.
   Tenterden TN30 .... 167 C1
Admiralty Terr. 1 ME4 .... 10 A7
Admiralty Wlk. CT5 .... 43 A7
Adrian Mews. CT8 .... 7 D1
Adrian Sq. CT8 .... 7 D1
Adrian St. CT16 & CT17 .... 166 D7
Aerodrome Rd.
   Bekesbourne CT3 & CT4 ...... 89 E3
Aerodrome Rd.
   Hawkinge CT18 .... 163 A4
Afghan Rd. Broadstairs CT10 .. 29 F8
Afghan Rd. Chatham ME4 .... 9 E4
Agester La. CT4 .... 129 A4
Ainsdale Cl. CT19 .... 178 B7
Aintree Ho. 1 ME15 .... 97 F6
Aintree Rd. ME5 .... 32 C3
Airedale Cl. CT9 .... 8 A1
Airfield View. ME12 .... 17 C8
Aisne Dr. CT1 .... 67 D1
Ajax Rd. ME1 .... 31 C8
Alamein Ave. ME5 .... 31 F7
Alamein Cl. CT16 .... 149 F3
Albany Dr. CT6 .... 22 D4
Albany Ho. 15 CT17 .... 166 D7
Albany Pl. CT17 .... 166 D7
Albany Rd. Capel-le-F CT18 .. 164 C1
Albany Rd. Chatham ME4 .... 10 B2
Albany Rd. Gillingham ME7 .... 10 D4
Albany Rd. Rochester ME1 .... 9 C4

Albany Rd. Sittingbourne ME10 .. 36 E3
Albany St. ME14 .... 75 B5
Albany Terr. Chatham ME4 .... 9 E4
Albany Terr. Gillingham ME7 .. 10 D4
Albemarle Rd. Ashford TN24 .. 139 F1
Albemarle Rd. Chatham ME5 .. 32 C2
Albert Costain Ct. 1 CT20 ... 178 D5
Albert Ct. 16 CT5 .... 20 D2
Albert La. CT21 .... 176 C1
Albert Manor. ME7 .... 10 B5
Albert Pl. ME13 .... 9 B7
Albert Rd. Ashford TN24 .... 139 B3
Albert Rd. Broadstairs CT10 .... 29 E8
Albert Rd. Canterbury CT1 ..... 88 B8
Albert Rd. Capel-le-F CT18 ... 164 C2
Albert Rd. Chatham ME4 .... 10 A3
Albert Rd. Deal CT14 .... 117 C6
Albert Rd. Dover CT16 .... 149 D1
Albert Rd. Folkestone CT19 .. 178 D6
Albert Rd. Gillingham ME7 ..... 10 C4
Albert Rd. Hythe CT21 .... 176 B1
Albert Rd. Margate CT9 .... 7 H2
Albert Rd. Ramsgate CT11 ..... 52 F7
Albert Rd. Rochester ME1 .... 9 C3
Albert St. Maidstone ME14 ..... 74 F6
Albert St. Ramsgate CT11 ...... 52 E6
Albert St. Whitstable CT5 ...... 20 D2
Albert Terr. Margate CT9 .... 7 I2
Albert Terr. Minster ME12 .... 5 A5
Alberta Cl. CT16 .... 149 B3
Albion Cl. CT6 .... 46 A8
Albion Hill. 6 CT11 .... 52 E6
Albion La. CT6 .... 46 A8
Albion Mews. CT11 .... 52 F6
Albion Mews Rd. 3 CT20 ...... 178 D4
Albion Pl. Ashford TN24 .... 156 E7
Albion Pl. Canterbury CT1 ...... 67 A1
Albion Pl. Faversham ME13 .... 62 C7
Albion Pl. Maidstone ME14 ..... 75 B4
Albion Pl. Newington ME9 ...... 35 B6
Albion Pl. Ramsgate CT11 ...... 52 E6
Albion Pl. Sheerness ME12 .... 1 D2
Albion Rd. Birchington CT7 .... 27 A7
Albion Rd. Broadstairs CT10 ... 29 F6
Albion Rd. Chatham ME5 .... 32 B2
Albion Rd. Deal CT14 .... 117 D8
Albion Rd. Eastry CT13 .... 93 A2
Albion Rd. Folkestone CT19 .. 178 D6
Albion Rd. Ramsgate CT11 ..... 52 F7
Albion Rd. St CT10 .... 30 B4
Albion Terr. ME10 .... 36 E6
Albion Villas. 6 CT20 .... 178 D4
Albuhera Sq. CT1 .... 67 D1
Albury Cl. ME5 .... 32 D2
Alchins Cotts. ME17 .... 96 E2
Alder Cl. ME12 .... 3 A8
Alder Rd. CT19 .... 178 C6
Aldergate La. CT21 & TN29 .. 174 C1
Alderney Gdns. CT10 .... 29 E5
Aldershot Rd. ME5 .... 32 A7
Aldington Cl. ME5 .... 32 B5

Aldington Cnr. TN25 .... 173 A6
Aldington
   Cty Prim Sch. TN25 .... 173 A5
Aldington La. ME14 .... 76 D8
Aldington Rd. Lympne CT21 .. 174 E3
Aldington Rd. Maidstone ME14 .. 75 F4
Aldon Cl. ME14 .... 75 C6
Aldon Ct. ME14 .... 75 C6
Aldred Rd. ME13 .... 62 C6
Aldridge Cl. CT6 .... 22 B3
Alexander Cl. ME13 .... 62 B8
Alexander Rd. Rochester ME2 .. 9 B8
Alexander Ct. 6
   Sittingbourne ME10 .... 36 E5
Alexander Dr. ME13 .... 62 B7
Alexandra Ave. ME7 .... 10 E4
Alexandra Cl. ME10 .... 36 E7
Alexandra Ct. CT21 .... 176 A1
Alexandra Gdns. CT20 .... 178 D4
Alexandra Glen. ME5 .... 32 A1
Alexandra Homes. CT9 .... 7 I1
Alexandra Hospl The. ME5 ..... 54 A8
Alexandra Pl. 1 CT16 .... 149 C1
Alexandra Rd.
   Birchington CT7 .... 27 A5
Alexandra Rd.
   Broadstairs CT10 .... 30 B4
Alexandra Rd.
   Capel-le-F CT18 .... 164 C2
Alexandra Rd. Chatham ME4 .. 10 B2
Alexandra Rd. Deal CT14 ...... 117 D2
Alexandra Rd.
   Kingsdown CT14 .... 134 C5
Alexandra Rd. Margate CT9 .... 28 E8
Alexandra Rd. Ramsgate CT11 .. 52 D8
Alexandra Rd. Sheerness ME12 .. 1 E2
Alexandra Rd. Whitstable CT5 .. 43 C8
Alexandra St. Folkestone CT19 .. 178 D6
Alexandra Terr. CT9 .... 7 I1
Alexandria Dr. CT6 .... 22 C5
Alfred Cl. Canterbury CT1 ...... 87 C6
Alfred Cl. Chatham ME4 .... 10 B2
Alfred Cotts. CT11 .... 52 E7
Alfred Rd. Ashford TN24 .... 156 D7
Alfred Rd. Birchington CT7 ..... 26 D8
Alfred Rd. Canterbury CT1 ..... 87 C6
Alfred Rd. Dover CT16 .... 149 B2
Alfred Rd.
   Littlestone-on-S TN28 .... 200 D3
Alfred Rd. Margate CT9 .... 8 B1
Alfred Row. CT14 .... 117 D7
Alfred Sq. CT14 .... 117 D7
Alicia Ave. CT9 .... 28 A8
Alison Cl. Birchington CT7 ...... 27 B8
Alison Cl. Whitfield CT16 ...... 149 A6
Alison Cres. CT16 .... 149 A7
Alkham Cl. CT9 .... 8 C2
Alkham Rd. Maidstone ME14 .. 75 C5
Alkham Rd.
   Temple Ewell CT15 & CT16 .. 148 C4
Alkham Valley Rd.
   Alkham CT15 .... 147 E1

Alkham Valley Rd.
   Hawkinge CT18 & CT15 ..... 163 E4
All Saints' Ave. CT9 .... 7 H1
All Saints' CE Prim Sch.
   Chatham ME4 .... 10 A3
All Saints CE Prim Sch.
   Maidstone ME15 .... 75 A3
All Saints' Cl. CT5 .... 20 F1
All Saints' Cl. CT15 .... 20 F1
All Saints Hospl. ME4 .... 10 A2
All Saints Ind Est. CT9 .... 7 I1
All Saints La. 2 CT1 .... 87 F8
All Saints Rd. ME10 .... 37 C4
All Saints View. ME13 .... 41 E2
All Souls CE Prim Sch. CT19 .. 177 E6
Allan Rd. CT5 .... 42 E6
Alland Grange La. CT12 .... 27 E2
Allen Ave. CT8 .... 27 D7
Allen Cl. ME5 .... 32 C6
Allen Ct. ME12 .... 4 A5
Allen Field. TN23 .... 155 F8
Allen St. ME14 .... 75 B5
Allenby Rd. CT14 .... 117 B5
Allenby Rd. CT12 .... 29 C2
Allenby Wlk. ME10 .... 36 B5
Allendale St. 2 CT19 .... 178 D6
Alliance Rd. CT11 .... 52 F6
Allington Prim Sch. ME16 ...... 74 C7
Allington Rd. ME8 .... 11 A3
Allington Way. ME16 .... 74 B6
Allison Ave. ME7 .... 10 E1
Allnutt Mill Cl. ME15 .... 74 E2
Allsworth Cl. ME9 .... 35 B6
Alma Pl. 2 Canterbury CT1 ..... 67 A1
Alma Pl. Ramsgate CT11 .... 52 E7
Alma Pl. Rochester ME2 .... 9 A7
Alma Rd. Folkestone CT20 .... 177 D5
Alma Rd. Herne Bay CT6 .... 23 C5
Alma Rd. Margate CT9 .... 7 J1
Alma Rd. Ramsgate CT11 .... 52 E8
Alma Rd. Sheerness ME12 .... 1 D2
Alma St. Canterbury CT1 .... 67 A1
Alma St. Sheerness ME12 .... 1 E2
Alma Street Pas. ME12 .... 1 E2
Almon Pl. ME1 .... 9 D5
Almond Cl. Ashford TN23 ...... 138 F5
Almond Cl. Broadstairs CT10 .. 29 C4
Almond Cl. Whitstable CT5 ..... 21 D1
Almond Gr. ME7 .... 33 A4
Almonds The. ME14 .... 76 A4
Almonry Rd. ME13 .... 104 C7
Almshouses. 7 ME1 .... 88 A8
Alpha Rd. Birchington CT7 ...... 27 A7
Alpha Rd. Ramsgate CT11 ...... 52 D6
Alsager Ave. ME11 .... 2 F3
Alsops Rd. TN24 .... 156 E7
Alston Cl. ME12 .... 4 C7
Altbarn Ind Est. ME5 .... 54 C8
Alvis Ave. CT6 .... 22 A4
Amage Rd. TN25 .... 141 C8
Amage Road Cotts. TN25 ...... 124 B1
Amanda Cl. ME5 .... 31 F3
Amber Cl. ME9 .... 38 D2

Amber La. ME17 .... 98 A1
Amber Way. ME17 .... 98 B1
Ambleside. Faversham ME13 .... 62 E6
Ambleside. Sittingbourne ME10 .... 37 C3
Ambley Gn. ME7 .... 33 A8
Ambley Rd. ME7 .... 33 B8
Ambrose Hill. ME4 & ME5 .... 10 C2
Amels Hill. ME9 .... 56 F8
Ames Ave. ME14 .... 76 A4
Amethyst Ave. ME5 .... 31 E6
Amherst Cl. Maidstone ME16 .... 74 D4
Amherst Cl. Margate CT9 .... 8 C1
Amherst Hill. ME4 .... 10 A6
Amherst Rd. ME1 .... 9 D3
Amherst Redoubt. ME4 .... 10 A5
Amies Ho. ME15 .... 96 F3
Amos Cl. Herne Bay CT6 .... 23 C4
Amos Cl. Sheldwich ME13 .... 83 C5
Amsa Cnr. CT16 .... 150 B1
Amsbury Rd. ME17 .... 96 B2
Amshurst Villas. ME15 .... 96 A4
Anchor Bsns Pk. ME10 .... 37 B6
Anchor Hill. 4 CT9 .... 7 J2
Anchor La. Deal CT14 .... 117 C6
Anchor La. Sheerness ME12 .... 1 B3
Anchor Rd. ME1 .... 9 C1
Ancress Cl. CT2 .... 67 A4
Andover Wlk. 12 ME14 .... 97 F6
Andrew Broughton Way. ME14 .... 75 B4
Andrew Manor. ME7 .... 10 C4
Andrews Wlk. ME10 .... 36 B5
Anerley Cl. ME16 .... 74 D7
Angel Cotts. ME8 .... 12 A2
Anglesey Ave. ME5 .... 97 A7
Anglesey Cl. ME5 .... 32 B7
Ann's Rd. CT11 .... 52 E8
Anna Pk. CT7 .... 26 F8
Anne Boleyn Cl. ME12 .... 5 E3
Anne Cl. CT7 .... 27 B7
Anne Green Wlk. 8 CT1 .... 67 B2
Anne Roper Cl. TN28 .... 200 E6
Anne's Rd. CT10 .... 30 C7
Ansell Ave. ME14 .... 10 A1
Anselm Cl. ME10 .... 36 E4
Anselm Rd. ME17 .... 166 A8
Anson Cl. Broadstairs CT10 .... 29 D3
Anson Cl. Chatham ME5 .... 32 C6
Anstee Rd. CT16 & CT17 .... 149 C1
Anthony Cres. CT5 .... 43 B6
Anthonys Way. ME2 .... 9 E8
Anvil Cl. CT7 .... 27 A6
Anzio Cres. CT16 .... 149 E2
Anzio Ho. 15 CT1 .... 67 B2
Apartments The. TN28 .... 200 E5
Apollo Ho. ME5 .... 32 A6
Appleby Rd. ME1 .... 31 D7
Appledore Ave. ME12 .... 3 B8
Appledore Cl. CT9 .... 8 C1
Appledore Cres. CT19 .... 177 D2
Appledore Cl. ME16 .... 74 C7
Appledore Rd.
    Appledore TN26 & TN30 .... 190 A7
Appledore Rd. Brattle TN26 .... 181 B8
Appledore Rd.
    Brattle TN26 & TN30 .... 181 C7
Appledore Rd. Gillingham ME8 .... 11 A3
Appledore Rd. Tenterden TN30 .... 179 E7
Appledown Way. CT1 .... 88 D5
Appleford Dr. ME12 .... 3 F7
Applegarth Pk. CT5 .... 43 A6
Approach Rd. Broadstairs CT10 .... 30 A4
Approach Rd. Dover CT17 .... 166 A6
Approach Rd. Margate CT9 .... 8 A2
Approach Rd.
    Shepherdswell CT15 .... 130 D5
April Rise. Birchington CT7 .... 26 D8
April Rise. Whitstable CT5 .... 43 B7
Apsley Cotts. CT4 .... 86 D3
Apsley St. TN23 .... 139 B2
Aragon Cl. TN23 .... 155 E7
Archbishop's
    CE Sec Sch The. CT2 .... 66 E3
Archcliffe Rd. CT17 .... 166 C5
Archer Rd. Chatham ME5 .... 32 B6
Archer Rd. Folkestone CT19 .... 178 D6
Archer's Court Rd.
    CT15 & CT16 .... 149 B7
Archers Court Sch. CT16 .... 149 B5
Archery Sq. CT14 .... 117 D3
Archway Ct. 1 ME2 .... 9 B7
Archway Rd. Ramsgate CT11 .... 52 E6
Archway Rd. Sheerness ME12 .... 1 B3
Arcon Cl. TN23 .... 156 A7
Arcon Rd. TN23 .... 156 A7
Arden Bsns Pk. ME2 .... 9 E8
Arden Cty Jun Sch. ME7 .... 10 D6
Arden Dr. TN24 .... 139 C3
Arden Rd. Faversham ME13 .... 62 E7
Arden Rd. Herne Bay CT6 .... 23 C2
Arden St. ME7 .... 10 C6
Ardenlee Dr. ME14 .... 75 B5
Arethusa Rd. ME1 .... 31 C8
Argent Bsns Pk. ME2 .... 9 E8
Argent Rd. ME11 .... 3 A2
Argyle Ave. CT9 .... 7 G1
Argyle Cl. ME1 .... 31 E8
Argyle Gdns. CT9 .... 7 G1
Argyle Rd. CT5 .... 20 D1
Argyll Dr. CT10 & CT11 .... 29 F1
Ark Cotts. CT18 .... 161 D4
Ark La. CT14 .... 117 D7
Arkley Rd. CT6 .... 22 F4
Arklow Sq. 4 CT11 .... 52 F7
Arlington. TN23 .... 155 F8

Arlington Gdns. CT9 .... 29 C8
Arlington Ho. CT9 .... 7 H2
Arlington Sq. CT9 .... 7 H2
Arlott Cl. ME14 .... 74 F6
Armada. TN28 .... 200 E5
Armada Ct. ME4 .... 9 F3
Armada Way. ME4 .... 9 F3
Armourers Wlk. CT16 .... 149 A3
Armstrong Rd. ME15 .... 75 A1
Armstrong Sq. CT6 .... 22 A3
Arnhem Dr. ME5 .... 31 F7
Arnold Rd. Chartham CT4 .... 86 C2
Arnold Rd. 5 Margate CT9 .... 7 J1
Arnolde Cl. ME2 .... 9 E7
Arran Mews. 4 CT1 .... 67 B2
Arran Rd. ME15 .... 97 A6
Arrowhead La. TN26 .... 191 D7
Arthur Kennedy Cl. ME13 .... 63 F3
Arthur Rd. Birchington CT7 .... 26 D8
Arthur Rd. Deal CT14 .... 117 A3
Arthur Rd. Gillingham ME8 .... 33 E7
Arthur Rd. Hythe CT21 .... 176 C1
Arthur Rd. Margate CT9 .... 8 A3
Arthur Rd. Rochester ME1 .... 9 D3
Arthur Salmon Cl. ME13 .... 62 B7
Arthur St. 2 Folkestone CT9 .... 178 E6
Arthur St. Sittingbourne ME10 .... 36 E4
Artillery Gdns. 12 CT1 .... 67 A1
Artillery Ho. 13 CT1 .... 67 A1
Artillery Rd. CT11 .... 52 F7
Artillery St. 11 CT1 .... 67 A1
Arundel Ave. ME10 .... 36 E1
Arundel Cl. ME5 .... 32 C1
Arundel Cl. Cliffs End CT12 .... 51 D7
Arundel Rd. Margate CT9 .... 8 B2
Arundel St. ME14 .... 74 F6
Ascot Cl. ME5 .... 32 C2
Ascot Gdns. CT8 .... 27 E7
Ascot Ho. 2 ME14 .... 97 F6
Ash Cl. Ashford TN23 .... 138 E3
Ash Cl. Broadstairs CT10 .... 29 C4
Ash Cl. Chatham ME5 .... 10 C1
Ash Cl. Gillingham ME8 .... 11 B3
Ash Cl. Herne Bay CT6 .... 22 F1
Ash Cl. River CT17 .... 148 E3
Ash Cres. CT3 .... 46 E1
Ash Gr. Elvington CT15 .... 114 B2
Ash Gr. Lydd TN29 .... 203 D7
Ash Gr. Maidstone ME16 .... 74 C6
Ash Meadows. TN24 .... 156 F7
Ash Rd. Aylesham CT3 .... 112 E5
Ash Rd. Sandwich CT13 .... 72 E2
Ash Tree Cl. TN29 .... 194 F3
Ash Tree La. ME5 .... 10 D1
Ash Tree Rd. 5 CT19 .... 178 E6
Ashbank Cotts. ME17 .... 99 B7
Ashbee Gdns. CT6 .... 23 C5
Ashborne Cl. TN24 .... 139 D6
Ashburn Gdns. CT6 .... 23 C5
Ashburnham Rd.
    Maidstone ME14 .... 75 B8
Ashburnham Rd.
    Ramsgate CT11 .... 52 C7
Ashburton Cl. TN24 .... 139 E2
Ashdale Hos. TN23 .... 139 C2
Ashdown Cl. Herne Bay CT6 .... 23 B2
Ashdown Cl. Maidstone ME16 .... 74 D3
Ashdown Cres. TN24 .... 139 C3
Ashdown Cres. TN28 .... 200 B6
Ashdown Rd. ME17 & ME9 .... 79 F3
Ashdown Cl. TN24 .... 139 C3
Ashen Tree Cotts. CT3 .... 70 B1
Ashen Tree La. CT16 .... 166 E8
Ashendene Gr. CT2 .... 68 A6
Ashentree La. TN29 .... 198 A5
Ashenden Cl. CT1 .... 87 C5
Ashford Bsns Pk. TN24 .... 157 A6
Ashford Bsns Point. TN24 .... 156 F5
Ashford Dr. ME17 .... 99 D3
Ashford East Stour
    Cty Prim Sch. TN24 .... 156 D6
Ashford Golf Course. TN24 .... 139 A6
Ashford Hospl. TN23 .... 139 C1
Ashford Int Sta. TN23 .... 139 C1
Ashford Rd.
    Bethersden TN26 & TN23 .... 153 C4
Ashford Rd.
    Chartham CT4 & CT1 .... 86 C3
Ashford Rd.
    Folkestone CT18 & CT19 .... 177 B7
Ashford Rd. Godmersham CT4 .... 107 C4
Ashford Rd. Great Chart TN23 .... 155 B8
Ashford Rd. Hamstreet TN26 .... 170 F1
Ashford Rd.
    Harrietsham ME17 .... 100 C6
Ashford Rd.
    Kingsnorth TN23 & TN26 .... 156 A4
Ashford Rd. Maidstone,Grove Green
    ME14 & ME15 .... 75 D4
Ashford Rd.
    Maidstone,Silver Hill ME14 .... 76 D3
Ashford Rd.
    New Romney TN28 .... 200 A6
Ashford Rd. Sellindge TN25 .... 159 B1
Ashford Rd. Sheldwich ME13 .... 83 C4
Ashford Rd. Tenterden TN30 .... 179 B8
Ashford Rd.
    Westenhanger TN25 .... 174 E6
Ashford Rd.Westenhanger
    CT21 & TN25 & CT18 .... 175 C6
Ashford Sch. TN23 .... 139 C2
Ashford Sta. TN23 .... 139 C1
Ashgrove. TN23 .... 139 C3
Ashington. ME10 .... 36 C5
Ashley Ave. CT19 .... 177 E6
Ashley Cl. Halfway Houses ME12 .... 3 E1
Ashley Cl. Ramsgate CT12 .... 29 B2
Ashley Dr. CT5 .... 43 A7
Ashley Ho. CT19 .... 177 E6

Ashley Mill Cotts. CT19 .... 177 E7
Ashley Rd. ME8 .... 11 C2
Ashmead Cl. ME5 .... 32 C3
Ashstead Dr. ME9 .... 37 D2
Ashton Cl. CT14 .... 116 D4
Ashtree Ho. ME10 .... 37 B3
Ashtrees. CT6 .... 23 B3
Ashurst Ave. CT5 .... 43 C6
Ashurst Gdns. CT9 .... 8 E3
Ashurst Rd. ME14 .... 75 C5
Askes Ct. TN23 .... 155 D8
Aspen Cl. CT10 .... 194 F3
Aspen Ho. 5 CT20 .... 178 D4
Aspen Way. 2 ME5 .... 31 E4
Aspian Dr. ME17 .... 96 D3
Asquith Rd. ME8 .... 33 C6
Association Wlk. ME1 .... 31 C7
Astley Ave. CT16 .... 149 C2
Astley St. ME14 .... 75 A4
Aston Cl. ME5 .... 32 A2
Astor Ave. CT17 .... 166 B8
Astor Cty Prim Sch. CT17 .... 166 B8
Astor Dr. CT14 .... 117 C5
Astor of Hever Sch The. ME16 .... 74 C3
Astor Rd. CT10 .... 29 F8
Astor Sch. Dover CT17 .... 166 A8
Astor Sch. Dover CT17 .... 166 B8
Astrid Rd. CT14 .... 117 A2
Athelstan Gn. ME17 .... 77 C2
Athelstan Pl. CT14 .... 117 C8
Athelstan Rd. Canterbury CT1 .... 87 C5
Athelstan Rd. Chatham ME4 .... 9 F2
Athelstan Rd.
    Faversham ME13 .... 62 C6
Athelstan Rd.
    Folkestone CT19 .... 178 D7
Athelstan Rd. Margate CT9 .... 8 A3
Athol Pl. ME13 .... 62 A8
Athol Rd. Ashford TN23 .... 155 F7
Athol Rd. Whitstable CT5 .... 20 F2
Athol Terr. CT16 .... 166 F8
Atlanta Ct. ME1 .... 9 D3
Attlee Ave. CT3 .... 112 E5
Attlee Way. ME10 .... 36 E8
Atwater Ct. ME17 .... 101 D5
Aubretia Wlk. ME10 .... 37 A3
Auckland Ave. CT12 .... 52 A8
Auckland Cres. CT16 .... 149 C3
Auckland Dr. ME10 .... 36 C3
Audley Ave. Gillingham ME7 .... 10 E1
Audley Ave. Margate CT9 .... 7 E1
Audley Cl. ME16 .... 74 B5
Audley Rd. CT20 .... 177 F5
Augusta Cl. 1 ME7 .... 10 C7
Augusta Gdns. CT20 .... 178 C4
Augusta Pl. 12 CT11 .... 52 F7
Augusta Rd. CT11 .... 52 F7
Augustine Rd. Minster, Minster
    CT12 .... 50 B6
Austell Manor. ME7 .... 10 C6
Austens Orch. 12 TN30 .... 179 A7
Austin Cl. Sittingbourne ME10 .... 37 A8
Austin Rd. TN23 .... 156 B6
Austins La. 4 CT13 .... 73 A1
Autumn Glade. ME14 .... 54 D8
Avebury Ave. CT11 .... 52 G8
Aveling Cl. 2 ME2 .... 9 B7
Avenue Gdns. CT9 .... 8 C1
Avenue of Remembrance.
    ME10 .... 36 F3
Avenue Rd. Dover CT16 .... 149 C1
Avenue Rd. Herne Bay CT6 .... 22 E5
Avenue Rd. Ramsgate CT11 .... 52 F7
Avenue The. Deal CT14 .... 117 C7
Avenue The. Hersden CT3 .... 46 E1
Avenue The. Hythe CT21 .... 176 C2
Avenue The.
    Kingsdown CT14 .... 134 D4
Avenue The. Margate CT9 .... 8 A1
Avenue The.
    St Margaret's at Cliffe CT15 .... 150 F6
Avenue The.
    Temple Ewell CT16 .... 148 E5
Averenches Rd. ME14 .... 75 F5
Avereng Gdns. CT19 .... 178 B6
Avereng Rd. CT19 .... 178 B6
Avery Cl. ME15 .... 74 F1
Avery La. ME15 .... 98 D6
Aviemore Gdns. ME14 .... 75 F4
Avington Cl. ME15 .... 74 F1
Avocet Wlk. ME5 .... 32 D2
Avon Cl. CT1 .... 88 C8
Avondale Cl. CT5 .... 44 A8
Avondale Rd. Capel-le-F CT18 .... 164 C2
Avondale Rd. Gillingham ME7 .... 10 D5
Axford Cl. ME8 .... 34 A8
Aycliffe Cty Prim Sch. CT17 .... 166 A4
Aylesford Cty Prim Sch. ME8 .... 11 B4
Aylesford Pl. TN24 .... 156 E7
Aylesham Cnr. CT3 .... 112 D3
Aylesham Cty Prim Sch. CT3 .... 112 E5
Aylesham Rd. CT15 & CT3 .... 113 A4
Aylesham Sta. CT3 .... 113 A5
Aylewyn Gn. ME10 .... 36 F8
Aynsley Cl. 1 CT13 .... 73 A1
Ayton Rd. CT11 .... 52 C6

Babs Oak Hill. CT2 & CT3 .... 68 B7
Back La. Marlpit ME17 .... 97 E1
Back La. Minster ME12 .... 4 D6
Back Rd W. CT16 .... 166 G8
Back St. Langley Heath ME17 .... 98 E6
Back St. Ringwould CT14 .... 133 F5
Backfields. ME1 .... 9 B4

Bad Munstereifel Rd.
    TN23 & TN24 .... 156 D5
Baddlesmere Rd. CT5 .... 21 A2
Baden Rd. ME7 .... 10 D7
Bader Cres. ME5 .... 32 A7
Badger Rd. ME5 .... 32 C1
Badgers Bridge. CT18 .... 161 D4
Badgers Cl. CT2 .... 66 A7
Badgers Oak. TN23 .... 155 D8
Badgers Rise. Deal CT14 .... 134 C8
Badgers Rise. River CT17 .... 148 D3
Badlesmere Cl. TN23 .... 155 E6
Baffin Cl. ME4 .... 9 F2
Bagham La. CT4 .... 107 D8
Bagham Rd. CT4 .... 107 C8
Bagshill Rd. ME13 .... 83 A3
Bailey Dr. ME7 .... 11 A1
Bailey Fields. TN26 .... 153 E4
Baileys Field. TN23 .... 138 F1
Baird's Hill. CT10 .... 29 F6
Bairdsley Cl. CT10 .... 29 F6
Bakenham Ho. 1 ME1 .... 9 C1
Baker Cl. ME9 .... 38 C2
Baker Rd. CT19 .... 177 E6
Baker St. ME1 .... 9 C3
Baker's La. CT4 .... 86 D2
Baker's Wlk. ME1 .... 9 C6
Bakers Cl. CT2 .... 87 C7
Balcomb Cres. CT9 .... 29 C8
Baldric Rd. CT20 .... 177 F5
Baldwin Rd.
    Greatstone-on-S TN28 .... 200 D1
Baldwin Rd. Minster ME12 .... 4 D7
Baldwin Terr. CT19 .... 178 D6
Balfour Ct. CT20 .... 178 B3
Balfour Cty Inf Sch. ME4 .... 9 E1
Balfour Cty Jun Sch. ME4 .... 9 E2
Balfour Rd. Chatham ME4 .... 9 E2
Balfour Rd. Deal CT14 .... 117 C2
Balfour Rd. Dover CT16 .... 149 C1
Baliol Rd. CT5 .... 20 E2
Baliol Rd. CT10 .... 29 E8
Balmer Cl. ME8 .... 33 D7
Balmoral Pl. 6 ME15 .... 97 F5
Balmoral Pl. 10 CT11 .... 52 F7
Balmoral Rd. Gillingham ME7 .... 10 D5
Balmoral Rd. Kingsdown CT14 .... 134 C6
Balmoral Rd. 4 Margate CT9 .... 28 B8
Bamford Way. CT14 .... 117 C4
Bank Cotts. ME17 .... 77 E3
Bank Rd. ME5 .... 172 E8
Bank Side. TN26 .... 183 A8
Bank St. Chatham ME4 .... 10 B3
Bank St. Faversham ME13 .... 62 C7
Bank St. Herne Bay CT6 .... 22 F5
Bank St. Hythe CT21 .... 176 C2
Bank St.
    Maidstone ME14 & ME15 .... 75 A4
Banks Rd. Ashford TN23 .... 156 A7
Banks Rd. Rochester ME2 .... 9 C8
Banks The. CT10 .... 29 F6
Banks Yd. 6 ME10 .... 36 F4
Bankside. Canterbury CT1 .... 88 D7
Bankside. Chatham ME5 .... 32 B8
Banky Fields Cl. ME8 .... 12 B1
Banner Way. ME12 .... 3 E6
Banning St. ME2 .... 9 B8
Banningbrook Cl. CT14 .... 117 D4
Bannister Hill. ME9 .... 36 B2
Bannister Hos. TN26 .... 120 A1
Bannister Rd. ME14 .... 75 A7
Bapchild & Tonge
    CE Prim Sch. ME10 .... 37 D3
Barbados Terr. 2 ME14 .... 75 A4
Barberry Ave. ME5 .... 31 E5
Barcham Ct. ME15 .... 96 F5
Barclay Ct. CT7 .... 7 C1
Bardell Terr. ME1 .... 9 D5
Barden Ct. ME14 .... 75 B5
Barfleur Manor. 6 ME4 .... 10 A6
Barfreston Cl. ME15 .... 74 F2
Barfrestone Rd. CT15 .... 114 A1
Bargates. TN23 .... 155 E6
Bargrove Rd. ME14 .... 75 C5
Barham CE Prim Sch. CT4 .... 128 F6
Barham Cl. ME15 .... 97 E5
Barham's Mill Rd. TN27 .... 118 B3
Barker Rd. ME16 .... 74 F3
Barkers Cl. ME10 .... 36 C4
Barkis Cl. ME1 .... 31 D7
Barler Pl. ME11 .... 3 A5
Barley Cl. Martin Mill CT15 .... 133 C2
Barley Fields. ME14 .... 75 D4
Barley Cl. ME5 .... 31 D1
Barleymow Cl. ME5 .... 32 C7
Barling Cl. ME5 .... 31 D1
Barlow Cl. ME8 .... 33 E5
Barn Cl. Borden ME9 .... 36 A2
Barn Cl. Hoath CT3 .... 46 E5
Barn Cl. Yorklets CT5 .... 43 A3
Barn Cres. CT9 .... 7 F1
Barn Platt. TN23 .... 156 A8
Barn The. ME9 .... 36 A2
Barnaby Terr. ME1 .... 9 D2
Barnard Ct. ME4 .... 10 A2
Barnberry Cl. TN23 .... 155 E8
Barncroft Dr. ME7 .... 32 F4
Barnes Ave. CT9 .... 7 F1
Barnes Cl. ME13 .... 62 B8

Barnes Ct. CT1 .... 87 D6
Barnesende Ct. CT14 .... 94 A8
Barnet's La. CT7 .... 67 D8
Barnett Ct. CT12 .... 29 B1
Barnett Field. TN23 .... 155 F8
Barnfield. Chatham ME5 .... 32 A8
Barnfield. Herne Bay CT6 .... 22 C2
Barnfield. St Michaels SN3 .... 167 C2
Barnfield Rd. Faversham ME13 .... 62 C8
Barnfield Oak. Folkestone CT19 .... 178 C7
Barnhouse La. TN29 .... 198 A8
Barnhurst La. CT18 .... 163 A5
Barnhurst Rd. ME14 .... 75 A8
Barnsley Cl. ME12 .... 1 F2
Barnsole Cty Inf Sch. ME7 .... 10 E4
Barnsole Cty Jun Sch. ME7 .... 10 E4
Barnsole Rd. Gillingham ME7 .... 10 E3
Barnsole Rd. Staple CT3 .... 92 B5
Barntye Cl. CT5 .... 149 E6
Barnwood Cl. ME1 .... 31 B8
Baron Cl. Gillingham ME7 .... 10 E7
Baron Cl. Maidstone ME14 .... 75 F5
Barrack Hill. CT21 .... 176 A2
Barrack Rd. ME4 .... 9 F5
Barrey Rd. TN24 .... 157 A6
Barrier Rd. ME4 .... 9 F5
Barrington Cl. ME5 .... 31 F5
Barrington Cres. CT7 .... 27 B7
Barrow Gr. ME8 .... 36 D3
Barrow Grove Cty Jun Sch.
    ME10 .... 36 D3
Barrow Hill.
    Ashford TN23 & TN24 .... 139 B2
Barrow Hill. Sellindge TN25 .... 174 D7
Barrow Hill Cotts. TN23 .... 139 A2
Barrow Hill Rise. TN25 .... 174 D7
Barrow Hill Terr. 1 TN23 .... 139 B3
Barrowfields. ME5 .... 32 D1
Barrowhill Pl. 2 TN23 .... 139 B3
Barrows Cl. CT7 .... 27 A6
Bartholomew Cl. CT21 .... 176 B3
Bartholomew La. CT21 .... 176 B3
Bartholomew St. 6
    Dover CT16 .... 149 C1
Bartholomew St. Hythe CT21 .... 176 B2
Bartlett Cl. ME5 .... 32 C1
Bartlett Dr. CT5 .... 21 A1
Bartletts Cl. ME12 .... 3 C5
Barton Bsns Pk. CT1 .... 88 D6
Barton Court Gram Sch. CT1 .... 88 B8
Barton Cty Jun Sch. CT16 .... 149 C2
Barton Field. CT18 .... 161 B7
Barton Hill Dr. ME12 .... 4 A5
Barton Mill Rd. CT1 .... 67 B2
Barton Rd. Canterbury CT1 .... 88 C6
Barton Rd. Dover CT16 .... 149 C2
Barton Rd. Maidstone ME15 .... 75 A2
Barton Rd. Rochester ME2 .... 9 A7
Barton View Terr. 2 CT16 .... 149 C1
Barton's Point
    Recn Ctr. ME12 .... 1 F2
Barville Rd. CT15 .... 114 E2
Barwick Rd. CT17 .... 148 F1
Bashford Barn La. ME9 .... 58 A4
Basing Cl. ME15 .... 75 B3
Baskerville. TN24 .... 139 B3
Basmere Cl. ME14 .... 75 C6
Bassett Cl. CT21 .... 176 E4
Bassett Gdns. CT21 .... 176 D4
Bassett Rd. ME10 .... 36 D4
Bastion Rd. CT17 .... 166 C6
Batchelor St. ME4 .... 10 A4
Bateman Cnr. TN26 .... 153 E6
Bates Cl. CT3 .... 91 F6
Bath Ct. CT20 .... 178 B3
Bath Hard. ME1 .... 9 D5
Bath Mews. TN24 .... 156 E6
Bath Pl. CT7 .... 7 J2
Bathurst Cl. CT12 .... 29 B1
Bathurst Rd. CT20 .... 178 A5
Batteries Cl. ME9 .... 60 B8
Batteries Terr. ME9 .... 60 B8
Battery Point. CT21 .... 177 B2
Battery Terr. TN29 .... 204 F2
Battle of Britain Homes. 17
    CT16 .... 166 D7
Bawden Cl. CT2 .... 67 A4
Baxendale Ct. TN24 .... 156 D7
Bay Banks. ME13 .... 61 E2
Bay Cotts. CT15 .... 151 C6
Bay Hill. CT15 .... 151 B6
Bay Hill. CT15 .... 151 A5
Bay Mus The. CT15 .... 151 B5
Bay View Gdns. ME12 .... 6 D2
Bay View Hts. CT7 .... 26 D8
Bay View Rd. CT10 .... 30 A2
Baye La. CT3 .... 69 D1
Bayfield. ME13 .... 61 E2
Bayford Rd. ME10 .... 37 A4
Bayhill. ME13 .... 61 E2
Bayle Ct. CT20 .... 178 E4
Bayle St. 16 CT20 .... 178 E5
Bayle The. CT20 .... 178 E4
Bayswater Dr. ME8 .... 33 E4
Bayview Rd. Kingsdown CT14 .... 134 C4
Bayview Rd. Whitstable CT5 .... 43 D7
Beach Alley. 9 CT5 .... 20 D2
Beach App. ME12 .... 6 E3
Beach Ave. CT7 .... 26 F8
Beach Flats. 2 CT21 .... 176 B2
Beach Ho's. CT7 .... 7 C1
Beach House Mews. CT8 .... 7 D1
Beach Marine. ME20 .... 177 F3
Beach Ho's. Dymchurch TN29 .... 187 A4
Beach Rd.
    St Margaret's at Cliffe CT15 .... 151 B5

Beach Rd.
Westgate-on-S CT8 & CT9 7 D1
Beach Rise. CT9 7 D1
Beach St. Deal CT14 117 D6
Beach St. Folkestone CT20 178 E4
Beach St. Herne Bay CT6 22 F5
Beach St. Sheerness ME12 1 C3
Beach Terr. ME12 1 C2
Beach The. CT14 117 D3
Beach Wlk. CT5 20 E3
Beachborough Rd.
CT19 & CT20 178 A5
Beachfield Lodge. ME12 1 D2
Beachmont Cl. TN29 204 E8
Beacon Ave. CT6 23 B5
Beacon Cl. ME8 33 D7
Beacon Hill. Chatham ME5 10 D2
Beacon Hill. Herne Bay CT6 23 B5
Beacon La. CT13 93 A6
Beacon Oak Rd. TN30 179 B8
Beacon Rd. Broadstairs CT10 29 F7
Beacon Rd. Chatham ME5 10 C2
Beacon Rd. Herne Bay CT6 23 A5
Beacon Rd. Lenham ME17 101 C5
Beacon Way. CT21 174 F3
Beacon Wlk. Herne Bay CT6 23 A5
Beacon Wlk. Tenterden TN30 167 B1
Beacons The. ME17 96 C2
Beaconsfield. CT5 42 F6
Beaconsfield Ave.
Dover CT16 149 C1
Beaconsfield Ave.
Gillingham ME7 10 E5
Beaconsfield Gdns. CT10 29 F5
Beaconsfield Rd.
Canterbury CT2 66 F2
Beaconsfield Rd. Chatham ME4 9 F3
Beaconsfield Rd. Deal CT14 117 D5
Beaconsfield Rd. Dover CT16 149 C1
Beaconsfield Rd.
Maidstone ME15 74 E2
Beaconsfield Rd.
Sittingbourne ME10 37 C4
Beamont Cl. CT12 27 F2
Beams The. ME15 75 F1
Bean Cl. TN23 138 C1
Beaney Inst
(Liby & Mus). CT1 87 F8
Beaney's La. CT4 & ME13 84 C1
Bear's La. TN26 137 E3
Bears End Ho. TN23 156 B8
Bearsted Cl. ME8 11 B3
Bearsted Green Bsns Ctr.
ME14 76 C4
Bearsted Rd. ME14 75 E6
Bearsted & Thurnham Sta.
ME14 76 B5
Beatrice Mews. TN28 204 E7
Beatrice Rd. Capel-le-F CT18 164 C2
Beatrice Rd. Margate CT9 28 E8
Beatty Ave. ME7 10 F4
Beatty Cl. CT19 178 E8
Beatty Rd. Chatham ME1 31 D8
Beatty Rd. Folkestone CT19 178 D8
Beauchamp Ave. CT14 117 A3
Beauchamp Cl. TN24 139 E5
Beauchamps La. CT15 113 D5
Beaufort Ave. CT12 52 B8
Beaufort Ct. ME2 9 E6
Beaufort Wlk. ME15 97 E4
Beaufoy Rd. CT17 149 A1
Beaufoy Terr. CT17 148 F1
Beauherne
Cty Prim Sch. CT2 87 D8
Beaulieu Rise. ME1 9 D1
Beaulieu Wlk. ME16 74 C7
Beaumanor. CT6 23 A3
Beaumont Davy Cl. ME13 62 C5
Beaumont Rd. ME16 74 B2
Beaumont St. CT6 22 C4
Beaumont Terr. ME13 62 D6
Beauvoir Dr. ME10 37 A8
Beauworth Pk. ME15 97 E8
Beauxfield. CT16 149 A7
Beaver Ct. TN23 156 A7
Beaver Green Cty Inf Sch.
TN23 155 E7
Beaver Ind Est. TN23 156 B7
Beaver La. Ashford TN23 138 E1
Beaver La.
Ashford, Beaver TN23 156 A7
Beaver Rd. TN23 156 B8
Beazley Ct. TN24 156 D7
Beckenham Dr. ME16 74 D7
Becket Ave. CT2 66 D1
Becket Cl. Ash CT3 71 D2
Becket Cl. Deal CT14 117 C8
Becket Cl. Whitstable CT5 21 B1
Becket Mews. CT2 66 F1
Becket's Cl. TN25 142 B6
Beckett St. 4 ME13 62 C7
Becketts Terr. CT21 176 B4
Beckley Mews. ME5 31 F5
Beckley Pl. TN25 175 B8
Beckley Rd. ME12 1 F2
Becksbourne Cl. ME14 75 A8
Beckwith Gn. CT20 177 E5
Beddow Way. ME20 53 B3
Bede Ho. CT14 117 D8
Bedford Ave. ME8 11 D1
Bedford Pl. ME16 74 E4
Bedford Sq. CT12 29 B2
Bedford Way. CT7 25 F1
Bedgebury Cl. Chatham ME1 31 D8
Bedgebury Cl. Maidstone ME14 75 C6
Bedingfield Way. CT18 161 B7
Bedlam Court La. CT12 50 C6
Bedlam La. TN12 135 A8
Bedson Wlk. ME8 12 B1
Bedwin Cl. ME1 31 D7
Beech Cl. Faversham ME13 62 B7
Beech Cl. Folkestone CT19 178 C6
Beech Ct. Canterbury CT1 88 A7
Beech Ct. Challock TN25 105 A1
Beech Dr. Broadstairs CT10 29 D4
Beech Dr. Elvington CT15 114 B2
Beech Dr. Hothfield TN26 138 A7
Beech Dr. Maidstone ME16 74 C5
Beech Gr. CT12 51 C5
Beech Green Cl. CT15 131 C7
Beech Hill. CT4 111 B8
Beechcroft. CT5 21 D1
Beechcroft Gdns. CT11 52 F8
Beechen Bank Rd. ME5 32 A1
Beeches The. ME5 32 A4
Beeching Rd. ME5 32 B3
Beechings Gn. ME8 11 C3
Beechings Way. ME8 11 C3
Beechmore Dr. ME5 32 A2
Beecholme Dr. TN24 139 C5
Beechwood Ave.
Chatham ME5 10 D2
Beechwood Ave. Deal CT14 117 C5
Beechwood Ave.
Sittingbourne ME10 36 E6
Beechwood Cl.
St Mary's Bay TN29 194 F3
Beechwood Cl.
Whitfield CT16 132 A1
Beechwood Ct. CT16 148 E4
Beecroft Cl. CT2 67 A4
Beer Cart La. CT1 87 F8
Beggars Cnr. CT3 48 D1
Beggarsbush La. TN29 198 D7
Begonia Ave. ME8 11 C2
Beke Rd. ME8 33 D4
Bekesbourne Hill. CT4 89 B5
Bekesbourne La.
Bekesbourne CT3 & CT4 89 E6
Bekesbourne La.
Canterbury CT1 & CT3 & CT4 88 F7
Bekesbourne La.
Littlebourne CT3 89 F6
Bekesbourne Rd. CT4 88 F2
Bekesbourne Sta. CT4 89 B5
Belcaire Cl. CT21 175 A3
Belgrave Cl. CT11 52 D7
Belgrave Rd. Dover CT17 166 B7
Belgrave Rd.
Halfway Houses ME12 3 C5
Belgrave Rd. Margate CT9 7 I2
Belinda Ct. CT19 178 B7
Bell Chapel Cl. TN23 156 C4
Bell Cnr. TN29 199 A4
Bell Cres. ME1 53 A8
Bell Farm La. ME12 5 A6
Bell Gr. CT3 113 A5
Bell La. Burham ME1 53 A8
Bell La. Maidstone ME14 76 A5
Bell La. Sandwich CT13 73 A1
Bell La. Westfield Sole ME14 54 B7
Bell Rd. Park Wood ME15 97 E5
Bell Rd. Sittingbourne ME10 36 F3
Bell Way. ME17 99 E2
Bell Wood Cty Inf Sch. ME15 97 E5
Bell Wood
Cty Jun Sch. ME15 97 E5
Bell's Cl. TN30 179 A7
Bell-Davies Dr. CT12 28 A1
Belle Friday Cl. ME9 38 C2
Belle Vue Rd. CT6 23 B5
Bellevue Ave. CT11 52 F7
Bellevue Rd. Minster ME12 4 C6
Bellevue Rd. Ramsgate CT11 52 F7
Bellevue Rd. Whitstable CT5 43 F8
Bellevue St. 5 CT20 178 D5
Bellgrove Ct. ME5 54 A8
Bellmeadow. ME15 97 E6
Bells La. 7 TN30 179 A7
Belmont. CT14 117 B1
Belmont Ct. CT11 52 D7
Belmont Farm
Bsns Ctr. TN26 137 A1
Belmont Pl. TN24 156 D7
Belmont Rd. Ashford TN24 139 D6
Belmont Rd. Broadstairs CT10 30 A4
Belmont Rd. Faversham ME13 62 C6
Belmont Rd. Gillingham ME7 10 C4
Belmont Rd.
Halfway Houses ME12 3 E6
Belmont Rd. Ramsgate CT11 52 D7
Belmont Rd.
Sittingbourne ME10 36 E3
Belmont Rd.
Westgate-on-S CT8 27 F8
Belmont Rd. Whitstable CT5 20 D1
Belmont St. CT11 52 E7
Belmont Terr. CT13 93 B3
Belmore Pk. TN24 139 B3
Belnor Ave. ME9 13 F1
Belsey La. CT15 147 D4
Belting Dr. CT6 23 E5
Beltinge Rd. CT6 23 B5
Belton Cl. CT5 43 E8
Belvedere Rd.
Broadstairs CT10 30 B4
Belvedere Rd.
Faversham ME13 62 D8
Benacre Rd. CT5 43 D6
Bench Hill. TN30 181 D5
Bench St. 10 CT16 166 D7
Bendon Way. ME8 33 D8
Benenden Manor. ME8 11 B3
Bengal Rd. CT12 29 A1
Benham Bsns Pk. TN25 174 F5
Bennells Ave. CT5 21 B3
Bennett Ct. 14 CT20 178 E5
Bennetts Cotts. ME7 55 A8
Bennetts Gdns. ME13 61 D8
Bennetts Mews. 11 TN30 179 A7
Benson Cl. CT18 162 F4
Benson La. CT18 162 F4
Bensted. TN23 155 F5
Bensted Gr. ME13 62 A7
Benstede Cl. CT6 23 A1
Bentham Sq. ME12 1 B3
Bentley Ave. CT6 22 B4
Bentley Cl. ME5 32 D2
Bentley Rd. TN24 156 F7
Bentlif Cl. ME16 74 D5
Berber Rd. ME2 9 B8
Berengrave La. ME8 11 F2
Berengrave Lane Chalk Pit
(Nature Reserve). ME8 12 A3
Beresford Ave. ME4 9 E2
Beresford Gap. CT7 26 F8
Beresford Gdns. CT9 8 C3
Beresford Rd. Gillingham ME7 10 D4
Beresford Rd. Kit's Coty ME20 53 D7
Beresford Rd. Ramsgate CT11 52 D6
Beresford Rd. River CT17 148 E3
Beresford Rd.
St Margaret's at Cliffe CT15 133 F1
Beresford Rd. Whitstable CT5 20 D1
Beresfords Hill. ME17 97 B4
Bergland Pk. ME2 9 D8
Berkeley Cl.
Boughton Street ME13 64 B3
Berkeley Cl. Chatham ME1 31 D8
Berkeley Cl. 2
Folkestone CT19 178 A7
Berkeley Ct. ME10 36 D3
Berkeley Mount. 1 ME4 9 F4
Berkeley Rd. CT7 26 F8
Berkshire Cl. ME5 32 C8
Bernard Sunley Hall. TN25 124 A2
Bernards Gdns. CT15 130 E5
Berridge Rd. ME12 1 D2
Berry St. ME10 36 F4
Berwick La. CT21 175 A3
Berwyn Gr. ME15 97 A6
Best La. CT1 87 F8
Best St. ME4 9 F4
Bethel Row. ME13 82 F1
Bethersden Ct. ME15 97 F7
Bethersden Cty Prim Sch.
TN26 153 D5
Bethersden Rd.
Bethersden TN27 & TN26 152 C5
Bethersden Rd.
Hothfield TN26 137 D4
Bethersden Rd.
Shadoxhurst TN26 154 E2
Bethersden Rd.
Woodchurch TN26 169 A6
Betony Gdns. ME14 75 F5
Betsham Rd. ME15 97 F6
Bettescombe Rd. ME8 33 E7
Betty Shelvey Ct. CT14 117 D4
Beult Meadow. TN27 135 A1
Bevan Way. CT3 112 E5
Beverley Cl. ME8 33 F8
Beverley Gdns. TN29 187 A4
Beverley Rd. Canterbury CT2 66 E2
Beverley Rd. Maidstone ME16 74 A1
Beverley Way. CT12 29 C1
Beverly Cl. CT7 27 B8
Bewsbury Cres. CT16 148 F7
Bewsbury Cross La. CT16 148 F7
Bexley St. CT5 20 D2
Bexon La. ME9 58 C4
Bicknor Cl. CT2 67 B4
Bicknor Court Cotts. ME9 57 C2
Bicknor La. ME9 57 D3
Bicknor Rd. ME15 97 F4
Biddenden Cl. Maidstone ME15 75 F3
Biddenden Cl. Margate CT9 8 C1
Biddenden Rd. TN26 167 A6
Bierce Ct. CT7 26 F7
Bifrons Gdns. CT4 89 B3
Bifrons Hill. CT4 89 B4
Bifrons Rd. CT4 89 B4
Bigbury Rd. CT2 & CT4 86 E7
Biggin St. CT16 166 D8
Biggins Wood Rd. CT19 177 E7
Bilberry Cl. ME14 75 E5
Bill Street Rd. ME2 9 C8
Billington Gdns. TN24 139 E6
Bilsington Cl. ME5 32 B5
Bilsington Cross. TN25 172 C1
Binbury La. ME14 56 A5
Bindon Blood Rd. CT16 149 A5
Bingley Rd. ME1 9 E4
Binland Gr. ME5 31 D5
Binnacle Rd. ME1 31 C8
Binnie Cl. CT10 29 F2
Birch Cl. Ashford TN24 139 F2
Birch Cl. Broadstairs CT10 29 C3
Birch Ct. CT4 128 F8
Birch Dr. ME5 32 D1
Birch Gr. ME7 33 A5
Birch Hill Ct. CT7 27 B7
Birch Ho. Sheerness ME12 1 C2
Birch Ho. Sittingbourne ME10 37 B3
Birch Rd. CT5 44 A8
Birch Tree Way. ME15 75 B3
Birches The. CT7 27 B7
Birchett. TN23 138 E1
Birchfield Cl. ME15 97 B6
Birchfields. ME5 32 A3
Birchington
CE Prim Sch. CT7 27 A6
Birchington Cl. ME14 75 C5
Birchington-on-Sea Sta. CT7 26 F7
Bircholt Forstal. TN25 158 E7
Bircholt Rd. ME15 97 F4
Birchwood Rd. ME16 74 C5
Birchwood Rise. CT17 166 C7
Birchwood Wlk. CT2 66 E2
Bird Farm. CT4 105 E4
Birds Ave. CT9 28 B7
Birdwood Ave. CT14 117 A5
Birkdale Ct. 3 ME16 74 E4
Birkdale Dr. CT19 178 A8
Birkdale Gdns. CT6 22 D2
Birkhall Cl. ME5 32 A5
Birling Ave. Gillingham ME8 11 E1
Birling Ave. Maidstone ME14 76 A4
Birling Cl. ME14 76 A4
Birling Rd. TN24 139 D1
Birnam Sq. 1 ME16 74 E4
Bishop Ct. 4 ME10 36 E5
Bishop Jenner Ct. CT3 70 C6
Bishop La. ME9 12 E3
Bishop's Ave. CT10 30 B6
Bishopbourne Gn. ME8 11 B4
Bishopden Ct. CT2 66 C4
Bishops Gn. TN23 155 E7
Bishops Way. Canterbury CT2 66 D1
Bishops Way. Maidstone ME15 74 F4
Bishops Wlk. ME1 9 C5
Bishopstone Dr. CT6 23 F6
Bishopstone La. CT6 23 F5
Black Bull Rd. CT19 178 D6
Black Griffin La. CT1 87 F8
Black Post. ME17 78 E4
Black Robin La. CT4 111 E3
Black Rock Gdns. ME7 33 B4
Blackburn Rd. CT6 22 B2
Blackdown Dr. TN24 139 B4
Blacketts Cotts. ME9 38 B7
Blacketts Rd. ME9 38 A6
Blackfriars St. 5 CT1 66 F1
Blackhouse Hill.
CT18 & CT21 176 D4
Blackhouse Rise. CT21 176 D3
Blackleys. ME13 84 F7
Blackmanstone Way. ME16 74 B7
Blacksmith Dr. ME14 75 D5
Blackstable Ct. CT5 43 D8
Blackthorn Ave. ME5 32 A3
Blackthorne Rd. ME8 34 B8
Blackwall Rd. TN24 & TN25 140 B4
Blake Cl. CT14 134 C8
Blake Ct. TN24 156 F8
Blakeney Cl. ME14 76 B4
Blaker Ave. ME1 9 E1
Blandford Gdns. ME10 36 E1
Blatcher Cl. ME12 4 B6
Blaxland Cl. ME13 62 B8
Bleak Ho. CT10 30 B4
Bleak Rd. TN29 203 C6
Bleakwood Rd. ME5 31 F4
Blean Bird Pk. CT2 65 F8
Blean Comm. CT2 66 A6
Blean Cty Prim Sch. CT2 66 B4
Blean Hill. CT2 66 A5
Blean Rd. ME8 11 C2
Blean Sq. ME14 75 C6
Blean View Rd. CT6 22 B2
Blendon Rd. ME14 75 C5
Blenheim Ave. Canterbury CT1 67 D1
Blenheim Ave.
Chatham ME1 & ME4 9 E2
Blenheim Ave.
Faversham ME13 62 E5
Blenheim Cl. Broadstairs CT10 29 D3
Blenheim Cl. Herne Bay CT6 23 A1
Blenheim Cl. Maidstone ME15 75 F3
Blenheim Dr. Dover CT16 149 C3
Blenheim Dr. Hawkinge CT18 163 A4
Blenheim Pl. CT20 177 F4
Blenheim Rd. Deal CT14 117 D5
Blenheim Rd.
Littlestone-on-S TN28 200 D6
Blenheim Rd.
Sittingbourne ME10 37 B2
Bleriot Meml. CT16 149 F1
Bliby Cnr. TN25 171 F8
Blind La. Bredhurst ME7 33 A1
Blind La. Challock TN25 105 C2
Blind La. Lidsing ME7 32 F1
Blind La.
Mersham TN24 & TN25 157 D5
Blind Mary's La. ME9 57 E4
Blindgrooms La. TN26 155 C1
Blindhouse La. TN25 160 B3
Blockmakers Ct. ME4 10 B1
Bloomsbury Rd. CT11 52 C6
Bloomsbury Way. TN24 139 B7
Bloors La. Gillingham ME8 11 D1
Bloors La. Gillingham ME8 11 E3
Bloors Wharf Rd. ME7 11 F4
Blowers Grove Wood. ME7 33 B3
Blue Boar La. ME1 9 D5
Blue House La. CT21 176 B8
Blue Line La. TN24 139 B3
Bluebell Cl. Gillingham ME7 10 F6
Bluebell Cl. Kingsnorth TN23 156 B4
Bluebell Rd. TN23 156 B4
Bluett St. ME14 75 A5
Blythe Cl. ME10 37 C5
Blythe Ct. CT21 176 D2
Blythe Rd. ME15 75 B4
Boarley Ct. ME14 53 F1
Boarley La. ME14 53 F2
Boarman's La. TN29 197 E8
Boat La. TN25 173 A4
Boathouse Rd. ME12 1 A3
Bob Amor Cl. ME13 62 E7
Bobbin Lodge Hill. CT4 86 B2
Bobbing Cty Prim Sch. ME10 36 B7
Bobbing Hill. ME10 & ME9 36 A6
Bockham Cotts. TN25 157 E8
Bockham La. Hinxhill TN25 141 A1
Bockham La.
Mersham TN24 & TN25 157 E8
Bockhanger La. TN24 139 C6
Bockingford La. ME15 96 F8
Bodenham Rd. CT20 178 A4
Bodiam Cl. ME8 11 C3
Bodsham CE Prim Sch. TN25 142 E8
Bodsham Cres. ME15 76 B3
Bogle Rd. ME9 60 C7
Bognor Dr. CT6 22 D4
Bogshole La. Herne Bay CT6 23 D3
Bogshole La. Whitstable CT5 43 E4
Boley Hill. ME1 9 C6
Boleyn Ave. CT9 7 E1
Bolner Cl. ME5 31 F2
Bolton Rd. CT19 178 D6
Bolton St. CT11 52 D8
Bolts Hill. CT4 86 C2
Bombay Ho. 1 ME15 97 E5
Bond La. TN23 156 A2
Bond Rd. Ashford TN23 156 B8
Bond Rd. Gillingham ME8 33 E5
Bonetta Ct. ME12 3 B8
Bonham Dr. ME10 37 B5
Bonners Alley. 13 CT5 20 D2
Bonnington Cross. TN25 172 E3
Bonnington Gn. ME8 11 C3
Bonnington Rd. ME14 75 C6
Bonny Bush Hill. CT4 111 D5
Bonsor Rd. CT19 178 D6
Booth Pl. CT9 7 J3
Booth Rd. ME4 9 F2
Borden CE Cty Prim Sch. ME9 35 F3
Borden Gram Sch for Boys.
ME10 36 F3
Borden La. ME10 & ME9 36 C3
Boresisle. TN30 167 B2
Bornefields. TN23 156 A7
Borough. CT1 67 A1
Borough Rd. Gillingham ME7 10 D4
Borough Rd. Queenborough ME11 3 B4
Borrowdale Ave. CT11 52 A7
Borstal Ave. CT5 43 D6
Borstal Hill. CT5 43 D7
Borstal HM Prison &
Youth Custody Ctr. ME1 9 B1
Borstal Rd. ME1 9 B3
Borstal St. ME1 9 A2
Boscombe Rd. CT19 178 C6
Bosney Banks. CT15 148 A7
Bossingham Rd. CT4 126 F3
Bossington Rd. CT3 90 E1
Boston Cl. 5 CT16 149 B3
Boston Gdns. ME8 11 C1
Boston Rd. ME5 32 C2
Botany Cl. ME12 1 C1
Botany Rd. CT10 & CT9 8 F2
Boteler Cotts. CT13 93 A2
Botolph's Bridge Rd. CT21 187 A6
Bottles La. ME9 59 A6
Bottlescrew Hill. ME17 97 B4
Bottom Pond Rd. ME9 58 D3
Boughton Ave. CT10 30 A2
Boughton Church Cotts. ME13 63 D1
Boughton Cl. ME8 11 B3
Boughton Cnr. TN25 123 C5
Boughton Field Cotts. ME13 63 A5
Boughton Golf Course. ME13 63 E2
Boughton Hill. ME13 64 C3
Boughton La. ME15 97 B6
Boughton Monchelsea
Cty Prim Sch. ME17 97 B2
Boughton Par. ME15 97 A7
Boughton Place Cotts. ME17 118 A8
Boughton Rd. ME17 101 B2
Boulevard Courrieres. CT3 112 E5
Boulevard The. TN24 156 F6
Boulogne Ct. 15 CT20 178 E5
Boundary Cl. ME12 4 E6
Boundary Ct. CT1 88 B6
Boundary Rd.
Chatham ME1 & ME4 9 E3
Boundary Rd. Hythe CT21 176 A2
Boundary Rd. Kingsdown CT14 134 D6
Boundary Rd. Ramsgate CT11 52 E7
Boundary The. CT1 87 D7
Bounds La. ME13 64 A3
Boundsgate Cnr. ME13 105 B7
Bourne. CT2 66 A7
Bourne Cotts. CT4 111 C5
Bourne Gr. ME10 36 C5
Bourne La. TN26 183 A8
Bourne Park Rd. CT4 111 A7
Bourne Rd. TN25 172 D5
Bourne View. CT4 88 F1
Bournemouth Dr. CT6 22 D4
Bournemouth Gdns. CT19 178 C6
Bournemouth Rd. CT19 178 C5
Bournes Cl. CT2 67 F7
Bournes Pl. TN26 169 A2
Bourneside Terr. ME17 77 D2
Bournewood. TN26 183 A8
Bournewood Cl. ME15 75 F1
Bournville Ave. ME4 9 F1
Bouverie Pl. 2 CT20 178 D4
Bouverie Rd. CT20 178 D4
Bouverie Rd W. CT20 178 C4
Bouverie Sq. 1 CT20 178 D4
Bow Hill. CT4 109 F2
Bowdell La. TN29 191 E3
Bowden Cres. CT20 177 C6
Bowen Rd. CT19 177 E6

Bowens Field. TN23 .... 139 B1
Bower Cl. ME16 .... 74 E4
Bower Gr. ME5 .... 32 C1
Bower Grove Sch. ME16 ...... 74 B2
Bower La. Maidstone ME16 ... 74 E2
Bower La. Maidstone ME16 ... 74 E3
Bower Mount Rd. ME16 .... 74 D4
Bower Pl. ME16 .... 74 E3
Bower Rd. TN25 .... 158 A3
Bower St. ME16 .... 74 E4
Bower Terr. ME16 .... 74 E3
Bowerland La. Chilham CT4 .... 85 E1
Bowerland La.
  Old Wives Lees CT4 .... 85 C2
Bowers Ho. ME7 .... 10 E7
Bowes Ave. CT9 .... 7 E1
Bowes La. CT6 .... 23 A2
Bowes La. CT6 .... 23 A3
Bowes Rd. ME2 .... 9 B8
Bowes Villas. CT14 .... 93 E4
Bowl Field. TN25 .... 142 B6
Bowl Rd. TN27 .... 103 D2
Bowland Cl. CT6 .... 23 C2
Bowles Well Gdns. CT19 ...... 178 F7
Bowley La. ME17 .... 118 D8
Bowling Green La. CT14 ...... 117 B5
Bowling Green Terr. ⑧ CT17 166 D7
Bowling St. CT13 .... 72 F1
Bowman Cl. ME5 .... 32 C5
Bowman Ct. CT17 .... 149 A1
Bowser Cl. CT14 .... 116 F4
Bowyer Rd. CT5 .... 42 F7
Boxley. TN23 .... 155 F8
Boxley Cl. Maidstone ME14 ... 75 B8
Boxley Cl. West Minster ME12 ... 3 B7
Boxley Rd. Chatham ME5 ...... 32 B2
Boxley Rd. Maidstone ME14 ... 75 B7
Boxmend Ind Est. ME15 .... 97 F3
Boxted La. ME9 .... 13 A1
Boyces Hill. ME9 .... 35 D6
Boyden Gate Hill. CT3 .... 47 B8
Boyes La. CT3 .... 91 D3
Boyke La. CT4 .... 144 C2
Boyne Rd. CT15 .... 134 A1
Boys Hall Rd. TN24 .... 156 F7
Boystown Pl. CT13 .... 93 C3
Brabazon Rd. ME12 .... 5 C1
Brabner Cl. CT19 .... 178 E8
Brabourne Ave. ME8 .... 11 C3
Brabourne
  CE Prim Sch. TN25 .... 159 A8
Brabourne Cl. CT2 .... 67 A4
Brabourne Gdns. CT20 .... 177 E5
Brabourne La. TN25 .... 142 F2
Brabourne Rd. TN25 .... 141 D8
Brack La. TN29 .... 191 B3
Bracken Cl. TN24 .... 139 C6
Bracken Ct. Broadstairs CT10 ... 29 E5
Bracken Ct. Sittingbourne ME10 ... 37 C2
Bracken Hill. ME5 .... 32 A1
Bracken Lea. ME5 .... 10 C1
Brackley. ME14 .... 75 C5
Brackwood Cl. ME8 .... 33 D5
Bradbridge Gn. TN23 .... 155 D8
Braddick Cl. ME15 .... 97 B6
Bradfield Ave. ME8 .... 38 D2
Bradfield Rd. TN24 .... 139 B5
Bradfields Ave. ME5 .... 31 F5
Bradfields Ave W. ME5 .... 31 F5
Bradfields Sch. ME5 .... 32 A6
Bradley Dr. ME10 .... 36 E2
Bradley Rd. Folkestone CT19 ... 178 F6
Bradley Rd. Ramsgate CT12 ... 29 C1
Bradshaw Cl. ME9 .... 12 E3
Bradstone Ave. CT19 .... 178 E6
Bradstone New Rd. ❸ CT20 ... 178 D5
Bradstone Rd. CT20 .... 178 D5
Bradstow Way. CT10 .... 30 A5
Brady Rd. CT18 .... 161 A7
Braeside. CT10 .... 30 B3
Braggs La. CT6 .... 45 E6
Brake Ave. ME5 .... 31 E5
Bramble Cl. Maidstone ME16 ... 74 B3
Bramble Cl. Wye TN25 .... 123 D3
Bramble La. TN25 .... 123 C3
Brambledown. Chatham ME5 ... 32 B8
Brambledown.
  Folkestone CT19 .... 178 D6
Bramblefield La. ME10 .... 14 E1
Bramblefields Cl. CT6 .... 23 B2
Bramblehill Rd. ME13 .... 62 C8
Brambles Wildlife Pk.
  CT2 & CT6 .... 45 D4
Brambley Cres. CT20 .... 177 E5
Bramley Ave. Canterbury CT1 ... 87 C6
Bramley Ave. Faversham ME13 ... 62 E6
Bramley Cl.
  Brabourne Lees TN25 .... 158 E6
Bramley Cl. Eastchurch ME12 ... 5 D3
Bramley Cl. Gillingham ME8 ... 34 B8
Bramley Cres. ME15 .... 75 F3
Bramley Gdns. Ashford TN23 ... 156 A6
Bramley Gdns. Coxheath ME17 ... 96 C3
Bramley Way. ME5 .... 5 D3
Bramling Gap. CT3 .... 90 C3
Bramling Rd. CT3 & CT4 ...... 90 B4
Bramshaw Rd. CT2 .... 66 E2
Bramshott Cl. ME16 .... 74 C6
Bramston Rd. ME12 .... 4 C6
Branch Ct. ME4 .... 107 C7
Branch St. CT16 .... 149 C1
Brandon Rd. CT12 .... 29 A1
Brandon Way. CT7 .... 27 B6
Bransgore Cl. ME8 .... 33 D7
Brasenose. ME7 .... 10 E4

Brasier Ct. ME12 .... 4 A5
Brassey Ave. CT10 .... 29 F3
Brattle. TN26 .... 181 B8
Bray Gdns. ME15 .... 96 F5
Breach La. ME9 .... 13 A2
Breadlands Cl. TN24 .... 156 E8
Breadlands Rd. TN24 .... 156 F8
Brecon Chase. ME12 .... 4 C7
Brecon La. TN24 .... 139 B4
Brecon Rise. TN24 .... 139 B4
Brecon Sq. CT12 .... 29 A1
Bredgar CE Prim Sch. ME9 ... 58 A5
Bredgar Cl. Ashford TN23 ... 155 F6
Bredgar Cl. Maidstone ME14 ... 75 C5
Bredgar Rd. ME8 .... 11 B4
Bredhurst CE Prim Sch. ME7 ... 33 B1
Bredhurst Cl. ME12 .... 3 B7
Bredhurst Rd. Gillingham ME8 ... 33 B4
Bredhurst Rd. Gillingham ME8 ... 33 C5
Bredlands La. CT3 & CT2 ..... 46 C1
Brenchley Ave. CT14 .... 116 F4
Brenchley Cl. Ashford TN23 ... 155 E6
Brenchley Cl. Chatham ME1 ..... 9 D2
Brenchley Cl. Gillingham ME8 ... 11 B2
Brenchley Rd. Maidstone ME15 ... 74 F2
Brenchley Rd.
  Sittingbourne ME10 .... 36 F2
Brendon Ave. ME5 .... 32 A3
Brendon Dr. ME5 .... 139 B3
Brenley Cnr. ME13 .... 63 B4
Brenley La. ME13 .... 63 C2
Brent Cl. ME5 .... 31 E5
Brent Hill. ME13 .... 62 C8
Brent Rd. ME13 .... 62 C8
Brents Ind Est. ME13 .... 40 D1
Brentwood. TN23 .... 155 F5
Brenzett Cl. ME5 .... 32 B5
Brenzett Cnr. TN29 .... 192 A3
Brenzett District
  CE Prim Sch. TN29 .... 192 A2
Breton Rd. ME1 .... 9 C2
Brett Wlk. ME8 .... 33 D4
Brewer St. Deal CT14 .... 117 D6
Brewer St. Maidstone ME14 ... 75 A5
Brewer's Hill. CT20 .... 177 D3
Brewery Cotts. CT14 .... 116 E4
Brewery La. CT4 .... 89 A1
Brewery Rd. ME10 .... 36 E6
Brewery Sq. CT3 .... 48 D2
Brewster Cotts. ME9 .... 59 E2
Brian Roberts Ho. CT6 .... 22 F5
Briar Cl. Ashford TN24 ...... 139 C6
Briar Cl. River CT17 .... 148 F2
Briar Fields. ME14 .... 75 E5
Briars Rd. TN29 .... 194 F3
Briars Wlk. CT10 .... 29 F3
Briary Cl. CT9 .... 28 A8
Brice Ave. CT4 .... 86 C1
Brices Alley. CT5 .... 20 D2
Brickfield Cotts. TN25 .... 123 B2
Brickfield La. ME13 .... 63 E2
Brickfield Rd. CT4 .... 128 F7
Brickmakers Ind Est. ME10 ... 37 B6
Brickwall Terr. TN26 .... 168 F3
Bridewell La. TN30 .... 179 A7
Bridewell Pk. CT5 .... 21 A1
Bridge App The. CT5 .... 20 F1
Bridge Cl. Hythe CT21 .... 176 A2
Bridge Cl. Woodchurch TN26 ... 181 B8
Bridge Cotts. Selling ME13 ... 84 E7
Bridge Cotts. Teynham ME9 ... 38 D2
Bridge Down. CT4 .... 111 B8
Bridge Hill. Bridge CT4 ...... 111 B8
Bridge Hill. Finglesham CT14 ... 116 C8
Bridge Ho. CT11 .... 52 C7
Bridge Mill Way. ME15 .... 74 D2
Bridge & Patrixbourne
  CE Prim Sch. CT4 .... 89 A2
Bridge Rd. Ashford TN23 .... 138 F2
Bridge Rd.
  Brabourne Lees TN25 .... 158 D5
Bridge Rd. Bridge CT4 .... 88 D1
Bridge Rd. Deal CT14 .... 117 D7
Bridge Rd. Faversham ME13 ... 62 D8
Bridge Rd. Gillingham ME7 ... 10 C7
Bridge Rd. Margate CT9 .... 7 E1
Bridge Rd. Rochester ME1 ..... 9 C2
Bridge Rd. Sheerness ME12 ... 1 C3
Bridge St. Dover CT16 .... 149 C1
Bridge St. Folkestone CT19 ... 178 E6
Bridge St. Loose ME15 .... 96 F5
Bridge St. Wye TN25 .... 123 C2
Bridge View Ind Est. ME11 ... 3 A2
Bridgefield Rd. CT5 .... 21 B3
Bridgeford Way. CT4 .... 89 A1
Bridges Cl. CT7 .... 25 E2
Bridgeside. CT14 .... 117 C6
Bridgewater Rd. ME12 .... 3 B8
Bridgeway. CT5 .... 20 F2
Bridle Way. CT21 .... 177 A3
Bridleway Gdns. CT10 .... 29 E3
Bridleway La. TN23 .... 156 B4
Brielle Way.
  Queenborough ME11 & ME12 ... 3 A6
Brielle Way. Sheerness ME12 ... 1 B2
Brier Cl. ME5 .... 32 C8
Brier Rd. ME10 & ME9 .... 36 B4
Bright Rd. ME4 .... 10 B2
Bright's Pl. CT11 .... 52 F7
Brightlingsea Rd. CT13 .... 93 F8
Brindle Way. ME5 .... 32 C1
Brinklow Terr. TN26 .... 155 F1
Brisbane Ave. ME10 .... 36 C4
Brisbane Dr. CT12 .... 29 B3
Brisbane Rd. ME4 .... 10 A3
Brishing Cl. ME15 .... 97 E5
Brishing La. ME17 .... 97 D4
Brishing Rd. ME15 & ME17 ... 97 F3
Brissenden Cl. TN28 .... 200 B8

Bristles Cnr. CT3 .... 46 E6
Bristol Pl. CT11 .... 52 D7
Bristol Rd. CT1 .... 87 F6
Britannia Ave. CT5 .... 43 B7
Britannia Cl. ME10 .... 36 E7
Britannia Rd. CT14 .... 117 D8
Briton Ct. ME12 .... 3 B8
Briton Rd. ME13 .... 62 C7
Britten Cl. CT21 .... 176 A3
Britton St. ME7 .... 10 B5
Broad La. CT14 .... 116 B7
Broad Oak Rd. CT2 .... 67 B3
Broad St. Canterbury CT1 ..... 67 A1
Broad St. Canterbury CT1 ..... 88 A8
Broad St. Deal CT14 .... 117 D6
Broad St. Margate CT9 .... 7 I3
Broad St. Ramsgate CT11 .... 52 E7
Broad St. Sheerness ME12 ..... 1 C2
Broad Street Hill.
  ME14 & ME17 .... 77 D7
Broadacre. Lydden CT15 ..... 147 F5
Broadacre. Teynham ME9 ..... 38 D2
Broader La. ME14 .... 55 B2
Broadfield Cres. TN24 .... 178 A5
Broadfield Rd.
  Folkestone CT20 .... 178 A5
Broadfield Rd.
  Maidstone ME15 .... 97 A8
Broadhurst Dr. TN24 .... 139 D7
Broadlands Ave. TN28 .... 200 B8
Broadlands Cres. TN28 ...... 200 B8
Broadlands Dr. ME5 .... 32 B4
Broadlands Ind Est. CT2 ...... 66 A7
Broadley Ave. CT7 .... 26 F5
Broadley Rd. CT9 .... 29 C7
Broadmead. TN23 .... 155 E6
Broadmead Rd. TN19 .... 178 C5
Broadmeadow. CT19 .... 178 B7
Broadoak Ave. ME15 .... 97 A8
Broadoak Ent Village. CT4 ... 58 F6
Broadoak Rd. ME9 .... 58 E6
Broadsole La. CT15 .... 164 E5
Broadstairs Rd. CT10 .... 29 E5
Broadstairs Sta. CT10 .... 30 A4
Broadview. CT20 .... 177 C6
Broadview Ave. ME8 .... 33 E8
Broadviews. CT21 .... 176 D1
Broadway. Gillingham ME8 .... 11 A3
Broadway. Maidstone ME16 ... 74 F4
Broadway. Petham CT4 .... 109 A2
Broadway. Sheerness ME12 ..... 1 D2
Broadway The.
  Broadstairs CT10 .... 30 A4
Broadway The. Herne Bay CT6 ... 22 C5
Broadway The. Minster ME12 ... 4 B7
Brockenhurst Ave. ME15 ..... 75 C1
Brockenhurst Cl.
  Canterbury CT2 .... 66 E2
Brockenhurst Cl.
  Gillingham ME8 .... 33 C7
Brockenhurst Rd. CT11 .... 52 G8
Brockhill Ctry Pk. CT21 .... 175 F4
Brockhill Park Sch
  (Lower Dept). CT21 .... 176 A3
Brockhill Park Sch
  (Upper Dept). CT21 .... 175 F4
Brockhill Rd. CT21 .... 176 B3
Brockley Rd. CT9 .... 8 A2
Brockman Cres. TN29 .... 187 B4
Brockman Rd. CT20 .... 178 C5
Brockman's Cl. CT12 .... 50 B7
Brogdale Farm Cotts. ME13 ... 62 A3
Brogdale Rd. ME13 .... 62 B5
Brogden Cres. ME17 .... 98 F7
Bromley Cl. Chatham ME5 ... 32 B4
Bromley Cl. Newington ME9 ... 35 A5
Bromley Green Rd. TN26 ... 171 A5
Brompton Hill. ME4 .... 9 F6
Brompton La. ME2 .... 9 A8
Brompton Rd. ME7 .... 10 B6
Brompton Villas. CT15 ...... 149 E6
Brompton-Westbrook
  Cty Prim Sch. ME7 .... 10 A5
Bromstone
  Cty Prim Sch. CT10 .... 29 D3
Bromstone Mews. CT10 .... 29 E3
Bromstone Rd. CT10 .... 29 E3
Bronington Cl. ME5 .... 32 A5
Brook. ME4 .... 10 A4
Brook Cl. Herne Bay CT6 ..... 22 C3
Brook Cl. Hythe CT21 .... 177 B3
Brook Cotts. Dean Street ME15 ... 96 C7
Brook Cotts. Teynham ME9 ... 39 A2
Brook Cty Prim Sch. TN25 ... 141 A4
Brook La. Cliffs End CT12 ... 50 F4
Brook La. Reculver CT6 ...... 24 B5
Brook La. Sellindge TN25 ... 159 E2
Brook La Cotts. TN25 .... 159 E2
Brook Rd. Whitstable CT5 ... 21 C3
Brook St. Eastry CT13 .... 93 C2
Brook St. Woodchurch TN26 ... 180 D8
Brookbank. Brook TN25 ..... 141 A5
Brookbank. Maidstone ME14 ... 75 A8
Brooke Ave. CT9 .... 28 B7
Brooke Rd. TN24 .... 139 B3
Brookes Pl. ME9 .... 35 B6
Brookfield Ave. CT16 .... 149 B2
Brookfield Ct. TN23 .... 155 F8
Brookfield Ind Pk. TN23 .... 138 F1
Brookfield Pl. CT16 .... 149 B2
Brookfield Rd. Ashford TN23 ... 155 F8
Brookfield Rd. Dover CT16 ... 149 A3
Brookland
  CE Prim Sch. TN29 .... 197 D8
Brooklands Cl. CT2 .... 67 A4
Brooklyn Paddock. ME7 .... 10 D6
Brooks Pl. ME14 .... 75 A4

Brooks Way. TN29 .... 203 C5
Brookside. St Mary's Bay TN29 ... 195 A5
Brookside. Temple Ewell CT16 ... 148 D5
Broom Rd. ME10 .... 37 C5
Broomcroft Rd. ME8 .... 11 F2
Broome Park Golf Course.
  CT4 .... 129 B6
Broomfield Cres. CT9 .... 8 F2
Broomfield Gate. CT5 .... 44 D5
Broomfield Rd.
  Broomfield ME17 .... 99 D4
Broomfield Rd.
  Faversham ME13 .... 62 E8
Broomfield Rd. Herne Bay CT6 ... 23 C2
Broomfield Rd. Herne Bay CT6 ... 177 E6
Brotherhood Cl. CT2 .... 66 D4
Broughton Ct. TN23 .... 138 E1
Brown St. ME8 .... 11 F1
Brownelow Copse. ME5 .... 32 B1
Brownhill Cl. ME5 .... 32 A4
Browning Pl. CT19 .... 178 E7
Brownings Orch. ME9 .... 59 A7
Broxhall Rd. CT4 .... 110 B3
Bruce Cl. CT14 .... 117 B4
Bruges Cl. ME10 .... 14 F1
Brundell Farm. CT4 .... 86 B2
Brunel Way. ME4 .... 10 A7
Brunswick Cotts. ME9 .... 38 E6
Brunswick Ct. ❸ CT11 .... 52 E7
Brunswick Field. ME9 .... 38 E6
Brunswick Gdns. ❸ CT16 ... 149 B3
Brunswick House
  Cty Prim Sch. ME16 .... 74 E5
Brunswick Ind Ctr. TN23 ... 138 F2
Brunswick Rd. Ashford TN23 ... 138 F2
Brunswick Rd. Birchington CT7 ... 27 A5
Brunswick Sq. CT6 .... 22 E5
Brunswick St. Maidstone ME15 ... 75 A3
Brunswick St. Ramsgate CT11 ... 52 E7
Brunswick St E. ME15 .... 75 A3
Bryant Rd. ME2 .... 9 A7
Bryant St. ME4 .... 10 A3
Brymore Cl. CT1 .... 67 B2
Brymore Rd. CT1 .... 67 B2
Bryony Sch (private). ME8 ... 33 F5
Buck St. TN25 .... 105 C2
Buckhurst Dr. CT9 .... 8 F2
Buckingham Rd. ❶
  Broadstairs CT10 .... 30 B4
Buckingham Rd.
  Gillingham ME7 .... 10 D5
Buckingham Rd. Margate CT9 ... 7 I1
Buckingham Rd.
  Whitstable CT5 .... 21 B2
Buckingham Row. ME15 ...... 97 E7
Buckland Ave. CT16 .... 149 B2
Buckland Cl. ME5 .... 32 A2
Buckland Cotts. ME13 .... 61 B8
Buckland Hill. ME16 .... 74 E5
Buckland Hospl. CT17 .... 149 A1
Buckland La. Maidstone ME16 ... 74 D6
Buckland La. Staple CT3 ..... 92 A4
Buckland Pl. ME16 .... 74 E4
Buckland Rd. ME16 .... 74 E4
Bucklers Cl. ME12 .... 6 E4
Buckmore Park
  (Scout Camp). ME5 .... 31 C3
Bucksford La. TN23 .... 155 C7
Buckthorn Cl. CT14 .... 117 C7
Budd's Farm Cotts. TN30 ... 188 F2
Budd's La. TN30 .... 188 F2
Buenos Ayres. CT9 .... 7 H2
Buffs Ave. CT20 .... 177 B6
Builders Sq. CT3 .... 90 A8
Bull Hill. ME7 .... 102 A1
Bull La. Bethersden TN26 ... 153 B4
Bull La. Boughton Street ME13 ... 63 F4
Bull La. Eccles ME20 .... 53 A6
Bull La. Stockbury ME9 ...... 34 E2
Bulldog Rd. ME5 .... 32 B2
Bulleid Pl. TN24 .... 156 D7
Buller Rd. ME4 .... 9 F2
Buller's Ave. CT6 .... 22 E4
Bullockstone Rd. CT6 .... 45 E7
Bulls Cotts. ❹ CT21 .... 176 B2
Bulltown Cnr. TN25 .... 141 F3
Bullwark St. CT17 .... 166 D5
Bulrush Cl. ME5 .... 31 F3
Bulrushes The. TN23 .... 155 D8
Bulwark Rd. CT14 .... 117 D7
Bumbles Cl. ME1 .... 31 D7
Bunce Court Rd.
  ME13 & ME17 .... 102 E7
Bungalow The. TN26 .... 137 F5
Bungalows The.
  Faversham ME13 .... 62 A4
Bungalows The.
  Tenterden TN30 .... 179 D7
Bungalows The.
  Woodnesborough CT13 .... 93 B5
Bunker's Hill. CT17 .... 149 B2
Bunkers Hill Ave. CT17 ..... 149 B1
Bunkers Hill Rd. CT17 ...... 149 A1
Bunkley Meadow. TN26 ...... 183 A7
Burberry La. ME17 .... 99 B5
Burch Ave. CT13 .... 93 F8
Burford's Alley. CT3 .... 71 D1
Burgate. CT1 .... 88 A8
Burgate La. ❹ CT1 .... 88 A8
Burgate Terr. TN25 .... 157 E4
Burgess Cl. Minster,Thanet CT12 ... 50 C7
Burgess Cl. Whitfield CT16 ... 149 B7
Burgess Gn. CT14 .... 116 C8
Burgess Hall Dr. ME17 ...... 98 F6
Burgess Rd. Aylesham CT3 ... 112 F6
Burgess Rd. Rochester ME2 ... 9 B7
Burgess Row. ❽ TN30 .... 179 A7

Burghclere Dr. ME16 .... 74 B2
Burgoyne Ct. ME14 .... 74 F7
Burgoyne Gr. CT16 .... 149 A5
Burgoyne Hts. CT16 .... 149 E3
Burkestone ME16 .... 37 A8
Burial Ground La. ME15 ..... 74 E7
Burkett Cl. ME10 .... 37 A8
Burleigh Dr. ME14 .... 53 F4
Burleigh Rd. TN27 .... 120 C7
Burley Rd. ME10 .... 36 C4
Burlington Dr. CT6 .... 23 D5
Burlington Gdns.
  Gillingham ME8 .... 33 E4
Burlington Gdns. Margate CT9 ... 28 C8
Burma Cres. CT1 .... 67 D1
Burma Way. ME5 .... 31 F6
Burmarsh Cl. ME5 .... 32 B5
Burmarsh Rd. Burmarsh TN29 ... 186 C3
Burmarsh Rd. Hythe CT21 ... 187 C8
Burn's Rd. ME7 .... 10 C7
Burnan Rd. CT5 .... 21 C2
Burnham Cl. ME10 .... 36 E8
Burnham Wlk. ME8 .... 33 E3
Burns Rd. ME16 .... 74 C2
Burnt House Hill. CT3 .... 69 B5
Burnt Oak Terr. ME7 .... 10 D6
Burnt Oast Rd. ME13 .... 64 A3
Burntwick Dr. ME9 .... 13 B3
Burnup Bank. ME10 .... 37 C5
Burrow Rd. CT19 .... 178 F6
Burrs The. ME10 .... 36 F3
Burrstock Way. ME8 .... 12 B2
Bursill Cres. CT12 .... 29 B1
Bursted Hill. CT4 .... 110 B2
Burston Rd. ME17 .... 96 B2
Burton Cl. CT19 .... 178 A7
Burton Fields. CT6 .... 23 B4
Burton Rd. TN24 .... 139 E6
Busbridge Rd. ME15 .... 96 E6
Bush Ave. CT12 .... 29 B1
Bush Cl. ME9 .... 57 F5
Bush Row. ME20 .... 53 A3
Bushey Cl. ME13 .... 63 F3
Busheyfields Rd. CT6 .... 45 F6
Bushmeadow Rd. ME8 .... 11 F2
Bushy Gr. ME17 .... 99 D2
Bushy Hill Rd. CT2 .... 68 D7
Bushy Royds. TN24 .... 156 D6
Bushy Ruff Cotts. CT16 ..... 148 D4
Butchers La. CT15 .... 113 E5
Butchery La. ❶ CT1 .... 88 A8
Butchery The. ❷ CT13 ...... 73 A1
Butler's Hill. ME13 .... 64 D7
Butt Field Rd. TN23 .... 155 E7
Butter St. CT15 .... 113 C4
Butterfly Ctr The. CT15 .... 146 B3
Buttermere. ME13 .... 62 E6
Buttermere Cl.
  Folkestone CT19 .... 178 B6
Buttermere Cl. Gillingham ME7 ... 11 A5
Buttermere Gdns. CT3 ...... 112 F6
Button La. ME15 .... 76 B2
Butts Ct. CT4 .... 110 A6
Butts Cty Prim Inf Sch The.
  ME10 .... 36 E6
Butts Hill. ME13 .... 63 F5
Butts Meadow. CT4 .... 110 A6
Butts The. Sandwich CT13 ... 72 F1
Butts The. Sittingbourne ME10 ... 36 F4
Buxton Cl. Chatham ME5 ..... 32 D1
Buxton Cl. Maidstone ME15 ... 97 A8
Buxton Rd. CT12 .... 29 B2
Bybrook Ct. TN24 .... 139 C4
Bybrook Cty Inf Sch. TN24 ... 139 D5
Bybrook Cty Jun Sch. TN24 ... 139 D5
Bybrook Field. CT20 .... 177 E3
Bybrook Rd. TN24 .... 139 C5
Bybrook Way. CT20 .... 177 E4
Bychurch Pl. ❻ ME15 .... 75 A3
Byllan Rd. CT17 .... 148 E3
Byron Ave. CT9 .... 7 J1
Byron Cl. CT1 .... 88 C7
Byron Cres. CT16 .... 149 B4
Byron Cty Prim Sch. ME7 ... 10 C3
Byron Rd. Gillingham ME7 ... 10 C3
Byron Rd. Maidstone ME14 ... 75 B7
Bysing Wood Cotts. ME13 ... 39 F1
Bysing Wood Cty Prim Sch.
  ME13 .... 62 A8
Bysing Wood Rd. ME13 ...... 39 F1
Bythorne St. ME8 .... 12 B1

C Ramp App. CT16 .... 166 G8
Cade Rd. TN23 .... 156 B7
Cades Orch. ME13 .... 61 E3
Cadnam Cl. CT2 .... 66 E3
Caernarvon Dr. ME15 .... 74 F1
Caesar's Way. CT19 .... 177 E7
Cage La. TN2 .... 135 A1
Calais Hill. CT2 .... 66 E6
Calcroft Mews. ❻ CT1 .... 67 B2
Calcutta Ho. ❸ ME15 .... 97 E5
Caldecot La. TN29 .... 199 D2
Caldecote Cl. ME8 .... 12 B1
Calder Rd. ME14 .... 74 E7
Caldew Ave. ME8 .... 11 C1
Caldew Gr. ME10 .... 37 A3
Caledon Terr. CT1 .... 88 A7
Caledonian St. ME8 .... 33 E8
Calehill Cl. ME14 .... 75 C6
Calgary Cres. CT19 .... 178 E8
California Row. CT3 .... 90 E6
Callams Cl. ME8 .... 33 D6
Calland. TN25 .... 158 E5
Callaways La. ME9 .... 35 B6
Calleywell La. TN25 .... 173 A7
Callis Court Rd. CT10 .... 29 F6
Callis Grange
  Cty Inf Sch. CT10 .... 29 F7

Calverden Rd. CT12 ... 29 A1
Camborne Manor. ME7 ... 10 C6
Cambourne Ave. CT8 ... 27 D8
Cambrai Ct. CT1 ... 67 D1
Cambridge Ave. CT13 ... 95 B7
Cambridge Cl. CT7 ... 27 B7
Cambridge Cres. ME15 ... 97 D7
Cambridge Gdns. CT20 ... 178 D5
Cambridge Ho. 3 ME15 ... 97 D7
Cambridge Rd. Canterbury CT1 ... 87 F6
Cambridge Rd. Deal CT14 ... 117 D3
Cambridge Rd.
  Dover CT16 & CT17 ... 166 D7
Cambridge Rd.
  Faversham ME13 ... 62 B6
Cambridge Rd. Gillingham ME8 ... 33 C6
Cambridge Rd. Rochester ME2 ... 9 A8
Cambridge Rd.
  Sittingbourne ME10 ... 37 B3
Cambridge Terr. Chatham ME4 ... 9 F4
Cambridge Terr. 11
  Dover CT16 ... 166 E7
Cambridge Terr. 11
  Folkestone CT20 ... 178 E5
Cambridge Terr. Margate CT9 ... 8 B1
Cambridge Way. CT1 ... 87 F6
Camden Cl. ME5 ... 32 B5
Camden Cres. CT16 ... 166 E7
Camden Rd. Broadstairs CT10 ... 29 D7
Camden Rd. Gillingham ME7 ... 10 D7
Camden Rd. Ramsgate CT11 ... 52 E7
Camden Sq. 7 CT11 ... 52 E7
Camden St. ME14 ... 75 A5
Camden Terr. TN24 ... 139 E1
Camellia Cl. Gillingham ME8 ... 33 D7
Camellia Cl. 2 Margate CT9 ... 28 B8
Cameron Cl. ME5 ... 32 B8
Cameron Ct. CT17 ... 166 A6
Camomile Dr. ME14 ... 75 F5
Camp Way. ME15 ... 97 C6
Campbell Cl. CT6 ... 23 C3
Campbell Rd. Deal CT14 ... 117 D4
Campbell Rd. Maidstone ME15 ... 75 A3
Campion Cl. ME5 ... 31 E3
Campleshon Rd. ME8 ... 33 D5
Campus Way. ME7 ... 33 A8
Canada Cl. CT18 & CT19 ... 177 C6
Canada Rd. CT14 ... 117 D3
Canada Terr. 3 ME14 ... 75 A7
Canadian Ave. ME7 ... 10 F4
Canal Rd. ME2 ... 9 C7
Canberra Gdns. ME10 ... 36 C4
Canning St. ME14 ... 75 A6
Cannon Appleton Ct. CT1 ... 87 E7
Cannon Rd. CT11 ... 52 D7
Cannon St. Deal CT14 ... 117 C7
Cannon St. Dover CT16 ... 166 D8
Cannon St. Lydd TN29 ... 203 C6
Cannon St. New Romney TN28 ... 200 B7
Cannonbury Rd. CT11 ... 52 D6
Cannongate Ave. CT21 ... 176 D3
Cannongate Cl. CT21 ... 176 E2
Cannongate Gdns. CT21 ... 176 E3
Cannongate Rd. CT21 ... 176 D3
Canon Cl. ME1 ... 9 B2
Canon Gn. CT3 ... 91 A7
Canon Woods Way. TN24 ... 139 F6
Canons Gate Rd. CT16 ... 166 E8
Canterbury Cl. CT10 ... 29 D5
Canterbury Coll. ... 88 A7
Canterbury Ct. TN24 ... 139 D2
Canterbury East Sta. CT2 ... 87 F7
Canterbury
  Equestrian Ctr. CT6 ... 22 D3
Canterbury Golf Course. CT2 ... 67 E2
Canterbury
  High Sch The. CT2 ... 87 D8
Canterbury Hill. CT2 ... 66 E5
Canterbury Ho. 2 ME15 ... 97 D7
Canterbury Ind Pk. CT2 ... 88 A7
Canterbury La. Canterbury CT1 ... 88 A8
Canterbury La.
  Gillingham ME8 & ME9 ... 12 C1
Canterbury Rd.
  Ashford, Bybrook TN24 ... 139 E5
Canterbury Rd.
  Ashford, S Willesborough TN24 ... 156 E6
Canterbury Rd. Barham CT4 ... 129 C5
Canterbury Rd. Boughton Aluph
  CT4 & TN25 & TN24 ... 123 C5
Canterbury Rd.
  Boughton Street ME13 ... 63 D4
Canterbury Rd.
  Brabourne TN25 ... 159 C8
Canterbury Rd.
  Brabourne Lees TN25 ... 158 F6
Canterbury Rd.
  Challock TN25 & TN27 ... 104 C1
Canterbury Rd. Chilham CT4 ... 85 E1
Canterbury Rd. Denton CT4 ... 129 A1
Canterbury Rd. Dunkirk ME13 ... 64 E2
Canterbury Rd. Elham CT4 ... 144 E3
Canterbury Rd.
  Etchinghill CT18 ... 161 D4
Canterbury Rd.
  Faversham ME13 ... 62 E5
Canterbury Rd.
  Folkestone CT19 ... 178 D7
Canterbury Rd.
  Folkestone, Foord CT19 ... 178 E6
Canterbury Rd. Hawkinge
  CT18 & CT19 & CT15 & CT4 ... 163 B4
Canterbury Rd. Herne CT3 & CT6 ... 45 E5
Canterbury Rd. Herne Bay CT6 ... 23 A3
Canterbury Rd. Littlebourne CT3 ... 89 C8
Canterbury Rd. Lydden CT15 ... 147 E7
Canterbury Rd. Lyminge CT18 ... 161 C7
Canterbury Rd. Sarre CT7 ... 48 C3

Canterbury Rd.
  Sittingbourne ME10 ... 37 B3
Canterbury Rd. Whitstable CT5 ... 43 D8
Canterbury Rd. Wingham CT3 ... 91 A7
Canterbury Rd E. CT11 & CT12 ... 52 A6
Canterbury Rd W. CT12 ... 51 D7
Canterbury Road Birchington.
  CT7 ...
Canterbury Road Cty Prim Sch.
  ME10 ... 37 B3
Canterbury Road Margate.
  CT9 ... 7 G1
Canterbury Road Westgate.
  CT8 & CT9 ... 27 E8
Canterbury St. ME7 ... 10 C4
Canterbury West Sta. CT2 ... 66 F1
Canute Rd. Birchington CT7 ... 26 D7
Canute Rd. Deal CT14 ... 95 C1
Canute Rd. Faversham ME13 ... 62 C6
Capel Cl. Broadstairs CT10 ... 8 F1
Capel Cl. Gillingham ME8 ... 33 D4
Capel Rd. Faversham ME13 ... 62 B7
Capel Rd. Petham CT4 ... 108 F3
Capel Rd.
  Ruckinge TN25 & TN26 ... 171 B4
Capel Rd. Sittingbourne ME10 ... 36 E2
Capel St. CT18 ... 164 B3
Capel-le-Ferne Cty Prim Sch.
  CT18 ... 164 C3
Capell Cl. ME17 ... 96 C3
Capetown Ho. 1 ME15 ... 97 F5
Capstan Row. CT14 ... 117 D7
Capstone Farm Country Pk.
  ME7 ... 32 D5
Capstone Rd. Chatham ME5 ... 10 D1
Capstone Rd. Gillingham ME7 ... 32 F6
Cardine Cl. ME10 ... 36 E7
Carey Cl. TN28 ... 200 B6
Carey Ho. 5 CT1 ... 87 F7
Caring La. ME15 ... 76 E1
Caring Rd. ME15 ... 76 C1
Carisbrooke Dr. ME16 ... 74 D4
Carlsden Cl. CT10 ... 149 A3
Carlton Ave. Broadstairs CT10 ... 30 A5
Carlton Ave. Gillingham ME7 ... 10 E4
Carlton Ave. Ramsgate CT11 ... 52 D6
Carlton Ave. Sheerness ME12 ... 1 C1
Carlton Cres. ME5 ... 32 D8
Carlton Gdns. ME15 ... 97 B8
Carlton Hill. CT6 ... 22 C4
Carlton Leas. CT20 ... 178 C4
Carlton Mansions. CT10 ... 8 A3
Carlton Rd. Ashford TN23 ... 139 A2
Carlton Rd. Kingsdown CT14 ... 134 C6
Carlton Rd. Whitstable CT5 ... 43 D2
Carlton Rd E. CT8 ... 27 D8
Carlton Rd W. CT8 ... 27 D8
Carlton Rise. CT8 ... 27 C8
Carman's Cl. ME5 & ME17 ... 96 F3
Carmel Ct. 2 CT7 ... 26 F8
Caroland Cl. TN25 ... 158 D5
Caroline Cl. CT5 ... 43 B6
Caroline Cres. Broadstairs CT10 . 29 E6
Caroline Cres. Maidstone ME16 ... 74 D7
Caroline Sq. CT9 ... 7 J3
Carpeaux Cl. ME4 ... 10 A4
Carpenters Cl. ME4 ... 9 E2
Carpinus Cl. ME5 ... 32 B1
Carriage Ho The. ME13 ... 83 D5
Carriage Mus. ME15 ... 75 A3
Carrie Ho. ME15 ... 74 E5
Carroway's Pl. CT9 ... 7 J2
Carter La. TN29 ... 191 E2
Carter's Rd. CT20 ... 177 F5
Carter's Wood. TN26 ... 183 B7
Carton Cl. ME1 ... 9 D2
Cartwright & Kelsey
  CE Prim Sch The. CT3 ... 71 C2
Carvoran Way. ME8 ... 33 C5
Caslocke St. 2 ME13 ... 62 C7
Cassino Ho. 16 CT1 ... 67 B2
Cassino Sq. CT16 ... 149 E2
Castalla Cotts. CT17 ... 117 D3
Castle Ave. Broadstairs CT10 ... 30 B6
Castle Ave. Dover CT16 ... 149 D1
Castle Ave. Hythe CT21 ... 176 B3
Castle Ave. Rochester ME1 ... 9 C4
Castle Bay. CT20 ... 177 D3
Castle Cl. 4 Folkestone CT20 ... 177 F3
Castle Cl. Lympne CT21 ... 174 F2
Castle Comm Sch. CT14 ... 117 C4
Castle Cotts. CT13 ... 72 E5
Castle Cres. CT21 ... 176 C4
Castle Dene. ME14 ... 74 F8
Castle Dr. CT16 ... 148 F7
Castle Hill.
  Folkestone CT19 & CT18 ... 178 A8
Castle Hill. Rochester ME1 ... 9 C4
Castle Hill. Thurnham ME14 ... 55 D1
Castle Hill Ave. CT20 ... 178 C4
Castle Hill Rd. CT16 ... 166 E8
Castle Mayne Ave. CT7 ... 27 F3
Castle Mews. CT14 ... 117 A4
Castle Rd. Chatham ME4 ... 10 B2
Castle Rd. Folkestone CT20 ... 177 F3
Castle Rd. Hythe CT21 ... 176 B4
Castle Rd. Maidstone ME16 ... 74 D7
Castle Rd. Sittingbourne ME10 ... 37 B5
Castle Rd. Whitstable CT5 ... 20 F2
Castle Rough La. ME10 ... 14 F1
Castle Row. CT1 ... 87 F7
Castle St. 6 Ashford TN23 ... 139 B2
Castle St. Canterbury CT1 ... 87 F8
Castle St. Dover CT16 ... 166 E8
Castle St. Queenborough ME11 ... 3 A5
Castle View Rd. ME2 ... 9 A7

Castle Wlk. CT14 ... 95 D1
Castleacres Ind Pk. ME10 ... 37 B6
Castlemaine Ave. ME7 ... 10 F6
Castlemere Ave. ME11 ... 3 B5
Castlemount Rd. CT16 ... 149 D1
Castlemount Sch. CT16 ... 149 E1
Castleview Ct. CT17 ... 149 B1
Cathedral View. CT2 ... 67 A2
Catherine Cl. ME16 ... 74 A3
Catherine St. ME1 ... 9 D3
Catherine Way. CT10 ... 30 A6
Catkin Cl. ME5 ... 31 F1
Catsole Hill. CT3 ... 91 D2
Catt's Hill. TN30 ... 189 E3
Catt's Wood Rd. CT4 ... 109 F4
Catterick Rd. ME5 ... 32 D2
Cattle Market. CT13 ... 72 F1
Cauldham Cl. CT18 ... 164 B1
Cauldham La. CT18 ... 164 B3
Causeway The. Canterbury CT2 ... 66 F1
Causeway The. Sandwich CT13 ... 72 D2
Cavalry Ct. CT17 ... 166 A2
Cave Hill. ME15 ... 74 F1
Cave La. CT3 ... 91 D3
Cavell Sq. CT14 ... 117 A3
Cavell Way. ME10 ... 36 D5
Cavenagh Rd. CT15 ... 151 B6
Cavendish Ave. ME7 ... 10 E6
Cavendish Ct. CT6 ... 23 A5
Cavendish Pl. 2 CT11 ... 52 E6
Cavendish Rd. Herne Bay CT6 ... 23 A5
Cavendish Rd. Rochester ME1 ... 9 D3
Cavendish St. CT11 ... 52 E6
Cavendish Way. ME15 ... 76 B3
Caversham Ave. ME8 ... 11 F1
Cavour Rd. Faversham ME13 ... 62 C7
Cavour Rd. Sheerness ME12 ... 1 D2
Caxton Rd. CT9 ... 28 C8
Cayser Dr. ME17 ... 99 E2
Cazeneuve St. ME1 ... 9 C5
Cecil Ave. Gillingham ME8 ... 11 A2
Cecil Ave. Rochester ME2 ... 9 B8
Cecil Ave. Sheerness ME12 ... 1 C1
Cecil Ct. Ashford TN24 ... 139 B3
Cecil Ct. Herne Bay CT6 ... 23 A4
Cecil Pk. CT6 ... 23 A4
Cecil Rd. Kingsdown CT14 ... 134 D7
Cecil Rd. Rochester ME1 ... 9 C3
Cecil Sq. CT9 ... 7 I2
Cecil St. CT9 ... 7 I2
Cecilia Gr. CT10 ... 29 F6
Cecilia Rd. CT11 ... 52 E8
Cedar Cl. Ashford TN23 ... 138 E3
Cedar Cl. Broadstairs CT10 ... 29 F7
Cedar Cl. Margate CT9 ... 28 B8
Cedar Cl. Sittingbourne ME10 ... 37 B2
Cedar Cres. TN29 ... 194 F3
Cedar Ct. Folkestone CT20 ... 177 E5
Cedar Ct. 10 Tenterden TN30 ... 179 A7
Cedar Gdns. ME8 ... 56 E8
Cedar Gr. ME7 ... 33 A5
Cedar Ho. ME12 ... 1 C2
Cedar Rd. CT2 ... 68 A6
Cedar Terr. ME13 ... 62 A4
Cedars Sch The.
  Maidstone ME16 ... 74 D4
Cedars Sch The.
  Rochester ME1 ... 9 C4
Cedars The. ME10 ... 37 C5
Cedarview. CT2 ... 66 C1
Cedarwood Ho. ME15 ... 96 B6
Cedric Rd. CT8 ... 7 C1
Ceil Villas. CT14 ... 94 B4
Celestine Cl. ME5 ... 32 A1
Cellar Hill. ME9 ... 60 C8
Celtic Rd. CT14 ... 117 A2
Cemetery La. TN24 ... 139 C4
Centenary Cl. TN27 ... 120 C8
Centenary Gdns. CT13 ... 93 A2
Central Ave. Gillingham ME4 ... 10 B8
Central Ave. Herne Bay CT6 ... 22 D4
Central Ave. Sittingbourne ME10 . 36 F4
Central Bsns Pk. ME2 ... 9 C7
Central Par. Herne Bay CT6 ... 22 E5
Central Par. Rochester ME1 ... 9 D2
Central Park Gdns. ME1 ... 9 E2
Central Rd. Ramsgate CT11 ... 52 D8
Central Rd. Rochester ME2 ... 9 A7
Central Service Rd. CT16 ... 166 H8
Centre 2000. Maidstone ME16 ... 74 C8
Centre 2000.
  Sittingbourne ME10 ... 37 A4
Centre Cl. ME2 ... 9 C7
Centre Rd. CT17 ... 166 C6
Centre The. Margate CT9 ... 7 I2
Centre The. Ramsgate CT12 ... 29 A1
Centurion Cl. ME7 ... 10 F1
Centurion Wlk. TN23 ... 156 B4
Century Rd. Faversham ME13 ... 62 E7
Century Rd. Gillingham ME8 ... 33 D8
Century Wlk. CT14 ... 117 C6
Ceres Ct. ME10 ... 37 C5
Chada Ave. ME7 ... 10 E3
Chaffe's La. ME9 ... 12 E3
Chaffes Terr. ME9 ... 12 E3
Chaffinch Cl. ME5 ... 32 A7
Chafy Cres. CT2 ... 67 C6
Chain Gate. TN27 ... 118 A8
Chain The. 6 CT13 ... 73 A1
Chalcroft Rd. CT20 ... 177 E4
Chalfont Dr. Gillingham ME8 ... 33 D6
Chalk Ave. TN30 ... 167 B2
Chalk Hill. CT11 & CT12 ... 51 F6
Chalk Hill Rd. CT14 ... 134 C5
Chalk Pit Hill. ME4 ... 10 A3

Chalk Pit La. CT13 & CT3 ... 92 C5
Chalk Rd. ME11 ... 3 C1
Chalkenden Ave. ME8 ... 11 A2
Chalkpit Hill. CT4 ... 89 D3
Chalksole Green La. CT15 ... 147 B2
Chalkwell Ct. CT17 ... 166 A7
Chalkwell Rd. ME10 ... 36 D5
Chalky Bank Rd. ME8 ... 11 F2
Challenger Cl. ME10 ... 36 E7
Challock Ct. CT9 ... 8 F2
Challock
  Cty Prim Sch. TN25 ... 105 B1
Challock Wlk. ME14 ... 75 C6
Chamberlain Ave. ME16 ... 74 C2
Chamberlain Ct. ME8 ... 33 B5
Chamberlain Dr. CT6 ... 22 B4
Chamberlain Rd.
  Chatham ME4 ... 10 B2
Chamberlain Rd. Dover CT16 ... 166 B8
Chance Meadow. CT15 ... 149 E6
Chancel Ct. CT2 ... 66 D1
Chancery La. ME15 ... 75 B3
Chanctonbury Chase. CT5 ... 43 A6
Chandos Rd. 16 CT10 ... 30 B4
Chandos Sq. 15 CT10 ... 30 B4
Channel Cl. CT19 ... 178 F7
Channel Lea. CT14 ... 117 C1
Channel Rd. CT9 ... 29 A6
Channel Sch The. CT19 ... 178 C7
Channel Tunnel Terminal.
  CT18 ... 177 B8
Channel View. 18 CT19 ... 178 E5
Channel View Ct. 16 CT11 ... 52 F7
Channel View Rd. CT17 ... 166 C5
Channel Watch. TN28 ... 200 E4
Channon Rd. ME29 ... 204 E7
Chantry Ct. 4 CT1 ... 66 F1
Chapel Cotts. ME17 ... 98 F5
Chapel Hill. Eythorne CT15 ... 131 C7
Chapel Hill. Margate CT9 ... 29 A6
Chapel Hill. CT9 ... 28 F7
Chapel La. Blean CT2 ... 66 A7
Chapel La. Broad Oak CT2 ... 67 D7
Chapel La. 18 Dover CT16 ... 166 D7
Chapel La. East Studdal CT15 ... 132 C6
Chapel La.
  Gillingham,Hempstead ME7 ... 33 A4
Chapel La.
  Gillingham,Lidsing ME7 ... 33 A2
Chapel La. Maidstone ME14 ... 76 A5
Chapel La. Newchurch TN29 ... 185 C4
Chapel La.
  Potter's Forstal TN27 ... 118 A2
Chapel La. Rhodes Minnis CT4 ... 144 B4
Chapel La. Ripple CT14 ... 133 D8
Chapel La.
  St Margaret's at Cliffe CT15 ... 150 F6
Chapel La. Staple CT3 ... 92 B6
Chapel La. Sturry CT2 ... 67 F5
Chapel Mews. TN23 ... 139 C2
Chapel Pl. 16
  Dover CT16 & CT17 ... 166 D7
Chapel Pl. Ramsgate CT11 ... 52 D7
Chapel Place La. CT11 ... 52 D7
Chapel Rd. Dymchurch TN29 ... 195 C7
Chapel Rd. Ram Lane TN26 ... 120 F1
Chapel Rd. Ramsgate CT11 ... 52 C7
Chapel Rd. Tilmanstone CT14 ... 115 A3
Chapel Rd. Whitfield CT16 ... 149 A8
Chapel Row. Herne CT6 ... 46 A8
Chapel Row. Kingsnorth TN23 ... 156 A3
Chapel Row. Ram Lane TN26 ... 120 F2
Chapel St. Deal CT14 ... 117 D6
Chapel St. Faversham ME13 ... 62 D6
Chapel St. Herne Bay CT6 ... 23 A5
Chapel St. Hythe CT21 ... 176 B2
Chapel St. Minster ME12 ... 4 B6
Chapel St. Sheerness ME12 ... 1 B2
Chapman Ave. ME15 ... 97 F8
Chapman Ho. CT14 ... 117 B3
Chapmans Cl. TN25 ... 105 C2
Chapmans Hill. CT15 & CT3 ... 113 B5
Chappell Way. ME10 ... 36 E6
Charing CE Prim Sch. TN27 ... 120 C8
Charing Cl. CT12 ... 52 C8
Charing Cres. CT21 ... 28 D7
Charing Heath Rd.
  Charing TN27 ... 119 F8
Charing Heath Rd.
  Coppins Corner TN27 ... 120 A6
Charing Hill. TN27 ... 103 E1
Charing Rd. ME8 ... 11 B3
Charing Sta. TN27 ... 120 B7
Charlbury Cl. ME16 ... 74 C3
Charlecote Ct. ME8 ... 33 D8
Charles Cobb Cl. TN29 ... 195 D8
Charles Cres. CT19 ... 177 E7
Charles Ct. CT8 ... 27 F8
Charles Dickens
  High Sch The. CT10 ... 29 E4
Charles Drayson Ct. ME13 ... 62 E7
Charles Ho. CT14 ... 117 B3
Charles Lister Ct. CT17 ... 149 B1
Charles Rd. Deal CT14 ... 117 B4
Charles Rd. Ramsgate CT11 ... 52 E8
Charles St. Chatham ME4 ... 9 E3
Charles St. Herne Bay CT6 ... 23 A5
Charles St. Maidstone ME16 ... 74 E3
Charles St. Rochester ME2 ... 9 A7
Charles St. Sheerness ME12 ... 1 B3
Charlesford Ave. ME17 ... 99 D3
Charleston Ct. CT10 ... 30 B3
Charlesworth Dr. CT7 ... 27 B7
Charlotte Cl. ME5 ... 32 B6
Charlotte Ct. CT11 ... 52 E6
Charlotte Dr. ME8 ... 11 C1
Charlotte Pl. 2 CT9 ... 7 J1

Charlotte Sq. 8 CT9 ... 7 J2
Charlotte St. 13
Charlotte St. ... 30 B4
Charlotte St. Folkestone CT20 ... 178 E5
Charlotte St.
  Sittingbourne ME10 ... 36 E5
Charlton Ave. CT16 ... 149 C1
Charlton CE Prim Sch. CT16 ... 149 C1
Charlton Cl. Ashford TN24 ... 157 A8
Charlton Cl. Ramsgate CT12 ... 29 B2
Charlton Ctr. 3 CT17 ... 166 C8
Charlton Gn. CT16 ... 149 C1
Charlton La. ME17 ... 99 C5
Charlton Manor. ME7 ... 10 B5
Charlton St. ME16 ... 74 C2
Charltons The. ME13 ... 63 F4
Charminster. TN23 ... 155 E6
Charnwood. CT5 ... 21 D1
Charnwood Rd. CT6 ... 23 B1
Chart Cl. ME13 ... 62 B7
Chart Cnr. ME17 ... 98 B1
Chart Hill Rd. ME17 ... 98 B1
Chart Pl. ME8 ... 33 C3
Chart Rd. Ashford TN23 ... 138 D1
Chart Rd. Ashford TN23 ... 155 D6
Chart Rd.
  Ashford, Godinton Park TN23 ... 138 F2
Chart Rd. Folkestone CT19 ... 177 F6
Chart Road Ind Est. TN23 ... 139 A3
Charter Ho. 9 CT16 ... 166 E7
Charter St. Chatham ME4 ... 9 F2
Charter St. Gillingham ME7 ... 10 C5
Chartham Cty Prim Sch. CT4 ... 86 C1
Chartham Downs Rd. CT4 ... 109 C2
Chartham Sta. CT4 ... 86 D3
Chartway St. ME17 ... 99 C1
Chartwell Ave. CT6 ... 23 D4
Chartwell Gr. ME10 ... 36 C3
Chase The. Chatham ME1 ... 9 D2
Chase The. Gillingham ME8 ... 11 A2
Chater Cl. CT14 ... 117 C4
Chatham Ct. CT11 ... 52 D8
Chatham Ho. ME4 ... 9 F1
Chatham Gram Sch for Boys.
  ME4 ... 31 F8
Chatham Gram Sch for Girls.
  ME5 ... 10 C2
Chatham Hill. ME4 ... 10 B3
Chatham Historic Dockyard.
  ME4 ... 10 A7
Chatham House
  Gram Sch for Boys. CT11 ... 52 E7
Chatham Pl. CT11 ... 52 E7
Chatham Rd. Chatham ME20 ... 53 D8
Chatham Rd. Kit's Coty ME20 ... 53 D6
Chatham Rd. Kit's Coty ME20 ... 53 D7
Chatham Rd. Maidstone ME14 ... 53 E1
Chatham Rd. Sandling ME14 ... 53 E4
Chatham Ski Ctr. ME7 ... 32 E6
Chatham South Sec Sch. ME4 ... 31 F8
Chatham St. CT11 ... 52 E7
Chatham Sta. ME4 ... 9 E4
Chatsworth Dr. ME10 ... 36 B5
Chatsworth Mews. ME11 ... 52 C6
Chatsworth Rd. ME7 ... 10 C6
Chattenden Ct. ME14 ... 75 B6
Chaucer Ave. CT5 ... 21 B1
Chaucer Cl. Canterbury CT1 ... 88 C7
Chaucer Cl. Rochester ME2 ... 9 E8
Chaucer Coll. CT2 ... 66 D3
Chaucer Cres. CT16 ... 149 B3
Chaucer Ct. CT1 ... 88 B7
Chaucer Hospl. CT1 ... 88 A4
Chaucer Rd. Broadstairs CT10 ... 30 A4
Chaucer Rd. Canterbury CT1 ... 67 C1
Chaucer Rd. Elvington CT15 ... 114 B2
Chaucer Rd. Gillingham ME7 ... 10 D3
Chaucer Rd. Sittingbourne ME10 . 36 D3
Chaucer Tech Coll. CT1 ... 88 C7
Cheddar Cl. TN24 ... 139 B4
Cheesmans Cl. CT12 ... 50 C5
Cheffins Ho. ME7 ... 10 E7
Chegwell Dr. ME5 ... 32 B4
Chegworth Gdns. ME10 ... 36 E1
Chegworth La. ME17 ... 100 A6
Chegworth Rd. ME17 ... 99 F5
Chelmar Rd. ME4 ... 10 B4
Chelsea Ct. CT21 ... 176 C1
Chelsea Rd. CT14 ... 67 C4
Cheltenham Cl. ME15 ... 97 F6
Cheney Cl. ME8 ... 33 D5
Cheney Hill. ME9 ... 59 A5
Cheney Rd. ME13 ... 62 F7
Chennels The. TN26 ... 167 C7
Chepstow Ho. 3 ME15 ... 97 F6
Chequer Cl. CT3 ... 71 D2
Chequer's Terr. ME12 ... 5 A5
Chequers Cl. ME5 ... 54 A8
Chequers Ctr. ME15 ... 75 A4
Chequers Hill. CT4 ... 109 C2
Chequers Orch. CT4 ... 109 D2
Chequers Pk. TN25 ... 123 E1
Chequers Rd. ME12 ... 4 E6
Chequertree. TN25 ... 172 A3
Cherbourg Cres. ME5 ... 31 F7
Cheriton Ave. CT12 ... 52 B8
Cheriton Court Rd. CT20 ... 177 C6
Cheriton Cty Prim Sch. CT18 . 177 C6
Cheriton Gdns. CT20 ... 178 C6
Cheriton High St.
  CT18 & CT19 & CT20 ... 177 D6
Cheriton Interchange. CT19 ... 177 C6
Cheriton Pl. Deal CT14 ... 117 D4

Cheriton Pl. Folkestone CT20 ... 178 D4
Cheriton Rd. Deal CT14 ...... 117 D4
Cheriton Rd.
   Folkestone CT19 & CT20 ...... 178 B5
Cheriton Rd.
   Folkestone, Morehall CT19 ...... 177 F6
Cheriton Rd. Gillingham ME8 ...... 33 D8
Cheriton Way. ME16 ...... 74 C7
Cheriton Wood Ho. CT19 ...... 177 D7
Cherries The. ME16 ...... 74 A2
Cherry Amber Cl. ME8 ...... 33 F8
Cherry Ave. CT2 ...... 66 D2
Cherry Cl. ME10 ...... 36 D6
Cherry Cl. Ashford TN23 ...... 139 B1
Cherry Ct. Folkestone CT19 ...... 178 A6
Cherry Dr. CT2 ...... 66 D2
Cherry Fields. ME10 ...... 36 A5
Cherry Garden Ave. CT19 ...... 178 A7
Cherry Garden Cres. TN25 ...... 123 F2
Cherry Garden La. Ash CT3 ...... 71 E1
Cherry Garden La.
   Folkestone CT19 ...... 177 F7
Cherry Garden La. Wye TN25 .. 123 F2
Cherry Garden Rd. CT2 ...... 66 D2
Cherry Gdns. Broadstairs CT10 .. 29 C3
Cherry Gdns. Elham CT4 ...... 144 F5
Cherry Gdns. Herne Bay CT6 ...... 22 F4
Cherry Gdns.
   Littlestone-on-S TN28 ...... 200 D6
Cherry Gdns. Teynham ME9 ...... 38 C2
Cherry Glebe. TN25 ...... 157 E3
Cherry Gr. CT15 ...... 114 B2
Cherry Hill Ct. ME9 ...... 35 B6
Cherry La. CT14 ...... 116 D3
Cherry Orch. Tenterden TN30 ... 179 A6
Cherry Orch. Whitstable CT5 ...... 44 C8
Cherry Orch. Woodchurch TN26 169 A3
Cherry Orchard La. TN25 ...... 172 E4
Cherry Orchard Way. ME16 ...... 74 B3
Cherry Tree Ave. CT16 ...... 149 C1
Cherry Tree Cl. Teynham ME9 .... 38 D2
Cherry Tree Cl.
   West Minster ME12 ...... 3 A8
Cherry Tree Dr. ME13 ...... 39 F3
Cherry Tree Gdns. CT12 ...... 29 B3
Cherry Tree Rd.
   Charing Heath TN27 ...... 119 E7
Cherry Tree Rd. Gillingham ME8 . 33 F8
Cherry View. ME17 ...... 97 B3
Cherry Waye. CT15 ...... 131 D7
Cherrybrook Rd. CT20 ...... 177 D6
Cherrygarden La. CT15 & CT3 .. 113 E7
Cherville La. CT3 ...... 90 C7
Chervilles. ME16 ...... 74 A2
Chesham Dr. ME8 ...... 33 E6
Cheshire Rd.
   Maidstone,Shepway ME15 ...... 97 C7
Cheshire Rd.
   Maidstone,Willington ME15 ...... 75 C2
Chessenden La. TN27 ...... 135 A1
Chester Ave. TN26 ...... 153 D5
Chester Rd. Gillingham ME7 ...... 10 D2
Chester Rd. Westgate-on-S CT8 .. 27 F8
Chestfield Cl. ME8 ...... 11 E2
Chestfield Rd. CT5 ...... 44 C7
Chestfield & Swalecliffe Sta.
   CT5 ...... 21 D2
Chestnut Ave. Blean CT2 ...... 66 A7
Chestnut Ave. Chatham ME5 ...... 31 F3
Chestnut Cl. Ashford TN23 ...... 138 E3
Chestnut Cl. Hythe CT21 ...... 187 E8
Chestnut Cl. Tenterden TN30 ... 167 C1
Chestnut Cl. Whitfield CT16 ... 149 A8
Chestnut Ct. ME13 ...... 64 A3
Chestnut Dr. Broadstairs CT10 .. 29 D4
Chestnut Dr. Coxheath ME17 .... 96 B3
Chestnut Dr. Herne Bay CT6 ...... 22 D3
Chestnut Dr. Kingswood ME17 .... 99 D2
Chestnut Dr. Sturry CT2 ...... 68 A7
Chestnut Dr. Worth CT14 ...... 94 A4
Chestnut La. TN23 ...... 156 C4
Chestnut Rd. CT17 ...... 166 B7
Chestnut St. ME9 ...... 35 E4
Chestnut Terr. TN17 ...... 176 A1
Chestnut Wood La. ME9 ...... 35 E3
Chestnuts The. TN25 ...... 158 D5
Chevalier Ct. CT17 ...... 166 A7
Chevening Cl. ME5 ...... 32 A5
Cheviot Ct. CT10 ...... 30 B5
Cheviot Gdns. ME15 ...... 76 A1
Cheviot Way. TN24 ...... 139 C4
Cheyne Cl. ME10 ...... 36 F8
Cheyne Mid Sch The. ME12 ...... 1 E2
Cheyne Rd. ME12 ...... 5 D3
Chicago Ave. ME7 ...... 10 F5
Chichester Cl. Ashford TN23 ... 139 B1
Chichester Cl. Gillingham ME8 .. 34 A8
Chichester Rd.
   Folkestone CT20 ...... 177 E4
Chichester Rd. Ramsgate CT12 .. 29 B1
Chickfield Gdns. ME5 ...... 10 C2
Chiddingfold Cl. ME12 ...... 4 D6
Chiddingstone Cl. ME15 ...... 97 F6
Chieftain Cl. ME7 ...... 10 C5
Childscroft Rd. ME8 ...... 11 F2
Chilham Ave. CT8 ...... 27 D7
Chilham Castle. CT4 ...... 107 B7
Chilham Cl. Chatham ME4 ...... 9 E3
Chilham Cl. West Minster ME12 .. 1 D4
Chilham Rd. Folkestone CT19 .. 177 E6
Chilham Rd. Gillingham ME8 ...... 11 A3
Chilham Rd. Maidstone ME16 .... 74 C7
Chilham Sta. CT4 ...... 107 D8
Chillington St. ME14 ...... 74 F6
Chilston Rd. ME17 ...... 101 D5

Chiltern Cl. ME15 ...... 75 F1
Chiltern End. TN24 ...... 139 B3
Chilton Ave. Kearsney CT16 ... 148 C4
Chilton Ave.
   Sittingbourne ME10 ...... 37 A3
Chilton Cl. ME8 ...... 11 E1
Chilton Cty Prim Sch. CT11 .... 52 A6
Chilton Field. CT3 ...... 71 D2
Chilton Gdns. CT3 ...... 71 D2
Chilton La. CT11 ...... 52 A6
Chilton Pl. CT3 ...... 71 D2
Chilton Sq. CT3 ...... 71 D2
Chilton Way. CT17 ...... 148 D3
Chimes The. Ashford TN24 ... 139 C3
Chimes The. Rochester ME1 ...... 9 C2
Chippendale Dr. ME5 ...... 31 F1
Chipstead Cl. ME16 ...... 74 D6
Chipstead Rd. ME8 ...... 33 D4
Chislehurst Cl. ME15 ...... 97 F6
Chislet CE Prim Sch. CT3 ...... 47 C5
Chislet Ct. CT6 ...... 22 E5
Chislet Park Cotts. CT3 ...... 46 F1
Chislet Wlk. ME8 ...... 33 D5
Chislett Cl. TN25 ...... 159 E2
Chisnall Rd. CT17 ...... 148 E4
Chitty La. CT3 ...... 47 D6
Christ Church Cath. CT1 ...... 88 A8
Christ Church CE High Sch.
   TN23 ...... 155 F5
Christ Church CE Jun Sch.
   Ramsgate CT11 ...... 52 C6
Christ Church CE Jun Sch.
   Ramsgate CT11 ...... 52 D6
Christ Church CE Prim Sch.
   CT20 ...... 178 C5
Christ Church Coll. CT1 ...... 88 B8
Christ Church Coll
   Post Graduate Ctr. CT2 ...... 67 F1
Christ Church Rd. CT20 ...... 178 C4
Christchurch CE Jun Sch.
   Chatham ME5 ...... 10 C2
Christchurch Ct. 1
   Dover CT17 ...... 166 D7
Christchurch Ho. 9 ME15 ...... 97 E5
Christchurch Rd. TN23 ...... 156 B8
Christchurch St. CT16 ...... 149 B3
Christen Way. ME15 & ME17 .... 97 F3
Christie Cl. ME5 ...... 32 B6
Christmas St. ME7 ...... 10 E7
Christopher's Row. ME9 ...... 60 A3
Chrysler Ave. CT6 ...... 22 B4
Chunnel Ind Est. TN23 ...... 139 B1
Church App. TN28 ...... 200 A6
Church Cl. Mersham TN25 ...... 157 E3
Church Cl. New Romney TN28 .. 200 B6
Church Cliff. CT14 ...... 134 D6
Church Cotts.
   Rodmersham ME9 ...... 59 D8
Church Cotts.
   St Michaels TN30 ...... 167 B3
Church Court Gr. CT10 ...... 29 E6
Church Cres. ME17 ...... 100 F6
Church Ct. CT18 ...... 161 C6
Church Farm Rd. ME9 ...... 12 E3
Church Field. TN25 ...... 160 B1
Church Gn. ME2 ...... 9 C8
Church Haven. CT5 ...... 44 B4
Church Hill.
   Boughton Street ME13 ...... 64 A5
Church Hill. Canterbury CT2 ...... 66 C1
Church Hill.
   Charing Heath ME17 & TN27 ... 119 C7
Church Hill. Chatham ME5 ...... 10 C2
Church Hill. Chilham CT4 ...... 107 B8
Church Hill. Doddington ME9 ...... 80 F8
Church Hill. Eythorne CT15 ...... 131 C8
Church Hill. High Halden TN26 .. 167 E7
Church Hill. Hythe CT21 ...... 176 C2
Church Hill.
   Kingsnorth TN23 & TN25 ...... 156 B2
Church Hill. Ramsgate CT11 .... 52 E7
Church Hill.
   Shepherdswell CT15 ...... 130 D4
Church Hill. Stockbury ME9 ...... 56 F7
Church Hill.
   Stone in Oxney TN30 ...... 189 F3
Church Hill. Sutton CT15 ...... 133 A7
Church Hill. Temple Ewell CT16 148 D5
Church Ho. CT14 ...... 117 C7
Church La. Adisham CT3 ...... 90 D1
Church La. Aldington TN25 ...... 173 D7
Church La.
   Boughton Aluph TN25 ...... 123 B4
Church La. Boyden Gate CT3 .... 47 C7
Church La. Brenzett TN29 ...... 192 A4
Church La. Brenzett TN29 ...... 192 A4
Church La. 21 Canterbury CT1 ... 67 A1
Church La. Canterbury CT1 ...... 87 F8
Church La. Challock TN25 ...... 122 B8
Church La. Chatham ME4 ...... 9 F6
Church La.
   Church Hougham CT15 ...... 165 B5
Church La. Deal CT14 ...... 117 B6
Church La. Harrietsham ME17 ... 100 E6
Church La. Kingston CT4 ...... 111 D3
Church La. Lower Hardres CT4 .... 88 B2
Church La. Lydden CT15 ...... 147 C5
Church La. Maidstone ME14 ...... 76 B4
Church La. New Romney TN28 .. 200 B6
Church La. Newington ME9 ...... 35 B6
Church La. Petham CT4 ...... 109 C3
Church La. Ringwould CT14 ...... 133 F5
Church La. Selling ME13 ...... 84 B6
Church La. Shadoxhurst TN26 .. 170 A7
Church La. Stockbury ME9 ...... 56 E8

Church La. Stowting TN25 ...... 160 A6
Church La. Sturry CT2 ...... 67 F5
Church La. Waltham CT4 ...... 125 F5
Church La. Westbere CT2 ...... 68 C7
Church La. Whitstable CT5 ...... 43 A6
Church La. Womenswold CT4 .... 112 D2
Church Meadows. CT14 ...... 117 A6
Church Mews. ME8 ...... 33 F8
Church Path. Deal CT14 ...... 117 B5
Church Path. Gillingham ME7 .... 10 E6
Church Rd. Ashford TN23 ...... 139 C2
Church Rd. Ashford TN24 ...... 157 A8
Church Rd.
   Boughton Malherbe ME17 ...... 118 A8
Church Rd. 1
   Broadstairs CT10 ...... 30 B4
Church Rd. Burmarsh TN29 ... 185 E4
Church Rd. Charing TN27 ...... 103 D2
Church Rd. Chart Sutton ME17 .. 98 C1
Church Rd. Coldred CT15 ...... 131 A3
Church Rd.
   Coldred Street CT15 ...... 130 F2
Church Rd. Dover CT17 ...... 166 A7
Church Rd. Eastchurch ME12 ...... 5 D2
Church Rd. Eastling ME13 ...... 82 B2
Church Rd. Faversham ME13 ...... 62 D7
Church Rd. Faversham ME13 ...... 62 D8
Church Rd. Folkestone CT20 ... 177 C6
Church Rd. Harrietsham ME17 .. 100 E6
Church Rd. Hoath CT3 ...... 46 E5
Church Rd. Hucking ME17 ...... 56 E1
Church Rd. Hythe CT21 ...... 176 C2
Church Rd. Kenardington TN26 .182 A5
Church Rd. Littlebourne CT3 .... 90 A8
Church Rd. Lydd TN29 ...... 203 C6
Church Rd. Lyminge CT18 ...... 161 C7
Church Rd.
   Maidstone,Shepway ME15 ...... 97 F7
Church Rd.
   Maidstone,Tovil ME15 ...... 74 E2
Church Rd. Margate CT9 ...... 7 J1
Church Rd. Mersham TN25 ...... 157 E3
Church Rd. Molash CT4 ...... 105 F5
Church Rd. New Romney TN28 .. 200 A6
Church Rd. Oare ME13 ...... 40 B3
Church Rd. Ramsgate CT11 ...... 52 E7
Church Rd. Sevington TN24 .... 157 A7
Church Rd. Sevington TN24 .... 157 B6
Church Rd. Sittingbourne ME9 .... 37 C5
Church Rd.
   Sittingbourne, Murston ME10 ...... 37 B5
Church Rd. Smeeth TN25 ...... 158 C4
Church Rd.
   Stalisfield Green ME13 ...... 103 F5
Church Rd. Tenterden TN30 ... 179 A7
Church Sq. 2
   Broadstairs CT10 ...... 30 B4
Church Sq. Lenham ME17 ...... 101 D5
Church St.
   Boughton Monchelsea ME17 .... 97 B2
Church St. Broadstairs CT10 .... 29 E6
Church St. Canterbury CT1 ...... 66 E1
Church St. Chatham ME4 ...... 10 A4
Church St. Deal CT14 ...... 117 B1
Church St. Dover CT16 ...... 166 D7
Church St. Eastry CT13 ...... 93 C2
Church St. Faversham ME13 ...... 62 D8
Church St. Folkestone CT20 ... 178 D4
Church St. Gillingham ME7 ...... 10 E6
Church St. Loose ME15 ...... 96 F5
Church St. Maidstone ME14 ...... 75 A4
Church St.
   Maidstone,Tovil ME15 ...... 74 E2
Church St. Margate CT9 ...... 7 J1
Church St. Minster,Thanet CT12 .. 50 C5
Church St. Nonington CT15 ...... 113 C5
Church St. Rochester ME1 ...... 9 D4
Church St. Rodmersham ME9 .... 59 C8
Church St. 7 Sandwich CT13 .... 73 A1
Church St. 5
   Sittingbourne ME10 ...... 36 E4
Church St. Sittingbourne ME10 .. 36 E5
Church St. Whitstable CT5 ...... 20 F1
Church St.
   Woodnesborough CT13 ...... 93 B6
Church St. Wye TN25 ...... 123 E2
Church Street St Mary's.
   CT13 ...... 72 F1
Church Street (St Pauls). 6
   CT1 ...... 88 A8
Church Terr. ME5 ...... 10 C2
Church View. Aldington TN25 ... 173 A6
Church View. Herne Bay CT6 .... 23 C4
Church View. Newchurch TN29 . 184 E3
Church View. Worth CT14 ...... 94 B5
Church Way. CT5 ...... 21 D3
Church Whitfield Rd. CT15 ... 149 B8
Church Wlk. CT4 ...... 144 F4
Church Wood Cl. CT2 ...... 66 B2
Church Yd. TN23 ...... 139 C2
Church Yard Pas. 10 TN23 ... 139 B2
Churchfield Pl. CT9 ...... 7 I2
Churchfield Way. TN25 ...... 123 E2
Churchfields. Broadstairs CT10 .. 29 F7
Churchfields. Margate CT9 ...... 7 J1
Churchfields Terr. ME1 ...... 9 B4
Churchill Ave. Chatham ME5 .... 32 A7
Churchill Ave. Deal CT14 ...... 117 C7
Churchill Ave. Folkestone CT19 178 C4
Churchill Ave. Herne Bay CT6 .... 23 D7
Churchill Cl. Bridge CT4 ...... 88 F1
Churchill Cl. Folkestone CT19 .. 178 D8
Churchill Cl.
   St Margaret's at Cliffe CT15 .. 150 F5
Churchill Cotts. ME17 ...... 98 F6
Churchill Ct. CT21 ...... 176 B1

Churchill Ho. 2
   Folkestone CT20 ...... 177 F5
Churchill Ho.
   Sittingbourne ME10 ...... 37 C4
Churchill Ho. Teynham ME9 .... 38 C3
Churchill Rd. Canterbury CT1 .... 88 C6
Churchill Rd. Minster ME12 ...... 4 D6
Churchill St. 7 CT16 ...... 149 C1
Churchill Way. ME13 ...... 40 B1
Churchill Wlk. CT18 ...... 162 F4
Churchlands Ho. TN28 ...... 200 B6
Churchlands The. TN28 ...... 200 B6
Churchwood Dr. CT5 ...... 21 D1
Chute Cl. ME14 ...... 33 D4
Cinder Path. CT10 ...... 30 A4
Cinnabar Cl. ME5 ...... 32 A1
Cinque Ports Ave. CT21 ...... 176 B1
Circular Rd. Dover CT16 ...... 150 B1
Circular Rd. Finglesham CT14 ... 116 B7
Circus The. CT6 ...... 22 C4
Citadel Cres. CT17 ...... 166 B6
Citadel Hts. CT17 ...... 166 B6
Citadel Rd. CT17 ...... 166 C6
Citroen Cl. CT6 ...... 22 B4
City Bsns Pk. CT1 ...... 67 C3
City View. CT2 ...... 87 C8
City Way. ME1 ...... 9 D2
Claire Cl. Birchington CT7 ...... 26 F7
Claire Cl. Broadstairs CT10 ...... 30 B5
Claire Ho. ME16 ...... 74 E5
Clandon Rd. ME5 ...... 32 D2
Clanwilliam Rd. CT14 ...... 117 D5
Clapham Hill. CT5 ...... 43 D5
Clapton Cl. ME8 ...... 33 D8
Clare Dr. CT6 ...... 22 C2
Clare Rd. CT5 ...... 20 E2
Claremont Cl. CT14 ...... 134 C6
Claremont Gdns. CT11 ...... 52 C7
Claremont Pl. CT1 ...... 87 F7
Claremont Rd. Deal CT14 ...... 117 B5
Claremont Rd.
   Folkestone CT20 ...... 178 C5
Claremont Rd.
   Kingsdown CT14 ...... 134 C6
Claremont St. CT6 ...... 22 C4
Claremont Terr. CT13 ...... 93 D7
Claremont Way. 1 ME4 ...... 9 F3
Clarence Ave. Margate CT9 ...... 8 D2
Clarence Ave. Rochester ME1 .... 9 C4
Clarence Cl. ME14 ...... 75 E4
Clarence Gdns. ME12 ...... 6 E3
Clarence Pl. Deal CT14 ...... 117 D7
Clarence Pl. Dover CT17 ...... 166 D5
Clarence Rd. Capel-le-F CT18 .. 164 B2
Clarence Rd. Chatham ME4 ...... 10 B2
Clarence Rd. Deal CT14 ...... 117 D3
Clarence Rd. Herne Bay CT6 .... 22 D5
Clarence Rd. Ramsgate CT11 .... 52 C6
Clarence Row. ME12 ...... 1 C2
Clarence St. Folkestone CT20 .. 178 D5
Clarence St. Herne Bay CT6 .... 22 E5
Clarendon Cl. Maidstone ME14 .. 76 A4
Clarendon Cl.
   Sittingbourne ME10 ...... 36 F1
Clarendon Gdns. 7 CT11 ...... 52 D6
Clarendon House Gram Sch.
   CT11 ...... 52 E6
Clarendon Mews.
   Broadstairs CT10 ...... 30 A4
Clarendon Mews.
   New Romney TN28 ...... 200 C8
Clarendon Pl. Dover CT17 ...... 166 C7
Clarendon Pl. Maidstone ME14 .. 75 A4
Clarendon Rd. Aylesham CT3 ... 112 F5
Clarendon Rd.
   Broadstairs CT10 ...... 30 A4
Clarendon Rd. Dover CT17 ...... 166 C7
Clarendon St. Dover CT17 ...... 166 C7
Clarendon St. Herne Bay CT6 .... 22 C4
Claridge Cl. ME7 ...... 32 F4
Claridge Mews. CT21 ...... 176 C2
Clarke Rd. ME8 ...... 200 E4
Clarke's Cl. CT14 ...... 116 F4
Clarklands. TN29 ...... 184 E3
Clavell Cl. ME8 ...... 33 E4
Claxfield Cotts. ME9 ...... 38 A2
Claxfield Rd. ME9 ...... 60 A8
Claygate. Ashford TN23 ...... 155 F5
Claygate. Maidstone ME15 ...... 75 D2
Clearmount Dr. TN27 ...... 120 C8
Cleave Rd. ME7 ...... 10 E3
Cleaver La. CT11 ...... 52 E7
Clematis Ave. ME8 ...... 33 B5
Clement Cl. CT1 ...... 67 B1
Clement Rd. ME16 ...... 74 D5
Clement's Rd. CT12 ...... 29 C2
Clementine Cl. CT6 ...... 23 D4
Clerke Dr. ME10 ...... 37 A8
Clermont Cl. ME7 ...... 33 A4
Cleveland Ct. TN25 ...... 105 B2
Cleveland Cl. CT16 ...... 149 B3
Cleveland Ho. ME16 ...... 74 B2
Cleveland Rd. ME7 ...... 10 C6
Cleveley Lodge. CT11 ...... 29 E2
Cleves Way. TN23 ...... 155 E8
Clewson Rise. ME14 ...... 75 B8
Cliff Ave. CT6 ...... 23 C5
Cliff Cl. CT17 ...... 176 D3
Cliff Dr. Herne Bay CT6 ...... 22 D4
Cliff Dr. Warden ME12 ...... 6 C4
Cliff Field. ME8 ...... 27 C8
Cliff Gdns. ME12 ...... 4 E7
Cliff Hill. ME17 ...... 97 D4

Cliff Hill Rd. ME17 ...... 97 C4
Cliff Prom. CT10 ...... 30 C7
Cliff Rd. Birchington CT7 ...... 26 F8
Cliff Rd. Broadstairs CT10 ...... 30 B7
Cliff Rd. Dover CT15 & CT16 .... 150 C1
Cliff Rd. Folkestone CT20 ...... 178 A3
Cliff Rd. Hythe CT21 ...... 176 E3
Cliff Rd. Whitstable CT5 ...... 20 F3
Cliff Sea Gr. CT6 ...... 22 C4
Cliff Terr. CT9 ...... 7 J3
Cliff View Gdns.
   Leysdown-on-S ME12 ...... 6 D1
Cliff View Gdns. Warden ME12 .. 6 E4
Cliff View Rd. CT12 ...... 51 D6
Cliffe Ave. CT9 ...... 7 F1
Cliffe Rd. CT20 ...... 178 A3
Cliffe Rd. Kingsdown CT14 ...... 134 D6
Cliffe Rd. Rochester ME2 ...... 9 B8
Cliffestone Ct. CT20 ...... 178 B5
Clifford Gdns. CT14 ...... 117 B2
Clifford St. CT5 ...... 43 F8
Cliffs End Gr. CT12 ...... 51 D5
Cliffs End Rd. CT12 ...... 51 E5
Cliffside Dr. CT10 ...... 30 A1
Clifftown Gdns. CT6 ...... 22 B4
Clifton Cl. ME14 ...... 75 B5
Clifton Cres. CT20 ...... 178 B3
Clifton Gdns. Canterbury CT2 ... 66 D2
Clifton Gdns. Folkestone CT20 .. 178 C4
Clifton Gdns. Margate CT9 ...... 7 J3
Clifton Lawn. CT11 ...... 52 D5
Clifton Mansions. 4 CT20 ...... 178 C4
Clifton Pl. CT20 ...... 8 A3
Clifton Rd. Folkestone CT20 ... 178 C4
Clifton Rd. Gillingham ME7 ...... 10 C7
Clifton Rd. Margate CT9 ...... 8 A2
Clifton Rd. Ramsgate CT11 ...... 52 D8
Clifton Rd. Whitstable CT5 ...... 20 D1
Clifton St. CT9 ...... 7 J3
Cliftonville Ave. Margate CT9 .... 8 A2
Cliftonville Ave. Ramsgate CT12 . 29 B1
Cliftonville Ct. CT9 ...... 8 A3
Cliftonville Cty Prim Sch. CT9 .. 8 C2
Cliftonville Mews. CT9 ...... 8 A3
Clim Down. CT14 ...... 134 D6
Clinton Cl. ME17 ...... 96 B3
Clints La. CT4 ...... 129 D4
Clipper Cl. ME2 ...... 9 E7
Clipper Ct. ME2 ...... 9 E7
Clive Dennis Ct. TN24 ...... 139 E1
Clive Rd. Cliffs End CT12 ...... 51 D6
Clive Rd. Margate CT9 ...... 29 A5
Clive Rd. Rochester ME1 ...... 9 A4
Clive Rd. Sittingbourne ME10 .... 36 B5
Clockhouse. TN23 ...... 138 F1
Clockhouse Pk. TN25 ...... 105 C2
Cloisterham Rd. ME1 ...... 31 D7
Cloisters The. 7
   Canterbury CT1 ...... 66 F1
Cloisters The. Lenham ME17 .... 101 C5
Cloisters The. Ramsgate CT11 .. 52 D5
Cloisters The. 7
   Sittingbourne ME10 ...... 36 E4
Close The. Ashford TN23 ...... 155 F7
Close The. Bridge CT4 ...... 88 F1
Close The. Canterbury CT2 ...... 66 F4
Close The. Faversham ME13 .... 62 C6
Close The. Folkestone CT19 ... 178 E8
Close The. Hythe CT21 ...... 176 B4
Close The. Lydden CT15 ...... 147 F8
Close The. Rochester ME1 ...... 9 C4
Close The. Wye TN25 ...... 123 E2
Close The (St Edmunds Sch).
   CT2 ...... 66 C3
Cloudesley Cl. ME1 ...... 9 B1
Clovelly. TN28 ...... 200 E6
Clovelly Dr. ME12 ...... 4 B8
Clovelly Rd. CT5 ...... 43 D7
Clover Bank View. ME5 ...... 32 B6
Clover Cl. ME10 ...... 37 B5
Clover Rise. CT5 ...... 21 B1
Clover St. ME4 ...... 9 F4
Clowes Ct. CT2 ...... 66 C4
Clubb's La. TN29 ...... 197 D2
Cluny Rd. ME13 ...... 62 F7
Clyde Cotts. ME1 ...... 1 E2
Clyde St. 1 Canterbury CT1 ...... 67 A1
Clyde St. Sheerness ME12 ...... 1 E2
Clynton Way. TN23 ...... 156 A7
Coach Dr. TN26 ...... 138 A7
Coach Rd. Densole CT18 ...... 162 F8
Coach Rd. Egerton TN27 ...... 118 E6
Coalpit La. ME9 ...... 80 A6
Coast Dr.
   Littlestone-on-S TN28 ...... 200 E3
Coast Dr. Lydd-on-S TN29 ...... 204 F2
Coast Dr. St Mary's Bay TN29 .. 194 F2
Coast Rd. TN28 & TN29 ...... 200 F7
Coastguard Alley. CT5 ...... 20 C1
Coastguard Cotts.
   Conyer ME9 ...... 38 E6
Coastguard Cotts.
   Dover CT16 ...... 166 G8
Coastguard Cotts.
   Herne Bay CT6 ...... 21 F4
Coastguard Cotts. Hythe CT21 . 176 B1
Coastguard Cotts.
   Kingsdown CT14 ...... 134 D4
Coastguard Cotts.
   Leysdown-on-S ME12 ...... 19 C4
Coastguard Cotts. Minster ME12 . 5 C5
Coastguard Cotts.
   Ramsgate CT11 ...... 52 A5
Coastguard Cotts. 18
   Ramsgate CT11 ...... 52 F7
Coastguard Cotts.
   Sandwich CT13 ...... 95 B7

Coastguard Cotts The. ME12 .... 1 I1
Coastguard Hos. ME12 .... 6 C5
Coats Ave. ME12 .... 3 A8
Cobay Cl. CT21 .... 176 D2
Cobb Ct. CT9 .... 7 I3
Cobb Wlk. ME13 .... 62 B8
Cobblers Bridge Rd. CT6 .... 22 D3
Cobblestones. ME7 .... 32 F5
Cobbs Hill. CT4 .... 85 C2
Cobbs Mews. 2 CT20 .... 178 C4
Cobbs Pl. CT9 .... 7 I3
Cobbs Wood Ind Est. TN23 .... 138 F2
Cobden Rd. 18 CT1 .... 67 A1
Cobden Rd. CT21 .... 176 B1
Cobdown Gr. ME8 .... 12 A2
Cobfield. ME17 .... 98 A1
Cobham Ave. ME10 .... 36 E1
Cobham Chase. ME13 .... 62 B8
Cobham Cl. Canterbury CT1 .... 88 C6
Cobham Cl. Maidstone ME16 .... 74 E4
Cobsden Cl. ME29 .... 195 A4
Cobsden Rd. TN29 .... 195 A4
Cobtree Cl. ME5 .... 32 C8
Cobtree Rd. ME17 .... 96 C3
Cobtree Wharf. ME20 .... 53 C2
Cock La. Elham CT4 .... 144 F4
Cock La. Hamstreet TN26 .... 183 A7
Cockering Rd. CT1 & CT4 .... 87 B4
Cockreed La. TN28 .... 200 B7
Codrington Rd. CT11 .... 52 D7
Cogans Terr. CT1 .... 87 E6
Coggan Ho. 7 CT1 .... 87 F7
Coinston Ave. CT11 .... 52 A7
Colburn Rd. CT10 .... 30 A2
Colchester Cl. ME5 .... 32 A4
Cold Harbour. CT1 .... 67 A2
Cold Harbour La. ME9 .... 35 F6
Cold Harbour Rd.
  ME13 & ME17 .... 103 A7
Coldblow. CT14 .... 117 A1
Coldblow La. Thurnham ME14 .... 56 A2
Coldblow La.
  Woodchurch TN26 .... 169 D4
Coldbridge La. TN27 .... 118 B5
Coldharbour La.
  Aylesford ME20 .... 53 A1
Coldharbour La.
  Bekesbourne CT4 .... 111 D7
Coldharbour La. Hucking ME14 .. 56 B1
Coldharbour La.
  Old Romney TN29 .... 198 C5
Coldharbour La.
  Sittingbourne ME10 .... 14 F1
Coldharbour La. Wye TN25 .... 124 A2
Coldred Hill. CT15 .... 130 F1
Coldred Rd. Coldred CT15 .... 131 B5
Coldred Rd. Park Wood ME15 .... 97 F4
Coldred Rd.
  Shepherdswell CT15 .... 130 E3
Coldswood Rd. CT12 .... 28 F2
Cole Rd. ME13 .... 62 E7
Cole Terr. ME17 .... 101 C4
Colegate Dr. ME14 .... 76 C4
Colegates Cl. ME13 .... 40 B2
Colegates Ct. ME13 .... 40 B2
Colegates Rd. ME13 .... 40 A2
Coleman Cres. CT12 .... 29 C1
Coleman's Stairs Rd. CT7 .... 27 A8
Coleman's Yd. 3 CT11 .... 52 E6
Colemans Cl. TN29 .... 203 D7
Coleridge Gdns. CT3 .... 112 F6
Coleshall Cl. ME15 .... 97 F6
Coleshall Cotts. ME9 .... 14 D3
Colette Cl. CT10 .... 8 G2
Coleville Cres. TN29 .... 204 E7
Colewood Rd. CT5 .... 21 E3
Colfe Way. ME10 .... 37 A8
Colin's Way. CT21 .... 177 A3
Collard Cl. CT6 .... 23 A4
Collard Rd. ME14 .... 157 A8
Collards Cl. CT12 .... 49 D7
Collards La. CT4 .... 144 E3
College Ave. Gillingham ME7 .... 10 B4
College Ave. Maidstone ME15 .... 74 F3
College Cotts. ME8 .... 74 F3
College Ct. Ashford TN23 .... 139 C2
College Ct. 5 Maidstone ME15 .. 75 A3
College Rd. Canterbury CT1 .... 67 B1
College Rd. Chatham ME4 .... 10 A7
College Rd. Deal CT14 .... 117 D8
College Rd. Maidstone ME15 .... 74 F2
College Rd. Margate CT9 .... 8 A1
College Rd. Margate CT9 .... 28 F8
College Rd. Ramsgate CT11 .... 29 E1
College Rd.
  Sittingbourne ME10 .... 36 D3
College Row. CT17 .... 166 B7
College Sq. 2 CT9 .... 7 J2
College Way. CT3 .... 91 A7
College Wlk. 3 CT9 .... 7 J2
College Yd. ME1 .... 9 C6
Collet Wlk. ME8 .... 33 D4
Collett Cl. TN25 .... 142 D8
Collingbourne. TN23 .... 155 E6
Collings Wlk. ME8 .... 33 D4
Collington Terr. ME15 .... 97 E4
Collingwood Cl.
  Broadstairs CT10 .... 29 E4
Collingwood Cl.
  Westgate-on-S CT8 .... 27 D7
Collingwood Ct. CT20 .... 177 E5
Collingwood Ind Ctr. ME17 .... 98 E2
Collingwood Rd.
  Kit's Coty ME20 .... 53 C7
Collingwood Rd.
  St Margaret's at Cliffe CT15 .... 150 F8
Collingwood Rd.
  Whitstable CT5 .... 20 C1

Collingwood Rd E.
  CT14 & CT15 .... 134 A1
Collingwood Rise. CT20 .... 177 E5
Collingwood Wlk. ME10 .... 36 B5
Collins Rd. CT6 .... 22 C2
Collis St. ME2 .... 9 A8
Collison Pl. TN30 .... 179 D7
Colman Ho. 2 ME14 .... 75 A4
Colombo Sq. CT12 .... 29 A1
Colonel's La. ME13 .... 64 A3
Colorado Cl. CT16 .... 149 B3
Colton Cres. CT16 .... 149 B4
Coltsfoot Dr. ME14 .... 75 F4
Columbia Ave. CT5 .... 43 B7
Command Rd. ME14 .... 74 F8
Commercial Rd. ME2 .... 9 A7
Commissioner's Rd. ME2 .... 9 C8
Commodore Rd. ME14 .... 75 C5
Common La. CT17 .... 148 E3
Common Rd. ME1 .... 31 B1
Common The. ME1 .... 9 C6
Common Way. ME14 .... 138 A7
Commonwealth Cl. ME10 .... 37 B3
Compass Cl. ME4 .... 9 C1
Compass Ctr. ME4 .... 10 B8
Compton Cl. ME5 .... 32 D2
Concord Ave. ME5 .... 31 E5
Conduit St. ME13 .... 62 D8
Conference Wlk. CT1 .... 88 C8
Conifer Ct. CT1 .... 7 D1
Conifer Dr. ME5 .... 32 D1
Coniston Cl. ME7 .... 11 A6
Coniston Dr. CT3 .... 112 F6
Coniston Rd. CT19 .... 178 B2
Connaught Barracks. CT16 .... 149 E1
Connaught Cl. ME15 .... 97 F4
Connaught Gdns. 9 CT9 .... 7 J1
Connaught Mews. ME4 .... 10 C2
Connaught Rd. Chatham ME4 .... 10 C2
Connaught Rd. Dover CT16 .... 149 D1
Connaught Rd.
  Folkestone CT20 .... 178 D5
Connaught Rd. Gillingham ME7 .. 10 B5
Connaught Rd. Margate CT9 .... 7 J1
Connaught Rd.
  Sittingbourne ME10 .... 36 E3
Conquest Ind Est. ME2 .... 9 A6
Conrad Ave. CT1 .... 67 C3
Conrad Cl. ME8 .... 33 D4
Consort Cl. ME4 .... 75 B5
Constable Rd. CT7 .... 27 A8
Constable's Rd. CT16 .... 166 E8
Constancia Ct. CT20 .... 178 C5
Constitution Hill. ME4 .... 10 B3
Constitution Rd. ME4 .... 10 C2
Consul Cl. CT6 .... 22 B4
Continental App. CT9 .... 28 F6
Convent Cl. CT15 .... 151 B6
Convent Rd. CT10 .... 8 G1
Convent Wlk. CT11 .... 52 B5
Conway Cl. CT7 .... 26 E7
Conway Mews. ME7 .... 10 A6
Conway Rd. ME16 .... 74 C6
Conyer Rd. ME9 .... 38 F4
Conyers Wlk. ME8 .... 33 D4
Conyngham Cl. CT12 .... 29 B2
Conyngham La. CT4 .... 89 A2
Conyngham Rd. Herne Bay CT6 .. 23 D5
Conyngham Rd. Minster, Thanet
  CT12 .... 50 C5
Cooden Cl. ME8 .... 12 A2
Cook Cl. ME5 .... 32 C6
Cook's Lea. CT13 .... 93 B2
Cookham Hill. ME1 .... 9 A2
Cookham Wood Rd. ME1 .... 31 B8
Cooks La. ME8 .... 36 F6
Cooling Cl. ME14 .... 75 C6
Coolinge La. CT20 .... 177 F4
Coolinge Rd. CT20 .... 178 D5
Coombe Cl. Chatham ME5 .... 32 B3
Coombe Cl. Dover CT17 .... 149 A1
Coombe Ct. CT17 .... 149 A1
Coombe Dr. ME10 .... 37 C4
Coombe La. Ash CT3 .... 92 E8
Coombe La. Tenterden TN30 .... 179 A7
Coombe Lands. TN30 .... 188 D4
Coombe Rd. Dover CT17 .... 148 F1
Coombe Rd. Dover CT15, CT17. 165 E8
Coombe Rd. Folkestone CT19 .... 177 F6
Coombe Rd. Maidstone ME15 .... 74 F2
Coombe Valley Rd. CT17 .... 149 A1
Coombe Way. CT18 .... 163 C4
Coombe Wlk. CT5 .... 43 A2
Coombe Wood La. CT18 .... 163 C4
Cooper Cl. ME5 .... 32 B3
Cooper Street Dro. CT3 .... 72 B4
Cooper's Hill. CT14 .... 22 F5
Cooper's La. TN25 .... 158 F2
Coopers La. CT1 .... 87 E7
Cooting La. CT3 .... 112 D8
Cooting Rd. CT3 .... 112 E4
Cop Street Dro. CT3 .... 71 D3
Copenhagen Rd. ME7 .... 10 C4
Copinger Cl. CT2 .... 67 A4
Copland Ave. ME12 .... 4 C6
Copper Tree Ct. ME15 .... 97 A5
Copper Tree Wlk. ME5 .... 32 C1
Copperfield. ME15 .... 2 F6
Copperfield Cl. TN24 .... 139 C6
Copperfield Ct. CT10 .... 30 B5
Copperfield Dr. ME17 .... 98 E4
Copperfield Ho. ME4 .... 10 A4
Copperfield Rd. ME1 .... 9 C2
Copperfields. TN29 .... 203 B6
Copperfields The. ME1 .... 9 B4
Coppergate. Canterbury CT2 .... 66 F2
Coppergate. Gillingham ME7 .... 32 F5
Copperhouse La. ME7 .... 11 B6

Copperhurst Wlk. CT9 .... 8 F2
Copperwood. TN24 .... 139 C4
Coppice Ct. ME7 .... 33 B4
Coppice Rd. ME5 .... 32 C2
Coppice The. CT3 .... 67 F6
Coppice View. ME14 .... 75 E6
Coppin St. CT14 .... 117 D6
Coppins La. ME9 .... 36 B2
Copse The. TN23 .... 138 D3
Copsewood Way. ME15 .... 76 A3
Copt Cl. CT2 .... 67 F7
Copthall Gdns. 10 CT20 .... 178 D5
Cordingham Rd. CT5 .... 43 A6
Cordova Ct. CT20 .... 178 A4
Corkwell St. ME4 .... 9 E3
Corner Cotts. TN26 .... 182 A6
Corner Field. TN23 .... 156 B5
Corner The. TN25 .... 173 A6
Cornerways. CT21 .... 176 B4
Cornflower Cl. ME14 .... 75 E4
Cornford Rd. CT7 .... 27 A7
Cornhill. 12 CT11 .... 52 E6
Corniche The. CT20 .... 177 C3
Cornwall Ave. CT11 .... 52 F8
Cornwall Cl. ME15 .... 97 E7
Cornwall Gdns.
  Canterbury CT1 .... 88 D7
Cornwall Gdns. Margate CT9 .... 8 B3
Cornwall Ho. Deal CT14 .... 117 A5
Cornwall Ho. 5 Dover CT17 .. 166 D7
Cornwall Rd. Deal CT14 .... 117 C3
Cornwall Rd. Gillingham ME7 .... 10 D6
Cornwall Rd. Herne Bay CT6 .... 22 B2
Cornwall Rd. Rochester ME1 .... 9 C3
Cornwallis Ave.
  Aylesham CT3 .... 112 F6
Cornwallis Ave. Chatham ME4 .... 9 E1
Cornwallis Ave.
  Folkestone CT19 .... 178 B6
Cornwallis Ave.
  Gillingham ME8 .... 11 A4
Cornwallis Ave. Herne Bay CT6 .. 23 C3
Cornwallis Circ. CT5 .... 20 C1
Cornwallis Cl. Ashford TN24 .... 157 B7
Cornwallis Cl. Folkestone CT19 . 178 B6
Cornwallis Cotts. ME17 .... 96 E2
Cornwallis Gdns. CT10 .... 30 A6
Cornwallis Rd. ME16 .... 74 D4
Cornwallis Sch The. ME15 .... 96 F2
Coronation Cl. CT10 .... 29 E7
Coronation Cotts. CT19 .... 177 D6
Coronation Cres. Margate CT9 .... 28 B8
Coronation Cres.
  Queenborough ME11 .... 2 F5
Coronation Dr.
  Great Chart TN23 .... 138 C1
Coronation Flats. 2 ME4 .... 9 F3
Coronation Rd. Chatham ME5 .... 10 C2
Coronation Rd. Ramsgate CT11 .. 52 D6
Coronation Rd.
  Sheerness ME12 .... 1 E1
Coronation Sq. TN29 .... 203 C6
Corone Cl. CT19 .... 178 A7
Corporation Rd. ME7 .... 10 D7
Corporation St. ME1 .... 9 C5
Corral Cl. ME5 .... 10 D2
Corrall Almshouses. 4 ME15. 75 A3
Corrance St. ME15 .... 97 A8
Corsican Wlk. CT6 .... 23 C3
Cortland Cl. ME10 .... 36 E6
Cortland Mews. ME10 .... 36 E6
Corunna Cl. CT21 .... 176 A2
Corunna Pl. CT16 .... 149 E3
Corylus Dr. CT5 .... 43 A7
Cossack St. ME1 .... 9 D3
Cossington Rd. Canterbury CT1 .. 88 A7
Cossington Rd. Chatham ME5 .... 32 B1
Cosway Cotts. TN25 .... 172 C1
Cotswold Cl. TN24 .... 139 B4
Cotswold Gdns. ME15 .... 76 A2
Cottage Rd. Chatham ME4 .... 9 F6
Cottage Rd. Ramsgate CT11 .... 52 E6
Cottage Row. CT13 .... 72 F1
Cottall Ave. ME4 .... 9 E3
Cottington Rd. CT12 .... 51 B5
Cotton Hill Wlk. TN26 .... 183 A7
Cotton Rd. CT1 .... 87 E7
Coulman St. ME7 .... 10 D5
Coulson Gr. CT14 .... 116 A5
Coulter Rd. CT6 .... 22 B2
Coulters Cl. ME14 .... 75 D5
Council Cotts. ME15 .... 96 A4
Countess Mountbatten Ct.
  .... 27 E8
Country's Field. TN29 .... 195 C8
County Rd. ME14 .... 75 A5
County Sq. 8 TN23 .... 139 B2
Court Cotts. CT17 .... 25 E2
Court Dr. ME16 .... 74 D4
Court Flats. CT3 .... 91 A7
Court Hall. ME11 .... 2 F5
Court Hill. CT3 .... 68 E2
Court Hill Ho. CT16 .... 148 E4
Court House Farm. CT15 .... 113 E5
Court La. Detling ME14 .... 55 C5
Court La. Preston CT3 .... 70 B6
Court Lodge Cotts. ME15 .... 96 A7
Court Lodge Rd.
  Appledore TN26 .... 190 C7
Court Lodge Rd.
  Gillingham ME7 .... 10 F6
Court Meadow. ME8 .... 11 B2
Court Meadows. CT3 .... 89 F8
Court Pl. CT20 .... 178 D5
Court Rd. Deal CT14 .... 117 B1
Court Rd. Eccles ME1 .... 53 A6
Court Rd. Sittingbourne ME10 .... 36 F7

Court Rd.
  St Nicholas at Wade CT7 .... 25 E2
Court St. ME13 .... 62 D7
Court Wurtin. TN23 .... 156 A7
Courtenay Rd.
  Boughton Street CT2 & ME13 .... 64 E5
Courtenay Rd. Deal CT14 .... 117 C8
Courtenay Rd. Maidstone ME15 .. 74 F2
Courteney Rd. Gillingham ME8 .. 33 B8
Courtfield Ave. ME5 .... 32 B3
Courtland Ave. CT16 .... 149 A6
Courtland Dr. CT16 .... 148 E4
Courtlands. Herne Bay CT6 .... 23 B3
Courtlands. Kingsdown CT14 .... 134 D6
Courtlands Way. CT8 .... 7 D1
Courts The. CT9 .... 7 E1
Courtyard The. Gillingham ME7 .. 33 A8
Courtyard The. Staple CT3 .... 92 A6
Coventina Ho. 1 .... 52 D7
Coventon La. CT13 & CT14 .... 94 A5
Coventry Gdns. CT6 .... 23 E5
Coverdale Ave. ME15 .... 97 D6
Coverdale Cl. ME5 .... 32 B7
Covert Rd. CT3 .... 138 E1
Covert Rd. CT3 .... 112 E4
Covert The. ME5 .... 32 B1
Covet La. CT4 .... 111 C2
Cow La. Canterbury CT1 .... 87 D7
Cow La. Dover CT17 .... 166 A7
Cowbeck Cl. ME8 .... 33 D6
Cowden Rd. ME4 .... 75 C5
Cowdray Rd. CT14 .... 117 A3
Cowdray Sq. CT14 .... 117 A3
Cowdrey Cl. Ashford TN24 .... 157 A7
Cowdrey Cl. Rochester ME1 .... 9 B2
Cowdrey Pl. CT1 .... 88 B6
Cowgate Hill. CT16 & CT17 .... 166 D7
Cowgate La. CT18 .... 163 C5
Cowley Rise. CT9 .... 29 C8
Cowper Cl. CT5 .... 21 D3
Cowper Rd. Deal CT14 .... 117 C5
Cowper Rd. Gillingham ME7 .... 10 D3
Cowper Rd. Margate CT9 .... 7 J1
Cowper Rd. River CT17 .... 148 E3
Cowper Rd. Sittingbourne ME10 .. 37 B4
Cowstead Rd. ME9 .... 34 D2
Cox St. ME14 .... 55 E6
Coxes Ave. CT12 .... 29 B3
Coxes La. CT12 .... 29 B3
Coxett Hill. ME13 .... 61 D5
Coxheath Cty Prim Sch. ME17 . 96 C3
Coxhill. CT15 .... 130 C3
Coxhill Cres. CT17 .... 148 D3
Coxhill Gdns. CT17 .... 148 D3
Cozenton Cl. ME8 .... 11 E1
Crabble Ave. CT17 .... 149 A2
Crabble Cl. CT17 .... 148 F2
Crabble Hill. CT16 & CT17 .... 149 A2
Crabble La. CT15 & CT17 .... 148 E1
Crabble Meadows. CT17 .... 149 A2
Crabble Rd. CT17 .... 149 A3
Crabble Water Mill. CT17 .... 148 F3
Crabtree La. ME17 .... 119 B8
Crabtree Rd. ME8 .... 33 D8
Crackstake. CT3 .... 71 D2
Craddock Dr. 8 CT1 .... 67 B1
Craddock Rd. CT1 .... 67 B1
Craddock Way. ME8 .... 33 D5
Cradle Bridge Dr. TN24 .... 139 F2
Cradles Rd. ME9 .... 34 C2
Crafford St. CT16 .... 149 D1
Cragie Wlk. ME8 .... 33 E4
Crampton Cl. CT10 .... 30 A4
Cranborne Ave. ME15 .... 75 C1
Cranbourne Ave. ME15 .... 97 B8
Cranbourne Cl. CT11 .... 52 F8
Cranbourne Wlk. CT2 .... 66 A2
Cranbrook Cl. Gillingham ME8 .... 11 C3
Cranbrook Cl. Maidstone ME15 .. 97 F7
Cranbrook Cl. Margate CT9 .... 8 E1
Cranbrook Dr. ME10 .... 36 D1
Cranbrooks. TN25 .... 157 D4
Cranford Cl. ME8 .... 11 D1
Cranleigh Dr. CT16 .... 149 B7
Cranleigh Gdns. Chatham ME5 .... 9 D3
Cranleigh Gdns.
  Maidstone ME16 .... 74 C7
Cranleigh Gdns.
  Whitstable CT5 .... 43 E8
Cranmer Ct. ME15 .... 97 B8
Cranswick Cotts. CT14 .... 133 C8
Craufurd Gn. CT20 .... 177 D5
Craven Cl. CT9 .... 28 C8
Crawford Gdns. CT9 .... 8 B2
Crawford Rd. CT10 .... 29 F5
Crayford Cl. ME14 .... 75 C6
Craythorne. TN30 .... 179 B8
Craythorne Cl. Hythe CT21 .... 177 B4
Craythorne Cl.
  New Romney TN28 .... 200 B8
Craythorne La. TN28 .... 200 B7
Cremer Cl. CT4 .... 86 C1
Cremer Pl. ME13 .... 62 A8
Cremers Rd. ME10 .... 37 B5
Crescent Rd. Birchington CT7 .... 27 A7
Crescent Rd. Broadstairs CT10 .. 30 C8
Crescent Rd. Faversham ME13 .. 62 D7
Crescent Rd. Margate CT9 .... 7 H2
Crescent Rd. Ramsgate CT11 .. 52 D7
Crescent St. 1 ME10 .... 36 E5
Crescent The. Aylesham CT15 .. 113 A3
Crescent The.
  Boughton Street ME13 .... 64 E5
Crescent The. Canterbury CT2 .... 66 F4
Crescent The. Chartham CT4 .... 86 D1
Crescent The.
  Folkestone CT20 .... 177 E3

Crescent The.
  Halfway Houses ME12 .... 3 E6
Crescent The.
  Lower Halstow ME9 .... 13 C3
Crescent The. Maidstone ME14 .. 74 F8
Crescent The. Sandwich CT13 .. 93 E6
Crescent The. Sheerness ME12 .... 1 D2
Crescent The.
  Sittingbourne ME10 .... 15 A1
Crescent The.
  St Margaret's at Cliffe CT15 .. 151 A5
Crescent The. Teynham ME9 .... 38 D3
Crescent Way. ME5 .... 31 D5
Cress Way. ME13 .... 62 A7
Cressey Ct. ME4 .... 9 E4
Cressfield. TN23 .... 138 F1
Crest Rd. ME1 .... 9 C1
Cresta Cl. CT6 .... 21 F4
Crestway. ME5 .... 32 B8
Crete Rd E. CT18 & CT19 .... 163 D1
Crete Rd W. CT18 .... 163 B1
Creteway Cl. CT18 .... 178 E8
Creve Coeur Cl. ME14 .... 76 A5
Cricketers Cl.
  Harrietsham ME17 .... 100 D6
Cricketers Cl. Hawkinge CT18 .. 163 B6
Cricketers Cl.
  Sittingbourne ME10 .... 36 F8
Crimond Ave. TN29 .... 187 A4
Criol La. TN26 .... 155 A2
Cripple Hill. TN26 .... 152 D1
Cripple St. ME15 .... 97 A3
Cripps Cl. CT3 .... 112 E5
Cripps' La. CT15 .... 150 F5
Crisfield Ct. TN30 .... 167 B2
Crismill La. ME14 .... 76 F4
Crismill Rd. ME14 .... 76 F3
Crispe Cl. ME8 .... 33 D4
Crispe Rd. CT7 .... 27 A5
Crispin Cl. ME13 .... 62 D8
Crispin Ct. ME17 .... 96 C3
Crittenden Bglws. ME15 .... 96 A4
Crittenden Cotts. ME15 .... 96 A4
Crocken Hill Rd. TN27 .... 118 C2
Crockham La. ME13 .... 64 B6
Crockham Rd. ME13 .... 64 C6
Crockshard Hill. CT3 .... 91 B4
Crockshard La. CT3 .... 91 B4
Croft Cl. ME5 .... 32 C1
Croft Gdns. ME17 .... 101 C4
Croft La. CT20 .... 177 F5
Croft Rd. TN24 .... 139 D2
Croft's Pl. 8 CT10 .... 30 B4
Crofters Cl. CT21 .... 187 E8
Crofters The. ME8 .... 33 F7
Crofton Cl. TN24 .... 139 C6
Crofton Ct. CT8 .... 27 E7
Croftwood. TN23 .... 155 D6
Croidene Ct. ME12 .... 4 A6
Cromer Rd. Rochester ME2 .... 9 B8
Cromer Rd. Sittingbourne ME10 .. 58 F8
Cromwell Park Pl. CT20 .... 177 D4
Cromwell Rd. Canterbury CT1 .... 88 A6
Cromwell Rd. Maidstone ME14 .. 75 B5
Cromwell Rd.
  West Minster ME11 & ME12 .... 2 F7
Cromwell Rd. Whitstable CT5 .... 20 E1
Cromwell Terr. ME4 .... 10 A3
Crook's Court La. CT15 .... 164 C5
Crooked S Rd. CT14 .... 133 E7
Crookenden Pl. CT4 .... 128 F8
Crosier Ct. ME9 .... 12 E3
Crosley Rd. ME7 .... 10 D3
Cross Dr. ME17 .... 99 B1
Cross Keys. ME14 .... 76 C4
Cross La. Faversham ME13 .... 62 C7
Cross La. 7 Faversham ME13 .... 62 D7
Cross La. Sittingbourne ME10 .... 36 E6
Cross La.
  Throwley Forstal ME13 .... 104 C7
Cross Rd. Birchington CT7 .... 27 B8
Cross Rd. Deal CT14 .... 117 A2
Cross Rd.
  St Margaret's at Cliffe CT15 .. 151 A4
Cross St. 2 Canterbury CT2 .... 66 E1
Cross St. Chatham ME4 .... 10 A4
Cross St. Gillingham ME7 .... 10 C6
Cross St. Herne Bay CT6 .... 22 D5
Cross St. Maidstone ME14 .... 75 A6
Cross St. Rochester ME2 .... 9 B8
Cross St. Sheerness ME12 .... 1 C2
Cross Stile. TN23 .... 155 F8
Cross The. CT13 .... 93 B2
Cross Way. ME1 .... 9 C3
Crossley Ave. CT6 .... 21 F4
Crossway. ME5 .... 31 E6
Crossways. Canterbury CT2 .... 66 F4
Crossways. Chart Sutton ME17 .... 98 B1
Crossways. Sittingbourne ME10 .. 36 F1
Crossways Ave. CT9 .... 29 A5
Crouch Cotts. ME13 .... 84 E8
Crouch Hill Ct. ME9 .... 13 C3
Crouch La. ME13 .... 84 E8
Crow Cnr. Ashford TN24 .... 156 F7
Crow Cnr. Brabourne TN25 .... 141 E1
Crow Cnr. Rochester ME1 .... 9 C5
Crow Hill. CT10 .... 30 B5
Crow Hill Rd. CT9 .... 28 B8
Crow La. CT4 .... 126 E3

Crown Quay. ME10 .... 36 F5
Crown Quay La. ME10 .... 37 A4
Crown Rd. ME10 .... 36 E6
Crown St. ME7 .... 10 D6
Crownfield Rd. TN23 .... 155 F8
Crownfields. ME14 .... 75 F4
Crows Camp Rd. CT4 .... 111 A5
Croydon Cl. ME5 .... 32 C4
Cruise Liner Terminal. CT17 .. 166 E4
Crundale. **2** ME14 .... 75 A5
Crundale Cl. TN23 .... 155 F6
Crundale Rd. ME8 .... 11 C3
Crundale Way. CT10 & CT9 ..... 8 E1
Crusader Cl. ME7 .... 33 B8
Cryalls Bsns Est. ME10 .... 36 C4
Cryalls La. ME10 & ME9 .... 36 C3
Cryol Rd. TN23 .... 156 A7
Crystal Bsns Ctr. CT13 .... 73 B2
Ctr for European Agricucultural
  Studies. TN25 .... 124 A1
Cubitt Ho. CT19 .... 178 D6
Cuckmere Ho. **3** ME15 .... 97 E8
Cuckold's Cnr.
  High Halden TN26 .... 168 B7
Cuckold's Cnr. Snargate TN29 .. 191 E7
Cuckolds Cnr. CT14 .... 114 A7
Cuckoo La. Ashford TN23 ... 155 D6
Cuckoo La. Ashford TN23 ... 155 E7
Cuckoo La. Postling CT21 ... 160 F2
Cuckoowood Ave. ME14 ...... 53 F1
Cudham Cl. ME14 .... 75 C6
Cudham Gdns. CT9 .... 8 E2
Cudworth Rd. TN24 .... 156 E7
Cullens Hill. CT4 .... 144 F4
Cullet Dr. ME11 .... 3 A3
Culling's Hill. CT4 .... 144 F4
Culmers Terr. ME13 .... 41 E1
Culpeper Cl.
  Hollingbourne ME17 .... 77 C2
Culpeper Cl. Rochester ME2 .... 9 E6
Culpeper Cl. CT2 .... 67 A4
Culpepper Rd. Coxheath ME17 .. 96 B3
Culpepper Rd. Gillingham ME8 .. 33 D4
Culter Field. TN23 .... 155 E8
Culver's La. TN23 .... 203 D4
Cumberland Ave.
  Broadstairs CT10 .... 30 A5
Cumberland Ave.
  Canterbury CT1 .... 88 D7
Cumberland Ave.
  Maidstone ME15 .... 97 D8
Cumberland Dr. ME9 .... 13 C3
Cumberland Rd.
  Gillingham ME4 & ME7 ...... 10 B7
Cumberland Rd.
  Gillingham ME8 .... 10 C7
Cumberland Rd. Margate CT9 .. 8 B3
Cumberland Rd. **1**
  Ramsgate CT11 .... 52 D6
Cundishall Cl. CT5 .... 43 C8
Cunningham Cres.
  Birchington CT7 .... 26 E7
Cunningham Cres.
  Chatham ME5 .... 32 A8
Cunningham Ho. ME1 .... 9 B4
Curlew Ave. ME9 .... 13 B3
Curlew Cl. CT6 .... 23 C2
Curlinge Cl. CT11 .... 52 A6
Curteis La. TN30 .... 167 B1
Curtis La. CT4 .... 126 D2
Curtis Rd. TN24 .... 156 E2
Curtis Way. **1** ME12 .... 62 C7
Curtis Wood Park Rd. CT6 .... 46 A4
Curtis Wood Rd. CT6 .... 45 F7
Curzon Cl. CT14 .... 117 C3
Curzon Ho. **5** CT11 .... 52 D6
Curzon Rd. Chatham ME4 ...... 9 F3
Curzon Rd. Dover CT17 ...... 166 B8
Curzon Rd. Maidstone ME14 .. 75 A6
Cushman Rd. CT1 .... 87 E7
Cutbush Almshouses. **2**
  ME15 .... 75 A3
Cutbush and Corrall Ct. ME14 .. 75 B4
Cuthbert Rd. CT8 .... 27 E8
Cuttings The. CT12 .... 52 C8
Cuxton. Park Wood ME15 .... 97 F5
Cuxton Rd. Rochester ME2 ..... 9 A7
Cygnet Rd. ME5 .... 32 C2
Cygnet Way. TN23 .... 138 F1
Cylinder Rd. CT21 .... 176 B4
Cypress Ave. TN23 .... 138 E2
Cypress Cl. CT5 .... 43 C7
Cypress Ct. ME7 .... 10 F6
Cypress Gr. CT15 .... 114 B2
Cyprus Rd. ME13 .... 62 E7

D'este Rd. CT11 .... 52 F7
D2 Trad Est. ME10 .... 37 B6
Daglish Cl. TN28 .... 200 B6
Dagmar Rd. ME4 .... 10 B2
Daimler Ave. CT6 .... 22 B3
Dalby Rd. CT9 .... 8 A3
Dalby Sq. CT9 .... 8 A3
Dale Rd. ME1 .... 9 C3
Dale St. ME4 .... 9 E2
Dale Wlk. TN24 .... 139 C2
Dalewood. ME4 .... 37 A2
Dallas-Brett Cres. CT19 .... 178 E8
Dallinger Rd. **1** CT7 .... 26 F8
Dalmatia Ct. CT17 .... 149 A1
Dalmeny Ave. CT9 .... 8 D1
Dalton Cl. **4** CT14 .... 52 E7
Dalton St. ME7 .... 10 C6
Dame Janet
  Cty Inf Sch. CT12 .... 29 B2

Dame Janet
  Cty Jun Sch. CT12 .... 29 B2
Damerham Cl. CT2 .... 66 E3
Damiem Cl. ME4 .... 10 A2
Dan Dr. ME13 .... 62 A8
Danaway Cotts. ME9 .... 35 C3
Dane Cl. Chatham ME5 .... 32 C2
Dane Cl. Hartlip ME9 .... 34 D6
Dane Court Gdns. CT10 .... 29 D5
Dane Court Gram Sch. CT10 .. 29 E4
Dane Court Rd. CT10 & CT9 .. 29 C6
Dane Cres. CT11 .... 52 E8
Dane Ct. ME17 .... 96 C2
Dane End Rd. CT8 .... 27 D8
Dane Gdns. CT9 .... 29 88
Dane Hill. CT9 .... 7 J3
Dane Hill Gr. CT9 .... 7 J2
Dane Hill Row. CT9 .... 7 J2
Dane John Ct. **3** CT1 .... 87 F7
Dane John Mews. **1** CT1 ..... 87 F7
Dane La. ME9 .... 34 D6
Dane Mount. CT9 .... 29 C8
Dane Park Rd. Margate CT9 .... 7 J2
Dane Park Rd. Ramsgate CT11 .. 52 E8
Dane Rd. Birchington CT7 .... 26 D7
Dane Rd. Margate CT9 .... 8 A2
Dane Rd. Ramsgate CT11 ...... 52 E8
Dane Valley Rd. CT10 & CT9 .. 29 C8
Danecourt Sch The. ME8 ...... 11 A2
Danedale Ave. ME12 .... 4 F6
Danefield Ct. ME14 .... 76 B4
Danehurst. CT7 .... 7 C1
Danemore. TN30 .... 179 B8
Danes Ct. CT16 .... 149 D2
Danes Dr. ME12 .... 6 D2
Danes Hill. ME7 .... 11 A6
Danes Mead. ME10 .... 14 F1
Danesmead Terr. CT9 .... 7 J2
Daniels Ct. CT5 .... 20 C1
Danley Mid Sch. ME12 .... 3 E7
Danley Rd. ME12 .... 3 E7
Danson Way. ME8 .... 11 D2
Danton La. CT18 & CT19 .... 162 C1
Darby Pl. CT20 .... 178 D5
Darby Rd. CT20 .... 178 D5
Darenth Cl. CT6 .... 23 B3
Darenth Ho. **2** ME15 .... 97 D8
Darenth Rise. ME5 .... 32 B3
Dargate Cl. ME16 .... 74 D7
Dargate
  Dargate CT2 & ME13 .... 64 F7
Dargate Rd. Yorklets CT5 ...... 43 A3
Dargets Rd. ME5 .... 32 A3
Dark Hill. ME13 .... 62 C8
Darland Ave. ME7 .... 10 E1
Darlinghurst Rd. CT19 .... 177 E7
Darlington Dr. ME12 .... 4 A4
Darlington St. CT20 .... 178 D5
Darnley Cl. Broadstairs CT10 .. 29 F3
Darnley Cl. Folkestone CT20 .. 177 F4
Darnley Rd. ME2 .... 9 A6
Darracott Cl. CT14 .... 117 B5
Darrell Cl. CT6 .... 22 C3
Darren Gdns. CT10 .... 29 F2
Darwin Coll. CT2 .... 66 E5
Darwin Rd. CT7 .... 26 F8
Daryngton Ave. CT7 .... 26 C7
Davenport Ave. ME7 .... 10 E7
David Ave. CT9 .... 8 D2
Davids Cl. CT10 .... 30 B3
Davidson Rd. CT2 .... 66 D1
Davie Cl. ME12 .... 3 B8
Davie Cl. ME12 .... 3 B8
Davington
  Cty Prim Sch. ME13 .... 62 C8
Davington Hill. ME13 .... 62 C8
Davis Ave. CT14 .... 117 A4
Dawbourns. TN30 .... 167 B3
Dawes Rd. CT2 & ME13 .... 64 C4
Dawes St. ME7 .... 10 C5
Dawn Rise. ME12 .... 5 F6
Dawson Rd. CT19 .... 178 D6
Dawson's Row. ME13 .... 62 A6
Dayton Rd. ME13 .... 83 C3
Daytona Way. CT6 .... 22 A4
De Burgh Hill. CT17 .... 149 C1
De Burgh St. **2** CT17 ...... 166 C8
De Havilland Cl. CT18 .... 163 B4
De L'angle Row. CT4 .... 86 D3
De Mere Cl. ME8 .... 33 D6
Deacon Est The. ME20 .... 53 A2
Deacon Trad Ctr. ME2 .... 9 A6
Deal Castle. CT14 .... 117 D5
Deal Castle Rd. CT14 .... 117 D5
Deal Parochial
  CE Prim Sch. CT14 .... 117 C5
Deal Rd. CT13 & CT14 .... 93 F5
Deal Sta. CT14 .... 117 C6
Dean Croft. CT6 .... 23 B2
Dean Ct. **14** CT1 .... 67 A1
Dean Hill. CT4 & TN25 ...... 126 B2
Dean Mead. CT19 .... 178 B7
Dean Rd. ME10 .... 36 E6
Dean St. ME15 .... 96 C6
Dean Wood
  Cty Prim Inf Sch. ME8 ...... 33 D3
Dean Wood
  Cty Prim Jun Sch. ME8 ..... 33 D4
Dean's Wlk. TN23 .... 155 F7
Deane Cl. CT5 .... 43 E7
Deans Hill Rd. ME9 .... 57 D5
Deans Mill Ct. CT2 .... 66 F1
Deansway Ave. CT2 .... 67 F7
Deanwood Cl. ME8 .... 33 D6
Deanwood Dr. ME8 .... 33 E4
Deanwood Rd. CT17 .... 148 E2
Deborah Cl. CT5 .... 43 F7
Deedes Cl. CT21 .... 176 C3

Deerhurst Gdns. ME16 .... 74 D4
Deerson La. CT3 .... 70 A4
Defiant Cl. ME5 .... 32 B6
Defoe Cl. ME5 .... 32 B6
Delacourt Cl. CT12 .... 51 D5
Delamark Rd. ME12 .... 1 D2
Delane Rd. CT14 .... 117 A5
Delaware Cl. CT2 .... 67 F6
Delce Cty Inf Sch. ME1 .... 9 D2
Delce Cty Jun Sch. ME1 .... 9 D3
Delce Rd. ME1 .... 9 D4
Delf St. CT13 .... 72 F1
Delfside. ME13 .... 94 A8
Delmaney Cl. CT10 .... 30 B5
Delmar Cl. CT2 .... 21 D3
Denbigh Ave. ME8 .... 11 D1
Denbigh Cl. ME10 .... 36 E7
Denbigh Rd. CT12 .... 29 A1
Dence Cl. CT6 .... 23 B5
Dence Pk. CT6 .... 23 B4
Dencora Way. TN23 .... 139 A1
Dene The. Bethersden TN26 .. 153 D5
Dene The. Canterbury CT1 .... 88 B5
Dene The. Hythe CT21 .... 176 C2
Dene Wlk. CT9 .... 28 F7
Dengemarsh Rd. TN29 .... 203 C3
Denham Cl. TN29 .... 187 B4
Denham Ho. ME10 .... 36 D5
Denham Rd. ME9 .... 35 B7
Denmark Rd. CT11 .... 52 E8
Denmark St. ST19 .... 178 E6
Denne Cl. CT2 .... 67 F7
Denne Manor La. CT4 .... 106 C8
Dennes La. TN29 .... 203 C8
Dennes Mill Cl. TN25 .... 123 D2
Denness Rd. TN23 .... 156 B7
Dennis Way. CT19 .... 177 E2
Dennis Willocks Cl. ME9 ..... 35 B6
Densole La. CT18 .... 163 A8
Densole Way. CT18 .... 163 A8
Denstead Cotts. CT4 .... 86 B8
Denstead Cl. CT2 .... 66 C4
Denstead La. CT4 & ME13 ... 86 C7
Denstead Oast. CT4 .... 86 B8
Denstead Wlk. **11** ME15 .... 97 F6
Denstroude La. CT2 .... 65 D8
Dent-De Lion Ct. CT9 .... 28 A8
Dent-De-Lion Rd.
  Margate CT9 .... 28 A8
Dent-De-Lion Rd.
  Westgate-on-S CT8 .... 7 C1
Dental St. CT21 .... 176 C2
Denton Cl. ME15 .... 97 E8
Denton Way. CT9 .... 8 C1
Derby Cl. ME10 .... 36 D6
Derby Rd. Chatham ME5 .... 10 E2
Derby Rd. Gillingham ME5 .... 10 E2
Derby Rd. Maidstone ME15 ... 97 C8
Dering Ct. Bridge CT4 .... 88 F1
Dering Cl.
  Chamber's Green TN27 .... 136 C4
Dering Rd. Ashford TN24 .... 139 D2
Dering Rd. Bridge CT4 .... 89 A1
Dering Rd. Herne Bay CT6 .... 22 F4
Dering Terr. TN27 .... 136 C3
Derings The. TN29 .... 203 B6
Deringwood Dr. ME15 .... 75 F1
Derringstone Downs. CT4 ... 128 F6
Derringstone Hill. CT4 ...... 128 F6
Derringstone St. CT4 .... 128 F7
Derville Ho. TN28 .... 200 B6
Derville Rd. TN29 .... 204 E7
Derwent Ave. CT11 .... 52 A7
Derwent Ho. **5** ME15 .... 97 E7
Derwent Way. Aylesham CT3 .. 112 F6
Derwent Way. Gillingham ME8 .. 33 D8
Desmond Cres. ME13 .... 63 A5
Detling Ave. CT10 .... 30 A1
Detling CE Prim Sch. ME14 ... 55 A1
Detling Cl. Maidstone ME8 ... 11 C2
Detling Cl. West Minster ME12 .. 3 B7
Detling Hill. ME14 .... 55 B2
Devon Ave. CT14 .... 117 C3
Devon Cl. Chatham ME5 .... 32 C7
Devon Cl. Gillingham ME8 .... 11 F1
Devon Ct. CT12 .... 29 B2
Devon Gdns. CT7 .... 26 F7
Devon Rd. Canterbury CT1 ... 88 D8
Devon Rd. Folkestone CT19 .. 178 D5
Devon Rd. Maidstone ME15 ... 97 C8
Devonshire Gdns. CT9 .... 8 C3
Devonshire Rd. Dover CT17 .. 166 B8
Devonshire Rd. Gillingham ME7 .. 10 D7
Devonshire Terr. CT10 .... 30 B5
Dhekelia Ct. ME14 .... 75 A7
Dial Cl. ME7 .... 10 F6
Dial Rd. ME7 .... 10 F6
Diamond Ct. ME12 .... 1 C1
Diamond Rd. CT5 .... 20 E2
Diana Gdns. CT14 .... 117 A5
Dibdin Rd. CT14 .... 117 D7
Dickens Ave. CT1 .... 67 D7
Dickens Cl. ME17 .... 98 E4
Dickens Ct. ME2 .... 9 F6
Dickens Rd. Broadstairs CT10 .. 30 B5
Dickens Rd. Maidstone ME14 .. 74 E8
Dickens Rd. Rochester ME1 .... 9 C2
Dickens Wlk. CT10 .... 30 B4
Dickley La. ME17 .... 101 A6
Dickson Ct. ME10 .... 37 B4
Dickson Rd. CT17 .... 166 C8
Dickson's Cnr. CT13 .... 95 A6
Dicksons Bourne. TN25 .... 172 F6
Dieu Stone La. CT16 .... 166 E8
Digby Rd. CT20 .... 177 E5
Dignals Cl. ME8 .... 11 F2
Dignash. TN25 .... 121 D2
Diligent Dr. ME10 .... 36 F7

Diocesan & Payne Smith
  CE Prim Sch. CT1 .... 67 A1
Discovery Wlk. CT1 .... 88 C7
Disraeli Cl. ME15 .... 97 E5
Dixon Cl. ME15 .... 74 F2
Dixwell Cl. ME8 .... 33 D5
Dixwell Rd. CT20 .... 178 A4
Dobbie Cl. ME10 .... 36 E6
Dock Exit Rd. CT16 .... 166 F8
Dock Head Rd. ME4 .... 10 A8
Dock Rd. Chatham ME4 .... 9 F6
Dock Rd. Gillingham ME4 ..... 10 A7
Doctor's La. CT15 .... 165 B5
Dodd's La. CT16 .... 149 A3
Doddington Ct. ME16 .... 74 D5
Doddington
  Cty Prim Sch. ME9 .... 80 F7
Doddington Rd. ME8 .... 11 D3
Does Alley. **4** ME10 .... 36 F4
Dog Kennel La. CT18 .... 161 B7
Doggerel Acre. CT5 .... 43 F7
Doggett's Sq. ME2 .... 9 C7
Dogwood Cl. ME5 .... 32 D1
Dola Ave. CT14 .... 117 B6
Dolphin Cl. CT10 .... 8 G3
Dolphin Dr. ME8 .... 33 E5
Dolphin Ho. **1** CT16 .... 166 E7
Dolphin La. CT16 .... 166 E7
Dolphin Pas. **2** CT16 .... 166 E7
Dolphin Pk. CT16 .... 37 B5
Dolphin Pl. **3** CT16 .... 166 E7
Dolphin Rd. Lydd TN29 ...... 203 C6
Dolphin Rd.
  Sittingbourne ME10 .... 37 B5
Dolphin St. Deal CT14 .... 117 D7
Dolphin St. Herne Bay CT6 ... 22 E5
Dolphins Rd. CT19 .... 178 D7
Dombey Cl. ME1 .... 9 C3
Domneva Rd. Minster, Thanet
  CT12 .... 50 B6
Domneva Rd.
  Westgate-on-S CT8 .... 27 D8
Donald Moor Ave. ME9 .... 38 C2
Doncaster Cl. **7** ME15 ...... 97 F6
Donegal Rd. CT1 .... 88 C8
Donemowe Dr. ME10 .... 36 F8
Donet Cl. ME8 .... 33 C5
Dongola Rd. ME2 .... 9 A8
Donkey La. CT3 .... 112 C8
Donkey St. CT21 & TN29 ... 186 E5
Donnahay Rd. CT12 .... 29 C3
Donnithorne Ho. CT6 .... 22 E5
Dorcas Gdns. CT10 .... 30 A6
Doric Ct. CT11 .... 52 C5
Dorman Ave N. CT3 .... 112 E6
Dorman Ave S. CT3 .... 112 F5
Dornden Gdns. ME5 .... 32 B2
Dorne Cotts. TN27 .... 118 E6
Dorothy Dr. CT12 .... 29 C2
Dorrit Way. ME1 .... 9 D2
Dorset Cl. CT5 .... 43 B7
Dorset Ct. Deal CT14 .... 117 D2
Dorset Ct. Ramsgate CT12 ... 29 B2
Dorset Gdns. Birchington CT7 .. 26 F7
Dorset Gdns. Deal CT14 ..... 117 C2
Dorset Pl. ME13 .... 62 C7
Dorset Rd. Canterbury CT1 ... 88 D7
Dorset Rd. West Minster ME12 .. 3 A8
Dorset Sq. ME8 .... 11 D1
Dorset Way. ME15 .... 97 C8
Dossett Cl. CT14 .... 117 A2
Dotterel Cl. ME5 .... 32 D2
Doubleday Dr. ME9 .... 37 E2
Douglas Almshouses. ME17 .. 101 D5
Douglas Ave. Hythe CT21 ... 176 C2
Douglas Ave. Whitstable CT5 .. 20 E1
Douglas Bglws. CT15 .... 132 E8
Douglas Cl. CT10 .... 29 E5
Douglas Rd. Deal CT14 ...... 117 A3
Douglas Rd. Dover CT17 ..... 166 B8
Douglas Rd. Herne Bay CT6 .. 23 A4
Douglas Rd. Lenham ME17 .. 101 D5
Douglas Rd. Maidstone ME16 .. 74 E3
Douglas Terr. CT14 .... 117 C5
Dour Side. CT17 .... 148 F3
Dour St. CT16 .... 166 D8
Douro Cl. CT1 .... 67 D1
Douro Pl. CT16 .... 166 E7
Dove Cl. Chatham ME5 .... 32 B6
Dove Cl. Hythe CT21 .... 187 D8
Dove Cl. Whitstable CT5 ...... 43 C7
Dove Lea Gdns. CT17 .... 148 E3
Dovedale. CT7 .... 27 B7
Dovedale Ct. CT7 .... 27 B7
Dover Castle. CT16 .... 166 F8
Dover Coll. Dover CT17 ...... 166 C8
Dover Coll. Dover CT16 ...... 166 D7
Dover Gram Sch for Boys.
  CT17 .... 166 A8
Dover Gram Sch for Girls.
  CT16 .... 149 C1
Dover Hill. CT19 .... 178 B6
Dover Pl. TN23 .... 139 C1
Dover Rd. Barham CT4 .... 112 A1
Dover Rd. Bishopsbourne CT4 .. 111 D5
Dover Rd.
  Folkestone CT19 & CT20 .. 178 E7
Dover Rd. Guston CT15 ...... 149 E4
Dover Rd. Sandwich CT13 .... 93 F6
Dover Rd.
  St Margaret's at Cliffe CT15 .. 150 D6
Dover Rd.
  Tilmanstone CT13 & CT14 .. 115 B5
Dover Rd.
  Woolage Green CT4 & CT15 .. 129 D6
Dover St. Canterbury CT1 ..... 88 A7

Dover St. Maidstone ME16 .... 74 C2
Dover St. **1**
  Sittingbourne ME10 .... 36 E4
Doves Cnr. CT14 .... 115 A4
Dowle Cl. TN29 .... 199 A7
Down Barton Rd. CT7 .... 25 E1
Down Court Rd. ME9 .... 59 C1
Down St. TN23 .... 155 E5
Downer Ct. ME4 .... 31 E8
Downhill Cl. CT16 .... 148 D6
Downings The. CT6 .... 23 A2
Downland Ct. TN24 .... 139 B3
Downlands. Deal CT14 .... 134 B8
Downlands.
  Harrietsham ME17 .... 100 F6
Downs Ave. CT5 .... 20 E1
Downs
  CE Prim Sch The. CT14 .... 117 B2
Downs Cl. Charing TN27 .... 120 C8
Downs Cl. East Studdal CT15 .. 132 D8
Downs Cl. Maidstone ME14 ... 75 B8
Downs Cl. Sittingbourne ME10 .. 36 D2
Downs Pk. CT6 .... 23 A5
Downs Rd. Canterbury CT2 ... 66 F4
Downs Rd. Deal CT14 .... 117 C3
Downs Rd. East Studdal CT15 .. 132 C8
Downs Rd. Folkestone CT19 .. 178 C2
Downs Rd. Maidstone ME14 ... 75 B8
Downs Rd. Ramsgate CT11 .... 52 B6
Downs The. Chartham CT4 .... 86 E1
Downs The. Chatham ME5 ..... 31 D1
Downs The. Preston CT3 ...... 70 C6
Downs View
  Cty Inf Sch. TN24 .... 139 E7
Downs View Rd. ME14 .... 75 B8
Downs Way. Charing TN27 .. 120 C8
Downs Way. Sellindge TN25 .. 159 C1
Downside. Bekesbourne CT4 .. 89 E3
Downside. Folkestone CT19 .. 178 C7
Downside. Rochester ME2 ...... 9 A7
Downside.
  St Margaret's at Cliffe CT15 .. 151 A6
Downsole Rd. CT16 .... 149 B7
Downsview. ME5 .... 32 C8
Dragonfly Cl. TN23 .... 155 D8
Dragoon Ho. **10** CT1 .... 67 A1
Drainless Rd. CT13 .... 93 A5
Drake Ave. ME2 .... 4 D5
Drake Rd. TN24 .... 157 B7
Drakes Cl. ME9 .... 12 E2
Drapers Almshouses. CT9 .... 29 A8
Drapers Ave. CT9 .... 28 F8
Drapers Cl. CT9 .... 29 A8
Drapers Mills
  Cty Prim Sch. CT9 .... 29 A8
Drapers Windmill (dis). CT9 .... 8 A1
Dray's Field. ME9 .... 79 A7
Dreadnought Ave. ME12 .... 4 B6
Drew La. CT14 .... 117 C4
Drewery Dr. ME8 .... 33 C5
Drill La. CT3 .... 69 B1
Drive The. Canterbury CT1 ... 88 B6
Drive The. Whitstable CT5 .... 44 B8
Drivers Rdbt. TN24 .... 139 A4
Drop Redoubt Rd. CT17 ..... 166 D7
Drove The. Fordwich CT2 ..... 68 A4
Drove The. Monkton CT12 ... 49 B6
Drove The. Northbourne CT14 .. 116 A5
Drove The. Whitfield CT16 .. 149 A8
Drove The. Whitstable CT5 .... 44 D8
Droveway Gdns. CT15 .... 151 A6
Droveway The. CT15 .... 151 B6
Drum La. TN23 .... 139 B2
Drury Rd. TN30 .... 179 B8
Drybeck Ave. CT11 .... 51 F7
Dryden Cl. CT1 .... 88 C7
Dryden Rd. CT16 .... 149 B3
Drywall Ind Est. ME10 .... 37 B6
Duchess Of Kent Dr. ME5 .... 32 B2
Duck La. Canterbury CT1 ...... 67 A1
Duck La. Shadoxhurst TN26 .. 169 F7
Duck St. CT14 .... 144 F4
Duckpit Rd. CT4 .... 126 A6
Duckworth Cl. TN24 .... 157 B7
Dudley Ave. CT8 .... 27 C8
Dudley Rd. Ashford TN24 ... 139 E5
Dudley Rd. Folkestone CT19 .. 178 E5
Duke of Clarence
  Trad Est The. ME12 .... 1 B3
Duke of York's
  Royal Military Sch. CT15 .. 149 F4
Duke St. Deal CT14 .... 117 D7
Duke St. Margate CT9 .... 7 I3
Dukes Meadow. TN26 .... 183 A7
Dukes Meadow Dr. ME7 ...... 32 F6
Dukes Wlk. **5** ME15 .... 75 A4
Dukeswood. CT5 .... 44 D6
Dully Rd. ME9 .... 59 E6
Dumergue Ave. ME11 .... 3 B5
Dumpton Gap Rd. CT10 ...... 30 A2
Dumpton La. CT11 .... 29 E1
Dumpton Park Dr.
  CT10 & CT11 .... 30 A2
Dumpton Park Rd. CT11 ...... 52 E8
Dumpton Park Sta. CT11 ..... 29 F1
Duncan Dr. CT7 .... 26 E8
Duncan Rd. Gillingham ME7 ... 10 D5
Duncan Rd. Ramsgate CT11 .. 52 D7
Duncan Rd. Whitstable CT5 ... 43 D7
Dundein Dr. CT16 .... 149 B3
Dundonald Rd. **11**
  Broadstairs CT10 .... 30 B4
Dundonald Rd. Ramsgate CT11 .. 52 C2
Dunedin Ho. ME16 .... 36 C3
Dunedin Rd. CT12 .... 29 A1
Dunera Dr. ME14 .... 75 A7
Dunes Rd. TN28 .... 200 D3

Dungeness Power Sta
  Visitor Ctr. TN29 .... 205 E6
Dungeness Rd. TN29 .... 204 C3
Dungeness Sta. TN29 .... 205 F6
Dunkery Rise. TN24 .... 139 B4
Dunkirk Cl. TN29 .... 195 B7
Dunkirk Cty Prim Sch. ME13 .... 64 D2
Dunkirk Dr. ME5 .... 31 F6
Dunkirk Rd.
  Boughton Street ME13 .... 64 B1
Dunkirk Rd.
  Boughton Street ME13 .... 64 B2
Dunkirk Sq. CT16 .... 149 F3
Dunlin Cl. TN29 .... 195 A3
Dunn Street Rd. ME7 .... 55 A8
Dunnett Rd. CT19 .... 177 E6
Dunning's La. ME1 .... 9 C4
Dunnings The. ME16 .... 74 A2
Dunoon Cl. CT11 .... 29 F1
Dunstall Cl. TN29 .... 195 A5
Dunstall Gdns. TN29 .... 195 A5
Dunstall La. TN29 .... 195 A5
Dunstan Ave. CT8 .... 27 D7
Dunston Ct. CT2 .... 66 E1
Dunston Ho. CT14 .... 117 D8
Durban Cl. CT12 .... 29 A2
Durban Cres. CT16 .... 149 C4
Durban Ho. 7 ME15 .... 97 E5
Durban Rd. CT9 .... 8 A1
Durham Cl. Canterbury CT1 ...... 87 F6
Durham Cl. 9 Dover CT17 ...... 166 D7
Durham Cl. Maidstone ME15 ..... 75 E1
Durham Hill. CT16 & CT17 ...... 166 D7
Durham Rd. ME8 .... 33 C7
Durling Cl. ME8 .... 12 A1
Durlock. CT12 .... 50 C5
Durlock Ave. CT11 .... 52 B5
Durlock Rd. CT3 .... 92 B7
Durlocks The. CT19 .... 178 E5
Durnford Cl. CT2 .... 66 E2
Durovernum Ct. CT1 .... 88 A7
Durrell Gdns. ME5 .... 10 C1
Duval Dr. ME1 .... 31 E8
Duvard's Pl. ME9 .... 35 F1
Dyke Rd. CT19 .... 178 E5
Dymchurch
  Cty Prim Sch. TN29 .... 195 C8
Dymchurch Ho. CT1 .... 88 B8
Dymchurch Rd. Hythe CT21 .... 176 A2
Dymchurch Rd.
  Hythe CT21 & TN29 .... 187 C6
Dymchurch Rd.
  St Mary's Bay TN29 & TN28 .... 195 A5
Dymchurch Sta. TN29 .... 195 A5
Dyngley Cl. ME10 .... 36 E2

Eagle Hill. CT11 .... 52 D7
Eagles Cl. ME10 .... 37 C4
Ealham Cl. Ashford TN24 .... 157 A8
Ealham Cl. Canterbury CT1 ...... 88 B5
Ealing Cl. ME5 .... 32 C4
Earl Cl. ME5 .... 32 B4
Earl St. ME14 .... 74 F4
Earl's Ave. CT20 .... 178 B4
Earls Ave. TN24 .... 139 F1
Earlsfield. TN25 .... 173 A6
Earlsfield Rd. CT21 .... 176 D2
Earlsmead Cres. CT12 .... 51 C5
Earlsworth Ct. TN24 .... 156 A6
Earlsworth Rd. TN24 .... 156 D6
Easole Hts. CT15 .... 113 D5
Easole St. CT15 .... 113 D5
East Borough
  Cty Prim Sch. ME14 .... 75 B5
East Cliff. Dover CT16 .... 166 F8
East Cliff. Folkestone CT19 .. 178 F6
East Cliff Gdns. 19 CT19 ...... 178 E5
East Cliff Golf Links. CT19 ... 178 G6
East Cliff Par. CT6 .... 23 A5
East Cliff Pas. 20 CT19 .... 178 E5
East Court
  (Sch for Dyslexics). CT11 ...... 52 G7
East Cross. TN30 .... 179 B7
East Farleigh
  Cty Prim Sch. ME15 .... 96 B6
East Gn. ME10 .... 15 A1
East Hall La. ME10 .... 37 C5
East Hill. Ashford TN23 & TN24 .. 139 C2
East Hill. Tenterden TN30 .... 179 B8
East Kent Light Railway.
  CT15 .... 131 C8
East La. ME12 .... 1 B2
East Langdon Rd. CT15 .... 149 F2
East Lodge Rd. TN23 .... 138 F3
East Mountain La. TN24 .... 139 F7
East Norman Rd. CT16 .... 149 E1
East Northdown Cl. CT9 .... 8 E1
East Park Rd. ME20 .... 74 A8
East Ramp. CT16 .... 166 G8
East Rd. Chatham ME4 .... 10 A7
East Rd. Folkestone CT20 ...... 177 D4
East Rd. Gillingham ME7 .... 10 A8
East Rd. Sandwich CT12 & CT13 .. 73 A8
East Rise. CT11 .... 29 B1
East Roman Ditch. CT16 .... 166 F8
East Row. ME1 .... 9 C5
East St. Ashford TN23 .... 139 B2
East St. Canterbury CT1 .... 67 C3
East St. Chatham ME4 .... 10 A3
East St. Dover CT17 .... 166 C8
East St. Faversham ME13 .... 62 D7
East St. Folkestone CT19 ...... 178 E6
East St. Gillingham ME7 .... 10 D6
East St. Harrietsham ME17 .... 100 E6
East St. Herne Bay CT6 .... 23 A5
East St. Hythe CT21 .... 176 D2
East St. Sittingbourne ME10 .... 37 A4

East Stour Ct. TN24 .... 139 D1
East View. Brookland TN29 .... 197 D8
East View. Hersden CT3 .... 46 F1
East Weald Dr. TN30 .... 167 B1
East Wootton Cotts. CT4 ...... 109 A4
Eastbridge Rd. TN29 .... 195 B8
Eastbrook Pl. CT16 .... 166 E8
Eastchurch
  CE Prim Sch. ME12 .... 5 D3
Eastchurch Rd. Margate CT9 ..... 8 E3
Eastchurch Rd. Minster ME12 ... 5 B5
Eastcourt Gn. ME8 .... 11 B4
Eastcourt La. Gillingham ME8 ... 11 B3
Eastcourt La.
  Lower Twydall ME7 & ME8 ...... 11 B4
Eastern Arm N. CT16 .... 166 H8
Eastern Arm S. CT16 .... 166 H8
Eastern Ave. Ashford TN23 .... 139 A2
Eastern Ave.
  Halfway Houses ME12 .... 3 D6
Eastern Ave.
  Queenborough ME11 .... 3 B4
Eastern Espl. Broadstairs CT10 .. 30 B5
Eastern Espl. Margate CT9 .... 8 B3
Eastern Gdns. TN24 .... 156 A8
Eastern Rd. Gillingham ME7 ... 10 F6
Eastern Rd.
  Leysdown-on-S ME12 .... 6 G2
Eastern Rd. Lydd TN29 .... 203 D7
Eastern Service Rd. CT16 ...... 166 H8
Eastfield Ho. ME14 .... 74 B2
Eastfield Rd. CT7 .... 27 A7
Eastfields. CT19 .... 178 D6
Eastgate. ME1 .... 9 D5
Eastgate Cl. CT6 .... 23 B3
Eastgate Ct. ME1 .... 9 C5
Eastgate Rd. TN30 .... 179 C8
Eastgate Terr. ME1 .... 9 C5
Eastling. ME8 .... 11 D3
Eastling Cty Prim Sch. ME13 .. 81 F5
Eastling Rd. Bayfield ME13 ...... 61 D2
Eastling Rd. Eastling ME13 ...... 81 F7
Eastmead Ave. TN23 .... 156 C8
Easton's Cnr. TN25 .... 172 F4
Eastry CE Prim Sch. CT13 .... 93 B2
Eastry Cl. Ashford TN23 .... 156 A6
Eastry Cl. Maidstone ME16 ...... 74 C7
Eastry Ct. CT3 .... 112 F5
Eastry Hospl. CT13 .... 93 B2
Eastry Park. CT13 .... 93 C1
Eastwell. 3 TN30 .... 179 A7
Eastwell Barn Mews. TN30 .... 179 A8
Eastwell Cl. Maidstone ME14 ... 75 C5
Eastwell Cl. Shadoxhurst TN26 .. 155 B1
Eastwell Meadows. TN30 ...... 179 A8
Eastwell Terr. TN25 .... 122 E3
Eastwood Cotts. ME9 .... 38 E6
Eastwood Rd. ME10 .... 36 D5
Eaton Hill. CT13 .... 7 I2
Eaton Rd. Dover CT17 .... 166 B7
Eaton Rd. Margate CT9 .... 7 I1
Eaves Rd. CT17 .... 166 A7
Ebbsfleet La. CT12 .... 51 A3
Ebony Cotts. TN30 .... 189 A6
Eccleston Rd. ME15 .... 74 F6
Echo Cl. ME15 .... 97 F6
Echo Ho. ME10 .... 37 B3
Echo Wlk. ME10 .... 4 D6
Eddington Cl. ME15 .... 97 D6
Eddington La. CT6 .... 22 F3
Eddington Way. CT6 .... 22 E3
Eden Ave. ME5 .... 32 A7
Eden Ho. TN23 .... 156 C8
Eden Rd. CT5 .... 43 A7
Edenbridge Dr. ME12 .... 3 B8
Edenbridge Ho. CT1 .... 88 B8
Edenfield. CT7 .... 27 B7
Edgar Cl. CT5 .... 21 D3
Edgar Ho. CT14 .... 117 B3
Edgar Rd. Canterbury CT1 .... 67 B1
Edgar Rd. Dover CT17 .... 149 B1
Edgar Rd. Margate CT9 .... 7 J3
Edgar Rd. Minster, Thanet CT12 .. 50 B6
Edge End Rd. CT10 .... 29 F4
Edgehill Cl. CT20 .... 177 D4
Edger Pl. 3 ME15 .... 75 A4
Edinburgh Ho. Deal CT14 ...... 117 A5
Edinburgh Ho. 7 Dover CT17 .. 166 D7
Edinburgh Pl. CT20 .... 178 B3
Edinburgh Rd.
  Ashford TN23 & TN24 .... 139 B2
Edinburgh Rd. Chatham ME4 ... 10 C2
Edinburgh Rd. Gillingham ME7 .. 10 D5
Edinburgh Rd. Margate CT9 .... 28 B8
Edinburgh Sq. Maidstone ME15 .. 97 C7
Edinburgh Sq. Maidstone ME15 .. 97 C6
Edinburgh Wlk. 5 CT9 .... 28 B8
Edith Rd. Faversham ME13 .... 62 C6
Edith Rd. Ramsgate CT11 .... 52 C6
Edith Rd. Westgate-on-S CT8 ..... 7 D1
Edmanson Ave. CT9 .... 7 E1
Edmund Cl. ME16 .... 74 A3
Edmund St. CT3 .... 91 A8
Edna Rd. ME14 .... 74 F8
Edred Rd. CT17 .... 166 B8
Edward Cl. ME5 .... 10 C1
Edward Dr. CT7 .... 28 B7
Edward Rd. Canterbury CT1 ..... 88 A8
Edward Rd. Folkestone CT19 .. 178 D6
Edward Rd. Kingsdown CT14 .. 134 C6
Edward Rd.
  Queenborough ME11 .... 3 B5
Edward Rd. Whitstable CT5 ...... 43 C5
Edward St. Chatham ME4 .... 10 A3
Edward St. Rochester ME2 .... 9 B7
Edward Terr. 8 CT20 .... 178 E6
Edwards Cl. ME8 .... 33 C5
Edwards Ct. ME16 .... 166 D8

Edwin Rd. ME8 .... 33 C8
Edwina Ave. ME12 .... 4 A7
Edwina Pl. ME9 .... 35 C7
Edyngham Cl. ME10 .... 37 A8
Effingham Cres. CT16 & CT17 .. 166 D8
Effingham St. Dover CT17 ..... 166 D8
Effingham St. Ramsgate CT11 .. 52 E6
Egbert Rd. Birchington CT7 ..... 26 D8
Egbert Rd. Faversham ME13 .... 62 C6
Egbert Rd. Minster, Thanet CT12 .. 50 B6
Egbert Rd. Westgate-on-S CT8 .... 7 C1
Egerton CE Prim Sch. TN27 ... 118 F3
Egerton Dr. CT9 .... 8 E2
Egerton House Rd. TN27 .... 118 E4
Egerton Rd. Maidstone ME14 ... 74 E7
Egerton Rd. Pluckley TN27 .... 119 B1
Egerton Rd. Temple Ewell CT16 .. 148 E5
Eggarton La. CT4 .... 107 C2
Eggringe. TN23 .... 138 E1
Egremont Rd. ME15 .... 75 F2
Eighteen Acre La. TN29 .... 198 D8
Elder. ME17 .... 99 D2
Elder Ct. ME8 .... 33 B6
Elders The. CT3 .... 68 F1
Eldon Pl. 4 CT10 .... 30 B4
Eldon St. ME4 .... 10 A4
Elfrida Cl. CT9 .... 29 C8
Elgar Pl. CT17 .... 149 B2
Elham CE Prim Sch. CT4 .... 144 F4
Elham Cl. Gillingham ME8 .... 11 B3
Elham Cl. Margate CT9 .... 8 C1
Elham Rd. CT1 .... 87 E6
Elham Way. CT10 .... 30 A2
Eling Cl. ME15 .... 97 A8
Eliot Coll. CT2 .... 66 E4
Elisans Wlk. CT1 .... 88 C3
Elizabeth Carter Ave. CT14 ... 116 F4
Elizabeth Ct. Broadstairs CT10 .. 30 B6
Elizabeth Ct. Chatham ME5 ...... 32 A7
Elizabeth Ct. Herne Bay CT6 .... 22 F5
Elizabeth Dr. CT18 .... 164 B2
Elizabeth Gdns. CT21 .... 176 B1
Elizabeth Ho. ME14 .... 75 A6
Elizabeth Kemp Ct. CT12 .... 29 C1
Elizabeth Rd. Dover CT17 ..... 166 C1
Elizabeth Rd. Ramsgate CT11 .. 52 F6
Elizabeth Way. CT6 .... 23 B3
Elizabethen Ct. TN27 .... 120 C7
Ellen Ave. CT11 .... 29 E2
Ellen's Hill. CT14 .... 116 E3
Ellen's Pl. ME9 .... 35 C6
Ellenden Ct. CT2 .... 66 C4
Ellens Rd. CT14 .... 116 F2
Ellenswood Cl. ME15 .... 76 A1
Ellesmere Mews. TN28 .... 200 C8
Ellingham Leas. ME15 .... 97 C7
Ellingham Way. TN23 .... 156 A5
Ellington Ave. CT9 .... 28 B8
Ellington Cty Inf Sch. CT11 ..... 52 C7
Ellington High Sch. CT11 .... 52 C7
Ellington Pl. CT11 .... 52 C7
Ellington Rd. CT11 .... 52 D7
Elliots Pl. ME13 .... 62 D7
Elliott Park Sch. ME12 .... 4 A7
Ellis Dr. CT14 .... 200 C8
Ellis Rd. CT5 .... 21 A3
Ellis Way. CT6 .... 23 C2
Ellison Cl. CT5 .... 21 C1
Ellison Ct. ME15 .... 62 E6
Ellison Way. ME8 .... 12 A2
Elm Cl. ME4 .... 9 E1
Elm Cl. TN27 .... 118 F3
Elm Cotts. TN25 .... 122 E3
Elm Court Ind Est. ME7 .... 32 E3
Elm Ct. ME8 .... 27 E8
Elm Fields. TN29 .... 199 A6
Elm Gdns. CT21 .... 176 E2
Elm Gr. Maidstone ME15 .... 75 B3
Elm Gr. Sittingbourne ME10 ..... 37 B4
Elm Gr. Westgate-on-S CT8 ...... 27 E8
Elm La. ME4 .... 4 E5
Elm La. 11 CT21 .... 176 B2
Elm Park Gdns. CT17 .... 165 F7
Elm Pl. TN23 .... 155 F7
Elm Rd. Aylesham CT3 .... 112 E5
Elm Rd. 6 Folkestone CT19 ... 178 E6
Elm Rd. Gillingham ME7 .... 10 E6
Elm Rd. St Mary's Bay TN29 .. 194 F3
Elm Tree Dr. ME1 .... 9 A2
Elm Wood Cl. CT5 .... 21 C2
Elm Wood W. CT5 .... 21 C2
Elmfield. Gillingham ME8 .... 11 A3
Elmfield. Tenterden TN30 ...... 179 B8
Elmfield Ct. Coxheath ME17 .... 96 C3
Elmfield Ct. Tenterden TN30 .. 179 B8
Elmhurst Gdns. ME1 .... 9 E3
Elmleigh Rd. CT3 .... 90 A8
Elmley Rd. ME11 .... 3 A2
Elmley Rd. ME12 .... 4 D3
Elmley Way. CT9 .... 28 F6
Elms Ave. CT11 .... 52 D6
Elms Hill. CT5 .... 165 D6
Elms The. Hersden CT3 .... 46 E1
Elms The. Teynham ME9 .... 39 A2
Elms Vale Rd. CT15 & CT17 .. 165 E7
Elmstead Pl. 10 CT20 .... 178 E5
Elmstone Cl. ME16 .... 74 B2
Elmstone Gdns. CT9 .... 8 E2
Elmstone Hole Rd. ME17 ...... 100 D1
Elmstone La. ME16 .... 74 B2
Elmstone Rd. Gillingham ME8 .. 33 C7
Elmstone Rd. Ramsgate CT11 .. 52 D7
Elmton La. CT15 .... 114 C1
Elmtree. TN26 .... 181 C1
Elmway. ME12 .... 5 F6
Elmwood Ave. CT10 .... 30 A8
Elmwood Cl. CT10 .... 30 A7

Elventon Cl. CT19 .... 177 E7
Elverland La. ME13 & ME9 ...... 61 B2
Elvington Cl. ME16 .... 74 D5
Elvington La. CT18 .... 162 C2
Elwick La. 13 TN23 .... 139 B2
Elwick Rd. TN23 .... 139 B2
Ely Cl. ME8 .... 11 E2
Embassy Cl. ME7 .... 10 F1
Emerald Cl. ME1 .... 31 D7
Emerald View. ME5 .... 32 B6
Emerson Gdns. CT5 .... 21 D3
Empire Terr. CT9 .... 28 E8
Empress Gdns. ME12 .... 6 D4
Emsworth Gr. ME14 .... 75 D6
Enbrook Rd. CT20 .... 177 E4
Enbrook Valley. CT20 .... 177 E5
Encombe. CT20 .... 177 D3
Enfield Rd. CT14 .... 117 D7
Engineers Ct. 1 TN23 .... 139 B2
English Martyrs'
  RC Prim Sch. ME2 .... 9 B8
Ennerdale. ME13 .... 62 E6
Ennerdale Gdns. CT3 .... 112 F6
Enterprise Bsns Est. ME2 .... 9 E7
Enterprise Cl. ME2 .... 9 B8
Enterprise Ctr The. ME5 .... 54 C8
Enterprise Rd. Maidstone ME15 .. 75 A1
Enterprise Rd. Margate CT9 ..... 29 A6
Enticott Cl. CT5 .... 21 A1
Epaul La. ME1 .... 9 C6
Epping Cl. CT6 .... 23 B2
Epple Bay Ave. CT7 .... 27 B8
Epple Bay Rd. CT7 .... 27 A8
Epple Rd. CT7 .... 27 B8
Epps Rd. ME10 .... 36 E3
Epsom Cl. ME15 .... 97 F6
Eric Rd. CT17 .... 149 B2
Erith Cl. ME14 .... 75 A8
Erith St. CT17 .... 149 B1
Ernest Dr. ME16 .... 74 B5
Ernest Rd. ME4 .... 10 A3
Ernwell Rd. CT19 .... 178 D6
Ersham Rd. CT1 .... 88 A7
Eskdale Ave. CT11 .... 52 A7
Esmonde Dr. CT12 .... 27 F2
Esplanade. Dover CT17 .... 166 D6
Esplanade. Rochester ME1 .... 9 B5
Esplanade.
  Westgate-on-S CT8 & CT9 .... 7 C1
Essella Pk. CT1 .... 139 E1
Essella Rd. TN24 .... 139 E1
Essetford Rd. TN23 .... 156 A7
Essex Ave. CT6 .... 22 B4
Essex Gdns. CT7 .... 26 F6
Essex Rd. Canterbury CT1 .... 88 D7
Essex Rd. Westgate-on-S CT8 ... 27 F8
Essex St. CT1 .... 43 D8
Estelle Cl. ME1 .... 31 D7
Esther Ct. ME10 .... 36 E8
Estuary Rd. ME12 .... 1 C1
Etchden Rd. TN26 .... 154 A8
Ethel Rd. CT10 .... 29 F5
Ethel-Maud Ct. ME7 .... 10 D7
Ethelbert Cres. CT9 .... 8 A3
Ethelbert Gdns. CT9 .... 7 J3
Ethelbert Rd. Birchington CT7 .. 26 D8
Ethelbert Rd. Canterbury CT1 .. 88 B6
Ethelbert Rd. Deal CT14 .... 95 C1
Ethelbert Rd. Dover CT17 ..... 166 C8
Ethelbert Rd. Faversham ME13 .. 62 C6
Ethelbert Rd.
  Folkestone CT19 .... 178 D7
Ethelbert Rd. Margate CT9 .... 7 J3
Ethelbert Rd. Ramsgate CT11 .. 52 D6
Ethelbert Rd. Rochester ME1 .... 9 C4
Ethelbert Road Cty Inf Sch.
  ME13 .... 62 C6
Ethelbert Sq. CT8 .... 7 C1
Ethelbert Terr. Margate CT9 ...... 8 A3
Ethelbert Terr.
  Westgate-on-S CT8 .... 7 C1
Ethelburga Dr. CT18 .... 161 B7
Ethelred Rd. ME13 .... 62 C6
Ethelred Ct. CT8 .... 7 C1
Eton Cl. ME5 .... 31 F4
Eurogate Bsns Pk. TN24 .... 139 B5
Eurolink Way. ME10 .... 36 F4
Eva Rd. ME7 .... 10 D3
Evans Rd. TN24 .... 157 A7
Evelings Alley. 12 CT5 .... 20 D2
Evelyn Ct. CT21 .... 177 A2
Evelyn Rd. ME14 .... 74 E3
Evenhill Rd. CT3 .... 89 E8
Everard Way. ME13 .... 62 B8
Everglades The. ME7 .... 32 F6
Evergreen Cl. Gillingham ME7 ... 33 A5
Evergreen Cl. Iwade ME9 .... 14 D4
Everist Ct. CT18 .... 161 C6
Eversley Cl. ME16 .... 74 C6
Eversley Coll. CT20 .... 177 F4
Eversley Rd. CT21 .... 177 B3
Eversley Way. CT20 .... 177 F5
Evison Cl. CT19 .... 149 B2
Ewart Rd. ME4 .... 9 E1
Exchange St. CT14 .... 117 D7
Exeter Cl. CT19 .... 177 D6
Exmoor Rise. TN24 .... 139 B4
Exmouth Rd. ME7 .... 10 C7
Exton Cl. ME5 .... 32 C2
Exton Gdns. ME14 .... 75 F5
Eyhorne St. ME17 .... 101 C6
Eylesden Court Sch. ME14 ...... 76 B4
Eynsford Cl. CT9 .... 8 F2
Eynsford Rd. ME16 .... 74 D5
Eythorn Court Barn. CT15 ..... 131 B7

Eythorne Cl. TN24 .... 139 D5
Eythorne Elvington
  Cty Prim Sch. CT15 .... 131 C8
Eythorne Rd. CT15 .... 130 E6
Eythorne Sta. CT15 .... 131 C8

Fagus Cl. ME5 .... 32 B1
Fair St. CT10 .... 29 E4
Fair View Jun & Inf Schs. ME8 .. 33 C5
Fairacre. CT10 .... 29 E4
Fairacres Cl. CT6 .... 23 C4
Fairbourne Heath Cotts.
  ME17 .... 100 B1
Fairbourne La. ME17 .... 100 C4
Fairfax Bsns Ctr. ME15 .... 97 F4
Fairfax Cl. Folkestone CT20 ... 177 D5
Fairfax Cl. Gillingham ME8 ...... 33 D5
Fairfax Dr. CT6 .... 23 F5
Fairfield. Deal CT14 .... 116 F6
Fairfield. Elham CT4 .... 144 F5
Fairfield Cl. CT18 .... 200 B7
Fairfield Pk. CT10 .... 29 E4
Fairfield Rd. Broadstairs CT10 .. 29 E4
Fairfield Rd. Minster, Thanet
  CT12 .... 50 B7
Fairfield Rd.
  New Romney TN28 .... 200 B7
Fairfield Rd. Ramsgate CT11 .... 29 E2
Fairfield Terr. TN26 .... 183 A7
Fairhurst Dr. ME15 .... 96 B4
Fairings The. TN30 .... 179 B8
Fairlawn. CT5 .... 21 D1
Fairlawn Rd. CT10 & CT12 ...... 29 B3
Fairlead Rd. ME1 .... 9 D1
Fairleas. ME10 .... 37 B2
Fairlight Ave. CT12 .... 52 B8
Fairlight Rd. CT21 .... 176 A3
Fairmeadow. ME14 .... 74 F4
Fairoaks. CT6 .... 23 B3
Fairservice Cl. ME10 .... 37 C5
Fairview Ave. ME8 .... 33 B5
Fairview Cl. CT9 .... 8 A2
Fairview Cotts. ME15 .... 96 F5
Fairview Gdns. Deal CT14 ...... 117 A2
Fairview Gdns. Sturry CT2 .... 68 A6
Fairview Ind Pk. TN26 .... 183 D7
Fairview Rd. Elvington CT15 .. 114 A3
Fairview Rd.
  Sittingbourne ME10 .... 37 A3
Fairway Ave. CT19 .... 178 A4
Fairway Cl. Rochester ME1 .... 9 C1
Fairway Cl. St Mary's Bay TN29 .. 194 F3
Fairway Cres. CT5 .... 43 A7
Fairway The. Deal CT14 .... 117 C8
Fairway The. Herne Bay CT6 .... 22 D2
Fairway The. Hythe CT21 ...... 176 C1
Fairway The.
  Littlestone-on-S TN28 .... 200 D6
Fairway The. Rochester ME1 ..... 9 C1
Fairway The.
  Sittingbourne ME10 .... 36 E1
Fairway The.
  St Mary's Bay TN29 .... 195 A5
Fairways The. ME13 .... 62 A6
Fairwood Ind Est. TN23 .... 139 A1
Falcon Cl. ME10 .... 37 A2
Falcon Gdns. ME12 .... 4 D7
Falcon Way. TN23 .... 155 E7
Falkland Pl. ME5 .... 31 E1
Fallowfield. Chatham ME5 .... 32 B8
Fallowfield. Sittingbourne ME10 .. 37 A2
Fallowfield CT. ME14 .... 75 E4
Fan The. CT16 .... 166 H8
Fanconi Rd. ME8 .... 32 B3
Fancy Row. ME14 .... 76 C5
Fane Way. ME8 .... 33 D4
Fans La. ME9 .... 14 D4
Fant La. ME16 .... 74 B2
Faraday Rd. ME14 .... 75 C7
Fareham Wlk. 10 ME15 .... 97 F6
Farleigh Cl. ME16 .... 74 A2
Farleigh Hill. ME15 .... 74 E1
Farleigh Hill Ret Pk. ME15 ...... 74 E1
Farleigh La. ME16 .... 74 A1
Farleigh Trad Est. ME16 .... 74 E1
Farley Cl. Chatham ME5 .... 32 D2
Farley Cl. Shadoxhurst TN26 .. 155 A1
Farley Rd. CT9 .... 28 F1
Farm Cl. CT21 .... 155 E7
Farm Cres. ME10 .... 37 A2
Farm House Cl. CT5 .... 43 F8
Farm La. CT14 .... 116 F6
Farm Rd. Chatham ME5 .... 31 E3
Farm Rd. Hamstreet TN26 ...... 183 A7
Farmer Cl. Hythe CT21 .... 176 D3
Farmer Cl. Leeds ME17 .... 99 A6
Farmhouse Cl. CT4 .... 128 F7
Farnborough Cl. ME16 .... 74 C2
Farncombe Way. CT16 .... 149 B7
Farne Cl. ME15 .... 97 A6
Farnham Cl. ME8 .... 12 B2
Farningham Cl. ME14 .... 75 C6
Farraday Cl. ME1 .... 31 D8
Farrar Rd. CT7 .... 27 A6
Farrers Wlk. TN23 .... 156 B4
Farrier Cl. Ashford TN23 .... 138 F5
Farrier Cl. Maidstone ME14 ..... 75 E5
Farrier St. CT14 .... 117 D7
Farriers Ct. ME8 .... 34 C8
Farrow Ct. TN23 .... 156 A6
Farthing Cnr. ME9 .... 33 E3
Farthingloe Ct. CT17 .... 166 A6
Farthingloe Rd. CT17 .... 166 A6
Farthings Cotts. ME14 .... 53 F1

Farthings Ct. CT2 .... 66 C4
Fauchon's Cl. ME14 .... 75 F3
Fauchon's La. ME14 .... 75 F4
Faulkners La. CT2 .... 66 A1
Faussett Hill. CT4 .... 109 F8
Faversham Cottage Hospl.
ME13 .... 62 C7
Faversham Rd.
Boughton Lees TN24 & TN25 ...... 122 E5
Faversham Rd. Charing TN27 .. 103 E1
Faversham Rd.
Faversham ME13 & ME9 .... 61 B5
Faversham Rd. Lenham ME17 .. 101 E7
Faversham Rd.
Paddock ME13 & TN25 & TN27 ... 104 C3
Faversham Rd.
Pested CT4 & ME13 & TN25 ...... 105 B4
Faversham Rd.
Wichling ME17 & ME9 .... 80 B4
Faversham Reach. ME13 .... 62 D8
Faversham Sta. ME13 .... 62 D6
Fawley Cl. ME14 .... 74 E7
Featherbed La. Selling ME13 .... 84 A7
Featherbed La.
Sittingbourne ME9 .... 14 E2
Featherby
Cty Prim Inf Sch. ME8 .... 11 A3
Featherby Jun Sch. ME8 .... 11 A3
Featherby Rd.
Gillingham,Lower Twydall ME7 .. 11 A3
Featherby Rd.
Gillingham,Twydall ME8 .... 11 A3
Felborough Cl. CT4 .... 107 C8
Felderland Cl.
Park Wood ME17 .... 97 C5
Felderland Cl. Sandwich CT14 ... 93 F5
Felderland Dr. ME17 .... 97 E5
Felderland La. CT13 & CT14 .... 93 E4
Felderland Rd. ME17 .... 97 E5
Feldspar Cl. ME5 .... 32 A1
Fellows Cl. ME8 .... 33 B6
Fenner Cl. CT20 .... 177 E4
Fenoulhet Way. CT6 .... 23 A5
Ferdi Lethert Ho. TN24 .... 139 E5
Ferguson Cl. CT20 .... 176 F2
Ferguson Rd. TN29 .... 202 D2
Fern Bank Cres. CT19 .... 178 D6
Fern Cl. Hawkinge CT18 .... 163 C6
Fern Cl. Whitstable CT5 .... 21 C1
Fern Ct. CT10 .... 30 B5
Fern Wlk. ME10 .... 37 C5
Fernbank Cl. ME5 .... 31 F2
Ferndale Cl. ME12 .... 3 D6
Ferndale Ct. CT7 .... 27 A6
Ferndale Rd. ME7 .... 10 E5
Ferndown. CT7 .... 26 D8
Ferndown Cl. ME7 .... 33 A5
Ferne La. CT15 .... 147 D3
Ferne Way. CT20 .... 177 E6
Fernfield. CT18 .... 163 C6
Fernfield La. CT18 .... 163 C7
Fernhill Rd. ME16 .... 74 A2
Fernlea Ave. CT6 .... 22 E4
Fernleigh Cl. ME13 .... 64 B3
Ferrier Cl. ME8 .... 33 E4
Ferry Rd. Iwade ME9 .... 14 E4
Ferry Rd.
Queenborough ME11 & ME12 ..... 3 D1
Ferry View. ME11 .... 2 F3
Fiddling La. TN25 .... 159 E6
Field Ave. CT5 .... 67 D3
Field Cl. ME5 .... 31 E6
Field End. ME4 .... 140 A1
Field End Pl. ME13 .... 64 A3
Field Mill Rd. ME7 .... 119 B5
Field View. Kingsnorth TN23 .. 156 B4
Field View. Whitstable CT5 ...... 43 B7
Field View. ME12 .... 3 C6
Field Way. CT2 .... 67 F5
Fielder Cl. ME10 .... 37 C5
Fielding St. ME13 .... 62 C7
Fieldings The. ME10 .... 36 E2
Fieldworks Rd. ME4 & ME7 ..... 10 A7
Fiesta Wlk. CT1 .... 88 C7
Fife Cl. CT6 .... 22 B3
Fifth Ave. CT9 .... 8 B3
Fig Tree Rd. CT10 .... 29 F7
Fiji Terr. ME14 .... 75 A7
Filer Rd. ME12 .... 3 E7
Filmer Rd. CT4 .... 88 F1
Finch Ct. ME14 .... 74 E7
Finch Gr. CT21 .... 187 D8
Finch Mews. CT14 .... 117 C4
Finches The.
Sittingbourne ME10 .... 36 F3
Finches The.
St Nicholas at Wade CT7 .... 25 E2
Findlay Cl. ME8 .... 33 D6
Findley St. ME8 .... 176 B2
Finglesham La. ME15 .... 97 C8
Finlay Cl. ME13 .... 62 B7
Finsbury Ct. CT11 .... 52 E8
Finsbury Rd. CT11 .... 52 E8
Fintonagh Dr. ME14 .... 75 B6
Finwell Rd. ME8 .... 12 A2
Fir Ct. TN24 .... 139 F1
Fir Tree Cl. CT11 .... 52 C6
Fir Tree Gr. Bredhurst ME7 ..... 33 B1
Fir Tree Gr. Chatham ME5 .... 32 D1
Fir Tree Hill. CT13 .... 93 B6
Firbank Gdns. CT9 .... 28 D7
Firbanks. CT5 .... 43 F8
Firethorn Cl. ME7 .... 10 E6
Firs Cl. CT19 .... 177 D7

Firs La. CT19 .... 177 D7
Firs Rd. CT4 .... 112 F1
Firs The. Deal CT14 .... 117 C8
Firs The. Hersden CT3 .... 46 E1
First Ave. Broadstairs CT10 ...... 8 F2
First Ave. Chatham ME4 .... 10 C2
First Ave. Eastchurch ME12 .... 5 E5
First Ave. Gillingham ME7 .... 10 E3
First Ave. Margate CT9 .... 8 B3
First Ave. Rushenden ME11 .... 2 F3
First Ave. Sheerness ME12 .... 1 D1
Firs The. ME15 .... 76 E2
Firtree Cl. CT2 .... 66 B3
Fish Market. CT19 .... 178 E5
Fisher Cl. CT21 .... 176 D1
Fisher Rd. Canterbury CT2 ...... 66 D1
Fisher Rd. Chatham ME5 .... 32 B7
Fisher St. Maidstone ME14 .... 75 A6
Fisher St. Sandwich CT13 .... 73 A1
Fisher Street Rd. ME13 .... 83 E2
Fishermans Ctyd. CT14 .... 117 D3
Fishmonger's La. CT16 .... 166 E7
Fitzgerald Ave. CT6 .... 22 C4
Fitzmary Ave. CT9 .... 7 E1
Fitzroy Ave. Broadstairs CT10 .... 8 G2
Fitzroy Ave. Margate CT9 .... 8 B1
Fitzroy Ave. Ramsgate CT12 ..... 29 B2
Fitzroy Cres. CT5 .... 20 F2
Fitzthorold Ho. ME7 .... 10 E7
Fitzwalter Ct. CT16 .... 149 B3
Fitzwilliam Rd. ME14 .... 75 F5
Five Acre Wood Sch. ME15 ..... 97 B7
Five Bells La. ME1 .... 9 D4
Five Vents La. TN29 .... 199 B8
Fiveways L Ctr. ME14 .... 10 A4
Fiveways Rise. CT14 .... 116 F5
Flamingo Cl. ME5 .... 32 A7
Flanders Cl. ME10 .... 14 F1
Flanders Field. TN25 .... 157 E4
Flax Court La. CT15 .... 131 C7
Flaxman Cl. ME7 .... 10 A6
Flaxman Dr. ME14 .... 74 C6
Flaxpond Rd. TN23 .... 155 F7
Fleet Ave. ME12 .... 1 C1
Fleet Rd. Rochester ME1 .... 9 D1
Fleet Rd.
St Margaret's at Cliffe CT15 .. 134 A1
Fleet Villas. TN24 .... 139 D7
Fleets La. CT2 .... 66 D7
Fleetwood Ave. CT6 .... 22 D4
Fleetwood Cl. ME12 .... 4 B6
Fleming Way. CT13 & CT3 ...... 92 D6
Fleming Way. CT19 .... 178 E8
Fletcher Rd. CT5 .... 21 B1
Flete Rd. CT9 .... 28 D5
Flimwell. TN23 .... 155 D6
Flint Gn. ME5 .... 32 C3
Flint La. ME17 .... 79 C1
Flood Hatch. ME15 .... 74 D2
Flood La. ME13 .... 62 C8
Flood St. TN25 .... 157 D2
Flora Rd. CT11 .... 52 E8
Florence Ave. CT5 .... 43 B7
Florence Cl. CT9 .... 8 B3
Florence Rd. Maidstone ME16 .. 74 E3
Florence Rd. Ramsgate CT11 ... 52 D6
Florence St. ME7 .... 9 B8
Florida Cl. CT16 .... 149 B3
Flower Rise. ME14 .... 74 F7
Flume End. ME16 .... 74 D2
Flying Horse La. CT16 .... 166 E7
Foads Hill. CT12 .... 51 D6
Foads La. CT12 .... 51 D5
Fodbury Ct. CT8 .... 7 C1
Foley Cl. TN24 .... 157 A7
Foley St. ME14 .... 75 A5
Folkestone Harbour Sta.
CT20 .... 178 E4
Folkestone Race Course.
TN25 .... 175 A6
Folkestone Rd.
Church Hougham CT15 .... 165 D4
Folkestone Rd.
Dover CT17 & CT15 .... 166 B7
Folkestone Rd.
East Guldeford TN31 .... 196 C3
Folkestone
Sch for Girls. CT20 .... 177 F4
Folkestone West Sta. CT18 .... 177 F5
Folkestone Ho. ME15 .... 97 F6
Folly Rd. CT20 .... 178 E6
Fonblanque Rd. ME12 .... 1 D2
Fontwell Cl. ME15 .... 97 F6
Foord Almshouses. ME1 .... 9 B3
Foord Rd. ME17 .... 101 D5
Foord Rd N. CT17 & CT20 ..... 178 D5
Foord Rd S. CT20 .... 178 D5
Foord St. ME1 .... 9 D4
Forbes Rd. ME13 .... 62 C6
Ford Cl. Bridge CT4 .... 88 F1
Ford Cl. Herne Bay CT6 .... 22 A4
Ford Hill. CT3 .... 46 E8
Ford Way. TN23 .... 138 F1
Ford Wlk. CT5 .... 43 A3
Fordcombe Cl. ME15 .... 97 F7
Fordingbridge Cl. ME16 .... 74 B5
Fordoun Rd. CT10 .... 29 F5
Fordwich Cl. ME16 .... 74 B7
Fordwich Gn. ME8 .... 11 C3
Fordwich Gr. CT10 .... 29 E7
Fordwich Pl. CT13 .... 93 F8
Fordwich Rd. CT7 .... 67 F4
Foreland Ave.
Folkestone CT19 .... 178 F6
Foreland Ave. Margate CT9 .... 8 D1
Foreland Ct. Ramsgate CT11 .... 52 D5
Foreland Rd.
St Margaret's at Cliffe CT15 .. 151 A5

Foreland Park Ho. CT10 .... 30 B7
Foreland Rd. CT15 .... 151 A4
Foreland Sch The. CT10 .... 30 A6
Foreland The. CT1 .... 88 B5
Forelands Sq. CT13 .... 117 B3
Foreness Cl. CT10 & CT9 .... 8 G3
Forest Cotts. TN25 .... 105 C2
Forest Dr. ME5 .... 31 F2
Forest Hill. ME15 .... 74 F1
Forestall Meadow. TN23 .... 156 B4
Forestdale Rd. ME5 .... 54 A8
Foresters Cl. ME5 .... 31 F2
Foresters Way. CT20 .... 178 D5
Forestry Cotts. CT4 .... 125 B7
Forge Cl. Eythorne CT15 .... 131 C7
Forge Cl. Sellindge TN25 ...... 159 D1
Forge Cl. Sturry CT2 .... 67 F5
Forge Cotts. CT3 .... 47 C8
Forge Field. CT15 .... 164 E5
Forge Hill. Aldington TN25 .... 173 A5
Forge Hill. Bethersden TN26 .. 153 E5
Forge Ho. Canterbury CT1 .... 87 E6
Forge Ho. Ickham CT3 .... 69 C1
Forge La. Ashford TN23 .... 139 B2
Forge La. Boxley ME14 .... 54 C2
Forge La. Boyden Gate CT3 ...... 47 C8
Forge La. Bredhurst ME7 .... 33 A1
Forge La. Dean Street ME15 ..... 96 C7
Forge La. Egerton Forstal TN27 .. 118 C1
Forge La. Gillingham ME7 .... 10 E7
Forge La. Leeds ME17 .... 98 F7
Forge La. Ramsgate CT12 .... 52 C7
Forge La. Sutton CT15 .... 133 A6
Forge La. Upchurch ME9 .... 12 F3
Forge La. Whitfield CT16 ...... 149 A8
Forge La. Whitstable CT5 .... 43 D8
Forge Lane Cty Inf Sch. ME7 .. 10 E6
Forge Meadow.
Harrietsham ME17 .... 100 D6
Forge Meadow.
Stone in Oxney TN30 .... 190 A4
Forge Meads. TN30 .... 188 E3
Forge Path. CT16 .... 149 A8
Forge Rd. ME10 .... 36 E6
Forgefield. TN26 .... 153 D5
Forgefields. CT6 .... 46 B8
Forrens The. CT1 .... 67 A1
Forrester Cl. CT20 .... 67 C2
Forson Cl. TN30 .... 179 B8
Forstal Cotts.
Lenham Heath ME17 .... 102 A1
Forstal Cotts.
Pratling Street ME20 .... 53 B2
Forstal La. ME17 .... 96 C4
Forstal Rd.
Egerton Forstal TN27 .... 118 C1
Forstal Rd. Forstal ME20 .... 53 C2
Forstal Rd.
Woolage Village CT4 .... 112 E1
Forstal The. Preston CT3 .... 70 B6
Forstal The. Wye TN25 .... 123 E2
Forsters. ME17 .... 98 E4
Fort Burgoyne (Casemated
Barracks). CT16 .... 149 E2
Fort Burgoyne Rd. CT16 .... 149 E1
Fort Cl. TN9 .... 204 E6
Fort Cres. CT9 .... 7 J3
Fort Hill. CT9 .... 7 I3
Fort Lower Prom. CT9 .... 7 J3
Fort Luton (Mus). ME4 .... 10 A1
Fort Paragon. CT9 .... 7 J3
Fort Pitt Gram Sch. ME1 .... 9 E4
Fort Pitt Hill. ME1 & ME4 .... 9 E4
Fort Pitt St. ME4 .... 9 E3
Fort Prom. CT9 .... 7 J3
Fort Rd. Broadstairs CT10 .... 30 B4
Fort Rd. Hythe CT21 .... 176 A2
Fort Rd. Margate CT9 .... 7 I3
Fort St. ME1 .... 9 D4
Fortuna Ct. CT11 .... 52 D7
Forty Acres Hill. ME12 .... 4 C4
Forty Acres Rd. CT2 .... 66 E2
Forum The. ME10 .... 36 F4
Fostall Gn. TN23 .... 155 F7
Fostall Rd. ME13 .... 40 C1
Foster Cl. CT19 .... 177 E7
Foster Clark Est. ME15 .... 75 B2
Foster St. ME15 .... 75 A3
Foster Way. CT14 .... 117 B5
Foster's Ave. CT10 .... 29 E7
Foster's Ct. CT13 .... 94 A7
Fostington Way. ME5 .... 31 F1
Foulds Cl. ME8 .... 33 B5
Fountain Ent Pk. ME15 .... 75 A1
Fountain Inn Ct. CT9 .... 7 I3
Fountain La. ME16 .... 74 A2
Fountain St.
Sittingbourne ME10 .... 36 E4
Fountain St. Whitstable CT5 .. 20 D2
Fountains Ct. TN24 .... 140 A1
Four Oaks. ME13 .... 61 B8
Four Turnings. CT3 .... 70 B3
Four Wents.
Langley Heath ME17 .... 98 E3
Four Wents. Marlpit ME17 .... 97 E2
Fouracre Cotts. ME9 .... 34 F6
Fourth Ave. Eastchurch ME12 .... 5 F5
Fourth Ave. Gillingham ME7 .... 10 E4
Fowey Cl. ME5 .... 32 C5
Fowler Cl. ME8 .... 33 C3
Fox Cl. CT18 .... 161 B7
Fox Hill. ME10 & ME9 .... 37 D3
Fox Holt Rd. CT15 .... 146 B2
Fox Way. CT4 .... 128 F3
Fox's Cross. CT5 .... 43 B4
Fox's Cross Hill. CT5 .... 43 A3

Fox's Cross Rd. CT5 .... 43 C3
Foxborough Cl. CT13 .... 93 B6
Foxborough Hill. CT13 .... 93 B5
Foxborough Cl. CT12 .... 50 C6
Foxburrow Cl. ME8 .... 33 D5
Foxden Dr. ME15 .... 75 F1
Foxdown Cl. CT2 .... 66 E2
Foxglove Cres. ME5 .... 31 E4
Foxglove Gn. TN24 .... 139 F2
Foxglove Rd. TN24 .... 139 E1
Foxglove Rise. ME14 .... 74 E7
Foxgrove. ME10 .... 36 E7
Foxgrove Rd. CT5 .... 21 A1
Foxhunter Pk The. CT12 .... 49 D6
Foxley Rd. ME11 .... 3 A5
Frampton Rd. CT21 .... 176 A2
France Rd. CT16 .... 149 A5
Frances Gdns. CT11 .... 52 F8
Francis Ave. CT13 .... 95 B7
Francis Dr. ME5 .... 32 A2
Francis La. ME15 .... 97 F5
Francis Rd. Ashford TN23 ..... 156 B8
Francis Rd. Broadstairs CT10 ... 30 B7
Frank Walters
Bsns Pk The. CT10 .... 29 D3
Frankapps Cl. ME9 .... 35 B6
Franklin Dr. ME14 .... 75 D4
Franklin Rd. ME7 .... 10 D5
Franklins Cotts. ME5 .... 96 C5
Franklyn Rd. CT2 .... 87 C8
Franks Ct. ME8 .... 11 B2
Freda Cl. CT10 .... 29 F1
Frederick Rd. Deal CT14 .... 117 A3
Frederick Rd. Gillingham ME7 .. 10 C4
Frederick St. ME10 .... 36 E4
Freedom The. CT15 .... 151 A7
Freeman Ct. ME10 .... 36 E4
Freeman Gdns. ME6 .... 9 F2
Freeman Way. ME15 .... 97 E7
Freeman's Cl. CT5 .... 43 A6
Freeman's Rd. CT12 .... 50 B6
Freemen's Way. CT14 .... 117 B3
Freesia Cl. ME7 .... 10 F6
Fremantle Rd. CT20 .... 177 C5
Fremlins Rd. ME14 .... 76 C4
French's Row. ME9 .... 38 D2
Frencham Cl. CT2 .... 67 A4
Frensham Cl. ME15 .... 37 B4
Frensham Wlk. ME5 .... 31 F1
Freshfield La. CT15 .... 176 B4
Freshland Rd. ME16 .... 74 B4
Freshlands. CT5 .... 23 E5
Freshwater Rd. ME5 .... 32 B7
Friars Ave. ME5 .... 31 F2
Friars Cl. CT5 .... 21 A1
Friars Sch. TN23 .... 155 B8
Friars The. CT1 .... 66 F1
Friars Way. CT16 .... 149 A3
Friary Pl. ME2 .... 9 B7
Friary Prec. ME2 .... 9 B7
Friary Way. CT2 .... 66 D2
Frid Cnr. TN27 .... 153 E7
Friendly Cl. CT9 .... 8 D1
Friends Ave. CT9 .... 29 D8
Frindsbury Rd. ME2 .... 9 B8
Frinstead Wlk. ME16 .... 74 B7
Frinsted Cl. ME8 .... 11 C3
Friston Way. ME1 .... 31 B8
Frith Rd. Aldington TN25 ...... 172 C6
Frith Rd. Dover CT16 .... 149 C1
Frithwood Cl. ME15 .... 75 F1
Frittenden Cl. TN23 .... 155 E6
Frobisher Cl. ME10 .... 36 E7
Frobisher Gdns. ME1 .... 9 C2
Frog Farm Cotts. ME9 .... 13 A4
Frog La. CT4 .... 111 C6
Frogmore Wlk. ME17 .... 101 C5
Frognal Cl. ME9 .... 38 B2
Frognal Gdns. ME9 .... 38 C2
Frognal La. ME9 .... 38 B2
Front Brents. ME13 .... 62 D8
Front Rd. TN26 .... 169 A1
Front St. CT14 .... 133 F5
Front The. CT15 .... 151 A4
Frost Cres. ME5 .... 32 A7
Froyle Cl. ME16 .... 74 C6
Fruiterer's Cl. ME9 .... 59 B7
Fulbert Dr. ME14 .... 75 F5
Fulbert Rd. CT16 .... 149 B5
Fulham Ave. CT9 .... 28 C7
Fullers Cl. ME14 .... 76 A4
Fulmar Ct. TN29 .... 194 F3
Fulsam Pl. CT9 .... 7 H1
Fulston Manor Sch. ME10 .... 36 F2
Fulston Pl. ME10 .... 37 A3
Furfield Cl. ME17 .... 97 E5
Furrell's Rd. ME1 .... 9 D5
Furze Hill Cres. ME12 .... 3 E6
Fusilier Ave. CT20 .... 177 B5
Fyndon Ho. CT1 .... 88 C7

Galena Cl. ME5 .... 32 A1
Gallants La. ME15 .... 96 A1
Galleon Cl. ME1 .... 31 C8
Galliard St. CT13 .... 94 A8
Gallow's Cnr. CT21 .... 176 A2
Galloways Rd. TN29 .... 203 C5
Gallwey Ave. CT7 .... 26 E7
Galway Rd. ME12 .... 1 D1
Gammon's Farm La. TN29 ..... 185 B3
Gandy's La. ME17 .... 97 C2
Gange Mews. ME13 .... 62 D7
Gann Rd. CT5 .... 20 F2
Gaol La. CT16 .... 166 D7
Gap House Sch. CT10 .... 30 B2
Gap The. Blean CT2 .... 66 A7
Gap The. Canterbury CT1 .... 88 B5
Garden Cl. Maidstone ME15 .... 97 E7
Garden Cl. Rough Common CT2 .. 66 A2
Garden Cotts. CT3 .... 91 A7
Garden Hall The. TN25 .... 124 A1
Garden of England Pk
(Mobile Home Pk). ME17 ...... 100 B7
Garden Rd. CT19 .... 178 D6
Garden St. ME7 .... 10 A6
Gardens The. Coxheath ME17 .. 96 C3
Gardens The. Ivychurch TN29 . 192 F4
Gardiner St. ME7 .... 10 C6
Garfield Pl. ME13 .... 62 D7
Garfield Rd. Gillingham ME7 ... 10 D6
Garfield Rd. Margate CT9 .... 7 H2
Garlinge Cty Inf Sch. CT9 ...... 28 C8
Garlinge Cty Jun Sch. CT9 ..... 28 B8
Garlinge Green Rd. CT4 .... 108 C6
Garrard Ave. CT9 .... 28 B8
Garrington Cl. ME14 .... 75 C6
Garrison Rd. ME12 .... 1 B3
Gas House Rd. ME1 .... 9 C6
Gas La. ME13 .... 63 F3
Gas Rd. Sittingbourne ME10 .... 36 F5
Gas Rd. Sittingbourne ME10 .... 37 C6
Gas St. CT1 .... 87 F7
Gasworks La. TN23 .... 139 B2
Gatcombe Cl. Chatham ME5 .... 32 A5
Gatcombe Cl. Maidstone ME16 . 74 B5
Gateacre Rd. CT5 .... 43 A6
Gatefield La. ME13 .... 62 D7
Gateway Cl. CT11 .... 52 F7
Gateway The. CT16 .... 166 E7
Gatland La. ME16 .... 74 B2
Gault Cl. ME15 .... 76 A2
Gaunt's Cl. CT14 .... 117 A4
Gayhurst Cl. ME8 .... 33 D6
Gayhurst Dr. ME10 .... 36 C5
Gaze Hill Ave. ME10 .... 37 A3
Gazedown. TN29 .... 194 F3
Gean Cl. ME5 .... 54 A8
Genesta Ave. CT5 .... 43 B7
Genesta Cl. ME10 .... 36 E7
Geneva Ave. ME5 .... 11 A2
Gentian Cl. Chatham ME5 .... 31 E4
Gentian Cl. Maidstone ME14 ... 75 E5
Geoffrey Ct. CT7 .... 27 A7
George Alley. CT14 .... 117 D6
George Cooper Ho. CT20 ...... 178 C4
George St. Ashford TN23 ...... 139 B1
George St. Deal CT14 .... 117 C7
George St. Dover CT17 .... 149 C1
George St. Maidstone ME15 .... 75 A3
George St. Ramsgate CT11 ..... 52 E7
George St. Sittingbourne ME10 . 37 B4
George Summers Cl. ME2 .... 9 E8
George V Ave. CT9 .... 28 C8
George Warren Ct. ME4 .... 7 J1
George Wood Cl. TN29 .... 203 C6
George's Ave. CT5 .... 43 A7
Georgian Cl. ME11 .... 3 A3
Georgian Dr. ME17 .... 96 D3
Georgian Way. ME8 .... 33 C4
Gerald Ave. ME4 .... 9 F2
Gerald Palmby Ct. CT14 .... 117 C7
Geraldine Rd. CT19 .... 177 F6
Gerrard Ave. ME1 .... 31 E8
Gerrards Dr. ME10 .... 36 F2
Gibbons Rd. ME10 .... 36 B5
Gibraltar Ave. ME7 .... 10 B7
Gibraltar Hill. ME4 .... 9 F4
Gibraltar La. Hawkinge CT18 .. 163 A2
Gibraltar La. Maidstone ME14 . 74 F8
Gibraltar Sq. CT16 .... 149 E3
Gibson St. ME10 .... 36 E4
Gidd's Pond Cotts. ME14 .... 75 E6
Giddyhorn La. ME16 .... 74 C5
Gifford Cl. ME8 .... 11 C3
Gigger's Green Rd. TN25 ...... 185 C7
Gilbert Cl. ME7 .... 33 A5
Gilbert Rd. Ashford TN23 ..... 139 B2
Gilbert Rd. Ramsgate CT11 ..... 52 D8
Gilbert Terr. ME14 .... 74 F7
Gilchrist Ave. CT6 .... 22 C2
Giles Gdns. CT9 .... 28 F8
Giles La. CT2 .... 66 C4
Gilford Rd. CT14 .... 117 D5
Gilham Gr. CT14 .... 117 B4
Gill La. Mersham TN25 .... 172 A8
Gill La. Ruckinge TN26 .... 171 C2

Gillett Rd. TN29 ...... 203 D7
Gillingham Gn. ME7 ...... 10 E6
Gillingham Rd. ME7 ...... 10 D5
Gillingham Sta. ME7 ...... 10 D5
Gillman Cl. CT18 ...... 162 F4
Gillon Mews. [9] CT1 ...... 67 B2
Gills Terr. ME8 ...... 12 C3
Ginsbury Cl. ME2 ...... 9 E6
Giraud Dr. ME13 ...... 62 B8
Glack Rd. CT14 ...... 116 F4
Glade The. Chatham ME5 ...... 32 A2
Glade The. Deal CT14 ...... 116 F6
Gladstone Dr. ME10 ...... 37 C4
Gladstone Rd. Ashford TN24 ...... 156 E7
Gladstone Rd. Broadstairs CT10 . 29 F4
Gladstone Rd. Chatham ME4 ...... 9 E2
Gladstone Rd. Deal CT14 ...... 117 C4
Gladstone Rd. Folkestone CT19 ...178 E6
Gladstone Rd. Maidstone ME14 ... 75 A6
Gladstone Rd. Margate CT9 ...... 7 I1
Gladstone Rd. Whitstable CT5 .... 20 D2
Gladwyn Cl. ME8 ...... 33 D4
Glamis Cl. ME5 ...... 32 A5
Glanville Rd. Gillingham ME7 ...... 10 D5
Glanville Rd. Rochester ME2 ...... 9 A8
Glasgow Ho. [7] ME15 ...... 97 E7
Gleaming Wood Dr. ME5 ...... 54 D8
Gleaners Cl. ME14 ...... 75 E4
Glebe Cl. Biddenden Green TN27 135 B2
Glebe Cl.
  St Margaret's at Cliffe CT15 ...... 150 F6
Glebe Cotts. ME13 ...... 81 E7
Glebe Ct. CT12 ...... 50 B5
Glebe Gdns. Lenham ME17 ...... 101 E5
Glebe Gdns. [6] Margate CT9 ...... 28 B8
Glebe La. Maidstone ME16 ...... 74 A1
Glebe La. Sittingbourne ME10 ...... 37 B2
Glebe Rd. Gillingham ME7 ...... 10 E3
Glebe Rd. Margate CT9 ...... 28 B8
Glebe The. TN27 ...... 120 D7
Glebe Way. Ashford TN24 ...... 139 D6
Glebe Way. Whitstable CT5 ...... 43 D8
Glebeland. TN27 ...... 118 F4
Glebelands. Alkham CT15 ...... 147 D1
Glebelands. Ash CT3 ...... 71 C2
Glebelands. Mersham TN25 ...... 157 E4
Glemsford Cotts. CT2 ...... 65 E1
Glen Ave. CT6 ...... 23 C5
Glen Gr. CT17 ...... 166 B7
Glen Iris Ave. CT2 ...... 66 C2
Glen Iris Cl. CT2 ...... 66 C2
Glen Rd. CT14 ...... 134 C6
Glen The. Minster ME12 ...... 4 B7
Glen The. Minster ME12 ...... 4 C7
Glen The. Shepherdswell CT15 .. 130 D5
Glen The. Upstreet CT3 ...... 47 D3
Glen Wlk. CT5 ...... 43 A3
Glenavon Ho. CT10 ...... 30 B7
Glenbervie Dr. CT6 ...... 23 E5
Glenbrook Cl. CT6 ...... 23 D5
Glenbrook Gr. ME10 ...... 36 E7
Glencoe Cty Inf Sch. ME4 ...... 10 A2
Glencoe Cty Prim Sch. ME4 ...... 10 A2
Glencoe Rd. Chatham ME4 ...... 10 A2
Glencoe Rd. Margate CT9 ...... 8 A1
Glendale Rd. ME12 ...... 4 B7
Gleneagles Ct. ME5 ...... 31 F2
Gleneagles Dr. ME15 ...... 75 A1
Glenfield Rd. CT16 ...... 149 B3
Glenside. CT5 ...... 44 A8
Glenside Ave. CT1 ...... 67 B2
Glenwood. TN30 ...... 167 B3
Glenwood Cl. Chatham ME5 ...... 10 C1
Glenwood Cl. Gillingham ME7 ...... 33 A7
Glenwood Cl. Maidstone ME14 ... 74 C5
Glenwood Cl. St Michaels TN30 167 B3
Glenwood Dr. ME12 ...... 4 C6
Glistening Glade. ME8 ...... 33 E6
Globe La. ME4 ...... 9 F5
Gloster Ropewalk. CT17 ...... 166 C5
Gloster Way. CT17 ...... 166 C5
Gloucester Ave.
  Broadstairs CT10 ...... 29 F3
Gloucester Ave. Margate CT9 ...... 8 D2
Gloucester Cl. ME8 ...... 34 A8
Gloucester Mews. TN28 ...... 200 C8
Gloucester Pl. [13] CT20 ...... 178 D5
Gloucester Rd.
  Maidstone ME15 ...... 97 D8
Gloucester Rd. Whitstable CT5 ... 20 F2
Glover Rd. TN24 ...... 139 E1
Glovers Cres. ME10 ...... 36 F3
Goad Ave. ME5 ...... 32 B3
Godden Rd. CT2 ...... 67 A4
Goddings Dr. ME1 ...... 9 A3
Goddington La. ME17 ...... 100 B6
Goddington Rd. ME2 ...... 9 B8
Godfrey Ho. CT5 ...... 43 E8
Godfrey Wlk. TN23 ...... 156 B8
Godfrey's Grave. ME13 ...... 64 B7
Godfreys Cotts. ME13 ...... 105 C8
Godinton
  Cty Prim Sch. TN23 ...... 138 D3
Godinton La. TN23 & TN26 ...... 138 D5
Godinton Park. TN23 ...... 138 C4
Godinton Rd. TN23 ...... 139 A2
Godinton Way. TN23 ...... 139 A2
Godwin Bglws. CT9 ...... 8 B3
Godwin Cl. ME10 ...... 14 F1
Godwin Cotts. CT9 ...... 8 A3
Godwin Rd. Canterbury CT1 ...... 87 C6
Godwin Rd. Dover CT16 ...... 166 F8
Godwin Rd. Margate CT9 ...... 8 A3
Godwyn Gdns. CT20 ...... 178 A4
Godwyn Rd. Deal CT14 ...... 117 C8
Godwyn Rd. Folkestone CT20 ... 178 A4
Godwyne Cl. CT16 ...... 166 D8
Godwyne Cl. CT16 ...... 149 D1

Godwyne Rd. CT16 ...... 149 D1
Gogway. CT4 ...... 126 B4
Gold Hill. TN25 ...... 121 D4
Goldcrest Wlk. CT5 ...... 43 B6
Golden Acre La. CT8 ...... 27 D7
Golden Cl. CT8 ...... 27 D7
Golden Hill. CT5 ...... 43 F6
Golden Sq. New Romney TN28 ... 200 A6
Golden Sq. Tenterden TN30 .... 179 B8
Golden St. CT14 ...... 117 D7
Golden Wood Cl. ME5 ...... 54 D8
Goldfinch Cl. Faversham ME13 ... 40 C1
Goldfinch Cl. Herne Bay CT6 .... 23 C2
Goldings The. Gillingham ME8 ... 33 C8
Goldings The. Monkton CT12 ..... 49 C7
Goldsmith Rd. ME8 ...... 33 E5
Goldstone Dro. CT3 ...... 71 E7
Goldstone Wlk. ME5 ...... 32 A1
Goldthorne Cl. ME4 ...... 75 C5
Goldups La. CT4 & ME13 ...... 84 C1
Goldups Lane Cotts. CT4 ...... 84 C1
Goldwell Cl. TN25 ...... 173 A6
Goldwell Hos. TN25 ...... 173 A6
Goldwell La. Aldington TN25 .... 173 B7
Goldwell La.
  Great Chart TN23 & TN26 ...... 154 F8
Golf Ct. CT14 ...... 95 C1
Golf Rd. CT14 ...... 117 C8
Golf Road Pl. CT14 ...... 117 C8
Good Hope. CT14 ...... 116 F4
Good Intent Cotts. TN27 ...... 119 A5
Goodall Cl. ME8 ...... 33 E5
Goodban Sq. CT3 ...... 71 D1
Goodcheap La. TN24 & TN25 .... 140 D2
Goodfellow Way. [3] CT16 ...... 166 D8
Goodnestone
  CE Prim Sch. CT3 ...... 91 C2
Goodnestone Hill. CT3 ...... 91 D2
Goodnestone Ho. CT3 ...... 91 C1
Goodnestone Rd.
  Sittingbourne ME10 ...... 37 B4
Goodnestone Rd. Wingham CT3 . 91 B5
Goodwin Ave. CT5 ...... 21 E2
Goodwin Dr. ME14 ...... 75 B8
Goodwin Rd. Ramsgate CT11 .... 52 B5
Goodwin Rd.
  St Margaret's at Cliffe CT15 .... 151 A4
Goodwood Cl. ME15 ...... 97 F6
Goose Cl. ME5 ...... 32 A7
Gordon Ave. ME11 ...... 3 A4
Gordon Cl. ME10 ...... 37 C4
Gordon Cotts. ME9 ...... 58 B6
Gordon Cl. ME17 ...... 96 E3
Gordon Cty Jun Sch. ME2 ...... 9 A8
Gordon Gr. CT7 ...... 7 C1
Gordon Rd. Canterbury CT1 ...... 87 F7
Gordon Rd. Chatham ME4 ...... 10 A2
Gordon Rd. Faversham ME13 .... 62 E8
Gordon Rd. Folkestone CT20 ... 177 D6
Gordon Rd. Gillingham ME7 ...... 10 E5
Gordon Rd.
  Gillingham,Brompton ME4 ...... 10 A7
Gordon Rd. Herne Bay CT6 ...... 22 F4
Gordon Rd. Margate CT9 ...... 8 A3
Gordon Rd.
  Margate,Westwood CT9 ...... 29 A5
Gordon Rd. Ramsgate CT11 .... 52 D8
Gordon Rd. Rochester ME2 ...... 9 A8
Gordon Rd. Whitfield CT16 ...... 149 A5
Gordon Rd. Whitstable CT5 ...... 43 D8
Gordon Sq. Birchington CT7 ..... 26 F7
Gordon Sq. Faversham ME13 .... 62 E7
Gordon Terr. ME1 ...... 9 C4
Gore Cl. CT13 ...... 93 B3
Gore Cotts. ME9 ...... 12 E1
Gore Court Rd.
  Park Wood ME15 ...... 97 F5
Gore Court Rd.
  Sittingbourne ME10 ...... 36 E2
Gore End Cl. CT7 ...... 26 F7
Gore La. CT13 ...... 93 B2
Gore Mews. [3] CT1 ...... 67 B2
Gore Rd. Eastry CT13 ...... 93 B3
Gore Rd. Silver Street ME9 ...... 57 F5
Gore St. CT12 ...... 49 A7
Gore Terr. CT13 ...... 93 B3
Gorely Ho. [14] CT17 ...... 166 D7
Goretop La. CT14 ...... 94 C6
Gorham Dr. ME15 ...... 76 A1
Gorrell Rd. CT5 ...... 20 E1
Gorse Ave. ME5 ...... 31 F5
Gorse La. CT6 ...... 23 C2
Gorse Mead. TN23 ...... 155 F8
Gorse Rd. ME10 ...... 37 C5
Goschen Rd. CT17 ...... 166 B8
Gosfield Rd. CT6 ...... 23 A4
Goss Hall La. CT3 ...... 72 A2
Gosselin St. CT5 ...... 43 E8
Goteley Mere. TN24 ...... 139 C7
Gothic Cl. CT14 ...... 117 B1
Gothic Cotts. TN25 ...... 121 A1
Goudhurst Cl. Canterbury CT2 ... 67 A4
Goudhurst Cl. Maidstone ME16 .. 74 F4
Goudhurst Rd. ME8 ...... 11 B3
Gough Rd. CT20 ...... 177 E3
Gould Rd. ME5 ...... 32 B3
Grace Ave. ME16 ...... 74 D6
Grace Ct. [12] CT20 ...... 178 D5
Grace Hill. CT20 ...... 178 D5
Grace Meadow. CT16 ...... 149 A7
Grace Rd. ME12 ...... 1 B1
Grace Wlk. CT14 ...... 117 A5
Grafton Ave. ME1 ...... 31 E8
Grafton Rd. Broadstairs CT10 .... 29 F8
Grafton Rd. Sittingbourne ME10 .. 36 F4
Grafton Rise. CT6 ...... 22 C4
Grain Rd. ME8 ...... 33 C3
Grainey Field. ME9 ...... 34 E4

Gram's Rd. CT14 ...... 134 C8
Grampian Way. ME15 ...... 76 A1
Grampion Cl. TN24 ...... 139 C4
Granada Ho. [6] ME15 ...... 75 A4
Granada St. [7] ME15 ...... 75 A4
Granary Cl. Gillingham ME8 ...... 11 F1
Granary Cl. Maidstone ME14 .... 75 E5
Granary Court Rd. TN25 ...... 159 A4
Granary Pl. CT5 ...... 43 D8
Grand Dr. CT6 ...... 22 C4
Grand Par. ME4 ...... 200 E5
Grange Cres. TN30 ...... 167 A3
Grange Ct. [1] CT20 ...... 178 C4
Grange Hill. ME4 ...... 10 B3
Grange Ho. ME16 ...... 74 A2
Grange La. ME5 ...... 54 A1
Grange Rd. Broadstairs CT10 .... 29 F6
Grange Rd. Deal CT14 ...... 117 B5
Grange Rd. Folkestone CT19 .... 177 E6
Grange Rd. Gillingham ME7 ...... 11 B5
Grange Rd. Herne Bay CT6 ...... 23 C4
Grange Rd. Hythe CT21 ...... 176 B4
Grange Rd. Ramsgate CT11 ..... 52 C6
Grange Rd. Rochester ME2 ...... 9 B7
Grange Rd. St Michaels TN30 ... 167 A3
Grange The.
  Shepherdswell CT15 ...... 130 D5
Grange The. Whitstable CT5 ..... 43 A6
Grange Way. Broadstairs CT10 .. 29 F2
Grange Way. Rochester ME1 ...... 9 C3
Grant Cl. Broadstairs CT10 ...... 29 E6
Grant Cl. Gillingham ME7 ...... 11 B1
Grant's Cotts. ME17 ...... 101 B5
Grantham Ave. CT14 ...... 117 A5
Grantley Cl. TN23 ...... 156 A8
Granville Ave. Broadstairs CT10 .. 30 B3
Granville Ave. Ramsgate CT12 ... 29 B1
Granville Cl. ME13 ...... 62 C7
Granville Dr. CT6 ...... 22 D5
Granville Farm Mews. [19] CT11 . 52 F7
Granville Marina. [17] CT11 ...... 52 F7
Granville Par. CT20 ...... 177 E3
Granville Pl. ME12 ...... 1 D2
Granville Rd. Broadstairs CT10 .. 30 B3
Granville Rd. Deal CT14 ...... 117 C2
Granville Rd. Gillingham ME7 .... 10 E5
Granville Rd. Kingsdown CT14 .. 134 D3
Granville Rd. Maidstone ME14 ... 75 A6
Granville Rd. Sheerness ME12 .... 1 D2
Granville Rd.
  St Margaret's at Cliffe CT15 .... 151 B6
Granville Rd E. CT20 ...... 177 F3
Granville St. Deal CT14 ...... 117 D5
Granville St. Dover CT16 ...... 149 C1
Grapple Rd. ME14 ...... 75 A7
Grasmere Ave. CT11 ...... 52 A7
Grasmere Gdns. CT19 ...... 178 B7
Grasmere Rd. Ashford TN24 .... 139 C6
Grasmere Rd. Whitstable CT5 ... 44 B8
Grasmere Way. CT12 ...... 112 F6
Grasslands. Ashford TN23 ...... 155 D7
Grasslands.
  Langley Heath ME17 ...... 98 E4
Grassmere. TN29 ...... 194 E3
Grassy Glade. ME7 ...... 33 B6
Gravel Castle Rd. CT4 ...... 129 A8
Gravel Hill. ME13 ...... 103 C8
Gravel La. CT15 ...... 165 A4
Gravel Wlk. [3] Ashford TN23 ... 139 B3
Gravel Wlk. [12] Canterbury CT1 .. 87 F8
Gravel Wlk. Rochester ME1 ...... 9 D5
Gravelly Bottom Rd. ME17 ...... 99 B2
Graveney Cty Prim Sch. ME13 . 41 E1
Graveney Rd. Faversham ME13 .. 62 F7
Graveney Rd. Maidstone ME15 .. 97 F7
Graylings Ct. ME10 ...... 36 C2
Grays Way. CT1 ...... 87 B6
Grayshott Cl. ME10 ...... 36 F3
Graystone Rd. CT5 ...... 21 A2
Great Basin Rd. ME12 ...... 1 A2
Great Burton Ho. TN24 ...... 139 E5
Great Chart
  Cty Prim Sch. TN23 ...... 155 D8
Great Conduit St. CT21 ...... 176 C2
Great Ivy Mill Cotts. ME15 ...... 96 F7
Great Lines. ME7 ...... 10 B5
Great South Ave. ME4 ...... 10 A1
Greatstone Halt. TN29 ...... 200 D3
Greatstone Prim Sch. TN28 ... 200 D2
Grebe Apartments. [13] ME15 .... 97 E5
Grebe Cl. CT18 ...... 163 A4
Grebe Cres. CT21 ...... 187 C8
Green Acres. CT15 ...... 131 D7
Green Acres Cl. CT3 ...... 23 B3
Green Bank Cl. ME7 ...... 33 A5
Green Cl. Bridge CT4 ...... 89 A1
Green Cl. Folkestone CT19 ...... 178 E7
Green Cloth Mews. [2] CT1 ...... 67 B2
Green Ct. Bridge CT4 ...... 89 A1
Green Ct. Folkestone CT19 ...... 178 E7
Green Dell. CT2 ...... 66 F4
Green Gates. CT16 ...... 149 A8
Green Hedges. TN30 ...... 179 B8
Green Hill. ME15 ...... 76 B1
Green Hill La. ME17 ...... 100 C1
Green Hills. CT4 ...... 128 D8
Green La. Ashford TN23 ...... 155 E5
Green La. Bethersden TN26 ...... 153 A2
Green La.
  Boughton Monchelsea ME17 ..... 97 C3
Green La. Bredhurst CT15 ...... 29 E5
Green La. Capel-le-F CT18 ...... 164 B3
Green La. Challock TN25 ...... 105 A2
Green La. Chilham CT4 ...... 85 C2
Green La. Deal CT14 ...... 117 B1
Green La. Dover CT15 ...... 149 B3
Green La. Ewell Minnis CT15 ... 147 D3

Green La. Eythorne CT15 ...... 131 D7
Green La. Folkestone CT19 ..... 178 E7
Green La. Goodnestone CT3 ..... 92 B3
Green La. Hythe CT21 ...... 176 A2
Green La. Langley Heath ME17 ... 98 E3
Green La. Margate CT9 ...... 29 E8
Green La. Platt's Heath ME17 ... 100 F2
Green La. Rhodes Minnis CT4 ... 143 E2
Green La. Rodmersham ME9 ..... 59 B7
Green La. Smarden TN27 ...... 135 A1
Green La.
  St Margaret's at Cliffe CT15 .... 133 F1
Green La. Stockbury ME9 ...... 34 F1
Green La. Temple Ewell CT16 ... 148 E6
Green La. Whitfield CT16 ...... 148 E7
Green La. Whitstable CT5 ...... 43 D8
Green Lane Ave. ME17 ...... 176 A2
Green Lane Cotts. ME17 ...... 98 E3
Green Leas. CT5 ...... 21 D1
Green Lees. ME13 ...... 61 E2
Green Meadows. TN29 ...... 186 D2
Green Porch Cl. ME10 ...... 36 F7
Green Rd. Birchington CT7 ...... 26 F8
Green Rd.
  Stalisfield Green ME13 ...... 103 C6
Green Sands. ME14 ...... 54 C8
Green St. ME7 ...... 10 C5
Green The. Blean CT2 ...... 66 A6
Green The. Burmarsh TN29 ..... 186 C4
Green The. Chartham CT4 ...... 86 D3
Green The. East Farleigh ME15 .. 96 B7
Green The. Harbledown CT2 ..... 65 E1
Green The. Hythe CT21 ...... 176 B4
Green The. Littlebourne CT3 .... 89 F7
Green The. Lower Halstow ME9 .. 13 B3
Green The. Lydd TN29 ...... 203 B5
Green The. Manston CT12 ...... 28 D1
Green The. Sheerness ME12 ...... 1 I1
Green The. Woodchurch TN26 ... 169 A2
Green The. Wye TN25 ...... 123 E2
Green Way. Lydd TN29 ...... 203 C5
Green Way. Maidstone ME16 .... 74 B3
Green's Cotts. ME15 ...... 96 A4
Greenacre. CT4 ...... 111 D3
Greenacre Cl. ME5 ...... 32 A5
Greenacre Dr. CT14 ...... 117 C1
Greenacre Sch. ME7 ...... 31 F5
Greenbank. Ashford TN24 ...... 139 D6
Greenbank. Chatham ME5 ...... 32 B8
Greenbanks. CT18 ...... 161 C6
Greenborough Cl. ME15 ...... 97 E6
Greencroft. TN23 ...... 155 E6
Greenfield Cl. ME20 ...... 53 A6
Greenfield Cotts.
  Canterbury CT1 ...... 87 F7
Greenfield Rd.
  Folkestone CT19 ...... 178 E7
Greenfield Rd. Gillingham ME7 .. 10 E6
Greenfield Rd. Ramsgate CT12 .. 29 C2
Greenfields. Maidstone ME15 .... 97 E8
Greenfields. Sellindge TN25 ..... 159 E2
Greenfinches. ME7 ...... 32 F6
Greenhill Bridge Rd. CT6 ...... 22 D3
Greenhill Cl. CT12 ...... 50 B7
Greenhill Gdns. Herne Bay CT6 .. 22 D3
Greenhill Gdns.
  Minster CT12 ...... 50 B7
Greenhill La. TN27 ...... 135 F3
Greenhill Rd. CT6 ...... 22 C2
Greenhithe. [3] ME15 ...... 75 A3
Greenhouse La. CT2 ...... 66 E2
Greenly Way. TN28 ...... 200 C6
Greensand Rd. ME15 ...... 76 A2
Greenside. High Halden TN26 .... 167 F7
Greenside. Maidstone ME15 ..... 75 B3
Greenvale Gdns. ME8 ...... 11 B2
Greenview Wlk. ME8 ...... 11 A4
Greenway. Chatham ME5 ...... 31 D6
Greenway. Faversham ME13 ..... 62 B8
Greenway Court Farm Cotts.
  ME17 ...... 78 A1
Greenway Court Rd. ME17 ...... 78 A1
Greenway La. ME17 ...... 100 A3
Greenways. Lower Halstow ME9 .. 13 A3
Greenways. Maidstone ME14 .... 75 F5
Greenways. Sittingbourne ME10 .. 37 A2
Greenwich Cl. Chatham ME5 .... 32 B4
Greenwich Cl. Maidstone ME16 .. 74 C5
Gregory Cl. Gillingham ME8 ...... 33 E4
Gregory Cl. Sittingbourne ME10 .. 37 A8
Gregory Ct. TN25 ...... 123 E2
Grenham Bay Ave. CT7 ...... 26 E8
Grenham Rd. CT7 ...... 26 E8
Grenville Gdns. CT7 ...... 26 E8
Grenville Way. CT10 ...... 29 E4
Gresham Ave. CT9 ...... 7 E1
Gresham Rd. ME17 ...... 96 D3
Greville Homes. CT13 ...... 93 B2
Grey Friars Cotts. [8] CT1 ...... 87 F8
Grey Wethers. ME14 ...... 53 E4
Grey Willow Gdns. TN23 ...... 155 E6
Greyfriars Cl. ME16 ...... 74 D5
Greyfriars Ct. CT10 ...... 8 F1
Greystones. ME15 ...... 76 A2
Greystones Sch. TN24 ...... 139 F1
Grieveson Ho. ME4 ...... 10 A4
Griffin Cotts. ME13 ...... 181 C2
Griffin St. CT14 ...... 117 C6
Griffin's Cnr. TN25 ...... 140 E7
Grimshill Ct. CT2 ...... 66 C4
Grimshill Rd. CT5 ...... 43 E8
Grimston Ave. CT20 ...... 178 B4
Grimston Gdns. CT20 ...... 178 B4
Grimthorpe Ave. CT5 ...... 43 C7
Grinsell Hill. CT12 ...... 50 E6
Grisbrook Farm Cl. TN29 ...... 203 B6
Grisbrook Rd. TN29 ...... 203 D6

Grizedale Cl. ME1 ...... 31 D8
Groombridge Sq. [13] ME15 ...... 97 F6
Grosvenor Ave. ME1 & ME4 ...... 9 E3
Grosvenor Gdns. CT9 ...... 7 I1
Grosvenor Hill. CT9 ...... 7 I2
Grosvenor Pl. CT9 ...... 7 I2
Grosvenor Rd. Ashford TN24 ... 139 E1
Grosvenor Rd. Broadstairs CT10 . 30 A4
Grosvenor Rd. Gillingham ME7 .. 11 A1
Grosvenor Rd. Ramsgate CT11 .. 52 C7
Grosvenor Rd. Whitstable CT5 ... 43 D7
Grotto Gdns. CT9 ...... 7 J2
Grotto Hill. CT9 ...... 7 J2
Grotto Rd. [5] CT9 ...... 7 J2
Grove Ave. ME12 ...... 6 G2
Grove Cl. ME13 ...... 62 A6
Grove Cotts. TN30 ...... 179 B6
Grove Court Farm. ME13 ...... 64 A3
Grove Ferry Hill. CT3 ...... 47 E3
Grove Ferry Rd. CT3 ...... 48 A2
Grove Gdns. [6] CT9 ...... 7 G1
Grove Green La. ME14 ...... 75 E5
Grove Green Rd. ME14 ...... 75 F5
Grove Ho. TN27 ...... 136 C3
Grove La. TN29 ...... 191 D3
Grove Park Ave. ME10 ...... 36 B5
Grove Park
  Cty Prim Sch. ME10 ...... 36 B6
Grove Pl. ME13 ...... 62 B6
Grove Rd. Chatham ME4 ...... 10 B2
Grove Rd. Deal CT14 ...... 117 C6
Grove Rd. Folkestone CT20 .... 178 E6
Grove Rd. Gillingham ME7 ...... 11 A6
Grove Rd. Maidstone ME15 ..... 97 C7
Grove Rd. Preston CT3 ...... 70 B8
Grove Rd. Ramsgate CT11 ...... 52 D6
Grove Rd. Rochester ME2 ...... 9 B8
Grove Rd. Selling ME13 ...... 84 B4
Grove Rd. Staple CT3 ...... 91 F6
Grove Rd. Wickhambreaux CT3 ... 69 D6
Grove Road Cotts.
  Wickhambreaux CT3 ...... 69 C2
Grove Road Cotts.
  Wickhambreaux CT3 ...... 69 C3
Grove Terr. CT1 ...... 87 F7
Grove The. Ashford TN24 ...... 139 E6
Grove The. Barham CT4 ...... 128 F8
Grove The. Deal CT14 ...... 117 C6
Grove The. Dover CT16 ...... 149 C1
Grove The. Herne Bay CT6 ...... 22 C4
Grove The. Maidstone ME16 .... 76 A3
Grove The. Westgate-on-S CT8 .. 27 F8
Grove Way. CT3 ...... 70 C7
Grovehurst Ave. ME10 ...... 14 F1
Grovehurst Rd. ME10 & ME9 ... 14 E2
Grovelands. ME17 ...... 101 E5
Groveway. ME12 ...... 6 F2
Grovewood Dr. ME14 ...... 75 E4
Grummock Ave. CT11 ...... 52 B8
Grundy's Hill. [10] CT11 ...... 52 E6
Guardian Ct. ME8 ...... 11 C1
Guildcount La. CT13 ...... 72 F1
Guildford Ave. CT8 ...... 27 E8
Guildford Lawn. [1] CT11 ...... 52 E6
Guildford Rd. CT6 ...... 87 F6
Guildhall St. [4] Canterbury CT1 .. 87 F8
Guildhall St. [14]
  Folkestone CT20 ...... 178 D5
Guildhall St N. CT19 & CT20 ... 178 D5
Guilford Ave. CT16 ...... 149 A8
Guilford Ct. CT14 ...... 117 D2
Guilford Rd. CT13 ...... 94 E8
Guilton. CT3 ...... 71 B1
Guldeford La. TN29 & TN31 .... 196 F3
Guldeford Lane Cnr. TN31 ...... 196 D2
Gullands. ME17 ...... 98 E4
Gun La. ME2 ...... 9 B7
Gundulph Rd. ME1 & ME4 ...... 9 E4
Gundulph Sq. ME1 ...... 9 C6
Gunnis Cl. ME8 ...... 33 D4
Gurling Rd. CT5 ...... 133 F1
Guston CE Prim Sch. CT16 .... 149 E8
Guston Rd. ME14 ...... 75 C6
Guy Cl. CT10 ...... 30 A7
Gwyn Rd. CT12 ...... 29 C2
Gypsy Cnr. CT12 ...... 44 D3

Hackfield. TN23 ...... 138 F1
Hackington Cl. CT2 ...... 66 E4
Hackington Pl. CT2 ...... 66 F2
Hackington Rd. CT2 ...... 66 F2
Hackington Terr. CT2 ...... 66 F2
Hacklinge Hill. CT14 ...... 94 B2
Hackney Rd. ME16 ...... 74 C2
Haddon Dene Sch. CT10 ...... 29 F4
Hadleigh Cl. ME7 ...... 33 B3
Hadleigh Gdns. CT6 ...... 23 B5
Hadley Gdns. ME17 ...... 77 E2
Hadlow Coll of Agriculture &
  Horticulture (Horticultural
  Unit). CT1 ...... 88 B8
Hadlow Dr. CT9 ...... 8 E2
Hadlow Rd. ME14 ...... 75 C5
Haffenden Meadow. TN27 ... 120 C8
Haffenden Rd. TN30 ...... 167 B1
Haig Ave. Chatham ME1 ...... 9 D1
Haig Ave. Chatham,Luton ME4 ... 10 A2
Haig Ave. Gillingham ME7 ...... 10 E4
Haine Hospl. CT12 ...... 29 A4
Haine Ind Est. CT12 ...... 28 F1
Haine Rd. CT12 & CT10 ...... 28 F2
Halden Cl. ME15 ...... 97 F6
Hales Cl. TN30 ...... 179 B8
Hales Ct. TN30 ...... 179 B8
Hales Dr. CT2 ...... 66 F3

Hales Rd. ME10 .... 36 D1
Haleys Pl. ME1 .... 53 A8
Halfmile Ride. CT9 .... 28 E6
Halford Cl. CT6 .... 23 B2
Halfpenny Cl. ME16 .... 74 A2
Halfway Houses
  Prim Sch. ME12 .... 3 D6
Halfway Rd. ME12 .... 3 D8
Halifax Cl. ME5 .... 32 B6
Hall Cl. ME10 .... 36 E6
Hall Cres. CT14 .... 116 F5
Hall Rd. ME5 .... 32 C3
Hallcroft Ct. CT11 .... 52 C7
Hallett Wlk. **10** CT1 .... 67 B2
Halliday Ct. CT21 .... 176 A2
Hallsfield Rd. ME5 .... 31 D2
Hallwood Cl. ME8 .... 33 D5
Hallwood Ho. ME5 .... 32 C2
Halstatt Rd. CT14 .... 117 A3
Halstead Cl. CT2 .... 67 B4
Halstead Gdns. CT9 .... 8 F3
Halstead Wlk. ME16 .... 74 C7
Halstow Cl. ME15 .... 97 B6
Halstow Way. TN23 .... 155 F8
Halt The. Elham CT4 .... 144 F4
Halt The. Whitstable CT5 .... 44 A7
Ham Farm Cotts. CT14 .... 93 F2
Ham La. Blean CT2 .... 32 E3
Ham La. Lenham ME17 .... 101 C5
Ham La. Snargate TN29 .... 191 F8
Ham Mill La.
  Warehorne TN26 & TN29 .... 183 A2
Ham Rd. ME13 .... 40 C1
Ham Shades La. CT5 .... 21 A1
Ham Street Sta. TN26 .... 183 A8
Hambledon Ct. ME16 .... 74 B3
Hambrook Cl. CT4 .... 107 B8
Hambrook Cl. CT4 .... 107 C8
Hambrook Wlk. ME10 .... 36 F8
Hamele The. CT2 .... 67 F5
Hamelin Rd. ME7 .... 32 F8
Hamilton Cl. CT21 .... 29 B1
Hamilton Cres. ME10 .... 36 C3
Hamilton Ho. ME17 .... 96 C3
Hamilton Rd. Ashford TN24 .... 156 D6
Hamilton Rd. Deal CT14 .... 117 C4
Hamilton Rd. Dover CT17 .... 166 B8
Hamilton Rd. Gillingham ME7 .... 10 D7
Hamilton Rd. Lydd TN29 .... 203 C6
Hamilton Rd. Whitstable CT5 .... 20 D1
Hammond Cl. CT15 .... 113 E5
Hammond's Cnr. TN29 .... 199 E6
Hammond's Rd. CT20 .... 177 E5
Hamond Hill. ME4 .... 9 E4
Hampden La. TN23 .... 156 A7
Hampden Mews. TN23 .... 156 A7
Hampden Rd. TN23 .... 156 A6
Hampshire Cl. ME5 .... 32 C7
Hampshire Dr. ME15 .... 97 C8
Hampshire Rd. CT1 .... 88 D7
Hampson Way. ME14 .... 76 A4
Hampton Cl. Chatham ME5 .... 32 A5
Hampton Cl. Herne Bay CT6 .... 22 A3
Hampton Cty Prim Sch
  (Jun & Inf). CT6 .... 22 C4
Hampton Gdns. CT6 .... 22 A3
Hampton La. TN25 .... 141 C3
Hampton Pier Ave. CT6 .... 22 B4
Hampton Rd. ME14 .... 75 C6
Hampton Vale. CT21 .... 177 B4
Hamstreet Rd.
  Bromley Green TN26 .... 170 E5
Hamstreet Rd.
  Hamstreet TN26 & TN26 .... 183 C7
Hamwick Gn. ME5 .... 32 C1
Hancocks Field. CT14 .... 117 A5
Hangman's La.
  Ringwould CT14 .... 133 F5
Hangman's La. Ripple CT14 .... 133 D5
Hanover Cl. Ashford TN23 .... 138 F2
Hanover Cl. Deal CT14 .... 117 D2
Hanover Cl. Margate CT9 .... 8 E2
Hanover Cl. Sittingbourne ME10 .... 36 E2
Hanover Ct. Faversham ME13 .... 62 B8
Hanover Ct. Hythe CT21 .... 176 C1
Hanover Ct. Maidstone ME14 .... 75 B5
Hanover Dr. ME8 .... 33 C4
Hanover Pl. CT2 .... 66 F2
Hanover Rd. ME7 .... 96 C3
Hanover Sq. CT6 .... 22 F5
Hanover St. CT6 .... 22 F5
Hanscomb Ho. CT2 .... 66 E2
Hanslett's La. ME13 .... 61 D3
Hanway. ME8 .... 11 A2
Harbledown Gdns. CT9 .... 8 E3
Harbledown Manor. ME8 .... 11 B3
Harbledown Pk. CT2 .... 66 C1
Harbour Approach Rd. CT20 .. 178 E4
Harbour Par. CT11 .... 52 E6
Harbour Point. CT11 .... 178 F5
Harbour Sch The. CT15 .... 165 E7
Harbour St. Broadstairs CT10 .... 30 B4
Harbour St. Folkestone CT20 .... 178 E5
Harbour St. Ramsgate CT11 .... 52 E6
Harbour St. Whitstable CT5 .... 20 D2
Harbour Twrs. **13** CT11 .... 52 E6
Harbour Way. CT20 .... 178 E5
Harbourne La. TN26 & TN30 .. 167 F5
Harcourt Dr. Canterbury CT2 .... 66 D2
Harcourt Dr. Herne Bay CT6 .... 22 B5
Harcourt Gdns. ME8 .... 33 E4
Harcourt Prim Sch. CT19 .... 177 E7
Harcourt Rd. CT19 .... 177 F7
Harden Rd. TN29 .... 203 D7

Hardinge Cl. ME8 .... 33 D4
Hardinge Rd. TN24 .... 139 C3
Hardres Court Rd.
  Lower Hardres CT4 .... 110 A3
Hardres Court Rd.
  Stelling Minnis CT4 .... 126 F6
Hardres Rd. CT11 .... 52 E8
Hardres St. CT11 .... 52 E7
Hardwick Ho. **1** ME15 .... 97 E8
Hardwick Rd. CT20 .... 178 A4
Hardwicke Rd. CT17 .... 166 B6
Hardy Cl. Ashford TN24 .... 157 A7
Hardy Cl. Canterbury CT2 .... 66 C1
Hardy Cl. Chatham ME5 .... 32 B6
Hardy Rd.
  St Margaret's at Cliffe CT15 .. 150 E8
Hardy St. ME14 .... 75 A6
Hare St. **2** ME4 .... 10 B3
Harebell Cl. **3** Chatham ME5 .. 31 F4
Harebell Cl. Maidstone ME14 .. 75 E5
Haredale Cl. ME1 .... 31 D7
Harkness Cl. ME10 .... 37 B4
Harkness Dr. CT2 .... 66 E2
Harman Ave. CT21 .... 174 F3
Harman Ct. ME5 .... 32 B3
Harmers Way. ME27 .... 118 F3
Harmsworth Gdns. CT10 .... 30 A5
Harnet St. CT13 .... 72 F1
Harold Ave. Gillingham ME7 .. 10 E4
Harold Ave. Westgate-on-S CT8 .. 27 E8
Harold Cl. CT2 .... 62 C6
Harold Rd. Birchington CT7 .... 26 E8
Harold Rd. Deal CT14 .... 117 D8
Harold Rd. Margate CT9 .... 8 B3
Harold Rd. Sittingbourne ME10 .. 37 B4
Harold St. Dover CT16 .... 166 B8
Harold St. Queenborough ME11 .. 3 A4
Harold's Rd. CT16 .... 166 E8
Harp Farm Rd. ME14 .... 54 C6
Harper Rd. TN23 .... 155 F8
Harple La. ME14 .... 54 F1
Harps Ave. ME12 .... 4 C6
Harpswood. ME17 .... 77 F1
Harpswood Ct. CT21 .... 176 A4
Harptree Dr. ME5 .... 31 F5
Harrier Dr. ME10 .... 37 A2
Harrietsham Sta. ME17 .... 100 D6
Harringe La. TN25 .... 174 A6
Harriot Cl. CT19 .... 178 B7
Harris Gdns. ME10 .... 37 C5
Harris Rd. ME12 .... 1 D2
Harris's Alley. CT3 .... 91 A7
Harrison Rd. **4** CT11 .... 52 D6
Harrison Terr. ME13 .... 40 A2
Harrow Ct. Chatham ME5 .... 32 C4
Harrow Ct. Stockbury ME9 .... 56 D8
Harrow Dene. CT10 .... 29 E6
Harrow Rd. ME7 .... 32 F6
Harrow Way. ME14 .... 75 E5
Harry Wells Rd. CT6 .... 22 B3
Harrys Rd. ME9 .... 38 D3
Hart Cl. CT18 .... 163 A4
Hart Hill. TN27 .... 103 A2
Hart St. ME16 .... 74 F3
Hart St Commercial Ctr. ME16 .. 74 F3
Hartington St. ME14 .... 10 A3
Hartley Cl. ME15 .... 97 F6
Hartlip Cl. ME12 .... 3 B7
Hartlip Endowed
  CE Prim Sch. ME9 .... 34 D5
Hartlip Hill. ME9 .... 34 F7
Hartnup St. ME16 .... 74 C2
Hartpiece Cl. ME8 .... 11 F2
Harts Cotts. TN26 .... 183 A8
Harts La. **6** CT5 .... 20 D2
Hartsdown Rd. CT9 .... 28 D8
Hartsdown Sch. CT9 .... 28 D8
Harty Ave. ME8 .... 33 C3
Harty Ferry Cotts. ME13 .... 40 C5
Harty Ferry Rd. ME12 .... 18 E4
Harty Terr. ME12 .... 5 A3
Harvest Way. TN23 .... 155 D7
Harvesters Cl. ME8 .... 33 E7
Harvesters Way. ME14 .... 75 D4
Harvey Dr. Sittingbourne ME10 .. 37 A2
Harvey Dr. Whitstable CT5 .... 21 B1
Harvey Gram Sch
  for Boys The. CT19 .... 178 B6
Harvey Pl. **18** Folkestone CT20 .. 178 D5
Harvey Pl. **7** Folkestone CT20 .. 178 E5
Harvey Rd. Ashford TN24 .... 139 F1
Harvey Rd. Gillingham ME8 .... 33 E8
Harvey St. CT20 .... 178 E5
Harville Rd. TN25 .... 123 C2
Harwich St. CT5 .... 43 D8
Harwick Dr. TN28 .... 200 C8
Harwood Ho. TN25 .... 123 E1
Harwood Rd. ME8 .... 12 B1
Hasborough Rd. CT19 .... 178 F6
Haskard Cl. CT18 .... 162 F4
Haslemere Est. ME15 .... 97 F5
Haslewood Cl. TN27 .... 135 B2
Hassall Reach. CT1 .... 87 B6
Hassell St. CT4 & TN25 .... 124 F2
Haste Hill Cl. ME17 .... 97 B3
Haste Hill Rd. ME17 .... 97 B3
Hasted Rd. ME9 .... 35 B7
Hasteds. ME17 .... 77 D2
Hastings Ave. CT9 .... 8 A1
Hastings Pl. CT13 .... 93 F8
Hastings Rd. ME15 .... 75 B3
Hatch La. CT4 .... 86 C5
Hatch Rd. ME17 .... 101 C3
Hatch St. **3** ME13 .... 62 C7
Hatfield Rd. Margate CT9 .... 7 G2

Hatfield Rd. Ramsgate CT11 .... 52 D7
Hatfield Rd. Rochester ME2 .... 9 A8
Hathaway Cl. Gillingham ME8 .. 33 D5
Hathaway Ct. Rochester ME1 .... 9 B5
Hatherall Rd. ME14 .... 75 B6
Hatherley Ct. CT9 .... 8 A3
Hatton Rd. ME5 .... 32 C3
Havant Wlk. **8** ME15 .... 97 F6
Havelock Pl. CT3 .... 71 E1
Havelock Rd. CT14 .... 117 C3
Havelock St. CT1 .... 67 A1
Haven Cl. ME1 .... 9 C2
Haven Dr. Hawkinge CT18 .... 163 A4
Haven Dr. Herne Bay CT6 .... 23 F6
Haven The. Ashford TN23 .... 155 F5
Haven The. Brenzett TN29 .... 192 A3
Haven The. Hythe CT21 .... 187 C8
Haventhorpe. TN24 .... 139 C3
Havisham Cl. ME1 .... 9 D2
Havock La. **1** ME14 .... 74 F4
Hawbeck Rd. ME8 .... 33 C3
Hawe Cl. CT2 .... 67 A4
Hawe Farm Way. CT6 .... 23 B2
Hawe La. CT2 & CT3 .... 68 A7
Hawes Ave. CT11 .... 52 B7
Hawk Cl. CT5 .... 43 C7
Hawk's La. CT1 .... 87 F8
Hawkesbury St. CT17 .... 166 D5
Hawkhurst Cl. CT7 .... 27 B8
Hawkhurst Rd. ME8 .... 11 B3
Hawkhurst Way. CT10 .... 30 A2
Hawkinge CP Sch. CT18 .... 163 B4
Hawkins Cl. Chatham ME4 .... 10 A6
Hawkins Cl. Sittingbourne ME10 .. 36 E7
Hawkins Rd. CT19 .... 177 D6
Hawkshall Activity Ctr. CT14 .. 134 C7
Hawkshill Rd. CT14 .... 134 C8
Hawkwood. ME16 .... 74 B5
Hawkwood Cl. ME1 .... 9 D5
Hawley Ct. ME16 .... 74 E4
Hawley Sq. CT9 .... 7 J2
Hawley St. CT9 .... 7 I2
Hawser Rd. ME1 .... 9 C1
Hawthorn. TN26 .... 190 D8
Hawthorn Ave. Canterbury CT2 .. 67 A2
Hawthorn Ave.
  West Minster ME12 .... 3 A8
Hawthorn Cl. Hythe CT21 .... 187 E8
Hawthorn Cl. Ramsgate CT11 .. 29 E1
Hawthorn Cl. River CT17 .... 148 E2
Hawthorn Cl.
  St Mary's Bay TN29 .... 194 F3
Hawthorn Cl.
  Womenswold CT3 .... 112 E4
Hawthorn Cnr. Herne Bay CT6 .. 24 A3
Hawthorn Cnr.
  Old Romney TN29 .... 198 E3
Hawthorn Ho. **5** ME5 .... 31 F5
Hawthorn Rd. Kingsnorth TN23 . 156 B4
Hawthorn Rd.
  Sittingbourne ME10 .... 36 E4
Hawthorne Ave. ME8 .... 11 C2
Hawthorne Cl. CT15 .... 131 D7
Hawthorns. ME5 .... 31 F1
Hawthorns The. CT10 .... 29 C4
Hay Hill. CT13 & CT14 .... 93 D2
Hay La. CT14 .... 93 F2
Hayes Alley. **11** CT5 .... 20 D2
Hayes La. ME8 .... 56 F6
Hayfields. ME5 .... 32 D2
Hayle Mill Cotts. ME15 .... 96 F8
Hayle Mill Rd. ME15 .... 96 F8
Hayle Rd. ME15 .... 75 A3
Haymakers La. TN23 .... 155 D8
Haymen St. ME4 .... 9 E3
Hayrick Cl. ME14 .... 75 E5
Haysel. ME10 .... 37 A2
Hayton Rd. TN25 .... 160 A2
Haywain Cl. ME14 .... 75 E4
Hayward Ave. ME2 .... 9 B8
Hayward Cl. Ashford TN24 .... 157 A4
Hayward Cl. Deal CT14 .... 117 A4
Hayward's Cl. TN28 .... 200 B6
Hayward's Hill. ME13 .... 82 C4
Hazebrouck Rd. ME13 .... 62 A7
Hazel Ave. ME16 .... 74 C5
Hazel Cl. CT15 .... 131 C7
Hazel Gr. Chatham ME5 .... 32 B8
Hazel Gr. Sheerness ME12 .... 1 H1
Hazel Street Rd. ME9 .... 57 A4
Hazel Wlk. CT10 .... 29 C4
Hazeldene. ME12 .... 5 F6
Hazeldown Cl. CT17 .... 148 E2
Hazelmere Dr. CT6 .... 23 D5
Hazels The. ME8 .... 33 B5
Hazelwood Dr. ME16 .... 74 B4
Hazelwood Meadow. CT13 .... 93 F7
Hazlemere Dr. ME7 .... 11 A5
Hazlemere Rd. CT15 .... 43 A7
Hazling Dane. CT15 .... 130 F5
Hazlitt Dr. ME16 .... 74 D5
Head Hill. ME13 .... 63 D7
Head Hill Rd. ME13 .... 63 D8
Head Race The. ME15 .... 74 D2
Headcorn Dr. CT2 .... 67 B4
Headcorn Gdns. CT9 .... 8 E2
Headcorn Rd. Gillingham ME8 .. 11 B4
Headcorn Rd. Sandway ME17 .. 101 A2
Headingley Rd. ME16 .... 74 B6
Heard Way. ME10 .... 37 B5
Heart In Hand Cnr. CT6 .... 23 F2
Heart In Hand Rd. CT6 .... 23 F2
Hearts Delight Rd. ME9 .... 36 B1
Heath Cl. CT2 .... 67 F7

Heath Ct. CT15 .... 150 F6
Heath Gr. ME16 .... 74 A2
Heath Ho. CT3 .... 46 E5
Heath Ho. Coxheath ME17 .... 96 C3
Heath Rd. Langley Heath ME17 .. 98 E4
Heath Rd. Maidstone ME16 .... 74 A2
Heath The. CT5 .... 21 B1
Heath Villas. TN26 .... 181 C2
Heather Cl. Chatham ME5 .... 31 F4
Heather Cl. Margate CT9 .... 28 C8
Heather Cl. Sittingbourne ME10 .. 37 A3
Heather Dr. Maidstone ME15 .. 75 B2
Heather Dr. St Michaels TN30 .. 167 B3
Heatherwood Cl. ME17 .... 99 E2
Heathfield. ME17 .... 98 E4
Heathfield Ave.
  Maidstone ME14 .... 75 C7
Heathfield Ave. Dover CT16 .. 149 B2
Heathfield Bglws. ME17 .... 102 B1
Heathfield Cl. Chatham ME5 .... 32 B8
Heathfield Cl. Maidstone ME14 .. 75 B7
Heathfield Rd. Ashford TN24 .. 139 C3
Heathfield Rd. Maidstone ME14 . 75 C7
Heathfield Way. CT4 .... 128 F8
Heathorn St. ME14 .... 75 B5
Heathside. TN26 .... 181 C1
Heathside Ave. ME17 .... 96 C4
Heathwood Dr. CT11 .... 29 E1
Heaton Rd. CT1 .... 87 F6
Hedgend Ind Est. CT7 .... 25 F3
Hedgerow The. ME14 .... 75 E5
Hedgerows. TN23 .... 155 D7
Hedges The. ME14 .... 75 A7
Hedley St. ME14 .... 75 A5
Heel La. CT2 .... 67 C8
Heel Rd. ME13 .... 104 B7
Heights Terr. CT17 .... 166 C6
Heights The. CT5 .... 43 C6
Helding Cl. CT6 .... 23 B2
Helena Ave. CT9 .... 28 E8
Helena Cl. CT9 .... 28 C8
Helena Corniche. CT20 .... 177 C3
Helena Rd. CT18 .... 164 C2
Helmdon Cl. CT12 .... 29 C2
Helvellyn Ave. CT11 .... 52 B7
Hempstead Cty Jun Sch ME7 .. 33 A5
Hempstead
  Cty Prim Sch. ME7 .... 33 A5
Hempstead La. ME9 .... 37 E3
Hempstead Rd. Gillingham ME7 .. 33 A5
Hempstead Rd. Gillingham ME7 .. 33 B6
Hempstead Valley Dr. ME7 .... 33 A4
Hempstead Valley
  Sh Ctr. ME7 .... 33 A3
Hempsted St. **11** TN23 .... 139 B2
Henbane Cl. ME14 .... 75 E5
Hendon Bsns Ctr. TN24 .... 139 D2
Hengest Ave. CT9 .... 8 B1
Hengist Rd. Birchington CT7 .... 26 C7
Hengist Rd. Westgate-on-S CT8 .. 27 E8
Henley Bsns Pk. ME2 .... 9 D7
Henley Cl. Chatham ME5 .... 32 A6
Henley Cl. Gillingham ME8 .... 33 D8
Henley Fields. Maidstone ME14 .. 75 E6
Henley Fields.
  St Michaels TN30 .... 167 B2
Henley Meadows. TN30 .... 167 A2
Henley View. TN30 .... 167 B2
Henniker Cl. CT16 .... 149 A5
Henry Ct. **9** CT1 .... 87 F7
Henry St. CT1 .... 87 F7
Henry St. Chatham ME4 .... 10 B3
Henry St. Gillingham ME8 .... 12 A1
Henwood. TN24 .... 139 D3
Hera Ho. ME12 .... 1 C2
Herbert Dane Ct. **10** ME13 .... 62 D7
Herbert Rd. Ashford TN24 .... 156 D6
Herbert Rd. Chatham ME4 .... 10 A3
Herbert Rd. Gillingham ME8 .... 33 E8
Herbert Rd. Ramsgate CT11 .... 52 C6
Herbert St. CT17 .... 149 B1
Herdson Rd. CT20 .... 178 A5
Hereford Cl. ME8 .... 11 D2
Hereford Gdns. CT7 .... 26 F6
Hereford Rd. ME15 .... 97 D7
Hereson Rd. CT11 .... 52 F8
Hereson Sch The. CT11 .... 52 F8
Hereward Ave. CT7 .... 26 E8
Heritage Dr. ME7 .... 10 F1
Heritage Rd. Chatham ME5 .... 32 A6
Heritage Rd. Folkestone CT20 .. 177 D6
Herman Terr. ME4 .... 10 A3
Hermitage Cl. CT21 .... 176 B2
Hermitage La. Detling ME14 .... 55 B4
Hermitage La. Maidstone ME16 . 74 A4
Herne Ave. CT6 .... 23 A4
Herne Bay
  Cty Prim & Inf Sch. CT6 .... 22 F4
Herne Bay Golf Course. CT6 .... 22 F2
Herne Bay High Sch. CT6 .... 22 D3
Herne Bay Jun Sch. CT6 .... 22 F4
Herne Bay Rd.
  Calcott CT3 & CT2 .... 45 E2
Herne Bay Rd. Whitstable CT5 .. 21 C3
Herne Bay Sta. CT6 .... 22 E3
Herne CE Inf Sch. CT6 .... 46 B8
Herne CE Jun Sch. CT6 .... 46 A8
Herne Ct. CT19 .... 177 C6
Herne Dr. CT6 .... 22 C2
Herne Rd. ME8 .... 11 C2
Herne St. CT6 .... 46 A8
Herneville Gdns. CT6 .... 23 B4
Hernhill CE Prim Sch. ME13 .. 64 B6
Hero Wlk. ME1 .... 31 C7
Heron Apartments. **3** ME15 .. 97 F5
Heron Cl. ME9 .... 13 B4
Heron Forestall Ave. CT18 .. 163 B4
Heron Way. ME5 .... 32 B7

Heron Wlk. TN23 .... 155 E8
Heron's Brook. TN25 .... 140 E6
Heron's Way. TN21 .... 187 D8
Heronden Rd. Eastry CT13 .... 92 F1
Heronden Rd. Park Wood ME15 . 97 F4
Herons Cl. CT14 .... 107 C8
Herschell Rd. CT7 .... 26 F8
Herschell Rd E. CT14 .... 117 C3
Herschell Rd W. CT14 .... 117 C3
Hersden Cty Prim Sch. CT3 .... 46 E1
Hertford Ho. **14** Ramsgate CT11 . 52 E6
Hertford Pl. CT11 .... 52 E6
Hertford Rd. CT9 .... 29 C8
Hertford St. CT11 .... 52 E6
Herts Cres. ME15 .... 96 F3
Hetford Ct. CT1 .... 88 C8
Hever Cl. ME15 .... 97 F6
Hever Gdns. ME16 .... 74 E3
Hever Pl. CT2 .... 67 A3
Hewitt Cl. ME7 .... 10 F6
Hewitt Rd. **1** CT16 .... 166 D8
Hewitts Pl. TN24 .... 139 F1
Hextable Cl. Ashford TN23 .... 155 F6
Hextable Cl. Maidstone ME16 .. 74 D7
Heyford Cl. CT18 .... 163 B4
Hibernia St. **5** CT11 .... 52 E6
Hickory Dell. ME7 .... 33 A5
Hicks Forstal Rd. CT3 & CT6 .... 46 B5
Higgins' La. ME4 .... 9 F5
High Banks. Loose ME15 .... 96 F5
High Banks. Rochester ME1 .... 9 D2
High Dewar Rd. ME8 .... 34 A8
High Elms. ME8 .... 11 E1
High Halden Parochial
  CE Prim Sch. TN26 .... 167 E7
High Knocke. TN29 .... 195 B6
High Meadow. CT17 .... 149 C1
High Minnis. CT4 .... 143 F8
High Oak Hill. ME9 .... 13 E1
High Snoad Wood. TN25 .... 105 A1
High St. Ashford TN23 .... 139 C2
High St. Aylesford ME20 .... 53 A2
High St. Bridge CT4 .... 89 A1
High St. Broadstairs CT10 .... 29 E5
High St.
  Broadstairs, St Peter's CT10 .. 30 A4
High St. Brookland TN29 .... 197 D8
High St. **8** Canterbury CT1 .... 67 A1
High St. Canterbury CT1 .... 87 F8
High St. Chatham ME4 .... 9 E4
High St. Chatham ME4 .... 10 A4
High St. Deal CT14 .... 117 D6
High St. Dover CT16 & CT17 .. 166 C6
High St. Dymchurch TN29 .... 195 C8
High St. Eastchurch ME12 .... 5 D3
High St. Eastry CT13 .... 93 B2
High St. Elham CT4 .... 144 F5
High St. Fordwich CT2 .... 68 A4
High St. Gillingham ME7 .... 10 B6
High St. Gillingham ME7 .... 10 C5
High St.
  Gillingham,Brompton ME4 .. 10 A6
High St. Gillingham,Rainham ME8 . 33 F8
High St. Herne Bay CT6 .... 22 F5
High St. Hythe CT21 .... 176 C2
High St. Lenham ME17 .... 101 D5
High St. Littlebourne CT3 .... 89 F7
High St. Lydd TN29 .... 203 B6
High St. Lyminge CT18 .... 161 C6
High St. Maidstone ME14 .... 74 F4
High St. Manston CT12 .... 51 D8
High St. Margate CT9 .... 7 I2
High St. Margate CT9 .... 7 J1
High St. Margate, Garlinge CT9 .. 28 B7
High St. Minster, Thanet ME12 .. 4 D6
High St. Minster CT12 .... 50 C6
High St. New Romney TN28 .. 200 B6
High St. Newington ME9 .... 35 C6
High St. Queenborough ME11 .. 2 F5
High St. Ramsgate CT11 .... 52 D7
High St. Rochester ME2 .... 9 B7
High St. Rochester ME1 .... 9 C6
High St. Rochester ME4 .... 9 E4
High St. Sandwich CT13 .... 73 A1
High St. Sheerness ME12 .... 1 B3
High St. Sheerness ME12 .... 1 D2
High St. Sittingbourne ME10 .... 36 A4
High St. Sittingbourne ME10 .... 36 E4
High St. Smarden TN27 .... 135 A1
High St.
  St Margaret's at Cliffe CT15 .. 150 F6
High St. Sturry CT2 .... 67 F5
High St. Temple Ewell CT16 .. 148 D5
High St. Tenterden TN30 .... 179 A7
High St. Whitstable CT5 .... 20 D2
High St. Wingham CT3 .... 91 A8
High St. Wye TN25 .... 123 E2
High St The. TN27 .... 120 C7
High Street St Lawrence
  CT11 .... 52 B7
High Trees Cl. TN24 .... 157 A8
High View Ave. CT6 .... 22 B5
Higham Cl. ME15 .... 74 E2
Higham La. CT4 .... 111 B8
Higham View. ME14 .... 53 E4
Highbury Gdns. CT12 .... 29 B3
Highbury La. TN30 .... 179 A7
Highbury Wlk. CT12 .... 29 B3
Highcroft Gn. ME15 .... 97 F4
Highfield Cl. Gillingham ME8 .. 33 D7
Highfield Cl. Hythe CT21 .... 176 A4
Highfield Cl. Ramsgate CT12 .. 29 B3
Highfield Cl. Rough Common CT2 66 B3
Highfield Ct. **5** Margate CT9 .. 8 B2
Highfield Ct. Ramsgate CT12 .. 29 B2
Highfield Gdns. CT9 .... 7 H1

Highfield Ind Est. CT19 ...... 178 F6
Highfield La. TN24 ...... 157 C6
Highfield Rd. Ashford TN24 ...... 157 A8
Highfield Rd. Gillingham ME8 .. 33 D7
Highfield Rd.
  Halfway Houses ME12 ...... 3 E6
Highfield Rd. Ramsgate CT12 ...... 29 B3
Highfields Ave. CT6 ...... 23 D4
Highfields View. CT6 ...... 23 C4
Highgate Rd. ME7 ...... 21 B1
Highgrove Rd. ME5 ...... 32 A5
Highland Cl. CT20 ...... 177 F4
Highland Court Annexe (Kent &
  Canterbury Hospl). CT4 ...... 111 C8
Highland Rd. Chatham CT4 ...... 86 D1
Highland Rd. Maidstone ME15 ... 97 E6
Highlands Cres. TN29 ...... 195 A4
Highlands Farm
  Rare Breeds Ctr. TN26 ...... 169 D1
Highpoint. TN24 ...... 139 D3
Highridge. Gillingham ME7 ...... 10 F1
Highridge. Hythe CT20 ...... 177 A3
Highridge Cl. ME14 ...... 75 F5
Highsted Rd. ME9 &10 ...... 36 F1
Highsted Sch. ME10 ...... 36 F2
Highsted Valley. ME9 ...... 58 F7
Highstreet Rd. Waterham ME13 . 42 D2
Highstreet Rd.
  Yorklets CT5 & ME13 ...... 42 C2
Highview Cl.
  Boughton Street ME13 ...... 64 B3
Highview Cl. Maidstone ME15 ... 97 A8
Highview Dr. ME5 ...... 31 D5
Highview Rd. ME12 ...... 4 C7
Highview Sch. CT19 ...... 178 D6
Highworth
  Gram Sch for Girls. TN24 ... 139 A3
Hilary Cl. CT6 ...... 23 C4
Hilda Rd. Chatham ME4 ...... 10 A3
Hilda Rd. Halfway Houses ME12 .. 3 D6
Hildenborough Cres. ME16 ...... 74 C7
Hildersham Cl. CT10 ...... 29 E5
Hill Ave. CT15 ...... 130 E5
Hill Brow. Maidstone ME5 ...... 76 A5
Hill Brow. Sittingbourne ME10 ... 36 D2
Hill Chase. ME5 ...... 31 E3
Hill Cres. Aylesham CT3 ...... 112 E5
Hill Cres. Lenham ME17 ...... 101 D5
Hill Crest. TN23 ...... 155 B8
Hill Ct. TN27 ...... 103 E1
Hill Dr. CT13 ...... 93 B3
Hill Green Rd. ME9 ...... 56 D8
Hill House Dr. CT12 ...... 50 C7
Hill La. CT18 ...... 162 B1
Hill Rd. Chatham ME1 ...... 31 A3
Hill Rd. Folkestone CT19 ...... 178 E7
Hill Rd. Folkestone CT19 ...... 178 E8
Hill Rd. Rochester ME1 ...... 9 A2
Hill The. Charing TN27 ...... 120 D8
Hill The. Littlebourne CT3 ...... 89 F8
Hill Top Cotts. ME17 ...... 96 E2
Hill Top Rd. CT6 ...... 23 B5
Hill View. Ashford TN24 ...... 139 C3
Hill View. Margate CT9 ...... 28 D7
Hill View Terr. CT18 ...... 161 D3
Hill View Way. ME5 ...... 31 E5
Hill's Terr. ME4 ...... 9 F3
Hillary Rd. ME4 ...... 75 A7
Hillborough Dr. CT6 ...... 23 F5
Hillborough Gr. ME5 ...... 32 A3
Hillborough Rd. CT6 ...... 23 B5
Hillbrow Ave. Herne Bay CT6 ...... 23 B2
Hillbrow Ave. Sturry CT2 ...... 67 F7
Hillbrow La. TN23 ...... 138 F1
Hillbrow Rd. Ashford TN23 ...... 139 A1
Hillbrow Rd. Ramsgate CT11 .. 52 D8
Hillcrest Cl. TN24 ...... 139 E6
Hillcrest Cl. Deal CT14 ...... 117 A2
Hillcrest Gdns. Ramsgate CT11 .. 52 B6
Hillcrest Rd. Chatham ME4 ...... 9 F2
Hillcrest Rd. Hythe CT21 ...... 176 B3
Hillcrest Rd. Kingsdown CT14 .. 134 D4
Hillcrest Rd. Littlebourne CT3 ... 89 E8
Hillcroft Rd. CT6 ...... 23 B3
Hillden Shaw. ME15 ...... 97 A8
Hiller Cl. CT10 ...... 30 A6
Hillfield Villas. TN26 ...... 167 F8
Hillman Ave. CT6 ...... 22 A4
Hillside. ■ CT20 ...... 177 E3
Hillside Ave. Canterbury CT2 ... 66 C2
Hillside Ave. Rochester ME2 ...... 9 B8
Hillside Ave. Rushenden ME11 .... 2 F3
Hillside Ct. Hythe CT21 ...... 176 C2
Hillside Ct. ■ Rochester ME2 .... 9 A7
Hillside Ind Est. CT20 ...... 177 E4
Hillside Rd. Chatham ME4 ...... 10 A4
Hillside Rd. Dover CT17 ...... 149 A2
Hillside Rd. Minster ME12 ...... 4 B7
Hillside Rd.
  Stalisfield Green ME13 ...... 103 E6
Hillside Rd. Whitstable CT5 ...... 21 A1
Hillside St. CT21 ...... 176 C2
Hilltop Rd. ME12 ...... 4 A5
Hillview Rd. Canterbury CT2 ... 66 C2
Hillview Rd. Whitstable CT5 ...... 43 D8
Hillyfield Rd. TN23 ...... 156 A8
Hillyfields Cty Jun Sch. ME7 ... 10 E6
Hillyfields Rise. TN23 ...... 139 A1
Hilton Bsns Ctr. TN23 ...... 156 B6
Hilton Dr. ME10 ...... 36 B6
Hilton Rd. TN23 ...... 138 F2
Hinchliffe Way. CT9 ...... 29 D8
Hind Cl. TN29 ...... 195 C8
Hinde Cl. ME10 ...... 36 F7
Hines Terr. ME4 ...... 10 C1
Hinton Cres. ME7 ...... 33 A6
Hinxhill Rd. TN24 & TN25 ...... 140 D1
Hirst Cl. CT16 ...... 149 B4

Hither Field. TN27 ...... 120 C7
Hoades Wood Rd. CT2 ...... 68 A7
Hoath Cl. ME7 ...... 33 B7
Hoath Cty Prim Sch. CT3 ...... 46 E5
Hoath La. ME8 ...... 33 B7
Hoath Rd. CT3 ...... 46 C3
Hoath Way. ME7 & ME8 .. 33 B5
Hobart Cres. CT16 ...... 149 C3
Hobart Gdns. ME10 ...... 36 C4
Hobart Rd. CT12 ...... 29 A1
Hockeredge Gdns. CT8 & CT9 ... 27 F8
Hockers Cl. ME14 ...... 76 A8
Hockers La. ME14 ...... 76 A7
Hodge's Gap. CT9 ...... 8 C3
Hodgson Rd. CT5 ...... 42 F7
Hog Gn. CT4 ...... 144 F4
Hog Hill. ME14 ...... 76 B5
Hogarth Cl. CT6 ...... 23 E5
Hogban La. ME17 ...... 79 A3
Hogben Cl. CT18 ...... 161 B7
Holbeam Rd. ME13 ...... 82 A1
Holborn La. ME4 ...... 9 F5
Holbourn Cl. CT6 ...... 46 B8
Holbrook Dr. CT12 ...... 29 B1
Holcombe Rd. Chatham ME4 ...... 9 F2
Holcombe Rd. Rochester ME1 .... 9 C3
Holdenhurst. TN23 ...... 155 E6
Holder Cl. ME8 ...... 32 C6
Holding St. ME8 ...... 11 F1
Holland Cl. Broadstairs CT10 ...... 8 G2
Holland Cl. Sheerness ME12 ...... 1 C1
Holland Ho. ME1 ...... 9 D5
Holland Rd. Chatham ME5 ...... 31 E4
Holland Rd. Maidstone ME14 ... 75 B5
Hollands Ave. CT19 ...... 178 F7
Hollicondane Rd. CT11 ...... 52 E8
Hollingbourne
  Cty Prim Sch. ME17 ...... 77 E2
Hollingbourne Hill. ME17 ...... 77 F4
Hollingbourne Rd. ME8 ...... 11 C2
Hollingbourne Sta. ME17 ...... 77 C3
Hollington Pl. TN24 ...... 139 B3
Hollington Sch. TN24 ...... 139 B3
Hollingworth Rd. ME15 ...... 97 F5
Hollow La. Canterbury CT1 ...... 87 E5
Hollow La. Hartlip ME9 ...... 34 E5
Hollow Rd. CT3 ...... 47 B6
Hollow St. CT3 ...... 47 C5
Hollow Wood Rd. CT17 ...... 165 E8
Hollowmede. CT1 ...... 87 E6
Holly Cl. Broadstairs CT10 ...... 29 C4
Holly Cl. Chatham ME5 ...... 32 C8
Holly Cl. Eastry CT13 ...... 93 B2
Holly Cl. Folkestone CT19 ...... 178 E7
Holly Cl. Gillingham ME7 ...... 10 E6
Holly Farm Rd. ME15 ...... 98 C6
Holly Gdns. CT9 ...... 8 C2
Holly Hill Rd. ME13 ...... 64 D5
Holly Ho. ME12 ...... 1 C2
Holly La. CT9 ...... 8 C2
Holly Rd. Ramsgate CT11 ...... 52 E8
Holly Rd. St Mary's Bay TN29 .. 194 F4
Holly Tree Cl. ME17 ...... 99 E2
Hollybrook Hill. ME10 ...... 36 D4
Hollybush Cnr. CT4 ...... 90 A3
Hollybush La. CT3 ...... 69 A4
Holm Mill La. ME17 ...... 100 B6
Holm Oak Cl. CT1 ...... 87 F6
Holm Oak Gdns. CT10 ...... 29 F4
Holmesdale Cl. ME15 ...... 96 F3
Holmestone Rd. CT15 & CT17 .. 148 E1
Holmlea Cl. TN24 ...... 139 E1
Holmoaks. Gillingham ME8 ...... 11 E2
Holmoaks. Maidstone ME14 ...... 75 C5
Holmscroft Rd. CT6 ...... 23 D5
Holmside. ME7 ...... 10 E3
Holmside Ave. ME12 ...... 3 D6
Holmwood Rd. TN23 ...... 155 E7
Holness Rd. CT3 ...... 71 D2
Holt St. CT15 ...... 113 C4
Holton Cl. CT7 ...... 27 A6
Holtwood Cl. ME8 ...... 33 D6
Holtye Cres. ME15 ...... 75 B2
Holy Cross
  RC High Sch The. CT10 ...... 30 A3
Holy Family
  RC Prim Sch The. ME15 ... 97 F4
Holy Trinity
  CE Prim Sch. CT10 ...... 30 A1
Holy Trinity & St John's
  CE Prim Sch. CT9 ...... 7 J2
Holyrood Dr. ME12 ...... 4 A5
Holywell Ave. CT10 ...... 178 D8
Holywell Cty Prim Sch. ME9 .. 12 F3
Holywell Ho. CT17 ...... 178 D8
Holywell La. ME9 ...... 12 F2
Home Farm Cotts. CT14 ...... 115 E6
Homebirch Ho. ■ CT7 ...... 26 F8
Homefield Ave. CT14 ...... 117 B6
Homefield Row. CT14 ...... 117 B6
Homefleet Ho. ■ CT11 ...... 52 F7
Homeleigh Rd. CT12 ...... 29 B3
Homepeak. ■ CT21 ...... 176 B2
Homeside Farm. CT14 ...... 126 F6
Homespire Ho. ■ CT1 ...... 67 A1
Homestall Cr. CT2 ...... 66 C4
Homestall La. ME13 ...... 63 B5
Homestead. TN23 ...... 155 D8
Homestead Cl. ■ CT9 ...... 7 J1
Homestead La. CT15 ...... 132 C7
Homestead Mews. ME9 ...... 36 B2
Homestead Village. CT5 ...... 52 C5
Homestreet
  Cty Prim Sch. TN26 ...... 182 F8
Homevale Ho. ■ CT20 ...... 177 E3
Homeview. ME10 ...... 37 B4

Homewood Ave. ME10 ...... 36 D3
Homewood Cty Inf Sch. ME10 .. 36 D4
Homewood Rd. Sturry CT2 ...... 68 A6
Homewood Rd.
  Tenterden TN30 ...... 167 B1
Homewood Sch. TN30 ...... 167 B1
Honduras Terr. ■ ME14 ...... 75 A7
Honey Bee Glade. ME8 ...... 33 E6
Honey Cl. ME7 ...... 33 A5
Honey Hill. CT2 & CT5 ...... 65 F8
Honey La. ME15 ...... 98 B6
Honeyball Wlk. ME9 ...... 38 C2
Honeycrock Hill. ME9 ...... 56 F8
Honeyfield. TN23 ...... 138 E1
Honeypot Cl. ME2 ...... 9 B8
Honeysuckle Cl. ■
  Chatham ME5 ...... 31 E4
Honeysuckle Cl. Gillingham ME7 32 F4
Honeysuckle Cl. Margate CT9 ... 28 C8
Honeysuckle Ct. ME10 ...... 37 B5
Honeysuckle Rd. CT11 ...... 52 F8
Honeysuckle Way. CT6 ...... 23 D2
Honeywood Cl. Canterbury CT1 .. 67 B2
Honeywood Rd. Lympne CT21 ... 175 A4
Honeywood Parkway. CT15 .. 149 B5
Honeywood Rd. CT15 & CT16 .. 149 A5
Honfleur Rd. CT13 ...... 93 F8
Honiton House Sch. CT9 ...... 8 B2
Honywood Rd. ME17 ...... 101 C4
Hook Cl. Chatham ME5 ...... 31 E5
Hook Cl. Folkestone CT20 ...... 177 F5
Hook La. Brookland TN29 ...... 197 C6
Hook La. Charing TN27 ...... 120 A7
Hook La. Harrietsham ME17 ...... 100 C6
Hook Wall. TN29 ...... 197 E5
Hookstead. TN26 ...... 167 C7
Hooper's Pl. ME1 ...... 9 C4
Hooper's Rd. ME1 ...... 9 C4
Hoopers La. CT6 ...... 23 D3
Hop Garden Way. CT1 ...... 87 E6
Hope La. New Romney TN29 .. 200 A8
Hope La. St Mary in the Marsh
  TN28 & TN29 ...... 193 F2
Hope Rd. CT14 ...... 117 D5
Hope St. Chatham ME4 ...... 10 A3
Hope St. Maidstone ME14 ...... 74 F6
Hope St. Sheerness ME12 ...... 1 C2
Hope's La. CT12 ...... 29 C3
Hopes Gr. TN26 ...... 167 D7
Hopeville Ave. CT10 ...... 29 E6
Hopewell Dr. ME5 ...... 32 C8
Hopewell Sch. TN23 ...... 155 B7
Hoppers Way. TN23 ...... 155 D8
Hopsons Pl. ME12 ...... 4 C5
Horn Hill. ME9 ...... 58 E2
Horn St. CT19 & CT20 & CT21 .. 177 B4
Hornash La. TN26 ...... 170 D8
Hornbeam Ave. ME5 ...... 32 B2
Hornbeam Cl. TN23 ...... 138 F3
Hornes Place Chapel. TN26 .. 181 D2
Hornet Cl. CT10 ...... 29 D3
Horsa Rd. Birchington CT7 ...... 26 D7
Horsa Rd. Deal CT14 ...... 117 D8
Horsebridge Rd. CT5 ...... 20 D2
Horselees Rd. ME13 ...... 64 A2
Horseshoe Cl. Gillingham ME7 .. 32 F5
Horseshoe Cl. Maidstone ME14 . 75 E5
Horseshoes La. ME17 ...... 98 E4
Horsewash La. ME1 ...... 9 C6
Horsford Wlk. ME13 ...... 62 A8
Horsham Hill. ME8 & ME9 ...... 12 E4
Horsham La. ME8 ...... 12 D3
Horshams The. CT6 ...... 23 D5
Horsley Cl. CT18 ...... 163 B4
Horsley Rd. ME1 ...... 9 B4
Horsted Ave. ME4 ...... 9 E1
Horsted Cty Inf Sch. ME4 ...... 31 D5
Horsted Cty Jun Sch. ME5 ...... 31 D5
Horsted Way. ME1 ...... 31 D7
Horton Cotts. CT4 ...... 86 E4
Horton Downs. ME15 ...... 75 F1
Horton Gdns. CT4 ...... 86 E4
Horton Rd. CT4 ...... 86 E4
Hoser Gdns. CT7 ...... 27 A7
Hospital Hill. CT20 & CT21 ...... 177 C3
Hospital La. Canterbury CT1 .. 87 F8
Hospital La. Chatham ME1 ...... 9 C4
Hospital Meadow Cotts. CT3 ... 91 D2
Hospital Rd. ME17 ...... 99 E8
Hotel Rd. Gillingham ME8 ...... 11 A2
Hotel Rd.
  St Margaret's at Cliffe CT15 .. 151 B6
Hothfield Common
  Nature Reserve. TN26 .. 137 F8
Hothfield
  Cty Prim Sch. TN26 ...... 138 A7
Hothfield Rd. ME8 ...... 11 F1
Hougham Court La. CT15 ...... 165 A3
Houghton Ave. ME7 ...... 33 B3
Houghton Ho. CT19 ...... 178 C5
House Field. TN24 ...... 139 F2
Housefield Rd. ME13 ...... 104 C6
Hovenden Cl. CT2 ...... 67 A4
Howard Ave. Rochester ME1 ...... 9 D3
Howard Ave. Sittingbourne ME10 36 D6
Howard Cl. ME1 ...... 4 C7
Howard Dr. ME16 ...... 74 B5
Howard Rd. CT10 ...... 30 A3
Howard Sch The. ME8 ...... 33 B8
Howbury Wlk. ME8 ...... 33 D4
Howfield La. CT4 ...... 86 E5
Howfield La. CT4 ...... 89 C5
Howletts Oast. CT4 ...... 89 C5
Howletts Zoo Pk. CT4 ...... 89 D6
Hoxton Cl. TN23 ...... 155 D8
Hoystings Cl The. CT1 ...... 88 A7
Hubbard's La. ME15 ...... 97 A3

Hubbards Cotts. ME8 ...... 12 C2
Hubbards Hill. ME17 ...... 102 B6
Hubble Dr. ME15 ...... 97 E7
Hubert Way. CT10 ...... 29 E6
Huckleberry Cl. ME5 ...... 32 B3
Hudson Cl. ■ Dover CT16 ...... 149 B3
Hudson Cl. Gillingham ME8 ...... 11 C1
Hudson Cl. Sturry CT2 ...... 67 F6
Hudson Rd. CT1 ...... 67 B2
Hugh Pl. ■ ME13 ...... 62 D7
Hugh Price Cl. ME10 ...... 37 C5
Hugin Ave. CT10 ...... 29 E7
Hull Pl. CT14 ...... 116 F6
Hull Rd. TN29 ...... 204 E6
Humber Ave. CT6 ...... 21 F4
Humber Ho. ■ ME15 ...... 97 E8
Hume Ct. CT21 ...... 176 D1
Humphrey Terr. CT18 ...... 162 F4
Hundreds Cl. CT18 ...... 27 D7
Hunger Hatch La. TN27 ...... 119 F4
Hunstanton Cl. ME8 ...... 33 E3
Hunt Cl. CT18 ...... 163 A4
Hunter Ave. TN24 ...... 156 E8
Hunter Cl. TN24 ...... 156 E8
Hunter Rd. TN24 ...... 139 E1
Hunters Chase. Herne Bay CT6 .. 23 C2
Hunters Chase. Whitstable CT5 .. 43 E7
Hunters Ct. ■ ME7 ...... 10 C7
Hunters Forstal Rd. CT6 ...... 23 C2
Hunters Way. Gillingham ME7 .. 10 E1
Hunters Way. Sheldwich ME13 .. 83 C5
Hunters Way W. ME5 & ME7 .... 10 E1
Hunters Wlk. CT14 ...... 117 B6
Huntersfield Cl. ME5 ...... 32 C1
Hunting Gate. CT7 ...... 26 F8
Hunting Rd. CT7 ...... 26 F7
Huntingdon Wlk. ■ ME15 ...... 97 E7
Huntington Rd. ME17 ...... 96 B3
Hunton Gdns. CT2 ...... 67 A4
Hunton Hill. ME15 ...... 96 A2
Huntsfield Ind Est. CT20 ...... 177 D4
Huntsman La. ME14 ...... 75 B4
Huntsman's Cnr. ME4 ...... 31 E8
Huntsmans Cl. ME4 ...... 9 E1
Huntswood. TN23 ...... 138 E1
Hurst Cl. ME5 ...... 31 E6
Hurst Gr. CT12 ...... 29 C1
Hurst Hill. ME5 ...... 31 E2
Hurst La. Capel-le-F CT18 ...... 164 B4
Hurst La. Charing Heath TN27 ... 119 E6
Hurst La. Sittingbourne ME10 ... 14 F1
Hurst Pl. ME8 ...... 33 F8
Hurst Rd. TN24 ...... 139 C7
Hurstford La. TN26 & TN27 ...... 120 C7
Hurstings The. ME16 ...... 74 D2
Hurstwood. ME5 ...... 31 E4
Hurstwood Rd. Bredhurst ME7 .. 33 B1
Hurstwood Rd. Detling ME14 ... 55 B7
Hurstwood Rd.
  Warren Street ME13 & ME17 .. 102 E8
Hutchings Cl. ME10 ...... 37 C5
Hutsford Cl. ME8 ...... 33 D5
Huxley Ct. ME1 ...... 9 D4
Hybrid Cl. ME1 ...... 9 D1
Hyde Ct. CT17 ...... 166 C2
Hyde Pl. CT3 ...... 112 F5
Hyde Rd. ME16 ...... 74 D6
Hyde The. CT4 ...... 86 B2
Hythe Cl. CT20 ...... 177 F5
Hythe Cty Inf Sch. CT21 ...... 176 B1
Hythe Light Railway
  Sta. CT21 ...... 176 A2
Hythe Pl. CT13 ...... 94 A8
Hythe Rd. Ashford TN24 ...... 139 E1
Hythe Rd. Dymchurch TN29 ... 186 E1
Hythe Rd. Pedlinge CT21 ...... 175 D4
Hythe Rd. Sittingbourne ME10 .. 36 D5
Hythe Rd. Smeeth TN25 & TN24 . 158 C3

Ian's Wlk. CT21 ...... 177 A3
Iden La. TN27 ...... 119 B4
Idenwood Cl. ME8 ...... 33 D6
Iffin La. CT1 & CT4 ...... 87 E2
Ifield Cl. ME15 ...... 97 F7
Ilex Rd. CT19 ...... 177 F6
Illustrious Cl. ME5 ...... 32 A6
Imbert Cl. ME5 ...... 200 C6
Imperial Ave. ME12 ...... 4 D7
Imperial Dr. ME12 ...... 6 E4
Imperial Rd. ME7 ...... 10 C3
Impton La. ME5 ...... 32 A1
Ince Rd. CT2 ...... 67 F7
Ingle Cl. CT7 ...... 27 B7
Ingle Rd. ME4 ...... 9 F2
Ingleden Cl. ME10 ...... 36 F8
Ingleden Park Rd. TN30 ...... 167 C1
Ingles La. ■ CT20 ...... 178 D5
Ingles Mews. ■ CT20 ...... 178 C4
Ingles Rd. CT20 ...... 178 C4
Ingoldsby Rd. Birchington CT7 .. 26 E7
Ingoldsby Rd. Canterbury CT1 .. 87 D6
Ingoldsby Rd. Folkestone CT19 . 178 E7
Ingram Rd. ME7 ...... 10 E6
Institute Rd. Chatham ME4 ...... 10 A4
Institute Rd. Faversham ME13 ... 62 D7
Inverary Ct. CT11 ...... 29 E1
Inverness Ho. ■ ME15 ...... 97 E7
Inverness Terr. CT10 ...... 30 A3
Invicta Cl. ME10 ...... 36 F7
Invicta Gram Sch for Girls.
  ME14 ...... 75 C4
Invicta Ho. Canterbury CT1 ...... 87 F7
Invicta Ho. Margate CT9 ...... 8 C1
Invicta Rd. Folkestone CT19 .. 178 D7
Invicta Rd. Lydd TN29 ...... 203 A2
Invicta Rd. Margate CT9 ...... 29 B8
Invicta Rd. Sheerness ME12 ...... 1 D2
Invicta Rd. Whitstable CT5 ...... 43 F8

Invicta Villas. ME14 ...... 76 C4
Inward Car Lanes. CT16 ...... 166 G8
Inward Freight Lanes. CT16 .. 166 G8
Iona Cl. ME5 ...... 32 D1
Iona Rd. ME15 ...... 97 A4
Irchester St. ■ CT11 ...... 52 F7
Ireland St. TN24 ...... 139 D2
Irene Astor Ct. ■ CT20 ...... 178 D5
Iris Cl. ME5 ...... 54 A8
Iron Bar La. ■ CT1 ...... 88 A8
Ironside Cl. ME5 ...... 32 A8
Irvine Dr. CT9 ...... 29 C8
Isis Cl. CT21 ...... 175 A3
Island Rd. Upstreet CT3 & CT7 ... 47 D2
Island Rd. Westbere CT2 & CT3 .. 68 C7
Island Wall. CT5 ...... 20 C1
Ivanhoe Rd. Herne Bay CT6 ...... 23 A4
Ivanhoe Rd. Westgate-on-S CT8 . 7 C1
Ivens Way. ME17 ...... 100 D6
Ivy Cl. Etchinghill CT18 ...... 161 D3
Ivy Cl. Kingswood ME17 ...... 99 D2
Ivy Cottage Hill. CT12 ...... 50 E7
Ivy Cotts. TN23 ...... 155 C8
Ivy House Rd. CT5 ...... 20 F1
Ivy La. Canterbury CT1 ...... 88 A8
Ivy La. Ramsgate CT11 ...... 52 D6
Ivy Pl. Canterbury CT1 ...... 87 E7
Ivy Pl. Deal CT14 ...... 117 D7
Ivy St. ME8 ...... 33 F8
Ivy Way. CT19 ...... 178 E2
Ivychurch Gdns. CT9 ...... 8 C2
Ivychurch Rd. TN29 ...... 192 B3
Iwade Cty Prim Sch. ME9 ...... 14 E2

Jaarlen Rd. TN29 ...... 203 B6
Jacklin Cl. ME5 ...... 31 F2
Jackson Ave. ME1 ...... 31 E8
Jackson Cl. ME8 ...... 11 C1
Jackson Rd. CT1 ...... 87 E7
Jacksons La. ■ TN30 ...... 179 A7
Jacob Cl. CT9 ...... 28 E7
Jacob Yd. ■ ME13 ...... 62 D7
Jacobs Ho. ME12 ...... 1 D2
Jaffa Ct. CT5 ...... 43 D8
Jamaica Terr. ME14 ...... 75 A7
James Cl. Ash CT3 ...... 71 D2
James Cl. Lyminge CT18 ...... 161 C7
James Cl. Folkestone CT20 .. 178 A4
James Ct. ■ Margate CT9 ...... 8 B2
James Hall Gdns. CT14 ...... 117 C3
James Morris Ct. ■ CT20 .. 177 F3
James St. Ashford TN23 ...... 139 A2
James St. Chatham ME4 ...... 9 F4
James St. Folkestone CT19 .. 178 D6
James St. Gillingham ME7 ...... 10 C6
James St. Maidstone ME14 ...... 75 A5
James St. ■ Ramsgate CT11 .. 52 D6
James St. Rochester ME1 ...... 9 C4
James St. Sheerness ME12 ...... 1 E2
James Whatman Way. ME14 ... 74 F5
Japonica Cl. ME5 ...... 32 C2
Jarman's Field. TN25 ...... 123 F2
Jarrett Ho. ■ CT20 ...... 178 C4
Jarrett's Ct. ME10 ...... 37 B4
Jarvis Dr. TN24 ...... 157 A7
Jarvis Pl. TN30 ...... 167 B3
Jarvist Rd. CT14 ...... 134 D6
Jasmine Cl. ■ ME5 ...... 31 F4
Jasper Ave. ME1 ...... 9 D2
Jayne Wlk. CT5 ...... 43 B6
Jefferson Cl. TN23 ...... 138 F1
Jefferson Dr. ME8 ...... 11 C1
Jefferson Rd. ME12 ...... 1 E2
Jefferstone Gdns. TN29 ...... 194 E4
Jefferstone La. TN29 ...... 194 E4
Jefferstone Lane Sta. TN29 .. 194 F4
Jeffery St. ME4 ...... 10 C6
Jeffrey St. ME14 ...... 75 A5
Jellicoe Cl. TN24 ...... 157 A7
Jemmett La. TN25 ...... 157 D3
Jemmett Rd. TN23 ...... 156 A8
Jenkins' Dale. ME4 ...... 9 F3
Jenkins Dr. ME15 ...... 97 E5
Jenner Rd. ME1 ...... 9 C4
Jenner's Way. TN29 ...... 194 F3
Jennifer Gdns. CT9 ...... 29 C8
Jersey La. CT4 ...... 109 C6
Jersey Rd. ME2 ...... 9 A8
Jesmond St. ■ CT19 ...... 178 D6
Jesse's Hill. CT4 ...... 111 B1
Jessica Mews. ■
  Canterbury CT1 ...... 67 B1
Jessica Mews.
  Sittingbourne ME10 ...... 36 E7
Jesuit Cl. CT2 ...... 67 A4
Jesus Hospl. CT1 ...... 67 A1
Jetty Rd. Sheerness ME12 ...... 1 B3
Jetty Rd. Warden ME12 ...... 6 E4
Jewry La. CT1 ...... 87 F8
Jeyes Rd. ME7 ...... 10 C4
Jezreels Rd. ME7 ...... 10 D3
Jillian Way. TN23 ...... 155 E7
Jiniwin Rd. ME1 ...... 31 D7
Joey's La. TN29 ...... 139 E2
Johannesburg Ho. ■ ME15 .. 97 F5
Johannesburg Rd. CT16 ...... 149 C4
John Anderson Ct. ■ ME13 .. 62 D7
John Bowley Ho. CT19 ...... 177 D4
John Graham Ct. CT1 ...... 88 A6
John Hall Cl. ME13 ...... 40 B4
John St. Broadstairs CT10 ...... 30 B4
John St. Maidstone ME14 ...... 75 A6

John St. Rochester ME1 .... 9 C4
John Tapping Cl. CT14 .... 117 B1
John Wilson Bsns Pk. CT5 .... 21 B1
John's Gn. CT13 .... 93 E6
Johnson Ave. ME7 .... 10 C2
Johnson Cl. TN24 .... 157 A7
Johnson Ct. ME13 .... 40 B1
Johnson Rd. ME10 .... 36 D4
Johnson Way. ME12 .... 4 A7
Joiners Cl. ME4 .... 10 B2
Jointon Rd. CT20 .... 178 B4
Jordan Cl. ME15 .... 97 E5
Joseph Conrad Ho. CT2 .... 66 D1
Joseph Wilson Ind Est. CT5 .... 44 A7
Joss Gap Rd. CT10 .... 8 H1
Joy La. CT5 .... 43 B8
Joy Lane
  Cty Prim Inf Sch. CT5 .... 43 C7
Joy Lane
  Cty Prim Jun Sch. CT5 .... 43 C7
Joyes Cl. Folkestone CT19 .... 178 E7
Joyes Cl. Whitfield CT16 .... 149 E7
Joyes Rd. Folkestone CT19 .... 178 E7
Joyes Rd. Whitfield CT16 .... 149 E7
Jubilee Cl. CT21 .... 187 D8
Jubilee Cotts. Throwley ME13 .... 82 D1
Jubilee Cotts. Worth CT14 .... 94 B4
Jubilee Cres. ME11 .... 2 F5
Jubilee Ct. 18 CT10 .... 30 B4
Jubilee Field. TN30 .... 188 E4
Jubilee Rd. Littlebourne CT3 .... 89 F8
Jubilee Rd. Sandwich CT13 .... 93 F8
Jubilee Rd. Worth CT14 .... 94 B4
Jubilee St. ME10 .... 36 E5
Jubilee Terr. ME7 .... 10 C6
Jubilee Way. Dover CT16 .... 166 G8
Jubilee Way.
  Guston CT15 & CT16 .... 150 A2
Judd Rd. ME13 .... 62 A7
Judkins Cl. ME5 .... 32 C6
Julian Rd. CT19 .... 178 B6
Julie Cl. CT10 .... 30 A7
Julien Pl. TN24 .... 157 A4
Junction Rd. Gillingham ME7 .... 10 D4
Junction Rd. Herne Bay CT6 .... 22 C2
Juniper Cl. Ashford TN23 .... 138 E2
Juniper Cl. Canterbury CT1 .... 88 A6
Juniper Cl. Chatham ME5 .... 32 A4
Juniper Cl. Whitstable CT5 .... 20 F1
Jury's Gap Coastguard Cotts.
  TN31 .... 201 B1
Jury's Gap Rd. TN29 .... 203 A5

Kake St. CT4 .... 125 E7
Katherine Ct. ME5 .... 32 B2
Kathleen Mews. 17 CT20 .... 178 D5
Kearsney Abbey. CT16 .... 148 D4
Kearsney Ct. ME16 .... 148 E4
Kearsney Ct. CT16 .... 148 D4
Kearsney Sta. CT16 .... 148 D4
Keat Farm Cl. CT6 .... 23 F5
Keddow's Cl. CT21 .... 187 D8
Keefe Cl. ME5 .... 31 D1
Keeper's Hill. CT4 .... 89 D2
Keith Ave. CT12 .... 52 A8
Kellaway Rd. ME5 .... 32 A2
Kelly Dr. ME7 .... 10 C7
Kelly Ho. ME1 .... 31 C7
Kelvedon Rd. CT14 .... 117 C2
Kemp Alley. 2 CT5 .... 20 D1
Kemp Cl. ME5 .... 31 E4
Kemp Rd. CT5 .... 21 C2
Kempes Pl. TN25 .... 123 E2
Kempton Cl. ME5 .... 32 C2
Kemsdale Rd. ME13 .... 63 F6
Kemsing Gdns. CT2 .... 67 B4
Kemsley Halt. ME10 .... 14 E1
Kemsley Street Rd. ME14 .... 33 C1
Kenardington Rd. TN26 .... 181 B3
Kenbrook. TN24 .... 139 C7
Kendal Cl. CT11 .... 52 B6
Kendal Rise. CT10 .... 30 A5
Kendal Way. ME8 .... 33 D8
Kendon Bsns Pk. ME2 .... 9 D8
Kenfield Rd. CT4 .... 109 A6
Kengate Ind Est. CT21 .... 175 F1
Kenilworth Cl. CT15 .... 151 A6
Kenilworth Ct. ME10 .... 36 C5
Kenilworth Dr. ME8 .... 33 D6
Kenilworth Gdns. ME8 .... 33 D7
Kenilworth Ho. ME16 .... 74 B2
Kennedy Cl. ME13 .... 62 D8
Kennedy Dr. CT14 .... 117 B2
Kennedy Ho. 6 CT11 .... 52 F7
Kennel Barn Rd. ME9 .... 57 C5
Kennel Hill. CT15 .... 131 E6
Kennelling Rd. ME13 & TN27 .... 103 D5
Kennett Dr. CT14 .... 117 A2
Kennett La. TN25 .... 175 B8
Kennett Lane Cotts. TN25 .... 175 B8
Kennington
  CE Jun Sch. TN24 .... 139 E7
Kennington Cl. Gillingham ME8 .... 11 B4
Kennington Cl.
  Maidstone ME15 .... 97 F7
Kennington Rd. TN24 .... 140 A1
Kensington Ho. ME16 .... 74 A2
Kensinton Ct. ME1 .... 67 C4
Kent Ave. Ashford TN24 .... 139 B3
Kent Ave. Canterbury CT1 .... 88 D8
Kent Ave. Maidstone ME15 .... 75 C1
Kent Ave. Minster ME12 .... 4 C6
Kent Ave. Sittingbourne ME10 .... 36 D3
Kent Battle of Britain Mus.
  CT18 .... 162 F4

Kent & Canterbury Hospl. CT1 .... 88 A5
Kent Cl. ME1 .... 31 C8
Kent Coll. CT2 .... 66 C3
Kent County Optholmic
  & Aural Hospl. ME14 .... 75 A4
Kent County Show Gd. ME14 .... 55 C3
Kent Gdns. CT7 .... 26 F7
Kent Ho. CT20 .... 178 B4
Kent Inst of Art & Design.
  Chatham ME1 .... 9 E4
Kent Inst of Art & Design.
  Maidstone ME16 .... 74 C3
Kent Int Bsns Pk. CT12 .... 27 D2
Kent International Airport.
  CT12 .... 28 B1
Kent Music Sch. CT2 .... 66 F1
Kent Pl. CT11 .... 52 F6
Kent Rd. Folkestone CT19 .... 177 E7
Kent Rd. Margate CT9 .... 29 B8
Kent Rd. Sheerness ME12 .... 1 C1
Kent St. CT5 .... 43 D8
Kent Terr. Gillingham ME8 .... 12 C2
Kent Terr. Ramsgate CT11 .... 52 F6
Kent View Dr. ME12 .... 5 D1
Kentmere Ave. CT11 & CT12 .... 51 F7
Kenton Gdns. CT12 .... 50 B6
Kenward Rd. ME16 .... 74 C5
Kenwood Ave. ME5 .... 32 A4
Kenya Terr. 7 ME14 .... 75 A7
Kenyon Wlk. ME8 .... 33 B3
Kerton Rd. TN29 .... 204 F3
Kestrel Cl. ME10 .... 37 A2
Kestrel Ho. 8 ME7 .... 10 B6
Kestrel Rd. ME5 .... 32 C2
Keswick Dr. ME16 .... 74 B5
Keswick Rd. ME10 .... 37 C3
Kettle Hill. ME13 .... 81 F4
Kettle Hill Rd. Eastling ME13 .... 81 F5
Kettle Hill Rd. Hockley ME13 .... 82 A4
Kevin Dr. CT11 .... 52 B6
Kewlands. ME14 .... 75 C6
Key St. ME10 .... 36 A5
Keycol Hill.
  Key Street ME10 & ME9 .... 36 A5
Keycol Hill. Sittingbourne ME9 .... 35 F5
Keycol Hospl. ME9 .... 35 E6
Keyes Ave. ME4 .... 9 F2
Keyes Pl. CT19 .... 178 E2
Keynes Coll. CT2 .... 66 D4
Keyworth Mews. 7 CT1 .... 67 B2
Khartoum Rd. Chatham ME4 .... 9 F5
Khartoum Rd. Gillingham ME4 .... 10 A6
Khartoum Sq. ME7 .... 149 A6
Khyber Rd. ME4 & ME7 .... 10 B7
Kilbride Ct. CT11 .... 29 F1
Kiln Cl. Challock TN25 .... 105 B1
Kiln Cl. Sittingbourne ME10 .... 37 A3
Kiln Cnr. CT21 .... 176 B4
Kiln Field. TN30 .... 179 C7
Kiln La. TN26 .... 153 F5
Kiln Rd. TN25 .... 172 F4
Kildown Cl. Ashford TN23 .... 155 E6
Kildown Cl. Maidstone ME16 .... 74 C7
Kildown Gdns. Canterbury CT2 .... 67 A4
Kildown Gdns. Margate CT9 .... 8 E2
Kimberley Cl. CT16 .... 149 C3
Kimberley Cnr. CT10 .... 29 F8
Kimberley Ct. CT7 .... 7 C1
Kimberley Gr. CT5 .... 42 F6
Kimberley Rd. Gillingham ME7 .... 10 D3
Kimberley Rd. Ramsgate CT12 .... 29 A1
Kimberly Terr. CT18 .... 161 C7
King Arthur Rd. CT12 .... 51 D7
King Charles Ct. CT14 .... 117 D2
King Edward Ave.
  Broadstairs CT10 .... 30 A4
King Edward Ave.
  Herne Bay CT6 .... 23 B4
King Edward Ct. CT6 .... 23 B4
King Edward Rd.
  Birchington CT7 .... 27 A5
King Edward Rd. Chatham ME4 .... 9 F2
King Edward Rd. Deal CT14 .... 117 D8
King Edward Rd.
  Gillingham ME7 .... 10 F6
King Edward Rd.
  Maidstone ME15 .... 74 F2
King Edward Rd.
  Ramsgate CT11 .... 52 C6
King Edward St. CT5 .... 20 D1
King Ethelbert Sch The. CT8 .... 27 C7
King George Rd. ME5 .... 31 E4
King George V Meml Hos.
  ME8 .... 11 C2
King George Villas. CT14 .... 94 B3
King Lear's Way. CT17 .... 166 B5
King St. Brookland TN29 .... 191 D2
King St. Canterbury CT1 .... 66 F1
King St. Chatham ME4 .... 10 A4
King St. Deal CT14 .... 117 D6
King St. Deal, Walmer CT14 .... 117 D3
King St. Dover CT16 .... 166 D7
King St. Fordwich CT2 .... 68 A4
King St. Gillingham ME7 .... 10 C6
King St. Maidstone ME14 & ME15 .... 75 A4
King St. Margate CT9 .... 7 J3
King St. Ramsgate CT11 .... 52 F7
King St. Rochester ME1 .... 9 C5
King St. Sandwich CT13 .... 73 A1
King St. Sheerness ME12 .... 1 B2
King William Rd. 5 ME7 .... 10 A2
King's Ave. Ashford TN23 .... 139 A2
King's Ave. Birchington CT7 .... 26 D7
King's Ave. Broadstairs CT10 .... 30 B6
King's Ave. Ramsgate CT12 .... 29 B1
King's Ave. Rochester ME1 .... 9 C3

King's Ave. Sandwich CT13 .... 95 A8
King's Ave. Whitstable CT5 .... 20 E1
King's Bastion. ME7 .... 10 A5
King's Cl. CT14 .... 134 D6
King's Head Alley. ME12 .... 1 B3
King's Orch. ME1 .... 9 C5
King's Pk. CT5 .... 67 B1
King's Pl. 4 CT11 .... 52 E6
King's Rd. Birchington CT7 .... 27 A6
King's Rd. Chatham ME5 .... 10 D1
King's Rd. Faversham ME13 .... 62 C7
King's Rd. Herne Bay CT6 .... 22 F5
King's Rd. Ramsgate CT11 .... 52 D8
King's Sch. Canterbury CT1 .... 67 A1
King's Sch. Rochester ME1 .... 9 C5
King's Sch. (Jun). CT2 .... 67 E5
Kingfisher Apartments. 11
  ME15 .... 97 E5
Kingfisher Ave. CT21 .... 187 D8
Kingfisher Cl. Margate CT9 .... 28 B8
Kingfisher Cl. Sevington TN24 .... 157 A7
Kingfisher Cl. Whitstable CT5 .... 43 C7
Kingfisher Cl. CT6 .... 22 D3
Kingfisher Dr. ME5 .... 32 C7
Kingfisher Drive
  Cty Prim Sch. ME5 .... 32 B7
Kingfisher Gdns. CT21 .... 187 C8
Kingfisher Wlk. CT10 .... 29 F5
Kings Acre. ME15 .... 76 A1
Kings Cotts. ME17 .... 98 F6
Kings Ct. CT14 .... 117 D3
Kings Meadow. TN24 .... 139 E7
Kings Mews. 7 CT1 .... 67 A1
Kings Mill Cl. ME10 .... 36 E5
Kings Par. 7 TN23 .... 139 B2
Kings Rd. Aylesham CT3 .... 112 F6
Kings Rd. Dover CT17 .... 166 A7
Kings Rd. Folkestone CT20 .... 177 D6
Kings Rd. Minster ME12 .... 4 D7
Kings Ropewalk. CT17 .... 166 B5
Kingsbridge Ct. 9 CT20 .... 178 E5
Kingsdale Ct. CT5 .... 10 C1
Kingsdown Cl. Gillingham ME7 .... 33 B8
Kingsdown Cl. Maidstone ME16 .... 74 E4
Kingsdown Hill. CT14 .... 134 D4
Kingsdown Hos. ME9 .... 59 E4
Kingsdown Pk. CT5 .... 20 F2
Kingsdown Rd.
  Erriottwood ME9 .... 59 D4
Kingsdown Rd.
  Kingsdown CT14 .... 134 D7
Kingsdown Rd.
  St Margaret's at Cliffe CT15 .... 151 A7
Kingsfield Rd. CT6 .... 23 B2
Kingsford Cl. TN25 .... 157 E4
Kingsford Ct. CT17 .... 149 B1
Kingsford St. TN24 & TN25 .... 157 D5
Kingsgate Ave. CT10 .... 8 F1
Kingsgate Bay Rd. CT10 .... 8 H2
Kingsgate Cl. ME16 .... 74 C4
Kingsgate Coll. CT10 .... 30 A8
Kingsgate La. TN30 .... 188 C5
Kingsland Gdns. CT14 .... 134 B8
Kingsland Hollow. TN29 .... 195 A4
Kingsland La. TN27 .... 118 C1
Kingsley Rd. Maidstone ME15 .... 75 A3
Kingsley Rd. Whitstable CT5 .... 43 E8
Kingsmarsh La. TN29 .... 199 C5
Kingsmead. CT19 .... 178 B8
Kingsmead
  Cty Prim Sch. CT1 .... 67 A1
Kingsmead Rd. CT1 & CT2 .... 67 A2
Kingsmead Stadium. CT1 .... 67 A2
Kingsnorth
  CE Prim Sch. TN23 .... 156 B3
Kingsnorth Ct. 2 CT20 .... 178 B5
Kingsnorth Gdns. CT20 .... 178 C5
Kingsnorth Rd. Ashford TN23 .... 156 A6
Kingsnorth Rd.
  Faversham ME13 .... 62 B7
Kingsnorth Rd. Gillingham ME8 .... 11 C4
Kingston Ave. CT9 .... 28 C7
Kingston Cl. Herne Bay CT6 .... 23 F5
Kingston Cl. Ramsgate CT12 .... 29 B2
Kingston Cl. River CT17 .... 148 F3
Kingston Cres. ME5 .... 32 C4
Kingston Dr. ME15 .... 97 A8
Kingstone Ct. 3 CT20 .... 178 B5
Kingsway. Chatham ME5 .... 10 D1
Kingsway. Dymchurch TN29 .... 186 E2
Kingsway. Gillingham ME7 .... 10 E1
Kingswood. TN24 .... 139 D5
Kingswood Ave. ME4 .... 9 F2
Kingswood
  Cty Prim Sch. ME17 .... 99 E2
Kingswood Rd. Gillingham ME7 .... 10 D6
Kingswood Rd.
  Kit's Coty ME1 & ME20 .... 53 D8
Kinross Cl. ME5 .... 32 B7
Kipling Rd. TN23 .... 139 B2
Kirby's La. CT2 .... 66 F1
Kirk Gdns. CT14 .... 117 B2
Kirkdale. ME15 .... 96 F5
Kirkdale Cl. ME15 .... 32 C1
Kirkdale Cotts. ME15 .... 96 F5
Kirkdale Rd. ME15 .... 96 F6
Kirkstone Ave. CT11 .... 51 F7
Kirkwood Ave. TN26 .... 169 A1
Kit Hill. ME13 .... 84 D8
Kit Hill Ave. ME5 .... 31 E3
Kit's Coty Ho. ME20 .... 53 C6
Kitchener Ave. ME4 .... 10 A1
Kitchener Cl. CT14 .... 128 F8
Kitchener Rd. Dover CT17 .... 166 A7
Kitchener Rd. Rochester ME2 .... 9 A8
Kitchener Sq. CT19 .... 178 E8
Kite Farm. CT5 .... 21 D3
Kitewell La. TN29 .... 203 D8

Kither Rd. TN23 .... 156 A7
Kitsbridge La.
  Hamstreet TN26 .... 183 C4
Kitsbridge La. Ruckinge TN26 .... 183 F5
Kitsbridge La.
  Ruckinge TN25 & TN26 .... 184 B6
Klondyke Ind Est. ME11 .... 2 F4
Knatchbull Way. TN25 .... 158 E5
Knavesacre Ct. ME8 .... 33 D5
Knight Ave. Canterbury CT2 .... 87 D8
Knight Ave. Gillingham ME7 .... 10 D7
Knight Rd. ME2 .... 9 A6
Knight's Ave. CT10 .... 30 B6
Knight's Rd. CT16 .... 166 E8
Knightrider Ct. ME15 .... 75 A3
Knightrider St. 1
  Maidstone ME15 .... 75 A3
Knights Alley. 14 CT5 .... 20 D2
Knights Ct. CT17 .... 149 B1
Knights Pk. ME2 .... 9 A6
Knights Templars. CT17 .... 166 C6
Knights Way. CT16 .... 149 A3
Knightsfield Rd. ME10 .... 36 D7
Knock Hill. TN30 .... 190 A2
Knock Rd. TN23 .... 156 A7
Knockholt Rd. CT9 .... 8 F3
Knockhurst Ct. TN30 .... 167 C1
Knockwood Rd. TN30 .... 167 C1
Knold Pk. CT9 .... 28 E8
Knole Rd. ME5 .... 32 C3
Knole The. ME13 .... 62 B7
Knoll Hill. TN25 .... 173 C3
Knoll La. TN23 .... 155 E7
Knoll Pl. CT14 .... 117 C2
Knoll Way. ME12 .... 6 D4
Knott Cres. TN24 .... 157 A7
Knott Ct. ME14 .... 74 F6
Knott's La. 20 CT1 .... 67 A1
Knotts La. CT15 .... 150 F5
Knotts Sq. TN23 .... 139 C2
Knowle Rd. ME14 .... 75 B6
Knowler Way. CT6 .... 23 C5
Knowlton Gdns. ME16 .... 74 B2
Knowlton Wlk. 1 CT1 .... 67 B1
Kohima Pl. CT16 .... 149 F2
Kyetop Wlk. ME8 .... 33 D6
Kymbeline Ct. CT14 .... 117 B4

La Belle Alliance Sq. 6
  Ramsgate CT11 .... 52 E7
La Belle Alliance Sq. 7
  Ramsgate CT11 .... 52 F7
La Galamina. TN28 .... 204 E8
La Rocca. TN28 .... 204 E8
La Tausco. TN28 .... 204 D8
La-Tene. CT14 .... 117 B2
Laburnum Ave. CT13 .... 93 F8
Laburnum Cl. CT16 .... 148 E4
Laburnum Gr. ME12 .... 1 I1
Laburnum Ho. ME12 .... 1 C2
Laburnum La. CT2 .... 68 B7
Laburnum Pl. ME10 .... 36 E4
Labworth Cl. ME12 .... 3 E6
Lacey Cl. ME17 .... 98 E4
Lachlan Ave. 2 CT20 .... 177 F3
Lacton Oast. TN24 .... 157 B8
Lacton Way. TN24 .... 157 A8
Ladds Cnr. ME7 .... 11 B5
Lade Fort Cotts. TN28 .... 204 E6
Lade Fort Cres. TN29 .... 204 E6
Lady Garne Rd. CT15 .... 164 F5
Lady J Thornhill's Endowed
  Prim Sch. TN25 .... 123 E2
Lady Wootton's Gn. 5 CT1 .... 88 A8
Ladyfields. Chatham ME5 .... 32 C2
Ladyfields. Herne Bay CT6 .... 23 D2
Ladysmith Gr. CT5 .... 42 F6
Ladysmith Rd. CT5 .... 43 C5
Ladywell. 7 CT16 .... 166 D8
Ladywell Ho. 2 CT16 .... 166 D8
Ladywood Rd. CT2 .... 67 F7
Lagos Ave. CT12 .... 29 A1
Lakelands. Harrietsham ME17 .... 100 E6
Lakelands. Maidstone ME15 .... 97 A7
Lakemead. TN23 .... 155 E8
Laker Rd. ME1 .... 31 C6
Lakeside. TN23 .... 155 E8
Lakeside Gdns. TN26 .... 120 F1
Lakeside Pk. ME2 .... 9 E7
Lakewood Dr. ME8 .... 33 C6
Laking Ave. CT10 .... 30 B7
Laleham Gdns. CT9 .... 8 B2
Laleham Rd. CT9 .... 8 B1
Laleham Sch. CT9 .... 8 B1
Laleham Wlk. CT9 .... 8 B1
Lamb's Wlk. CT5 .... 43 C6
Lambard Ho. 6 ME14 .... 75 A5
Lambden Rd. ME17 .... 136 C6
Lamberhurst Gn. ME8 .... 11 B3
Lamberhurst Rd. ME14 .... 74 B7
Lamberhurst Way. CT9 .... 8 F3
Lambert Ho. CT14 .... 117 B3
Lambeth Cl. ME5 .... 32 B4
Lambeth Rd. CT1 .... 67 C4
Lambourn Way. ME5 .... 32 C2
Lambourne Pl. ME8 .... 12 A2
Lambourne Rd. ME15 .... 75 F2
Lambourne Wlk. CT1 .... 88 C8
Lambsfrith Gr. ME7 .... 33 B3
Lamington Rd. CT17 .... 149 A1
Laming Cl. CT7 .... 27 B6
Lammas Dr. ME10 .... 36 E6
Lamplighters Cl. ME7 .... 32 F5
Lancashire Rd. ME15 .... 97 E7
Lancaster Ave. CT18 .... 164 C5
Lancaster Cl. CT12 .... 29 B1
Lancaster Ct. ME8 .... 33 C7

Lancaster Gdns.
  Birchington CT7 .... 26 F6
Lancaster Gdns.
  Herne Bay CT6 .... 23 D5
Lancaster Ho. Deal CT14 .... 117 A5
Lancaster Ho. 3 Dover CT17 .... 166 D7
Lancaster Rd. Canterbury CT1 .... 87 D5
Lancaster Rd. Dover CT17 .... 166 D7
Lancet La. ME15 .... 97 A6
Lanchester Cl. CT6 .... 22 A3
Landbury Wlk. TN23 .... 138 F4
Landon Rd. CT6 .... 23 C4
Landor Ct. ME7 .... 33 A3
Landrail Cl. ME9 .... 13 B3
Landway The. ME14 .... 76 A4
Lane End. CT15 .... 149 F6
Lane The. CT15 .... 149 F6
Lane's Wlk. CT5 .... 20 E2
Lanes The. CT12 .... 50 D6
Lanfranc Gdns. CT2 .... 66 C1
Lanfranc Ho. 5 CT1 .... 67 A1
Lang Ct. CT5 .... 21 C3
Langdale. TN23 .... 155 E8
Langdale Ave. CT11 .... 52 A7
Langdale Cl. ME8 .... 11 D1
Langdale Rise. ME16 .... 74 C5
Langdon Ave. CT3 .... 71 F1
Langdon Cl. CT15 .... 150 F5
Langdon Cross. CT15 .... 150 C7
Langdon City Prim Sch. CT15 .... 133 A1
Langdon Rd. Folkestone CT19 .... 177 D7
Langdon Rd. Rochester ME1 .... 9 C4
Langham Cl. CT9 .... 7 F1
Langham Gr. ME15 .... 74 C4
Langholm Rd. TN23 .... 156 A7
Langhorne Gdns. 5 CT20 .... 178 C4
Langley Gdns. CT9 .... 8 E3
Langley Rd. ME10 .... 36 F7
Langney Dr. TN23 .... 155 E6
Langport Rd. TN28 .... 200 C6
Langton Cl. ME14 .... 75 C5
Langton Cotts. CT3 .... 70 B5
Langton La. CT1 .... 88 A4
Lankester Parker Rd. ME1 .... 31 C6
Lansdown Rd. Canterbury CT1 .... 88 A7
Lansdown Rd.
  Sittingbourne ME10 .... 37 C4
Lansdowne Ave. ME15 .... 97 C6
Lansdowne Ct. 2 ME4 .... 9 F4
Lansdowne
  Cty Prim Sch. ME10 .... 37 C3
Lansdowne Rd. ME4 .... 9 E2
Lanthorne Rd. CT10 .... 30 A6
Lapwing Dr. ME9 .... 13 B3
Larch Cl. CT10 .... 29 D4
Larch Rd. CT15 .... 114 B1
Larch Terr. ME12 .... 3 A8
Larch Wlk. TN24 .... 139 C6
Larch Wood Cl. ME5 .... 32 D1
Larchcroft. ME5 .... 32 A4
Larches The. Faversham ME13 .... 62 A8
Larches The. Whitstable CT5 .... 43 C8
Larkey View. CT4 .... 86 C4
Larkfield Ave. Gillingham ME7 .... 10 E4
Larkfield Ave.
  Sittingbourne ME10 .... 36 E6
Larksfield Rd. ME13 .... 40 C1
Larkspur Rd. ME5 .... 31 E4
Lascelles Rd. CT17 .... 166 A6
Laser Quay. ME2 .... 9 D6
Latchgate. CT20 .... 177 C3
Lathe Barn (Mus). TN29 .... 186 D5
Latimer Cl. CT6 .... 22 B2
Latimer Pl. 8 ME7 .... 10 C7
Launder Way. ME15 .... 74 E2
Laundry Rd. CT12 .... 50 D7
Laureate Cl. CT9 .... 8 B2
Laurel Ave. TN29 .... 194 F4
Laurel Cl. CT20 .... 177 E6
Laurel Gr. ME17 .... 99 D2
Laurel Ho. ME12 .... 1 C2
Laurel Rd. ME7 .... 10 C7
Laurel Wlk. ME8 .... 33 E6
Laurels The. ME16 .... 74 C2
Laureston Pl. CT16 .... 166 E8
Laurie Gray Ave. ME5 .... 31 D1
Lauriston Cl. CT11 .... 52 A5
Lauriston Mount. CT10 .... 30 A5
Lausanne Ct. CT9 .... 7 J2
Lausanne Terr. 11 CT9 .... 7 J2
Lavenda Cl. ME7 .... 33 A4
Lavender Cl. 1 Chatham ME5 .... 31 E4
Lavender Cl. Margate CT9 .... 28 C8
Lavender Cl. Whitstable CT5 .... 21 C2
Lavender Ct. ME10 .... 37 A3
Laverstoke Rd. ME16 .... 74 C8
Lawley Cl. CT12 .... 29 C1
Lawn Cl. ME4 .... 10 B2
Lawn Rd. Broadstairs CT10 .... 30 A4
Lawn Rd. Deal CT14 .... 117 C1
Lawns The. 13 CT11 .... 52 F7
Lawrence Cl. Folkestone CT19 .... 177 F6
Lawrence Cl. Maidstone ME15 .... 97 A7
Lawrence Ct. CT19 .... 178 E6
Lawrence Gdns. CT6 .... 23 C4
Lawrence St. ME7 .... 10 C5
Laws La. TN25 .... 172 D7
Lawson Cl. CT4 .... 86 D2
Laxey The. ME15 .... 74 E1
Laxton Cl. ME15 .... 75 F3
Laxton Dr. ME17 .... 98 A1
Laxton Way. Canterbury CT1 .... 88 C7
Laxton Way. Faversham ME13 .... 62 E8
Laxton Way. Sittingbourne ME10 .... 36 D6
Lay La. CT3 .... 71 D2
Layfield Rd. ME7 .... 10 F7
Laylam Cl. CT10 .... 29 D5

Lea Cl. CT21 .... 176 B4
Lea Ct. ME4 .... 9 E1
Leacon Cotts. TN27 .... 120 E4
Leacon Cotts The. TN27 .... 120 E4
Leacon Rd. TN23 .... 138 F2
Leafield. TN25 .... 159 D1
Leafy Glade. ME8 .... 33 B6
Leahurst Ct. CT16 .... 148 E4
Leander Rd. ME1 .... 31 C7
Learoyd Rd. TN28 .... 200 C6
Leas Gn. CT10 .... 29 D4
Leas Rd. CT14 .... 117 B4
Leas The. Faversham ME13 .. 62 B8
Leas The. Folkestone CT20 . 178 C4
Leas The. Kingsdown CT14 .. 134 D3
Leas The. Minster ME12 .... 4 C8
Leas The. Sheerness ME12 .. 1 I1
Leas The. Whitstable CT5 .. 21 D1
Leaside Cotts. CT21 .... 176 B3
Leatt Cl. CT10 .... 29 F4
Leaveland Cl. Ashford TN23 155 E6
Leaveland Cl. Ashford TN23 155 F6
Leaveland Cotts. ME13 ..... 83 B2
Leda Cotts. TN25 .... 120 F3
Leeds & Broomfield
  CE Prim Sch. ME17 .... 99 A7
Leeds Castle. ME17 .... 99 D7
Leeds Rd. ME17 .... 98 E3
Leeds Sq. ME8 .... 11 B3
Leelands Ho. CT14 .... 117 B1
Lees Cl The. TN25 .... 158 D5
Lees Court Rd. ME13 .... 83 C5
Lees Rd. Ashford TN24 ..... 140 A1
Lees Rd. Branbourne Lees TN25 158 E6
Lees Terr. CT4 .... 85 C2
Lees The. Herne Bay CT6 ... 23 C5
Lees The. Herne Bay CT6 ... 23 D5
Leet Cl. ME7 .... 10 E6
Leeward Cl. ME1 .... 9 C1
Leggett's La. CT5 .... 20 D2
Leicester Ave. CT9 .... 8 C2
Leicester Gdns. ME12 ...... 6 E3
Leicester Rd. ME15 .... 97 D7
Leigh Ave. ME15 .... 97 B6
Leigh Ct. ME12 .... 3 F5
Leigh Green Ind Est. TN30 . 179 E6
Leigh Rd. CT12 .... 28 F1
Leighton Cl. CT16 .... 149 C1
Leighton Rd. CT16 .... 149 C1
Leighville Dr. CT14 .... 22 D4
Leivers Rd. CT14 .... 117 A3
Len Valley Wlk. ME15 ...... 75 F1
Lenacre Ave. CT16 .... 148 F7
Lenacre La. CT16 .... 148 F8
Lenacre St. TN25 .... 122 B2
Lenfield Ave. ME14 .... 75 B4
Length The. CT7 .... 25 F2
Lenham Cl. CT10 .... 30 A2
Lenham Cty Prim Sch. ME17 101 C5
Lenham Forstal Rd. ME17 ... 119 B8
Lenham Gdns. CT9 .... 28 B8
Lenham Heath Rd. ME17 ..... 101 C2
Lenham Ho. ME17 .... 101 E5
Lenham Rd. ME17 .... 100 C1
Lenham Sta. ME17 .... 101 C4
Lenham Way. ME8 .... 11 A3
Lennard Ct. CT20 .... 178 E5
Lennard Rd. CT20 .... 178 E5
Lenside Dr. ME15 .... 76 A2
Leona Ct. CT9 .... 8 B2
Leonard Cl. ME16 .... 74 B6
Leonard Rd. Chatham ME4 ... 10 B3
Leonard Rd.
  Greatstone-on-S TN29 .... 204 E7
Leonard's Ave. CT11 .... 29 E1
Leopold Rd. Chatham ME4 ... 10 A3
Leopold Rd. Ramsgate CT11 . 52 E6
Leopold St. CT11 .... 52 E6
Lerryn Gdns. CT10 .... 29 F8
Les Spickett Cl. ME13 ..... 62 E6
Lesley Ave. CT1 .... 88 A6
Leslie Ave. CT9 .... 28 B8
Leslie Cres. TN30 .... 167 B2
Leslie Pl. ME16 .... 74 E5
Leslie Rd. Birchington CT7 27 A8
Leslie Rd. Gillingham ME7 . 10 D7
Leslie Smith Dr. ME13 ..... 62 C7
Lested La. ME17 .... 98 B2
Lester Rd. ME4 .... 10 A3
Letchworth Ave. ME4 .... 9 F1
Lewis Ave. ME8 .... 11 B2
Lewis Cl. ME13 .... 62 A7
Lewis Court Dr. ME17 ...... 97 C3
Lewis Cres. CT9 .... 8 B3
Lewis Cl. TN23 .... 155 F7
Lewisham Rd. CT17 .... 148 C3
Lewson Street Rd. ME9 ..... 60 E8
Leybourn Rd. CT10 .... 30 B2
Leybourne Cl. ME5 .... 32 A2
Leybourne Dr. CT9 .... 28 B8
Leyburne Rd. CT16 .... 166 D8
Leycroft Cl. CT2 .... 66 E3
Leys The. CT12 .... 28 D1
Leysdown Rd. Eastchurch ME12 5 E3
Leysdown Rd.
  Leysdown-on-S ME12 ...... 6 C1
Leyton Ave. ME7 .... 10 E1
Libya Terr. ME14 .... 75 A7
Lichfield Ave. CT1 .... 88 B6
Lichfield Cl. ME8 .... 11 D2
Lidsing Rd. ME14 .... 54 E6
Liege Cl. ME4 .... 14 F1
Lighthouse Rd. CT15 .... 151 A5
Lilac Ho. ME12 .... 1 C2
Lilk Hill. ME14 .... 76 C3
Lillian Rd. CT11 .... 52 F8
Lilyvale Cotts. TN25 ...... 158 F4

Lime Cl. TN23 .... 138 F3
Lime Ct. ME8 .... 33 C3
Lime Gr. Halfway Houses ME12 3 D5
Lime Gr. Sittingbourne ME10 37 A4
Lime Kiln Rd. CT1 .... 87 F6
Lime Kiln Wharf. ME11 ..... 3 A5
Lime Villas. CT4 .... 144 F5
Limekiln Rdbt. CT17 .... 166 D6
Limekiln St. CT17 .... 166 D5
Limepits Cross. ME9 .... 35 F3
Limes Cl. TN30 .... 179 C8
Limes Pl. ME13 .... 62 D7
Limes Rd. Dover CT16 ...... 149 C1
Limes Rd. Folkestone CT19 . 177 F6
Limes The. Lenham ME17 .... 101 D5
Limes The. Old Romney TN29 199 A4
Limetree Cl. ME5 .... 32 B8
Limetree Terr. ME17 .... 101 C6
Linces The. CT16 .... 149 B4
Lincoln Ave. CT1 .... 88 B7
Lincoln Cl. CT5 .... 21 D3
Lincoln Gdns. CT7 .... 26 F7
Lincoln Rd. ME15 .... 97 D8
Lincon Rd. ME7 .... 10 D7
Linden Ave. Broadstairs CT10 30 B5
Linden Ave. Herne Bay CT6 . 22 E4
Linden Ave. Whitstable CT5 20 F1
Linden Chase. CT2 .... 66 E1
Linden Cl. Sittingbourne ME10 36 D3
Linden Cl. Westgate-on-S CT8 27 E7
Linden Cres. CT19 .... 178 D6
Linden Dr. ME12 .... 3 A7
Linden Gr. CT2 .... 66 E1
Linden Grove
  Cty Prim Sch. TN23 ...... 155 F6
Linden Ho. ME5 .... 31 F4
Linden Rd. Ashford TN24 ... 139 D1
Linden Rd. Coxheath ME17 .. 96 C4
Linden Rd. Gillingham ME7 . 10 E5
Linden Rd. Westgate-on-S CT8 27 F8
Lindens. CT21 .... 176 D2
Lindenthorpe Rd. CT10 ..... 30 A6
Lindfield Cotts. ME13 ..... 62 A6
Lindridge Cl. CT6 .... 46 A8
Lineacre Cl. ME8 .... 33 D6
Lines Terr. ME4 .... 10 A4
Linington Rd. ME14 .... 27 A6
Link Hill La. TN27 .... 118 D3
Link La. CT1 .... 88 A8
Link Rd. Broadstairs CT10 . 29 F7
Link Rd. Tyler Hill CT2 ... 66 E6
Link The. TN23 .... 155 E7
Links Cl. CT6 .... 23 A3
Links Cl. CT6 .... 23 A3
Links Cres. TN29 .... 195 A4
Links Ct. CT14 .... 95 C1
Links Rd. CT14 .... 117 C8
Links The. ME5 .... 32 B8
Linksway. ME8 .... 200 D6
Linksfield Rd. CT8 .... 27 D7
Linksway. CT19 .... 178 B8
Linksway Ct. CT19 .... 178 B8
Linkway. ME9 .... 14 D4
Linley Ho. CT10 .... 29 E2
Linley Rd. CT10 .... 29 E2
Linnet Ave. CT5 .... 43 B6
Linton Gore. ME17 .... 96 D3
Linton Hill. ME17 .... 96 E1
Linton Hospl. ME17 .... 96 C2
Linton Rd. ME15 .... 96 F4
Lion Field. ME13 .... 62 B7
Lion Yd. Faversham ME13 ... 62 A6
Lion Yd. Sittingbourne ME10 36 F4
Lion's Rd. TN28 .... 200 A6
Lionard Ho. CT2 .... 66 E1
Liphook Way. ME16 .... 74 C8
Lisa Ct. CT5 .... 21 A2
Lismore Cl. ME15 .... 97 A7
Lismore Rd. Herne Bay CT6 . 23 D5
Lismore Rd. Whitstable CT5 44 B8
Liss Rd. CT13 .... 93 A1
List The. CT3 .... 69 C2
Lister Cl. Deal CT14 ...... 117 C5
Lister Cl. Dover CT17 ..... 149 B1
Lister Ho. CT9 .... 29 A8
Lister Rd. CT9 .... 29 A8
Lister Way. CT20 .... 177 F3
Listmas Rd. ME4 .... 10 B3
Listways Cotts. CT3 .... 113 B6
Little Ave. CT14 .... 116 F3
Little Brook Rd. TN23 ..... 139 A3
Little Buckland Ave. ME16 74 D6
Little Charles St. CT6 .... 22 F5
Little Chequers. TN25 ..... 123 E2
Little Cl. ME16 .... 74 D2
Little Glovers. ME10 ...... 36 F3
Little Hempen. TN23 .... 155 D8
Little Hill. TN30 .... 167 B2
Little John Ave. ME5 ...... 31 F2
Little Kit's Coty La. ME20 53 C5
Little Knoll. TN23 .... 155 F8
Little Meadow. CT2 .... 65 E1
Little Orch. ME13 .... 96 D3
Little Paddocks. CT5 ...... 44 D7
Little Stone Stile Cotts. ME13 84 F4
Little Walton. CT13 .... 93 C3
Littlewood. ME5 .... 32 B1
Littlebourne Ave. ME8 ..... 11 B4
Littlebourne CE Prim Sch. CT3 89 E8
Littlebourne Rd.
  Canterbury CT1 & CT3 .... 88 E8
Littlebourne Rd.
  Maidstone ME14 .... 75 C6
Littlebrook Cl. TN23 ...... 139 A3
Littlemead. CT19 .... 178 A7
Littlestone Golf Course.
  TN28 .... 200 E8
Littlestone Rd. TN28 ...... 200 D6
Liverpool Lawn. CT11 ...... 52 E6

Liverpool Rd. CT14 .... 117 D2
Livingstone Circ. ME7 ..... 10 D5
Livingstone Cl. TN29 ...... 187 B4
Livingstone Rd.
  Broadstairs CT10 .... 29 E6
Livingstone Rd. Gillingham ME7 10 E5
Livingstone Wlk. ME15 ..... 97 F5
Llamas Gate. ME13 .... 62 D8
Lloyd Rd. CT10 .... 30 A4
Lloyds Gn. TN30 .... 188 D4
Loach Ho. ME13 .... 64 A3
Loading Bay App. CT12 & CT13 73 A8
Loaland Bsns Ctr. ME2 ..... 9 D8
Lobelia Cl. ME7 .... 10 E6
Locarno Ave. ME8 .... 11 A2
Lock La. ME14 & ME16 ...... 53 D1
Lock St. ME7 .... 10 C5
Lockenden Cotts. CT3 ...... 89 D6
Lockholt Cl. TN23 .... 138 E3
Lockington Gr. ME1 .... 9 C5
Locksley Cl. ME5 .... 31 E2
Lockswood. ME16 .... 74 D7
Loddington La. ME17 .... 97 A1
Loder Ho. ME17 .... 101 B5
Lodge Cl. CT2 .... 66 A7
Lodge Rd. ME14 .... 75 D5
Lodge The. TN24 .... 139 D7
Lomas Rd. ME10 & ME9 ...... 37 D4
Lombard St. CT7 .... 7 I3
Lombardy Cl. ME7 .... 33 A6
Lombardy Dr. ME14 .... 75 C5
London Rd. Canterbury CT2 66 D1
London Rd.
  Dover CT16 & CT17 .... 149 B1
London Rd.
  Faversham ME13 & ME9 .... 61 C7
London Rd.
  Faversham ME13 .... 63 A5
London Rd.
  Faversham, Ospringe ME13 62 B6
London Rd. Gillingham ME8 . 11 C1
London Rd.
  Hartlip Hill ME8 & ME9 .. 34 D7
London Rd. Hythe CT21 ..... 175 F3
London Rd. Maidstone ME16 74 C6
London Rd. Newington ME9 .. 35 A6
London Rd. Ramsgate CT11 .. 52 B6
London Rd. Rochester ME2 .. 9 A7
London Rd. Sittingbourne ME10 36 C4
London Rd.
  Temple Ewell CT15 & CT16 148 B6
London Rd. Teynham ME9 .... 38 C1
London Road (River).
  CT16 & CT17 .... 148 F4
London Road Temple Ewell.
  CT16 .... 148 D5
London Road Trad Est. ME10 36 D4
London St. CT13 .... 178 E6
Lone Barn Rd. ME17 .... 102 B8
Lonefield. TN26 .... 155 B1
Long Acre Cl. CT2 .... 66 E2
Long Barrow The. TN24 .... 156 E6
Long Beech. TN23 .... 138 E1
Long Catlis Rd. ME8 ...... 33 D4
Long Dr. CT13 .... 93 C2
Long Hill. CT4 .... 85 C1
Long La. CT15 .... 130 D7
Long Length. TN23 .... 155 D4
Long Market. CT1 .... 88 A8
Long Meadow Way. CT2 ..... 67 A4
Long Reach Cl. CT5 .... 43 C6
Long Rede La. ME16 .... 74 A3
Long Rock. CT5 .... 21 C3
Long Row. TN25 .... 157 D2
Long Wlk. TN23 .... 138 E4
Long's Acre. TN25 .... 123 E1
Longacre. CT5 .... 21 D1
Longacre Rd. TN23 .... 155 D7
Longage Hill. CT18 & CT4 . 144 A1
Longbridge. TN24 .... 140 B1
Longbridge Terr. CT21 .... 175 F1
Longfellow Rd. ME7 .... 10 C3
Longfield. TN30 .... 179 A6
Longfield Cl. CT5 .... 21 D3
Longfield Pl. ME15 .... 97 C8
Longfield Rd. CT17 .... 166 B7
Longfields Dr. ME14 ...... 76 A5
Longford Cl. ME8 .... 34 A8
Longford Ct. ME8 .... 34 A8
Longford Terr. CT20 ...... 178 D4
Longford Way. CT20 .... 178 D4
Longham Copse. ME15 ...... 75 F1
Longhill Ave. ME7 .... 10 B3
Longhurst Dr. ME5 .... 31 F4
Longley Rd. Gillingham ME8 11 F1
Longley Rd. Rochester ME1 9 C4
Longmead Cl. CT3 .... 22 C3
Longmete Rd. CT3 .... 70 C5
Longmore Dr. ME12 .... 5 C1
Longparish Cl. ME15 ...... 97 F6
Longport. CT1 .... 88 B8
Longridge. ME10 .... 37 B2
Longsfield. TN25 .... 173 A6
Longshaw Rd. ME15 .... 97 F5
Longtye Dr. CT5 .... 44 C7
Lonsdale Ave. CT9 .... 8 C3
Lonsdale Dr. Gillingham ME8 11 B4
Lonsdale Dr. Herne Bay CT6 22 B5
Lonsdale Dr.
  Sittingbourne ME10 ...... 36 C5
Lookers La. CT21 .... 176 B3
Loop Court Mews. CT13 .... 72 F1
Loop St. CT13 .... 72 F1
Loose Cty Prim Sch. ME15 . 96 F4
Loose Down Rd. ME13 ...... 104 F7
Loose Rd. ME15 .... 97 A7
Lord Romney's Hill. ME14 . 75 F3

Lord Warden Ave. CT14 ..... 117 D2
Lord Warden Sq. CT17 ...... 166 C5
Lords Cl. ME9 .... 37 E2
Lords Cotts. ME13 .... 83 C4
Lords Wood Cl. ME5 .... 32 B3
Lords Wood La. ME5 .... 32 B3
Lordswood Cty Prim Sch. ME5 32 B3
Lordswood Ind Est. ME5 .... 54 C8
Lorina Rd. CT12 .... 52 C8
Lorne Cotts. CT17 .... 117 C7
Lorne Rd. Dover CT16 ...... 149 B2
Lorne Rd. Ramsgate CT11 ... 52 C6
Lorraine Cl. CT19 .... 178 E6
Loudon Ct. TN23 .... 138 E3
Loudon Path. TN23 .... 138 E3
Loudon Way. TN23 .... 138 E3
Loughborough Ct. CT1 ..... 52 E7
Louisville Ave. ME7 ...... 10 D4
Love La. Adisham CT3 ..... 90 F2
Love La. Canterbury CT1 .. 88 A8
Love La. Faversham ME13 .. 62 F6
Love La. Margate CT9 ..... 7 I3
Love La. Minster ME12 .... 4 D7
Love La. Rochester ME1 ... 9 C5
Love Street Cl. CT6 ...... 22 C2
Lovelace Cl. ME8 .... 33 D4
Lovelace Ct. TN26 .... 153 C5
Lovell Rd. Minster ME12 .. 4 A5
Lovell Rd. Rough Common CT2 66 B3
Lower Blackhouse Hill. CT21 176 D3
Lower Boxley Rd. ME14 .... 75 A5
Lower Bridge St. CT1 ..... 88 A8
Lower Chantry La. CT1 .... 88 A8
Lower Denmark Rd. TN23 ... 156 C8
Lower East Rd. ME4 .... 10 B8
Lower Ensden Rd. CT4 ..... 85 D4
Lower Fant Rd. ME16 ...... 74 D7
Lower Gore La. CT13 ...... 93 B3
Lower Halstow
  Cty Prim Sch. ME9 ...... 13 B2
Lower Hartlip Rd. ME9 .... 34 E5
Lower Herne Rd. CT6 ...... 45 E8
Lower Lees Rd. CT4 .... 85 D2
Lower Mill La. CT14 ...... 117 C5
Lower Northdown Ave. CT9 . 8 B2
Lower Rainham Rd.
  Gillingham ME8 .... 12 A3
Lower Rainham Rd.
  Gillingham, Lower Twydall ME7 11 D5
Lower Rd. East Farleigh ME15 96 B7
Lower Rd. Faversham ME13 . 61 C8
Lower Rd. Maidstone ME15 . 75 B3
Lower Rd. Minster ME12 ... 3 E4
Lower Rd. Minster ME12 ... 4 E4
Lower Rd. River CT16 & CT17 148 E3
Lower Rd. Staple CT3 ..... 92 B6
Lower Rd. Temple Ewell CT16 148 D5
Lower Rd. Teynham ME9 .... 38 B3
Lower Rd.
  Teynham ME9 & ME13 ..... 38 E2
Lower Rd. Wittersham TN30 189 D5
Lower Rd. Woodchurch TN26 169 B1
Lower Rd E. CT16 .... 166 H8
Lower Rd W. CT16 .... 166 G8
Lower Sandgate Rd. CT20 .. 178 C3
Lower Sands. TN29 .... 186 E2
Lower Santon La. CT3 ..... 70 D7
Lower St. Eastry CT13 .... 93 B1
Lower St. Leeds ME17 ..... 99 A7
Lower St. Tilmanstone CT14 115 A2
Lower Stone St. ME15 ..... 75 A3
Lower Tovil. ME15 .... 74 E2
Lower Twydall La. ME7 & ME8 11 C4
Lower Vicarage Rd. TN24 .. 139 D7
Lower Wall Rd.
  CT21 & TN29 & TN25 ..... 186 D8
Lower Warren Rd.
  ME5 & ME14 .... 53 E6
Lower Woodlands Rd. ME7 .. 11 A4
Lowfield Rd. ME12 .... 3 E6
Lowslip Hill. CT15 .... 165 A5
Lowther Rd. CT17 .... 166 B8
Loxwood Cl. CT16 .... 149 B7
Lubbock Cl. ME15 .... 97 E5
Lubbock Wlk. ME8 .... 33 D5
Lucerne Cl. CT5 .... 42 F6
Lucerne Dr. CT5 .... 42 F6
Lucerne La. CT15 .... 133 C2
Lucerne St. ME14 .... 75 A5
Luckhurst Gdns. CT9 ...... 8 E3
Luckhurst Rd. Ashford TN24 157 A2
Luckhurst Rd. River CT17 . 148 E3
Lucknow Cl. CT16 .... 149 F3
Lucy Ave. CT19 .... 178 B7
Lucy's Hill. CT21 .... 176 B2
Luddenham Cl. Ashford TN23 155 F6
Luddenham Cl.
  Maidstone ME14 .... 75 C6
Luddenham
  Cty Prim Sch. ME13 ..... 39 E1
Ludgate Rd. ME9 .... 59 F5
Lukes Cl. CT17 .... 149 B1
Lullingstone Cl. ME7 ..... 33 B3
Lullingstone Ct. CT1 ..... 87 F8
Lullingstone Rd. CT16 .... 74 C7
Lumsden Terr. ME4 .... 9 E4
Lushington Rd. ME14 ...... 74 E7
Luton Ave. CT9 .... 29 F3
Luton Ct. CT10 .... 29 F3
Luton Cty Inf Sch. ME5 ... 10 C2
Luton Cty Jun Sch. ME4 ... 10 C2
Luton High St. ME5 .... 10 C2
Luton Rd. Chatham ME4 .... 10 B2
Luton Rd. Faversham ME13 . 62 E7
Lyall Way. ME8 .... 33 E4
Lychfield Dr. ME2 .... 9 A8
Lydbrook Cl. ME10 .... 36 D4
Lydd Airport. TN28 .... 204 A7

Lydd Cty Prim Sch. TN29 .. 203 C6
Lydd Golf Course. TN29 ... 199 F1
Lydd Rd. Camber TN31 ..... 201 C1
Lydd Rd. Chatham ME5 ..... 32 B5
Lydd Rd. New Romney TN28 . 199 F6
Lydd Town Crossing. TN29 . 203 D8
Lydden Cty Prim Sch. CT15 147 F8
Lydden Hill. CT15 .... 130 C1
Lydden International
  Motor Racing Circuit. CT4 129 F3
Lydia Rd. CT14 .... 117 A2
Lydos Cl. TN29 .... 204 E5
Lyeat Ct. CT2 .... 66 C4
Lyell Cl. CT21 .... 174 F2
Lyell Ct. ME15 .... 176 A1
Lyell Cl. CT7 .... 26 F8
Lyell Cl. CT7 .... 26 F8
Lyle Ct. ME2 .... 9 B8
Lyle Ct. ME16 .... 74 C5
Lyminge CE Prim Sch. CT18 161 C7
Lyminge Cl. ME8 .... 11 C2
Lyminge Way. CT10 .... 8 C1
Lymington Ct. ME15 .... 97 F4
Lymington Rd. CT8 .... 27 E7
Lympne Castle. CT21 ...... 174 F2
Lympne CE Prim Sch. CT21 . 175 A3
Lympne Hill. CT21 .... 175 A2
Lympne Ind Est. CT21 ..... 174 E3
Lyndhurst Ave. Gillingham ME8 33 C7
Lyndhurst Ave. Margate CT9 8 B2
Lyndhurst Cl. CT2 .... 66 E3
Lyndhurst Gr. ME10 .... 36 E2
Lyndhurst Rd. Broadstairs CT10 30 A6
Lyndhurst Rd.
  Dymchurch TN29 .... 195 C8
Lyndhurst Rd. Maidstone ME15 97 C8
Lyndhurst Rd. Ramsgate CT11 52 F7
Lyndhurst Rd. River CT17 . 148 E2
Lyndon Way. CT18 .... 161 C7
Lyngate Ct. CT9 .... 8 D2
Lynmouth Dr. ME12 .... 4 C7
Lynsted Ho. ME16 .... 74 A1
Lynsted Cl. ME15 .... 155 F6
Lynsted La. ME9 .... 60 B7
Lynsted & Norton
  Cty Prim Sch. ME9 ...... 60 B7
Lynsted Rd. Gillingham ME8 11 B3
Lynsted Rd. Halfway Houses ME12 3 E1
Lynton Court Mansions. CT9 8 B3
Lynton Dr. ME5 .... 32 B3
Lynton Pl. CT4 .... 89 A1
Lynton Rd. CT21 .... 176 C1
Lynwood. CT19 .... 178 C7
Lysander Cl. Broadstairs CT10 29 C3
Lysander Cl. Littlebourne CT4 89 E4
Lysander Wlk. CT18 .... 163 A4
Lytham Ave. CT6 .... 22 D1

Mabledon Ave. TN24 .... 139 D1
Mabledon Cl. TN28 .... 200 B6
Macdonald Par. CT5 .... 43 A6
Macdonald Rd. Dover CT17 . 149 A1
Macdonald Rd. Gillingham ME7 10 D6
Mace Ind Est. TN24 .... 139 C3
Mace La. TN23 & TN24 ..... 139 C2
Mace Terr. TN26 .... 155 A1
Mackenders Cl. ME20 ...... 53 A6
Mackenders Gn. ME20 ...... 53 A6
Mackenders La. ME20 ...... 53 A6
Mackenzie Dr. CT20 .... 177 E5
Mackeson Ct. CT1 .... 176 B2
Macklands Way. ME8 .... 12 A2
Madden Ave. ME5 .... 31 E5
Madeira Ct. CT20 .... 178 B3
Madeira Rd.
  Littlestone-on-S TN28 .. 200 E6
Madeira Rd. Margate CT9 .. 8 A2
Madeira Wlk. CT11 .... 52 E6
Madginford Cl. ME15 ...... 76 A2
Madginford Park
  Cty Inf Sch. ME15 ...... 76 A2
Madginford Park
  Cty Jun Sch. ME15 ...... 76 A2
Madginford Rd. ME15 ...... 75 F2
Madras Ho. ME15 .... 97 E5
Mafeking Rd. ME5 .... 31 F3
Magazine Rd. TN24 .... 139 B3
Magdala Rd. Broadstairs CT10 29 E6
Magdala Rd. Dover CT17 ... 149 B1
Magdala Rd. ME8 .... 33 A4
Magdalen Ct. Broadstairs CT10 30 A6
Magdalen Ct. Canterbury CT1 88 B7
Magness Rd. CT14 .... 117 C4
Magnolia Ave. Gillingham ME8 33 B5
Magnolia Ave. Margate CT9 8 D2
Magnolia Rise. CT6 .... 23 D2
Magpie Cl. ME12 .... 4 A6
Magpie Hall Rd. Chatham ME4 10 A2
Magpie Hall Rd.
  Stubb's Cross TN26 ..... 155 E2
Magpie La. Rhodes Minnis CT4 144 B3
Magpie La.
  Yelstead ME9 & ME14 .... 33 F1
Magwitch Cl. ME1 .... 9 B4
Maida Rd. ME4 .... 10 B2
Maidstone Barracks Sta. ME16 74 E5
Maidstone East Sta. ME14 74 F5
Maidstone Gram Sch. ME15 75 B2
Maidstone Gram Sch
  for Girls. ME16 .... 74 E5
Maidstone Hospl The. ME16 74 A4
Maidstone Ind Est. ME14 .. 74 F5
Maidstone Mus & Art Gallery.
  ME14 .... 74 F5
Maidstone Rd. Ashford
  TN23 & TN24 & TN25 & TN26 138 D7

Maidstone Rd.
Charing TN25 & TN26 & TN27 ... **120** D6
Maidstone Rd. Chatham ME4 .... **9** F2
Maidstone Rd.
Chatham,Walderslade ME5 .... **31** D4
Maidstone Rd.
Chestnut Street ME9 .... **35** D4
Maidstone Rd. Five Wents ME17 **98** E2
Maidstone Rd. Gillingham ME8 ... **33** C6
Maidstone Rd.
Gillingham,Bredhurst ME7 .... **33** B2
Maidstone Rd. Lenham ME17 ... **101** D5
Maidstone Rd. Rochester ME1 ...... **9** C3
Maidstone St Francis Sch.
ME14 .... **75** A5
Maidstone West Sta. ME16 ...... **74** F3
Mailyns The. ME8 .... **33** D7
Main Gate Rd. ME4 .... **9** F7
Main Rd.
Queenborough ME11 & ME12 .... **3** B5
Main Rd. Sheerness ME12 .... **1** B3
Maine Cl. CT16 .... **149** B3
Maison Des Fleurs. ME16 ...... **74** C2
Maison Dieu Pl. 4 CT16 ...... **166** D8
Maison Dieu Rd. CT16 .... **166** D8
Maitland Cl. ME13 .... **40** B1
Makenade Ave. ME13 .... **62** E6
Malcolm Sargent Rd. TN23 ... **156** B5
Malden Dr. ME14 .... **75** A8
Mall The. ME13 .... **62** C6
Mallard Apartments. 12 ME15 .. **97** E5
Mallard Cl. ME12 .... **4** A6
Mallards. TN23 .... **156** D7
Mallards Way. ME15 .... **76** A1
Malling Terr. ME16 .... **74** C4
Mallings Dr. ME14 .... **76** C4
Mallings La. ME14 .... **76** C4
Mallory Cl. CT12 .... **29** C2
Mallow Way. 1 ME5 .... **31** F4
Mallows The. ME14 .... **74** E7
Malmains Rd. CT17 .... **166** A6
Malt House La. TN30 .... **179** A7
Malta Ave. ME5 .... **32** A7
Malta Ho. 17 CT1 .... **67** B2
Malta Terr. 5 ME14 .... **75** A7
Malthouse Cl. ME17 .... **101** D5
Malthouse Cotts. ME14 .... **75** A5
Malthouse Hill. 10 Hythe CT21 . **176** B2
Malthouse Hill. Loose ME15 ...... **96** F4
Malthouse La.
Boughton Aluph TN25 .... **123** A4
Malthouse La.
Hamstreet TN26 .... **170** D1
Malthouse Rd. CT2 .... **66** F2
Maltings The. Faversham ME13 .. **62** D8
Maltings The. Gillingham ME8 ..... **34** A8
Maltings The. Littlebourne CT3 ... **89** F7
Maltings The. Maidstone ME14 ... **75** E5
Maltings The. Ramsgate CT11 .. **52** D7
Maltings The.
The Quarries ME17 .... **97** B4
Malus Cl. ME5 .... **32** B1
Malvern Meadow. CT16 .... **148** E5
Malvern Pk. CT6 .... **23** D4
Malvern Rd. Ashford TN24 .... **139** B4
Malvern Rd. Dover CT17 .... **166** C7
Malvern Rd. Gillingham ME7 ..... **10** E3
Malvern Rd. Temple Ewell CT16 **148** E5
Mamignot Cl. ME14 .... **76** A5
Manchester Cl. ME5 .... **32** C6
Manciple Cl. CT2 .... **87** C8
Mandeville Ct. 1 ME14 .... **75** A5
Mandeville Rd. CT2 .... **66** E2
Mangers La. CT16 .... **149** A3
Mangers Pl. CT16 .... **149** A3
Mangravet Ave. ME15 .... **97** C7
Manktelow Ct. TN30 .... **29** F2
Manley Cl. CT16 .... **149** A7
Mannock Ho. 6 CT1 .... **67** B1
Manns Hill. CT4 .... **127** A6
Manor Ave. CT14 .... **117** B4
Manor Cl. Canterbury CT1 .... **87** C5
Manor Cl. Deal CT14 .... **117** A4
Manor Cl. Herne Bay CT6 .... **23** F6
Manor Cl. Maidstone ME14 ...... **76** B3
Manor Cl. Rushenden ME11 .... **3** A3
Manor Cotts. Hernhill ME13 ..... **64** B6
Manor Cotts. Langley ME17 ..... **98** C5
Manor Ct. Canterbury CT1 .... **87** F7
Manor Ct. Gillingham ME7 ...... **11** C4
Manor Ct. Maidstone ME14 .... **76** B3
Manor Dr. CT7 .... **26** F6
Manor Gdns. ME5 .... **31** F4
Manor Gr. ME10 .... **36** E3
Manor Ho. 8 ME7 .... **10** A6
Manor House Dr. ME16 .... **74** D3
Manor La. ME1 .... **9** A2
Manor Lea Rd. CT7 .... **25** F1
Manor Mews. CT14 .... **133** F5
Manor Pound La. TN25 .... **158** F7
Manor Rd. Broadstairs CT10 ..... **30** A4
Manor Rd. Chatham ME4 .... **9** F4
Manor Rd. Deal CT14 .... **117** A4
Manor Rd. Dover CT17 .... **166** A6
Manor Rd. Folkestone CT20 .... **178** C4
Manor Rd. Herne Bay CT6 .... **23** F6
Manor Rd. Lydd TN29 .... **203** C6
Manor Rd. Milstead ME9 .... **58** F2
Manor Rd. Monkton CT12 & CT7 . **49** A8
Manor Rd. Rushenden ME11 ...... **3** A3
Manor Rd. Whitstable CT5 .... **21** A2
Manor Rise. Dover CT17 .... **166** A6
Manor Rise. Maidstone ME14 ..... **76** B3

Manor St. ME7 .... **10** A6
Manor Way. Ashford TN23 .... **138** F4
Manor Way.
Leysdown-on-S ME12 .... **6** H2
Manor Way. Warden ME12 .... **6** D6
Manorfield. Ashford TN23 ...... **155** E8
Manorfield. Elham CT4 .... **144** F4
Manse Field. TN25 .... **158** E5
Mansel Dr. ME1 .... **9** A2
Mansell La. CT15 .... **146** B4
Mansfield Ct. CT4 .... **89** A1
Mansfield Wlk. ME16 .... **74** E2
Mansion Gdns. CT16 .... **149** A4
Mansion Row. ME7 .... **10** A6
Mansion St. CT9 .... **7** I3
Manston Court Cotts. CT12 ...... **28** C2
Manston Court Rd. CT12 & CT9 . **28** D3
Manston Park Bglws. CT12 .... **27** F2
Manston Rd. Acol CT12 & CT7 ... **27** D4
Manston Rd. Lydden CT12 & CT9 . **28** C4
Manston Rd.
Ramsgate CT11 & CT12 .... **52** A8
Mantles Hill. CT14 .... **116** D1
Manwood Ave. CT2 .... **66** F3
Manwood Cl. ME10 .... **36** F2
Manwood Cl. CT13 .... **94** A8
Maple Ave. Gillingham ME7 .... **10** E6
Maple Ave. Maidstone ME16 ..... **74** C6
Maple Cl. Ashford TN23 .... **138** E3
Maple Cl. Rough Common CT2 .... **66** B3
Maple Ct. CT3 .... **68** E8
Maple Dr. ME29 .... **194** F4
Maple Gdns. CT3 .... **68** E8
Maple St. ME12 .... **1** D1
Maples The. Broadstairs CT10 .... **29** D4
Maples The. Minster ME12 .... **4** A6
Maplesden Noakes Sch The.
ME16 .... **74** E6
Maplins Cl. ME8 .... **11** F1
Marathon Paddock. ME7 .... **10** D4
Mardale Cl. ME8 .... **12** A1
Marden Ave. CT12 .... **52** B8
Mardol Rd. TN24 .... **139** C5
Maresfield Ct. CT16 .... **149** B2
Margaret Ct. CT6 .... **22** F4
Margaret St. 8 CT20 .... **178** E5
Margarets Ct. CT15 .... **134** A1
Margate Cl. ME7 .... **10** E6
Margate Hill. CT7 .... **27** C4
Margate Rd. Herne Bay CT6 ..... **23** C3
Margate Rd.
Herne Bay, Broomfield CT6 .... **23** D2
Margate Rd.
Ramsgate CT10 & CT12 & CT11 .. **29** B3
Margate Sta. CT9 .... **7** H2
Marian Ave. ME12 .... **4** A7
Marilyns Cres. CT7 .... **27** B7
Marina Cl. CT14 .... **117** D8
Marina Dr. ME12 .... **4** A7
Marina Espl. CT11 .... **52** F7
Marina Rd. CT11 .... **52** F7
Marina The. CT14 .... **117** D8
Marine Ave. TN29 .... **186** F3
Marine Cres. 7
Folkestone CT20 .... **178** D4
Marine Cres. Whitstable CT5 ..... **21** B3
Marine Ct. 13 CT14 .... **166** E7
Marine Dr. Broadstairs CT10 ...... **8** G3
Marine Dr. Margate CT9 .... **7** H2
Marine Gap. CT5 .... **20** C1
Marine Gdns. CT9 .... **7** I2
Marine Par. Dover CT16 .... **166** E7
Marine Par. Dover CT16 .... **166** F8
Marine Par. Folkestone CT20 .. **178** E4
Marine Par. Hythe CT21 .... **176** C1
Marine Par.
Littlestone-on-S TN28 .... **200** E5
Marine Par. Sheerness ME12 ...... **1** F2
Marine Par. Whitstable CT5 ...... **21** A3
Marine Parade Mews. CT20 ... **178** E4
Marine Point. CT20 .... **178** A3
Marine Rd. CT14 .... **117** D4
Marine Terr. Folkestone CT20 . **178** E4
Marine Terr. Margate CT9 .... **7** H2
Marine Terr. Whitstable CT5 ..... **20** C1
Marine Walk St. CT21 .... **176** C1
Marion Cl. ME5 .... **32** A2
Marion Cres. ME15 .... **97** B8
Maritime Cl. ME2 .... **9** D8
Maritime Way. ME4 .... **10** A8
Marjan Cl. CT17 .... **149** A1
Mark Ave. CT11 .... **52** B5
Market Bldgs. 4 ME14 .... **74** F4
Market Colonnade. 3 ME14 ... **74** F4
Market Hill. CT17 .... **176** C2
Market La. 12 TN23 .... **139** B2
Market Pl. Aylesham CT3 .... **112** F5
Market Pl. Charing TN27 .... **120** C7
Market Pl. 1 Faversham ME13 .. **62** D7
Market Pl. 16 Folkestone CT20 . **178** D5
Market Pl. Margate CT9 .... **7** I3
Market Sq. 12 CT16 .... **166** D7
Market St. Deal CT14 .... **117** D6
Market St. Faversham ME13 ..... **62** D7
Market St. Herne Bay CT6 .... **22** F5
Market St. 2 Maidstone ME14 ... **74** F4
Market St. Margate CT9 .... **7** I3
Market St. Sandwich CT13 .... **73** A1
Market View. CT3 .... **112** F5
Market Way. CT2 .... **67** A2
Markland Rd. CT15 & CT17 .. **165** F7
Marlborough Cl.
Broadstairs CT10 .... **29** E3
Marlborough Cl.
Littlestone-on-S TN28 .... **200** D6
Marlborough Ct.
Folkestone CT20 .... **178** B4
Marlborough Ct. Hythe CT21 .. **176** D1

Marlborough Ho. ME8 .... **33** F8
Marlborough Rd. Deal CT14 .. **117** A2
Marlborough Rd.
Dover CT15 & CT17 .... **165** F7
Marlborough Rd.
Gillingham ME7 .... **10** B5
Marlborough Rd. Margate CT9 ... **7** I1
Marlborough Rd. 6
Ramsgate CT11 .... **52** D6
Marlborough Rd.
Whitstable CT5 .... **43** D5
Marlborough Way. TN24 ...... **139** F7
Marler Rd. CT19 .... **177** E6
Marley Ct. CT2 .... **66** C4
Marley La. Chislet CT3 .... **47** A5
Marley La. Finglesham CT14 ... **116** A8
Marley La. Kingston CT4 .... **111** B1
Marley La. Westwood CT14 .... **127** F8
Marley Rd. ME17 .... **100** F6
Marley Way. ME1 .... **9** C2
Marlow Cl. CT5 .... **21** B1
Marlow Copse. ME5 .... **31** F1
Marlowe Arc. 11 CT1 .... **87** F8
Marlowe Ave. CT1 .... **87** F8
Marlowe Ct. 13 CT1 .... **87** F8
Marlowe Rd. Ashford TN23 ... **139** B2
Marlowe Rd. Dover CT16 ...... **149** B3
Marlowe Rd. Margate CT9 .... **29** C8
Marlpit Cotts. ME17 .... **97** E2
Marquis Dr. ME7 .... **33** B3
Marr Cl. ME12 .... **3** F7
Marrose Ave. CT12 .... **29** B3
Marrowbone Hill. ME12 .... **5** B5
Marsh Cres. TN28 .... **200** B6
Marsh Farm Rd. CT12 .... **50** B4
Marsh La. CT14 .... **117** A7
Marsh St. ME2 .... **9** B7
Marsh View. CT21 .... **187** C8
Marshall Cres.
Broadstairs CT10 .... **29** E4
Marshall Cres. Rushenden ME11 ... **2** F3
Marshall Rd. ME8 .... **33** C8
Marshall St. CT19 .... **178** E7
Marshalls Land. TN30 .... **167** A3
Marsham Cres. ME17 .... **98** A3
Marsham St. ME14 .... **75** A4
Marshborough Rd. CT13 .... **93** B7
Marshlands. ME7 .... **195** B7
Marshlands Cl. TN29 .... **195** B7
Marshwood Cl. CT1 .... **67** C3
Marstan Cl. ME9 .... **12** E2
Marston Cl. ME5 .... **31** E3
Marston Dr. ME14 .... **75** C5
Marston Wlk. ME5 .... **31** E3
Martello Cotts. CT21 .... **187** E8
Martello Dr. CT21 .... **175** F1
Martello Ind Ctr. CT19 .... **178** F6
Martello Rd. Folkestone CT20 . **178** E6
Martello Rd.
Folkestone, Sandgate CT20 ... **177** E3
Martello Terr. 1 CT20 .... **177** F3
Marten Rd. CT20 .... **178** B5
Martha Cl. CT19 .... **178** B7
Martin Ct. ME7 .... **33** A3
Martin Dale Cres. CT15 .... **133** C4
Martin Ho. TN25 .... **123** E2
Martin Mill Sta. CT15 .... **133** C2
Martin Rd. ME2 .... **9** B8
Martin's Cl. CT12 .... **29** C2
Martin's Way. CT21 .... **187** D8
Martindale Cl. CT1 .... **88** A7
Martindown Rd. CT5 .... **43** C7
Martins Cl. ME10 .... **179** C8
Martins The. TN26 .... **168** A8
Martyrs' Field Rd. CT1 .... **87** F7
Mary Green Wlk. 5 CT1 .... **67** B2
Mary Haugham Almshouses.
CT14 .... **117** D7
Mary Rd. CT14 .... **117** A3
Maryland Ct. ME8 .... **33** E5
Mason's Rise. CT10 .... **30** A5
Masons Rd. CT17 .... **149** B1
Mate Hall Villas. ME14 .... **76** C4
Matfield Cres. ME14 .... **75** C5
Matilda Cl. ME7 .... **33** B8
Matthew's Pl. 9 CT16 .... **149** C1
Matthews Cl. CT14 .... **117** C6
Matthews Rd. ME15 .... **22** C7
Mattinson Pl. ME9 .... **78** F7
Matts Hill Rd. ME9 .... **33** E2
Maugham Ct. CT5 .... **43** D8
Maundene Cty Prim Sch. ME5 . **32** B5
Maunders Cl. ME8 .... **32** C8
Maunsell Pl. TN24 .... **156** D7
Maxine Gdns. CT10 .... **29** F5
Maxted Ct. CT6 .... **23** C4
Maxton Cl. Dover CT17 .... **166** A6
Maxton Cl. Maidstone ME14 .... **75** F5
Maxton Ct. CT17 .... **166** A6
Maxton Rd. CT17 .... **166** A6
Maxwell Dr. ME8 .... **34** B6
Maxwell Pl. CT14 .... **117** C4
Maxwell Rd. ME7 .... **10** A6
May Lodge. CT14 .... **117** D5
May Rd. Gillingham ME7 .... **10** C4
May Rd. Rochester ME1 .... **9** C3
May St. CT6 .... **23** F4
May Terr. 2 ME14 .... **74** F4
Maybrook Ind Est. CT1 .... **67** C3
Maydowns Rd. CT5 .... **21** D2
Mayers Rd. CT14 .... **117** A1
Mayfair. ME2 .... **9** C8
Mayfair Ave. ME15 .... **97** A8
Mayfield Cl. CT16 .... **149** C2
Mayfield Cl. Chatham ME5 .... **32** A1
Mayfield Cl. Gillingham ME8 ..... **11** E2
Mayfield Ct. 3 CT16 .... **149** B2
Mayfield Gdns. CT16 .... **149** C2

Mayfield Rd. Herne Bay CT6 .... **23** A3
Mayfield Rd. Lyminge CT18 ... **161** C6
Mayfield Rd. Whitfield CT16 .. **149** A7
Mayfly Dr. CT18 .... **163** A4
Mayford Rd. ME5 .... **32** D2
Mayforth Gdns. CT11 .... **52** B6
Mayhew Cl. TN23 .... **156** A8
Maymills Cotts. CT13 .... **93** B2
Maynard and Cotton's Spital. 9
CT1 .... **87** F8
Maynard Ave. CT9 .... **28** B8
Maynard Pl. ME5 .... **10** D2
Maynard Rd. CT1 .... **87** E7
Mayor's Pl. 9 TN30 .... **179** A7
Maypits. TN23 .... **155** F8
Maypole La. CT3 .... **46** E6
Maypole Rd. CT3 .... **46** E6
Mays Rd. CT11 .... **52** C6
Maystreet Cross. CT6 .... **23** C7
Mayton La. CT2 .... **45** C1
Maytree Cotts. CT14 .... **133** D8
Mayville Rd. CT10 .... **29** E6
Mayweed Ave. ME5 .... **31** E4
Mc Kenzie Rd. ME5 .... **32** A3
McAlpine Cres. ME15 .... **96** F3
McCarthy Ave. CT2 .... **67** F7
McClean Wlk. ME12 .... **17** C8
McCudden Row. 4 ME4 .... **10** A6
McKinlay Ct. CT7 .... **26** D8
Mead Rd. Ashford TN24 .... **156** F7
Mead Rd. Folkestone CT19 ... **178** D6
Mead Way. CT2 .... **66** E1
Mead Wlk. TN23 .... **155** E8
Meade The. CT18 .... **162** F4
Meadow Bank. ME13 .... **61** F2
Meadow Brook Ct. CT20 ...... **177** E4
Meadow Cl. Bagham CT4 ...... **107** E8
Meadow Cl. Bridge CT4 .... **89** A1
Meadow Cl. Chatham ME5 .... **31** F5
Meadow Cl. Herne Bay CT6 ..... **23** C4
Meadow Cl. Iwade ME9 .... **14** D4
Meadow Cotts.
East Studdal CT15 .... **132** D8
Meadow Cotts.
Goodnestone CT3 .... **92** A2
Meadow Ct. TN25 .... **175** B6
Meadow Dr. CT5 .... **44** D8
Meadow Gr. TN25 .... **174** D8
Meadow Rd. Ashford TN23 ... **139** A4
Meadow Rd. Canterbury CT2 ... **66** C2
Meadow Rd. Margate CT9 .... **7** F1
Meadow Rd. Sturry CT2 .... **67** F6
Meadow Rise. ME9 .... **14** D4
Meadow View. TN26 .... **138** A6
Meadow View Industries.
TN26 .... **183** C7
Meadow View Rd.
Boughton Monchelsea ME17 ... **97** B3
Meadow View Rd.
Shepherdswell CT15 .... **130** E5
Meadow Wlk. Maidstone ME15 ... **75** B3
Meadow Wlk. Whitstable CT5 .... **43** C6
Meadowbank Rd. ME4 .... **10** A4
Meadowbrook. CT20 .... **177** E4
Meadowbrook Cl. TN24 .... **139** D6
Meadowbrook Rd. TN24 ...... **139** D6
Meadowdown. ME14 .... **75** A4
Meadowdown Cl. ME7 .... **33** A4
Meadows The. Herne Bay CT6 .. **23** D2
Meadows Way. TN29 .... **194** E3
Meadows The.
Sittingbourne ME10 .... **36** F2
Meads Ave The. ME10 .... **36** D7
Meads Way. TN29 .... **194** E3
Meadside Wlk. ME5 .... **31** F6
Meadway. CT17 .... **148** E3
Medina Ave. CT5 .... **43** B7
Medlar Cl. ME9 .... **58** A6
Medlar Gr. ME7 .... **33** A4
Medlars The. ME14 .... **75** D6
Medway Cl. ME10 .... **36** D4
Medway Com Coll. ME4 .... **10** A1
Medway Ent Ctr. ME2 .... **9** D8
Medway Gdns. ME4 .... **9** F7
Medway Heritage Ctr. ME4 ...... **9** F5
Medway Ho. 1 ME15 .... **97** D8
Medway Hospl. ME7 .... **10** B4
Medway Rd. Gillingham ME7 ... **10** C7
Medway Rd.
Gillingham,Rainham ME8 .... **11** F1
Medway Rd. Sheerness ME12 .... **1** C1
Medway Service Area. ME8 ... **33** F3
Medway St. Chatham ME4 .... **9** F5
Medway St. Maidstone ME14 ... **74** F4
Medway Trad Est. ME16 .... **74** F3
Medway Villas. ME15 .... **96** B7
Meehan Rd. ME12 .... **200** E4
Meehan Rd S. TN28 .... **200** E3
Meeres Court La. ME10 .... **37** C5
Meeson's Cl. ME13 .... **81** E6
Meeting House La. ME4 .... **9** F4
Meeting St. CT11 .... **52** E7
Megby Cl. ME8 .... **33** D6
Megone Cl. CT18 .... **163** A4
Meirs Court La. ME8 .... **33** E6
Melbourne Ave. Dover CT16 . **149** C4
Melbourne Ave. Ramsgate CT12 **29** B3
Melbourne
Cty Prim Sch. CT16 .... **149** C4
Melbourne Rd. ME4 .... **10** A3
Melbury Mews. TN28 .... **200** C8
Melford Dr. ME16 .... **74** C4
Mellanby Cl. CT7 .... **27** A6
Mellor Row. ME10 .... **14** F1
Melody Cl. Milstead ME9 .... **33** C4
Melody Cl. Warden ME12 .... **6** E4
Melon La. TN26 & TN29 .... **193** B6
Melrose Cl. ME15 .... **97** A7

Melsetter Cl. CT7 .... **27** B7
Melville Ct. ME4 .... **9** F6
Melville Lea. CT13 .... **93** C7
Melville Rd. ME15 .... **75** A3
Memorial (General) Hospl.
ME10 .... **36** F3
Mendfield St. 5 ME13 .... **62** C7
Mendip Rise. TN24 .... **139** B4
Menin Rd. ME10 .... **14** F1
Mentmore Ho. CT12 .... **29** C3
Mentmore Rd. CT10 & CT12 ... **29** C3
Menzies Ave. CT14 .... **117** B1
Menzies Cl. ME12 .... **4** A5
Mercer Dr. ME17 .... **100** F6
Mercer Way. ME17 .... **98** B1
Mercery La. 5 CT1 .... **87** F8
Merchants Way. CT2 .... **87** C8
Mercury Cl. ME1 .... **9** A3
Mere Gate. CT9 .... **7** I1
Meredale Cty Inf Sch. ME8 .... **12** A1
Meresborough Cotts. ME8 ...... **33** F5
Meresborough La. ME8 & ME9 . **34** B5
Meresborough Rd. ME8 .... **34** A7
Mereworth Cl. ME8 .... **11** A3
Meridian Ho. TN23 .... **155** E7
Meridian Pk. ME2 .... **9** E6
Merivale Gr. ME5 .... **32** B4
Merleburgh Dr. ME10 .... **36** F8
Merlin Cl. ME10 .... **37** A3
Mermaid Cl. ME5 .... **32** A6
Merritt Rd. TN28 .... **200** E2
Mersham Cty Prim Sch. TN25 **157** E3
Merton Cl. ME5 .... **32** C5
Merton La. CT1 & CT4 .... **87** F4
Merton Rd. ME15 .... **75** F2
Meryl Gdns. CT14 .... **117** C1
Metcalfe Mews. 1 CT1 .... **67** B2
Meteor Ave. CT5 .... **43** B7
Metropole Rd E. CT20 .... **178** B3
Metropole Rd W. CT20 .... **178** B3
Meverall Ave. CT12 .... **51** E5
Mews The. Maidstone ME16 ..... **74** E5
Mews The. Sittingbourne ME10 .. **36** E2
Meyrick Rd. ME12 .... **1** D2
Micawber Cl. ME5 .... **32** A1
Michael Ave. CT11 .... **52** G8
Michelle Gdns. CT9 .... **28** A8
Mickleburgh Ave. CT6 .... **23** B4
Mickleburgh Hill. CT6 .... **23** B4
Mid Kent Coll (City Way Ctr.).
ME1 .... **9** E4
Mid Kent Coll of H & F Ed.
ME16 .... **74** E3
Mid Kent Coll of H & F Ed.
Maidstone,Cherry Orchard ME16 . **74** C3
Mid Kent Coll of Higher
& F Ed. ME1 & ME4 .... **31** E6
Mid Kent Sch for Girls. ME14 .. **75** A5
Mid Kent Sh Ctr The. ME16 .... **74** C7
Middelburg Ho. CT20 .... **177** D6
Middelburg Sq. CT20 .... **178** D4
Middle Cl. TN23 .... **138** C1
Middle Deal Rd. CT14 .... **117** B5
Middle Mead. CT14 .... **117** B6
Middle Row. Ashford TN23 ... **139** C2
Middle Row. 2
Faversham ME13 .... **62** D7
Middle Row. 6
ME15 .... **74** F4
Middle St. Ashford TN23 ...... **139** B2
Middle St. Deal CT14 .... **117** D6
Middle St. 5 Gillingham ME4 ... **10** A6
Middle Wall. CT5 .... **20** D2
Middle Way. ME10 .... **37** B3
Middlefields. ME8 .... **34** A8
Middlesex Rd. ME15 .... **97** D7
Middleton Cl. ME8 .... **33** E4
Middleton Cotts. TN25 .... **122** E3
Middleton Cl. 8 ME10 .... **36** E4
Middletune Ave. ME10 .... **36** E7
Midhurst Cl. ME15 .... **75** A3
Midley Cl. ME16 .... **74** C7
Midsummer Hill. TN24 .... **139** D6
Miers Court
Cty Prim Sch. ME8 .... **33** F7
Mierscourt Cl. ME8 .... **34** A8
Mierscourt Rd. ME8 .... **33** E6
Mikyle Cl. CT1 .... **88** A6
Milbourne Gr. ME10 .... **36** E7
Milburn Rd. ME7 .... **10** C7
Mildred Cotts. CT19 .... **177** F7
Mile Rd. CT12 & CT3 .... **48** F6
Miles Cl. CT3 .... **91** A8
Miles Pl. ME1 .... **9** D3
Miles Way. CT7 .... **26** F7
Milestone Cl. CT19 .... **178** A7
Milestone Rd. CT14 .... **117** B5
Milford Cl. ME16 .... **74** D5
Military Rd. Canterbury CT1 .... **67** A1
Military Rd. Canterbury CT1 .... **67** B1
Military Rd. Chatham ME4 .... **9** F5
Military Rd. 2 Dover CT17 ... **166** D7
Military Rd. Folkestone CT20 . **177** E4
Military Rd. Hythe CT21 .... **52** E6
Military Rd. Ramsgate CT11 ... **52** E6
Military Rd.
Stone in Oxney TN26 & TN30 ... **190** B4
Mill Bank. TN29 .... **203** B6
Mill Bank Cotts. CT13 .... **93** A2
Mill Bay. CT20 .... **178** E5
Mill Cl. Lenham ME17 .... **101** C4
Mill Cl. River CT17 .... **148** F2
Mill Cl. Sandwich CT13 .... **72** E2
Mill Cotts. Ramsgate CT11 ..... **52** D6
Mill Cotts. Worth CT14 .... **94** A4
Mill Ct. ME10 .... **37** A3
Mill Field. Ash CT3 .... **71** E1
Mill Field. Broadstairs CT10 .... **29** F5

Mill Fields Rd. CT21 .... 175 F2
Mill Gn. CT13 .... 93 A2
Mill Hamlet. CT3 .... 69 C2
Mill Hill. CT14 .... 117 A3
Mill La. Aldington TN25 .... 172 E5
Mill La. Ashford TN24 .... 140 A1
Mill La. Bagham CT4 .... 107 D7
Mill La. Biddenden Green TN27 ... 135 A2
Mill La. Birchington CT7 .... 26 F6
Mill La. Bridge CT4 .... 88 F1
Mill La. Canterbury CT1 .... 66 F1
Mill La.
Canterbury, Harbledown CT2 .... 87 C8
Mill La.
Chatham,Bluebell Hill ME5 ...... 31 D1
Mill La. Chatham,Luton ME5 ...... 10 C1
Mill La. Coxheath ME17 .... 96 D4
Mill La. 8 Dover CT16 .... 166 E7
Mill La. Eastry CT13 .... 93 B2
Mill La. Hartlip Hill ME9 .... 34 E6
Mill La. Hawkinge CT18 .... 163 B5
Mill La. Herne Bay CT6 .... 23 B2
Mill La. Lynsted ME9 .... 60 C5
Mill La. Maidstone ME14 .... 74 F6
Mill La. Margate CT9 .... 7 I2
Mill La. Nonington CT15 .... 113 F4
Mill La. Northbourne CT14 ...... 115 F4
Mill La. Preston CT3 .... 70 D6
Mill La. Shepherdswell CT15 ...... 130 F5
Mill La. Stelling Minnis CT4 ...... 126 F2
Mill La. Tenterden TN30 .... 167 B1
Mill La. Whitfield CT16 .... 149 A8
Mill La. Worth CT14 .... 94 A4
Mill Lane Cotts. CT14 .... 116 A4
Mill Mews. CT14 .... 117 B4
Mill Pl. ME13 .... 62 D8
Mill Rd. Bethersden TN26 ...... 153 E5
Mill Rd. Bramling CT3 .... 90 E6
Mill Rd. Deal CT14 .... 117 C4
Mill Rd. Dymchurch TN29 ...... 195 B7
Mill Rd. Gillingham ME7 ...... 10 C6
Mill Rd. Hoath CT3 .... 46 F5
Mill Rd. Hythe CT21 .... 176 D2
Mill Rd. Lydd TN29 .... 203 D7
Mill Rd. Rochester ME2 ...... 9 B8
Mill Rd. Staple CT3 .... 92 B5
Mill Rd. Sturry CT2 .... 67 F5
Mill Row. CT7 .... 26 F6
Mill St. Loose ME15 .... 96 F5
Mill St. Maidstone ME15 .... 74 F4
Mill St. Sittingbourne ME10 ...... 36 E5
Mill St. Temple Ewell CT16 ...... 148 D5
Mill Terr. Bridge CT4 .... 88 F1
Mill Terr. Chartham CT4 .... 86 D3
Mill View. Ashford TN24 .... 156 F8
Mill View. Woodchurch TN26 ...... 169 A3
Mill View Rd. CT6 .... 23 A1
Mill Wall Pl. CT13 .... 94 A8
Mill Way. ME10 .... 36 F6
Mill Wlk. ME16 .... 74 A3
Millais Rd. CT16 .... 149 C1
Millbank La. TN29 .... 198 E7
Millbank Rd. TN23 .... 155 F5
Millbrook. CT21 .... 176 D2
Millbrook Cl. ME15 .... 74 F1
Millbrook Meadow. TN23 ...... 138 E1
Milldale Ct. CT14 .... 117 B4
Millen Rd. ME10 .... 36 E5
Millen's Row. ME13 .... 83 B3
Miller Ave. CT2 .... 87 D8
Miller Cl. ME10 .... 37 A8
Miller Ct. ME12 .... 4 A5
Millers Ct. CT5 .... 43 D7
Millers La. CT12 .... 49 C7
Millers Wharf. ME16 .... 74 E2
Millfield. Ashford TN23 .... 155 D8
Millfield. Folkestone CT20 ...... 178 D5
Millfield. Hawkinge CT18 .... 163 C6
Millfield. High Halden TN26 ...... 167 D3
Millfield. Sittingbourne ME10 ... 37 A3
Millfield.
St Margaret's at Cliffe CT15 .... 150 F7
Millfield Cl. CT18 .... 163 B5
Millfield Manor. CT5 .... 20 E1
Millfield Rd. Faversham ME13 ... 62 E7
Millfield Rd. Ramsgate CT12 ... 29 B3
Millfields. Chatham ME5 ...... 32 C1
Millfields. Shepherdswell CT15 .. 130 E4
Millmead Ave. CT9 .... 8 D1
Millmead Gdns. CT9 .... 8 C1
Millmead Rd. CT9 .... 8 C1
Millpond Cl. ME2 .... 9 B8
Mills Cl. ME12 .... 3 F6
Mills Terr. ME4 .... 10 A3
Millstock Terr. ME15 .... 74 E2
Millstream Cl. Faversham ME13 . 62 C7
Millstream Cl. Whitstable CT5 .... 20 E1
Millstrood Rd. CT5 .... 43 E8
Milne Rd. TN24 .... 156 F8
Milner Cl. CT15 .... 114 B1
Milner Cres. CT3 .... 112 E5
Milner La. CT2 .... 67 F5
Milner Rd. Elvington CT15 ...... 114 B1
Milner Rd. Gillingham ME7 ...... 10 D7
Milner Rd. Whitstable CT5 ...... 43 A6
Milstead Cl. Maidstone ME14 .... 75 C5
Milstead Cl. West Minster ME12 ... 3 B7
Milstead & Frinstead
CE Prim Sch. ME9 .... 58 E1
Milsted Rd. ME8 .... 11 C3
Milton Ave. CT7 .... 7 J1
Milton Cl. Canterbury CT1 ...... 88 C6
Milton Cl. Dover CT16 .... 149 B4
Milton Rd. Ashford TN23 ...... 139 B2
Milton Rd. Canterbury CT1 ...... 88 A6
Milton Rd. Dover CT16 .... 149 B4
Milton Rd. Gillingham ME7 ...... 10 C3
Milton Rd. Sittingbourne ME10 ... 36 E4

Milton Sq. 4 CT9 .... 7 J1
Milton St. ME16 .... 74 C2
Mincers Cl. ME5 .... 32 C2
Minerva Ave. CT11 .... 149 C2
Minerva Ho. CT11 .... 52 D7
Minerva Rd. ME2 .... 9 A8
Minnis Field. CT4 .... 126 E2
Minnis Gn. CT4 .... 126 E2
Minnis La. CT15 & CT17 ...... 148 C2
Minnis Rd. CT7 .... 26 E7
Minnis Terr. CT17 .... 149 A2
Minnis Way. CT14 .... 94 B5
Minster Abbey. Minster ME12 ...... 4 D6
Minster Abbey. Minster,Thanet
CT12 .... 50 C5
Minster CE Prim Sch. CT12 ...... 50 B5
Minster Cl. CT10 .... 30 A2
Minster Coll. ME12 .... 3 F6
Minster Dr. Herne Bay CT6 ...... 22 D4
Minster Dr. Minster ME12 ...... 4 B8
Minster Lodge. CT11 .... 52 C6
Minster Rd. Acol CT12 & CT7 ... 27 C2
Minster Rd. Faversham ME13 ... 62 E7
Minster Rd. Gillingham ME8 ...... 11 C3
Minster Rd. Minster ME12 ...... 4 B6
Minster Rd. Ramsgate CT11 ...... 52 B5
Minster Rd. Westgate-on-S CT8 ... 27 F7
Minster (Thanet) Sta. CT12 ...... 50 C5
Minster-in-Sheppey
Cty Prim Sch. ME12 .... 4 C7
Mint The. CT2 .... 66 C1
Mintching Wood La. ME9 ...... 58 F2
Minter Ave. CT18 .... 162 F7
Minter Cl. CT18 .... 162 F7
Minterne Ave. ME10 .... 36 D2
Minterne Cty Jun Sch. ME10 ... 36 D2
Miranda Ct. ME12 .... 1 C1
Misling La. CT4 & TN25 ...... 143 C7
Missenden Cl. 6 CT20 .... 178 D5
Mitcham Rd. TN29 .... 195 C8
Mitchell Ave. ME4 .... 9 F2
Mitchell Cl. ME17 .... 101 C5
Mitchell St. CT19 .... 177 D6
Mitre Rd. ME1 .... 9 B4
Mittell Ct. TN29 .... 203 B6
Moat Farm Cl. CT19 .... 178 C7
Moat Farm Rd. CT19 .... 178 C7
Moat Ho. Canterbury CT1 ...... 87 F7
Moat Ho. Charing TN27 .... 120 C7
Moat La. Ash CT3 .... 71 E1
Moat La. Fordwich CT2 & CT3 .. 68 A3
Moat La. Rough Common CT2 ... 66 B4
Moat Pk. CT7 .... 120 C6
Moat Sole. CT13 .... 72 F1
Moat The. TN27 .... 120 C7
Moat Way. ME11 .... 3 A5
Moatfield Meadow. TN23 ...... 156 B4
Mock La. TN23 .... 155 B6
Mockett Cl. 4 ME10 .... 36 E4
Mockett Dr. CT10 .... 29 F7
Molehill Copse
Cty Prim Sch. ME15 .... 97 D7
Molehill Rd.
Herne Bay CT6 & CT5 .... 22 A1
Molehill Rd.
Whitstable CT5 & CT6 .... 44 E8
Molineux Rd. CT12 .... 50 B6
Molland Cl. CT3 .... 71 C2
Molland La. Ash CT3 .... 71 C2
Molland La. Westmarsh CT3 ... 71 D6
Molland Lea. CT3 .... 71 C2
Molloy Rd. TN26 .... 155 B1
Monarch Cl. ME5 .... 32 A6
Monastery St. CT1 .... 88 A8
Monckton's Ave. ME14 .... 74 F7
Monckton's Dr. ME14 .... 74 F7
Moncktons La. ME14 .... 74 F7
Moncrif Cl. ME14 .... 76 B4
Mongeham Church Cl. CT14 . 116 D3
Mongeham
Cty Prim Sch. CT14 .... 116 F4
Mongeham Rd. CT14 .... 116 E3
Monins Rd. CT17 .... 166 B7
Monkdown. ME5 .... 76 A1
Monkery La. ME13 & TN25 ...... 104 D2
Monks Cl. Canterbury CT2 ...... 67 A2
Monks Cl. Faversham ME13 ... 62 B8
Monks Way. CT16 .... 149 A3
Monks Wlk. TN27 .... 120 C7
Monkshill Rd. ME13 .... 42 B2
Monkton CE Prim Sch. CT12 ... 49 D7
Monkton Court La. CT15 ...... 131 D7
Monkton Gdns. CT9 .... 8 E3
Monkton Manor. CT12 .... 49 B7
Monkton Pl. CT11 .... 52 D7
Monkton Rd. CT12 .... 50 A6
Monkton Rdbt. CT12 .... 49 D8
Monkton St. CT12 .... 49 D7
Monkwood Cl. ME1 .... 31 B8
Monmouth Cl. ME8 .... 11 D2
Mons Ct. ME10 .... 14 F1
Montacue Ct. ME12 .... 1 C1
Montague Cl. ME12 .... 1 C1
Montague Rd. CT11 .... 52 E8
Montague St. CT6 .... 22 D5
Montefiore Ave. CT11 .... 29 F1
Montefiore Cotts. CT11 .... 52 F8
Montfort Cl. Ashford TN23 .... 155 F7
Montfort Cl. Canterbury CT2 ... 67 A4
Montfort Rd. Chatham ME5 ... 31 F2
Montfort Rd. Rochester ME2 ... 9 A8
Montgomery GM Sch. CT3 ... 68 C8
Montgomery Rd. ME7 .... 10 C3
Montgomery Way. CT19 ...... 178 E8
Montpelier Ave. CT5 .... 43 D6
Montpelier Bsns Pk. TN23 ... 138 F1

Montpelier Gate. ME16 .... 74 B5
Montreal Cl. 8 CT16 .... 149 B3
Montrose Ave. ME5 .... 10 E2
Monument Way. TN24 .... 156 F5
Moon Hill. CT15 .... 130 E4
Moonstone Dr. ME5 .... 32 B2
Moor La. Ivychurch TN29 ...... 192 D4
Moor La.
Woodchurch TN26 & TN30 .... 180 E6
Moor Lane Cotts. TN26 .... 181 C2
Moor Park Cl. ME8 .... 34 A8
Moor St. ME8 .... 34 B8
Moore St. ME2 .... 9 A8
Moorfield. CT2 .... 66 F4
Mooring Rd. ME1 .... 9 D1
Moorings The. ME9 .... 38 E6
Moorstock La. TN25 .... 159 C2
Moorwell Dr. CT15 .... 130 D5
Moray Ave. CT7 .... 26 F8
Mordaunt Ave. CT8 .... 27 E8
Morehall Cl. CT19 .... 177 F6
Morehall Cty Prim Sch. CT19 . 177 F6
Morella Wlk. ME17 .... 101 C5
Morello Cl. ME9 .... 38 C2
Moreton Terr. TN26 .... 155 A1
Morgan Kirby's Gdn. ME13 ... 83 D5
Morris Ave. CT6 .... 21 F4
Morris Court Cl. ME9 .... 37 D2
Morrison Rd. CT20 .... 178 E6
Morry La. ME17 .... 99 D1
Mortimer Cl. TN23 .... 156 B7
Mortimer Rd. CT18 .... 166 F8
Mortimer St. CT5 .... 22 F5
Mossbank. ME5 .... 32 A3
Mossend Mews. CT11 .... 29 E2
Mossy Glade. ME8 .... 33 E6
Mostyn Rd. ME14 .... 75 C4
Mote Ave. ME15 .... 75 B3
Mote Pk. ME15 .... 75 D2
Mote Rd. ME15 .... 75 A3
Motney Hill Rd. ME8 .... 12 A4
Mouat Ct. ME5 .... 32 A3
Mount Charles Wlk. CT4 ...... 88 F1
Mount Dr. ME14 .... 76 B4
Mount Ephraim. ME13 .... 64 A4
Mount Field. Faversham ME13 .. 62 B6
Mount Field.
Queenborough ME11 .... 3 A5
Mount Green Ave. CT12 ...... 51 D5
Mount La. Hartlip ME9 .... 34 D4
Mount La. Maidstone ME14 .... 76 B4
Mount Lodge. ME14 .... 9 B2
Mount Pleasant.
Aldington ME25 .... 173 A6
Mount Pleasant.
Aylesford ME20 .... 53 A3
Mount Pleasant. Blean CT2 ... 66 A6
Mount Pleasant.
Gillingham ME4 .... 10 B3
Mount Pleasant.
Kingsdown CT14 .... 134 D5
Mount Pleasant. Oare ME13 ... 40 B2
Mount Pleasant.
Tenterden TN30 .... 179 C8
Mount Pleasant Dr. ME14 ...... 76 A5
Mount Pleasant Rd. 4 CT20 .. 178 D5
Mount Pleasant Terr. ME17 ... 100 E2
Mount Rd. Canterbury CT1 ...... 88 C6
Mount Rd. Chatham ME4 ...... 9 F3
Mount Rd. Dover CT17 .... 166 A6
Mount Rd. Rochester ME1 ...... 9 B2
Mount St. CT21 .... 176 C2
Mount View. ME15 .... 62 A5
Mount View Rd. CT6 .... 23 A2
Mountain St. CT4 .... 107 B6
Mountbatten Ave. ME5 .... 32 A7
Mountbatten Way. TN25 ...... 158 E6
Mounts Cl. CT14 .... 117 A5
Mountsfield Cl. ME16 .... 74 D5
Moyle Cl. ME8 .... 33 D4
Mozart Ct. ME4 .... 9 E3
Muddy Bush Cnr. CT3 .... 90 F2
Muir Rd. Maidstone ME15 ...... 75 A2
Muir Rd. Ramsgate CT11 ...... 52 D8
Mulberry Cl. Gillingham ME7 ... 33 A4
Mulberry Cl. Ramsgate CT11 ... 52 F8
Mulberry Ct. Canterbury CT1 ... 87 F8
Mulberry Ct.
Littlestone-on-S TN28 .... 200 E5
Mulberry Field. CT13 .... 72 F1
Mulberry Hill. CT4 .... 85 D1
Munday Bois Cotts. TN27 ... 135 F8
Munday Bois Rd. TN27 ...... 118 E1
Mundella
Cty Prim Sch. CT19 .... 178 D6
Mungeham Ho. ME1 .... 9 C4
Munn's La. ME9 .... 34 E6
Murrain Dr. ME15 .... 76 A1
Murray Rd. ME2 .... 9 C8
Murston Cty Inf Sch. ME10 .... 37 B4
Murston Jun Sch. ME10 ...... 37 B5
Murston Rd. ME10 .... 37 B4
Murthwaite Ct. ME12 .... 4 A5
Murton Pl. ME13 .... 41 E1
Museum of Kent Rural Life.
ME14 .... 53 D1
Musgrave Cl. CT12 .... 27 F2
Musgrave Rd. ME10 .... 36 F6
Musgrove. TN23 .... 156 A8

Musket La.
Eyhorne Street ME17 .... 77 B2
Musket La. Silver Hill ME17 ... 77 A2
Mustards Rd. ME12 .... 6 D2
Mutrix Gdns. CT9 .... 7 E1
Mutrix Rd. CT9 .... 28 E8
Mutton La. ME13 .... 62 A6
Mymms Cl. CT5 .... 44 C8
Mynn Cres. ME14 .... 76 A4
Myrtle Cres. ME5 .... 31 F5
Myrtle Rd. 4 CT19 .... 178 E6
Mystole Cl. CT4 .... 108 C8
Mystole Rd. CT4 .... 108 A8

Nacholt Cl. CT5 .... 21 A2
Nackington Ct. CT1 .... 88 B6
Nackington Pk. CT1 .... 88 A4
Nackington Rd. CT1 & CT4 .... 88 A3
Nag's Head La. ME1 .... 9 D4
Nagpur Ho. 4 ME15 .... 97 E5
Nags Head La. ME1 .... 9 D4
Nailbourne Cl. ME9 .... 111 D3
Nailbourne Ct. CT18 .... 161 C7
Naildown Cl. CT21 .... 177 A3
Naildown Rd. CT21 .... 177 A3
Nairne Cl. TN26 .... 170 A8
Namur Pl. CT16 .... 149 F3
Napchester Rd. CT15 & CT16 .. 149 A8
Napier Cl. ME10 .... 36 C4
Napier Ct. ME14 .... 74 F7
Napier Cty Prim Sch. ME7 ...... 10 D4
Napier Gdns. CT21 .... 176 C1
Napier Rd. Broadstairs CT10 ... 29 E6
Napier Rd. Dover CT16 .... 149 B2
Napier Rd. Gillingham ME7 ...... 10 D4
Napleton Cl. CT11 .... 52 C6
Napleton Rd. Faversham ME13 .. 62 C7
Napleton Rd. Ramsgate CT11 ... 52 C6
Napoleon Wlk. ME17 .... 101 C5
Napwood Cl. ME8 .... 33 D6
Nares Rd. ME8 .... 33 D4
Nargate Cl. CT3 .... 90 A8
Nargate St. CT3 .... 90 A8
Narrabeen Rd. CT19 .... 177 E6
Narrowbush La. TN29 .... 198 B7
Naseby Ave. CT20 .... 177 D5
Nash Cl. ME5 .... 32 C2
Nash Court Gdns. CT9 .... 28 F8
Nash Court Rd. CT9 .... 28 F8
Nash Gdns. CT10 .... 30 B4
Nash Hill. CT18 .... 161 D6
Nash La. CT9 .... 28 F7
Nash Rd. CT9 & CT10 .... 28 F7
Nashenden Farm La. ME1 .... 31 A8
Nasmyth Rd. CT7 .... 27 A8
Nat's La. TN25 .... 141 A5
Natal Rd. Chatham ME4 ...... 10 A3
Natal Rd. Dover CT16 .... 149 C4
Nativity Cl. ME10 .... 36 E4
Nautilus Cl. ME12 .... 4 A6
Nautilus Dr. ME12 .... 4 A6
Naval Terr. ME12 .... 1 B3
Naylands. CT9 .... 7 H1
Naylor's Cotts. ME14 .... 33 B1
Neal's Place Rd. CT2 .... 66 C3
Neale St. ME4 .... 9 F2
Neame Rd. CT7 .... 27 A7
Neames Forstal. ME13 .... 84 E7
Neason Ct. CT19 .... 178 F6
Neason Way. CT19 .... 178 F6
Neath Ct. 2 ME15 .... 97 E8
Neath Rd. TN29 .... 202 A2
Neatscourt Cotts. ME12 ...... 3 C4
Nelson Ave. ME12 .... 4 D5
Nelson Cl. Ashford TN24 ...... 157 B8
Nelson Cl. West Minster ME12 .. 3 A8
Nelson Cres. CT11 .... 52 E6
Nelson Ct. CT7 .... 26 E8
Nelson Ho. 5 ME15 .... 97 E5
Nelson Park Rd. CT15 .... 150 E8
Nelson Pl. CT10 .... 30 B5
Nelson Rd. Gillingham ME7 ... 10 D4
Nelson Rd. Whitstable CT5 ...... 20 D1
Nelson St. Deal CT14 .... 117 D7
Nelson St. Faversham ME13 ... 62 C6
Nelson Terr. ME5 .... 10 C1
Nelson Wlk. ME10 .... 36 B5
Neptune Bsns Pk. ME2 ...... 9 E7
Neptune Cl. ME2 .... 9 E7
Neptune Terr. ME12 .... 1 E2
Nesbit Rd. TN29 .... 194 F4
Ness Rd. TN29 .... 203 C6
Ness The. CT1 .... 88 B5
Nether Ave. TN28 .... 200 D6
Nethercourt Cir. CT12 .... 52 A6
Nethercourt Farm Rd. CT11 ... 52 B7
Nethercourt Gdns. CT11 ...... 52 B6
Nethercourt Hill. CT11 .... 52 B6
Nethergong Hill. CT3 .... 47 D3
Netherhale Farm Rd. CT7 ... 26 B3
Nethersole Cl. CT2 .... 67 A4
Nethersole Rd. CT4 .... 112 F1
Netley Cl. ME14 .... 75 D6
Nettlefield. ME14 .... 139 E5
Nettlepole La. TN27 .... 119 D1
Nevill Gdns. CT14 .... 117 B1
Neville Cl. ME14 .... 75 B8
Neville Rd. ME4 .... 9 E2
New Barns Rd. ME14 .... 75 A4
New Beverley Ho. CT2 .... 66 F2
New Bridge. 5 CT16 .... 166 E7
New Cotts. Guston CT15 ...... 149 E6
New Cotts. Harbledown CT2 ... 65 E1
New Cotts. Teynham ME9 ...... 38 A4
New Covenant Pl. ME1 ...... 9 B4
New Cross. CT9 .... 7 I2
New Cut. Chatham ME4 ...... 9 F4
New Cut. Dean Street ME15 .. 96 C1

New Cut Rd.
Chilham CT4 & ME13 .... 85 A3
New Cut Rd. Maidstone ME14 ... 75 D5
New Delhi Ho. 5 ME15 ...... 97 E5
New Dover Rd.
Canterbury CT1 & CT4 .... 88 C6
New Dover Rd.
Capel-le-F CT18 .... 164 C2
New Forest La. CT4 & ME13 ... 85 B3
New Gardens Rd. ME9 ...... 38 C2
New Hall Cl. TN29 .... 195 C8
New Hall Mus. TN29 .... 195 C8
New House Cl. CT1 .... 87 E4
New House La. CT1 & CT4 .... 87 C2
New Inn Cotts. ME15 .... 96 C7
New La. Calcott CT2 & CT6 ...... 45 C4
New Rd. Chatham ME1 .... 9 D4
New Rd. Chatham ME4 .... 9 F4
New Rd. Egerton TN27 .... 119 A2
New Rd. Elham CT4 .... 144 F4
New Rd. Eythorne CT15 ...... 131 C7
New Rd.
Harbledown CT2 & ME13 ...... 65 D3
New Rd. Hythe CT21 .... 176 B1
New Rd. Hythe, Saltwood CT21 ... 176 B4
New Rd. Langley ME17 ...... 98 C5
New Rd. Minster ME12 .... 4 C6
New Rd. Rough Common CT2 ... 66 B3
New Rd. Sheerness ME12 ...... 1 B1
New Rectory La. TN23 ...... 156 B4
New Rents. 5 TN23 .... 139 B2
New Road Ave. ME4 .... 9 E4
New Road Cotts. CT6 .... 45 E5
New Road Cty Prim Sch. ME4 .. 10 A3
New Road Hill. TN25 .... 172 F4
New Road Ind Est. ME12 ...... 1 B1
New Romney CE Jun Sch.
TN28 .... 200 B7
New Romney Cty Inf Sch.
TN28 .... 200 B7
New Romney Pl. CT13 .... 93 F8
New Romney Sta. TN28 ...... 200 C6
New Ruttington La. CT1 ...... 67 B2
New St. Ash CT3 .... 71 E1
New St. Ashford TN23 & TN24 ... 139 B2
New St. Canterbury CT2 ...... 66 E1
New St. Canterbury CT1 ...... 87 E7
New St. Chatham ME4 .... 9 E3
New St. Deal CT14 .... 117 D7
New St. Dover CT16 .... 166 D8
New St. Folkestone CT20 ...... 178 D5
New St. Herne Bay CT6 .... 22 F5
New St. Lydd TN29 .... 203 C6
New St. Margate CT9 .... 7 I2
New St. Sandwich CT13 ...... 94 A8
New Strs. Sheerness ME12 ...... 1 C1
New Strs. 2 Whitstable CT5 ...... 20 D2
New Strs. ME4 .... 9 F6
New Town Gn. TN24 .... 156 D8
New Town St. Canterbury CT1 ... 67 B2
New Town St. Chartham CT4 ... 86 C5
New Villas. ME15 .... 96 C7
Newark Ct. 1 ME2 .... 9 B7
Newark Yd. ME2 .... 9 B7
Newbridge Ave. ME10 ...... 36 E7
Newbury Ave. ME16 .... 74 C6
Newbury Cl. Birchington CT7 ... 27 B6
Newbury Cl. Dover CT17 ...... 165 F7
Newbury Cl. Folkestone CT20 ... 177 D5
Newcastle Hill. 5 CT11 ...... 52 E7
Newchurch La. TN29 & TN26 .. 193 A7
Newchurch Rd. ME15 .... 75 A1
Newcomen Rd. ME12 .... 1 D2
Newenden Cl. Ashford TN23 ... 155 F6
Newenden Cl. Maidstone ME14 .. 75 D6
Newgate Gap. CT9 .... 8 A3
Newgate Lower Prom. CT9 ... 8 A3
Newgate Prom. CT9 .... 8 A3
Newham St. ME4 .... 10 B3
Newhouse Cnr. CT3 .... 48 D1
Newhouse La. ME13 .... 83 D7
Newing Cl. CT3 .... 89 E8
Newington CE Prim Sch. ME9 ... 35 B7
Newington Cty Inf Sch. CT12 ... 52 B8
Newington Ent Ctr. ME9 ...... 35 C8
Newington Ind Est. ME9 ...... 34 F6
Newington Jun Sch. CT12 ...... 52 A8
Newington Rd.
Newington CT18 .... 177 A8
Newington Rd.
Ramsgate CT12 & CT11 ...... 29 B1
Newington Sta. ME9 .... 35 B6
Newington Wlk. ME14 ...... 75 D6
Newland Green La. TN27 ... 135 D8
Newland Rd. ME12 .... 2 F7
Newlands. Ashford TN23 ...... 155 D6
Newlands. St Mary's Bay TN29 .. 194 F3
Newlands. Whitfield CT16 ...... 149 B6
Newlands Ave. ME10 .... 36 B5
Newlands Cty Prim Sch. CT11 . 29 E1
Newlands Dr. CT11 .... 134 B8
Newlands Farm Cotts. ME13 . 104 C4
Newlands Rd. ME15 .... 29 E2
Newlands Rd. CT11 .... 29 E2
Newlands Rd. Charing TN27 ... 119 F5
Newlands Rd.
Ramsgate CT11 & CT12 ...... 29 D1
Newlyn Ct. 1 ME14 .... 75 A4
Newlyn's Meadow. CT15 ...... 147 A8
Newman Dr. ME10 .... 37 A8
Newman Rd. ME14 .... 112 E5
Newnham Cl. ME8 .... 11 C3
Newnham La. ME13 & ME9 ... 81 D7
Newport Ct. CT1 .... 88 B6

Newton Cl. Chatham ME5 .... 32 C2
Newton Cl. **1** Maidstone ME16 .. 74 E3
Newton Rd. Faversham ME13 ...... 62 D7
Newton Rd. Whitstable CT5 .... 21 B2
Newtown Rd. Ashford TN23 ...... 156 C8
Newtown Rd.
   Ashford TN23 & TN24 .... 156 D7
Nicholas Cl. ME16 .... 74 A3
Nicholas Dr. CT12 .... 51 D5
Nicholas Rd. TN24 .... 139 B6
Nicholls Ave. CT10 .... 29 F2
Nicklaus Dr. ME5 .... 31 F3
Nickle Cotts. CT4 .... 86 A3
Nickleby Cl. ME1 .... 9 C2
Nickley Wood Rd. TN26 .... 170 C6
Nightingale Ave. Hythe CT21 .... 187 D8
Nightingale Ave.
   Whitstable CT5 .... 43 B6
Nightingale Cl. Chartham CT4 .... 86 C6
Nightingale Cl. Gillingham ME8 .. 33 E6
Nightingale Cl. Sevington TN24 157 B7
Nightingale La. CT13 .... 113 C2
Nightingale Rd. Dover CT16 .... 149 C2
Nightingale Rd.
   Faversham ME13 .... 62 C7
Nile Rd. ME7 .... 10 C4
Nine Acres. TN24 .... 139 C5
Nine Ash La. ME13 .... 63 D3
Ninn La. TN23 & TN26 .... 138 B2
Nixon Ave. CT12 .... 29 C1
No Name St. **3** CT13 .... 73 A1
Noah's Ark Rd. CT17 .... 166 A8
Noah's Ark Terr. CT17 .... 166 B8
Noakes Meadow. TN23 .... 156 A8
Nobel Cl. ME9 .... 38 C2
Nobel Ct. ME13 .... 62 C7
Noble Cl. CT9 .... 28 A8
Noble Gdns. CT9 .... 28 A8
Nonington
   CE Prim Sch. CT15 .... 113 C5
Nonsuch Cl. CT1 .... 88 C8
Nore Cl. ME7 .... 10 E1
Noreen Ave. ME12 .... 4 A6
Norfolk Cl. Chatham ME5 .... 32 C3
Norfolk Cl. Gillingham ME8 ...... 11 D2
Norfolk Dr. TN23 .... 139 A2
Norfolk Rd. Canterbury CT1 ...... 87 E6
Norfolk Rd. Lydden CT15 .... 28 D5
Norfolk Rd. Maidstone ME15 .... 97 C8
Norfolk Rd. Margate CT9 .... 8 B3
Norfolk Sq. CT12 .... 29 B2
Norfolk St. CT5 .... 43 D8
Norman Cl. Gillingham ME8 ...... 33 B5
Norman Cl. Maidstone ME14 ...... 75 B6
Norman Rd. Ashford TN23 ...... 156 B7
Norman Rd. Broadstairs CT10 .... 29 F6
Norman Rd. Canterbury CT1 ...... 88 A7
Norman Rd. Faversham ME13 .... 62 C7
Norman Rd. Ramsgate CT11 ...... 52 B6
Norman Rd.
   St Margaret's at Cliffe CT15 .. 151 B6
Norman Rd. Warden ME12 .... 6 A6
Norman Rd.
   Westgate-on-S CT8 & CT9 ...... 7 D1
Norman Rd. Whitstable CT5 ...... 43 E8
Norman St. **8** CT16 & CT17 .. 166 B4
Norreys Rd. ME8 .... 33 E7
Norrie Rd. CT7 .... 27 A6
Norrington Mead. **3** CT19 .... 178 A7
Norrington Rd. ME15 .... 97 B6
North Ave. CT11 .... 52 D6
North Barrack Rd. CT14 .... 117 D4
North Borough
   Cty Jun Sch. ME14 .... 75 A6
North Camber Way. CT16 .... 150 B1
North Cl. CT20 .... 177 D4
North Close Bsns Ctr. CT20 .. 177 D4
North Court Cl. CT3 .... 91 A8
North Court La. CT14 .... 115 A4
North Court Rd. CT3 .... 91 A8
North Cres. ME17 .... 96 D4
North Ct. Deal CT14 .... 117 C7
North Ct. Ramsgate CT12 .... 29 B2
North Dane Way. ME5 .... 32 C4
North Downs Cl. CT4 .... 85 C2
North Eastling Rd. ME13 & ME9 81 F8
North Exit Rd. CT16 .... 166 H8
North Foreland Ave. CT10 .... 30 B7
North Foreland Golf Course.
   CT10 .... 30 A8
North Foreland Hill. CT10 .... 30 B8
North Foreland Rd. CT10 .... 30 B7
North Holmes Rd. CT1 .... 88 B8
North La. Boughton Street ME13 .. 84 F8
North La. Canterbury CT2 .... 66 F1
North La. Faversham ME13 .... 62 C8
North La. **7** Folkestone CT20 .. 177 E3
North Lea. CT14 .... 117 C7
North Lockside Rd. ME4 .... 10 D8
North Lyminge La. CT18 .... 161 C7
North Military Rd. CT17 .... 166 C7
North Pasley Rd. ME4 .... 10 B7
North Pends. TN24 .... 139 E5
North Pondside Rd. ME4 .... 10 A8
North Rd. Dover CT17 .... 166 C8
North Rd. Folkestone CT20 ...... 177 D4
North Rd. Gillingham ME4 & ME7 .. 10 B7
North Rd. Hythe CT21 .... 176 B2
North Rd. Kingsdown CT14 ...... 134 D6
North Rd. Queenborough ME11 .... 2 F5
North Rd. Richborough CT13 .... 51 A1
North Rd. Sandwich CT13 .... 95 A7
North Rd W. CT21 .... 176 A3
North Return Rd. CT16 .... 166 G8

North Sch The. TN24 .... 139 D1
North Side Three Rd. ME4 .... 10 C8
North St. Ashford TN23 .... 139 C2
North St. Ashford TN24 .... 139 C3
North St. Deal CT14 .... 117 D7
North St. Dover CT17 .... 166 B7
North St. Folkestone CT19 ...... 178 E5
North St. Herne Bay CT6 .... 23 A5
North St. New Romney TN28 .... 200 A6
North St. Rochester ME2 .... 9 B7
North St. Sittingbourne ME10 .... 36 F7
North St. Sutton Valence ME17 .. 98 E1
North View. Hersden CT3 .... 46 F1
North View. Maidstone ME15 .... 75 B1
North View Cotts. ME15 .... 96 C7
North Way. Finglesham CT14 .. 116 A7
North Way. Maidstone ME14 .... 75 B7
Northbourne
   CE Prim Sch. CT14 .... 115 F5
Northbourne Court Gdns.
   CT14 .... 116 B5
Northbourne Park Sch
   (Annexe). CT14 .... 115 D6
Northbourne Park Sch
   (Prep). CT14 .... 115 C6
Northbourne Rd.
   East Studdal CT14 & CT15 .... 115 E1
Northbourne Rd.
   Gillingham ME8 .... 11 B4
Northbourne Rd.
   Great Mongeham CT14 .... 116 C4
Northbrooke Way. CT9 .... 8 E2
Northbrooke. TN24 .... 139 C3
Northbrooke La. TN24 .... 139 C3
Northcliffe Gdns. CT10 .... 30 A7
Northcote Rd. Deal CT14 .... 117 D5
Northcote Rd. Kingsdown CT14 134 D4
Northcote Rd. Rochester ME2 ...... 9 A7
Northdown. Ashford TN24 .... 139 C4
Northdown. Doddington ME9 .... 80 F7
Northdown. Stockbury ME9 .... 56 D8
Northdown Ave. CT9 .... 8 B2
Northdown Cl.
   East Studdal CT15 .... 132 B6
Northdown Cl. Maidstone ME14 .. 75 B7
Northdown Cty Prim Sch. CT9 .. 8 C1
Northdown Hill. CT10 & CT9 ...... 29 C7
Northdown Park Rd. CT9 .... 8 C1
Northdown Rd. Broadstairs CT10 29 E6
Northdown Rd. Margate CT9 ...... 8 B2
Northdown View. ME17 .... 100 F6
Northdown Way. CT9 .... 8 C1
Northern By-Pass. TN27 .... 120 C8
Northfleet CT14 .... 75 C8
Northgate. Canterbury CT1 .... 67 A1
Northgate. Rochester ME1 .... 9 C6
Northleigh Cl. ME15 .... 97 A6
Northpoint Bsns Est. ME2 .... 9 D8
Northumberland Ave.
   Ashford TN24 .... 139 D5
Northumberland Ave.
   Gillingham ME8 .... 11 E1
Northumberland Ave.
   Margate CT9 .... 8 C2
Northumberland Ct.
   Maidstone ME15 .... 97 D7
Northumberland Ct.
   Margate CT9 .... 8 C3
Northumberland Rd. ME15 .... 97 D8
Northwall Cl. CT14 .... 117 C7
Northwall Mews. CT14 .... 117 C7
Northwall Rd. CT14 .... 117 B8
Northwood Dr. ME10 .... 36 F1
Northwood Rd. Broadstairs,
   Ramsgate CT10 & CT12 .... 29 C3
Northwood Rd. Whitstable CT5 .. 20 F2
Norton Ave. CT6 .... 46 A8
Norton Dr. CT12 .... 50 B6
Norton Gr. ME5 .... 31 E3
Norton Knatchbull Sch The.
   TN24 .... 139 E2
Norton La. TN26 .... 153 D5
Norton Rd. Five Wents ME17 .... 98 D1
Norton Rd. Lynsted ME13 & ME9 . 60 E5
Norview Rd. CT5 .... 43 B7
Norway Dro. CT15 .... 151 A8
Norway Terr. **4** ME14 .... 75 A7
Norwood Gdns. TN23 .... 139 B2
Norwood La. TN29 .... 193 E7
Norwood Rise. ME12 .... 4 C7
Norwood St. TN23 .... 139 B2
Norwood Wlk E. ME10 .... 36 C5
Norwood Wlk W. ME10 .... 36 B5
Notley St. CT1 .... 67 A1
Notley Terr. **3** CT1 .... 67 A1
Nottingham Ave. ME15 .... 97 D7
Nottingham Rd. CT7 .... 26 F5
Nouds Rd. ME9 .... 60 D7
Nunnery Fields. CT1 .... 88 A7
Nunnery Fields Hospl. CT1 ...... 88 A6
Nunnery Rd. CT1 .... 87 F7
Nursery Ave. Maidstone ME16 .. 74 B6
Nursery Ave.
   Maidstone,Bearsted ME14 ...... 76 B3
Nursery Cl. Densole CT18 .... 163 A7
Nursery Cl. Ramsgate CT11 ...... 52 C7
Nursery Cl. Sheerness ME12 ...... 1 E1
Nursery Cl. Whitstable CT5 .... 21 A1
Nursery Fields. Acol CT7 .... 27 B3
Nursery Fields. Hythe CT21 .... 176 A2
Nursery La. Densole CT18 .... 163 A7
Nursery La. Sheldwich ME13 .... 83 B6
Nursery La. Whitfield CT16 ...... 148 F7
Nursery Rd. ME8 .... 33 D8
Nursery Wlk. CT6 .... 22 F3
Nurserylands. CT6 .... 22 F3
Nutberry Cl. ME9 .... 38 D2

Nutfield Cl. ME5 .... 32 B8
Nutfields. ME10 .... 37 B3
Nutley Cl. TN24 .... 139 C3
Nutts Ave. ME12 .... 6 G2
Nutwood Cl. ME14 .... 75 A4

Oak Ave. Eythorne CT15 .... 131 D5
Oak Ave. Gillingham ME7 .... 10 E6
Oak Ave. Minster ME12 .... 4 F6
Oak Bglws. TN29 .... 203 C6
Oak Caer. TN25 .... 172 F4
Oak Cotts. East Studdal CT15 .... 132 E8
Oak Cotts. Selindge TN25 ...... 174 D7
Oak Cotts. Selling ME13 .... 84 D4
Oak Dr. Boughton Street ME13 .. 64 A3
Oak Dr. Hawkinge CT18 .... 163 B5
Oak Dr. St Mary's Bay TN29 .... 194 F3
Oak Gr. CT5 .... 114 B2
Oak Hall Pass. CT21 .... 176 C2
Oak Hill. CT13 .... 93 B6
Oak Ho. **6** ME5 .... 31 F4
Oak La. Lydd TN29 .... 203 B6
Oak La. Minster ME12 .... 4 F7
Oak La. Upchurch ME9 .... 12 D2
Oak Lodge Rd. TN28 .... 200 B7
Oak Rd. ME10 .... 37 C5
Oak Ridge. TN25 .... 183 F8
Oak St. CT14 .... 117 D6
Oak Tree Ave. ME15 .... 97 C7
Oak Tree Cty Prim Sch. TN25 155 F8
Oak Tree Gr. CT9 .... 28 A8
Oak Tree Rd. TN25 .... 155 F8
Oak Trees Cty Prim Sch. ME15 97 C7
Oak Wlk. TN25 .... 176 C2
Oakapple La. ME16 .... 74 A3
Oakdale Rd. CT6 .... 23 A4
Oakdene Rd. CT12 .... 29 C1
Oakenpole. TN23 .... 138 E1
Oakfield Cl. CT12 .... 52 B8
Oakfield Rd. TN24 .... 139 D5
Oakfields. ME10 .... 36 C3
Oakhurst Cl. ME5 .... 31 F3
Oakland Cl. ME5 .... 31 F3
Oakland Ct. CT6 .... 22 E5
Oaklands. Ashford TN23 .... 138 F1
Oaklands. Mersham TN25 .... 157 E4
Oaklands Ave. CT10 .... 29 E5
Oaklands Cty Prim Sch. ME5 .. 31 F4
Oaklands Way. CT2 .... 68 B7
Oakleigh Cl. ME5 .... 31 E2
Oakleigh Ho. TN23 .... 155 E8
Oakleigh La. CT4 .... 89 B5
Oakleys The. CT15 .... 130 D5
Oakridge. CT10 .... 8 G1
Oaks Ave. CT6 .... 22 D2
Oaks Bsns Village The. ME5 .... 32 C1
Oaks Cty Inf Sch The. ME10 .... 36 D2
Oaks Dene. ME5 .... 31 F1
Oaks Pk. CT2 .... 66 B3
Oaks Rd. Folkestone CT20 ...... 177 D6
Oaks Rd. Tenterden TN30 .... 179 B8
Oaks The. Broadstairs CT10 ...... 29 F7
Oaks The. Hersden CT3 .... 46 F1
Oaks The.
   St Nicholas at Wade CT7 .... 25 F2
Oaks View. CT21 .... 187 C8
Oakside Rd. CT3 .... 112 E5
Oaktree Ho. ME10 .... 37 B3
Oakum Ct. ME4 .... 10 B2
Oakvale Cl. CT17 .... 166 B7
Oakwood Cl. ME16 .... 74 D3
Oakwood Dr. CT5 .... 21 A1
Oakwood Hospl. ME16 .... 74 B3
Oakwood Park Gram Sch.
   ME16 .... 74 C3
Oakwood Rd. Maidstone ME16 .. 74 D3
Oakwood Rd. Sturry CT2 .... 68 A7
Oare Rd. ME13 .... 40 C1
Oast Cotts. Dargate ME13 .... 64 D8
Oast Cotts. Sheldwich ME13 .... 83 C8
Oast Ct. Margate CT9 .... 28 F8
Oast Ct. Sittingbourne ME10 .... 36 E2
Oast Ho. CT4 .... 85 C2
Oast La. ME13 .... 104 E6
Oast Meadow. TN24 .... 139 F1
Oast Paddock The. CT3 .... 92 A4
Oast The. Canterbury CT1 .... 88 B6
Oast The. Staple CT3 .... 92 A6
Oasthouse Field. TN29 .... 192 F4
Oasts The. ME14 .... 76 C4
Oastview. ME8 .... 34 A8
Oaten Hill. CT1 .... 88 A7
Oaten Hill Pl. CT1 .... 88 A7
Occupation Rd. TN25 .... 123 F2
Ocean Cl. CT7 .... 27 B8
Ocean View. Broadstairs CT10 .. 30 A1
Ocean View. Herne Bay CT6 ...... 23 F6
Octavia Cl. ME5 .... 32 B3
Octavian Dr. CT21 .... 175 A3
Odiham Dr. ME16 .... 74 C7
Odo Rd. CT17 .... 166 C8
Officers' Rd. ME4 .... 10 B8
Offley Cl. CT9 .... 8 C1
Ogilvy Cl. CT10 .... 29 E7
Okehampton Cl. TN24 .... 139 F7
Olantigh Ct. CT7 .... 27 A7
Olantigh Rd. TN25 .... 123 F3
Olave Rd. CT9 .... 8 B1
Old Ash La. TN24 .... 139 C5
Old Ashford Rd. Charing TN27 . 120 C7
Old Ashford Rd. Lenham ME17 . 101 E5
Old Badgins Rd. ME13 .... 83 B6
Old Bakery Cl. TN29 .... 194 F4
Old Bakery The. ME12 .... 3 F5
Old Barn Cl. ME7 .... 32 F6
Old Billet La. ME12 .... 5 C6
Old Boundary Rd. CT9 .... 7 D1
Old Bridge Rd. CT5 .... 20 E1

Old Carriageway The. ME7 .... 32 F4
Old Castle Wlk. ME8 .... 33 D4
Old Charlton Rd. CT16 .... 149 D2
Old Chatham Rd.
   Kit's Coty ME20 .... 53 D6
Old Chatham Rd.
   Maidstone ME14 .... 53 F1
Old Court Hill. CT15 .... 113 C6
Old Crossing Rd. **1** CT9 .... 28 B8
Old Dairy Cl. **3** CT11 .... 52 F7
Old Dover Rd. Barham CT4 ...... 112 B1
Old Dover Rd. Canterbury CT1 .. 88 B6
Old Dover Rd. Capel-le-F CT18 . 164 C1
Old Dr. ME15 .... 96 F6
Old Dungeness Lighthouse.
   TN29 .... 205 F6
Old Farm Cl. CT5 .... 43 C6
Old Farm Rd. CT7 .... 26 D7
Old Ferry Rd. ME9 .... 14 E2
Old Fold. CT15 .... 44 C8
Old Folkestone Rd. CT17 .... 166 A4
Old Forge La. ME9 .... 56 F3
Old Gate Rd. ME13 .... 62 B8
Old Green Rd. Broadstairs CT10 29 F7
Old Green Rd. Margate CT9 .... 8 C1
Old Hall Dr. CT12 .... 51 C5
Old Ham La. ME17 .... 101 A4
Old High St The. CT20 .... 178 E5
Old Hockley Rd. ME13 .... 82 C2
Old Hook Rd. ME12 .... 4 F2
Old House Rd. ME9 .... 34 E4
Old Kingsdown Cl. CT10 .... 29 E3
Old Lain. ME17 .... 100 F6
Old London Rd. CT21 .... 175 F2
Old Loose Hill. ME15 .... 96 F4
Old Mead. CT19 .... 178 A7
Old Mill La. ME20 .... 53 C3
Old Mill Rd. ME17 .... 76 F1
Old Oast Bsns Ctr The. ME20 .. 53 A1
Old Orch. TN23 .... 155 D8
Old Orch The. ME8 .... 34 A8
Old Park Ave. CT1 .... 67 C2
Old Park Cl. CT16 .... 149 A4
Old Park Cl. CT1 .... 67 C2
Old Park Hill. CT16 .... 149 B4
Old Park Rd. CT16 .... 149 B2
Old Park Way. CT16 .... 149 A3
Old Pattens La. ME1 .... 9 D2
Old Pond Rd. TN23 .... 155 F8
Old Railway Works
   (Ind Est). TN24 .... 156 D8
Old Rd. Chatham ME4 .... 9 F4
Old Rd. Elham CT4 .... 144 F4
Old Rectory Cl. CT18 .... 163 B4
Old Rectory The. TN25 .... 122 E2
Old Roman Rd. CT15 .... 133 C1
Old Ruttington La. CT1 .... 67 A1
Old Saltwood La. CT21 .... 176 B4
Old Saw Mill The. TN26 .... 153 E6
Old School Cl. ME17 .... 101 D4
Old School Ct. Egerton TN27 .... 118 F3
Old School Ct. Folkestone CT20 178 B4
Old School Gdns. CT3 .... 8 A1
Old School Mews. CT4 .... 86 C2
Old School The. TN24 .... 156 D8
Old Surrenden Manor Rd.
   TN26 .... 154 C5
Old Tovil Rd. ME15 .... 75 A2
Old Trafford Cl. ME16 .... 74 B6
Old Tree La. ME17 .... 97 D3
Old Tree Rd. CT3 .... 47 B7
Old Valley Rd. CT4 .... 128 F7
Old Vicarage The. CT13 .... 93 C7
Old Way. TN26 .... 190 D7
Oldborough Manor Com Coll.
   ME15 .... 97 B6
Oldchurch Ct. **3** ME16 .... 74 E3
Oldfield Cl. Gillingham ME8 ...... 33 D8
Oldfield Cl. Maidstone ME15 .... 75 E1
Oldhawe Hill. CT3 & CT6 .... 46 D7
Oldhouse La. TN29 .... 191 E1
Oldstairs Rd. CT14 .... 134 D4
Oliver Cl. ME4 .... 10 B2
Oliver Twist Cl. ME1 .... 9 B4
Olivers Cotts. ME14 .... 76 C4
Olivine Cl. ME5 .... 54 A8
Olliffe Cl. ME5 .... 31 F2
Omer Ave. CT9 .... 8 C2
Onslow Rd. ME1 .... 9 D3
Ontario Way. CT16 .... 149 B3
Opal Gn. ME5 .... 32 B2
Orache Dr. ME4 .... 75 E5
Orange St. CT1 .... 87 F8
Orange Terr. ME1 .... 9 D5
Orbit Ct. ME5 .... 54 A8
Orchard Ave. CT14 .... 117 B5
Orchard Bank. ME17 .... 98 B1
Orchard Bsns Ctr. ME16 .... 74 C8
Orchard Cl. Canterbury CT2 ...... 66 F4
Orchard Cl. Coxheath ME17 ...... 96 C3
Orchard Cl. Langley Heath ME17 . 98 E4
Orchard Cl. Littlebourne CT3 .... 89 F7
Orchard Cl. Mersham TN25 .... 157 E3
Orchard Cl. Minster,Thanet CT12 50 B7
Orchard Cl. Ramsgate CT12 ...... 29 B3
Orchard Cl. Whitfield CT16 .... 148 F8
Orchard Cl. Whitstable CT5 ...... 20 F3
Orchard Cl. Wingham CT3 .... 91 A7
Orchard Cotts. ME16 .... 96 A4
Orchard Ct. Chillenden CT3 .... 113 F4
Orchard Ct. Herne Bay CT6 ...... 22 F1
Orchard Dr. Ashford TN23 ...... 138 F4
Orchard Dr.
   Littlestone-on-S TN28 .... 200 E6
Orchard Dr. Newington ME9 .... 35 A5
Orchard Dr. River CT17 .... 148 E3
Orchard Dr. Wye TN25 .... 123 F1
Orchard Field. TN26 .... 153 D4

Orchard Fields. CT21 .... 160 E2
Orchard Flats. CT1 .... 88 D7
Orchard Gdns. CT9 .... 28 A8
Orchard Gr. ME12 .... 4 C6
Orchard Hts. TN23 .... 138 F5
Orchard Ind Est. ME15 .... 97 F3
Orchard La. Ashford TN24 ...... 139 F6
Orchard La. Challock TN25 ...... 105 B2
Orchard Mews. CT14 .... 117 D5
Orchard Pk. CT6 .... 23 D4
Orchard Pl. Faversham ME13 .... 62 D7
Orchard Pl. **2** Maidstone ME16 . 74 E3
Orchard Pl. Sittingbourne ME10 . 37 A3
Orchard Rd. Eastry CT13 .... 93 B3
Orchard Rd. Herne Bay CT6 ...... 22 F3
Orchard Rd. Maidstone ME15 .... 75 E4
Orchard Rd. Margate CT9 .... 28 A8
Orchard Rd.
   St Mary's Bay TN29 .... 195 A5
Orchard Rd. St Michaels TN30 . 167 A3
Orchard Residences The. CT1 . 88 A5
Orchard Row. CT6 .... 23 A1
Orchard Sch. CT1 .... 87 F6
Orchard St. Canterbury CT2 ...... 66 E1
Orchard St. Gillingham ME8 ...... 33 E8
Orchard St. Maidstone ME15 .... 75 A3
Orchard The. ME14 .... 76 B4
Orchard Valley. CT21 .... 176 A2
Orchard View. Ash CT3 .... 71 F1
Orchard View.
   Tenterden TN30 .... 179 C8
Orchard View. Teynham ME9 .... 38 C3
Orchard Villas. CT16 .... 148 E4
Orchard Way. ME12 .... 5 D1
Orchard Way. CT4 .... 144 F4
Ordnance St. ME4 .... 9 E3
Ordnance Terr. ME4 .... 9 E4
Orgarswick Ave. TN29 .... 195 C7
Orgarswick Way. TN29 .... 195 C7
Oriel Rd. TN23 .... 138 F4
Orient Pl. CT2 .... 66 F1
Orion Rd. ME1 .... 31 C7
Orion Way. TN24 .... 156 E8
Ormonde Ct. CT21 .... 176 C1
Ormonde Rd. **10**
   Folkestone CT20 .... 178 E6
Ormonde Rd. Hythe CT21 ...... 176 C1
Ormsby Gn. ME8 .... 33 E3
Orwell Ho. **6** ME15 .... 97 E8
Osborne Gdns. CT6 .... 23 D4
Osborne Rd. Ashford TN24 .... 156 F8
Osborne Rd. Gillingham ME7 .... 10 C5
Osborne Rd. Kingsdown CT14 . 134 C6
Osborne Terr. 7 J1
Osbourn Ave. CT8 .... 27 E8
Osbourne Rd. CT10 .... 29 F4
Oscar Rd. CT10 .... 30 B4
Osier Field. TN24 .... 139 E7
Osier Rd. ME9 .... 38 E3
Osprey Ave. ME5 & ME7 .... 10 E2
Osprey Cl. CT5 .... 43 C7
Osprey Ct. **2** Dover CT16 ...... 149 B4
Osprey Ct. Sittingbourne ME10 . 37 A3
Ospringe CE Prim Sch. ME13 .. 62 A6
Ospringe Rd. ME13 .... 62 B6
Ospringe St. ME13 .... 62 B7
Ostend Ct. ME10 .... 14 F1
Ostlers La. CT17 .... 48 D6
Oswald Pl. CT17 .... 149 B2
Oswald Rd. CT17 .... 149 B2
Otham Cl. CT2 .... 67 A4
Otham La. ME15 .... 76 C2
Otham St. Maidstone ME15 ...... 76 C2
Otham St. Otham ME15 .... 98 B7
Ottawa Cres. CT16 .... 149 C3
Ottawa Way. CT16 .... 149 B3
Otterbourne Pl. ME15 .... 75 E1
Otterden Cl. TN23 .... 155 F6
Otterden Rd. ME13 .... 81 D3
Otterham Quay La. ME8 .... 12 B2
Otteridge Rd. ME14 .... 76 A3
Otterpool La. CT21 & TN25 .... 174 D4
Otway Cl. ME4 .... 10 A3
Otway Terr. **1** ME4 .... 10 A3
Out Elmstead La. CT4 .... 111 F2
Oval The. TN29 .... 186 D1
Overland La. CT3 .... 71 A3
Owen Sq. CT14 .... 117 B2
Owen's Cl. CT21 .... 177 B3
Owens Court Cotts. ME13 .... 83 F8
Owens Way. ME7 .... 11 A6
Owl's Hatch Rd. CT6 .... 22 C1
Ox La. TN30 .... 167 B2
Oxen Lease. TN23 .... 155 E8
Oxenden Cnr. CT3 .... 23 F1
Oxenden Cres. CT3 .... 91 A8
Oxenden Park Dr. CT6 .... 22 E4
Oxenden Rd. CT20 .... 177 E4
Oxenden St. CT6 .... 22 E5
Oxenden Way. CT4 .... 128 F8
Oxenturn Rd. TN25 .... 140 E8
Oxford Ct. CT1 .... 87 F7
Oxford Rd. Canterbury CT1 ...... 87 F7
Oxford Rd. Gillingham ME7 ...... 10 D3
Oxford Rd. Maidstone ME15 .... 97 D8
Oxford St. **6** Margate CT9 .... 7 J1
Oxford St. Whitstable CT5 .... 20 D1
Oxford Terr. CT20 .... 178 D4
Oxney Cl. CT7 .... 26 F7
Oxney Cotts. TN30 .... 190 A4
Oyster Cl. ME10 .... 36 E6

Packer Pl. ME5 .... 32 A8
Packer's La. CT1 .... 52 E7
Pad's Hill. ME15 .... 75 A4
Padbrook La. CT3 .... 70 D6
Paddock Cl. Deal CT14 .... 116 F5

Paddock Cl. Folkestone CT20 ..... 177 F5
Paddock Cl. Lydd TN29 .... 203 B6
Paddock Cl. Ashford TN23 .... 155 E7
Paddock Rd. Birchington CT7 .... 27 A7
Paddock The. Chatham ME4 .... 9 F4
Paddock The. Chilham CT4 .... 85 C2
Paddock The. Dover CT16 .... 166 B8
Paddock View. CT5 .... 43 E7
Paddocks The.
  Broadstairs CT10 .... 29 F7
Paddocks The. Gillingham ME7 ..... 33 A5
Paddocks The.
  Great Chart TN23 .... 138 C1
Paddocks The. Herne Bay CT6 ..... 23 F5
Padsole La. ME15 .... 75 A4
Padstow Manor. ME7 .... 10 C6
Padwell La. TN23 .... 155 C8
Paffard Cl. CT2 .... 67 F6
Paffard Ct. CT2 .... 67 F6
Page Pl. CT19 .... 178 D8
Paget Row. ME7 .... 10 C5
Paget St. ME7 .... 10 C5
Pagitt St. ME4 .... 9 E3
Paine Ave. TN29 .... 203 C6
Painesfield Cl. TN29 .... 186 C4
Painter's Forstal Rd. ME13 .... 61 D3
Palace Ave. ME15 .... 75 A4
Palace Cl. CT5 .... 21 B2
Palace Cotts. ME9 .... 80 F8
Palace Ct. Chatham ME5 .... 10 D2
Palace Ct. Hythe CT21 .... 176 C2
Palace Ind Est. ME15 .... 97 F4
Palace St. 17 CT1 .... 67 A1
Palace Wood
  Cty Inf Sch. ME16 .... 74 C6
Palace Wood
  Cty Jun Sch. ME16 .... 74 C6
Palm Bay Ave. CT9 .... 8 D3
Palm Bay Cty Prim Sch. CT9 ...... 8 D3
Palm Bay Gdns. CT9 .... 8 C3
Palm Tree Cl. CT15 .... 131 D7
Palm Tree Way. CT18 .... 161 B7
Palmar Rd. ME16 .... 74 D6
Palmarsh Ave. CT21 .... 187 D7
Palmarsh Cres. CT21 .... 187 D7
Palmarsh
  Cty Prim Sch. CT21 .... 187 D8
Palmbeach Ave. CT21 .... 187 D8
Palmer Cl. CT6 .... 46 B8
Palmer Cres. CT9 .... 29 C8
Palmer Rd. CT3 .... 91 A8
Palmers Cross Hill. CT2 .... 66 A1
Palmerston Ave.
  Broadstairs CT10 .... 30 B3
Palmerston Ave. Deal CT14 .... 117 C2
Palmerston Ct. CT12 .... 117 D2
Palmerston Rd. ME4 .... 9 F1
Palmerston St. 4 CT19 .... 178 D6
Palmerston Wlk. ME10 .... 37 C4
Palting Way. CT20 .... 178 B4
Pantemy La. ME9 .... 37 E2
Panton Cl. ME5 .... 32 C4
Papion Gr. ME5 .... 31 E2
Papworth Pl. 1 CT19 .... 178 A7
Parade. CT1 .... 87 F8
Parade Rd. CT20 .... 177 F3
Parade The. Birchington CT7 ..... 26 D8
Parade The. Folkestone CT20 ... 178 E5
Parade The.
  Greatstone-on-S TN28 & TN29 .. 204 E7
Parade The. Margate CT9 .... 7 I3
Parade The. Sevington TN24 .... 156 F5
Paradise. CT11 .... 52 D7
Paradise Cotts. ME9 .... 34 E5
Paradise Row. CT13 .... 72 F1
Paragon. CT11 .... 52 E5
Paragon St. CT11 .... 52 D5
Paraker Way. CT21 .... 177 B4
Pardoner Cl. CT2 .... 87 C7
Pardoners Way. CT16 .... 149 A3
Parfitt Way. CT16 .... 149 B2
Parham Cl. CT1 .... 67 B2
Parham Rd. Canterbury CT1 ...... 67 B2
Parham Rd. Chatham ME4 .... 9 F2
Paris Cnr. TN26 .... 153 F6
Parish Rd. Chartham CT4 .... 86 C3
Parish Rd. Minster ME12 .... 4 A5
Park Ave. Birchington CT7 .... 27 A6
Park Ave. Broadstairs CT10 .... 29 E2
Park Ave. Deal CT14 .... 117 C5
Park Ave. Dover CT16 .... 149 D1
Park Ave. Gillingham ME7 .... 10 D3
Park Ave. Leysdown-on-S ME12 ... 6 G1
Park Ave. Loose ME17 .... 96 E2
Park Ave. Maidstone ME14 .... 75 B6
Park Ave. Queenborough ME11 .... 3 B4
Park Ave. Sittingbourne ME10 .... 36 E1
Park Ave. Whitstable CT5 .... 20 F3
Park Barn Rd. ME17 .... 99 C5
Park Chase. CT10 .... 29 E2
Park Cl. CT9 .... 8 D1
Park Cotts. CT11 .... 29 E2
Park Cres. ME4 .... 31 F8
Park Crescent Rd. CT9 .... 8 A1
Park Ct. ME13 .... 62 E7
Park Dr. Hothfield TN26 .... 138 A6
Park Dr. Sittingbourne ME10 .... 36 D1
Park Farm Cl.
  Shadoxhurst TN23 .... 155 A1
Park Farm Cl. Tyler Hill CT2 ..... 66 E6
Park Farm Prim Sch. CT19 ...... 178 C6
Park Farm Rd. CT19 .... 178 C7
Park Gate. CT10 .... 29 F2
Park Ho. ME14 .... 75 B6
Park La. Bethersden TN26 ...... 154 C8
Park La. Birchington CT7 .... 27 A6
Park La. Bishopsbourne CT4 ..... 111 C5

Park La. Cock Street ME17 .... 97 D2
Park La. Elham CT4 .... 144 F5
Park La. Maidstone ME14 .... 74 F7
Park La. Margate CT9 .... 8 A2
Park Lea. CT14 .... 117 C5
Park Mall. 2 TN23 .... 139 B2
Park Manor. ME7 .... 10 B5
Park Mews. 6 CT16 .... 166 D8
Park Pl. Ashford TN24 .... 156 F8
Park Pl.
  Ashford, Willesborough TN23 ... 156 B7
Park Pl. Dover CT16 .... 166 D8
Park Pl. Herne CT6 .... 46 A8
Park Pl. Margate CT9 .... 7 I1
Park Rd. Ashford TN24 .... 139 D6
Park Rd. Broadstairs CT10 .... 30 B6
Park Rd. Dover CT16 .... 149 B2
Park Rd. Faversham ME13 .... 62 D7
Park Rd.
  Folkestone CT19 & CT20 ...... 177 E6
Park Rd. Herne Bay CT6 .... 22 F4
Park Rd. Hythe CT21 .... 176 B1
Park Rd. Littlestone-on-S TN28 .. 200 E5
Park Rd. Margate CT9 .... 8 A2
Park Rd. Preston CT3 .... 70 D7
Park Rd. Queenborough ME11 ..... 2 F5
Park Rd. Ramsgate CT11 .... 52 C7
Park Rd. Sheerness ME12 .... 1 E1
Park Rd. Sittingbourne ME10 .... 36 E3
Park Rd. Temple Ewell CT16 .... 148 D5
Park Rd.
  Westgate-on-S CT7 & CT8 & CT9 .. 27 C6
Park Rd N. TN24 .... 139 B3
Park St. Ashford TN23 & TN24 .. 139 C2
Park St. Deal CT14 .... 117 D6
Park St. Dover CT16 .... 166 D8
Park St. Lydd TN29 .... 203 C6
Park Terr.
  Woodnesborough CT13 .... 93 D7
Park Vale. TN24 .... 139 D6
Park View. Folkestone CT19 .... 178 E7
Park View. Sturry CT2 .... 67 F6
Park View Cl. CT3 .... 91 D2
Park View Ct. ME15 .... 75 E1
Park View Rise. CT15 .... 113 D4
Park Way. Coxheath ME17 .... 96 D3
Park Way. Maidstone ME15 .... 75 B1
Park Way
  Cty Prim Sch. ME15 .... 75 B1
Park Wood Cl. TN23 .... 156 B5
Park Wood
  Cty Prim Schs. ME8 .... 33 E5
Park Wood Gn. ME8 .... 33 D5
Park Wood Par. ME15 .... 97 F5
Park Wood Trad Est. ME15 ...... 97 F4
Parker Cl. Folkestone CT19 .... 178 C6
Parker Cl. Hamstreet TN26 ..... 183 A7
Parkfield Rd. Folkestone CT19 .. 178 C6
Parkfield Rd. Gillingham ME8 .... 11 F1
Parkland Ct. CT10 .... 29 F6
Parkside Cty Prim Sch. CT1 .... 67 D2
Parkway The. CT7 .... 27 B7
Parkwood Cl. CT10 .... 29 F2
Parr Ave. ME7 .... 10 D6
Parrs Head Mews. ME1 .... 9 C6
Parsonage Chase. ME12 .... 3 F5
Parsonage Cotts. ME9 .... 58 A5
Parsonage Farm
  (Rural Heritage Ctr) CT4 .... 145 A6
Parsonage Fields. CT12 .... 49 C7
Parsonage La. Bobbing ME9 ..... 14 A1
Parsonage La. Rochester ME2 .... 9 C8
Parsonage Rd. CT6 .... 23 A3
Parsonage Stocks Rd. ME13 ..... 82 F5
Parsonage Villas. CT15 .... 165 C5
Partridge La. ME13 .... 62 D7
Pasley Rd. ME7 .... 10 A7
Pasley Rd E. ME7 .... 10 B7
Pasley Rd W. ME4 .... 10 A7
Pasture The. TN24 .... 139 D6
Patchways. TN24 .... 184 E3
Path Field Cotts. CT15 .... 164 E5
Patricia Way. CT10 .... 29 D3
Patrixbourne Ave. ME8 .... 11 C2
Patrixbourne Rd. CT4 .... 89 B2
Pattens Gdns. ME4 .... 9 E2
Pattens La. ME4 .... 9 E1
Pattens Pl. ME1 .... 9 D2
Paul's Pl. 8 CT16 .... 149 C1
Pavement The. TN30 .... 167 B3
Pavilion Ct. CT20 .... 178 E4
Pavilion Dr. ME10 .... 14 F1
Pavilion Meadow. CT17 .... 148 E4
Pavilion Rd. CT19 .... 178 D6
Pay St. CT18 .... 162 F7
Payden St. ME17 & ME9 .... 102 D8
Payers Pk. CT20 .... 178 D5
Payne's La. ME15 .... 97 A7
Pays La. TN25 .... 104 D1
Payton Cl. CT9 .... 29 A7
Payton Mews. 4 CT1 .... 67 B1
Peacock Mews. 7 ME16 .... 74 E4
Peacock Pl. ME13 .... 84 A6
Peafield Wood Rd. CT4 .... 127 E4
Pean Court Rd. CT5 .... 43 D3
Pean Hill. CT5 .... 43 D2
Pear Tree Alley. 2 ME10 .... 36 E5
Pear Tree Cl. CT10 .... 29 C4
Pear Tree La.
  Dymchurch TN29 .... 186 D1
Pear Tree La. Gillingham ME7 .. 32 E7
Pear Tree La. Maidstone ME15 .. 97 B6
Pear Tree Wlk. ME9 .... 35 A5
Pearmain Wlk. CT1 .... 88 C7
Pearman Ct. ME8 .... 12 A1

Pearson's Way. CT10 .... 29 E7
Peartree Cotts. ME8 .... 34 B8
Peartree Rd. CT6 .... 23 C3
Peckham Cl. ME2 .... 9 C8
Pedding Hill. CT3 .... 71 A1
Pedding La. CT3 .... 92 A8
Peel Dr. ME10 .... 37 C4
Peel St. ME14 .... 75 A6
Peene Cotts. CT18 .... 162 B1
Pegwell Ave. CT11 .... 52 A5
Pegwell Cl. CT11 .... 52 A5
Pegwell Rd. CT11 .... 52 B5
Pegwell Rd. CT11 .... 52 B5
Pelham Gdns. CT20 .... 178 A4
Pelwood Rd. TN31 .... 201 A2
Pemberton Cl. CT21 .... 177 B3
Pemberton Rd. TN24 .... 139 D2
Pemberton Sq. ME2 .... 9 C8
Pembroke. ME4 .... 10 B8
Pembroke Ave. CT9 .... 7 F1
Pembroke Ct. Chatham ME4 .... 10 A4
Pembroke Ct. 1
  Ramsgate CT11 .... 52 E7
Pembroke Gdns. ME8 .... 33 E4
Pembroke Mews. TN28 .... 200 C8
Pembroke Rd. ME7 .... 96 C3
Pembury Ct. 6 ME10 .... 36 E4
Pembury Gdns. ME16 .... 74 D3
Pembury Dr. ME10 .... 36 E4
Pembury Way. ME8 .... 11 E2
Pencester Ct. CT16 .... 166 E8
Pencester Rd. CT16 .... 166 D8
Penderel Mews. TN30 .... 179 B8
Penenden Ct. ME14 .... 75 B7
Penenden Heath Rd. ME14 ...... 75 C7
Penenden St. ME14 .... 75 A6
Penfield Cl. ME9 .... 59 A4
Penfold Cl. Chatham ME5 .... 32 B7
Penfold Cl. Park Wood ME15 .... 97 C5
Penfold Gdns. CT15 .... 130 E5
Penfold Hill. ME17 .... 99 B8
Penfold Rd. CT19 .... 178 F6
Penfold Way. ME15 .... 96 F6
Penhurst Cl. ME14 .... 75 F5
Penlee Point. TN24 .... 139 D5
Penn Cl. ME10 .... 37 B2
Penn Hill. TN23 .... 155 E6
Pennant Rd. ME1 .... 31 C7
Pennine Way. Ashford TN24 ... 139 B4
Pennine Way. Maidstone ME15 .. 76 A1
Pennington Cl. CT2 .... 68 C7
Penny Pot La. CT4 .... 108 B4
Pennypot Ind Est. CT21 .... 175 F1
Penrose Ct. CT21 .... 176 C1
Penryn Manor. ME7 .... 10 C6
Pensand Ho. CT21 .... 176 D1
Penshurst Cl. Canterbury CT2 .. 67 A3
Penshurst Cl. Gillingham ME8 .. 11 E2
Penshurst Gdns. CT9 .... 8 F2
Penshurst Rd. CT11 .... 52 F7
Penshurst Rise. ME13 .... 62 B8
Penstocks The. ME16 .... 74 D2
Pent Vale Cl. CT19 .... 178 A6
Pent Valley High Sch. CT19 .... 177 F7
Pent Valley Sch (annexe).
  CT19 .... 177 F6
Pepys Ave. ME12 .... 1 C2
Percival Terr. CT17 .... 166 B7
Percy Ave. CT10 .... 8 F2
Percy Rd. Broadstairs CT10 ...... 29 F5
Percy Rd. Margate CT9 .... 8 A3
Percy Rd. Ramsgate CT11 .... 52 D8
Peregrine Dr. ME10 .... 37 A2
Peri Ct. CT1 .... 87 E6
Perimeter Rd. CT16 .... 166 G8
Periwinkle Cl. ME10 .... 36 E5
Periwinkle Ct. 5 ME10 .... 36 E5
Perkins Ave. CT9 .... 28 F8
Perries Mead. CT9 .... 178 B7
Perry Court
  Rudolf Steiner Sch. CT4 ...... 108 E7
Perry Rd. CT3 .... 70 C3
Perry St. Chatham ME4 .... 9 E3
Perry St. Maidstone ME14 .... 74 F6
Perryfield St. ME14 .... 74 F6
Perth Gdns. ME10 .... 36 C4
Perth Way. CT16 .... 149 C3
Pested Bars Rd. ME17 .... 97 D5
Pested La. CT4 & CT5 .... 105 C4
Petchell Mews. 11 CT1 .... 67 B2
Peter St. Deal CT14 .... 117 D7
Peter St. Dover CT16 & CT17 .. 166 D8
Peter St. Folkestone CT20 ..... 178 E5
Petfield Cl. ME15 .... 97 D6
Petham Cty Prim Sch. CT4 .... 109 C3
Petham Gn. ME8 .... 11 C2
Pett Bottom Rd. CT4 .... 110 C5
Pett Hill. CT4 .... 88 F1
Pett La. TN27 .... 120 D7
Pett's Cres. CT12 .... 50 B5
Pettfield Hill Rd. ME13 .... 82 B1
Pettitts Row. ME13 .... 62 B7
Pettman Cl. CT6 .... 22 C3
Pettmans Mews. CT5 .... 20 C2
Petts La. CT3 .... 91 A8
Peverel Dr. ME14 .... 76 A5
Peverel Gn. ME8 .... 33 D4
Peverell Rd. CT16 .... 149 B4
Pheasant La. ME15 .... 97 B8
Pheasant Rd. ME4 .... 10 C2
Pheasants' Hall Rd. CT4 .... 110 F2
Philip Corby Cl. CT9 .... 8 B2
Philippa Ho. CT19 .... 178 F6
Phillip Rd. CT19 .... 177 E6
Phillipine Village Craft Ctr.
  TN29 .... 197 A6
Phillippa Ct. ME10 .... 36 E8
Phillips Ct. ME8 .... 11 B2

Phillips Rd. CT7 .... 27 A6
Phoenix Ind Est. ME2 .... 9 D7
Phoenix Pk. ME15 .... 97 F4
Phoenix Rd. ME5 .... 32 B2
Piccadilly. 4 ME4 .... 10 B3
Pickelden La. CT4 .... 107 F8
Pickering St. ME15 .... 97 B6
Pickhill Oast. TN30 .... 179 B4
Pickneybush La. TN29 .... 194 A7
Pickwick Cres. ME1 .... 9 C3
Picton Rd. CT11 .... 52 C7
Pier Approach Rd. ME7 .... 10 D7
Pier Ave. Herne Bay CT6 .... 22 E4
Pier Ave. Whitstable CT5 .... 21 A2
Pier Rd. ME7 .... 10 E7
Pier Rd Ind Est. ME7 .... 10 D7
Pier The. CT16 .... 148 F8
Pierpoint Rd. CT5 .... 43 D7
Pierremont Ave. CT10 .... 30 A4
Pigeon La. CT6 .... 23 A2
Pigtail Cnr. ME12 .... 4 E6
Pike Cl. CT19 .... 178 A7
Pike Rd. CT14 & CT15 .... 114 E4
Pikefields. ME8 .... 11 C2
Pilckem Cl. CT1 .... 67 D1
Pilgrim Spring. CT19 .... 178 D8
Pilgrims. CT27 .... 120 C7
Pilgrims La. Chilham CT4 .... 85 E1
Pilgrims La. Whitstable CT5 ..... 43 B4
Pilgrims Lakes. ME17 .... 100 E5
Pilgrims Rd. CT1 .... 88 C7
Pilgrims View. ME14 .... 53 E3
Pilgrims Way. Boxley ME14 ...... 54 E3
Pilgrims' Way.
  Brabourne TN25 .... 159 E8
Pilgrims Way.
  Broad Street ME14 & ME17 ... 77 C8
Pilgrims Way. Canterbury CT1 ... 88 C7
Pilgrims Way. Charing TN27 ... 120 E8
Pilgrims Way. Detling ME14 ..... 55 B1
Pilgrims Way. Dover CT16 ...... 149 A3
Pilgrims Way. Eccles ME20 ...... 53 B6
Pilgrims Way.
  Hollingbourne ME17 .... 77 F3
Pilgrims Way. Lenham ME17 ... 101 B7
Pilgrims Way. Westwell TN25 .. 121 D5
Pilgrims Way
  Cty Prim Sch The. CT1 .... 88 C7
Pilot Rd. ME1 .... 31 C8
Pilot's Farm Rd. CT4 .... 110 A4
Pilots Ave. CT14 .... 117 A4
Pimp's Court Cotts. ME15 .... 96 E6
Pimp's Court Farm Ctr. ME15 .. 96 E6
Pimpernel Cl. ME14 .... 76 B4
Pimpernel Way. ME5 .... 31 E4
Pin Hill. CT1 .... 87 F7
Pine Cotts. ME14 .... 74 E8
Pine Gr. Gillingham ME7 .... 33 A5
Pine Gr. Maidstone ME14 .... 75 B6
Pine Ho. 3 ME5 .... 31 F5
Pine Lodge. ME14 .... 74 C3
Pine Tree Ave. CT2 .... 66 E2
Pine Way. CT19 .... 177 D7
Pine Wlk. CT6 .... 23 E5
Pineham Rd. CT15 .... 149 D6
Pines Gdns The. CT15 .... 151 B5
Pines The. CT10 .... 29 A8
Pineside Rd. CT3 .... 89 E8
Pinetree Cl. CT5 .... 20 F5
Pinewood Cl. CT12 .... 29 C1
Pinewood Dr. ME14 .... 54 D8
Pink's Cnr. ME14 .... 14 E3
Pinks Cnr. CT12 .... 50 D6
Pinners Hill. CT15 .... 113 C6
Pinners La. CT15 .... 113 C5
Pinous Ho. ME10 .... 36 D5
Pintail Way. CT6 .... 23 C2
Pioneer Rd. CT16 .... 149 A3
Pippin Ave. CT4 .... 111 B8
Pippin Cl. Coxheath ME17 .... 96 B2
Pippin Cl. Sittingbourne ME10 .. 36 D6
Pippin Croft. ME7 .... 33 A6
Pirbright Cl. ME5 .... 32 D2
Pitstock Rd. ME9 .... 59 B5
Pitt Rd. Langley Heath ME17 .... 99 A2
Pitt Rd. Maidstone ME16 .... 74 B1
Pittlesden. TN30 .... 179 A7
Pittlesden Pl. 1 TN30 .... 179 A7
Pittock Ho. CT14 .... 117 B3
Pivington La. TN27 .... 119 C2
Pivington Mill Ind Est. TN27 .. 119 C2
Pixwell La. CT14 .... 116 D3
Place La. Hartlip ME9 .... 34 D4
Place La. Woodchurch TN26 ... 169 B3
Place The. CT4 .... 112 F1
Plain Rd. Brabourne Lees TN25 . 158 F5
Plain Rd. Folkestone CT20 ..... 178 B4
Plains Ave. ME15 .... 75 C1
Plains Of Waterloo. CT11 .... 52 F7
Plaistow Sq. ME14 .... 75 C6
Plantation Cl. TN26 .... 138 A7
Plantation La. ME14 .... 76 A3
Plantation Rd. Faversham ME13 . 62 C7
Plantation Rd. Gillingham ME7 .. 11 A6
Plantation Rd. Whitstable CT5 .. 21 D2
Platt's Heath
  Cty Prim Sch. ME17 .... 100 F2
Platters The. ME8 .... 33 C7
Playstool Cl. ME9 .... 35 B6
Playstool Rd. ME9 .... 35 A6
Plaza Ct. ME10 .... 37 A4
Pleasance Rd N. TN29 .... 204 E5
Pleasance Rd S. TN29 .... 204 F2
Pleasance Road Central.
  TN29 .... 204 F3
Pleasant Row. 2 ME4 .... 10 A6
Pleasant Pl. ME12 .... 3 E6
Plenty Brook Dr. CT6 .... 22 F3

Plewis Ho. ME7 .... 10 E7
Pleydell Cres. CT2 .... 67 F7
Pleydell Gdns. CT20 .... 178 D4
Plimsoll Ave. CT19 .... 178 E8
Plomley Cl. ME8 .... 33 D4
Plough Cotts. ME17 .... 98 E2
Plough Ct. CT6 .... 23 D2
Plough Hill. CT15 .... 165 C4
Plough La. CT6 .... 21 D3
Plough Rd. ME12 .... 5 C5
Plough Wents Rd. ME17 .... 98 B2
Ploughmans Way.
  Chatham ME5 .... 32 A1
Ploughmans Way.
  Gillingham ME8 .... 33 E6
Plover Cl. ME5 .... 32 D1
Pluckley CE Prim Sch. TN27 .. 136 D7
Pluckley Cl. ME8 .... 11 C3
Pluckley Gdns. CT9 .... 8 E2
Pluckley Rd.
  Bethersden TN26 & TN27 .... 153 D7
Pluckley Rd. Charing TN27 .... 120 B5
Pluckley Rd. Hothfield TN26 ... 137 B4
Pluckley Rd.
  Maltman's Hill TN27 .... 135 D2
Pluckley Sta. TN27 .... 136 C3
Plum Tree Gdns. TN26 .... 169 B1
Plum Tree Rd. ME9 .... 56 B8
Plumford Rd. ME13 .... 62 A2
Plumpton Wlk. 5
  Canterbury CT1 .... 67 B1
Plumpton Wlk. 9
  Maidstone ME15 .... 97 F6
Plumpudding La. ME13 .... 42 F1
Plumstone Rd. CT7 .... 26 F1
Plumtree Gr. ME7 .... 33 A4
Plumtrees. ME14 .... 74 A2
Plurenden Manor Farm Cotts.
  TN26 .... 168 E7
Plurenden Rd. TN26 .... 168 E7
Poachers Cl. ME5 .... 32 C5
Podkin Wood. ME5 .... 53 F8
Poets Cnr. CT9 .... 7 J1
Poets Wlk. CT14 .... 117 C1
Poison Cross. CT13 .... 93 B4
Poldark Ct. 14 CT11 .... 52 F7
Poles The. ME9 .... 12 E4
Polhill Dr. ME5 .... 31 F2
Pollard Cl. TN23 .... 155 F8
Pollard Ct. ME4 .... 10 C5
Polo Way. CT5 .... 21 D1
Pomfret Ho. CT4 .... 86 D1
Pomfret Rd. CT4 .... 86 D1
Pommeus La. CT14 .... 133 D7
Poncia Rd. TN23 .... 156 A7
Pond Cotts. Herne Bay CT6 ..... 23 D2
Pond Cotts. Sittingbourne ME10 . 58 D8
Pond Dr. ME10 .... 37 A2
Pond Farm La. Hucking ME17 ... 56 D1
Pond Farm Rd. Oad Street ME9 . 35 F1
Pond Hill. CT3 .... 90 D1
Pond Hill Rd. CT20 .... 177 C5
Pond La.
  St Margaret's at Cliffe CT15 .. 150 D7
Pond La.
  Womenswold CT3 & CT4 ...... 112 D3
Pondfield. TN25 .... 139 C8
Poorhole La. CT10 .... 29 B5
Poot La. ME9 .... 12 E5
Pope House La. TN30 .... 167 B4
Pope St. Godmersham CT4 ..... 107 E4
Pope St. Maidstone ME16 .... 74 C2
Popes La. CT2 .... 67 F7
Poplar Cl. TN23 .... 138 F3
Poplar Dr. Elvington CT15 .... 114 B2
Poplar Dr. Herne Bay CT6 ...... 22 D2
Poplar Field. TN30 .... 188 D4
Poplar Gr. ME16 .... 74 C5
Poplar Ho. ME12 .... 1 C2
Poplar La. TN29 .... 203 D7
Poplar Rd. Broadstairs CT10 .... 29 E6
Poplar Rd. Ramsgate CT11 ...... 52 D7
Poplar Rd. Wittersham TN30 ... 188 D4
Poplar View. ME13 .... 63 E3
Poplars. TN26 .... 182 A7
Poplars The. Ashford TN23 .... 156 A7
Poplars The. Bethersden TN26 .. 153 E5
Poplars The. Hersden CT3 .... 46 F1
Poppy Cl. ME7 .... 10 E5
Popsal Cl. CT3 .... 91 B6
Porchester Cl. ME15 .... 97 A6
Port Cl. Chatham ME5 .... 32 B3
Port Cl. Maidstone ME14 .... 76 A5
Port Lympne Zoo. CT21 .... 174 C2
Portal House Sch. CT15 .... 151 A6
Portbello Cl. CT14 .... 117 D7
Porter Cl. ME12 .... 4 A6
Porters Wlk. ME17 .... 98 E4
Portland Ave. ME10 .... 37 C4
Portland Cl. Ashford TN24 .... 139 C7
Portland Cl. Hythe CT21 ...... 176 B2
Portland Ct. 3 Hythe CT21 .... 176 B2
Portland Ct. Ramsgate CT11 .... 52 E7
Portland Rd. Gillingham ME7 ... 10 E6
Portland Rd. Hythe CT21 .... 176 B2
Portland St. ME4 .... 10 B2
Portland Terr. Ripple CT14 .... 133 D8
Portland Terr. Sheerness ME12 .. 1 D2
Portsdown Cl. ME16 .... 74 B2
Portus Cl. CT9 .... 43 C8
Post Barn Rd. ME4 .... 9 F2
Postley Commercial Ctr. ME15 . 75 A2
Postley Rd. ME15 .... 75 A1

Postling. TN23 .... 138 E1
Postling Rd. CT19 .... 177 E7
Postling Wents. CT21 .... 175 F8
Postmill Dr. ME15 .... 74 F1
Potten Street Rd. CT7 .... 25 E3
Potter St. CT13 .... 73 A1
Potters Cl. TN24 .... 138 E6
Potters Cnr. TN24 .... 138 E6
Pottery Cotts. TN25 .... 140 E5
Potyn Ho. ME1 .... 9 C4
Pouces Cotts. CT12 .... 27 F1
Poulders Gdns. CT13 .... 93 E8
Poulders Rd. CT13 .... 93 E8
Poulsen Cl. ME10 .... 37 B4
Poulton Cl. CT17 .... 165 F8
Poulton Close Bsns Pk. CT17 . 148 E1
Poulton La. CT3 .... 92 C8
Pound Ct. TN23 .... 156 A3
Pound Farm Cotts. CT18 ...... 177 A7
Pound Ho. TN23 .... 156 B8
Pound La. Ashford TN23 ...... 155 F4
Pound La.
  Brabourne Lees TN25 .... 158 F5
Pound La.
  Canterbury CT1 & CT2 .... 66 F1
Pound La. Elham CT4 .... 144 F4
Pound La. Molash CT4 .... 105 F4
Poundhurst Rd. TN26 .... 171 C3
Powell Cl. ME20 .... 53 C4
Powell Cotton Dr. CT7 .... 27 B6
Powell Cotton Mus. CT7 .... 27 B6
Powell Sch (Prim) The. CT16 . 149 B4
Power Station Rd. ME12 .... 1 A7
Pratling St. ME20 .... 53 C4
Precincts The. [16]
  Canterbury CT1 .... 67 A1
Precincts The. Canterbury CT1 .. 88 A8
Prentis Cl. ME10 .... 36 C5
Prentis Quay. ME10 .... 36 E5
Prescott Cl. CT15 .... 149 E6
Prescott Ho. TN28 .... 200 A7
Prestedge Ave. CT10 & CT11 ... 29 E2
Preston Ave. Faversham ME13 ... 62 E6
Preston Ave. Gillingham ME7 ... 10 E1
Preston Gr. ME13 .... 62 D6
Preston Hall Gdns. ME12 ...... 6 E4
Preston Hill. CT3 .... 70 B1
Preston La. Faversham ME13 ... 62 E6
Preston La. Preston CT3 ...... 70 B5
Preston Malt Ho. ME13 ...... 62 D6
Preston Par. CT5 .... 42 F7
Preston Pk. ME13 .... 62 D6
Preston Rd. Manston CT12 ...... 28 E2
Preston Rd. Stourmouth CT3 ... 48 D1
Preston Rd. Wingham CT3 ...... 70 B2
Preston St. ME13 .... 62 D7
Preston-next-Wingham
  Cty Prim Sch. CT3 .... 70 C6
Pretoria Ho. [8] ME15 .... 97 E5
Pretoria Rd. Canterbury CT1 ... 88 B8
Pretoria Rd. Chatham ME4 ...... 9 F2
Pretoria Rd. Gillingham ME7 ... 10 D3
Price's Ave. Margate CT9 ...... 8 B2
Price's Ave. Ramsgate CT11 ... 52 C6
Priest Ave. CT12 .... 87 C7
Priest Fields. CT6 .... 23 F5
Priest & Sow Cnr. CT5 ...... 21 B3
Priest Wlk. CT5 .... 21 C3
Priestfield Rd. ME7 .... 10 E5
Priestfield Stad
  (Gillingham FC). ME7 .... 10 E5
Priestfields. ME1 .... 9 B3
Primrose Ave. ME8 .... 33 B5
Primrose Cl. ME1 .... 31 E7
Primrose Dr. TN23 .... 156 B4
Primrose Gr. ME9 .... 58 A6
Primrose Hill. CT4 .... 86 B7
Primrose La. ME9 .... 58 A6
Primrose Pl. CT17 .... 149 B1
Primrose Rd. CT17 .... 149 A1
Primrose Way. Cliffs End CT12 ... 51 C5
Primrose Way. Whitstable CT5 ... 21 C1
Prince Andrew Rd. CT10 ...... 29 E7
Prince Arthur Rd. ME7 ...... 10 B6
Prince Charles Ave.
  Chatham ME5 .... 32 B4
Prince Charles Ave.
  Minster ME12 .... 4 C6
Prince Charles Ave.
  Sittingbourne ME10 .... 37 C3
Prince Charles Rd. CT10 ...... 29 E7
Prince of Wales Rdbt. CT17 .. 166 B6
Prince Of Wales Terr. CT14 ... 117 D5
Prince's Ave. CT12 .... 29 B1
Prince's Gdns. CT9 .... 8 C2
Prince's Golf Links. CT13 ...... 73 E5
Prince's Rd. CT11 .... 52 D8
Prince's St. Margate CT9 ...... 7 J2
Prince's St. [7] Ramsgate CT11 .. 52 E6
Prince's St. Rochester ME1 ...... 9 C4
Prince's Wlk. CT9 .... 8 D3
Princes Ave. Chatham ME5 ... 32 B5
Princes Ave. Minster ME12 ... 4 D7
Princes Cl. CT7 .... 26 D7
Princes Cres. [10] CT9 .... 7 J2
Princes Dr. Sandwich CT13 ... 73 F2
Princes Dr. Sandwich CT13 ... 95 A8
Princes Par. CT21 .... 176 E2
Princes St. Deal CT14 .... 117 D7
Princes St. [11]
  Dover CT16 & CT17 .... 166 D7
Princes St. Maidstone ME14 ... 75 A5
Princes Terr. CT21 .... 175 F1
Princes Way. Canterbury CT2 ... 66 E1
Princes Way. Detling ME14 ... 55 A1

Princess Anne Rd. CT10 ...... 29 E7
Princess Cl. CT5 .... 21 C3
Princess Margaret Ave.
  Margate CT9 .... 8 E2
Princess Margaret Ave.
  Ramsgate CT12 .... 29 A1
Princess Mary Ave. ME7 ...... 10 B7
Princess Mary's
  Day Hospl. CT9 .... 8 A2
Princess Rd. CT5 .... 21 C3
Princess St. CT19 .... 178 E6
Prinys Dr. ME8 .... 33 C4
Prior Rd. TN29 .... 204 E8
Prior's Lees. [8] CT20 ...... 178 D4
Prioress Rd. CT17 .... 87 D8
Priory Cl. Broadstairs CT10 ... 29 F3
Priory Cl. East Farleigh ME15 .. 96 B8
Priory Cl. New Romney TN28 .. 199 F6
Priory Ct. Gillingham ME8 ...... 11 A2
Priory Ct. Leysdown-on-S ME12 .. 6 G1
Priory Cty Inf Sch.
  Ramsgate CT11 .... 52 D6
Priory Cty Inf Sch.
  Ramsgate CT11 .... 52 D7
Priory Gate. [4] ME14 .... 75 A5
Priory Gate Rd. CT17 .... 166 C8
Priory Gdns. CT20 .... 178 D4
Priory Gr. CT17 .... 166 C8
Priory Hill. CT16 & CT17 ...... 166 C8
Priory Ho. CT17 .... 166 C7
Priory La. Herne Bay CT6 ...... 23 A3
Priory La. Sellindge TN25 ...... 159 D4
Priory of St Jacob. CT1 ...... 87 E6
Priory Rd. Bilsington TN25 .... 172 C4
Priory Rd. Dover CT16 & CT17 .. 166 D8
Priory Rd. Faversham ME13 ... 62 C8
Priory Rd. Gillingham ME8 ...... 11 A2
Priory Rd. Maidstone ME15 ... 75 A3
Priory Rd. Ramsgate CT11 ...... 52 D6
Priory Rd. Rochester ME2 ...... 9 A6
Priory Row. ME13 .... 62 C8
Priory St. [10] CT16 & CT17 ...... 166 C8
Priory Sta. CT17 .... 166 C8
Priory Station Approach Rd.
  CT17 .... 166 C7
Priory Way. TN30 .... 179 C7
Progress Est The. ME15 ...... 98 A4
Promenade. Birchington CT7 .. 26 F8
Promenade. Deal CT14 ...... 117 D3
Promenade The. ME12 ...... 6 G2
Prospect Ave. ME2 .... 9 B8
Prospect Cl. CT8 .... 27 E7
Prospect Cotts.
  Boughton Lees TN25 ...... 122 B4
Prospect Cotts.
  Harbledown CT2 .... 65 E1
Prospect Gdns. CT12 .... 50 B7
Prospect Hill. CT6 .... 23 A5
Prospect Mews. CT21 ...... 176 C2
Prospect Pl. [7]
  Broadstairs CT10 .... 30 B4
Prospect Pl. Canterbury CT1 ... 88 A7
Prospect Pl. Dover CT17 ...... 149 B1
Prospect Pl. Eastling ME13 ...... 81 E6
Prospect Pl. Maidstone ME16 .. 74 E3
Prospect Pl.
  St Nicholas at Wade CT7 ...... 25 E1
Prospect Rd. Birchington CT7 .. 26 F7
Prospect Rd. Broadstairs CT10 .. 30 B4
Prospect Rd. Folkestone CT20 .. 177 D3
Prospect Rd. Hythe CT21 ...... 176 C2
Prospect Rd. Minster CT12 ...... 50 B6
Prospect Row. Chatham ME4 .... 10 A3
Prospect Row. Gillingham ME4 .. 10 A6
Prospect Terr. Elham CT4 ...... 144 F4
Prospect Terr. [17]
  Ramsgate CT11 .... 52 E6
Prospect Way. TN23 .... 158 E5
Provender Rd. ME13 & ME9 .. 61 A6
Provender Way. ME14 ...... 75 E5
Providence La. ME1 .... 9 C5
Providence St. TN23 ...... 156 C8
Puckle La. CT1 .... 88 A6
Pudding La. Ash CT3 .... 71 D1
Pudding La. Maidstone ME14 .. 74 F4
Pudding Rd. ME8 .... 33 F8
Pullman Cl. CT12 .... 52 C8
Pump La. Gillingham ME8 ...... 11 D2
Pump La. Gillingham ME7 & ME8 . 11 D3
Pump La. [1] Margate CT9 ...... 7 J2
Purbeck Rd. ME4 .... 9 E2
Purchas Ct. CT2 .... 66 C4
Purchase La. TN26 .... 154 E8
Purr Wood. CT4 .... 107 B2
Purser Way. ME7 .... 10 C7
Puttney Dr. ME10 .... 37 A8
Pyatt Mews. [3] CT1 .... 67 B1
Pye Alley La. CT5 .... 43 C3
Pym Ho. TN27 .... 120 D7
Pyrus Cl. ME5 .... 54 A8
Pyson's Rd. CT10 & CT12 ...... 29 D3
Pyson's Road Ind Est. CT10 ... 29 D3

Quain Ct. CT20 .... 178 C4
Quantock Dr. TN23 & TN24 ... 139 B4
Quantock Gdns. CT12 ...... 29 B3
Quarries The. ME17 .... 97 C4
Quarrington La. TN25 ...... 158 A7
Quarry Cotts. TN30 .... 189 C3
Quarry Rd. Hythe CT21 ...... 176 B3
Quarry Rd. Maidstone ME15 .. 75 A2
Quarry Sq. ME14 .... 75 A5
Quarry View. TN12 .... 155 D7
Quarry Wlk. CT21 .... 177 A3
Quarry Wood. TN25 .... 173 A6
Quay Cotts. ME9 .... 38 E6
Quay La. Faversham ME13 ...... 62 D8
Quay La. Sandwich CT13 ...... 73 A1

Quay The. ME9 .... 38 E6
Quayside. ME4 .... 10 B8
Queen Anne Rd. ME14 ...... 75 B4
Queen Bertha Rd. CT11 ...... 52 C6
Queen Bertha's Ave.
  CT7 & CT8 .... 27 C8
Queen Elizabeth Ave. CT9 ...... 8 D1
Queen Elizabeth Rd. CT16 ... 166 F8
Queen Elizabeth Sq. ME15 ... 97 D6
Queen Elizabeth the
  Queen Mother Hospl. CT9 ... 28 F8
Queen Elizabeth's Sch. ME13 . 62 D8
Queen Mother Ct The. ME1 ... 9 B4
Queen St. Ashford TN23 ...... 139 B2
Queen St. Chatham ME4 ...... 10 A4
Queen St. Deal CT14 .... 117 D6
Queen St. Dover CT16 ...... 166 D7
Queen St. Folkestone CT20 ... 178 E5
Queen St. Herne Bay CT6 ...... 22 F5
Queen St. Margate CT9 ...... 7 I2
Queen St. Ramsgate CT11 ...... 52 E6
Queen St. Rochester ME1 ...... 9 C4
Queen Victoria Meml Hospl.
  CT6 .... 23 B4
Queen's Ave. Birchington CT7 .. 26 D7
Queen's Ave. Broadstairs CT10 .. 30 B6
Queen's Ave. Maidstone ME6 .. 74 D5
Queen's Ave. Margate CT9 ...... 7 I1
Queen's Ave. Ramsgate CT12 .. 29 B1
Queen's Gate Rd. CT11 ...... 52 C8
Queen's Gdns. CT16 .... 166 D8
Queen's Lea. CT15 .... 164 E5
Queen's Prom. CT9 .... 8 B3
Queen's Rd. Ash CT3 .... 71 D2
Queen's Rd. Ashford TN24 ... 140 A1
Queen's Rd. Broadstairs CT10 .. 30 B4
Queen's Rd. Chatham ME5 ... 10 D1
Queen's Rd. Faversham ME13 . 62 B7
Queen's Rd. Gillingham ME7 ... 10 C4
Queen's Rd.
  Littlestone-on-S TN28 ...... 200 D6
Queen's Rd. Lydd TN29 ...... 203 C6
Queen's Rd. Maidstone ME6 .. 74 C4
Queen's Rd. Ramsgate CT11 ... 52 F7
Queen's Rd. Westgate-on-S CT8 . 27 F8
Queen's Rise. CT14 .... 133 F5
Queen's Way. ME12 .... 3 A8
Queenborough
  Cty Prim Sch. ME11 ...... 3 B5
Queenborough Dr. ME12 ...... 4 B7
Queenborough Rd.
  Halfway Houses ME12 ...... 3 C6
Queenborough Rd.
  Queenborough ME11 & ME12 .. 3 C4
Queenborough Sta. ME11 ...... 3 A5
Queendown Ave. ME8 ...... 33 D5
Queendown Rd. CT7 .... 28 A3
Queens Ave. Canterbury CT2 ... 66 E1
Queens Ave. Dover CT17 ...... 166 A7
Queens Ave. Herne Bay CT6 ... 23 D5
Queens Ave. Hythe CT20 ...... 177 B6
Queens Ct. Ashford TN24 ...... 139 C3
Queens Ct. Hythe CT21 ...... 176 B1
Queens Ct. Margate CT9 ...... 8 A3
Queens Gdns. Broadstairs CT10 . 30 B3
Queens Gdns. Herne Bay CT6 .. 22 F5
Queens Mews. CT14 .... 117 D6
Queens Par. [12]
  Faversham ME13 .... 62 D7
Queens Par. Margate CT9 ...... 8 A3
Queens Par. West Minster ME12 . 75 A3
Queens Rd. Ashford TN24 ...... 139 C3
Queens Rd. Aylesham CT3 ...... 112 F5
Queens Rd. Minster ME12 ...... 4 D7
Queens Rd. Whitstable CT5 ... 21 A2
Queens Way. ME14 .... 55 A1
Queensbridge Dr. CT6 ...... 22 C4
Queensdown Rd. CT14 ...... 134 D4
Queensway. Dymchurch TN29 .. 186 E2
Queensway. Lydd TN29 ...... 203 C6
Queenswood Rd. ME20 ...... 53 D7
Quern Rd. CT14 .... 117 A2
Quern The. ME15 .... 74 E1
Querns Pl. CT1 .... 88 B8
Querns Rd. CT1 .... 88 C8
Quested Rd. CT19 .... 177 E6
Quested Way. ME17 .... 100 C6
Quetta Rd. CT12 .... 28 F1
Quex Rd. CT8 .... 27 F8
Quex View Rd. CT7 .... 27 A5
Quickthorn Cres. ME5 ...... 31 E5
Quince Orch. TN26 .... 183 A7
Quinion Cl. ME5 .... 54 A8
Quinnell St. ME8 .... 11 E1
Quinton Rd. ME10 .... 36 C7

Rabbit Hole. CT4 .... 129 A7
Radfall Cnr. CT5 .... 44 C6
Radfall Gate. CT5 .... 44 C6
Radfall Hill. CT5 .... 44 D5
Radfall Rd. CT2 & CT5 & CT6 .. 44 D4
Radfall Ride. CT5 .... 44 C5
Radleigh Gdns. ME4 ...... 9 E1
Radley Cl. CT10 .... 30 A6
Radnor Bridge Rd.
  CT19 & CT20 .... 178 E5
Radnor Cl. CT6 .... 23 B1
Radnor Cliff. CT20 .... 178 A3
Radnor Cliff Cres. CT20 ...... 178 A3
Radnor Park Ave. CT19 ...... 178 C6
Radnor Park Cres. CT19 ...... 178 C6
Radnor Park Gdns. CT19 ...... 178 C6
Radnor Park Rd. CT19 ...... 178 C6
Radnor Pk W. CT19 .... 178 B6
Radnor St. CT19 .... 178 E5
Raggatt Pl. ME15 .... 75 B2
Raglan Pl. [10] CT10 .... 30 B4
Ragstone Hollow. TN25 ...... 173 A6

Ragstone Rd. ME15 .... 76 A2
Railway Ave. CT5 .... 20 E1
Railway Cotts. ME9 .... 38 D3
Railway Hill. CT4 .... 128 E8
Railway Rd. ME12 .... 1 C2
Railway St. Chatham ME4 ...... 9 F4
Railway St. Gillingham ME7 ... 10 D6
Railway Terr. Margate CT9 ...... 7 H1
Railway Terr.
  Queenborough ME11 ...... 3 A5
Rainham Cl. ME15 .... 75 A1
Rainham Mark
  Gram Sch. ME8 .... 11 D2
Rainham Rd. ME5 & ME7 ...... 10 C3
Rainham Sch for Girls. ME8 .. 33 C8
Rainham Sh Ctr. ME8 ...... 33 F8
Rainham Sta. ME8 .... 11 F1
Raleigh Cl. Ashford TN24 ...... 157 A3
Raleigh Cl. Chatham ME5 ...... 32 A6
Raleigh Way. ME7 .... 32 E3
Ralph Grimshaw Ct. CT8 ...... 27 E8
Ram La. TN26 .... 137 C8
Ramillies Cl. ME5 .... 32 A6
Ramp A. CT16 .... 166 H8
Ramp B. CT16 .... 166 H8
Ramp C. CT16 .... 166 G8
Rampart Rd. CT21 .... 176 B2
Rampion Cl. ME14 .... 75 E5
Ramsey Cl. CT12 .... 66 E1
Ramsey Ho. [8] CT1 ...... 87 F7
Ramsgate Hospl (Geriatric).
  CT11 .... 52 D6
Ramsgate Rd.
  Broadstairs CT10 & CT11 ...... 29 F2
Ramsgate Rd. Broadstairs CT10 . 30 B4
Ramsgate Rd.
  Margate CT10 & CT9 ...... 29 A6
Ramsgate Rd.
  Sandwich CT12 & CT13 ...... 73 A7
Ramsgate Sch The. CT12 ...... 29 A2
Ramsgate Sta. CT12 .... 52 C8
Ramstone Cl. TN25 .... 158 E5
Rancorn Rd. CT9 .... 7 G1
Randall Ave. ME9 .... 9 E1
Randall St. ME14 .... 74 F6
Randalls Row. ME15 .... 96 F5
Randolph Cl. CT1 .... 88 A7
Randolph Gdns. ME14 ...... 139 E5
Randolph Ho. [13] CT20 ...... 178 E5
Randolph Rd. Dover CT17 ... 149 B1
Randolph Rd. Gillingham ME7 . 10 C5
Randolph Sq. CT9 .... 7 J3
Ranelagh Gdns. CT10 ...... 29 E5
Ranelagh Gr. CT10 .... 29 E5
Ranelagh Rd. Deal CT14 ...... 117 D5
Ranelagh Rd. Sheerness ME12 . 1 D2
Range Cl. Eastchurch ME12 ... 5 D1
Range Rd. Hythe CT21 ...... 176 B1
Range Road Ind Est. CT21 ... 176 B1
Ransley Gn. TN26 .... 183 F8
Raspberry Hill La. ME9 ...... 14 D6
Ratling Rd. CT3 .... 112 F7
Rattington St. CT4 .... 86 E2
Ravenlea Rd. CT20 .... 178 A5
Ravens Dane Cl. ME15 ...... 76 A1
Ravensbourne Ave. CT10 ...... 8 B3
Ravenscourt Rd. Deal CT14 ... 117 C5
Ravenscourt Rd.
  Rough Common CT2 ...... 66 B3
Ravenswood Ave. ME2 ...... 9 B8
Rawdon Rd. Maidstone ME15 .. 75 A3
Rawdon Rd. Ramsgate CT11 ... 52 C6
Rawling St. ME9 .... 58 F3
Rayham Rd. CT5 .... 44 A8
Raymer Rd. ME14 .... 75 B8
Raymond Ave. CT1 .... 88 A6
Raymoor Ave. TN29 .... 195 A4
Rayners Hill. ME17 .... 102 C5
Reach Cl. CT15 .... 150 F5
Reach Meadow. CT15 ...... 151 A6
Reach Rd. Lympne CT21 ...... 174 D2
Reach Rd.
  St Margaret's at Cliffe CT15 .. 150 F5
Reachfields. CT21 .... 176 A1
Reading Cl. CT14 .... 117 B1
Reading Rd. CT17 .... 165 F7
Reading St. Broadstairs CT10 .. 29 F8
Reading St. Tenderden TN30 ... 180 C2
Reading Street Rd. CT10 & CT9 . 29 E8
Readscroft Rd. ME8 ...... 33 D5
Rebecca Ct. [6] CT9 .... 8 B2
Recreation Cl. ME4 .... 75 B6
Recreation Ground Rd. TN30 . 179 B7
Rectory Bglws. TN26 ...... 169 F8
Rectory Cl. TN26 .... 169 A2
Rectory Gdns. CT5 .... 21 D2
Rectory Grange. ME1 ...... 9 C2
Rectory La. Barham CT4 ...... 112 A1
Rectory La. Harrietsham ME17 . 100 F5
Rectory La. Hythe CT21 ...... 176 B5
Rectory La. Lyminge CT18 ... 161 C6
Rectory La. Maidstone ME16 ... 74 A1
Rectory Rd. Broadstairs CT10 .. 30 B5
Rectory Rd. Deal CT14 ...... 116 F4
Rectory Rd. Sittingbourne ME10 . 37 B3
Rectory Rd.
  St Mary in the Marsh TN29 .. 194 B4
Rectory Way. TN24 .... 139 C5
Reculver Ave. CT7 .... 26 E8
Reculver CE Prim Sch. CT6 ... 24 A4
Reculver Cl. CT6 .... 23 F5
Reculver Dr. CT6 .... 23 E5
Reculver La. CT6 .... 24 B6
Reculver Rd. CT6 .... 23 D5
Reculver Wlk. Maidstone ME15 . 97 F7
Reculvers Rd. CT8 .... 27 F7

Red Lion La. [5] CT5 .... 20 D2
Red Lion Sq. [7] CT21 ...... 176 B2
Red Rd. CT2 & ME13 .... 64 D5
Red Robin Cotts. ME9 ...... 35 B6
Red Tree Orch. TN23 ...... 155 E7
Redbridge Cl. ME5 .... 32 C4
Redbrook St. TN26 .... 168 D5
Redbrooks Way. CT21 ...... 175 F2
Redcliffe La. ME14 .... 75 B7
Redcot La. CT2 & CT3 ...... 68 B7
Redfern Ave. ME7 .... 10 E5
Redgates. CT6 .... 23 A5
Redhill Rd. CT8 .... 27 E8
Redhouse La. CT4 .... 109 D6
Redhouse Wall. CT14 ...... 95 B1
Redington. TN24 .... 139 C3
Redland Shaw. ME4 .... 9 E1
Redlands Ct. CT17 .... 148 E4
Redmill Cl. CT20 .... 177 E5
Redoubt Way. TN29 .... 187 B4
Redyear Ct. TN24 .... 140 A1
Redyear Cotts. TN24 ...... 140 A1
Reed Ave. CT1 .... 67 D3
Reed Cres. TN23 .... 156 C3
Reedland Cres. ME13 ...... 62 C5
Reedmace Cl. TN23 .... 155 D8
Reeds Cl. CT6 .... 23 C4
Reeves Alley. [1] CT5 ...... 20 D1
Reeves Pas. [7] ME13 ...... 62 C7
Reeves Way. CT5 .... 21 C2
Reform Ct. ME4 .... 10 B2
Regency Cl. Gillingham ME8 .. 33 C3
Regency Cl. Sheerness ME12 .. 1 B3
Regency Cl. Whitstable CT5 ... 43 F7
Regency Ct. ME10 .... 36 D4
Regency Pl. CT1 .... 67 B2
Regency Villas. CT4 ...... 129 C5
Regent Dr. ME15 .... 97 A8
Regent Ho. ME7 .... 10 C4
Regent St. CT5 .... 20 D2
Regents Pl. TN23 .... 139 B2
Regents Wlk. CT6 .... 23 D5
Reginald Rd. ME16 .... 74 E3
Regis Cres. ME10 .... 36 F7
Regis Manor
  Cty Prim Sch. ME10 ...... 36 E7
Reglvlbivm Roman Fort. CT6 . 24 D7
Reinden Gr. CT4 .... 75 F1
Remston Mews. [12] CT1 ...... 67 B2
Renault Cl. CT6 .... 22 A4
Rendezvous St. CT20 ...... 178 D5
Rendezvous The. CT9 ...... 7 I3
Renown Rd. ME5 .... 32 C2
Rentain Rd. CT4 .... 86 D2
Repton Cl. CT10 .... 29 F6
Repton Manor Rd. TN23 ...... 139 A3
Repton Way. ME5 .... 31 F4
Resolution Cl. ME5 .... 32 A6
Resrvoir Rd. CT5 .... 20 E2
Rest Harrow. ME13 .... 83 D6
Restharrow Rd. ME14 ...... 75 E4
Retreat The. Birchington CT7 .. 27 B8
Retreat The. Doddington ME9 .. 80 D7
Retreat The. Ramsgate CT12 .. 52 B8
Revenge Rd. ME5 .... 54 C8
Reynolds Cl. CT6 .... 23 B4
Rhee Wall. TN26 .... 190 D7
Rheims Ct. CT2 .... 66 D1
Rheims Way. CT1 & CT2 ...... 87 E8
Rhodaus Cl. CT1 .... 87 F7
Rhodaus Ho. CT1 .... 87 F7
Rhodaus Town. CT1 .... 87 F7
Rhode St. ME4 .... 10 A4
Rhodes Gdns. CT10 ...... 30 A6
Rhodes Ho. ME5 .... 10 C2
Rhodewood Cl. ME15 ...... 76 A1
Richard St. [7] CT9 .... 8 B2
Richard St. Chatham ME4 ...... 9 F4
Richard St. Rochester ME1 ...... 9 C3
Richborough Bsns Pk. CT13 ... 73 A3
Richborough Castle. CT13 ...... 72 E5
Richborough Rd. CT8 ...... 27 F7
Richbourgh Rd. CT13 ...... 72 E3
Richdore Rd. CT4 .... 125 C6
Richmond Ave. CT9 .... 8 B1
Richmond Cl. ME5 .... 32 B4
Richmond Ct. CT16 .... 149 D1
Richmond Cty Inf Sch. ME7 .. 10 E5
Richmond Cty Prim Sch. ME12 . 1 E2
Richmond Dr. Herne Bay CT6 .. 23 E5
Richmond Dr.
  New Romney TN28 .... 200 C8
Richmond Dr.
  Sittingbourne ME10 .... 36 E7
Richmond Gdns. CT2 ...... 66 C2
Richmond Rd. Gillingham ME7 . 10 C7
Richmond Rd. Ramsgate CT11 . 52 D6
Richmond Rd. Whitstable CT5 .. 21 B1
Richmond St. Folkestone CT19 . 177 D6
Richmond St. Herne Bay CT6 .. 22 F5
Richmond St. Sheerness ME12 .. 1 E2
Richmond Way. ME15 ...... 97 A8
Riddles Rd. ME10 & ME9 ...... 36 C3
Ridge Meadow
  Cty Prim Sch. ME5 ...... 31 F6
Ridge The. TN24 .... 139 E6
Ridgeway. Lympne CT21 ...... 175 A3
Ridgeway. Whitstable CT5 ...... 21 C1
Ridgeway Cliff. CT6 .... 22 C5
Ridgeway Rd. CT6 .... 46 A7

Ridgeway Terr. TN25 .... 158 C5
Ridgeway The.
  Boughton Street ME13 .... 64 A3
Ridgeway The.
  Broadstairs CT10 .... 29 F3
Ridgeway The. Chatham ME4 .... 31 E7
Ridgeway The. Gillingham ME7 .. 10 C7
Ridgeway The. Margate CT9 .... 8 B1
Ridgeway The. River CT17 ...... 148 E2
Ridgeway The. Smeeth TN25 .... 158 B5
Ridgeway Wlk. CT6 .... 46 A7
Ridgway. ME16 .... 74 B2
Ridham Ave. ME10 .... 15 A1
Riding Hill. TN24 .... 139 C6
Ridings The. ⬛ Canterbury CT1 .. 67 B1
Ridings The. Margate CT9 .... 8 F3
Ridings The. Whitstable CT5 .... 21 D1
Ridlands. CT1 .... 88 A5
Ridley Cl. CT6 .... 46 A8
Ridley Rd. ME1 .... 9 C4
Rigden Rd. TN23 .... 156 B7
Rigshill Rd. ME13 .... 103 B6
Riley Ave. CT14 .... 21 F4
Ring Wall. CT14 .... 94 E2
Ringlestone Cres. ME14 .... 74 F8
Ringlestone Rd. ME17 .... 78 D4
Ringold Ave. CT12 .... 52 A8
Ringsloe Ct. CT7 .... 26 D8
Ringwood Cl. Canterbury CT2 .. 66 E3
Ringwood Cl. Gillingham ME8 .. 33 D8
Ringwood Rd. ME15 .... 97 C8
Ringwould Rd.
  Kingsdown CT14 .... 134 B5
Ringwould Rd.
  Ringwould CT14 & CT15 ..... 133 D4
Ripley Rd. TN24 .... 157 A8
Ripon Cl. ME8 .... 11 D3
Ripper's Cross. TN26 .... 137 D4
Ripple Cross. CT14 .... 133 F6
Ripple Cty Prim Sch. CT14 .... 133 D8
Ripple Rd. CT14 .... 133 F7
Ripplevale Sch. CT14 .... 133 E8
Risborough La. CT19 & CT20 .. 177 D5
Risborough Way. CT20 .... 177 E6
Risdon Cl. CT2 .... 67 F6
Rise The. Ashford TN23 .... 155 E7
Rise The. Borden ME9 .... 36 B2
Rise The. Gillingham ME7 .... 33 A3
Rise The. Halfway Houses ME12 .. 3 C5
Rise The. Kingsdown CT14 ..... 134 D5
Rise The. Rochester ME1 .... 9 D3
Rise The.
  St Margaret's at Cliffe CT15 .. 151 B6
Rising Rd. TN23 .... 139 A1
River Cl. ME15 .... 96 A2
River Ct. Chartham CT4 .... 86 D3
River Ct. River CT17 .... 148 E2
River Cty Prim Sch. CT17 ...... 148 E3
River Dale. CT17 .... 148 F3
River Dr. CT17 .... 148 F2
River Meadow. CT17 .... 148 F3
River St. ⬛ Gillingham ME4 ...... 10 A6
River St. River CT17 .... 148 E3
River Valley Golf Course.
  ME8 & ME9 .... 12 D2
River View. Gillingham ME8 ..... 11 D3
River View. Maidstone ME15 .... 74 F2
River View. Rushenden ME11 ...... 2 F3
River View. Sturry CT2 .... 67 F7
Riverdale Rd. CT7 .... 67 B2
Riverhead Cl. Maidstone ME16 .. 74 D6
Riverhead Cl. Margate CT9 .... 8 B1
Riverhead Cl.
  Sittingbourne ME10 .... 36 C3
Rivers Rd. ME7 .... 38 D2
Rivers Wlk. ME17 .... 101 C5
Riversdale Rd. Ashford TN23 .. 156 C8
Riversdale Rd. Ramsgate CT12 .. 29 B1
Riverside. CT4 .... 86 C3
Riverside Bsns Pk. TN24 .... 139 D2
Riverside Cl. Bridge CT4 .... 89 A1
Riverside Cl. Kingsnorth TN23 .. 156 A4
Riverside Ct. ⬛ CT2 .... 66 F1
Riverside Ctry Pk. ME7 .... 11 D5
Riverside Ind Est. CT21 .... 175 B1
Riverside Mews. CT4 .... 89 A1
Riverside Rd. CT12 .... 51 A1
Riverside Sch. TN23 .... 138 F1
Riverview. TN23 .... 138 E1
Riviera Ct. ⬛ CT20 .... 177 E3
Riviera Rd. CT20 .... 178 A3
Riviera The. CT20 .... 177 F3
Roach St. ME2 .... 9 A7
Road Five. CT20 .... 177 C3
Road of Remembrance. CT20 .. 178 D4
Robert Napier Sch The. ME7 ... 10 E3
Robert St. CT14 .... 117 D7
Roberts Cl. ME10 .... 36 D7
Roberts Rd. Gillingham ME8 .... 33 E8
Roberts Rd.
  Greatstone-on-S TN28 .... 200 E1
Roberts Rd. Whitstable CT5 ..... 42 F6
Robeshaw. ME9 .... 58 E2
Robin Ho. ⬛ ME16 .... 74 E4
Robin Hood La. Chatham ME5 .. 31 D1
Robin Hood La. Lydd TN29 .... 203 C5
Robin Hood Lane
  (Lower). ME5 .... 31 F2
Robin Hood Lane
  (Upper). ME5 .... 31 E1
Robin La. TN29 .... 203 C6
Robin's Cl. CT21 .... 187 C8
Robins Ave. ME17 .... 101 C5
Robins Cl. ME17 .... 101 C4
Robins Ct. ME14 .... 75 B7
Robson's Yd. CT17 .... 166 C8
Robus Cl. CT18 .... 161 C7
Robus Terr. CT18 .... 161 C7

Rochester Airport. ME1 & ME5 .. 31 C6
Rochester Ave. Canterbury CT1 .. 88 B7
Rochester Ave. Rochester ME1 .. 9 C4
Rochester Cath. ME1 .... 9 C6
Rochester Ct. ME2 .... 9 E8
Rochester Gram Sch
  for Girls The. ME1 .... 9 C2
Rochester Ho. ⬛ ME1 .... 97 D7
Rochester Rd. Chatham ME5 .... 31 C4
Rochester Rd.
  Pratling Street ME20 .... 53 B4
Rochester St. ME4 .... 9 E5
Rochester Sta. ME1 .... 9 D5
Rock Ave. ME4 .... 10 C3
Rock Hill Rd. TN27 .... 118 E2
Rock Rd. Maidstone ME14 .... 75 A6
Rock Rd. Sittingbourne ME10 .. 36 E4
Rocky Bourne Rd. TN25 .... 172 D5
Rocky Hill. ME16 .... 74 E4
Rocky Hill Terr. ⬛ ME16 .... 74 E4
Rodmer Cl. ME12 .... 4 C8
Rodmersham Cty Prim Sch.
  ME9 .... 59 B7
Rodmersham Gn. ME9 .... 59 B7
Rodney St. CT11 .... 52 D6
Roebuck Rd. Faversham ME13 .. 62 A7
Roebuck Rd. Rochester ME1 ...... 9 C5
Roentgen Ho. ME10 .... 36 D5
Roethorne Gdns. TN30 .... 179 B8
Roffen Rd. ME1 .... 9 C2
Rogersmead. TN30 .... 179 A7
Rokesley Rd. CT16 .... 149 B5
Rolfe La. TN28 .... 200 B7
Roll's Ave. ME12 .... 5 C1
Rolvenden Ave. ME8 .... 11 C3
Rolvenden Dr. ME10 .... 36 B5
Roly Eckhoff Ho. CT16 .... 149 B3
Roman Cl. Chatham ME5 .... 31 D1
Roman Cl. Deal CT14 .... 117 B6
Roman Hts. ME4 .... 75 C6
Roman Rd. East Studdal CT15 .. 132 C5
Roman Rd. Faversham ME13 .... 62 C7
Roman Rd. Ramsgate CT12 ...... 29 C2
Roman Rd. Whitfield CT15 .... 149 D8
Roman Sq. ME10 .... 36 F3
Roman Way. Elvington CT15 .. 114 B2
Roman Way. Folkestone CT19 .. 177 C6
Roman Way. Kingsnorth TN23 .. 156 C4
Roman Way.
  St Margaret's at Cliffe CT15 .. 150 F5
Romany Ct. ME5 .... 10 D1
Romany Rd. ME8 .... 11 C2
Romden Rd. TN27 .... 135 D1
Rome House Cnr. TN28 .... 200 A6
Rome Rd. TN28 .... 200 A6
Romilly Gdns. CT12 .... 29 C2
Romney Ave. CT20 .... 177 F5
Romney Cl. Birchington CT7 .... 27 A7
Romney Cl. Maidstone ME14 ... 76 A3
Romney Cl. ME10 .... 36 E5
Romney Marsh Rd. TN23 ...... 156 B6
Romney Pl. ME15 .... 75 A4
Romney Rd. Ashford TN24 .... 139 E1
Romney Rd. Chatham ME5 ...... 32 B5
Romney Rd. Hamstreet TN26 .. 183 A7
Romney Rd. New Romney TN29 .. 199 C7
Romney Sands
  Holiday Village. TN28 .... 204 D8
Romney Sands Sta. TN28 ..... 204 E8
Romney Warren
  Golf Course. TN28 .... 200 E7
Romney Way. CT21 .... 175 F1
Ronalds Cl. ME10 .... 37 A4
Rook La. ME9 .... 35 F6
Rookery Cl. Ashford TN24 .... 139 D7
Rookery Cl. Bredgar ME9 .... 58 A6
Rookston Cnr. CT3 .... 48 D1
Roonagh Ct. ME10 .... 36 E2
Roosevelt Ave. ME5 .... 32 A8
Roosevelt Rd. CT16 .... 149 B3
Rope Walk Mews. CT13 .... 93 F8
Rope Wlk. ME4 .... 9 F5
Ropemakers Ct. ME4 .... 10 A1
Roper Cl. Canterbury CT1 .... 66 E1
Roper Cl. Gillingham ME8 .... 33 C3
Roper Rd. Canterbury CT2 ...... 66 E1
Roper Rd. Teynham ME9 .... 38 D3
Rose Acre Rd. CT3 .... 89 F7
Rose Cotts. Hythe CT21 .... 176 B4
Rose Cotts.
  Lenham Heath ME17 .... 119 B8
Rose Ct. ME17 .... 96 D1
Rose Gdns. Birchington CT7 .... 26 F6
Rose Gdns. Eythorne CT15 ... 131 D7
Rose Gdns. Herne Bay CT6 ...... 23 C4
Rose Gdns. Minster CT12 ...... 50 B6
Rose Hill. ⬛ Ramsgate CT11 ... 52 E6
Rose Hill. Wittersham TN30 .. 189 B5
Rose La. Bishopsbourne CT4 .. 111 C6
Rose La. Canterbury CT1 .... 87 F8
Rose La. Lenham Heath ME17 .. 119 B8
Rose St. Rochester ME1 .... 9 D3
Rose St. Sheerness ME12 .... 1 C2
Rose Street
  Cty Prim Sch. ME12 .... 1 C2
Rose Terr. ME13 .... 62 D5
Rose Yd. ME14 .... 75 A4
Roseacre Cl. CT2 .... 66 E1
Roseacre Cl. ME9 .... 8 E2
Roseacre Gdns. CT4 .... 76 A4
Roseacre Jun Sch. ME14 .... 76 A4
Roseacre La. ME14 .... 76 A4
Rosebery Ave. Herne Bay CT6 .. 23 E5
Rosebery Ave. Ramsgate CT11 .. 29 F1
Rosebery Cl. ME10 .... 37 D4
Rosebery Rd. Chatham ME4 ...... 9 E2

Rosebery Rd. Gillingham ME7 .. 10 D7
Rosedale Rd. CT9 .... 8 A1
Roseholme. ME4 .... 74 D2
Roselands. CT14 .... 117 C1
Roselands Gdns. CT2 .... 66 D2
Roselawn Gdns. ⬛ CT9 .... 28 B8
Roselea Ave. CT6 .... 22 F3
Roseleigh Ave. ME16 .... 74 C5
Roseleigh Rd. ME10 .... 36 D2
Rosemary Ave.
  Broadstairs CT10 .... 30 A3
Rosemary Ave.
  Halfway Houses ME12 .... 3 D6
Rosemary Cl. ⬛ ME5 .... 31 F4
Rosemary Cnr. TN29 .... 197 D8
Rosemary Gdns.
  Broadstairs CT10 .... 29 F2
Rosemary Gdns.
  Whitstable CT5 .... 44 A8
Rosemary La. ⬛ CT1 .... 87 F8
Rosemary Rd. ME15 .... 76 A3
Rosemount Cl. ME15 .... 96 F4
Rosetower Ct. CT10 .... 29 F8
Rosiers Ct. ⬛ CT2 .... 66 E1
Ross Gdns. CT2 .... 66 B3
Ross St. ME1 .... 9 D4
Ross Way. CT20 .... 177 E5
Rossendale Cl. ⬛ CT20 .... 178 E6
Rossendale Gdns. ⬛ CT20 .... 178 E6
Rossendale Rd. CT20 .... 178 E6
Rossetti Rd. CT7 .... 26 F8
Rossland Rd. CT12 .... 52 A8
Rosslyn Dr. ME16 .... 74 B5
Rothbrook Dr. TN24 .... 139 C7
Rother Ho. ⬛ ME15 .... 97 D8
Rother Vale. ME5 .... 32 C3
Rothley Cl. TN30 .... 179 B8
Rothsay Ct. CT11 .... 29 F1
Rough Common Rd. CT2 .... 66 B3
Roundel Cl. ME9 .... 38 D2
Roundel The. ME10 .... 36 F2
Roundwell. ME14 .... 76 D3
Rover Rd. ME5 .... 32 B2
Row The. Ash CT3 .... 71 E5
Row The. Elham CT4 .... 144 F5
Rowan Cl. Ashford TN23 ...... 138 E2
Rowan Cl. Staple CT3 .... 92 A6
Rowan Cl. Sturry CT3 .... 67 F6
Rowan Ct. CT10 .... 30 A5
Rowan Ho. ⬛ Chatham ME5 .... 31 F5
Rowan Ho. Sheerness ME12 ..... 1 C2
Rowan Lea. ME5 .... 10 B1
Rowan Wlk. ME4 .... 9 E3
Rowans The. ME12 .... 4 B7
Rowbrocke Cl. ME8 .... 33 D3
Rowe Cl. CT7 .... 28 F7
Rowena Rd. CT8 .... 7 C1
Rowetts Way. ME12 .... 5 D3
Rowland Ave. ME7 .... 10 E2
Rowland Cl. ME5 .... 10 E1
Rowland Cres. CT6 .... 23 E5
Rowland Dr. CT6 .... 22 C2
Roxburgh Rd. CT8 .... 7 D1
Royal Ave. CT5 .... 43 C5
Royal Cinque Ports
  Golf Links. CT13 .... 95 B4
Royal Cl. CT10 .... 29 F4
Royal Cres. Margate CT9 .... 7 H2
Royal Cres. Ramsgate CT11 .... 52 D5
Royal Eagle Cl. ME2 .... 9 E7
Royal Engineers' Rd. ME14 .... 74 F7
Royal Espl. Margate CT9 .... 7 F1
Royal Espl. Ramsgate CT11 .... 52 C5
Royal Military Ave. CT20 ...... 177 D5
Royal Military Rd.
  Aldington TN25 .... 173 D1
Royal Military Rd.
  Hythe CT21 .... 175 D1
Royal Par. CT11 .... 52 E6
Royal Rd. Ramsgate CT11 ...... 52 D5
Royal Rd. Sheerness ME12 .... 1 D2
Royal Sch for
  Deaf Children. CT9 .... 7 J2
Royal Sea Bathing Hospl. CT9 .. 7 J2
Royal Sovereign Ave. ME7 .... 10 B7
Royal St George's
  Golf Links. CT13 .... 73 E2
Royal Star Arc. ⬛ ME14 .... 74 F4
Royal Victoria Hospl. CT19 .. 178 C6
Royal Victoria Pl. ⬛ CT16 ... 166 D8
Royds Rd. TN24 .... 156 D6
Royston Gdns. CT15 .... 150 F6
Royston Rd. ME15 .... 76 A3
Roystons Cl. ME8 .... 11 F2
Royton Ave. ME17 .... 101 D5
Rubery Dro. CT3 .... 72 C7
Ruckinge Cnr. TN25 .... 183 B4
Ruckinge Rd. TN26 .... 183 A7
Ruckinge Way. ME8 .... 11 C3
Rudge Cl. ME5 .... 32 D2
Rugby Cl. Broadstairs CT10 .... 29 F5
Rugby Cl. Chatham ME5 .... 31 F4
Rugby Gdns. TN23 .... 156 C8
Rugby Rd. CT17 .... 166 A6
Ruins Barn Rd. ME10 & ME9 .. 58 D6
Rule Ct. ME12 .... 3 B8
Rumfields Rd. CT10 .... 29 D4
Rumstead La. ME17 & ME 9 .. 56 D4
Rumstead Rd. ME9 .... 56 E4
Rumwood Ct. ME17 .... 98 B5
Runcie Ho. ⬛ ME7 .... 87 F7
Runcie Pl. CT2 .... 67 F4
Runham Cl. ME17 .... 100 E3
Running Horse Rndbt The.
  ME20 .... 53 E1
Rush Cl. Chatham ME5 .... 32 A3
Rush Cl. Dymchurch TN29 .... 195 B6
Rusham Rd. CT3 .... 70 C1

Rushenden Ct. ME11 .... 2 F3
Rushenden Rd. ME11 .... 3 A4
Rushmead Cl. CT2 .... 66 D2
Rushmead Dr. ME15 .... 97 A7
Russel Dr. CT5 .... 21 D3
Russel Cl. ME10 .... 36 C3
Russell Cl. ME4 .... 10 B3
Russell Pl. ME13 .... 40 B3
Russell Rd. ⬛ Folkestone CT19 .. 178 D6
Russell Rd. Kit's Coty ME20 .... 53 D7
Russell St. Dover CT16 .... 166 E7
Russell St. Sheerness ME12 ..... 1 C2
Russells Ave. ME8 .... 34 A8
Russet Ave. ME17 .... 62 E5
Russet Ct. ME17 .... 96 C3
Russet Rd. CT1 .... 88 C8
Russets The. Maidstone ME16 .. 74 B5
Russets The. Whitstable CT5 ... 21 D1
Ruth Ho. ME16 .... 74 E5
Rutherford Coll. CT2 .... 66 E4
Rutherford Rd. TN24 .... 139 E5
Rutland Ave. CT9 .... 8 C2
Rutland Cl. CT1 .... 88 D7
Rutland Gdns. Birchington CT7 .. 26 F7
Rutland Gdns. Margate CT9 ..... 8 C2
Rutland Ho. ⬛ CT16 .... 8 B2
Rutland Pl. ME8 .... 33 C3
Rutland Rd. CT16 .... 149 B3
Rutland Way. ME15 .... 97 E8
Ryan Dr. ME15 .... 76 A2
Rycaut Cl. ME8 .... 33 D3
Rydal Ave. CT11 .... 52 B7
Ryde St. CT2 .... 66 E1
Ryder's Ave. CT8 .... 27 D8
Rye Ct. Maidstone ME16 .... 74 B5
Rye Rd. TN30 .... 189 A2
Rye Wlk. CT6 .... 23 C2
Ryecourt Cl. ⬛ ME16 .... 74 E3
Ryeglass Cl. ME5 .... 32 C6
Ryegrass Cl. ME5 .... 32 C6
Ryland Ct. ⬛ CT20 .... 178 E5
Ryland Pl. ⬛ CT20 .... 178 E5
Rylands Rd. TN24 .... 139 D5
Rype Cl. TN29 .... 203 C5
Ryswick Mews. TN28 .... 200 C8

Sabre Ct. ME7 .... 11 A1
Sackett's Gap. CT9 .... 8 C3
Sacketts Hill. CT10 .... 29 C6
Sackville Cl. TN26 .... 138 A7
Sackville Cres. TN23 .... 139 A2
Saddler's Wall La. TN29 ...... 191 B1
Saddlers Cl. ME14 .... 75 E5
Saddlers Hill. CT13 .... 91 D2
Saddlers Mews. CT5 .... 21 D1
Saddlers Rd. TN23 .... 156 B5
Saddleton Gr. CT5 .... 43 D8
Saddleton Rd. CT5 .... 43 D8
Sadlers Cl. ME5 .... 31 D2
Saffron Way. ⬛ Chatham ME5 .. 31 F5
Saffron Way.
  Sittingbourne ME10 .... 36 F7
Saffron's Pl. ⬛ CT20 .... 178 E5
Sailfield Ct. ME4 .... 9 F7
Sailmakers Ct. ME4 .... 10 B2
St Agnes Gdns. ME12 .... 1 D1
St Alban's Rd. CT13 .... 46 E1
St Albans Rd. ME7 .... 10 E7
St Alphege CE Inf Sch. CT5 .... 20 D1
St Alphege Cl. CT5 .... 43 B7
St Alphege La. ⬛ CT1 .... 66 F1
St Alphege Rd. ⬛ CT16 .... 149 C1
St Ambrose Gn. ME25 .... 123 E2
St Andrew Rd. ME7 .... 10 D7
St Andrew Terr. CT17 .... 149 A2
St Andrew's Cl.
  Maidstone ME16 .... 74 A2
St Andrew's Cl. Whitstable CT5 .. 43 E7
St Andrew's Gdns. CT15 ...... 130 E5
St Andrew's Lees. CT13 .... 94 A8
St Andrew's Rd. Deal CT14 ... 117 C6
St Andrew's Rd.
  Littlestone-on-S TN28 .... 200 E6
St Andrew's Rd.
  Maidstone ME16 .... 74 A3
St Andrews Cl.
  Ramsgate CT11 .... 52 F8
St Andrews. CT19 .... 178 E5
St Andrews Cl. Canterbury CT1 .. 87 E7
St Andrews Cl. Herne Bay CT6 .. 23 A4
St Andrews Cl. Margate CT9 .... 28 F7
St Andrews Gdns. CT17 .... 149 B2
St Andrews Way. CT14 .... 115 A3
St Ann's Rd. Dymchurch TN29 .. 195 B7
St Ann's Rd.
  Faversham ME13 .... 62 B7
St Anne Ct. ME14 .... 74 E4
St Anne's Ct. ⬛ Dover CT16 .. 149 B2
St Anne's Ct. Herne Bay CT6 ... 22 E5
St Anne's Dr. CT6 .... 22 D4
St Anne's Gdns. CT9 .... 28 F8
St Anne's Rd. Ashford TN23 .. 155 F7
St Anne's Rd. Whitstable CT5 ... 20 F2
St Anselm's
  Catholic Comp Sch. CT1 ...... 88 C5
St Anthony's Sch. CT9 .... 8 C1
St Anthony's Way. CT1 .... 8 C1
St Augustine of Canterbury
  RC Prim Sch. CT1 .... 33 D3
St Augustine's Abbey. CT1 .... 52 D5
St Augustine's Ave. CT9 .... 28 F8
St Augustine's Coll. CT1 .... 88 A8
St Augustine's Cres. CT5 .... 21 D3
St Augustine's Ct. CT1 .... 88 B8
St Augustine's Golf Course.
  CT12 .... 51 C4
St Augustine's Pk. CT11 .... 52 C6

St Augustine's RC Prim Sch.
  CT1 .... 176 E2
St Augustine's Rd.
  Canterbury CT1 .... 88 B7
St Augustine's Rd. Deal CT14 .. 116 C4
St Augustine's Rd.
  Ramsgate CT11 .... 52 D5
St Barnabas Cl. Ashford TN23 .. 155 F7
St Barnabas Cl. Gillingham ME7 .. 10 D3
St Barnabas Cl.
  Maidstone ME16 .... 74 C8
St Bart's Rd. CT13 .... 93 F8
St Bartholomew's Hospl. ME1 ... 9 E4
St Bartholomew's La. ME1 ...... 9 E4
St Bartholomew's Sch. ME10 .. 36 F7
St Bartholomew's Terr. ME1 .... 9 E4
St Benedict's Lawn. CT11 ...... 52 D5
St Benedicts
  RC Prim Sch. ME5 .... 32 C2
St Benet's Rd. CT8 .... 27 E7
St Benets Cl. TN30 .... 179 B8
St Benets Way. TN30 .... 179 B8
St Catherine's Dr. ME13 .... 62 D6
St Catherine's Gr. CT12 .... 28 D1
St Catherine's Hospl. ME1 .... 9 D4
St Catherines. TN29 .... 199 A7
St Catherines Ct. CT11 .... 29 F1
St Christopher Dr. CT9 .... 29 D8
St Christopher's Sch. CT1 ...... 88 B6
St Christophers Gn. CT10 .... 29 F5
St Clare Rd. CT14 .... 117 C1
St Clement's Ct. CT6 .... 23 A3
St Clement's Ho. ME1 .... 9 D5
St Clement's Rd. CT8 .... 7 C1
St Clements. ⬛ CT13 .... 73 A1
St Clements Cl. ME12 .... 6 D2
St Clements Ct. CT10 .... 29 E6
St Clements Rd. ME12 .... 6 E3
St Cosmus Cl. TN25 .... 105 B1
St Crispin's Cty Inf Sch. CT8 .. 27 E7
St Crispin's Rd. CT8 .... 27 E7
St David's Cl. Birchington CT7 .. 27 B8
St David's Cl. Whitstable CT5 .. 43 E8
St David's Rd. Deal CT14 ...... 117 C6
St David's Rd. Ramsgate CT11 .. 29 C6
St Davids Ave. CT17 .... 166 A5
St Denys Rd. CT18 .... 163 B5
St Dunstan's Cl. CT2 .... 66 E1
St Dunstan's Ct. CT9 .... 8 A2
St Dunstan's St. CT2 .... 66 E1
St Dunstan's Terr. CT2 .... 66 E1
St Eanswythe Way. ⬛ CT20 .. 178 D5
St Eanswythe's
  CE Prim Sch. CT20 .... 178 D4
St Edmund's RC Sch. CT16 .... 149 D2
St Edmund's Rd. CT14 .... 116 C4
St Edmunds Rd. CT1 .... 87 F8
St Edmunds Way. ME8 .... 12 B1
St Edward's
  RC Prim Sch. ME12 .... 1 C2
St Ethelbert's
  RC Prim Sch. CT11 .... 52 F8
St Faith's La. ME14 .... 76 B4
St Faith's St. ME14 .... 74 F4
St Faiths Sch. CT3 .... 71 C1
St Francis Cl. Deal CT14 ...... 116 F4
St Francis Cl. Margate CT9 ..... 29 D8
St Francis
  RC Prim Sch. ME14 .... 75 B7
St Francis Rd. CT19 .... 177 F6
St Francis Sch. ME14 .... 75 B7
St Gabriel's. ⬛ CT20 .... 178 E6
St George's Ave.
  Herne Bay CT6 .... 22 D4
St George's Ave.
  Sheerness ME12 .... 1 C1
St George's Bsns Ctr. TN28 .. 138 F2
St George's
  CE High Sch. CT11 .... 29 C5
St George's CE Mid Sch. ME12 .. 1 B8
St George's Cl. CT5 .... 43 E7
St George's Ct. ME12 .... 3 B8
St George's Lees. CT13 .... 94 A8
St George's Pass. CT14 .... 117 D6
St George's Pl. Canterbury CT1 .. 88 A8
St George's Pl. Hythe CT21 .. 187 D8
St George's Rd.
  Broadstairs CT10 .... 30 A4
St George's Rd. Deal CT14 ... 117 D6
St George's Rd.
  Folkestone CT19 .... 177 F6
St George's Rd.
  Gillingham ME7 .... 10 C6
St George's Rd.
  Ramsgate CT11 .... 52 F8
St George's Sch. CT13 .... 94 A8
St George's Sq. ⬛
  Ashford TN23 .... 139 B2
St George's Sq.
  Maidstone ME16 .... 74 E3
St George's St. CT1 .... 88 A8
St George's Terr. CT6 .... 22 E5
St Georges Ave. ME12 .... 5 D2
St Georges Cres. CT17 .... 166 B5
St Georges Ct. CT12 .... 149 A2
St Georges La. CT1 .... 88 A8
St Georges Pl. CT15 .... 150 F6
St Georges St. CT1 .... 88 A8
St Giles Cl. CT17 .... 166 B5
St Giles Rd. CT17 .... 166 B5
St Giles Wlk. CT17 .... 166 B5
St Gregory's. ⬛ CT1 .... 67 A1
St Gregory's Cl. CT14 .... 116 F4

St Gregory's
RC Prim Sch. CT9 .... 28 E8
St Gregory's Rd. CT1 .... 67 B1
St Helen's Rd. ME12 .... 1 E1
St Helier's Cl. ME16 .... 74 B2
St Hilda Rd. CT19 .... 177 E6
St Hilda's Rd. CT21 .... 176 B1
St Jacob's Pl. CT1 .... 87 D6
St James' Ave.
Broadstairs CT10 .... 29 E5
St James' Ave. Ramsgate CT12 .. 29 B1
St James Cl. ME12 .... 6 E4
St James' Gdns. CT5 .... 43 D8
St James La. 5 CT5 .... 166 E7
St James' Park Rd. CT9 .... 28 A8
St James Rd. CT14 .... 134 D5
St James St. CT5 .... 166 E7
St James's Terr. CT7 .... 27 B8
St Jean's Rd. CT8 .... 27 E7
St John Fisher
Cath Comp Sch. ME4 .... 9 E3
St John Fisher
Cath Sch (Lower Sch). ME4 .. 9 F2
St John's Ave. Ramsgate CT12 .. 29 A1
St John's Ave.
Sittingbourne ME10 .... 37 B3
St John's CE Inf Sch. ME4 .... 9 E4
St John's
CE (VA) Prim Sch. ME14 ... 75 E4
St John's Church Rd. CT19 .. 178 C6
St John's Cl. CT18 .... 163 A7
St John's Commandery
(rems of). CT15 .... 146 E4
St John's Cl. TN24 .... 157 A6
St John's Hospl. 6 CT1 .... 67 A1
St John's La. Ashford TN23 ... 139 C2
St John's La. Canterbury CT1 .. 87 F8
St John's Pl. CT1 .... 67 A1
St John's Rd. Dover CT17 .. 166 C7
St John's Rd.
Faversham ME13 .... 62 D7
St John's Rd. Gillingham ME7 .. 10 C3
St John's Rd. Margate CT9 .. 7 J2
St John's Rd.
New Romney TN28 .... 200 A6
St John's Rd. Whitstable CT5 .. 21 D3
St John's St. Folkestone CT20 .. 178 D5
St John's St. 7 Margate CT9 .. 7 J2
St John's Way. CT18 .... 163 A7
St Johns Cres. CT2 .... 66 D6
St Johns Rd. Elvington CT15 .. 114 B2
St Johns Rd. Hythe CT21 .. 176 A3
St Johns Way. ME1 .... 9 A2
St Joseph's
RC Prim Sch. CT3 .... 113 A5
St Julien Ave. CT1 .... 67 D1
St Katherine Rd. ME12 .... 3 E7
St Laurence Ave. ME16 .... 74 C8
St Laurence CE Jun Sch. CT12 52 B8
St Laurence Cl. ME9 .... 37 D2
St Laurence Cl. CT11 .... 52 C7
St Laurence Ave. CT11 .... 52 B5
St Laurence Cl. CT11 .... 88 B6
St Laurence Coll. CT11 .... 52 D8
St Laurence Coll
(Jun Sch). CT11 .... 52 E8
St Laurence Ct. TN28 .... 200 A6
St Laurence Forstal. CT1 .... 88 B6
St Lawrence Gd
(Kent Cty Cricket Club). CT1 88 B6
St Lawrence Ind Est. CT11 .... 52 B7
St Lawrence Rd. CT1 .... 88 B6
St Leonard's
CE Jun Sch. CT21 .... 176 B2
St Leonards Ave. ME4 .... 9 F2
St Leonards Cl. CT21 .... 176 B1
St Leonards Rd. Hythe CT21 176 B1
St Leonards Rd.
Maidstone ME16 .... 74 C8
St Louis Gr. CT6 .... 22 C4
St Luke's Ave. Maidstone ME14 .. 75 B5
St Luke's Ave. Ramsgate CT11 .. 52 B5
St Luke's Cl. CT8 .... 27 E8
St Luke's Cl. Maidstone ME14 .. 75 B5
St Luke's Rd. Ramsgate CT11 .. 52 B8
St Luke's Wlk. CT18 .... 162 F4
St Lukes Cl. CT5 .... 43 E7
St Lukes Cl. TN23 .... 155 F7
St Magnus Cl. CT7 .... 27 A8
St Margaret's at Cliffe
Cty Prim Sch. CT15 .... 151 A6
St Margaret's at Troy Town
CE Prim Sch. ME1 .... 9 C4
St Margaret's Banks. ME1 .... 9 D5
St Margaret's CE Inf Sch. ME8 33 E8
St Margaret's
CE Jun Sch. ME8 .... 33 E8
St Margaret's Cl. CT5 .... 43 A6
St Margaret's Mews. ME1 .... 9 C5
St Margaret's
St Margaret's at Cliffe CT15 .. 151 A5
St Margaret's Rd.
Westgate-on-S CT8 .... 27 E7
St Margaret's St.
Canterbury CT1 .... 87 F8
St Margaret's St.
Rochester ME1 .... 9 C5
St Margarets Cl. ME16 .... 74 B2
St Margarets Cl. 1 CT20 .... 178 E5
St Margarets Dr. Deal CT14 .. 134 B8
St Margarets Rd.
Gillingham ME8 .... 33 C5
St Margarets Rd. CT7 .... 27 F3
St Mark's Cl. CT20 .... 177 D5

St Marks Cl. CT5 .... 43 E8
St Marks Ho. ME7 .... 10 C5
St Martin's
CE Prim Sch. CT18 .... 177 B5
St Martin's Cl. Detling ME14 .. 55 A1
St Martin's Cl. Dover CT17 .. 166 B5
St Martin's
Cty Prim Sch. CT17 .... 166 A7
St Martin's Hill. CT1 .... 88 C8
St Martin's Hospl. CT1 .... 88 D8
St Martin's Pl. CT1 .... 88 B8
St Martin's Rd. Canterbury CT1 .. 67 B1
St Martin's Rd. Deal CT14 .. 116 F4
St Martin's Rd. Guston CT15 .. 149 E4
St Martin's Terr. CT1 .... 88 B8
St Martin's View. CT6 .... 46 A8
St Martins Ave. CT1 .... 88 B8
St Martins Cl. Canterbury CT1 .. 88 B8
St Martins Cl. Newington ME9 .. 35 C7
St Martins Rd.
Folkestone CT20 .... 177 D6
St Martins Rd.
New Romney TN28 .... 200 B6
St Mary Cl. 13 ME13 .... 62 D7
St Mary of Charity
CE Inf Sch. ME13 .... 62 D7
St Mary of Charity
CE Jun Sch. ME13 .... 62 D7
St Mary's Ave. CT9 .... 8 D1
St Mary's CE Prim Sch.
Ashford TN23 .... 139 A3
St Mary's CE Prim Sch.
Chilham CT4 .... 107 B8
St Mary's CE Prim Sch.
Dover CT16 .... 166 E8
St Mary's CE Prim Sch.
Folkestone CT19 .... 178 F6
St Mary's Church. CT5 .... 24 D7
St Mary's Cl. Eastry CT13 .... 93 C2
St Mary's Cl. Hamstreet TN26 .. 183 A8
St Mary's Cl. Nonington CT15 .. 113 C5
St Mary's Cl.
Woodnesborough CT13 .... 93 B6
St Mary's Coll.
Folkestone CT20 .... 178 A5
St Mary's Coll. Herne Bay CT6 .. 22 E4
St Mary's Cty Prim Sch. ME9 .. 9 B7
St Mary's Gdns. Gillingham ME7 . 10 B7
St Mary's Bay TN29 .... 195 A5
St Mary's Gdns. Upstreet CT3 .. 47 E3
St Mary's Gr.
Tilmanstone CT14 .... 115 A4
St Mary's Gr. Whitstable CT5 .. 42 F7
St Mary's Hospl. CT18 .... 161 D3
St Mary's Meadow. CT3 .... 91 A8
St Mary's Pl. ME9 .... 35 C7
St Mary's RC Prim Sch.
Deal CT14 .... 116 F3
St Mary's RC Prim Sch.
Gillingham ME7 .... 10 D6
St Mary's RC Prim Sch.
Whitstable CT5 .... 20 F2
St Mary's Rd. 5
Broadstairs CT10 .... 30 B4
St Mary's Rd. Deal CT14 .. 117 C1
St Mary's Rd. Elham CT4 .. 144 F4
St Mary's Rd. Faversham ME13 .. 62 D7
St Mary's Rd. Gillingham ME7 .. 10 C6
St Mary's Rd. Minster CT12 .. 50 B6
St Mary's Rd. Patrixbourne CT4 .. 89 B3
St Mary's Rd. Rochester ME2 .. 9 B7
St Mary's Rd. St Mary
in the Marsh TN28 & TN29 ..... 196 F3
St Mary's Rd. West Hythe TN21 175 B1
St Mary's Row. ME12 .... 4 A6
St Mary's St. CT1 .... 87 F8
St Mary's View. ME9 .... 35 C7
St Marys Gn. TN24 .... 139 E7
St Marys Mews. TN24 .... 156 F8
St Matthew's
CE (VC) Inf Sch. ME1 .... 9 A2
St Matthew's Cl. ME9 .... 35 C7
St Matthews Dr. ME1 .... 9 A2
St Michael's Alley. 11 CT11 .. 52 E6
St Michael's CE Inf Sch. ME16 . 74 E3
St Michael's
CE Jun Sch. ME16 .... 74 E3
St Michael's
CE Prim Sch. TN30 .... 167 A3
St Michael's Cl. Chatham ME4 .. 9 F3
St Michael's Cl. 5
Sittingbourne ME10 .... 36 F4
St Michael's Ct. 6
Folkestone CT20 .... 178 E5
St Michael's Ct. Rochester ME2 .. 9 B8
St Michael's Pl. CT2 .... 66 E2
St Michael's
RC Prim Sch. ME4 .... 9 F3
St Michael's Rd.
Canterbury CT2 .... 66 E2
St Michael's Rd.
Maidstone ME16 .... 74 D3
St Michael's Rd.
Sittingbourne ME10 .... 36 E4
St Michael's Rd.
Sittingbourne ME10 .... 37 A4
St Michael's St. CT20 .... 178 E5
St Michael's Terr. TN30 .. 167 B3
St Michael's Wlk. CT18 .. 162 F4
St Michaels Ave. CT9 .... 29 D8
St Michaels Cl. Canterbury CT2 .. 66 A1
St Michaels Cl.
Pratling Street ME14 & ME20 .. 53 C3
St Mildred's Ave.
Birchington CT7 .... 26 E8

St Mildred's Ave.
Broadstairs CT10 .... 30 A4
St Mildred's Ave.
Ramsgate CT11 .... 52 B5
St Mildred's Cl. 2 TN30 .... 179 A7
St Mildred's CE Inf Sch. CT10 .. 30 A4
St Mildred's Gdns. CT8 & CT9 .. 7 D1
St Mildred's Rd. Margate CT9 .. 8 A2
St Mildred's Rd. Minster CT12 .. 50 B5
St Mildred's Rd.
Ramsgate CT11 .... 52 C6
St Mildred's Rd.
Westgate-on-S CT8 .... 7 C1
St Mildreds Ct. Canterbury CT1 .. 87 E8
St Mildreds Ct. Deal CT14 .. 117 C1
St Mildreds Pl. CT1 .... 87 E7
St Monicas CT17 .... 166 C7
St Monicas Rd. CT14 .... 134 D6
St Nicholas at Wade
CE Prim Sch. CT7 .... 25 E2
St Nicholas CE Inf Sch. ME2 .. 9 A7
St Nicholas Cl. Deal CT14 .. 116 F4
St Nicholas Cl. Sturry CT2 .. 67 F7
St Nicholas Cnr. CT7 .... 25 F1
St Nicholas Hospl. CT2 .... 66 C1
St Nicholas Rd. Canterbury CT1 . 87 D6
St Nicholas Rd.
Faversham ME13 .... 62 A7
St Nicholas Rd. Hythe CT21 .. 176 A2
St Nicholas Rd.
Littlestone-on-S TN28 .... 200 E6
St Nicholas Rdbt. CT7 .... 26 B2
St Nicholas Sch. CT1 .... 87 F6
St Nicholas & St John's
CE Prim Sch. CT14 .... 134 C5
St Nicholas Terr. 1 CT21 .. 176 B2
St Patrick's Cl. Deal CT14 .. 117 C6
St Patrick's Cl. Whitstable CT5 .. 43 E7
St Patrick's Rd. Deal CT14 .. 117 C6
St Patrick's Rd. Ramsgate CT11 . 52 F8
St Patricks Rd. CT17 .... 166 A4
St Paul's Ave. ME13 .... 62 A7
St Paul's Ct. CT20 .... 177 E4
St Paul's Rd. CT9 .... 8 A3
St Paul's St. 1 ME10 .... 36 E5
St Paul's Way. CT20 .... 177 F4
St Pauls Cres. ME13 .... 64 A3
St Pauls Cty Inf Sch. ME14 .. 75 A7
St Pauls Rd. ME13 .... 64 A3
St Pauls Terr. CT1 .... 88 A8
St Peter St. ME1 .... 9 D4
St Peter's Bridge. ME16 .... 74 F4
St Peter's CE Prim Sch.
Aylesford ME20 .... 53 A3
St Peter's CE Prim Sch.
Folkestone CT19 .... 178 E5
St Peter's Cl. ME13 .... 3 D6
St Peter's Ct. Broadstairs CT10 .. 29 F5
St Peter's Ct. Faversham ME13 .. 62 A7
St Peter's Cty Inf Sch. ME1 .. 9 C3
St Peter's Footpath.
Margate CT9 .... 7 J1
St Peter's Footpath.
Margate CT9 .... 29 A8
St Peter's Gr. CT1 .... 87 F8
St Peter's La. CT1 & CT2 .... 66 F1
St Peter's Meth Prim Sch. CT1 87 F8
St Peter's Park Rd. CT10 .... 29 F5
St Peter's Path. ME1 .... 9 D5
St Peter's Pl. CT1 & CT2 .... 87 F8
St Peter's RC Prim Sch.
Sittingbourne ME10 .... 36 D2
St Peter's RC Prim Sch.
Sittingbourne ME10 .... 36 E4
St Peter's Rd.
Boughton Street ME13 .... 64 A3
St Peter's Rd. Broadstairs CT10 .. 29 F5
St Peter's Rd. Margate CT9 .... 7 J1
St Peter's Rd. Whitstable CT5 .. 20 D2
St Peter's St.
Canterbury CT1 & CT2 .... 87 F8
St Peter's St. Sandwich CT13 .. 73 A1
St Peter's Way. TN26 .... 170 A8
St Philip Howard
RC Prim Sch. CT6 .... 22 F5
St Philip's Ave. ME15 .... 75 B2
St Philip's CE Prim Sch. ME15 . 75 A3
St Radigund's
Cty Prim Sch. CT17 .... 149 A1
St Radigund's Pl. CT17 .... 67 A1
St Radigund's Rd. CT17 .. 149 A1
St Radigunds St. 22 CT1 .. 67 A1
St Richard's
RC Prim Sch. CT16 .... 149 D1
St Richard's Rd. CT14 .... 116 F3
St Richard's Wlk. CT17 .. 166 A4
St Ronan's Cl. ME15 .... 97 C7
St Saviour's Cl. ME13 .... 62 E7
St Saviour's Hospl. CT21 .. 176 F2
St Saviours CE Jun Sch. CT8 .. 27 E8
St Saviours Cl. CT19 .... 178 D7
St Saviours Rd. ME15 .... 97 D6
St Simon of England
RC Prim Sch. TN23 .... 156 A8
St Simon Stock RC Sch. ME16 . 74 C4
St Stephen's CE Inf Sch. ME15 74 E2
St Stephen's Cl. Canterbury CT2 66 F2
St Stephen's Cl. Newington ME9 35 C7
St Stephen's Ct. CT2 .... 66 F2
St Stephen's Cty Inf Sch. CT2 . 66 F3
St Stephen's Cty Jun Sch. CT1 66 F2
St Stephen's Fields. CT2 .... 66 F1
St Stephen's Gn. CT2 .... 66 F3
St Stephen's Hill. CT2 .... 66 E4

St Stephen's Lodge. CT2 .... 66 F2
St Stephen's Rd. CT2 .... 66 F2
St Stephen's Sq. ME15 .... 74 E2
St Stephen's Way. CT2 .... 177 F4
St Stephen's Wlk. TN23 .. 155 F7
St Swithin's Rd. CT5 .... 21 B3
St Teresa's
RC Prim Sch. TN24 .... 139 B4
St Theresa's Cl. TN24 .... 139 B3
St Thomas' Cross. TN26 .. 170 E3
St Thomas Hill. CT2 .... 66 D3
St Thomas More
RC Prim Sch. ME5 .... 32 A5
St Thomas of Canterbury
Cath Prim Sch. ME8 .... 11 B2
St Thomas' RC Prim Sch. CT1 . 67 A1
St Thomas's Hospl. CT13 .... 72 F1
St Thomas's Sch. ME10 .... 36 E7
St Vincent Rd. CT15 .... 150 F7
St Vincent's Cl. Littlebourne CT3 68 F1
St Vincent's Cl. Whitstable CT5 .. 43 E7
St Welcume's Way. ME17 .. 100 E6
St Winifred Rd. CT19 .... 177 F6
Salem St. ME15 .... 75 A3
Salisbury Ave. Broadstairs CT10 .. 29 F2
Salisbury Ave. Gillingham ME8 .. 33 D8
Salisbury Ave. Ramsgate CT11 .. 52 F8
Salisbury Cl. ME10 .... 37 C4
Salisbury Ho. 5 ME15 .... 97 D7
Salisbury Rd. Canterbury CT2 .. 66 E2
Salisbury Rd. Chatham ME4 .. 10 A3
Salisbury Rd. Deal CT14 .. 117 B2
Salisbury Rd. Dover CT16 .. 149 D1
Salisbury Rd. Folkestone CT19 .. 177 E7
Salisbury Rd. Herne Bay CT6 .. 23 C5
Salisbury Rd. Kit's Coty ME20 .. 53 D7
Salisbury Rd. Maidstone ME14 .. 75 A6
Salisbury Rd.
St Margaret's at Cliffe CT15 .. 151 B6
Salisbury Rd. Whitstable CT5 .. 43 D8
Sally Port. ME7 .... 10 A6
Sally Port Gdns. ME7 .... 10 B6
Salmestone
Cty Prim Sch. CT9 .... 28 E8
Salmestone Grange. CT9 .. 28 E8
Salmestone Rd. CT9 .... 28 F8
Salmestone Rise. CT9 .... 28 E8
Salmon Cres. ME12 .... 3 F6
Salt Marsh La. 15 CT5 .... 20 D2
Salt's Ave. ME15 .... 96 F3
Salt's Dr. CT10 .... 29 E5
Salter's La. TN29 .... 197 C8
Salters La. ME13 .... 62 D4
Salthouse Cl. TN29 .... 197 D8
Saltings The.
Littlestone-on-S TN28 .... 200 E5
Saltings The. 10 Whitstable CT5 .. 20 D2
Salts Cl. CT5 .... 20 D1
Salts La. ME15 .... 97 A4
Saltwood CE Prim Sch. CT21 .. 176 B4
Saltwood Gdns. CT9 .... 8 E2
Saltwood Rd. ME15 .... 74 F1
Samara Cl. ME5 .... 32 A1
Samian Cres. CT19 .... 177 C6
Samphire Cl. ME14 .... 75 E4
Sancroft Ave. CT2 .... 66 C1
Sanctuary Cl. CT10 .... 29 F2
Sanctuary Rd. ME8 .... 11 A3
Sand Ct. ME12 .... 6 G2
Sandbanks Rd. ME13 .... 41 C2
Sandbourne Dr. ME14 .... 53 F1
Sanders Cl. ME12 .... 4 A5
Sandford Rd. ME10 .... 36 B5
Sandgate St. ME8 .... 33 F4
Sandgate
Cty Prim Sch. CT20 .... 177 F4
Sandgate Espl. CT20 & CT21 .. 177 D2
Sandgate High St. CT20 .. 177 E3
Sandgate Hill. CT20 .... 178 A4
Sandgate Rd. Folkestone CT20 .. 178 C4
Sandgate Rd. Folkestone CT20 .. 178 D4
Sandhurst Cl. Canterbury CT2 .. 67 A4
Sandhurst Cl. Gillingham ME8 .. 11 C3
Sandhurst Rd. CT9 .... 8 F2
Sandilands. TN24 .... 139 E2
Sandle's Rd. CT7 .... 26 F7
Sandlewood Dr. CT7 .... 25 F1
Sandling Cl. TN23 .... 155 F6
Sandling Cty Prim Sch. ME14 .. 75 B8
Sandling La. ME14 .... 75 A8
Sandling Rd. Hythe CT21 .. 175 F6
Sandling Rd. Maidstone ME14 .. 74 F6
Sandling Rd.
Maidstone,Ringlestone ME14 .. 74 F7
Sandling Sta. CT21 .... 175 F6
Sandown Cl. CT14 .... 95 D1
Sandown Cotts. Margate CT9 .. 8 A3
Sandown Cotts. Teynham ME9 .. 38 E1
Sandown Ct. CT14 .... 117 C7
Sandown
Cty Prim Sch. CT14 .... 117 C7
Sandown Dr. Gillingham ME8 .. 33 D7
Sandown Dr. Herne Bay CT6 .. 22 D4
Sandown Lees. CT13 .... 94 D8
Sandown Rd. Deal CT14 .. 117 D8
Sandown Rd. Sandwich CT13 .. 94 B8
Sandpiper Cl. 3
Birchington CT7 .... 26 F8
Sandpiper La. Margate CT9 .... 7 13
Sandpiper Rd. Chatham ME5 .. 32 D2
Sandpiper Rd. Whitstable CT5 .. 43 B7
Sandpit Hill. CT3 .... 47 C4
Sandringham Ho. ME1 .... 9 B4
Sandringham Rd. ME8 .... 33 E3

Sandstone Ct. CT20 .... 178 A3
Sandstone Rise. ME14 .... 54 C8
Sandway ME17 .... 100 F4
Sandway Bay
Bird Obsy. CT13 .... 94 E7
Sandwich Cl. CT20 .... 177 F5
Sandwich Cty Inf Sch. CT13 .. 72 F1
Sandwich Cty Jun Sch. CT13 .. 93 F7
Sandwich Hill. CT3 .... 70 B1
Sandwich Ind Est. CT13 .... 73 B1
Sandwich Rd. Ash CT3 .... 71 F1
Sandwich Rd. Ash CT3 .... 72 A2
Sandwich Rd. Cliffs End CT12 .. 51 D4
Sandwich Rd. Eastry CT13 .. 93 C3
Sandwich Rd. Eythorne CT15 .. 131 C8
Sandwich Rd.
Nonington CT15 & CT3 .... 113 F6
Sandwich Rd. Sandwich CT13 .. 93 D7
Sandwich Rd.
Tilmanstone CT14 & CT15 .. 115 B2
Sandwich Rd. Whitfield CT15 .. 132 A2
Sandwich Rd. Whitfield CT16 .. 149 A7
Sandwich Rd.
Woodnesborough CT13 .... 93 D5
Sandwich Sta. CT13 .... 94 A8
Sandwich Tech Sch. CT13 .. 93 F6
Sandwood Rd. Ramsgate CT11 .. 29 F1
Sandwood Rd. Sandwich CT13 .. 93 F8
Sandy Dell. ME7 .... 33 A3
Sandy La. Ashford TN24 .... 140 B1
Sandy La. Daniel's Water TN26 .. 154 E6
Sandy La. Hythe CT20 & CT21 .. 177 B3
Sandy La.
Maidstone,Harbourland ME14 .. 75 C8
Sandy La.
Maidstone,Penenden Heath ME14 75 C7
Sandy La.
Maidstone,Ware Street ME14 .. 76 B5
Sandy La. Tenterden TN30 .. 179 B7
Sandy Mount. ME14 .... 76 B5
Sandy Pl. TN25 .... 158 D5
Sandyhurst La.
TN24 & TN25 & TN23 .... 139 B8
Sangro Pl. CT1 .... 67 D1
Sanspareil Ave. ME12 .... 4 A6
Santon La. CT3 .... 70 E8
Saracen Cl. ME7 .... 11 A1
Saracen Fields. ME5 & ME14 .. 54 C8
Sarah Gdns. CT9 .... 29 D8
Sark Cl. TN29 .... 195 C8
Sarre Ct. CT7 .... 48 D6
Sarre Mill. CT7 .... 48 D7
Sarre Pl. CT13 .... 93 F8
Sarsen Hts. ME5 .... 31 F1
Satis Ave. ME10 .... 36 E7
Satmar La. CT15 & CT18 .... 164 E4
Saunders La. CT3 .... 71 F1
Saunders St. ME7 .... 10 C6
Saunders Way. TN31 .... 201 A2
Savage Rd. ME5 .... 32 B3
Savernake Dr. CT6 .... 23 B2
Saw Lodge Field. TN23 .. 156 C4
Sawpit Rd. ME9 .... 59 B2
Sawyers Ct. ME4 .... 10 B2
Saxon Ave. ME12 .... 4 B6
Saxon Cl. CT21 .... 176 E2
Saxon Rd. Bridge CT4 .... 89 A1
Saxon Rd. Faversham ME13 .. 62 C7
Saxon Rd. Ramsgate CT11 .. 52 B6
Saxon Rd. Westgate-on-S CT8 .. 7 D1
Saxon St. 9 CT17 .... 166 D8
Saxons Cl. CT14 .... 117 C8
Saxons Dr. ME14 .... 75 B7
Saxton Rd. TN29 .... 204 E5
Saxton St. ME7 .... 10 C5
Sayer Rd. TN27 .... 120 C8
Sayers La. 4 TN30 .... 179 A7
Scanlons Bridge Rd. CT21 .. 176 A2
Scarborough Dr. ME12 .... 4 C8
Scarlett Cl. ME5 .... 32 C5
Scene Cotts. CT21 .... 176 E4
Sceptre Way. CT5 .... 43 B7
School Ave. ME7 .... 10 E4
School Cl The. CT8 .... 7 C1
School Hill. CT4 .... 107 B8
School La. Bapchild ME9 .... 37 D2
School La. Bekesbourne CT4 .. 89 C4
School La. Blean CT2 .... 66 A6
School La. Borden ME9 .... 35 F4
School La.
Boughton Street ME13 .... 63 F3
School La. Fordwich CT2 .... 68 A4
School La. Goodnestone CT3 .. 91 D2
School La. Herne Bay CT6 .... 23 B1
School La. Hoath CT3 .... 46 E6
School La. Ickham CT3 .... 90 C8
School La. Iwade ME9 .... 14 C4
School La. Lower Halstow ME9 .. 13 B2
School La. Lower Hardres CT4 .. 110 B6
School La. Maidstone ME15 .. 75 E1
School La. Newington ME9 .. 35 B7
School La. Platt's Heath ME17 .. 100 F2
School La. Ramsgate CT11 .. 52 E7
School La.
Stalisfield Green ME13 .... 103 D6
School La. Staple CT3 .... 92 A6
School La. Stourmouth CT3 .. 48 E2
School La. Wingham CT3 .... 91 A7
School Rd. Appledore TN26 .. 181 C1
School Rd. Ash CT3 .... 71 C2
School Rd. Bethersden TN26 .. 153 D4
School Rd. Charing TN27 .. 120 C8
School Rd. Densole CT18 .. 162 F2
School Rd. Faversham ME13 .. 62 C6
School Rd. Hothfield TN26 .. 138 A2
School Rd. Hythe CT21 .. 176 B4
School Rd. Sandwich CT13 .. 72 F1

School Rd. Sittingbourne ME10 .... 37 B3
School Rd. Tilmanstone CT14 .... 114 F4
School View. ME9 .... 58 C8
Scimitar Cl. ME7 .... 11 A1
Scocles Cotts. ME12 .... 4 C5
Scocles Rd. ME12 .... 4 C5
Scoggers Hill. ME13 .... 85 A7
Scot's La. TN25 .... 159 F8
Scotby Ave. ME5 .... 32 B4
Scott Ave. ME8 .... 12 A1
Scott St. ME14 .... 74 F6
Scott's Terr. ME4 .... 9 F3
Scotteswood Ave. ME4 .... 9 F2
Scotton St. TN25 .... 123 F2
Scragged Oak Rd.
  Detling ME14 .... 55 C5
Scragged Oak Rd.
  Hucking ME14 .... 56 C1
Scraps Hill. ME9 .... 37 F4
Scrapsgate Rd. ME12 .... 4 A7
Scrubbs La. ME16 .... 74 D4
Sea App. ME12 .... 6 E4
Sea Rd. Hythe CT21 .... 177 A2
Sea Rd. Kingsdown CT14 .... 134 D6
Sea Rd. Westgate-on-S CT7 & CT8 ... 7 C1
Sea St. Herne Bay CT6 .... 22 C3
Sea St.
  St Margaret's at Cliffe CT15 .... 151 A6
Sea St. Whitstable CT5 .... 20 D2
Sea View Ave. CT7 .... 26 E8
Sea View Cl. CT18 .... 164 B1
Sea View Gdns. ME12 .... 6 E3
Sea View Hts. CT7 .... 26 D8
Sea View Rd. Birchington CT7 .... 26 E8
Sea View Rd. Broadstairs CT10 ... 30 A6
Sea View Rd. Cliffs End CT12 .... 51 D6
Sea View Rd. Herne Bay CT6 .... 23 C5
Sea View Rd.
  St Margaret's at Cliffe CT15 .... 150 F4
Sea View Sq. CT6 .... 22 F5
Sea View Terr.
  Folkestone CT20 .... 177 D3
Sea View Terr. Margate CT9 ...... 7 G2
Sea View Terr. Minster ME12 .... 5 A5
Sea Wall. Dymchurch TN29 ...... 195 D8
Sea Wall. Whitstable CT5 .... 20 D2
Seabourne Way. TN29 .... 195 B7
Seabrook Cl. CT21 .... 177 B3
Seabrook Gdns. CT21 .... 177 B2
Seabrook Gr. CT21 .... 177 A2
Seabrook Rd. CT21 .... 176 E2
Seabrook Vale. CT21 .... 177 B4
Seacroft Rd. CT10 .... 30 A1
Seadown Cl. CT21 .... 177 A4
Seafield Rd. Broadstairs CT10 ... 30 A4
Seafield Rd. Ramsgate CT11 .... 52 C6
Seafield Rd. Whitstable CT5 .... 21 B3
Seaford Ct. ME15 .... 9 B5
Seagar Rd. ME13 .... 40 B1
Seager Rd. ME12 .... 1 F2
Seagrave Cres. CT19 .... 178 F6
Sealand Ct. ME15 .... 9 B5
Seamark Cl. CT12 .... 49 D7
Seamark Rd. CT12 & CT7 .... 26 D2
Seapoint Rd. CT10 .... 30 B3
Seaview Ave. ME12 .... 6 H1
Seaview Cotts. CT10 .... 30 B4
Seaview Cl. CT10 .... 30 B3
Seaview Rd. Gillingham ME7 .... 10 C4
Seaview Rd.
  Greatstone-on-S TN28 .... 200 E1
Seaville Dr. CT6 .... 23 E5
Seaway Cres. TN29 .... 194 F4
Seaway Gdns. TN29 .... 194 F4
Seaway Rd. TN29 .... 195 A4
Second Ave. Broadstairs CT10 .... 8 G2
Second Ave.
  Chatham ME4 & ME5 .... 10 C1
Second Ave. Eastchurch ME12 .... 5 F5
Second Ave. Gillingham ME7 .... 10 E3
Second Ave. Margate CT9 .... 8 B3
Second Ave. Rushenden ME11 .... 2 F3
Second Ave. Sheerness ME12 .... 1 C1
Secretan Rd. ME1 .... 9 B1
Sedge Cres. ME5 .... 31 E4
Sedley Cl. ME8 .... 33 C3
Seesalter Cross. CT5 .... 43 A6
Seeshill Cl. CT5 .... 43 E8
Segrave Rd. CT19 .... 178 F5
Selbey Cl. CT6 .... 23 C4
Selborne Rd. CT19 .... 29 B8
Selbourne Rd. ME7 .... 10 D7
Selbourne Wlk. ME15 .... 97 F6
Selby Rd. ME15 .... 97 F4
Selkirk Rd. ME13 .... 149 B3
Sellens Cotts. ME12 .... 1 E2
Sellindge
  Cty Prim Sch. TN25 .... 159 C1
Selling CE Prim Sch. ME13 ...... 84 B5
Selling Ct. ME13 .... 84 C5
Selling Rd. Chilham CT4 .... 85 B3
Selling Rd. Faversham ME13 .... 84 E6
Selling Rd. Selling ME13 .... 84 E6
Sellinge Gn. ME8 .... 11 C3
Selsea Ave. CT6 .... 22 D4
Selstead Cl. ME8 .... 11 C2
Selsted CE Prim Sch. CT15 .... 146 C6

Selway Ct. CT14 .... 117 B3
Selwood Rd. ME12 .... 3 E6
Selwyn Cl. CT10 .... 29 F5
Selwyn Dr. CT10 .... 29 F5
Semaphore Rd. CT7 .... 26 F8
Semple Cl. CT12 .... 50 C7
Semple Gdns. ME4 .... 9 E3
Senacre La. ME15 .... 97 E6
Senacre Sq. ME15 .... 97 F7
Senacre Tech Coll. ME15 .... 97 D6
Senacre Wood
  Cty Prim Sch. ME15 .... 97 F7
Sene Pk. CT21 .... 176 D3
Sene Valley
  Golf Course. CT21 .... 176 E4
Senlac Cl. CT11 .... 52 B6
Serene Ct. [12] CT10 .... 30 B4
Serene Pl. [9] CT10 .... 30 B4
Setford Rd. ME5 .... 32 C6
Setterfield Ho. CT21 .... 176 D2
Setterfield Rd. CT9 .... 7 J1
Settington Ave. ME5 .... 10 C1
Sevastopol Pl. CT1 .... 67 D1
Seven Stones Dr. CT10 .... 30 A1
Sevenacre Rd. ME13 .... 62 C8
Sevenscore Farm Cotts. CT12 ... 51 A5
Severn Rd. ME5 .... 32 C5
Sevington La. TN24 .... 157 A7
Sevington Pk. ME15 .... 96 F6
Sewell Cl. CT7 .... 27 A6
Sexburga Dr. ME12 .... 4 B8
Sextant Pk. ME9 .... 9 E6
Seymour Ave.
  Westgate-on-S CT9 .... 7 D1
Seymour Ave. Whitstable CT5 .... 20 E1
Seymour Cl. CT6 .... 23 B1
Seymour Pl. CT1 .... 87 E7
Seymour Rd. [1] Chatham ME4 ... 10 B3
Seymour Rd. Gillingham ME8 .... 12 C1
Seymour Rd.
  St Margaret's at Cliffe CT15 .... 150 F8
Shackleton Cl. ME5 .... 32 B6
Shadoxhurst Rd. TN26 .... 169 C7
Shaftesbury Ave. CT19 .... 177 E7
Shaftesbury Ct. CT14 .... 117 D2
Shaftesbury Dr. ME16 .... 74 C4
Shaftesbury Rd. Canterbury CT2 ... 66 F3
Shaftesbury Rd. Hersden CT3 .... 46 E1
Shaftesbury Rd. Whitstable CT5 .... 20 D1
Shaftsbury St. CT11 .... 52 F7
Shah Pl. CT11 .... 52 D7
Shakespeare Ct. CT17 .... 166 B7
Shakespeare Pas. CT9 .... 7 H2
Shakespeare Rd.
  Birchington CT7 .... 27 A8
Shakespeare Rd. Dover CT17 .... 166 B6
Shakespeare Rd.
  Gillingham ME7 .... 10 C3
Shakespeare Rd. Margate CT9 .... 7 J1
Shakespeare Rd.
  Sittingbourne ME10 .... 37 A4
Shakespeare Terr. [8] CT20 .... 178 C4
Shalder Ho. ME7 .... 10 D7
Shalloak Rd. CT2 .... 67 D6
Shallows Rd. CT10 .... 29 D6
Shalmsford Ct. CT4 .... 86 C2
Shalmsford Rd. CT4 .... 85 E2
Shalmsford St. CT4 .... 86 B2
Shamel Bsns Ctr. ME2 .... 9 C7
Shamley Rd. ME5 .... 32 D2
Shamrock Ave. CT5 .... 43 B7
Shanklin Cl. ME5 .... 32 C8
Shapland Cl. CT6 .... 23 C3
Share and Coulter Rd. CT5 .... 21 D1
Sharon Cres. ME5 .... 31 F4
Sharsted Hill. ME9 .... 81 C8
Sharsted Way. Gillingham ME7 ... 33 A3
Sharsted Way. Maidstone ME14 .... 76 B5
Shatterlocks
  Cty Inf Sch. CT17 .... 149 B2
Shaw Cross. TN24 .... 139 D5
Shawdon Ave. CT13 .... 95 A7
Shaws Way. ME1 .... 9 C3
Shawstead Rd. ME7 & ME7 ...... 32 D5
Sheal's Cres. ME15 .... 75 A2
Sheals Ct. ME15 .... 75 A2
Shear Way. TN29 .... 186 C5
Shearers Cl. ME14 .... 75 E4
Shearwater. ME16 .... 74 B5
Shearwater Ave. CT5 .... 43 C7
Shearwater Ct. ME12 .... 3 B8
Shearwater Ho. TN29 .... 195 A3
Shearway Rd. CT19 .... 177 F8
Sheepfold La. TN23 .... 156 C4
Sheerness Golf Course. ME12 .... 3 E6
Sheerness Harbour Est. ME12 ... 1 A3
Sheerness-on-Sea
  (Terminus). ME12 .... 1 C2
Sheerstone. ME9 .... 14 D4
Sheerwater Rd. CT3 .... 70 F5
Sheerways. ME13 .... 62 A6
Sheet Glass Rd. ME11 .... 3 A3
Shelden Dr. ME8 .... 33 F8
Sheldon Bsns Ctr. ME2 .... 9 D8
Sheldon Cl. CT3 .... 113 A6
Sheldwich Cl. TN23 .... 156 A6
Shellbeach. ME12 .... 19 D6
Shelley Ave. CT1 .... 67 C2
Shelley Rd. ME16 .... 74 C2
Shellness Rd. ME12 .... 19 D7
Shellons St. CT20 .... 178 D5
Shelvin La. CT4 .... 129 C3
Shenley Gn. ME14 .... 53 F2
Shepherd Dr. TN24 .... 157 A8
Shepherd's Close Rd. CT4 ...... 89 E1
Shepherd's Cres. CT15 .... 132 B1
Shepherds Gate. ME7 .... 32 F5
Shepherds Gate Dr. ME14 ...... 75 E6

Shepherds Way.
  Langley Heath ME17 .... 98 E4
Shepherds Way.
  Whitstable CT5 .... 44 C8
Shepherds Well Sta. CT15 ...... 130 D5
Shepherds Wlk. Hythe CT21 .... 175 E1
Shepherds Wlk. Whitstable CT5 . 44 C8
Shepherdsgate. CT2 .... 66 F1
Shepherdsgate Dr. CT6 .... 46 A8
Shepherdswell Rd. CT15 .... 131 A7
Shepperton Cl. ME5 .... 32 C4
Sheppey Cotts. ME12 .... 1 E2
Sheppey Hospl. ME12 .... 4 C7
Sheppey Rd. ME15 .... 97 A7
Sheppey St. ME12 .... 1 B2
Sheppey Terr. ME12 .... 4 F5
Sheppey View. CT5 .... 43 C6
Sheppey Way.
  Bobbing ME9 & ME9 .... 36 B7
Sheppey Way. Iwade ME9 .... 14 F6
Sheppey Way.
  Queenborough ME12 & ME9 ..... 3 D2
Shepway. TN24 .... 139 E5
Shepway Cl. CT19 .... 178 D6
Shepway Cross. CT21 .... 175 B3
Shepway Cty Inf Sch. ME15 .... 97 C8
Shepway Cty Inf Sch. ME15 .... 97 E8
Shepway Cty Jun Sch. ME15 .... 97 E8
Sheraton Ct. ME5 .... 31 F1
Sherbourne Dr. ME16 .... 74 B2
Sheridan Cl. Chatham ME5 ...... 32 C7
Sheridan Cl. Maidstone ME14 ... 74 E8
Sheridan Rd. CT16 .... 149 B3
Sheriff Dr. ME5 .... 32 A2
Sherman Cl. ME7 .... 11 B1
Shernold Sch. ME16 .... 74 D5
Shernolds. ME15 .... 97 B7
Sheron Cl. CT14 .... 117 A5
Sherriffs Court La. CT12 ...... 49 E6
Sherwood Ave. ME5 .... 32 A2
Sherwood Cl. Ashford TN24 .... 139 D7
Sherwood Cl. Faversham ME13 .... 40 B1
Sherwood Cl. Herne Bay CT6 ... 23 C2
Sherwood Cl. Whitstable CT5 .... 43 C6
Sherwood Ct. CT8 .... 7 C1
Sherwood Dr. CT5 .... 43 C6
Sherwood Gdns. CT11 .... 29 E1
Sherwood Ho. ME5 .... 32 A3
Sherwood Rd. CT7 .... 26 F5
Shillingheld Cl. ME14 .... 75 F5
Ship Cl. TN29 .... 195 C8
Ship La. ME1 .... 9 E4
Ship St. CT19 .... 178 D6
Shipland Hos. TN27 .... 136 D8
Shipley Ct. ME4 .... 75 A4
Shipman Ave. CT2 .... 87 C8
Shipmans Way. TN16 .... 149 A3
Shipwrights Ave. ME4 .... 10 B2
Shipwrights Lee. CT5 .... 20 C2
Shire La. ME13 .... 103 C6
Shireway Cl. CT19 .... 178 A7
Shirley Ave. Chatham ME5 ...... 31 D5
Shirley Ave. Ramsgate CT11 .... 29 E1
Shirley Way. ME15 .... 76 A3
Shoebury Terr. ME12 .... 5 A5
Sholden Bank. CT14 .... 116 E4
Sholden New Rd. CT14 .... 116 E4
Shooter's Hill. [5] CT16 & CT17 .... 149 C1
Shooters Hill. CT15 .... 131 C8
Shorefields. ME8 .... 12 B2
Shoregate La. ME9 .... 12 F6
Shoreham La. TN30 .... 167 A3
Shoreham Wlk. ME15 .... 97 F7
Shoreland Ct. ME1 .... 9 B5
Shorncliffe Cres. CT20 .... 177 E5
Shorncliffe Ind Est. CT20 .... 177 D4
Shorncliffe Rd.
  Folkestone CT20 .... 177 F5
Shorncliffe Rd.
  Folkestone CT20 .... 178 B5
Short La. Alkham CT15 .... 147 D1
Short La. Gillingham ME7 ...... 11 A6
Short La. Snargate TN29 ...... 191 D6
Short St. [3] Chatham ME4 .... 10 B3
Short St. Chillenden CT3 ...... 114 A8
Short St. [5] Sandwich CT13 ... 73 A1
Short St. Sheerness ME12 ...... 1 C2
Short's Prospect. ME12 .... 17 C8
Shortlands Gn. ME15 .... 97 F5
Shortlands Rd. ME10 .... 37 B4
Shorts Way. ME1 .... 9 A3
Shottendane Rd.
  CT9 & CT7 & CT9 .... 28 C7
Shottenden Rd. Gillingham ME7 . 10 D7
Shottenden Rd.
  Leaveland CT4 & ME13 .... 105 D8
Shottenden Rd. Shottenden CT4 . 84 B1
Shrimpton Cl. CT4 .... 85 B3
Shropshire Terr. [3] ME15 .... 97 E7
Shrub Hill Rd. CT5 .... 44 D7
Shrubbery The. Barham CT4 .... 111 F1
Shrubbery The. Deal CT14 ...... 117 C1
Shrubcote. TN30 .... 179 C7
Shrubsole Ave. ME12 .... 1 D1
Shrubsole Dr. ME14 .... 53 F3
Shuart La. CT7 .... 25 F4
Shurland Ave.
  Leysdown-on-S ME12 .... 6 H1
Shurland Ave. Minster ME12 .... 4 B6
Shurland Ave.
  Sittingbourne ME10 .... 36 F1
Shuttle Rd. CT10 .... 30 B5
Sibert's Cl. CT15 .... 130 F5
Sibertswold
  CE Prim Sch. CT15 .... 130 E4
Sibton Park Prep Sch. CT18 .... 161 B8

Sidings The. CT18 .... 161 C7
Sidney Rd. Gillingham ME7 .... 10 C7
Sidney Rd. Rochester ME1 .... 9 A7
Sidney St. Folkestone CT19 .... 178 E7
Sidney St. Maidstone ME16 .... 74 C2
Silchester Ct. ME14 .... 75 C7
Silecroft Ct. TN23 .... 138 E1
Silvanus Ho. CT11 .... 52 D7
Silver Ave. CT7 .... 27 B6
Silver Bank. ME5 .... 32 A6
Silver Birch Gr. TN23 .... 155 E6
Silver Birches. Chatham ME5 ... 32 A3
Silver Birches. Ruckinge TN26 . 171 A5
Silver Birches. Sheerness ME12 . 1 H1
Silver Hill. Chatham ME4 .... 9 F3
Silver Hill. Tenterden TN30 .... 167 B1
Silver Hill Gdns. Ashford TN24 . 140 A1
Silver Hill Gdns. Chatham ME4 .... 9 F3
Silver Hill Rd. TN24 .... 140 A1
Silver St. Deal CT14 .... 117 D7
Silver St. Silver Street ME9 .... 57 F5
Silver Tree. ME5 .... 32 B1
Silverdale. ME16 .... 74 A2
Silverdale Ave. ME12 .... 4 A6
Silverdale Dr. Gillingham ME8 . 33 F7
Silverdale Dr. Herne Bay CT6 .. 23 D2
Silverdale Gr. ME10 .... 36 D3
Silverdale Rd. CT11 .... 52 A5
Silverlands Rd. CT18 .... 161 C7
Silvers The. CT10 .... 29 C4
Silverspot Cl. ME8 .... 33 F7
Silverweed Rd. ME5 .... 31 F4
Simmonds La. ME15 .... 98 B6
Simmonds Rd. CT1 .... 87 E7
Simon Ave. CT9 .... 8 D2
Simon Langton
  Sch for Boys. CT1 .... 88 A4
Simon Langton
  Sch for Girls. CT1 .... 88 C5
Simon's Ave. TN23 .... 155 F7
Simone Weil Ave. TN24 .... 139 B4
Simpson Rd. ME10 .... 36 C5
Sinclair Cl. ME8 .... 33 E5
Singapore Dr. ME7 .... 10 B5
Singer Ave. CT6 .... 22 B4
Singledge Ave. CT16 .... 148 F6
Singledge La. CT15 .... 131 C2
Singleton Cl. CT12 .... 50 B6
Singleton Ctr The. TN23 ...... 155 D8
Singleton Hill. TN23 .... 155 D8
Singleton Rd. TN23 .... 138 C1
Sion Hill. CT11 .... 52 E6
Sir Evelyn Rd. ME1 .... 9 B1
Sir John Hawkins Way. ME4 .... 9 F4
Sir John Moore Ave. CT21 .... 176 E2
Sir John Moore Ct. [5] CT20 .. 177 E3
Sir Joseph Williamson's
  Mathematical Sch. ME1 .... 9 C1
Sir Roger Manwood's Sch.
  CT13 .... 94 B8
Sir William Nottidge
  Tech Sch. CT5 .... 43 F8
Siskin Cl. ME20 .... 162 F4
Sissinghurst Dr. ME16 .... 74 B4
Sittingbourne
  Comm Coll. ME10 .... 37 C2
Sittingbourne & Kemsley
  Light Rly. ME10 .... 37 A7
Sittingbourne Rd.
  Maidstone,Detling ME14 ...... 75 E8
Sittingbourne Rd. Maidstone,
  Penenden Heath ME14 .... 75 B6
Six Fields Path. TN30 .... 179 A7
Sixth Ave. ME15 .... 6 A5
Skeete Rd. CT18 & TN25 ...... 160 E7
Skene Cl. ME8 .... 12 A1
Skinner Rd. TN29 .... 203 C6
Skinner St. Chatham ME4 .... 9 F3
Skinner St. Gillingham ME7 .... 10 C5
Skinner St. Gillingham ME7 .... 10 C6
Skinner Street
  Cty Prim Sch. ME7 .... 10 C6
Skinner's Alley. [3] CT5 ...... 20 D1
Skinner's Way. ME17 .... 98 E4
Skinners Cl. ME20 .... 53 A6
Skye Cl. ME15 .... 97 A7
Slade Cl. ME5 .... 32 B6
Slade Rd. ME17 & ME9 & ME13 . 102 D8
Slades Cl. CT15 .... 44 C8
Slatin Rd. ME2 .... 9 B8
Sleigh Rd. CT2 .... 67 F6
Slicketts Hill. ME4 .... 10 A4
Slip La. CT15 .... 147 C2
Slip Rd. ME4 .... 10 A8
Slipway Rd. ME12 .... 1 A3
Sloe La. CT10 & CT9 .... 29 B6
Slough Rd. ME9 .... 59 A3
Smack Alley. ME13 .... 62 D8
Small Hythe Rd. TN30 .... 179 C3
Smallhythe Rd. TN30 .... 179 A6
Smarden Cty Prim Sch. TN27 ... 135 A1
Smarden Rd. TN27 .... 136 B6
Smarden Wlk. ME8 .... 12 B1
Smarts Cotts. ME14 .... 76 C4
Smeed Cl. ME10 .... 37 A4
Smeed-Dean Ctr The. ME10 .... 37 A4
Smeeth Cty Prim Sch. TN25 ... 158 D5
Smith Rd. ME5 .... 32 B3
Smith St. ME2 .... 9 A6
Smuggler's Way. CT7 .... 27 A8
Snakes Hill. CT3 .... 91 A5
Snargate La. TN29 .... 191 C5
Snargate St. CT17 .... 166 D7
Snell Gdns. CT6 .... 22 A6
Snodhurst Ave. ME5 .... 31 E5
Snow Ho. ME7 .... 10 C7
Snowball Rd. TN23 .... 156 B4

Snowdon Ave. ME14 .... 75 B5
Snowdon Cl. ME5 .... 32 B7
Snowdown Caravan Site.
  CT15 .... 113 A4
Snowdown Ct. CT3 .... 112 F5
Snowdown Sta. CT15 .... 113 B3
Snowdrop Cl. CT19 .... 178 C8
Sobraon Way. CT1 .... 67 D1
Sole Street Cotts. CT4 .... 125 B7
Solent Gdns. ME5 .... 32 B8
Soleshill Rd. CT4 .... 84 E1
Solihull Cotts. CT12 .... 49 E6
Solomon Ho. CT14 .... 117 B3
Solomon Rd. ME8 .... 12 A1
Solomons La. ME13 .... 62 D7
Solomons Rd. ME4 .... 9 F4
Somerfield Barn Ct. TN25 .... 174 C8
Somerfield Rd. ME16 .... 74 D5
Somerfield Hospl The. ME16 ... 74 E5
Somerfield La. ME16 .... 74 D4
Somerfield Rd. ME16 .... 74 D4
Somerset Cl. Chatham ME5 .... 32 C8
Somerset Cl.
  Sittingbourne ME10 .... 36 C4
Somerset Cl. Whitstable CT5 .... 43 B7
Somerset Ct. Deal CT14 ...... 117 B3
Somerset Ct. Ramsgate CT12 .. 29 B2
Somerset Rd.
  Ashford TN23 & TN24 .... 139 B3
Somerset Rd. Canterbury CT1 . 88 D8
Somerset Rd. Deal CT14 ...... 117 C3
Somerset Rd. Folkestone CT19 . 177 E6
Somerset Rd. Maidstone ME15 . 97 C8
Somme Ct. CT1 .... 67 D1
Sommerville Cl. ME13 .... 62 E7
Somner Cl. CT2 .... 66 D1
Somner Wlk. ME15 .... 97 F4
Sondes Cl. CT6 .... 23 A2
Sondes Rd. CT14 .... 117 D5
Sorrell Rd. ME5 .... 31 F4
Sotherton. TN24 .... 156 E7
Souberg Cl. CT14 .... 117 C8
South Ave. Aylesham CT15 .... 113 A3
South Ave. Gillingham ME8 .... 11 B2
South Ave. Sittingbourne ME10 . 37 A3
South Avenue
  Cty Jun & Inf Schs. ME10 .... 37 A3
South Barham Rd. CT4 .... 128 C8
South Borough
  Cty Prim Sch. ME15 .... 75 A2
South Brooks Rd. TN29 .... 202 F2
South Bush La. ME8 .... 34 B6
South Camber Way. CT16 ...... 150 B1
South Canterbury Rd. CT1 .... 88 A6
South Cl. CT1 .... 88 A8
South Cliff Par. CT10 .... 30 B1
South Court Dr. CT3 .... 91 A7
South Cres. ME17 .... 96 C4
South Ct. Deal CT14 .... 117 D6
South Ct. Ramsgate CT12 ...... 29 B2
South Cty Prim Sch. TN23 .... 156 A8
South Deal
  Cty Prim Sch. CT14 .... 117 B4
South Eastern Rd.
  Ramsgate CT11 .... 52 D7
South Eastern Rd.
  Rochester ME2 .... 9 C7
South Exit Rd. CT16 .... 166 G8
South Goodwin Ct. CT14 ...... 117 D8
South Green La. ME9 .... 56 F6
South Kent Coll of Tech.
  Ashford TN23 .... 139 C1
South Kent Coll of Tech.
  Ashford TN23 .... 156 A8
South Kent Coll of Tech.
  Dover CT16 .... 166 D8
South Kent Coll of Tech.
  Folkestone CT20 .... 178 B5
South Lea. TN23 .... 156 A3
South Lodge Cl. CT5 .... 20 E3
South Military Rd. CT17 ...... 166 C5
South Motto. TN23 .... 156 B5
South of England
  Rare Breeds Ctr The. TN26 ... 169 D1
South Park
  Bsns Village. ME15 .... 75 A1
South Park Rd. ME15 .... 75 C1
South Pondside Rd. ME4 ...... 10 A8
South Rd. Dover CT17 .... 166 B8
South Rd. Faversham ME13 .... 62 C7
South Rd. Gillingham ME7 .... 10 A7
South Rd. Gillingham ME7 .... 10 B7
South Rd. Herne Bay CT6 ...... 23 A5
South Rd. Hythe CT21 .... 176 D1
South Rd. Kingsdown CT14 .... 134 D5
South Rd.
  Sandwich CT12 & CT13 .... 73 A8
South Side Three Rd. ME4 .... 10 C8
South St. Boughton Street ME13 . 84 F8
South St. Canterbury CT1 .... 67 C2
South St. Deal CT14 .... 117 D6
South St. Lydd TN29 .... 203 C4
South St. Queenborough ME11 . 2 F5
South St. Whitstable CT5 ...... 44 A7
South Stour Ave. TN23 .... 156 C8
South Street Crossing. CT5 .... 44 A7
South View. TN23 .... 46 F1
South View Gdns. ME12 .... 1 D1
South View Rd. CT5 .... 43 D6
South Wall. CT14 .... 117 B7
Southall Cl. CT12 .... 50 C7
Southbourne. TN23 .... 155 E5
Southbourne Gr. ME5 .... 32 A4
Southbourne Rd. CT19 .... 178 E5

Southdown Rd. ME12 .... 3 E6
Southenay La. TN25 .... 159 C4
Southernwood Rise. CT20 .... 177 F4
Southfields. ME1 .... 9 C3
Southgate Rd. TN30 .... 179 C7
Southill Rd. ME4 .... 9 F3
Southlands Comm
   Comp Sch. TN28 .... 200 B7
Southlees La. ME9 .... 56 F3
Southmead Rd. CT19 .... 178 A6
Southover Ct. 2 CT20 .... 177 E3
Southsea Ave. ME12 .... 4 C8
Southsea Dr. CT6 .... 22 D4
Southwall Rd. CT14 .... 117 B6
Southward Gdns. CT11 .... 52 B7
Southwold Pl. CT8 .... 27 E7
Southwood Gdns. CT11 .... 52 B6
Southwood Rd. Ramsgate CT11 . 52 C6
Southwood Rd. Whitstable CT5 . 21 B2
Sovereign Bvd.
   Gillingham ME7 .... 10 F2
Sovereign Bvd.
   Gillingham,Twydall ME8 .... 11 A2
Sovereigns The. ME16 .... 74 D4
Sowell St. CT10 .... 29 F5
Spade La. ME8 & ME9 .... 34 C6
Spanton Cres. CT21 .... 176 A3
Sparrow Castle. 3 CT9 .... 7 J1
Spearhead Rd. ME14 .... 74 F7
Spearpoint Cnr. TN24 .... 139 F5
Spectrum Bsns Cnr. ME12 ...... 9 E8
Spectrum Bsns Est. ME15 .... 97 F4
Speedwell Ave. ME5 .... 31 F4
Speedwell Cl. Gillingham ME7 . 10 E5
Speedwell Cl. Maidstone ME14 . 75 E5
Speke Rd. CT10 .... 29 E6
Spekes Rd. ME7 .... 33 B6
Speldhurst Cl. TN23 .... 155 E5
Speldhurst La. ME16 .... 74 D4
Speldhurst Gdns. CT9 .... 8 F3
Spencer Cl. ME5 .... 32 A5
Spencer Flats. ME5 .... 32 B8
Spencer Ho. 3 CT20 .... 177 F5
Spencer Rd. CT7 .... 27 A8
Spencer Sq. CT11 .... 52 E6
Spencer St. 9 CT11 .... 52 D6
Spencer Way. ME15 .... 97 E7
Spenlow Dr. ME5 .... 54 A8
Spenser Rd. CT6 .... 22 F4
Spicer Homes. ME10 .... 36 F2
Spicer's Pl. CT3 .... 69 C2
Spiers The. ME7 .... 11 C5
Spillett Cl. ME13 .... 62 B6
Spillway The. ME15 .... 74 D2
Spindle Glade. ME14 .... 75 C5
Spindlewood Cl. ME5 .... 32 B3
Spinnaker Ct. 3 ME1 .... 9 C1
Spinners Acre
   City Jun Sch. ME15 .... 32 C1
Spinney La. Aylesham CT3 .... 112 A4
Spinney La. Aylesham CT3 .... 112 F5
Spinney The. Ashford TN23 .. 138 E3
Spinney The. Chatham ME5 ... 32 B1
Spinney The. Maidstone ME15 . 75 B2
Spinney The. Margate CT9 ...... 8 E1
Spinney The. River CT17 ..... 148 C2
Spire Ave. CT5 .... 44 A8
Spires The. ME16 .... 74 D4
Spitalfield La. TN28 .... 199 F6
Spitfire Cl. ME5 .... 31 F4
Spitfire & Hurricane
   Meml Mus. CT12 .... 28 A7
Split La. CT4 .... 127 A5
Sportsfield. ME14 .... 75 B5
Spot La. ME15 .... 76 A2
Spratling La. CT12 .... 28 F1
Spratling St. CT12 .... 28 E1
Sprig The. ME14 .... 76 A4
Spring Farm Rd. TN29 .... 192 C5
Spring Ho. CT12 .... 176 C2
Spring Hollow. TN29 .... 195 A4
Spring La. Canterbury CT1 .... 88 C7
Spring La. Fordwich CT2 .... 68 A4
Spring La. Hythe CT21 .... 177 A4
Spring Vale. ME16 .... 74 E4
Spring Wlk. CT5 .... 43 C7
Springett Way. ME17 .... 96 B3
Springfield Ave.
   Maidstone ME14 .... 74 F7
Springfield Ave.
   St Michaels TN30 .... 167 C2
Springfield Cl. CT11 .... 29 E2
Springfield Pass. CT21 .... 176 B2
Springfield Rd. Dover CT16 .. 149 B2
Springfield Rd. Gillingham ME7 . 10 E6
Springfield Rd. Margate CT9 ... 8 E3
Springfield Rd.
   Sittingbourne ME10 .... 36 D5
Springfield Way. CT21 .... 177 B3
Springhead Rd. ME13 .... 40 D1
Springside Terr. CT18 .... 161 C6
Springvale. Gillingham ME8 ... 33 C6
Springvale. Iwade ME9 .... 14 D4
Springwood. Ashford TN23 .. 138 E3
Springwood Cl.
   Maidstone ME16 .... 74 A3
Springwood Ct. TN28 .... 200 B6
Springwood Dr. TN23 .... 138 E3
Springwood Rd. ME16 .... 74 A3
Sprotlands Ave. TN24 .... 139 F1
Sprowgay. ME4 .... 76 A4
Spurgeons Cotts. ME17 .... 96 E2
Spurway. ME4 .... 76 A4
Square Hill. ME15 .... 75 B4
Square Hill Rd. ME14 & ME15 . 75 B4

Square The. Birchington CT7 ... 27 A7
Square The. Chilham CT4 .... 107 B8
Square The. Elham CT4 .... 144 F4
Square The. Lenham ME17 ... 101 D5
Square The. Selling ME13 ..... 84 A6
Square The. Sittingbourne ME10 . 14 F1
Squeeze Gut Alley. 8 CT5 ... 20 D2
Squire Ave. CT2 .... 87 C8
Squire Cl. ME12 .... 5 E3
Squires Way. CT16 .... 149 A3
Stable Cl. ME5 .... 32 C5
Stable Cl. ME13 .... 62 D6
Stable Mews. CT18 .... 161 D4
Stablemead. CT19 .... 178 A7
Stace Cl. TN30 .... 179 C8
Staceys St. ME14 .... 74 F5
Stade St. CT21 .... 176 C1
Stade The. CT19 .... 178 E5
Staffa Rd. ME15 .... 97 A7
Stafford Cl. TN23 .... 138 F2
Stafford St. ME7 .... 10 C5
Staffordshire St. 6 CT11 ...... 52 E7
Stag Rd. ME5 .... 32 B5
Staines Hill. CT2 .... 68 B7
Staines Pl. CT10 .... 30 B5
Stalham St. ME7 .... 33 B4
Stalin Ave. ME5 .... 32 B8
Stalisfield Cl.
   Charing ME13 & TN27 .... 103 E3
Stalisfield Rd. Stalisfield Green
   ME13 & ME17 & TN27 .... 103 C5
Stalisfield Rd.
   Throwley, Eastling ME13 ..... 82 C6
Stampers The. ME15 .... 74 D2
Stanbury Cres. CT19 .... 178 F7
Stancomb Ave. CT11 .... 52 C5
Standard Ave. 1 CT6 .... 22 A4
Standen Cl. ME14 .... 33 E4
Standen La. CT18 .... 163 E5
Staner Ct. CT12 .... 52 A8
Staner Hill. CT12 .... 51 F8
Stanford Dr. ME16 .... 74 C3
Stanhope Ave. ME10 .... 37 A3
Stanhope Cl. ME14 .... 55 E7
Stanhope Rd. Ashford TN23 . 155 F7
Stanhope Rd.
   Ashford, Stanhope TN23 .... 155 E6
Stanhope Rd. Deal CT14 ...... 117 D6
Stanhope Rd. Dover CT16 ... 149 C2
Stanhope Rd. Rochester ME2 .. 9 A7
Stanhope Sq. TN23 .... 155 F6
Stanley Ave. Minster ME12 .... 4 D7
Stanley Ave.
   Queenborough ME11 .... 3 A4
Stanley Cl. TN29 .... 187 B4
Stanley Gdns. CT6 .... 22 F3
Stanley Pl. Broadstairs CT10 . 30 A4
Stanley Pl. Ramsgate CT11 ... 52 E7
Stanley Rd. Broadstairs CT10 . 30 A6
Stanley Rd. Chatham ME5 .... 32 C6
Stanley Rd. Deal CT14 .... 117 D5
Stanley Rd. Folkestone CT19 . 177 E6
Stanley Rd. Gillingham ME7 ... 10 C6
Stanley Rd. Herne Bay CT6 ... 22 F4
Stanley Rd. Margate CT9 .... 8 A3
Stanley Rd. Ramsgate CT11 .. 52 D8
Stanley Rd. Whitstable CT5 ... 43 D7
Stanley Sykes Cl. CT9 .... 29 B8
Stanmore Ct. CT1 .... 88 B7
Stansted Cl. ME16 .... 74 D7
Staple Cl. ME10 .... 36 E5
Staple Rd. CT3 .... 91 C6
Staple St. ME13 .... 63 F5
Staple Vineyard. CT3 .... 91 F5
Staplehurst Ave. CT10 .... 30 A2
Staplehurst Gdns. CT9 .... 8 E2
Staplehurst Rd. Gillingham ME8 . 11 B3
Staplehurst Rd.
   Sittingbourne ME10 .... 36 D5
Staplers St. ME14 .... 75 B8
Staplestreet Rd. ME13 .... 64 A4
Star Hill. ME1 .... 9 D5
Star La. Folkestone CT19 .... 177 D7
Star La. Gillingham ME7 .... 33 A7
Star La. Margate CT10 & CT9 .. 29 A5
Star Mill Ct. ME5 .... 10 D2
Star Mill La. ME5 .... 10 D2
Star Rd. TN24 .... 139 D2
Starle Cl. CT1 .... 67 B1
Starnes Ct. 5 ME14 .... 75 A5
Starvation Cnr. 1 CT5 .... 20 D2
Station App. Adisham CT3 ... 112 B8
Station App. Birchington CT7 . 26 F7
Station App. Maidstone ME16 . 74 F3
Station App. Martin Mill CT15 . 133 C2
Station App. Minster,Thanet
   CT12 .... 50 C5
Station App.
   New Romney TN28 .... 200 C6
Station Approach Rd. CT11 ... 52 D8
Station Cotts. ME13 .... 84 E7
Station Dr. CT14 .... 117 A1
Station Rd. Adisham CT3 ...... 90 E1
Station Rd. Ashford TN23 .... 139 C2
Station Rd. Birchington CT7 .. 27 A7
Station Rd. Bridge CT4 .... 88 F2
Station Rd. Charing TN27 .... 120 C7
Station Rd. Deal CT14 .... 117 B1
Station Rd. Dymchurch TN29 . 195 B7
Station Rd. East Farleigh ME15 . 96 A7
Station Rd. Faversham ME13 . 62 D6
Station Rd. Folkestone CT19 . 177 F5
Station Rd. Gillingham ME8 ... 12 A2
Station Rd. Harrietsham ME17 . 100 D6
Station Rd. Herne Bay CT6 .... 22 F4
Station Rd. Hythe CT21 ...... 176 D3
Station Rd. Lydd TN29 .... 203 D7
Station Rd. Lyminge CT18 ... 161 C6

Station Rd. Maidstone ME14 .. 74 F5
Station Rd. Margate CT9 .... 7 H2
Station Rd. Martin Mill CT15 . 133 D1
Station Rd. Minster CT12 ..... 50 C5
Station Rd. New Romney TN28 . 200 C6
Station Rd. Newington ME9 ... 35 B6
Station Rd. Patrixbourne CT4 . 89 C4
Station Rd. Pluckley TN27 ... 136 C5
Station Rd. Rochester ME2 ..... 9 C7
Station Rd.
   Shepherdswell CT15 .... 130 D5
Station Rd. Smeeth TN25 .... 158 B3
Station Rd.
   St Margaret's at Cliffe CT15 . 150 E8
Station Rd. Tenterden TN30 . 179 A7
Station Rd. Teynham ME9 ..... 38 F1
Station Rd. Westgate-on-S CT8 . 7 D1
Station Rd. Whitstable CT5 ... 20 E2
Station Rd E. CT1 .... 87 F7
Station Rd W. CT1 .... 66 F1
Station Row. ME9 .... 38 D3
Station St. ME10 .... 36 F4
Stede Hill. ME17 .... 78 F3
Steed Cl. CT6 .... 46 B8
Steeds Cl. TN23 .... 156 A1
Steeds La. TN23 & TN26 ...... 156 B1
Steele St. ME1 .... 9 A8
Steerforth Cl. ME1 .... 9 C2
Stella Maris
   RC Prim Sch. CT19 .... 178 C6
Stelling Minnis
   CE Prim Sch. CT4 .... 126 F6
Stembrook. CT16 .... 166 D8
Stembrook Ct. 4 CT16 .... 166 D7
Step Style. ME10 .... 37 B2
Stephen Cl. CT10 .... 30 A4
Stephen Cl. 2 CT20 .... 178 D5
Stephen's Cl. CT9 .... 28 B7
Stephens Cl. Faversham ME13 . 62 B8
Stephens Cl. Ramsgate CT11 . 52 C8
Stephenson Rd. CT2 .... 66 F3
Steps Hill Rd. ME9 .... 56 D6
Sterling Ave. ME16 .... 74 C5
Sterling Cl. CT10 .... 29 E5
Sterling Rd. Queenborough ME11 . 3 A5
Sterling Rd. Sittingbourne ME10 . 36 D1
Stevens Cl. ME15 .... 74 F3
Stickfast La. ME9 .... 14 A1
Stiles Cl. CT19 .... 178 A7
Stirling Cl. Gillingham ME8 ... 33 E4
Stirling Cl. Rochester ME1 ..... 9 A3
Stirling Way. CT12 .... 29 A2
Stirling Rd. TN24 .... 156 D7
Stisted Way. TN27 .... 118 F3
Stock La. TN25 .... 158 A4
Stockbury Dr. ME16 .... 74 D7
Stockbury Gdns. CT9 .... 8 E2
Stockdale Gdns. CT14 .... 117 C4
Stocker's Hill. ME13 .... 63 C4
Stockers Brow. ME9 .... 59 A7
Stockers Hill. ME10 & ME9 ... 59 A7
Stockett La. ME15 .... 96 B6
Stockham Ct. CT19 .... 177 E7
Stockton Cl. ME14 .... 75 B8
Stockwood Chase. CT2 .... 66 A2
Stoddard Rd. CT19 .... 177 E6
Stodmarsh National
   Nature Reserve. CT3 .... 69 D8
Stodmarsh Rd. CT3 .... 68 C3
Stombers La. CT15 .... 163 C6
Stonar Cl. Ramsgate CT11 ... 29 E1
Stonar Cl. Sandwich CT13 .... 73 A1
Stonar Gdns. CT13 .... 73 A2
Stone Abbage. TN27 .... 136 D4
Stone Barn Ave. CT7 .... 27 A6
Stone Bay Sch. CT10 .... 30 B6
Stone Cnr. ME13 .... 189 A6
Stone Cross Lees. CT13 .... 93 F7
Stone Gdns. CT10 .... 30 B5
Stone Gn. TN30 .... 189 F4
Stone Hill. TN25 .... 159 A2
Stone Hill Rd. TN27 .... 118 F2
Stone Ho. CT10 .... 30 B7
Stone Rd. CT10 .... 30 B5
Stone St. Faversham ME13 ... 62 C7
Stone St. Lympne CT21 & TN25 . 175 A4
Stone St. Stanford TN25 ..... 160 C3
Stone St. Stelling Minnis
   CT4 & CT18 & TN25 .... 126 D4
Stone St. Westenhanger TN25 . 175 B6
Stoneacre Cl. ME8 .... 33 D5
Stoneacre La. ME15 .... 98 B7
Stoneacre (NT). ME15 .... 98 B7
Stonebridge Cotts. TN23 .... 156 B8
Stonebridge Green Rd. TN27 . 119 A4
Stonebridge Way. ME13 .... 62 B7
Stonecross Lea. ME5 .... 10 C1
Stonedane Ct. ME13 .... 62 C8
Stonehall Rd. CT15 .... 147 F8
Stoneheap Rd. CT14 .... 115 E1
Stonestile Farm Rd. TN27 .. 103 A3
Stoney Bank. ME7 .... 10 F1
Stoney Rd. ME13 .... 64 B3
Stony La. ME5 .... 31 C5
Stonyway La. CT15 .... 165 C5
Stopford Rd. ME7 .... 10 D4
Storehouse Wharf. ME12 .... 1 A3
Stour Cl. Ashford TN23 .... 138 C1
Stour Cl. Chartham CT4 .... 86 D2
Stour Cres. CT1 .... 67 D3
Stour Ct. 7 Canterbury CT1 ... 87 F8
Stour Ct. Sandwich CT13 ...... 72 F1
Stour Ho. 4 ME15 .... 97 D8
Stour Rd. CT14 .... 86 D2
Stour St. CT1 .... 87 F8
Stour Valley Cl. CT3 .... 47 D3

Stourmouth Rd. CT3 .... 70 C8
Stourside Studios. 2 CT2 ..... 66 F1
Stowting CE Prim Sch. TN25 . 160 B8
Stowting Hill. TN25 .... 143 A1
Straight La. TN29 .... 191 F1
Strakers Hill. CT15 .... 132 D8
Strand Approach Rd. ME7 .... 10 E7
Strand St. CT13 .... 72 F1
Strand The. CT14 .... 117 D4
Stranger's Cl. CT1 .... 87 C6
Stranger's La. CT1 .... 87 C6
Strangford Pl. CT6 .... 23 B2
Strangford Rd. CT5 .... 20 F2
Strasbourg St. CT9 .... 29 A6
Stratford Ave. ME8 .... 33 D8
Stratford La. ME8 .... 33 F8
Straw Mill Hill. ME15 .... 74 E1
Stream Wlk. CT5 .... 20 D2
Street End. CT3 .... 71 E1
Street End Rd. ME5 .... 10 B1
Street The. Acol CT7 .... 27 B3
Street The. Adisham CT3 .... 112 C8
Street The. Appledore TN26 . 190 D8
Street The. Ash CT3 .... 71 D1
Street The. Ashford TN24 ... 157 B8
Street The.
   Ashford, Kennington TN24 . 139 E6
Street The. Bapchild ME9 ..... 37 E3
Street The. Barfrestone CT15 . 113 D1
Street The. Barham CT4 ...... 111 F1
Street The. Bethersden TN26 . 153 D5
Street The. Bishopsbourne CT4 . 111 C6
Street The. Borden ME9 .... 36 B2
Street The. Bossingham CT4 . 127 A7
Street The.
   Boughton Street ME13 ...... 64 A3
Street The. Boxley ME14 ...... 54 C3
Street The. Brabourne TN25 . 159 C8
Street The. Bredgar ME9 ...... 58 A5
Street The. Bredhurst ME7 ... 33 B1
Street The. Brook TN25 ...... 141 B6
Street The. Chilham CT4 .... 107 B8
Street The. Deal CT14 .... 116 F6
Street The. Denton CT4 ...... 129 B3
Street The. Detling ME14 ..... 55 A1
Street The. Doddington ME9 . 80 E7
Street The. East Langdon CT15 . 133 A1
Street The. Eastling ME13 .... 81 E6
Street The. Egerton TN27 ... 118 F3
Street The. Eythorne CT15 .. 131 D7
Street The. Finglesham CT14 . 116 B8
Street The. Godmersham CT4 . 107 B2
Street The. Goodnestone CT3 . 91 D2
Street The. Great Chart TN23 . 138 C1
Street The. Guston CT15 ..... 149 E6
Street The. Hamstreet TN26 . 183 C1
Street The. Hartlip ME9 .... 34 D5
Street The. Hastingleigh TN25 . 142 B6
Street The. Hawkinge CT18 . 163 B5
Street The. Hothfield TN26 .. 138 A6
Street The. Ickham CT3 .... 69 C2
Street The. Iwade ME9 .... 14 E4
Street The. Kingston CT4 .... 111 D3
Street The. Lower Halstow ME9 . 13 B3
Street The. Lympne CT21 .... 174 F2
Street The. Lynsted ME9 ...... 60 A6
Street The. Maidstone ME14 . 76 C4
Street The. Martin CT15 ..... 133 B3
Street The. Mersham TN25 .. 157 E4
Street The. Newington CT18 . 177 A7
Street The. Newnham ME9 ... 81 C8
Street The. Northbourne CT14 . 116 A5
Street The. Oare ME13 .... 40 B2
Street The. Patrixbourne CT4 . 89 B3
Street The. Petham CT4 ...... 109 B3
Street The. Postling CT21 ... 160 F2
Street The. Preston CT3 ...... 70 C6
Street The. Shadoxhurst TN26 . 170 A8
Street The. Silver Street ME9 . 57 F5
Street The.
   St Nicholas at Wade CT7 ... 25 F2
Street The. Staple CT3 .... 91 B6
Street The.
   Stone in Oxney TN30 .... 190 A5
Street The. Stourmouth CT3 . 48 E1
Street The. Upchurch ME9 .... 12 F4
Street The.
   West Hougham CT15 .... 164 F5
Street The. Wickhambreaux CT3 . 69 C1
Street The. Wittersham TN30 . 188 D3
Street The. Womenswold CT4 . 112 D2
Street The.
   Woodnesborough CT13 ...... 93 C7
Street The. Wormshill ME9 ... 79 A7
Street The. Worth CT14 .... 94 B5
Streete Court Rd. CT8 .... 27 E8
Streete Ct. CT8 .... 27 F8
Streetfield. CT6 .... 46 B8
Streetfield Rd. ME8 .... 11 F1
Stringer Dr. CT7 .... 27 A6
Strode Cres. ME12 .... 1 D2
Strode Park Rd. CT6 .... 23 A2
Strond St. CT17 .... 166 D6
Strood Sta. ME2 .... 9 C7
Strouts Rd. TN23 .... 155 C7
Strover St. ME7 .... 10 C7
Stuart Cl. ME14 .... 75 C6
Stuart Ct. CT17 .... 166 C8
Stuart Ho. CT14 .... 117 A5
Stuart Rd. Folkestone CT19 . 178 A6
Stuart Rd. Gillingham ME7 ... 10 D3
Studds Cotts. CT6 .... 22 A3
Studfall Cl. CT21 .... 187 D8
Studio Cl. TN24 .... 139 C2
Stumble La. TN23 & TN26 ... 156 B1
Stuppington Court Farm. CT1 . 87 D7
Stuppington La. CT1 .... 87 C5
Sturdee Ave. ME7 .... 10 E4

Sturdy Cl. CT21 .... 176 D2
Sturges Rd. TN24 .... 139 B3
Sturla Rd. ME4 .... 10 A3
Sturmer Cl. CT2 .... 88 C7
Sturry CE Prim Sch. CT2 ...... 68 A7
Sturry Court Mews. CT2 .... 67 F5
Sturry Hill. CT2 .... 67 F5
Sturry Rd. CT1 & CT2 .... 67 C3
Sturry Sta. CT2 .... 67 F5
Sturry Way. ME8 .... 11 C2
Stutfall Castle
   (rems of). CT21 .... 174 F1
Style Cl. ME8 .... 33 E4
Sudbury Pl. CT8 .... 27 E7
Suffolk Ave. Gillingham ME8 . 11 F1
Suffolk Ave. Westgate-on-S CT8 . 7 D1
Suffolk Dr. TN23 .... 139 A2
Suffolk Gdns. CT17 .... 165 F7
Suffolk Rd. Canterbury CT1 .. 88 D8
Suffolk Rd. Maidstone ME15 . 97 D8
Suffolk St. CT5 .... 43 D8
Sugarloaf Wlk. CT19 .... 178 D8
Sultan Rd. ME5 .... 32 C2
Summer Cl. Hythe CT21 ...... 175 F2
Summer Cl. Tenterden TN30 . 167 C5
Summer Ct. CT2 .... 66 C1
Summer Hill. CT2 .... 66 C1
Summer Hill Pk. TN24 .... 157 C7
Summer La. CT2 .... 66 E6
Summer Leeze. TN24 .... 156 E8
Summer Leeze Gdns. TN24 . 156 E8
Summer Rd. CT7 .... 25 E1
Summerfield Ave. CT5 .... 20 F1
Summerfield Rd. CT9 .... 8 E2
Summerhill. TN23 .... 155 E6
Summerville Ave. ME12 .... 4 A5
Sumpter Way. ME13 .... 61 F7
Sun La. Hythe CT21 .... 176 C2
Sun La. St Nicholas at Wade CT7 . 25 F2
Sun St. CT1 .... 87 F8
Sun Terr. ME5 .... 32 B4
Sunbeam Ave. CT6 .... 21 F4
Sunderland Cl. ME1 .... 9 A3
Sunderland Dr. ME8 .... 34 A8
Sunderland Ho. 2 ME7 .... 10 C7
Sundew Gr. CT11 .... 52 E8
Sundridge Cl. CT2 .... 67 A4
Sundridge Dr. ME5 .... 32 A4
Sunningdale Ave. 4 CT19 ... 178 A7
Sunningdale Cl. ME8 .... 33 D6
Sunningdale Cl. ME15 .... 75 B4
Sunningdale Dr. ME8 .... 33 D6
Sunningdale Wlk. CT6 .... 22 D1
Sunny Bank. Hythe CT21 .... 175 F2
Sunny Bank.
   Sittingbourne ME10 .... 37 B5
Sunny Cnr. CT17 .... 166 B5
Sunnyfields Cl. ME8 .... 33 E8
Sunnyfields Dr. ME12 .... 3 C6
Sunnyhill Rd. CT6 .... 22 C4
Sunnymead. CT2 .... 66 D7
Sunnymead Ave. ME7 .... 10 E5
Sunnyside. Doddington ME9 . 80 E7
Sunnyside.
   Littlestone-on-S TN28 ...... 200 D6
Sunnyside. Lydd TN29 .... 203 B6
Sunnyside Ave. ME12 .... 4 A6
Sunnyside Cl. CT14 .... 116 D1
Sunnyside Gdns. CT13 .... 93 E8
Sunnyside Rd. CT20 .... 177 D3
Sunray Ave. CT5 .... 43 B7
Sunrise
   Ind Pre-Prep Sch. ME17 .... 98 D4
Sunset Cl. Eastchurch ME12 ... 5 F6
Sunset Cl. Whitstable CT5 .... 43 C6
Superabbey Est. ME20 .... 53 B2
Surf Cres. ME12 .... 5 F6
Surrenden. TN27 .... 136 F7
Surrenden Rd. CT19 .... 177 F6
Surrey Gdns. CT7 .... 26 F7
Surrey Rd. Canterbury CT1 ... 88 D7
Surrey Rd. Maidstone ME15 . 97 D8
Surrey Rd. Margate CT9 .... 8 B3
Susan's Hill. TN26 .... 168 E3
Sussex Ave. Ashford TN24 .. 139 B3
Sussex Ave. Canterbury CT1 . 88 D7
Sussex Ave. Margate CT9 ...... 7 J1
Sussex Cl. CT6 .... 22 B4
Sussex Dr. ME5 .... 32 A4
Sussex Gdns. Birchington CT7 . 26 F7
Sussex Gdns. Herne Bay CT6 . 22 B4
Sussex Gdns.
   Westgate-on-S CT8 .... 7 D1
Sussex Mansions. CT8 .... 7 D1
Sussex Rd. 5
   Folkestone CT19 .... 178 D6
Sussex Rd. Maidstone ME15 . 97 D8
Sussex Rd. New Romney TN28 . 200 A6
Sussex St. CT11 .... 52 E7
Sussex Wlk. CT1 .... 88 D7
Sutherland Cl. CT21 .... 176 A2
Sutherland Gdns. ME8 .... 33 E6
Sutherland Rd. CT14 .... 117 C6
Sutton Cl. Folkestone CT19 . 178 A7
Sutton Cl. Gillingham ME8 ... 34 A8
Sutton Cotts. ME13 .... 84 C3
Sutton La. Ringwould CT14 . 133 F5
Sutton La. Ripple CT14 ...... 133 C8
Sutton Rd. Hersden CT3 ...... 46 E1
Sutton Rd. Langley ME17 .... 98 C5
Sutton Rd. Maidstone ME15 . 97 D6
Sutton Rd. Maidstone ME14 . 76 D4
Suttons The. TN31 .... 201 A1
Swadelands Cl. ME17 .... 101 C5
Swadelands Sch. ME17 .... 101 C5
Swain Rd. Gillingham ME8 ... 33 B6
Swain Rd. St Michaels TN30 . 167 D3

Swakeley Wlk. CT5 .... 21 D3
Swale Ave. Rushenden ME11 ...... 2 F3
Swale Ave. Sheerness ME12 ...... 1 C1
Swale Cl. CT6 .... 23 A3
Swale Halt. ME9 .... 15 A7
Swale Ho. **1** ME15 .... 97 E7
Swale View. ME13 .... 64 B6
Swalecliffe Ave. CT5 .... 22 B4
Swalecliffe Court Dr. CT5 ...... 21 D3
Swalecliffe Cty Prim Sch. CT5 . 21 B2
Swalecliffe Rd. CT5 .... 21 B2
Swallow Ave. CT5 .... 43 B6
Swallow Cl. CT9 .... 28 C8
Swallow Ho. **4** ME16 .... 74 E4
Swallow Rise. ME5 .... 32 A5
Swallowfield. TN24 .... 156 F7
Swamp Rd. TN29 .... 199 B4
Swan Apartments. **10** ME15 ...... 97 E5
Swan Cl. ME10 .... 37 B4
Swan Cotts. TN30 .... 188 D4
Swan Gn. TN25 .... 159 D1
Swan La. TN25 .... 159 E2
Swan St. TN30 .... 188 C3
Swanfield Rd. CT5 .... 43 D8
Swanstree Ave. ME10 .... 37 B2
Swanton La. Canterbury CT3 ...... 68 D2
Swanton La. Lydden CT15 ...... 147 C6
Swanton Mill. TN25 .... 157 B2
Swarling Hill Rd. CT4 .... 109 C7
Swaynes Way. CT13 .... 93 B2
Sweechbridge Rd. CT6 .... 23 F3
Sweechgate. CT2 & CT3 .... 67 E7
Sweetbriar La. CT15 .... 114 B2
Sweetlove Pl. CT3 .... 91 A8
Sweyn Rd. CT9 .... 8 A3
Swift Cres. ME5 .... 32 C6
Swift Ho. **6** ME16 .... 74 E4
Swinburne Ave. CT10 .... 30 A3
Swinford Gdns. CT9 .... 29 C8
Swingate Cl. ME5 .... 32 B2
Swingate Cty Inf Sch. ME5 ...... 32 C1
Sycamore Ave. CT3 .... 112 E5
Sycamore Cl. Broadstairs CT10 .. 29 C4
Sycamore Cl.
  Dymchurch TN29 .... 195 C8
Sycamore Cl. Herne Bay CT6 ...... 23 C5
Sycamore Cl. Hythe CT21 ...... 175 E1
Sycamore Cl. Lydd TN29 ...... 203 D7
Sycamore Cl. Margate CT9 ...... 28 E7
Sycamore Cres. ME5 .... 74 C5
Sycamore Gdns. TN29 .... 195 C8
Sycamore Ho. ME12 .... 1 C2
Sycamore The. CT3 .... 68 E8
Sydcot Dr. CT14 .... 117 D8
Sydenham Rd. CT14 .... 117 D7
Sydenham St. CT5 .... 20 D2
Sydney Ave. ME10 .... 36 C4
Sydney Cooper Cl. CT2 .... 66 B2
Sydney Rd. Chatham ME4 ...... 10 A3
Sydney Rd. Deal CT14 .... 117 A1
Sydney Rd. Ramsgate CT11 ...... 52 F8
Sydney Rd. Whitstable CT5 ...... 43 E8
Sydney St. TN23 .... 156 C8
Sylewood Cl. ME1 .... 31 B8
Sylvan Glade. ME5 .... 54 A8
Sylvan Rd. ME8 .... 33 C8
Symmonds Dr. ME10 .... 37 A6
Symons Ave. ME4 .... 10 A2
Syndale Pl. **1** CT11 .... 52 F7

Tabret Cl. TN24 .... 139 D6
Tadburn Gn. ME5 .... 32 B4
Taddington Wood La. ME5 .. 31 E2
Taddy Gdns. CT9 .... 29 C8
Tadley Ct. ME7 .... 10 F6
Tadworth Rd. TN24 .... 139 D5
Tail Race The. ME15 .... 74 E2
Taillour Cl. ME10 .... 36 F7
Talavera Rd. CT1 .... 88 D8
Talbot Ave. CT6 .... 22 B3
Talbot Rd. Maidstone ME16 ...... 74 C6
Talbot Rd. Margate CT9 ...... 8 B2
Tall Trees Cl. ME17 .... 99 D2
Tally Ho Rd. TN26 .... 155 C2
Tamar Ho. **4** ME15 .... 97 E8
Tamarind Cl. ME7 .... 33 A4
Tamarisk. ME12 .... 19 E5
Tame La. TN29 .... 185 F6
Tamley Gdns. 4 D6
Tams Gdns. 4 D6
Tangier Ct. CT16 .... 149 E3
Tanglewood Cl. ME8 ...... 33 C6
Tangmere Cl. ME7 .... 10 F5
Tanker Hill. ME8 .... 33 D6
Tankerton Cir. CT5 .... 20 F3
Tankerton Cl. CT5 .... 21 B3
Tankerton Mews. CT5 .... 20 E3
Tankerton Rd. CT5 .... 20 F3
Tanner's Hill. CT21 .... 176 C3
Tanner's Hill Gdns. CT21 ...... 176 C3
Tanners St. ME13 .... 62 C7
Tannery Ct. **3** ME10 .... 36 E5
Tannery La. TN23 & TN24 ...... 139 C2
Tapleys Hill. CT14 .... 110 B5
Target Bsns Ctr. ME15 ...... 97 F4
Target Firs. CT16 .... 148 D5
Tariff Reform Cotts. ME13 .. 62 D5
Tartane La. TN29 .... 195 C8
Tasker Cl. ME15 .... 76 B3
Tassell's Wlk. CT5 .... 21 D3
Taswell Ct. CT16 .... 166 E8
Taswell Rd. ME8 .... 12 A1
Taswell St. CT16 .... 166 E8
Tatler Cl. ME5 .... 32 D2
Tatsfield Cl. ME8 .... 11 A2
Taunton Cl. ME15 .... 97 F6
Taverners Rd. ME8 .... 33 E7
Tavistock Cl. Chatham ME5 ...... 31 F1

Tavistock Cl. Gillingham ME8 ...... 33 E7
Tavistock Cl.
  Sittingbourne ME10 .... 36 D4
Tavistock Rd. CT11 .... 29 E1
Tay Cl. ME5 .... 32 B5
Taylor Rd. Folkestone CT19 .... 177 E6
Taylor Rd. Lydd-on-S TN29 .... 204 E6
Taylor Rd. Minster CT12 ...... 50 B6
Taylor's La. 9 B7
Taylors Cl. TN29 .... 194 F3
Taylors Hill. CT4 .... 107 B8
Taylors La. TN29 .... 194 F3
Taylors Yd. TN29 .... 123 E2
Taywood Rd. TN24 .... 139 F1
Teasaucer Hill. ME15 .... 96 F8
Teasel Cl. ME14 .... 75 F4
Teasel Rd. ME5 .... 31 F4
Teddars Leas Rd. CT18 ...... 161 E4
Tedder Ave. ME5 .... 32 A7
Teddington Cl. CT1 .... 67 B2
Teelin Cl. TN29 .... 195 A4
Tees Ho. **9** ME15 .... 97 E7
Telegraph Rd. CT14 .... 117 B3
Telford Cl. Folkestone CT19 .... 178 E6
Telford Cl. Herne Bay CT6 ...... 22 C2
Telford Ho. **1** ME14 .... 75 A6
Telford St. CT6 .... 22 E5
Telham Ave. CT12 .... 52 B8
Templar Rd. CT16 .... 148 D5
Templar St. CT17 .... 166 C8
Temple Cl. CT16 .... 148 D6
Temple Ct. CT16 .... 66 D1
Temple Ewell
  CE Prim Sch. CT16 ...... 148 D5
Temple Gdns. Rochester ME2 .. 9 A6
Temple Gdns.
  Sittingbourne ME10 .... 37 B3
Temple Mews. **10** CT1 ...... 87 F8
Temple Rd. CT2 .... 66 D1
Temple Side. CT16 .... 148 D6
Temple Way. CT14 .... 94 A4
Templeman Liby. CT2 .... 66 E4
Ten Acre Way. ME8 .... 12 B1
Ten Perch Cl. ME5 .... 31 F4
Tennyson Ave. CT1 .... 67 D3
Tennyson Gdns. CT3 .... 112 F6
Tennyson Pl. CT19 .... 178 E7
Tennyson Rd. Ashford TN23 .. 156 A6
Tennyson Rd. Gillingham ME7 .. 10 C3
Tenterden CE Jun Sch. TN30 . 179 B7
Tenterden Cty Inf Sch. TN30 . 179 B7
Tenterden Dr. CT2 .... 67 A4
Tenterden Rd.
  Appledore TN26 & TN30 .... 181 B1
Tenterden Rd. Chatham ME5 .... 32 B5
Tenterden Town Sta. TN30 .... 179 A8
Tenterden Way. CT9 .... 8 C1
Terence Rd. ME4 .... 10 A2
Terminus Dr. CT6 .... 23 D5
Terminus Rd. ME16 .... 74 A2
Terrace Cotts. CT4 .... 127 A6
Terrace Rd. Elvington CT15 .... 114 B1
Terrace Rd. Maidstone ME16 .. 74 B3
Terrace Rd. Sittingbourne ME10 .. 37 B3
Terrace The. Canterbury CT2 .... 66 F3
Terrace The. Chatham ME4 ...... 9 F7
Terrace The. Faversham ME13 .. 62 A7
Terrace The. Little Chart TN26 .. 120 A1
Terrace The. Rochester ME1 .... 9 C5
Terrace The.
  Shepherdswell CT15 .... 130 D5
Terry's La. CT5 .... 20 D2
Teynham Cl. CT9 .... 8 F2
Teynham Dr. CT5 .... 20 F2
Teynham Gn. ME8 .... 11 A4
Teynham Parochial
  CE Prim Sch. ME9 .... 38 C2
Teynham Rd. CT5 .... 20 F2
Teynham Sta. ME9 .... 38 D3
Thames Ave. Gillingham ME8 .. 33 E8
Thames Ave. Sheerness ME12 .. 1 C1
Thames Ct. ME12 .... 6 G2
Thames Ho. **3** ME15 .... 97 D8
Thames View
  Cty Inf Sch. ME8 .... 11 D2
Thames View
  Cty Prim Sch (Jun). ME8 .. 11 D2
Thanet Cl. CT10 .... 30 B5
Thanet Coll. Broadstairs CT10 .. 30 A3
Thanet Coll. Margate CT9 ...... 7 I2
Thanet Gdns. CT19 .... 178 F6
Thanet Place Gdns. CT10 .... 30 B6
Thanet Rd. Broadstairs CT10 .. 30 A4
Thanet Rd. Margate CT9 ...... 7 J2
Thanet Rd. Ramsgate CT11 .... 52 F7
Thanet Rd. Westgate-on-S CT8 .. 27 D8
Thanet Terr. TN26 .... 138 A6
Thanet View. Eythorne CT15 .. 131 B8
Thanet View.
  St Nicholas at Wade CT7 .... 25 F2
Thanet Way.
  Boughton Street ME13 ...... 63 D6
Thanet Way.
  Hawthorn Cnr CT3 & CT6 & CT7 .. 24 C4
Thanet Way.
  Herne Bay CT6 & CT5 ...... 22 D3
Thanet Way. Whitstable CT5 .. 21 C2
Thanet Way. Whitstable CT5 .. 43 D6
Thanet Way.
  Yorklets CT5 & ME13 ...... 42 E2
Thanington Rd. CT1 .... 87 C6
Thatchers The. ME16 .... 74 B5
Theatre Sq. **5** TN30 .... 179 A7
Theatre St. CT21 .... 176 C2
Theodore Pl. ME7 .... 10 C5
Theresa Rd. CT21 .... 176 B1
Third Ave. Chatham ME4 & ME5 .. 10 C1
Third Ave. Eastchurch ME12 .... 5 F6

Third Ave. Gillingham ME7 ...... 10 F4
Third Ave. Margate CT9 ...... 8 B3
Thirlmere. TN24 .... 139 D6
Thirlmere Ave. CT11 .... 52 A7
Thirlmere Cl. ME7 .... 11 A5
Thirlmere Gdns. CT3 .... 112 F6
Thistle Wlk. ME10 .... 37 B5
Thistlebank. ME5 .... 32 A3
Thistledown. ME14 .... 75 F4
Thistledown Cl. ME7 .... 33 A4
Thomas Aveling
  Sch The. ME1 .... 31 C8
Thomas Cl. ME10 .... 37 B4
Thomas Rd. Faversham ME13 .. 62 D7
Thomas Rd.
  Sittingbourne ME10 .... 37 B4
Thomas St. ME1 .... 9 C3
Thompson Cl. Deal CT14 .... 134 B8
Thompson Cl. Folkestone CT19 .. 178 B7
Thompson Cl. Gillingham ME8 .. 34 B8
Thorn Cl. ME5 .... 31 D1
Thorn Est The. TN27 .... 136 B6
Thorn Gdns. CT11 .... 29 E1
Thorn Hill Rd. ME12 .... 6 D4
Thorn La. CT4 .... 126 C2
Thorn Wlk. ME10 .... 37 C5
Thornbridge Rd. CT14 .... 117 B2
Thorndale. ME5 .... 31 D4
Thornden Cl. CT6 .... 22 B2
Thornden Ct. CT2 .... 66 C4
Thornden Wood Rd.
  Herne Bay CT6 .... 22 B1
Thornden Wood Rd.
  Whitstable CT2 & CT6 ...... 44 E4
Thorndike Cl. ME4 .... 31 F8
Thorndike Rd. TN29 .... 186 C4
Thorne Hill. CT12 .... 51 A6
Thorne Rd. CT12 .... 50 B6
Thorney Croft Cl. ME17 ...... 99 D2
Thorneycroft Rd. ME13 ...... 103 D5
Thornham Rd. ME8 .... 11 C3
Thornhill Pl. ME14 .... 75 A6
Thornhurst. CT6 .... 23 D4
Thornlea. TN23 .... 138 E2
Thornton La. CT13 & CT14 .... 114 E7
Thornton's La. **7** CT16 ...... 166 E7
Thorold Rd. ME4 .... 10 B3
Thorpe Wlk. ME8 .... 33 D3
Thrale Way. ME8 .... 33 E4
Thread La. ME13 .... 64 B4
Three Acres Site. CT19 ...... 178 B8
Three King's Yd. CT13 ...... 73 A1
Threshers Dr. ME14 .... 75 E5
Throwley Dr. CT6 .... 22 C4
Throwley Rd. ME13 .... 82 D5
Thrupp Paddock. CT10 ...... 8 G1
Thrush Cl. ME5 .... 32 B7
Thruxted La. CT4 .... 86 B1
Thunderland Rd. CT6 .... 23 B4
Thurlow Ave. CT6 .... 23 C5
Thurnham CE Inf Sch. ME14 . 76 A4
Thurnham La. ME14 .... 76 C6
Thurston Pk. CT5 .... 20 E1
Thurstone Ct. ME14 .... 74 F6
Tiber Cl. CT19 .... 177 C6
Tichborne Cl. ME4 .... 31 C8
Tickham La. ME9 .... 60 C5
Tickner's La. TN29 .... 192 B1
Tideway The. ME1 .... 31 C8
Tilbury Rd. ME8 .... 12 A2
Tilden Cl. TN26 .... 167 D7
Tilden Gill Rd. TN30 .... 179 C7
Tile Fields. ME17 .... 77 D2
Tile Ho The. CT21 .... 176 C2
Tile Kiln Hill. CT2 .... 66 B5
Tile Kiln La. CT19 .... 177 F7
Tile Kiln Rd. TN24 .... 139 C2
Tile Lodge Cotts. TN27 ...... 119 E8
Tile Lodge Rd. TN27 .... 119 E8
Tilford Ct. CT4 .... 109 B3
Tillery La. TN29 .... 198 A8
Timber Tops. ME14 .... 54 D8
Timberbank. ME5 .... 32 A6
Timperley Cl. CT14 .... 117 B6
Tina Gdns. CT10 .... 30 A6
Tinbridge Pk. ME13 .... 63 A5
Tintagel Manor. ME7 .... 10 C6
Tintern Rd. ME16 .... 74 D7
Titchfield Cl. **5** ME15 ...... 97 F6
Titchfield Rd. ME15 .... 97 F6
Tithe Barn La. TN23 .... 155 D8
Tithe Yd. ME17 .... 101 D5
Tivoli Brooks. CT9 .... 7 I1
Tivoli Park Ave. CT9 .... 7 H1
Tivoli Rd. CT9 .... 28 E8
Tobruk Way. ME5 .... 31 F6
Toby Rd. TN29 .... 204 E6
Todd Cres. ME10 .... 31 D1
Toddington Cres. ME5 ...... 31 D3
Toke Cl. TN23 .... 138 C1
Tolgate La. ME2 .... 9 B7
Tolgate Way. ME4 .... 53 E4
Toll Gate. CT14 .... 117 A4
Toll La. TN27 .... 120 F7
Tollemache Cl. CT12 .... 27 F2
Tollgate Cl. CT5 .... 43 D7
Tolsford Cl. Etchinghill CT18 .. 161 D3
Tolsford Cl. Folkestone CT19 .. 177 D6
Tomay Cotts. CT6 .... 24 A3
Tomlin Dr. CT9 .... 29 C8
Tonbridge Ct. ME16 .... 74 D3
Tonford La. Canterbury CT1 .... 87 B6
Tonford La. Harbledown CT2 .. 87 B7
Tong Rd. ME10 .... 37 B4
Tonge Rd. ME10 .... 37 A4
Tontine St. CT20 .... 178 E5
Tookey Rd. TN28 .... 200 B6
Top Rd. TN30 .... 189 E3

Tormore Mews. CT14 .... 117 A4
Tormore Pk. CT14 .... 117 A4
Toronto Cl. **6** CT16 .... 149 B3
Toronto Rd. ME7 .... 10 C4
Torrington Cotts. CT12 ...... 50 D7
Torrington Rd. TN23 .... 156 C8
Tothill St. CT12 .... 50 C7
Tournay Cl. TN23 .... 155 F8
Tourney Cl. CT21 .... 174 F3
Tourney Rd. TN29 .... 203 C5
Tourtel Rd. CT1 .... 67 A1
Tovil Gn. ME15 .... 74 E2
Tovil Green Bsns Pk. ME15 .... 74 E1
Tovil Hill. ME15 .... 74 E2
Tovil Rd. ME15 .... 74 F2
Tower Bglws. CT7 .... 27 A8
Tower Ct. **4** CT20 .... 177 E3
Tower Est. TN29 .... 186 E2
Tower Gdns. Hythe CT21 ...... 176 C1
Tower Gdns. Maidstone ME14 .. 76 B4
Tower Hamlets Rd. CT17 .... 166 C8
Tower Hamlets St. **1** CT17 .. 166 C8
Tower Hill. Dover CT16 ...... 166 C8
Tower Hill. Whitstable CT5 .... 20 E3
Tower La. ME14 .... 76 B4
Tower Par. CT5 .... 20 E3
Tower Rd. CT5 .... 20 E2
Tower St. CT17 .... 166 C8
Tower Way. **1** CT1 .... 87 F8
Towers Sch The. TN24 ...... 139 D3
Towers The. TN27 .... 103 E1
Towers View. TN27 .... 139 C7
Town La. CT4 .... 86 C6
Town Rd. CT4 .... 109 C5
Town Wlk. CT20 .... 178 D4
Townley St. CT11 .... 52 D6
Townsend Farm Rd. CT15 .... 150 F6
Townsend Terr. CT17 .... 166 B5
Townwall St. CT16 .... 166 E7
Tracies The. ME9 .... 35 C6
Trafalgar Pl. ME12 .... 4 B6
Trafalgar Rd. CT7 .... 27 F3
Trafalgar St. ME7 .... 10 C5
Tram Rd The. CT20 .... 178 E5
Transom Ho. **2** ME1 .... 9 C1
Trapfield Cl. ME14 .... 76 C4
Trapfield La. ME14 .... 76 C4
Trapham Rd. ME16 .... 74 D5
Travers Gdns. ME9 .... 57 F5
Travers Rd. CT14 .... 117 A5
Travertine Rd. ME5 .... 32 B1
Treasury View. CT5 .... 90 C8
Trefoil Cl. ME9 & ME13 ...... 60 E6
Trefor Jones Ct. CT16 ...... 149 B2
Trelawn Cres. ME5 .... 32 B2
Trent Ho. **2** ME15 .... 97 E7
Trent Rd. ME5 .... 32 B5
Trenton Cl. ME16 .... 74 B7
Trevale Rd. ME1 .... 9 B1
Trevino Dr. ME5 .... 31 F2
Trevor Dr. ME16 .... 74 C5
Tribune Cl. ME14 .... 3 B8
Tribune Dr. ME10 .... 36 F6
Trident Cl. ME2 .... 9 D7
Trigg's Row. ME9 .... 38 D2
Trimworth Rd. CT19 .... 177 F6
Trinity Cres. CT20 .... 178 B4
Trinity Ct. Aylesford ME20 ...... 53 A3
Trinity Ct. Margate CT9 ...... 7 J3
Trinity Gdns. CT20 .... 178 C4
Trinity Homes. CT11 .... 117 C1
Trinity Pl. Deal CT14 .... 117 A4
Trinity Pl. Ramsgate CT11 ...... 52 F7
Trinity Rd. Ashford TN24 ...... 139 B6
Trinity Rd. Folkestone CT20 .. 178 B4
Trinity Rd. Gillingham ME7 .... 10 C6
Trinity Rd. Sheerness ME12 .... 1 D2
Trinity Rd. Sittingbourne ME10 .. 36 F7
Trinity Sq. CT10 .... 29 F7
Trinity Trad Est. ME10 ...... 36 F6
Trinty Hill. CT17 .... 7 J3
Trinty Sq. CT9 .... 7 J3
Tritton Cl. TN24 .... 139 F7
Tritton Fields. TN24 .... 139 F7
Tritton Gdns. TN29 .... 186 D1
Tritton La. TN28 .... 200 B6
Troodos Hill. ME14 .... 74 F8
Trotts Hall Gdns. ME10 ...... 36 F3
Trotwood Cl. ME5 .... 54 A8
Troubridge Cl. ME14 ...... 157 B7
Troughton Mews. CT9 ...... 7 H1
Trove Ct. **5** CT11 .... 52 F7
Troy Town La. TN25 .... 141 B5
Troys Mead. ME17 .... 77 D2
Trueman Cl. CT2 .... 66 A7
Trumpet Ho. TN23 .... 156 B8
Truro Cl. ME8 .... 11 D3
Truro Rd. CT11 .... 52 F7
Tudor Ave. Dymchurch CT9 .. 186 D1
Tudor Ave. Maidstone ME14 .. 75 B6
Tudor Byway. TN24 .... 139 D6
Tudor Cl. CT7 .... 27 B8
Tudor Dr. TN24 .... 139 D5
Tudor Gr. ME8 .... 33 F8
Tudor Rd. Ashford TN24 ...... 139 D5
Tudor Rd. Canterbury CT1 ...... 87 E7
Tudor Rd. Folkestone CT19 .. 177 D6
Tufa Cl. ME5 .... 32 B1
Tufton Rd. Ashford TN24 ...... 139 D2
Tufton Rd. Gillingham ME8 .... 11 F1
Tufton Rd. Hothfield TN26 .. 138 A7
Tufton St. Ashford TN24 ...... 139 D2
Tufton St. Maidstone ME14 .. 75 A4
Tufton Wlk. **9** ME15 .... 139 B2
Tunbury Ave. Chatham ME5 .. 31 F1
Tunbury Ave. Chatham ME5 .. 31 F2
Tunbury Ave S. ME5 .... 31 F1

Tunbury Cty Prim Sch. ME5 .... 31 F1
Tunis Ct. CT1 .... 67 D1
Tunis Row. CT10 .... 30 B5
Tunstall CE Prim Sch. ME9 .... 58 C8
Tunstall Rd. Canterbury CT2 .. 67 A4
Tunstall Rd.
  Sittingbourne ME10 & ME9 .. 58 D8
Tupman Pl. ME4 .... 9 B4
Turgis Cl. ME17 .... 98 E4
Turketel Rd. CT20 .... 178 A4
Turmine Ct. ME12 .... 4 A5
Turnagain La. **3** CT1 ...... 87 F8
Turnden Gdns. CT9 .... 8 E2
Turner Cl. ME2 .... 37 A7
Turner Ct. **5** Folkestone CT20 .. 177 F5
Turner Ct. Margate CT9 ...... 8 A2
Turner St. CT11 .... 52 E7
Turners Ave. TN30 .... 179 B8
Turners Cl. ME2 .... 1 D1
Turnpike Cl. CT21 .... 176 A2
Turnpike Hill. CT21 .... 176 A3
Turnstone Ct. TN29 .... 195 A3
Turnstone Rd. ME5 .... 32 C1
Tuscan Dr. ME5 .... 32 C1
Twelve Acres. TN24 .... 156 F8
Twiss Ave. CT21 .... 176 D2
Twiss Gr. CT21 .... 176 D2
Twiss Rd. CT21 .... 176 D2
Two Chimneys
  Holiday Pk. CT7 .... 27 E5
Twydall Cty Inf Sch. ME8 .... 11 B2
Twydall
  Cty Prim Jun Sch. ME8 .... 11 B2
Twydall Gn. ME8 .... 11 B3
Twydall La. ME8 .... 11 B2
Twyford Cl. ME8 .... 12 A2
Twyford Rd. ME14 .... 75 D6
Twyne Cl. CT2 .... 68 A6
Tydeman Rd. ME15 .... 75 F2
Tydeman's Ave. CT5 .... 21 C1
Tyland La. ME14 .... 53 F3
Tyler Cl. CT2 .... 66 F3
Tyler Dr. ME8 .... 33 E4
Tyler Hill Rd. CT2 .... 66 C6
Tyler Way. CT5 .... 21 E3
Tyndale Pk. CT6 .... 23 B5
Tyne Cl. ME5 .... 32 C5
Tyne Ho. **10** ME15 .... 97 E7
Tysoe Ct. CT14 .... 7 E1
Tyson Ave. CT9 .... 7 E1
Tyson Rd. CT19 .... 178 E7

Uden Rd. TN29 .... 187 B4
Uffington Ct. CT3 .... 91 A2
Ufton Cl. ME15 .... 75 C1
Ufton La. ME10 .... 36 E3
Ulcombe Gdns. CT2 .... 67 A3
Ulcombe Hill. ME17 .... 99 F1
Ulcombe Rd. ME17 .... 98 E3
Ulley Rd. TN24 .... 139 D7
Ullswater Gdns. CT3 .... 112 F6
Ulster Rd. CT9 .... 28 F8
Undercliff. CT20 .... 177 E3
Undercliffe Rd. CT14 .... 134 D5
Underdown Ave. ME4 .... 9 F1
Underdown La. CT6 .... 22 F2
Underdown Rd. Dover CT17 .. 166 B7
Underdown Rd. Herne Bay CT6 .. 22 F5
Underhill Cotts. CT18 .... 177 B8
Underhill Rd. CT20 .... 177 B5
Underwood. CT18 .... 163 C6
Underwood Cl. Ashford TN24 .. 139 D6
Underwood Cl. Canterbury CT1 .. 88 B5
Underwood Cl.
  Maidstone ME15 .... 74 F2
Underwood Ct. CT1 .... 88 B6
Unicorn Cotts. CT4 .... 89 B5
Unicumes La. ME16 .... 74 C2
Union Cres. CT9 .... 7 J2
Union Pk. ME5 .... 97 F4
Union Pl. **4** CT1 .... 67 A1
Union Rd. Bridge CT4 .... 88 F1
Union Rd. Deal CT14 .... 117 D6
Union Rd. Minster ME12 ...... 4 C7
Union Rd. Ramsgate CT11 ...... 52 F8
Union Row. CT9 .... 7 J2
Union Sq. **3** CT10 .... 30 B4
Union St. Canterbury CT1 ...... 67 A1
Union St. Chatham ME4 ...... 10 A3
Union St. Dover CT17 .... 166 D6
Union St. Faversham ME13 .... 62 C7
Union St. Maidstone ME14 .... 75 A5
Union St. **9** Ramsgate CT11 .. 52 F7
Union St. Rochester ME1 ...... 9 C5
Union St. Sheerness ME12 .... 1 B2
Unity Pl. **2** CT11 .... 52 F7
Unity St. Sheerness ME12 .... 1 E2
Unity St. Sittingbourne ME10 .. 36 E3
Univ of Kent at Canterbury.
  CT2 .... 66 D3
University Rd. CT2 .... 66 D3
Unwin Cl. ME20 .... 53 A3
Upbury Manor High Sch. ME7 .. 10 A4
Upbury Rd. ME4 .... 10 A4
Upchurch Wlk. CT9 .... 8 E2
Uphill. CT18 .... 163 B4
Uplands. CT2 .... 66 F4
Uplands Way. ME12 .... 3 C5
Uplees Cotts. ME13 .... 39 F5
Uplees Rd. ME13 .... 40 A3
Upnor Rd. ME2 .... 9 D8
Upper Approach Rd. CT10 .... 30 A3
Upper Brents. ME13 .... 62 D8
Upper Bridge St.
  Canterbury CT1 .... 88 A8

Upper Bridge St. Wye TN25 ..... 123 F2
Upper Britton Pl. ME7 .... 10 B5
Upper Chantry La. CT1 .... 88 A7
Upper Corniche. CT20 .... 177 C3
Upper Dane Rd. CT6 .... 8 B1
Upper Denmark Rd. TN23 ..... 156 B8
Upper Dumpton Park Rd.
CT11 .... 52 E8
Upper East Rd. ME4 .... 10 B8
Upper Fant Rd. ME16 .... 74 D2
Upper Field Rd. ME10 .... 37 B5
Upper Free Down. CT6 .... 23 B2
Upper Gore La. CT13 .... 93 A2
Upper Gr. CT9 .... 7 J2
Upper Hunton Hill. ME15 .... 96 A3
Upper Luton Rd. ME4 & ME5 .. 10 C2
Upper Malthouse Hill. TN21 .. 176 B2
Upper Rd. Dover CT15 & CT16 .. 150 C2
Upper Rd. Dover CT16 .... 166 H8
Upper Rd. Maidstone ME15 ..... 75 D2
Upper St. Hollingbourne ME17 ... 77 E3
Upper St. Kingsdown CT14 .... 134 D5
Upper St. Leeds ME17 .... 98 F5
Upper St. Tilmanstone CT14 .. 115 A3
Upper St Ann's Rd. ME13 .... 62 B6
Upper Stone St. ME15 .... 75 A3
Upper Strand St. CT13 .... 73 A1
Upper Tickham Cotts. ME9 ..... 60 D6
Upper Vicarage Rd. TN24 ..... 139 D7
Upstreet. CT18 .... 161 D3
Upton Cl. CT19 .... 178 A7
Upton Cty Jun Sch. CT10 .... 29 F4
Upton Rd. CT10 .... 29 F5
Urquhart Cl. ME5 .... 32 A5
Ursuline Dr. CT8 .... 27 D7

Vale Cotts. ME9 .... 57 A8
Vale Dr. ME5 .... 31 E6
Vale Pl. CT11 .... 52 D6
Vale Rd. Broadstairs CT10 ...... 29 F4
Vale Rd. Loose ME15 .... 96 E4
Vale Rd. Ramsgate CT11 .... 52 D6
Vale Rd. Ripple CT14 & CT15 .. 133 B8
Vale Rd. Whitstable CT5 .... 43 D8
Vale Sq. CT11 .... 52 D6
Vale The. CT10 .... 30 A4
Vale View
Cty Prim Sch. CT17 .... 166 B7
Vale View Rd. Aylesham CT3 .. 112 E5
Vale View Rd. Dover CT17 .... 166 B7
Valebrook Cl. CT20 .... 177 C3
Valence Ho. ME15 .... 97 C7
Valenciennes Rd. ME10 .... 36 E3
Valentine Cl. ME7 .... 11 A1
Valentine Rd. ME15 .... 97 E1
Valerian Cl. ME5 .... 31 E4
Valestone Cl. CT20 & CT21 .... 177 B4
Valiant Rd. ME5 .... 32 C2
Valkyrie Ave. CT5 .... 43 C7
Vallance The. ME9 .... 60 A6
Valley Cotts. Alkham CT15 .... 147 C1
Valley Cotts.
Stalisfield Green ME13 .... 103 D8
Valley Dr. ME15 .... 96 F6
Valley Rd. Barham CT4 .... 111 E2
Valley Rd. Canterbury CT1 ...... 87 E6
Valley Rd. Folkestone CT20 ... 177 C3
Valley Rd. Gillingham ME7 ..... 10 E4
Valley Rd. Lydden CT9 .... 28 E4
Valley Rd. River CT17 .... 148 E3
Valley Rise. ME5 .... 31 F1
Valley The. ME17 .... 96 D3
Valley View. CT15 .... 131 C8
Valley View Rd. ME1 .... 9 B1
Valley Wlk. CT17 .... 177 B3
Vancouver Dr. ME8 .... 11 C1
Vancouver Rd. CT16 .... 149 C3
Vange Cottage Mews. ME1 ...... 9 B4
Vanity La. ME17 .... 96 D1
Vanity Rd. ME12 .... 6 F2
Varne Ct. 6 CT20 .... 177 F3
Varne Lodge. 5 CT20 .... 177 F3
Varne Pl. CT19 .... 178 F5
Varne Rd. CT19 .... 178 F5
Vaughan Dr. ME10 .... 36 F8
Vauxhall Ave. Canterbury CT1 .. 67 C3
Vauxhall Ave. Herne Bay CT6 .. 22 A3
Vauxhall Cres. CT1 .... 67 C3
Vauxhall Industrial Rd. CT1 ..... 67 D4
Vauxhall Lakes
(Nature Reserve). CT1 .... 67 B3
Vauxhall Rd. CT1 & CT2 .... 67 C4
Vectis Dr. ME10 .... 36 F8
Ventnor Cl. ME5 .... 32 C8
Ventnor La. 12 CT9 .... 7 J2
Venture Cl. TN29 .... 186 D1
Vere Rd. CT10 .... 30 A4
Vereth Rd. 2 CT11 .... 52 D6
Vernon Holme (Kent Coll
Inf & Jun Sch). CT2 .... 66 A1
Vernon Pl. Canterbury CT1 ..... 88 A7
Vernon Pl. Deal CT14 .... 117 D8
Verwood Cl. CT2 .... 66 E2
Vesper Ct. TN27 .... 135 A1
Vestey Ct. CT8 .... 7 C1
Viaduct Cl. CT12 .... 52 C8
Viaduct Terr. TN26 .... 182 F7
Viaduct The. CT17 .... 166 D5
Viburnum Cl. TN23 .... 138 E2
Vicarage Cl. ME20 .... 53 A3
Vicarage Cres. 8 CT9 .... 7 J1
Vicarage Ct. ME9 .... 35 B7
Vicarage Gdn. CT12 .... 49 C7
Vicarage Gdns. CT3 .... 91 A7
Vicarage Hill. CT4 .... 109 B4

Vicarage La. Ashford TN23 .... 139 C2
Vicarage La. Blean CT2 .... 66 A6
Vicarage La. Deal CT14 .... 116 F5
Vicarage La.
East Farleigh ME15 .... 96 B6
Vicarage La. Elham CT4 .... 144 F4
Vicarage La. Faversham ME13 .. 62 A4
Vicarage La.
Lower Halstow ME9 .... 13 C3
Vicarage La. Nonington TN15 .. 113 C5
Vicarage La. Sandwich CT13 .. 72 F1
Vicarage La. Selling ME13 ..... 84 C6
Vicarage La. Tilmanstone CT14 .. 115 A3
Vicarage Pl. CT9 .... 7 J1
Vicarage Rd. Folkestone CT20 .. 177 F3
Vicarage Rd. Gillingham ME7 .. 10 C5
Vicarage Rd. Minster ME12 ...... 4 D7
Vicarage Rd. Rochester ME2 .... 9 B8
Vicarage Rd.
Sittingbourne ME10 .... 36 E6
Vicarage St. Broadstairs CT10 .. 29 E5
Vicarage St. Faversham ME13 .. 62 D8
Vicary Way. ME16 .... 74 D5
Vickers Cl. CT18 .... 163 A4
Victor Ave. CT9 .... 8 D2
Victoria Ave. Broadstairs CT10 .. 29 E8
Victoria Ave. Hythe CT21 .... 176 B2
Victoria Ave. Margate CT9 .... 8 B1
Victoria Ave.
St Margaret's at Cliffe CT15 .. 151 B6
Victoria Ave.
Westgate-on-S CT8 .... 27 E8
Victoria Cl. ME5 .... 31 D2
Victoria Cres. Ashford TN23 .. 139 B1
Victoria Cres. Dover CT16 .... 166 D8
Victoria Ct. Hythe CT21 .... 176 C3
Victoria Ct. 6 Maidstone ME16 .. 74 E3
Victoria Dr. CT6 .... 22 C5
Victoria Gr. 9
Folkestone CT20 .... 178 D5
Victoria Gr. Hythe CT21 .... 177 B2
Victoria Ho. 7 CT5 .... 20 D2
Victoria Hospl. CT14 .... 117 B5
Victoria Par. Broadstairs CT10 .. 30 B4
Victoria Par. Ramsgate CT11 .. 52 F7
Victoria Pk. Dover CT16 .... 166 E8
Victoria Pk. Herne Bay CT6 .... 23 A5
Victoria Pl. Faversham ME13 .. 62 C7
Victoria Pl. Hythe CT21 .... 176 B4
Victoria Rd. Ashford TN23 ... 139 B1
Victoria Rd. Broadstairs CT10 .. 29 E6
Victoria Rd. Canterbury CT1 .. 87 E7
Victoria Rd. Capel-le-F CT18 .. 164 B1
Victoria Rd. Chatham,Luton ME4 .. 10 B2
Victoria Rd.
Chatham,Walderslade ME5 .... 31 C3
Victoria Rd. Deal CT14 .... 117 D5
Victoria Rd. Folkestone CT19 .. 178 C5
Victoria Rd. Hythe CT21 ...... 176 C1
Victoria Rd. Kingsdown CT14 .. 134 C4
Victoria Rd.
Littlestone-on-S TN28 .... 200 E5
Victoria Rd. Lydden CT9 .... 28 D4
Victoria Rd. Margate CT9 .... 7 J2
Victoria Rd. Ramsgate CT11 .. 52 F7
Victoria Rd. Sittingbourne ME10 .. 36 D4
Victoria Rd W. TN28 .... 200 E5
Victoria Road Cty Prim Sch.
TN23 .... 139 B1
Victoria Row. CT1 .... 67 A1
Victoria St. Dover CT17 .... 149 B1
Victoria St. Gillingham ME7 ... 10 D6
Victoria St. Maidstone ME16 .. 74 E3
Victoria St.
New Romney TN28 .... 200 A6
Victoria St. Rochester ME2 ...... 9 B7
Victoria St.
Rochester,Troy Town ME1 ...... 9 D5
Victoria St. Sheerness ME12 .... 1 D1
Victoria St. Whitstable CT5 ..... 20 D2
Victoria Terr. Minster ME12 ..... 5 A5
Victoria Terr. Rochester ME1 .... 9 A2
Victoria Terr.
Sittingbourne ME10 .... 36 D4
Victory Pk. ME2 .... 9 E7
Victory St. CT15 .... 133 F1
Victory St. ME12 .... 1 C2
Vidal Manor. ME7 .... 10 C5
Vigo Terr. ME9 .... 38 B1
Viking Cl. CT7 .... 26 D8
Viking Ct. Broadstairs CT10 ... 30 B3
Viking Ct. Canterbury CT2 ...... 66 F2
Viking Ct. Margate CT9 .... 8 A2
Village Way. TN26 .... 183 A7
Villas The. CT3 .... 47 A1
Villiers Ct. CT17 .... 166 C2
Villiers Ho. CT10 .... 30 B7
Villiers Rd. CT1 .... 67 D1
Vincent Cl. Broadstairs CT10 .. 29 C3
Vincent Cl. Folkestone CT20 .. 177 E5
Vincent Ct. ME12 .... 1 D1
Vincent Gdns. ME12 .... 1 D1
Vincent Rd. Kit's Coty ME20 ... 53 C7
Vincent Rd. Lydden CT9 .... 28 C4
Vincent Rd. Sittingbourne ME10 .. 37 C3
Vine Cl. CT11 .... 29 E2
Vine End. CT11 .... 29 E2
Vine Lands. TN29 .... 203 B6
Vineries The. ME7 .... 10 E5
Viners Cl. ME10 .... 36 F1
Vines La. ME1 .... 9 C5
Viney's Gdns. TN30 .... 167 C1
Vineyard Cres. ME8 .... 12 B1
Vinson Cl. ME13 .... 41 D1
Vinten Cl. CT6 .... 46 B8
Vinters Rd. ME14 .... 75 B4
Vinters Sch for Boys. ME14 .... 75 C4
Vintners Way. ME14 .... 75 E4

Violet Ave. CT12 .... 29 C2
Violet Cl. ME5 .... 54 A8
Virginia Rd. Gillingham ME7 ... 10 C7
Virginia Rd. Whitstable CT5 .... 44 A8
Vlissingen Dr. CT14 .... 117 C8
Vixen Cl. ME5 .... 32 C6
Volante Dr. ME10 .... 36 E7
Vulcan Cl. Chatham ME5 .... 32 B7
Vulcan Cl. Whitstable CT5 ...... 43 C7

Wacher Cl. CT2 .... 66 F2
Waddenhall Farm. CT4 .... 126 B6
Waddle Cnr. TN30 .... 189 D3
Wades Cl. TN29 .... 194 B4
Wadham Pl. ME10 .... 37 B2
Waghorn St. ME4 .... 10 B3
Waghorn St. ME14 .... 75 E4
Wain Ct. ME12 .... 4 A5
Wainwright Pl. TN24 .... 156 D8
Wake Rd. ME1 .... 31 C8
Wakefield Way. CT21 .... 176 B1
Wakefield Wlk. CT21 .... 176 D1
Wakehurst Cl. ME17 .... 96 B3
Wakeley Cty Jun Sch. ME8 ..... 12 A1
Wakeley Rd. ME8 .... 12 A1
Wakeleys Cotts. ME8 .... 34 B8
Walcheren Cl. CT14 .... 117 C8
Waldens The. ME17 .... 99 E2
Waldershare Ave. CT13 .... 95 A7
Waldershare Rd. CT15 .... 132 A5
Walderslade
Cty Prim Sch. ME5 .... 32 A3
Walderslade Girls Sch. ME5 ... 31 F5
Walderslade Rd. ME5 .... 31 F6
Walderslade Woods.
Chatham ME5 .... 31 E2
Walderslade Woods.
Chatham ME5 & ME14 .... 54 B8
Waldron Dr. ME15 .... 96 F6
Waldron Rd. CT10 .... 30 B2
Walk The. ME17 .... 99 E2
Walker La. CT7 .... 26 D8
Walkers Outland
(RSPB Reserve). TN28 .... 204 B1
Wall Rd. TN24 .... 139 B3
Wall The. ME10 .... 36 E5
Wallace Mews. CT19 .... 178 D7
Wallace Rd. ME1 .... 31 E8
Wallace Way. CT10 .... 29 E4
Wallbridge La. ME8 & ME9 .... 12 D7
Waller Rd. TN29 .... 204 E7
Wallers Rd. ME13 .... 62 A7
Wallis Ave. ME15 .... 97 E5
Wallis Rd. TN24 .... 139 D2
Wallwood Rd. CT11 .... 52 F8
Walmer Castle. CT14 .... 117 D1
Walmer Castle Rd. CT14 ...... 117 C1
Walmer Ct. 3 ME14 .... 75 A5
Walmer Gdns. Cliffs End CT12 .. 51 D5
Walmer Gdns. Deal CT14 ..... 117 A2
Walmer Gdns.
Sittingbourne ME10 .... 36 D5
Walmer & Kingsdown
Golf Links. CT14 .... 134 D2
Walmer Rd. CT5 .... 43 E8
Walmer Sch. CT14 .... 117 B2
Walmer Sta. CT14 .... 117 A1
Walmer Way. CT14 .... 117 A2
Walmsley Rd. 3 CT19 .... 178 E6
Walmsley Rd. CT10 .... 29 F5
Walmer Gdns. TN28 .... 200 B7
Walner La. TN28 .... 200 B7
Walnut Cl. Ashford TN29 ..... 139 D6
Walnut Cl. Chatham ME5 .... 32 B8
Walnut Ridge. TN25 .... 173 A6
Walnut Tree Ave. ME15 .... 97 A5
Walnut Tree Cotts. ME13 .... 84 E8
Walnut Tree Dr. ME10 .... 36 D5
Walnut Tree La. Loose ME15 .. 97 A5
Walnut Tree La. Westbere CT2 .. 68 D7
Walpole Rd. CT9 .... 7 J3
Walsby Dr. ME10 .... 37 A8
Walseley Terr. TN29 .... 203 C5
Walsham Rd. ME5 .... 31 F1
Walshaw Ho. 2 ME14 .... 75 A6
Walsingham Cl. ME8 .... 33 D3
Walsingham Ho. 3 ME14 .... 75 A6
Waltham Cl. CT1 .... 8 E2
Waltham Rd. Gillingham ME8 .. 11 C3
Waltham Rd. Waltham CT4 ... 108 F1
Walton Gdns. CT19 .... 178 D7
Walton Manor Cl. CT19 .... 178 D7
Walton Rd. CT19 .... 178 D6
Waltons The. CT19 .... 178 C8
Wanden La. TN27 .... 135 C8
Wanstall Ct. CT7 .... 27 A7
Wansted House Sch. CT9 .... 8 A3
Wantsum Mews. CT13 .... 72 F1
Wantsum Way. CT7 .... 25 E3
Wantsume Lees. CT13 .... 72 E2
Warblers Cl. ME2 .... 9 A7
Warden Bay Rd. ME12 .... 6 E3
Warden Rd. Rochester ME1 ...... 9 C2
Warden Rd. Warden ME12 .... 6 E4
Warden Terr. ME12 .... 5 A6
Warden View Gdns. ME12 .... 6 D1
Warden Way. ME12 .... 6 B5
Wardour Cl. CT10 .... 30 B4
Wards Hill Rd. ME12 .... 4 A2
Wardwell La. ME9 .... 13 C1
Ware St. ME14 .... 76 A5
Warehorne Rd. TN26 .... 183 A7
Warlingham Cl. ME8 .... 12 A1
Warmlake. ME17 .... 98 F1

Warmlake Est. ME17 .... 98 E1
Warmlake Rd. ME17 .... 98 C1
Warner St. ME4 .... 9 F3
Warnford Gdns. ME15 .... 97 A8
Warre Ave. CT11 .... 52 C5
Warren Cl. Folkestone CT19 .. 178 F6
Warren Cl. Sittingbourne ME10 .. 37 B2
Warren Dr. CT10 .... 29 E5
Warren Dr The. CT8 .... 27 D7
Warren Hos. TN27 .... 119 E8
Warren Hts. TN25 .... 158 E5
Warren La.
Ashford TN23 & TN24 .... 139 A4
Warren La. Hartlip ME9 .... 34 C3
Warren La. Lydden CT14 ...... 147 D6
Warren Rd. Folkestone CT19 .. 178 F6
Warren Rd.
Kit's Coty ME5 & ME20 .... 53 D7
Warren Rd.
Littlestone-on-S TN28 .... 200 D6
Warren Ret Pk. TN24 .... 139 B4
Warren St.
Stalisfield Green TN27 .... 103 A3
Warren St.
Warren Street ME17 .... 102 D7
Warren The.
Brabourne Lees TN25 .... 158 E5
Warren The. Whitstable CT5 ... 43 C6
Warren View. TN23 .... 138 F4
Warren Way. CT19 .... 178 F6
Warren Wood
Cty Prim Sch. ME1 .... 31 C8
Warren Wood Rd. ME1 .... 31 C7
Warten Rd. CT10 & CT11 .... 29 E1
Warwick Cres. ME10 .... 36 C5
Warwick Dr. CT11 .... 52 B5
Warwick Pl. ME16 .... 74 E3
Warwick Rd. Ashford TN24 ... 139 E5
Warwick Rd. Canterbury CT1 .. 88 C8
Warwick Rd. Deal CT14 .... 117 D2
Warwick Rd. Margate CT9 .... 8 B2
Warwick Rd. Whitstable CT5 .. 20 D2
Washford Farm Rd. TN23 .... 155 E5
Washington Cl. 4 CT16 .... 149 B3
Washington La. TN29 .... 198 C6
Wass Dro. CT3 .... 71 B7
Wat Tyler Way. ME15 .... 75 A4
Watchester Ave. CT11 .... 52 C5
Watchester La. CT12 .... 50 B5
Water Farm. CT14 .... 144 F4
Water La. Bayfield ME13 .... 61 C4
Water La. Canterbury CT1 ...... 87 F8
Water La. 6 Faversham ME13 .. 62 C7
Water La. Harrietsham ME17 .. 100 B5
Water La. Kingswood ME17 ..... 99 F3
Water La. 4 Maidstone ME15 .. 75 A4
Water La.
Maidstone,Bearsted ME14 .... 76 E6
Water La. Smarden TN2 .... 135 A2
Water St. CT14 .... 117 D7
Watercress La. TN23 .... 155 F8
Waterditch La. ME17 & TN27 .. 102 E5
Waterfall Rd. TN26 .... 138 B6
Waterham Rd. ME13 .... 42 C1
Waterlock Cotts. CT3 .... 91 A7
Waterloo Cres. CT16 & CT17 .. 166 E7
Waterloo Hill. ME12 .... 4 D6
Waterloo Mansions. 12
CT16 & CT17 .... 166 E7
Waterloo Pl. 8 CT11 .... 52 F7
Waterloo Rd. Folkestone CT20 .. 177 D5
Waterloo Rd. Gillingham ME7 .. 10 C4
Waterloo Rd.
Sittingbourne ME10 .... 36 D5
Waterloo Rd. Whitstable CT5 .. 20 D2
Waterloo St. ME15 .... 75 A3
Waterloo Terr. ME12 .... 5 A5
Waterlow Rd. ME14 .... 75 A6
Waterman Ho. TN23 .... 156 B8
Watermead Cl. TN23 .... 155 F7
Watermeadow Cl. ME7 .... 32 F6
Watermill Cl. Maidstone ME16 .. 74 B5
Watermill Cl. Rochester ME2 .... 9 C8
Waters Edge. ME15 .... 74 F2
Waters Pl. ME7 .... 33 A6
Watersend. CT16 .... 148 D5
Watershed. CT16 .... 139 F1
Waterside. ME12 .... 6 E4
Waterside Ct. 5 CT21 .... 176 B2
Waterside Dr. CT8 .... 7 D1
Waterside La. ME7 .... 10 F7
Waterside View. ME12 .... 6 E4
Waterstone Pl. ME13 .... 62 A6
Waterworks Hill. CT15 .... 133 B3
Waterworks La. CT15 .... 133 B3
Watery La. CT4 .... 109 C5
Watkin Rd. CT19 .... 178 C6
Watling Ave. ME5 .... 10 D2
Watling Pl. ME10 .... 37 A3
Watling St. Canterbury CT1 .... 87 F8
Watling St.
Chatham ME5 & ME7 .... 10 D2
Watling St.
Gillingham ME5 & ME7 .... 10 D2
Watson Ave. ME5 .... 31 D5
Watsons Cl. TN25 .... 139 C4
Watsons Hill. ME10 .... 36 C5
Wattle Cnr. TN30 .... 189 D3
Watts' Ave. ME1 .... 9 C4
Watts Cotts. TN24 .... 139 D7
Watts' St. ME4 .... 9 F3
Watts Yd. CT1 .... 72 F1
Wauchope Rd. CT5 .... 42 F6
Wave Crest. CT5 .... 20 C1
Waveney Ho. 7 ME15 .... 97 E8
Waverley Ave. ME4 .... 4 B7
Waverley Cl. Chatham ME5 ..... 32 C6
Waverley Cl. Coxheath ME17 .. 96 C3
Waverley Rd. CT9 .... 28 C8

Way Farm Cotts. CT12 .... 50 D4
Way Hill. CT12 .... 50 E8
Wayborough Hill. CT12 .... 50 D7
Wayfield Cty Prim Sch. ME5 ... 32 A7
Wayfield Rd. ME5 .... 32 A7
Wayne Cl. CT10 .... 29 E5
Wayside. TN30 .... 167 B3
Wayside Ave. TN30 .... 167 B3
Wayside Flats. TN30 .... 167 B2
Weald Cl. ME15 .... 97 C6
Weald Ct. ME10 .... 36 D2
Weald The. TN24 .... 139 C3
Wealden Ave. TN30 .... 167 B1
Wealden Cl. 5 ME4 .... 10 B3
Wealden Forest Pk. CT2 &CT6 .. 45 D4
Wealdhurst Pk. CT10 .... 29 D5
Wear Bay Cres. CT19 .... 178 F6
Wear Bay Rd. CT19 .... 178 F5
Weatherly Cl. ME1 .... 9 C4
Weatherly Dr. CT10 .... 29 F2
Weavering Cotts. ME14 .... 75 E3
Weavering St. ME14 .... 75 F4
Weavers The. ME16 .... 74 B5
Weavers Way. Ashford TN23 .. 155 F2
Weavers Way. Dover CT16 .... 149 A3
Webb Cl. CT19 .... 178 A3
Webster Rd. ME8 .... 11 F1
Weddington La. CT3 .... 71 E2
Wedgewood Cl. ME16 .... 74 B5
Wedgewood Dr. ME5 .... 32 A7
Weeds Wood Rd. ME5 .... 31 F4
Week St. ME14 .... 75 A4
Weeks Ct. ME11 .... 3 A5
Weigall Pl. CT1 .... 52 C7
Weighbridge Way. CT16 ...... 166 H8
Welcombe Ct. ME8 .... 33 D8
Well Cl. CT2 .... 68 A6
Well La. Bayfield ME13 .... 61 B3
Well La. Fordwich CT2 & CT3 .. 68 A3
Well La.
St Margaret's at Cliffe CT15 .. 150 F4
Well Rd. Lyminge CT18 .... 161 C6
Well Rd. Maidstone ME14 .... 75 A5
Well Rd. Queenborough ME11 .. 3 A5
Well Rd. Rushenden ME11 .... 2 F3
Well St. ME8 & ME17 .... 96 E4
Well Winch Rd. ME10 .... 36 D5
Welland Ho. 8 ME15 .... 97 E8
Weller Ave. ME1 .... 9 D2
Wellesley Ave. CT14 .... 117 C3
Wellesley Cl. Broadstairs CT10 .. 29 E3
Wellesley Cl.
Westgate-on-S CT8 .... 27 E7
Wellesley Rd. Ashford TN23 .. 139 C2
Wellesley Rd. Dover CT16 .... 166 E7
Wellesley Rd. Margate CT9 ...... 8 B1
Wellesley Rd. Sheerness ME12 .. 1 E2
Wellesley Rd.
Westgate-on-S CT8 .... 27 E7
Wellesley Villas. TN24 .... 139 C3
Wellfield Rd. CT20 .... 178 A5
Wellington Cl. CT8 .... 7 C1
Wellington Cres. CT11 .... 52 F6
Wellington Ct. CT14 .... 117 D3
Wellington Gdns. 2
Dover CT16 .... 149 B3
Wellington Gdns. Margate CT9 .. 7 J3
Wellington Ho. 6 ME15 .... 97 E5
Wellington Par.
Kingsdown CT14 .... 134 D7
Wellington Par.
Kingsdown CT14 .... 134 E6
Wellington Pl.
Folkestone CT20 .... 177 D3
Wellington Pl. Maidstone ME14 .. 74 F4
Wellington Pl. Deal CT14 ..... 117 D5
Wellington Rd.
Folkestone CT20 .... 177 D5
Wellington Rd. Gillingham ME7 .. 10 C4
Wellington Rd. Lydden CT9 .... 28 D4
Wellington Rd.
Sittingbourne ME10 .... 36 B5
Wellington Rd.
Temple Ewell CT16 .... 148 D5
Wellington Rd.
Westgate-on-S CT8 .... 27 E7
Wellington St. CT5 .... 43 C5
Wellington St. CT5 .... 43 D5
Wellington Terr. CT20 .... 177 D3
Wellis Gdns. CT9 .... 7 G1
Wells Ave. CT1 .... 88 B7
Wells Cl. New Romney TN28 .. 200 C6
Wells Cl. Tenterden TN30 .... 179 B8
Wells Ho. ME10 .... 37 B4
Wells Rd. CT19 .... 177 F6
Wells Way. ME13 .... 40 B1
Welsdene Rd. CT9 .... 28 B8
Welson Rd. CT20 .... 178 A5
Wemmick Cl. ME1 .... 31 D7
Wemyss Pl. 13 CT1 .... 67 B2
Wemyss Ho. 14 CT1 .... 67 B2
Wemyss Way. CT1 .... 67 C1
Wenham's La. TN29 .... 192 E2
Wents Wood. ME14 .... 75 F5
Wentworth Ave. CT9 .... 7 E1
Wentworth Cl. CT18 .... 161 C6
Wentworth Dr. Gillingham ME8 .. 33 E7
Wentworth Dr. Ramsgate CT12 .. 29 A1
Wentworth Dr.
Sittingbourne ME10 .... 36 C5
Wentworth Gdns. CT6 .... 22 D2
Wentworth Ho. ME10 .... 36 C5
Wesley Terr. CT1 .... 161 C7
West Beach. CT5 .... 20 C1
West Borough
Cty Prim Sch. ME16 .... 74 B3
West Cliff. CT5 .... 20 D1
West Cliff Arc. 8 CT11 .... 52 E6

West Cliff Ave. CT10 .... 30 B3
West Cliff Dr. CT6 .... 22 B4
West Cliff Gdns.
Folkestone CT20 .... 178 D4
West Cliff Gdns.
Herne Bay CT6 .... 22 B4
West Cliff Prom. CT11 .... 52 D5
West Cliff Rd. Broadstairs CT10 .. 30 B3
West Cliff Rd. Ramsgate CT11 .. 52 D6
West Cliff Terr. CT11 .... 52 B5
West Dr. ME5 .... 31 D5
West Dumpton La.
CT10 & CT11 .... 29 E1
West End. TN26 .... 168 F3
West End Cotts. ME9 .... 80 D7
West Gn. ME10 .... 14 F1
West Hill Rd. CT6 .... 22 C5
West Hythe Rd. CT21 .... 187 A8
West La. Sheerness ME12 .... 1 B2
West La. Sittingbourne ME10 .. 37 A4
West Lane Trad Est. ME10 .. 37 A4
West Lawn Gdns. CT20 .... 177 D3
West Lea. CT14 .... 117 C7
West Minster
Cty Prim Sch. ME12 .... 3 B8
West Norman Rd. CT16 .... 166 E8
West Par. CT21 .... 176 B1
West Park Ave. CT9 .... 8 D1
West Park Farm North
Ret Pk. CT19 .... 178 B8
West Park Rd. ME15 .... 75 B2
West Pas. ME12 .... 1 B2
West Pl. TN29 .... 197 D8
West Ramp. CT16 .... 166 G8
West Rd. Folkestone CT20 .... 177 C4
West Rd. Gillingham ME4 .... 10 A7
West Rd. Sandwich CT13 .... 51 A1
West Ridge. ME10 .... 36 D3
West Rise. CT12 .... 29 B1
West Side. CT15 .... 133 A1
West St. Ashford TN23 .... 139 B2
West St. Deal CT14 .... 117 D6
West St. Dover CT17 .... 166 C8
West St. Faversham ME13 .... 62 C7
West St. Gillingham ME7 .... 10 D6
West St. Harrietsham ME17 .... 100 C6
West St. Hothfield TN26 .... 137 F7
West St. Lenham ME17 .... 79 E1
West St. New Romney TN28 .. 200 A6
West St. Queenborough ME11 .. 2 F5
West St. Sheerness ME12 .... 1 B2
West St. Sittingbourne ME10 .. 36 E4
West Street Cotts. CT13 .... 94 A1
West Terr. CT20 .... 178 D4
West View. CT19 .... 178 D8
West View Cl. CT6 .... 22 C2
West Wlk. ME16 .... 74 B3
West Wood Rd. ME9 .... 56 B8
Westbere La. CT2 .... 68 B7
Westbourne. TN23 .... 155 D6
Westbourne Gdns. CT20 .... 178 B4
Westbourne St. ME10 .... 36 E4
Westbrook Ave. CT9 .... 7 G1
Westbrook Cotts. CT9 .... 7 G1
Westbrook Gdns. CT9 .... 7 G1
Westbrook House Sch. CT20 .. 178 B5
Westbrook La. CT6 .... 22 B3
Westbrook Prom. CT9 .... 7 G2
Westbrook Rd. CT9 .... 7 G2
Westbrook Wlk. 8 ME13 .... 62 C7
Westbrooke Cl. ME4 .... 10 A2
Westbury Cres. CT17 .... 166 B6
Westbury Hts. CT17 .... 166 B6
Westbury Rd. Dover CT17 .. 166 B6
Westbury Rd.
Westgate-on-S CT8 .... 27 E8
Westcliff Dr. ME12 .... 4 D8
Westcliff Gdns. CT9 .... 7 F1
Westcliff Ho. 4 CT20 .... 178 D4
Westcliff Rd. CT9 .... 7 G1
Westcourt La. CT15 .... 130 C5
Westcourt Rd. ME4 .... 10 A6
Westdean Cl. CT18 .... 148 E2
Westenhanger Sta. TN25 .. 175 B7
Westerham Cl. Broadstairs CT9 .. 8 F1
Westerham Cl. Canterbury CT2 .. 67 A4
Westerham Cl. Gillingham ME8 .. 11 B3
Westerham Rd. ME10 .... 36 C3
Westerhill Rd. ME17 .... 96 C1
Westerhout Cl. CT14 .... 117 C8
Western Ave. Ashford TN23 .. 139 A4
Western Ave. Bridge CT4 .... 89 A1
Western Ave.
Halfway Houses ME12 .... 3 D6
Western Ave. Herne Bay CT6 .. 22 E4
Western Cl. CT17 .... 166 C6
Western Espl.
Broadstairs CT10 .... 30 B2
Western Espl. Herne Bay CT6 .. 22 C5
Western Gdns. TN24 .... 156 E8
Western Heights Rdbt. CT17 .. 166 C5
Western Ho. CT14 .... 117 C7
Western Link. ME13 .... 62 A8
Western Rd. Deal CT14 .... 117 C7
Western Rd. Maidstone ME16 .. 74 C1
Western Rd. Margate CT9 .... 29 C8
Western Service Rd. CT16 .. 166 G8
Western Undercliff. CT11 .. 52 C5
Westfield. CT2 .... 66 A6
Westfield Bsns Ctr. ME2 .... 9 C7
Westfield Cotts. ME9 .... 13 A2
Westfield La. CT18 .... 161 C3
Westfield Rd. Birchington CT7 .. 27 A8
Westfield Rd. Margate CT9 .... 28 C8
Westfield Sole Rd. ME14 .. 54 D8
Westfields. TN27 .... 136 D8
Westgate Ave. CT7 .... 28 A4
Westgate Bay Ave. CT8 & CT9 .. 7 C1

Westgate & Birchington
Golf Course. CT7 .... 27 C8
Westgate Cl. CT2 .... 66 C1
Westgate Court Ave. CT2 .. 66 D1
Westgate Garden Flats. CT2 .. 87 E8
Westgate Gr. CT2 .... 66 F1
Westgate Hall Rd. 3
CT1 & CT2 .... 66 F1
Westgate Rd. ME13 .... 62 E7
Westgate Terr. CT5 .... 20 E2
Westgate-on-Sea Sta. CT8 .. 27 F7
Westlands Ave. ME10 .... 36 B4
Westlands
High Sch The. ME10 .... 36 B4
Westlands Rd. CT6 .... 22 C3
Westleigh Rd. CT8 .... 27 D8
Westmarsh Cl. ME15 .... 97 F7
Westmeads Cty Inf Sch. CT5 .. 20 E2
Westmeads Rd. CT5 .... 20 E2
Westminster Rd. CT1 .... 67 C4
Westminster Wlk. CT12 .... 29 C1
Westmoors. TN23 .... 155 E6
Westmoreland Dr. ME9 .... 13 C3
Westmorland Cl. ME15 .... 97 E7
Westmorland Gn. ME15 .... 97 E7
Westmorland Rd. ME15 .... 97 E7
Westmount Ave. ME4 .... 9 F3
Westmount Ho. 4 CT9 .... 8 B2
Weston Rd. ME9 .... 9 A8
Westonville Ave. CT9 .... 7 F1
Westover Gdns. CT10 .... 29 E7
Westover Rd. CT10 .... 29 E6
Westree Rd. ME16 .... 74 E3
Westway. ME17 .... 96 C3
Westwell La.
Charing TN25 & TN27 .. 120 F5
Westwell La.
Potters Corner TN24 & TN25 .. 138 E7
Westwell La. Westwell TN25 .. 121 B4
Westwood Ind Est. CT9 .... 29 A6
Westwood Pl. ME13 .... 62 D5
Westwood Rd.
Broadstairs CT10 .... 29 C4
Westwood Rd.
Maidstone ME15 .... 97 A7
Wetheral Dr. ME5 .... 32 B4
Wey Cl. ME5 .... 32 C5
Wey St. TN26 .... 183 D3
Weybridge Cl. ME5 .... 32 C4
Weyburn Dr. CT12 .... 29 A1
Weyhill Cl. ME14 .... 75 C6
Weymouth Cl. CT19 .... 177 D7
Weymouth Rd. CT19 .... 177 D6
Weymouth Terr. CT19 .... 177 D7
Wharf Rd. Gillingham ME7 .. 10 C7
Wharf Rd. Maidstone ME15 .. 74 E2
Wharfedale Rd. CT9 .... 8 A1
Wharton Gdns. TN24 .... 156 E8
Whatman Cl. ME14 .... 75 C6
Whatmer Cl. CT2 .... 68 A6
Wheatcroft Cl. ME10 .... 37 B4
Wheatcroft Gr. ME8 .... 33 F7
Wheatear Way. ME5 .... 32 B7
Wheatfields. ME9 .... 32 D2
Wheatfields. Maidstone ME14 .. 75 D4
Wheatley Rd. Ramsgate CT12 .. 29 C1
Wheatley Rd. Whitstable CT5 .. 20 E2
Wheatsheaf Cl.
Boughton Street ME13 .... 64 A3
Wheatsheaf Cl.
Maidstone ME15 .... 97 B8
Wheatsheaf Gdns. ME12 .... 1 C1
Wheeler St. ME14 .... 75 A5
Wheelers The. ME8 .... 33 B6
Wheelwrights Way. CT13 .... 93 B2
Wheler Rd. TN27 .... 120 C8
Whewell Terr. 1 CT20 .. 178 E5
Whiffen's Ave. CT9 .... 9 F5
Whiffen's Ave W. ME4 .... 9 F5
Whigham Cl. TN23 .... 155 D7
Whimbrel Cl. ME9 .... 36 F8
Whimbrel Wlk. ME5 .... 32 C1
Whinfell Ave. CT19 .... 51 F7
Whinless Rd. CT17 .... 166 A8
Whiston Ave. TN26 .... 153 C4
Whitby Rd. CT20 .... 177 D6
Whitchurch Cl. ME16 .... 74 E4
Whitcombe Cl. ME5 .... 32 C3
White Acre Dr. CT14 .... 134 B8
White Cliffs. 11 CT20 .... 178 D4
White Cliffs Bsns Pk. CT16 .. 149 A6
White Ct. 8 CT20 .... 177 E3
White Hart Mansions. CT9 .. 7 I3
White Hill.
Boughton Aluph TN25 & CT4 .. 123 B6
White Hill. Challock TN25 .. 105 E1
White Hill Cl. ME14 .... 110 A8
White Hill Rd. ME14 .... 33 D1
White Horse La. 6
Canterbury CT1 .... 87 F8
White Horse La.
Otham Hole ME15 .... 98 A6
White Horse La.
Rhodes Minnis CT4 .... 144 A3
White House Farm Ct. CT15 .. 113 E5
White Marsh Ct. CT5 .... 20 E2
White Mill Folk Mus. CT13 .. 72 E2
White Post. ME17 .... 78 B5
White Post Gdns. CT3 .... 71 E1
White Rd. ME4 .... 10 A8
White Rock Ct. ME16 .... 74 E3
White Rock Pl. 5 ME16 .. 74 E3
White Rock Rd. CT13 .... 93 B1
Whiteacre La. CT4 .... 125 E4
Whitebeam Dr. ME17 .... 96 B3
Whitecliff Way. CT19 .... 178 F6
Whitefriars Meadow. CT13 .. 94 A8

Whitefriars Way. CT13 .... 72 F1
Whitehall. TN29 .... 197 E8
Whitehall Bridge Rd. CT2 .. 87 E8
Whitehall Cl. CT5 .... 87 E8
Whitehall Dr. ME17 .... 99 D3
Whitehall Gdns. CT2 .... 66 E1
Whitehall Rd.
Broad Street ME14 .... 77 A6
Whitehall Rd. Canterbury CT2 .. 87 D7
Whitehall Rd. Canterbury CT2 .. 87 E8
Whitehall Rd. Ramsgate CT2 .. 29 C1
Whitehall Rd.
Sittingbourne ME10 .... 36 E2
Whitehall Way. TN25 .... 159 D1
Whiteheads La. ME14 .... 76 B4
Whitehorse Hill. ME4 .... 10 B3
Whitehouse Cres. ME1 .... 53 A8
Whitehouse Dro. CT13 & CT3 .. 72 D7
Whitelocks Cl. CT4 .... 111 D3
Whitenbrook. CT21 .... 177 A3
Whiteness Gn. CT10 .... 8 F1
Whiteness Rd. CT10 .... 8 G1
Whites Hill. CT14 .... 115 B2
Whitfield Ave.
Broadstairs CT10 .... 29 E7
Whitfield Ave. Dover CT16 .. 149 B2
Whitfield Cotts. TN23 .... 156 B8
Whitfield Cty Prim Sch. CT16 .. 149 A7
Whitfield Hill.
Temple Ewell CT16 .... 148 F4
Whitfield Hill. Whitfield CT16 .. 148 F5
Whitfield Rdbt. CT16 .... 149 A6
Whitgift Ct. CT2 .... 66 D1
Whiting Cres. ME13 .... 62 A8
Whiting Ho. TN29 .... 203 C5
Whitmore St. ME16 .... 74 F3
Whitstable Cty Jun Sch. CT5 .. 20 D1
Whitstable Rd. Canterbury CT2 .. 66 D2
Whitstable Rd.
Faversham ME13 .... 62 E7
Whitstable Rd.
Faversham, Goodnestone ME13 .. 63 B6
Whitstable Rd.
Herne Bay CT5 & CT6 .... 21 F3
Whitstable Rd.
Herne Bay, Studd Hill CT6 .. 22 B3
Whitstable Rd.
Rough Common CT2 .... 66 B4
Whitstable & Seasalter
Endowed CE Jun Sch. CT5 .. 20 D1
Whitstable & Tankerton
Hospl. CT5 .... 21 A2
Whitstable & Tankerton Sta.
CT5 .... 20 E1
Whittaker St. ME4 .... 10 A4
Whittington Terr. CT15 .... 130 D4
Whybornes Chase. ME12 .... 4 C7
Whyman Ave. ME4 .... 10 A1
Whytecliffs. CT10 .... 30 A2
Wichling Cl. CT2 .... 67 A3
Wick La. CT4 .... 129 E7
Wicken Ho. ME16 .... 74 E4
Wicken La. TN25 & TN27 .. 120 E6
Wickenden Cres. TN24 .... 157 A8
Wickets The. TN24 .... 156 F7
Wickham Ave. CT11 .... 52 G8
Wickham Cl. ME9 .... 35 B6
Wickham Court La. CT3 .... 69 B3
Wickham La. CT3 .... 69 B1
Wickham Mill. CT3 .... 69 C2
Wickham Pl. ME17 .... 101 D5
Wickham Rd. CT3 .... 69 B2
Wickham St. ME1 .... 9 D3
Wickhambreaux
CE Prim Sch. CT3 .... 69 C2
Widred Rd. CT17 .... 166 C8
Wierton La. ME17 .... 97 E1
Wife Of Bath Hill. CT2 .... 87 C8
Wigmore La. CT15 .... 131 C8
Wigmore Rd. Gillingham ME8 .. 33 B4
Wigmore Rd. Gillingham ME8 .. 33 B5
Wigwam Paddocks. CT7 .... 27 A8
Wihtred Rd. ME9 .... 37 D2
Wilberforce Rd.
Coxheath ME17 .... 96 D3
Wilberforce Rd.
Folkestone CT20 .... 177 E3
Wilbrough Rd. CT7 .... 27 A7
Wilcox Cl. CT3 .... 112 D5
Wilderness Hill. CT9 .... 8 A2
Wildfell Cl. ME14 .... 54 C8
Wildish Rd. ME13 .... 62 A8
Wildman Cl. ME8 .... 33 D3
Wildwood Cl. ME17 .... 99 E2
Wildwood Glade. ME7 .... 33 B4
Wildwood Rd. CT2 .... 67 F6
Wiles Ave. TN28 .... 200 B6
Wiles Ho. TN28 .... 200 B6
Wilfred Rd. CT11 .... 52 C8
Wilgate Green Rd. ME13 .. 82 F6
Wilkes Rd. CT10 .... 29 E4
Wilkie Rd. CT7 .... 27 A8
Will Adams Ct. ME7 .... 10 C6
Will Adams Way. ME7 .... 10 F1
Willement Rd. ME13 .... 62 B7
Willesborough Ct. TN24 .. 140 A2
Willesborough
Cty Inf Sch. TN24 .... 157 A8
Willesborough Ind Pk.
TN24 .... 140 A1
Willesborough Rd. TN24 .. 139 F4
Willetts Hill. CT12 .... 49 D2
William Ave. Folkestone CT19 .. 178 B7

William Ave. Margate CT9 .... 29 C8
William Gibbs Ct. 14 ME13 .. 62 D7
William Harvey Hospl The.
TN24 .... 140 C1
William Judge Cl. TN30 .. 179 D7
William Pitt Ave. CT14 .. 117 B6
William Pitt Cl. CT21 .... 176 D2
William Rd. TN23 .... 156 B8
William St. Faversham ME13 .. 62 D7
William St. Gillingham ME8 .. 12 A1
William St. Herne Bay CT6 .. 22 F5
William St. Sittingbourne ME10 .. 36 E4
William St. Whitstable CT5 .. 20 D2
Williamson Rd. TN29 .... 204 E5
Willingdon. TN23 .... 155 E5
Willingdon Pl. CT14 .... 117 C1
Willington Gn. ME15 .... 97 E7
Willington St. ME15 .... 75 F2
Willis Ct. ME12 .... 3 F5
Willis Ho. ME1 .... 9 C4
Willop Cl. TN29 .... 186 F3
Willop Way. TN29 .... 186 F3
Willoughby Ct. 14 CT1 .... 87 F8
Willow Ave. Broadstairs CT10 .. 29 D4
Willow Ave. Faversham ME13 .. 62 A7
Willow Cl. Canterbury CT2 .. 67 A2
Willow Cl. Hythe CT21 .... 175 E1
Willow Cl. Margate CT9 .... 8 C2
Willow Ct. Broadstairs CT10 .. 30 A5
Willow Ct. Folkestone CT20 .. 177 E4
Willow Dr. Hamstreet TN26 .. 183 A7
Willow Dr. St Mary's Bay TN29 .. 194 F3
Willow Ho. 2 Chatham ME5 .. 31 F5
Willow Ho. Sheerness ME12 .. 1 C2
Willow Ho. Sittingbourne ME10 .. 37 B3
Willow Rd.
Great Mongeham CT14 .. 116 C3
Willow Rd. Whitstable CT5 .. 43 C5
Willow Rise. ME15 .... 75 F1
Willow Tree Cl. Ashford TN24 .. 139 F1
Willow Tree Cl.
Herne Bay CT6 .... 23 D5
Willow Way. Maidstone ME15 .. 75 B3
Willow Way. Margate CT9 .. 28 C8
Willow Way. Whitstable CT5 .. 44 C8
Willow Waye. CT15 .... 131 D7
Willowbank Cl. TN29 .... 195 A4
Willowby Gdns. ME8 .... 33 E4
Willows Cl. CT2 .... 66 C4
Willows The. Gillingham ME8 .. 11 E2
Willows The. Newington ME9 .. 35 B6
Willows The. Sheerness ME12 .. 1 I1
Willows The.
Sittingbourne ME10 .... 14 F1
Willson's Rd. CT11 .... 52 D6
Wilmecote Ct. ME8 .... 33 D8
Wilmington Way. ME8 .... 11 B2
Wilmott Pl. CT13 .... 93 B2
Wilson Ave. Chatham ME1 .. 31 E7
Wilson Ave. Deal CT14 .... 116 F4
Wilson Cl. Ashford TN24 .. 140 A1
Wilson Cl. Maidstone ME15 .. 97 E7
Wilsons La. ME15 .... 96 A5
Wiltie Gdns. CT19 .... 178 C5
Wilton Cl. CT14 .... 117 C5
Wilton Rd. Folkestone CT19 .. 178 B6
Wilton Rd. Margate CT12 .. 28 F1
Wilton Terr. ME10 .... 36 B5
Wiltshire Cl. ME5 .... 32 C8
Wiltshire Way. ME15 .... 97 E8
Wimborne Pl. CT12 .... 52 B8
Wimbourne Dr. ME8 .... 33 D6
Win Pine Ho. CT21 .... 176 A1
Winant Way. CT16 .... 149 B3
Wincheap. CT1 .... 87 E7
Wincheap Ind Est. CT1 .... 87 D7
Wincheap Prim Sch. CT1 .. 87 E7
Winchelsea Ct. CT17 .... 166 C7
Winchelsea Rd. Chatham ME5 .. 32 B5
Winchelsea Rd. Dover CT17 .. 166 B7
Winchelsea St. CT17 .... 166 B7
Winchelsea Terr. CT17 .... 166 B7
Winchester Ave. ME5 .... 31 F4
Winchester Gdns. CT1 .... 88 A6
Winchester Ho. 4 ME15 .. 97 D7
Winchester Pl. 7 ME14 .. 75 A5
Winchester Way. ME8 .... 34 A8
Wind Hill. TN27 .... 119 E7
Wind Hill La. TN27 .... 119 E7
Windermere. ME13 .... 62 E6
Windermere Ave. CT11 .... 52 A7
Windermere Ct. TN24 .... 139 C4
Windermere Dr. ME8 .... 33 D7
Windermere Gdns. CT3 .... 112 F6
Windermere Gr. ME10 .... 36 D3
Winding Hill. ME13 .... 83 F6
Windmill Ave. CT12 .... 29 B3
Windmill Cl. Ashford TN24 .. 140 A1
Windmill Cl. Bridge CT4 .... 89 A1
Windmill Cl. Canterbury CT1 .. 88 C8
Windmill Cl. Herne Bay CT6 .. 23 A2
Windmill Ct.
Boughton Monchelsea ME17 .. 97 B3
Windmill Hill. Whitstable CT5 .. 43 C7
Windmill Hill. ME17 .... 100 B1
Windmill Hts. ME14 .... 76 B4
Windmill Quay Rd. ME2 .. 4 E2
Windmill Rd. Canterbury CT1 .. 88 C8
Windmill Rd. Gillingham ME7 .. 10 C4
Windmill Rd. Herne Bay CT6 .. 23 A2
Windmill Rd.
Sittingbourne ME10 .... 36 D6
Windmill Rd. Whitstable CT5 .. 43 D7
Windmill Rise. ME12 .... 4 E6
Windmill Row. ME17 .... 98 C2
Windmill St. CT21 .... 176 B1
Windmill View. CT9 .... 29 A8

Windmill Wlk. CT12 .... 29 B1
Windsor Ave. Chatham ME4 .. 9 F2
Windsor Ave. Margate CT9 .. 8 B1
Windsor Cl. Broadstairs CT10 .. 29 E5
Windsor Cl. Maidstone ME14 .. 75 B6
Windsor Cl. Deal CT14 .... 117 C5
Windsor Ct. Margate CT9 .. 8 B1
Windsor Dr. ME10 .... 36 D2
Windsor Gdns. Herne Bay CT6 .. 22 B3
Windsor Gdns. Warden ME12 .. 6 H2
Windsor Ho. Deal CT14 .... 117 A5
Windsor Ho. 6 Dover CT17 .. 166 D7
Windsor Ho. Whitstable CT5 .. 20 D1
Windsor Mews. 9
Margate CT9 .... 7 J2
Windsor Mews.
New Romney TN28 .... 200 C8
Windsor Rd. Canterbury CT1 .. 87 C6
Windsor Rd. Cliffs End CT12 .. 51 D7
Windsor Rd. Gillingham ME7 .. 10 D5
Windward Rd. ME1 .... 9 C1
Windyridge. ME1 .... 10 E1
Winehouse La. CT18 .... 164 D3
Wineycock. ME9 .... 81 C8
Wing Ho. ME12 .... 6 H1
Wing Rd. ME12 .... 6 H1
Wingate Rd. CT19 .... 178 D7
Wingham Bird Pk. CT3 .... 70 C1
Wingham Cl. Gillingham ME8 .. 11 C3
Wingham Cl. Maidstone ME15 .. 97 F7
Wingham Cty Prim Sch. CT3 .. 91 F2
Wingham Rd. CT3 .... 90 D8
Wingrove Dr. Maidstone ME14 .. 75 E5
Wingrove Dr. Rochester ME2 .. 9 C8
Wingrove Hill. CT17 .... 148 E2
Wings Ct. CT10 .... 30 B5
Winifred Ave. CT12 .... 29 C2
Winifred Rd. ME15 .... 75 F3
Winnipeg Cl. CT16 .... 149 C3
Winstanley Cres. CT11 .. 52 D8
Winstanley Rd. ME12 .... 1 D2
Winston Cl. CT1 .... 88 C7
Winston Ct. CT7 .... 27 A8
Winston Gdns. CT6 .... 23 D4
Winston Ho. 4 CT20 .... 177 F5
Winterage La. CT18 .... 162 C7
Winterstoke Cres. CT11 .. 52 G8
Winterstoke Way. CT11 .. 52 F8
Winton Way. TN29 .... 195 A5
Wirrals The. ME5 .... 32 A4
Wises La. ME10 & ME9 .... 36 A4
Wish The. TN29 .... 181 F6
Wissenden La. TN26 .... 153 B6
Witherdane Cotts. TN25 .. 124 A2
Witley Wlk. CT16 .... 149 B7
Wittersham
CE (VA) Prim Sch. TN30 .. 188 D2
Wittersham Cl. ME5 .... 32 B5
Wittersham Rd.
Stone in Oxney TN30 .... 189 C3
Wittersham Rd.
Wittersham TN30 .... 188 C5
Wivenhoe. TN23 .... 155 E5
Wivenhoe Cl. ME8 .... 12 A2
Wolfe Rd. ME16 .... 74 B2
Wollaston Cl. ME8 .... 33 D3
Wollaston Rd. CT14 .... 117 D4
Wolmer Way. 1 CT20 .... 177 F5
Wolseley Ave. CT6 .... 22 A4
Wolseley Pl. 4 TN24 .... 139 B3
Wood Ave. CT19 .... 178 E7
Wood Cottage La. CT19 .. 177 D7
Wood Hill. CT2 .... 66 E6
Wood Rd. CT21 .... 176 B1
Wood St. Dover CT16 .... 166 D8
Wood St. Gillingham ME7 .. 10 A6
Wood St. Lynsted ME9 .... 59 F8
Wood St. Sheerness ME12 .. 1 D2
Wood View. CT3 .... 46 E5
Wood Yd. CT14 .... 117 D6
Wood's Pl. CT17 .... 149 B2
Woodberry Dr. ME10 .... 37 C3
Woodbridge Dr. ME15 .... 74 F1
Woodbrook. TN27 .... 120 D7
Woodbury La. TN30 .... 179 A7
Woodbury Rd. ME5 .... 31 F1
Woodchurch
CE Prim Sch. TN26 .... 169 A2
Woodchurch Cl. ME5 .... 32 B5
Woodchurch Cres. ME8 .. 11 C2
Woodchurch Ho. ME8 .... 11 C2
Woodchurch Rd.
Appledore TN26 & TN30 .. 181 C4
Woodchurch Rd.
Margate CT7 & CT9 .... 28 A5
Woodchurch Rd.
Shadoxhurst TN26 .... 155 A1
Woodchurch Rd.
Tenterden TN30 .... 179 D8
Woodchurch Rd.
Westgate-on-S CT12 & CT7 .. 27 F3
Woodcock Gdns. CT18 .... 163 A4
Woodcote. CT5 .... 21 D1
Woodcourt Cl. ME10 .... 36 E2
Woodcut. ME14 .... 75 A8
Woodfield Ave. CT19 .... 177 E7
Woodfield Cl. CT19 .... 177 E7
Woodford Ave. CT11 & CT12 .. 29 D1
Woodford Rd. CT7 .... 27 A7
Woodford Rd. ME16 .... 74 B2
Woodgate. CT4 .... 110 E3
Woodgate Cl. ME13 .... 62 C8
Woodgate Ct. ME13 .... 84 E7
Woodgate La. ME9 .... 35 C2
Woodhall Terr. ME11 .... 3 A5

Woodhurst. ME5 .... 31 D4
Woodland Ave. Aylesham CT3 .. 112 E5
Woodland Ave.
  Birchington CT7 .... 27 B6
Woodland Cl. CT17 .... 148 E2
Woodland Cotts. CT18 .... 161 B7
Woodland Dr. ME12 .... 4 B7
Woodland Rd. Herne Bay CT6 .... 22 B2
Woodland Rd.
  Lyminge CT18 & TN25 .... 160 E8
Woodland View. TN30 .... 188 E4
Woodland Way.
  Broadstairs CT10 .... 8 G1
Woodland Way.
  Canterbury CT2 .... 66 D4
Woodland Way.
  Dymchurch TN29 .... 187 A5
Woodland Way.
  Maidstone ME14 .... 75 B7
Woodland Way.
  Woodnesborough CT13 .... 93 C6
Woodlands. Blean CT2 .... 65 F7
Woodlands. Chatham ME5 .... 32 A2
Woodlands. Coxheath ME17 ...... 96 B3
Woodlands. Hernhill ME13 .... 64 C7
Woodlands Cl. ME14 .... 75 B7
Woodlands Cty Prim Sch. ME7 10 F4
Woodlands Dr. CT21 .... 177 A4
Woodlands High Sch. ME7 ...... 10 F4
Woodlands Rd. Adisham CT3 ... 112 C8
Woodlands Rd. Ashford TN24 ... 139 F2
Woodlands Rd. Gillingham ME7 .. 10 F4
Woodlands Rd.
  Sittingbourne ME10 .... 37 B3
Woodlawn St. CT5 .... 20 D2
Woodlea. TN24 .... 139 C3
Woodman Ave. CT5 .... 21 E3
Woodnesborough La. CT13 ...... 93 B3
Woodnesborough Rd. CT13 ...... 93 E7

Woodpecker Glade. ME8 .... 33 D6
Woodrow Chase. CT6 .... 23 A1
Woodruff Cl. ME8 .... 12 D4
Woods Hill. CT4 .... 125 C5
Woods Ley. CT3 .... 71 D2
Woodshale Cotts. ME9 .... 14 D1
Woodside. Ashford TN23 .... 155 E6
Woodside.
  Boughton Street ME13 .... 64 B2
Woodside. Gillingham ME8 .... 33 C6
Woodside Ave. CT4 .... 86 D2
Woodside Cl. CT16 .... 148 E4
Woodside Gdns. ME10 .... 36 D2
Woodside Rd. Maidstone ME15 .. 97 C7
Woodside Rd. Sturry CT2 .... 67 F7
Woodstock Rd. Deal CT14 .... 117 C4
Woodstock Rd. Rochester ME2 .... 9 A7
Woodstock Rd.
  Sittingbourne ME10 .... 36 E1
Woodstock Way. TN24 .... 139 C6
Woodvale Ave. CT5 .... 44 C8
Woodville Cl. CT1 .... 87 D6
Woodville Rd. Maidstone ME15 .. 75 A2
Woodville Rd. Ramsgate CT12 .... 29 C1
Woolaston Cl. ME15 .... 74 F1
Woolcomber St. CT16 .... 166 E7
Wooldeys Rd. ME8 .... 11 F2
Woolett Rd. ME10 .... 36 C5
Woollets Cl. CT6 .... 22 C3
Woollett St. ME14 .... 75 A5
Woolley Rd. ME15 .... 97 F7
Woolmer Dr. TN24 .... 157 A7
Woolpack Hill. TN25 .... 158 D5
Woolreeds Rd. TN23 .... 156 A7
Woolwich Cl. ME5 .... 32 A7
Wootton Gn. ME8 .... 11 D3
Wootton La. CT15 & CT4 .... 146 C7
Wopsle Cl. ME1 .... 31 D7
Worcester Cl. Faversham ME13 .. 62 E6
Worcester Cl. Minster ME12 ...... 4 C6
Worcester Dr. ME10 .... 36 D6
Worcester La. CT3 & CT4 .... 88 E7

Worcester Rd. ME15 .... 97 D7
Wordsworth Cl. ME5 .... 32 C7
Wordsworth Gdns. CT3 .... 112 F6
Wordsworth Rd. ME14 .... 75 B7
Workhouse La. ME15 .... 96 C4
Workhouse Rd.
  Sutton Valence ME17 .... 99 A1
Workhouse Rd. Throwley ME13 .. 82 F1
World's End. ME9 .... 60 E7
Wormdale Hill. ME9 .... 35 B3
Wormdale Rd. ME9 .... 35 B4
Worth Cty Prim Sch. CT14 .... 94 B5
Worth La. CT20 .... 177 E3
Worthgate Pl. **2** CT1 .... 87 F7
Worthington St. **11** CT16 ...... 166 D8
Wotton Cl. ME15 .... 97 E5
Wotton Rd. TN23 .... 156 B6
Wraightsfield Ave. TN29 .... 195 D8
Wraik Hill. CT5 .... 43 C5
Wrangleden Cl. ME15 .... 97 E5
Wrangleden Rd. ME15 .... 97 E5
Wreight Ct. ME13 .... 40 B1
Wren Ind Est. ME15 .... 97 F4
Wren Way. ME5 .... 32 B6
Wrens Ct. ME9 .... 58 A8
Wrens Rd. ME9 .... 58 A7
Wrentham Ave. CT6 .... 22 B2
Wright Cl. ME8 .... 11 C2
Wright's Way. ME12 .... 17 C8
Wrights Cl. TN30 .... 179 A8
Wrotham Ave. **19** CT10 .... 30 B4
Wrotham Rd. CT10 .... 30 B4
Wyatt Ho. **2** ME2 .... 9 A7
Wyatt Pl. ME2 .... 9 A7
Wyatt St. ME14 .... 75 A4
Wych Elm Way. CT21 .... 187 E8
Wycherley Cres. CT16 .... 149 B4
Wye Coll (Univ of London).
  TN25 .... 123 F2
Wye Gdns. CT9 .... 8 F2
Wye High Sch (Prep). TN25 ... 123 E2
Wye Rd. TN25 .... 122 F3

Wye Sta. TN25 .... 123 D2
Wyke Manor Rd. ME14 .... 75 A4
Wykeham Cl. ME11 .... 2 F3
Wykeham Cotts. ME17 .... 96 F2
Wykeham Gr. ME17 .... 99 A7
Wykeham Rd. ME10 .... 37 B4
Wykeham St. ME2 .... 9 B8
Wyles Rd. ME4 .... 9 E2
Wyles St. ME7 .... 10 C7
Wyllie Ct. ME10 .... 36 E7
Wynd The. TN27 .... 103 D1
Wyndam Rd. ME4 .... 9 E2
Wyndham Ave. CT9 .... 8 B2
Wyndham Rd. CT17 .... 166 B8
Wynn Ellis Ho. CT5 .... 20 E3
Wynn Rd. CT5 .... 21 A2
Wytchlings The. ME17 .... 99 D2
Wytherling Cl. ME14 .... 75 F5
Wyvern Way. TN24 .... 139 E3
Wyvill Cl. ME8 .... 33 E5

Yard The. CT4 .... 111 F1
Yardhurst Gdns. CT9 .... 8 F3
Yardley Ho. CT10 .... 30 B7
Yarrow Cl. CT10 .... 30 A3
Yarrow Ct. ME14 .... 75 F5
Yarrow Rd. ME5 .... 31 F4
Yates Cl. TN31 .... 201 A2
Yaugher La. ME9 .... 34 C3
Yeates Dr. ME10 .... 37 A8
Yellow Sands. ME12 .... 19 E5
Yelsted La. Chatham ME14 .... 54 D7
Yelsted La. Yelsted ME9 .... 34 A1
Yelsted Rd. ME9 .... 56 A7
Yeoman Ct. ME14 .... 76 B3
Yeoman Dr. ME7 .... 10 F1
Yeoman Gdns. TN24 .... 157 B8
Yeoman La. ME14 .... 76 B4
Yeoman Way. ME15 .... 76 A2
Yeomans Sq. TN23 .... 155 D8
Yevele Cl. ME11 .... 3 A5
Yew Cl. TN23 .... 138 E2

Yew Tree Cl. Broadstairs CT10 ... 29 D4
Yew Tree Cl. Chatham ME5 .... 32 D1
Yew Tree Cl. Deal CT14 .... 117 A4
Yew Tree Cl. Stanford TN25 ...... 160 B1
Yew Tree Cotts. ME14 .... 53 F1
Yew Tree Farm. CT3 .... 114 A8
Yew Tree Gdns. Birchington CT7 27 A7
Yew Tree Gdns. Fordwich CT2 ... 68 A4
Yew Tree Pl. ME7 .... 33 B1
Yew Tree Rd. TN29 .... 194 F3
Yewhedges. ME13 .... 81 E4
Yewtree Cross. CT18 .... 161 C8
Yoakes La. TN29 .... 192 F1
Yoakley Sq. CT9 .... 28 F8
York and Albany Cl. CT14 ...... 117 B1
York Ave. **17** Broadstairs CT10 ... 30 B4
York Ave. Chatham ME5 .... 31 F3
York Ave. Gillingham ME7 .... 10 C4
York Cl. CT6 .... 22 D4
York Hill. ME4 .... 10 C2
York Ho. **10** CT17 .... 166 D7
York Mews. CT19 .... 177 E7
York Rd. Ashford TN24 .... 139 D5
York Rd. Canterbury CT1 .... 87 E7
York Rd. Deal CT14 .... 117 D4
York Rd. Herne Bay CT6 .... 22 D5
York Rd. Maidstone ME15 .... 75 C2
York Rd. Rochester ME1 .... 9 C3
York St. Broadstairs CT10 .... 30 B4
York St. Dover CT16 & CT17 .... 166 D7
York St. Ramsgate CT11 .... 52 E6
York Street Rdbt. CT16 .... 166 D7
York Terr. CT7 .... 27 B7
Young Cl. CT14 .... 117 B6
Young's Pl. CT15 .... 164 F5
Ypres Ct. CT1 .... 67 D1
Ypres Dr. ME10 .... 14 F1

Zarena Ct. **8** CT20 .... 177 F3
Zealand Rd. CT1 .... 87 F6
Zetland Ave. ME7 .... 10 E2
Zion Pl. CT9 .... 7 J3

OS Ordnance Survey

STREET ATLASES on CD-ROM

The Interactive Street Atlases are CD-ROM versions of the Ordnance Survey/Philip's Street Atlases. They have a wide range of software features, additional levels of mapping, and are remarkably easy to use.

Searches can be carried out for street names and buildings, towns and villages, National Grid references, Postcode districts and sectors, and for page-grid references from the printed Atlases.

You can move around the mapping with no breaks at page boundaries, and scale bars, keys and locator maps can be displayed or hidden. You can measure distances along complex routes, add bookmarks,

draw over the mapping with a range of tools, and create hotspots connected to database tables. You can print sections of mapping, and the price includes a licence to make 1,500 prints.

The Interactive Street Atlases can be used effectively together with the printed atlases – for example, you can always see on which page of the printed Atlas a section of electronic mapping appears.

Mapping includes:

◆ **General Map for orientation**

◆ **County Map showing major routes**

◆ **Road Map showing the majority of roads and streets, and highlighting through routes**

◆ **Street Map, the full mapping from the printed Street Atlases, which forms a "seamless" map of the whole region and can be magnified**

Available now:

◆ **Berkshire** (£150 + VAT)
◆ **Hertfordshire** (£150 + VAT)

More titles coming soon!

Network licences and discounts for bulk purchases are available. Prices subject to change without notice.

You can obtain the Atlases by mail order direct from the publisher:

Tel: 01933 443863
Fax: 01933 443849

Philip's Direct,
27 Sanders Road, Wellingborough,
Northants NN8 4NL

OS Ordnance Survey

Updated annually

MOTORING ATLAS Britain

The best-selling *OS Motoring Atlas Britain* uses unrivalled and up-to-date mapping from the Ordnance Survey digital database. The exceptionally clear mapping is at a large scale of 3 miles to 1 inch (Orkney/Shetland Islands at 5 miles to 1 inch).

A special feature of the atlas is its wealth of tourist and leisure information. It contains comprehensive directories, including descriptions and location details, of the properties of the National Trust in England and Wales, the National Trust for Scotland, English Heritage and

Historic Scotland. There is also a useful diary of British Tourist Authority Events listing more than 300 days out around Britain during the year.

Available from all good bookshops or direct from the publisher:
Tel: 01933 443863

The atlas includes:

◆ **112 pages of fully updated mapping**
◆ **45 city and town plans**
◆ **8 extra-detailed city approach maps**
◆ **route-planning maps**
◆ **restricted motorway junctions**
◆ **local radio information**
◆ **distances chart**
◆ **county boundaries map**
◆ **multi-language legend**

STREET ATLASES ORDER FORM

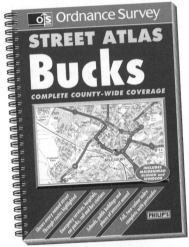

All Street Atlases contain Ordnance Survey mapping and provide the perfect solution for the driver who needs comprehensive, detailed regional mapping in a choice of compact and easy-to-use formats. They are indispensable and are ideal for use in the car, the home or the office.

The series is available from all good bookshops or by mail order direct from the publisher. Before placing your order, please check by telephone that the complete range of titles are available. Payment can be made in the following ways:

By phone Phone your order through on our special Credit Card Hotline on 01933 443863 (Fax: 01933 443849). Speak to our customer service team during office hours (9am to 5pm) or leave a message on the answering machine, quoting your full credit card number plus expiry date and your full name and address.

By post Simply fill out the order form (you may photocopy it) and send it to: **Philip's Direct, 27 Sanders Road, Wellingborough, Northants** NN8 4NL.

COLOUR EDITIONS

	HARDBACK	SPIRAL	POCKET	£ Total
	Quantity @ £10.99 each	Quantity @ £8.99 each	Quantity @ £4.99 each	£ Total
BERKSHIRE	☐ 0 540 06170 0	☐ 0 540 06172 7	☐ 0 540 06173 5	➤ ☐
MERSEYSIDE	☐ 0 540 06480 7	☐ 0 540 06481 5	☐ 0 540 06482 3	➤ ☐
	Quantity @ £12.99 each	Quantity @ £8.99 each	Quantity @ £4.99 each	£ Total
SURREY	☐ 0 540 06435 1	☐ 0 540 06436 X	☐ 0 540 06438 6	➤ ☐
	Quantity @ £12.99 each	Quantity @ £9.99 each	Quantity @ £4.99 each	£ Total
BUCKINGHAMSHIRE	☐ 0 540 07466 7	☐ 0 540 07467 5	☐ 0 540 07468 3	➤ ☐
DURHAM	☐ 0 540 06365 7	☐ 0 540 06366 5	☐ 0 540 06367 3	➤ ☐
HERTFORDSHIRE	☐ 0 540 06174 3	☐ 0 540 06175 1	☐ 0 540 06176 X	➤ ☐
EAST KENT	☐ 0 540 07483 7	☐ 0 540 07276 1	☐ 0 540 07287 7	➤ ☐
WEST KENT	☐ 0 540 07366 0	☐ 0 540 07367 9	☐ 0 540 07369 5	➤ ☐
EAST SUSSEX	☐ 0 540 07306 7	☐ 0 540 07307 5	☐ 0 540 07312 1	➤ ☐
WEST SUSSEX	☐ 0 540 07319 9	☐ 0 540 07323 7	☐ 0 540 07327 X	➤ ☐
TYNE AND WEAR	☐ 0 540 06370 3	☐ 0 540 06371 1	☐ 0 540 06372 X	➤ ☐
SOUTH YORKSHIRE	☐ 0 540 06330 4	☐ 0 540 06331 2	☐ 0 540 06332 0	➤ ☐
	Quantity @ £12.99 each	Quantity @ £9.99 each	Quantity @ £5.50 each	£ Total
GREATER MANCHESTER	☐ 0 540 06485 8	☐ 0 540 06486 6	☐ 0 540 06487 4	➤ ☐
	Quantity @ £12.99 each	Quantity @ £9.99 each	Quantity @ £5.99 each	£ Total
NORTH HAMPSHIRE	☐ 0 540 07471 3	☐ 0 540 07472 1	☐ 0 540 07473 X	➤ ☐
SOUTH HAMPSHIRE	☐ 0 540 07476 4	☐ 0 540 07477 2	☐ 0 540 07478 0	➤ ☐

COLOUR EDITIONS

	HARDBACK	SPIRAL	POCKET	£ Total
	Quantity @ £12.99 each	Quantity @ £9.99 each	Quantity @ £5.99 each	
OXFORDSHIRE	☐ 0 540 07512 4	☐ 0 540 07513 2	☐ 0 540 07514 0	➤ ☐
WEST YORKSHIRE	☐ 0 540 06329 0	☐ 0 540 06327 4	☐ 0 540 06328 2	➤ ☐
	Quantity @ £14.99 each	Quantity @ £9.99 each	Quantity @ £5.99 each	£ Total
LANCASHIRE	☐ 0 540 06440 8	☐ 0 540 06441 6	☐ 0 540 06443 2	➤ ☐

BLACK AND WHITE EDITIONS

	HARDBACK	SOFTBACK	POCKET	£ Total
	Quantity @ £10.99 each			
WARWICKSHIRE	☐ 0 540 05642 1	—	—	➤ ☐
	Quantity @ £12.99 each	Quantity @ £9.99 each	Quantity @ £4.99 each	£ Total
BRISTOL AND AVON	☐ 0 540 06140 9	☐ 0 540 06141 7	☐ 0 540 06142 5	➤ ☐
CARDIFF, SWANSEA & GLAMORGAN	☐ 0 540 06186 7	☐ 0 540 06187 5	☐ 0 540 06207 3	➤ ☐
CHESHIRE	☐ 0 540 06143 3	☐ 0 540 06144 1	☐ 0 540 06145 X	➤ ☐
DERBYSHIRE	—	☐ 0 540 06138 7	☐ 0 540 06139 5	➤ ☐
EDINBURGH & East Central Scotland	☐ 0 540 06180 8	☐ 0 540 06181 6	☐ 0 540 06182 4	➤ ☐
EAST ESSEX	☐ 0 540 05848 3	☐ 0 540 05866 1	☐ 0 540 05850 5	➤ ☐
WEST ESSEX	☐ 0 540 05849 1	☐ 0 540 05867 X	☐ 0 540 05851 3	➤ ☐
NOTTINGHAMSHIRE	—	☐ 0 540 05859 9	☐ 0 540 05860 2	➤ ☐
STAFFORDSHIRE	☐ 0 540 06134 4	☐ 0 540 06135 2	☐ 0 540 06136 0	➤ ☐
	Quantity @ £12.99 each	Quantity @ £9.99 each	Quantity @ £5.99 each	£ Total
GLASGOW & West Central Scotland	☐ 0 540 06183 2	☐ 0 540 06184 0	☐ 0 540 06185 9	➤ ☐

Post to: Philip's Direct,
27 Sanders Road,
Wellingborough, Northants,
NN8 4NL

◆ Free postage and packing

◆ All available titles will normally be dispatched within 5 working days of receipt of order but please allow up to 28 days for delivery

◆ Please tick this box if you do not wish your name to be used by other carefully selected organisations that may wish to send you information about other products and services

Registered Office: 25 Victoria Street, London SW1H 0EX.

Registered in England number: 3396524

I enclose a cheque / postal order, for a **total** of ☐

made payable to *Reed Book Services,* or please debit my

☐ Access ☐ American Express ☐ Visa ☐ Diners

account by ☐

Account no
☐☐☐☐ ☐☐☐☐ ☐☐☐☐ ☐☐☐☐

Expiry date ☐☐ ☐☐

Signature...

Name...

Address..

....

....POSTCODE

STREET ATLASES ORDER FORM